Edited by **Les Gasser**
Distributed Artificial Intelligence Group
University of Southern California, Los Angeles

and **Michael N. Huhns**
Artificial Intelligence Laboratory
MCC, Austin, Texas

Distributed Artificial Intelligence

Volume II

Pitman, London

Morgan Kaufmann Publishers, Inc., San Mateo, California

PITMAN PUBLISHING
128 Long Acre, London WC2E 9AN

A Division of Longman Group UK Limited

© Les Gasser and Michael N. Huhns 1989

Copyright of the volume as a whole is the Editors',
although copyright of an individual paper within the volume
is retained by its author(s).

First published 1989

Available in the Western Hemisphere from
MORGAN KAUFMANN PUBLISHERS, INC.,
2929 Campus Drive, San Mateo, California 94403

ISSN 0268-7526

British Library Cataloguing in Publication Data

Distributed artificial intelligence.—(Research notes
    in artificial intelligence, ISSN 0268-7526)
    Vol. 2, edited by Michael Huhns and Les Gasser
    1. Distributed artificial intelligence
    I. Huhns, Michael N.   II. Gasser, Les   III. Series
    006.3

ISBN 0 273 08810 6

Library of Congress Cataloging in Publication Data
(Revised for volume 2)

Distributed artificial intelligence.

    (Research notes in artificial intelligence,
ISSN 0268-7526)
    Includes bibliographies and indexes.
    Vol. 2 edited by Les Gasser and Michael N. Huhns.
    1. Artificial intelligence.   2. Electronic data
processing—Distributed processing.   3. Problem
solving—Data processing.   I. Gasser, Leslie George,
1949–   .   II. Huhns, Michael N.   III. Series:
Research notes in artificial intelligence (London,
England)
Q335.D57   1987   006.3   86-33259
ISBN 0-934613-38-9 (pbk. : v. 1)

ISBN 1-55860-092-2 (v. 2)

Reproduced and printed by photolithography
in Great Britain by Biddles Ltd, Guildford

CONTENTS

Preface

The last several years have witnessed a rapidly growing interest in Distributed Artificial Intelligence (DAI). This interest has been international in scope; we now know of strong DAI research teams in at least eleven countries around the world. The continued development of DAI is chronicled here, and this book attests to the quality and diversity of recent research.

The American Association for Artificial Intelligence has sponsored eight workshops on DAI during the period from 1980 through 1988. In 1987, one of us edited a collection of papers [Huhns 1987], most of which were based on work presented at the 1985 DAI Workshop at Sea Ranch, California, USA. This book, the second in the series of collected papers on DAI, had its genesis with the 1988 DAI workshop held in May 1988 at Lake Arrowhead, California. Contained herein are 19 papers, most of which are revised versions of papers first presented at Lake Arrowhead. The remainder have been contributed by other prominent researchers in the field.

We are grateful to the authors of the chapters in this book for their ideas, insights, and experimental results that are at the forefront of the development of distributed artifical intelligence. Their enthusiasm for this research area is evident and inspiring. The reviewers, Miro Benda, Phil Cohen, Dan Corkill, Lee Erman, Vic Lesser, Uttam Mukhopadhyay, Joe Nunes, and Larry Stephens, deserve our thanks for their insightful comments and criticisms that insured the high caliber of the published papers.

—Les Gasser and Michael N. Huhns

Themes in Distributed Artificial Intelligence Research

Les Gasser and Michael N. Huhns

There is ideally a synergy between the desire to gain new knowledge and the desire to apply the knowledge to solve real-world problems. DAI has recently been benefiting from such a synergy. Ideas from DAI are becoming important to research in fields such as distributed databases, distributed and parallel computing, human-computer interaction, computer supported cooperative work, computer-aided design and manufacturing, and concurrent engineering. At the same time, the need to attack large problems with knowledge from numerous simultaneous perspectives, coupled with advances in concurrent and parallel computing, have inspired many new ideas in DAI. Among these new ideas are several major research themes that have become apparent to us over the last year. We find these central to further developments in DAI and exciting in their own right.

First, new problem-solving architectures for DAI have begun to appear. In earlier periods of DAI research, three types of interaction architectures predominated: (1) blackboard systems, (2) systems in which task allocation was based on contracting or negotiating among problem-solvers, and (3) multiagent planning frameworks in which single agents constructed detailed plans for a collection of agents. Over time, these mainstays of DAI have been only marginally extended. Lesser and his colleagues extended blackboard architectures with both goal and data blackboards [Lesser *et al.* 1982], and several researchers experimented with added control blackboards (cf. [Hayes-Roth 1985]). Parunak applied the contract net to manufacturing control [Parunak 1987]. Georgeff, Lansky, and others refined models of action in multiagent planning theory [Georgeff and Lansky 1987]. The new architectures, by contrast, incorporate a wider array of control and interaction models, including distributed, interacting truth-maintenance systems [Chapter 13], blackboard systems with concurrency at several levels [Chapter 14], and new negotiation frameworks that involve agents' goals, values, and plans [Chapters 6 and 10].

Second, new avenues of research have emerged recently, filling important gaps in DAI literature and practice. To date, there has been insufficient research on multiagent systems that improve their performance over time. Huhns and colleagues developed simple learning techniques that improved the performance of networks of problem solvers cooperating in information retrieval [Huhns *et al.* 1987]. Corkill, Lesser, and colleagues have been developing self-organizing problem solvers, but their work along these lines is as yet incomplete [Corkill 1982], [Pattison *et al.* 1987]. Here, Shaw and Whinston provide interesting new learning techniques by introducing a market mechanism through which agents can compete and an evolution mechanism through which the characteristics of successful agents can propagate [Chapter 16].

Another omission from prior DAI research, being rectified herein, is consideration of the social behavior of a large collection of agents. In Chapter 1, Werner develops a unified theory of communication, cooperation, and social structure that fulfills a necessary condition for the design of cooperating complex agents. Star suggests basing DAI on a social metaphor, using boundary objects as the data structure for interaction [Chapter 2]. In Chapter 3, Gasser and colleagues develop a new framework for representing and revising organizational knowledge. The modeling of potentially chaotic systems by Kephart *et al.* begins to reveal constraints on the behavior of individual problem solvers that are needed to avoid chaotic behavior *en masse* [Chapter 4].

Third, new theories, both pragmatic and abstract, are also emerging from recent work. Sathi and Fox apply constraint-directed reasoning to negotiations about resource allocation in scheduling problems [Chapter 8]. By examining probabilistic communication-free interactions among agents, John Breese and Jeff Rosenschein [Chapter 5] extend earlier work of [Rosenschein *et al.* 1986] on models of rationality and cooperation without communication. In addition, several researchers represented both in this book and elsewhere (e.g., Gasser in Chapter 3, Star in Chapter 2, and Hewitt in [Hewitt 1988]), have begun to urge that DAI researchers use social theories (especially constructivist and interactionist ones) as a methodological and epistemological foundation for DAI. Again, new theories of large-scale dynamic systems [Chapter 4], market and genetic systems [Chapter 16], and human organizations [Chapters 2 and 3] promise global insights for systems that can be modeled realistically in simple terms. These represent the beginnings of DAI systems that may someday be developed from the integrated perspectives of sociology, psychology, and economics. They also provide needed movement toward strong underlying behavioral theories for DAI, and steps toward what has been called an "ethology" or "sociology" of intelligent machines (e.g., [Woolgar 1985]).

Fourth, there is now a wide range of perspectives on planning in multiagent worlds, which can be organized along a spectrum from those dealing with simple, mathematically characterizable agents working in abstracted, constrained worlds [Chapters 5 and 9], to experimentally useful but theoretically uncharacterized multiagent planners [Chapters 10, 11, and 12], and on to more qualitative models or "situated" theories of cooperative planning, like those of [Agre 1988], [Cohen and Levesque 1988], [Grosz and Sidner 1988], [Suchman 1987], and Werner [Chapter 1].

Fifth, researchers are beginning to define carefully their objects of study, units of analysis, and research methods, using clear comparative studies, in order to strengthen the scientific basis for DAI [Gasser 1987]. Five fundamental questions for DAI research have been posed in [Bond and Gasser 1988]. Linking DAI research to basic questions provides one way to make DAI research comparable across projects and problems. Another means for comparison is provided by Decker, Durfee, and Lesser in this volume [Chapter 19]: they provide a collection of 73 dimensions along which to describe any particular DAI system or theory, as well as a metric for each dimension. Their scheme allows different systems to be described and compared in a large feature space; for example, they compare their method of partial global planning with the contract net system of [Davis and Smith 1983].

Finally, an array of methodological approaches are appearing and being debated in DAI research. Due to many years of effort in building problem solving architectures, distributed object-oriented languages, and programming environments, it is now much easier to use careful experimental methods in DAI. Most papers in this book discuss implementations or simulations of DAI systems, and many of them report on the performance of these systems under experimental conditions. A number of research methods new to DAI appear here as well. The dynamic models of very large systems with which Kephardt *et al.* have experimented are one example [Chapter 4]. Nii and coworkers have reported numerous experimental studies to evaluate their multilevel concurrency control mechanisms in CAGE and POLIGON [Chapter 14]. Star suggests the "Durkheim test" for *social utility* to replace the Turing test for individual intelligence [Chapter 2]. Her earlier investigations of the construction of robust knowledge in scientific practice suggest ways of refining the units of analysis and objects of study for DAI. We paraphrase her by saying that, to explain their systems and insights, researchers in DAI must have "open theories" that recognize the inherently multiperspective nature of knowledge and account for the processes of theory revision. Such open theories could provide the boundary objects through which systems would interact.

Despite the variety and vitality manifested in the papers included here, there are several currents in contemporary DAI research and development that are not well represented in this volume, but that we believe are important to mention. These include:

Shared Knowledge as a Basis for Cooperation. There is an ongoing investigation of the hypothesis that a base of common knowledge is *necessary* for multiagent cooperation to occur, i.e., neither humans nor machines can cooperate if they know nothing in common [Huhns *et al.* 1988]. The problem-solving architecture that is resulting from this investigation employs the large common-sense knowledge base, CYC, to provide globally consistent semantics among the problem-solving agents. This underlying common-sense knowledge relates terms that are common among the agents and serves as the "glue" that interconnects them.

Distributed, Multiperspective Diagnosis. Several researchers have begun to investigate the distributed modeling and diagnosis of systems [Geffner and Pearl 1987]. Preliminary work on modeling and diagnosing problem-solving system behavior has been reported [Hudlicka *et al.* 1986], [Hudlicka and Lesser 1987], and several theories of distributed debugging and program analysis have been advanced. Usually these approaches have relied on a single global view of the system being diagnosed, and have not allowed multiple agents with multiple perspectives to perform the diagnosis. More recently, some researchers have begun investigating techniques to permit numerous diagnosers to cooperate in analyzing and categorizing faults in concurrent systems.

Human-Computer Interaction. A number of researchers are working with DAI techniques, such as distributed and multiagent planners, to provide intelligent assistance in such domains as office support, computer supported cooperative work, and software development. Others are constructing knowledge-based models of multiagent processes in these domains plus manufacturing and engineering [Chapter 18].

Technology Platforms for DAI. Development has continued on technology platforms for DAI research. There are now a number of programming environments, blackboard shells, and distributed, object-oriented languages for building DAI systems, and more are on the way. Some of these have been designed specifically for DAI applications, while others are more general purpose programming tools. Discussion of numerous concurrent object-based systems can be found in a special issue of ACM SIGPLAN Notices [Agha *et al.* 1989], and in [Bond and Gasser 1988]. The merits and shortcomings of concurrent programming languages and constructs used for DAI research, such as Linda [Carriero and Gelernter 1989] and Concurrent Logic Programming [Kahn *et al.* 1988], are being hotly debated. The concurrent knowledge representation language *Mering IV* is being designed expressly for building DAI systems [Ferber 1988].

Issues for Research

We believe there are a number of timely research issues in DAI. These are important issues not only in which research is urgently needed, but also in which much of the groundwork has been done and advances are likely. The issues are:

Methodology. Distributed AI (like AI in general) needs much more discussion and debate about its foundations and its research methods. It seems that the authors of every recent survey, report, and taxonomy have advanced their own perspective on the central problems of the field, and their own way of interpreting results and progress (a bibliography including a list of collections and surveys can be found in [Bond and Gasser 1988]; see also [Hern 1988]). But no clear consensus has yet emerged on the central problems of DAI. Bond and Gasser have proposed five basic questions for DAI in [Bond and Gasser 1988], and these and others should be debated, revised, and extended. Lesser and colleagues' evaluation metrics [Chapter 19] provide one definition of progress in the field—will it prove to be a useful and pragmatic one? The appropriateness and clarity of economic, sociological, and computational metaphors and techniques for discourse in DAI are open to question (see, e.g., Chapters 1, 2, and 3 in this volume). These discussions can be fruitful, as they refine the premises upon which DAI research rests, and provide definitions of the arenas in which problems can be solved.

Deep Theories of Coordination. Researchers in DAI have developed several weak and highly constrained theories of coordination, which provide guidance and some techniques for designing DAI systems. In general, these are still too specialized and project-specific. We still have no broadly useful definitions of terms such as *coordination*, *cooperation*, or *interaction*. To be sure, we do have the "cooperation without communication," "rational deal-making," and "probabilistic interaction" theories of Rosenschein, Genesereth, Breese, and Ginsberg (e.g., [Chapter 5]), but these are bound by highly restrictive assumptions. The promising "metalevel control" and "partial global planning" techniques of Lesser and colleagues have not yet become full-fledged coordination theories that can guide us to other new practical coordination techniques. We have a plethora of interaction frameworks and architectures as noted above, but no deep theories that would integrate some large percentage of them in an explanatory framework. Such theories could lead directly to new architectures with better performance, or could help explain the limitations of known architectures.

Representations of Collective Action. The problems of reasoning about action and time have been recognized issues in AI for many years. Most formal approaches to reasoning about action address the actions of individual actors, in both single-agent and multiagent environments. To reason effectively about coordination and organizational activity, however, we need representations of action that address higher-order units of analysis—for example, collective action, which is different from the action of individuals. The action of "a hive of bees making honey," or "computer science organization producing research reports," or "300 brokers trading stocks" is at once multifaceted, multiported (there are numerous simultaneous interaction points), multiperspective, and complex.

Learning. Beyond the early learning research in DAI by Huhns *et al.* is the new approach that Shaw and Whinston have begun to explore. However, we still need much more. We would especially like to reach the DAI research goal first stated by Corkill, Lesser, and their colleagues: adaptive organization self-design by a collection of problem-solvers or intelligent agents.

Multigrain Concurrency. There are opportunities for concurrency in AI at many levels. One focus of DAI research should be on integrating different types of concurrency in the same system, thereby exploiting the best techniques for the job. For example, we would like guidance on how to integrate reasoning and representation methods of different granularities and styles, such as neural networks and high-level distributed symbolic reasoning. Such research could lead directly to better coordination theories, as well as to needed techniques for decomposing and composing knowledge and action to different levels of granularity. Steps are being made in these directions, notably in the "calculus of actor configurations" of [Agha and Hewitt 1985], in the boundary objects of Star [Chapter 2], in the agent compositions of [Gasser *et al.* 1987], in research into integrated heterogeneous operating systems and problem-solvers such as ABE [Erman *et al.* 1988] and AGORA [Bisiani 1986], in the modular decomposition of intelligence in BB* by Hayes-Roth [Chapter 15], and in the multilevel parallelism experiments of Nii and colleagues [Chapter 14]. But much more needs to be done.

Modeling and Explaining Problem-Solving Behavior. Developing and maintaining systems of coordinated problem solvers can be complex and frustrating, especially without automated support [Bond and Gasser 1988], [Hudlicka and Lesser 1987]. Conventional AI systems with a single thread of control and execution can be difficult enough, but systems of coordinated problem solvers add several dimensions to the complexity. Modeling the relationships among asynchronously unfolding goals, knowledge, and actions in different contexts requires new methods and tools. We need what amounts to a set of "qualitative theories" (cf. [Bobrow 1985]) that can serve as the basis of explanation, behavioral prediction, and analysis. Beyond development, better models will be also useful as bases for organization self-design and coordination.

Hypothetical Worlds. DAI offers an appealing approach to hypothetical worlds, whereby multiple agents each explore alternatives and form hypotheses, and then negotiate to resolve any differences of opinion that may arise. Little research has been done on this approach to date.

Real-Time AI. Cooperative and competitive computation in DAI holds promise for real-time AI systems [Lesser *et al.* 1988]. Different agents with different techniques, perspectives, and resource requirements can be run simultaneously on the same problem to provide opportunistically efficient solutions. Heuristic techniques for exploiting "combinatorial implosion" need further investigation [Davis 1982].

Epistemology and Emergent Knowledge. The relationships between knowledge and action have been a central focus of AI research for twenty years or more; discussions date back at least to the original "procedural/declarative" debates in the early 1970's. Now, in coordination with recent work in the sociology of knowledge and the sociology of science, DAI research presents exciting opportunities to investigate the collaborative construction and use of knowledge by multiple agents in open systems. For example, questions of how any knowledge can be "shared" knowledge; how discrepancies in knowledge and action can be settled without global perspective, control, or authority; how meanings and representations can be made to change or be kept stable across space and time; how multiple perspectives affect metalevel architectures and representations; and so on.

These are just a few of the deep practical and theoretical questions that DAI research can help to address. As interest in DAI grows, we hope to see greater collaborative effort; as Hayes-Roth stated early on, "All real systems are distributed" [Davis 1980].

References

[Agha and Hewitt 1985] Gul Agha and Carl Hewitt, "Concurrent Programming Using Actors: Exploiting Large-Scale Parallelism," *Proceedings of the 5th Conference on Foundations of Software Technology and Theoretical Computer Science*, Springer-Verlag, 1985.

[Agha *et al.* 1989] Gul Agha, Peter Wegner, and Akinori Yonezawa, editors, "Proceedings of the ACM SIGPLAN Workshop on Object-Based Concurrent Programming," *SIGPLAN Notices*, vol. 24, no. 4, April 1989.

[Agre 1988] Philip Agre, "The Dynamic Structure of Everyday Life," Ph.D. thesis, Department of Computer Science, Massachusetts Institute of Technology, 1988.

[Bisiani 1986] Roberto Bisiani, "A Software and Hardware Environment for Developing AI Applications on Parallel Processors," *Proceedings AAAI-86*, Philadelphia, PA, 1986, pp. 742–747.

[Bobrow 1985] Daniel G. Bobrow, *Qualitative Reasoning about Physical Systems*, MIT Press, Cambridge, MA, 1985.

[Bond and Gasser 1988] Alan H. Bond and L. Gasser, editors, *Readings in Distributed Articficial Intelligence*, Morgan Kaufmann, San Mateo, CA, 1988.

[Carriero and Gelernter 1989] Nicholas Carriero and David Gelernter, "Linda in Context," *Communications of the ACM*, vol. 32, no. 4, April 1989, pp. 444–458.

[Cohen and Levesque 1988] Philip R. Cohen and Hector J. Levesque, "On Acting Together: Joint Intentions for Intelligent Agents," in [Gasser (to appear)].

[Corkill 1982] Daniel D. Corkill, *A Framework for Organization Self-Design in Distributed Problem Solving Networks*, Ph.D. thesis, Department of Computer and Information Science, University of Massachusetts, Amherst, MA, 1982.

[Davis 1980] Randall Davis, "Report on the Workshop on Distributed AI," *SIGART Newsletter*, Issue 73, October, 1980, pp. 42–52.

[Davis 1982] Randall Davis, "Report on the Second Workshop on Distributed AI," *SIGART Newsletter*, Issue 80, April, 1982, pp. 13–23.

[Davis and Smith 1983] Randall Davis and Reid G. Smith, "Negotiation as a Metaphor for Distributed Problem Solving," *Artificial Intelligence*, vol. 20, no. 1, 1983, pp. 63–109.

[Erman *et al.* 1988] Lee D. Erman, Jay S. Lark, and Frederick Hayes-Roth, "ABE: An Environment for Engineering Intelligent Systems," *IEEE Transactions on Software Engineering*, vol. SE-14, no. 1, December, 1988, pp. 1758–1770.

[Ferber 1988] Jacques Ferber and Jean-Pierre Briot, *Design of a Concurrent Language for Distributed Artificial Intelligence*, Technical Report Number LITP-88-57-RXF, Laboratoire Informatique, Theorique, et Programmation (LITP), Universite Paris VI, 4 Place Jussieu, Paris, France, 1989.

[Gasser 1987] Les Gasser, "Report on the 1985 Workshop on Distributed Artificial Intelligence," *AI Magazine*, vol. 8, no. 2, Summer 1987, pp. 91–97.

[Gasser *et al.* 1987] Les Gasser, Carl Braganza, and Nava Herman, "MACE: A Flexible Testbed for Distributed Artificial Intelligence Research," in [Huhns 1987].

[Gasser (to appear)] Les Gasser, *Report on the 1988 Workshop on Distributed Artificial Intelligence*, Technical Report Number CS-89-05, Computer Science Department, University of Southern California, Los Angeles, CA, June, 1988. (To appear in *AI Magazine*).

[Geffner and Pearl 1987] Hector Geffner and Judea Pearl, "Distributed Diagnosis of Systems with Multiple Faults," *Proceedings Third IEEE Conference on Artificial Intelligence Applications*, 1987, pp. 156–162.

[Georgeff and Lansky 1987] Michael P. Georgeff and Amy L. Lansky, editors, *Reasoning about Actions and Plans: Proceedings of the 1986 Workshop*, Morgan Kaufmann Publishers, San Mateo, CA, 1987.

[Grosz and Sidner 1988] Barbara J. Grosz and Candace L. Sidner, "Distributed Know-How and Acting: Research on Collaborative Planning," in [Gasser (to appear)].

[Hayes-Roth 1985] Barbara Hayes-Roth, "A Blackboard Architecture for Control," *Artificial Intelligence*, vol. 26, 1985, pp. 251–321.

[Hern 1988] Luis Eduardo Castillo Hern, "On Distributed Artificial Intelligence," *The Knowledge Engineering Review*, vol. 3, part 1, March 1988, pp. 21–57.

[Hewitt 1988] Carl Hewitt, "Organizational Knowledge Processing," in [Gasser (to appear)].

[Hudlicka *et al.* 1986] Eva Hudlicka, Victor R. Lesser, Jasmina Pavlin, and Anil Rewari, *Design of a Distributed Diagnosis System*, Technical Report Number COINS-TR-86-63, Department of Computer and Information Science, University of Massachusetts, Amherst, MA, December 1986.

[Hudlicka and Lesser 1987] Eva Hudlicka and Victor R. Lesser, "Modeling and Diagnosing Problem Solving System Behavior," *IEEE Transactions on Computers*, vol. SMC-17, no. 3, May/June 1987, pp. 407–419.

[Huhns 1987] Michael N. Huhns, editor, *Distributed Artificial Intelligence*, Pitman, London, 1987.

[Huhns *et al.* 1987] Michael N. Huhns, Uttam Mukhopadhyay, Larry M. Stephens, and Ronald D. Bonnell, "DAI for Document Retrieval: The MINDS Project," in M. N. Huhns, ed., *Distributed Artificial Intelligence*, Pitman, London, 1987.

[Huhns *et al.* 1988] Michael N. Huhns, Larry M. Stephens, and Douglas B. Lenat, *Cooperation for DAI through Common-Sense Knowledge (Extended Abstract)*, MCC Technical Report Number ACA-AI-060-88, MCC, Austin, TX, February 1988.

[Kahn *et al.* 1988] Kenneth Kahn, Eric D. Tribble, Mark S. Miller, and Daniel S. Bobrow, "VULCAN: Logical Concurrent Objects," in *Procedings of the 1986 ACM Conference on Object-Oriented Programming, Systems and Languages*, Portland, Oregon, 1986.

[Lesser *et al.* 1982] Victor R. Lesser, Daniel D. Corkill, and Eva Hudlicka, "Unifying Data-directed and Goal-directed Control: An Example and Experiments," *Proceedings of AAAI-82*, Pittsburgh, PA, August 1982, pp. 143–147.

[Lesser *et al.* 1988] Victor R. Lesser, Jasmina Pavlin, and Edmund Durfee, "Approximate Processing in Real-Time Problem-Solving," *AI Magazine*, vol. 9:1, Spring, 1988, pp. 49–61.

[Parunak 1987] H. Van Dyke Parunak, "Manufacturing Experience with the Contract Net," in [Huhns 1987].

[Pattison *et al.* 1987] H. Edward Pattison, Daniel D. Corkill, and Victor R. Lesser, "Instantiating Descriptions of Organizational Structures," in [Huhns 1987].

[Rosenschein *et al.* 1986] Jeffrey S. Rosenschein, M. Ginsberg, and Michael R. Genesereth, "Cooperation without Communication," *Proceedings of AAAI-86*, Philadelphia, PA, August 1986, pp. 51–57.

[Suchman 1987] Lucy Suchman, *Plans and Situated Actions: The Problem of Human-Machine Communication*, Cambridge University Press, New York, 1987.

[Woolgar 1985] Steve Woolgar, "Why Not a Sociology of Machines? The Case of Sociology and Artificial Intelligence," *Sociology*, vol. 19, no. 4, Novembe 1985, pp. 557–572.

Part I

Societies of Agents

Chapter 1

Cooperating Agents: A Unified Theory of Communication and Social Structure

Eric Werner

Abstract

We aim at providing a general theoretical framework for designing agents with a communicative and social competence. Thereby, we develop the foundations for the design of systems of agents that behave as a social unit or group. A unified theory of communication, cooperation, and social structure is presented. First, a theory of the cognitive states, the information and intentional states, of an agent is given. A theory of communication is developed that gives a formal account of how messages affect the intentions or plans of an agent. The theory of intentions is used to define the concepts of social role and social structure. The unified theory of communication, intention, and social structures is used to develop a theory of social cooperation for multiagent systems. This fulfills a necessary condition for the design of complex agents that cooperate as a group. We apply the theories with an analysis of two examples: the contract net protocol and a Wittgensteinian language game.

1.1 Introduction

How is it possible for a group of independent agents, such as humans, robots, or processes in a distributed environment, to achieve a social goal? By a *social goal* we mean a goal that is not achievable by any single agent alone but is achievable by a group of agents. The key element that distinguishes social goals from other goals is that they require cooperation;

social goals are not, in general, decomposable into separate subgoals that are achievable independently of the other agent's activities. In other words, one agent cannot simply proceed to perform its action without considering what the other agents are doing. Examples include the operation of a factory, the construction of a ship, or the lifting of a couch.

The attainment of social goals appears to require a coordination of agent actions. What makes coordination possible? If we imagine independent agents with pure self-interest, the achievement of social goals would be purely accidental. It seems that coordination of social activity requires that the agents cooperate. How is such cooperation achieved? These questions lie at the foundation of distributed artificial intelligence (DAI) [Genesereth *et al.* 1986, Rosenschein 1986].

We argue that cooperation is made possible through communication and social organization. What sort of communication is necessary to achieve cooperation? What is a social organization? What are the requirements for an agent to be able to communicate and take a place in a social organization? If we want to design and construct agents with a communicative and social competence, we must develop a unified theory that answers these questions.

In this paper we extend the work of [Werner 1988a] by looking at communication and social structure in more detail. Our aim is to develop a global computational theory of cooperation, communication, and social structure as a foundation for the design of the achitecture of agents with communicative and social competencies. The relationship between language and social cooperation is achieved by a communication theory that links meaning to changes in the cognitive states of the agents. We do this by examining and formally describing how messages affect the planning process, thereby relating communication to the intentions of the agents. A theory of cooperation and social structure is outlined. It is shown how this is related to communication and the distribution of social roles. This serves as a foundation for the design of agents that act in harmony as a group.

The theory we present is formal and abstract, quite distant from an actual artificial social agent. However, such a unified formal theory that ties together several, traditionally distinct, disciplines is an important step in the direction of a deeper understanding of not only distributed systems, but also ourselves, our linguistic abilities, and our social nature.

1.2   Problems of Cooperation

There are two central interrelated themes or problems in achieving multiagent cooperation and coordination: one is the communication problem, which is concerned with the role and nature of communication in cooperation. The other is the organization problem, which is concerned with the nature and function of social organization in facilitating cooperation. The first half of the paper investigates the communication problem and the second half considers social organization.

After looking at previous approaches in Section 1.3, we distinguish types of information and cooperation in Sections 1.4 and 1.5. We then develop a formal theory of the cognitive structure of an agent in Section 1.6, focusing on intentions. We outline the communication theory in Section 1.7. A description of types of social cooperation through communication is given in Section 1.8. Section 1.9 presents a formal theory of social roles. This is followed by a theory of social structure and dynamic social groups in Section 1.10. We then apply our theory by giving a formal analyis of the contract net protocol in Section 1.11, and analyzing a Wittgensteinian language game in Section 1.12. We finish in Section 1.13 with a discussion of the approaches of Gasser, Lesser, Corkill, and Durfee, and relate their work to ours.

1.3 Previous Approaches to the Communication Problem

The possible solutions to the communication problem range between two poles: from those involving no communication to those involving high-level, sophisticated communication. The solutions implicit in previous research fall somewhere in between. However, none of the previous approaches develop the solution adopted by human agents, namely, that of using high-level linguistic communication to achieve complex social action. This is the solution we will investigate. First, we look more specifically at previous approaches.

Previous research in computer science on multiagent action, e.g., in operating systems theory, distributed systems, parallel processing, and distributed artificial intelligence, has implicitly or explicitly taken a position with regard to the problem of how cooperative social action is to be achieved. They have been limited to the following kinds of communication.

1.3.1   No Communication

In this case the agent rationally infers the other agents' intentions (plans) without communicating with them [Genesereth *et al.* 1986, Rosenschein 1986]. However, there are difficulties inherent in this approach: first, the solution fails to work when there are several optimal paths to the same goal. For then there is by definition no general rational way of deciding which choice to make, and communication is necessary to resolve the uncertainty. Second, rationally inferring the decisions of the other agents requires knowledge of the other agents' beliefs. How does the agent get that knowledge except by some form of communication? Third, if the other agents are themselves speculating on what the others are going to do, the result is a potentially infinite nesting of beliefs. Finally, irrespective of the above difficulties even if cooperation were possible by pure mutual rational deduction, the computational cost of rationally deducing the other agents' intentions would be enormous for cooperative activity of even mild complexity. We are not saying rational deduction is not used in cooperative behaviour. Indeed, often it is necessary: see related work on helpful responses [Allen 1979, Allen and Perrault 1980]. Our claim is that it is inadequate for achieving sophisticated cooperative action.

One could postulate the existence of a preestablished harmony. Each agent has a plan that fits in with the other agents' plans. One problem is that if the environment changes, a new plan would have to be constructed and that plan would no longer necessarily fit with the other agents' plans. Another problem is that it is not specified how the agents get their plans. Presumably, communication of some form is necessary. But that communication may be limited to the user giving instructions in the form of a program to the agent.

1.3.2 Primitive Communication

In this case, communication is restricted to some finite set of fixed signals (usually two) with fixed interpretations [Dijkstra 1968, Hoare 1978]. [Georgeff 1983] has applied this work to multiagent planning to achieve avoidance of conflict between plans for more than one agent. It has also been applied in robotics to coordinate parallel activity (for a review see [Lozano-Pérez 1983]).

The coordination made possible by these means is limited, being primarily used to avoid conflicts between sequential processes. Sophisticated cooperative action is virtually impossible. The reason is that the direct reference to one of a large repertoire of actions is not possible due to the limited number and types of signals available. Arbitrarily complex actions cannot be formed since there is no syntax of signals to build up complex actions. Hence, arbitrarily complex commands, requests, and intentions cannot be expressed. It is somewhat analogous to the distinction between machine-level and task-level robot programming [Lozano-Pérez 1983].

1.3.3 Plan and Information Passing

An agent A communicates its total plan to agent B and B communicates its total plan to A. Whichever plan arrives first is accepted [Rosenschein 1986]. While this method can achieve cooperative action, it has several problems. First, total plan passing is computationally expensive. Second, there is no guarantee that the resulting plan will be warranted by the recipient's database [Rosenschein 1986]. In addition to Rosenschein's criticisms, there are general problems with any form of total plan passing.

First, total plan passing as a communication strategy is unfeasible. In any real world application there is a great deal of uncertainty about the present state of the world, as well as its future. Hence, for real life situations total plans cannot be formulated in advance, let alone be communicated. At best, general strategies are communicable to the agent with more specific choices being computed with contextual information. Similar difficulties arise with preformulated linguistic intentions [Grosz 1985].

Second, a given agent will usually have additional goals distinct from the sender. The sender must somehow guess the additional goals that the recipient wants if he is to choose the correct plan. A mutually satisfactory plan is guaranteed only if abstract goals, not just total plans, can be communicated. Finally, and most importantly, how the plan is passed is left open, i.e., there is no theory of communication given.

As for information passing in isolation [Rosenschein 1986], it suffers from all the problems mentioned in Section 1.3.1, except the second; since there is no explicit communication of intentions, these must be deduced.

1.3.4   Message Passing

[Hewitt 1977] has, we believe, the fundamentally correct intuition that control of multiagent environments is best looked at in terms of communication structures. However, he gives no formal syntax, semantics, or pragmatics for such communication structures. Furthermore, the agents Hewitt investigates have an extremely simple structure. His theory is not and was never intended to be a theory of communication between complex agents. Thus no systematic account or theory of communication for message passing between agents is given.

1.3.5   High-level Communication

A great deal of work has been done on speech act planning [Cohen and Perrault 1979], [Allen and Perrault 1980], [Appelt 1985]. It would seem this work would be ideal for our purposes. What is lacking is that those works are restricted to the planning by a single agent of some communicative act to another agent. They do not give an explicit formal theory of how complex intentional states are formed by the process of communication. The reason is that they do not explicate the conventional meaning of the speech act and how that is related to planning and intention formation. No systematic theory of the semantics or pragmatics of a language fragment is developed.

[Appelt 1985] implicitly describes an information state I by Know and Belief operators.

Similarly, the intentional state S, described below, is implicitly described by an Intends operator. However, no explicit formal theory of these structures is given. [Grosz 1985] takes an important step in this direction when she clearly recognizes these structures for discourse theory. She does not make any attempt at formalization.

In summary, in none of the above studies is a formal computational theory given as to how it is possible to communicate incrementally, or to tailor and adjust plan communication to fit an uncertain world of changing circumstances. Therefore, no complex communication of strategic information is possible. In this paper we investigate complex communication among agents that use a high-level language. This, together with the theory of social roles and social structures we develop, makes possible the coordination of arbitrarily complex social activity.

1.4 Information Required for Cooperation

What sort of information is required for cooperation? In previous papers [Werner 1988a], [Werner 1988c] we distinguished *three kinds of information*: process information, state information, and evaluative information. *Process information* is information about the intentions of an agent. It modifies the intentional state of an agent. *State information* is information about the state of the world. *Evaluative information* is information about the evaluations a given agent makes. While state and evaluative information are important to an account of agent action, they are not as central as process information.

1.4.1 Common Knowledge

[Halpern and Moses 1984] have sucessfully argued that common knowledge is an important concept in the analysis of distributed systems. What is missing in their account is the crucial notion of process information and how that updates the intentional states of agents. The problem is that without the concept of intention we do not get an account of cooperation. Nor do we get an account of how communication achieves coordinated action. The question of common knowledge is independent of the question of the type of information or knowledge involved. Agents can have common kowledge of state, process, and evaluative information. Therefore, we view the work of Halpern and Moses as complementary to ours.

1.4.2 Common Knowledge of State

Because Halpern and Moses fail to differentiate process, state and evaluative information, their examples often contain messages that are clearly process information, e.g., one general sending to another the message, *I will attack at dawn*. Yet, the semantics of knowledge

[Halpern 1987] describes is of the Hintikka variety that corresponds to the semantics of messages that give state information [Hintikka 1962]. The problem is that intentional or process information is not reducible to state information. Moreover, state information, even if it is common knowledge, is not sufficient to achieve coordinated action. My telling you the stove is in the kitchen does not tell you what I want you to do in the kitchen. Hence, you will not be able to adjust your intentions to mine to achieve some social goal, such as helping me move the stove to the living room.

1.4.3   Evaluative Information and Rationality

Evaluative information combined with some notion of rationality based on that information is also too weak to insure coordination. The utility function for agent A may give two possible courses of action the same value (e.g., two optimal paths). In that case, no rational procedure based on utility maximization will tell agent A what to do. Neither will an evaluative message, sent by agent A to agent B, about A's evaluations of the two courses of action tell agent B what A will do.

1.4.4   Process Information

In summary, in spite of the fact that they are necessary, state information, evaluative information, and common knowledge are not sufficient to achieve cooperation. What is needed is a theory of process information together with a theory of intentional states. To see why, we need to look more closely at the nature of cooperation.

1.5   Two Types of Cooperation

For independent agents in the form of parallel programs, or simple robots acting in parallel, and being controlled by independently running programs, the traditional problem is to design the programs in such a way that the processes do not get into each other's way. There are *critical regions* that only one agent (process or robot) is allowed to occupy at one time (e.g., a printer, a space occupied by a robot arm). This idea is based on an *assumption of negative cooperation*: Cooperation is negative only in that two processes try to avoid doing some subprocess simultaneously. Critical regions are treated as *zones of exclusion*.

More complex cooperative activities, e.g., lifting a heavy object or fitting several parts together at once, may demand *positive cooperation*. In positive cooperation one agent may want to perform processes of some type only if one or more other agents are performing processes of a complementary type. In such activities the issue is not that of avoidance, but of need. One agent needs another to accomplish some goal. In cases of positive cooperation there are *zones of cooperation* in addition to zones of exclusion.

The communication required for coordination of processes depends on the type of cooperation, negative or positive, required by the processes. The negative cooperation assumption allows one to make a further assumption: the *assumption of limited knowledge*, i.e., knowledge of the state or region of another process is required only if that process is in a critical region. A process needs only the information that the other process is or is not, wants or does not want to be, in a critical region. Since the knowledge required is so limited, it is natural that we then hold an *assumption of limited communication*: the communication requirements for processes of this variety are limited and expressible by semaphores [Dijkstra 1968]. Their semantic interpretation is limited to declarations of state: *I am not in critical region X* or *I am in critical region X*. There are also declarations of wants (requests): *I want to be in critical region X* or *I do not want to be in critical region X*.

If, however, we allow positive cooperation, then a process needs much more sophisticated information. If, for example, the goal can be achieved only by a series of complex interwoven and simultaneous actions of several agents, then the agents need knowlege of the other agents' future actions. More generally, the agents need knowledge of the other agents' intentions. For it is the intentions, consisting of the active plans that guide a given agent, that determine what an agent will do and when he will do it. Intentions, insofar as they require other parallel intentions to achieve a given goal, we call *social intentions* [Werner 1988c].

Intentions are formed incrementally through the communication of process information. Furthermore, as we will see below, intentional states allow us to define the notions of social role and social structure which are necessary for understanding efficient and more permanent social cooperation. It is for these reasons that process information and intentional states are the central components in a theory of cooperation based on communication and social structure.

We now investigate the cognitive and, in particular, the intentional state of an agent in more detail. Then we outline our theory of communication, cooperation, and social structure.

10

1.6　A Theory of Cognitive States

1.6.1　Representational States

Let P, $P_1, \ldots$, be *properties*, and R^n, R_1^n, $\ldots$, be *n-ary relations* for $n \geq 2$. Let O be the set of *individuals*. Let T be the set of *time instants* ordered by a relation $<$. The elements of T will be denoted by t, t', t_1, etc. Let TP be the set of *time periods*. The elements of TP will be denoted by τ, τ', etc.

A *situation* s is a set of objects in O that have properties P and that stand in various relations R^n to one another. For example, $s = \{Pa; yes. \; Qa; no. \; R(a,b); yes.\}$ is a situation where property P holds of a, a does not have the property Q, nothing is said about b's properties, and a is related to b by the relationship R. Let $Sits$ be the set of all possible situations.

A *state* σ is a complete situation where all properties and relations are specified. Let Σ be the set of all states. *Histories* or *Worlds* are series of states. More formally, a *history* H is a function from times T to the set of states Σ. Let H_t be the value of the function H at t. H_t is state of the world H at time t. Let Ω be the set of all possible *histories* or *worlds* H. Let H^t be the *partial history* of H up to and including the time $t \in T$. Let $Hist(\Omega)$ be the set of possible *partial histories* H^t for all times $t \in T$. Partial histories H^t are then partial functions where $H_{t_0}^t$ is the state of the partial history at time t_0. *Events* are situations over a time period τ, i.e., events are functions taking times $t \in \tau$ to situations $s \in Sits$. *Actions* a are events with agents given by the function $Agent(a)$. $Time(event)$ is the time period of the event. An event e is *realized* in H at τ if e is contained in H and the domain of e is time period τ (See [Barwise and Perry 1983]).

An *information state* I is a set of partial histories that are possible given the available information. Each information set I has an associated set of alternatives or choices $Alt(I)$. Each *alternative* is a set of possible histories leaving I. $Time(I)$ is the time indicated by the information I. We assume $Time(I)$ is unique. The possible information states of an agent A in the environment Ω form an *information partition* Ξ_A (see [Werner 1989a]). A *strategy* π is a function from information states I to the alternatives at I. STRAT is the set of all possible strategies. π^* is the set of possible histories consistent with the strategy π, i.e., $\pi^* = \{H : H \in \pi_A(I), \forall I \in \Xi_A(H)\}$. $\Xi_A(H) = \{I : I \in \Xi_A \text{ and } \exists t \in T, H^t \in I\}$.

The *cognitive* or *representational state* R of an agent is described by three components $R = <I, S, V>$. I is the *information state* of the agent. S is the *intentional state* of the agent. S is a set of possible strategies that guide the actions of the agent. V is the *evaluative state* of the agent. V represents the agent's evaluation and focus on situations. The representational state R_A may include the agent A's representation of B's representation, R_A^B. It may also include the agent A's representation of B's representation of A's representation, R_A^{BA}. Thus we can represent arbitrary levels of nesting of representations. Let INF, INT, and EVAL be the set of all possible information, intentional, and evaluative states, respectively. Let the *representational capacity*, *Rep*, be the set of all possible representational states of an agent. For the theoretical foundations and some of the principles interrelating intention, information, and ability, see [Werner 1988d].

1.6.2   Properties of Information States

An information state gives the partial information that the agent has at a given time. A partial history H^t is in the information state I if H^t is possible given the information available to the agent. An increase of information leads to a reduction of the possibilities allowed by I. An increase of information thus leads to a reduction of uncertainty. At the same time it leads to an increase in the abilities of the agent in the sense of increasing what that agent can do [Werner 1988d]. Note that information states are inherently dynamic changing with the communication of messages or with sensory data.

We have defined information states extensionally, i.e., in terms of the possible states that are consistent with the information available to the agent. Viewed extensionally an increase of information leads to a decrease in the size of the information set I (the set of possibilities). A loss of information leads to an increase in the size of the information set I. We could also define information states positively. Viewed positively an increase in information leads to a building up of the core situation that the possibilities in I have in common. A loss of information leads to a decrease of the core situation. Thus, the positive representation of information through the core situation reflects the intuitive properties of gain and loss of information that we associate with information states. There are advantages and disadvantages with both of these approaches to representing knowledge (see [Werner 1989c]). Similar remarks apply to thedefinition of intentional and evaluative states.

1.6.3   Evaluative States

Traditionally the evaluations of agent's are modelled by an *evaluation function E*. The domain of E is the set of possible histories Ω. For $H \in \Omega$, $E(H)$ is some numerical value called the *utility* of H. When combined with a probability distribution p the *expected utility* is definable as $\sum_{H \in \Omega} p(H)E(H)$. However, when looking at the internal structure of a history H as composed of a series of states σ, we might want evaluations of objects in O, substituations s, as well as events. Furthermore, in AI systems we may not want such detailed knowledge of evaluations to be represented. Instead of numerical evaluations the evaluations might be symbolic, e.g., *WANT*(Agent, s) versus $E_{Agent}(s) = 0.75$. Still, one can interpret *WANT*, *NOT-WANT*, and *INDIFFERENT* as a simple ordering of three values, and, thereby, an instance of the numerical view of evaluations. Viewed this way, symbolic representations of evaluations are just coarse grained evaluation functions.

Formally, we can define an *evaluative state V* as a class of utility functions E. The uncertainty and ambivalence of agent evaluations is then representable since different evaluation functions in V may have conflicting values. The grain size of the values is an independent dimension of the evaluation functions.

While evaluations guide rational decision making as well as the selection of strategies, and intention formation, they are, nevertheless, distinct from intentional states.

1.6.4 Properties of Intentional States

The way we have defined it, an intentional state is a class of strategies that guide the actions of a given agent. $\pi \in S_A$ means that agent A, who is governed by the intentional state S_A, may possibly be using π as his strategy. If π is not in S_A then we know agent A is not using strategy π. Thus, if several strategies are in S there may be several alternatives still open at I given S. A strategy class generates a partial strategy that for any given information state I gives the subset of alternatives at I consistent with the agent's intentions (see [Werner 1988d] for details).

This way of defining intentions has the following desirable *global and local properties*:

1. Intentions can *combine globally* to form *super-intentions*. This property of intentions is fundamental to the understanding of social cooperation since the intentional super-state of a set of multiple agents forces the social goal.

2. Furthermore, intentions can be *operated on* by the pragmatic interpretation of a linguistic message. Such a property of intentions is fundamental to a theory of communication. It accounts for how communication forms and modifies intentions.

3. Intentions are *dynamic*, changing through communication and agent rationality. This is because the intentional and information states are time dependent.

4. Intentions can be *partially specified*; the agent need not have a response in advance to every possible situation. It allows for the fact that our agents have a limited representational capacity. Furthermore, our theory allows for *uncertainty* in one agent's representation of another agent's intentions: agent A's representation of B's intentions S_A^B may be incomplete.

13

5. Intentions *guide individual and group action* since the strategy given in the intentional state S determines the action the agent is to perform at the time t given information state I.

6. Intentions of a single agent *combine locally* to form composite intentions subject to constraints. Intentions *constrain* the adoption of new intentions. If the agent is in an intentional state S, then the formation of new intentions must not conflict with the given ones in S. If they do conflict, then the new intention must be rejected or some form of backtracking must occur to modify S. New intentions are the imputs to a rational process which generates a modified intentional state.

7. Since the agent can have linguistic strategies, our formal definition of intention allows the agent to have *linguistic intentions*. These will have all of the above properties of regular intentions.

8. We will see that *roles* and social structures can be defined using our notion of intention. Thus intentions form the basis of a theory of social cooperation. Since roles are a type of intentional state, roles share all of the properties of intentions. Thus roles govern behaviour and are composable, dynamic, linguistically modifiable, and partial. Linguistic roles are also possible.

Our formal theory of intention, although developed independently, is close to Bratman's informal philosophical account [Bratman 1987]. Bratman attempts to analyze agent rationality in the context of an agent's intentions, and where an intention is having a plan. As Bratman states "Plans ... are intentions writ large. They share the properties of intentions ... they resist reconsideration ... they are conduct controllers ... they provide crucial inputs for further practical reasoning and planning ... plans are typically partial ... plans typically have a hierarchical structure" [Bratman 1987, p. 29]. Note, in our formal theory, intentional states not only have these *local, agent-centered properties* of intentions of a single agent, but intentional states also have the complementary *global, interagent properties* of intentions for groups of agents given above.

1.6.5   Connectionist versus Symbolic Intentional States

The way we have defined intentional states has left open how these intentional states might be realized in the form of software or hardware. Thus the intentions may be represented symbolically as *Want* and *Intend* contexts in an *Assertion Box* in a KL-TWO like representation [Villain 1985], as rule sets in a robot planner data base [Genesereth and Nilsson 1987], as the planning component in a subsumption architecture [Brooks 1986], or, perhaps by dynamic equations in a connectionist achitecture. The global and local properties of intentional states should be the same in any of these realizations. The power of our theory of intention is that it allows various realizations of strategic agent behavior.

Given a subsumption architecture [Brooks 1986], our approach would also allow for a mixture of low level connectionist robotic strategies (intentions) with high level (symbolic or nonsymbolic) strategies (intentions). Thus, in the case of a communicating robot, a command might first be processed by a high level structure (symbolically or nonsymbolically) in order to integrate it and make conflict adjustments (perhaps with some negotiation) before giving a low level connectionist translation of the high level intentions. Given a subsumption architecture, low level and high level intention formation and execution can occur in parallel.

1.7 Communication Theory

1.7.1 Syntax

To illustrate how the representational semantics works we develop the pragmatic interpretation for a small temporal propositional language fragment we will call L_{Pt}. The language L_{Pt} will include logical and temporal connectives: $\wedge$ (= and), $\vee$ (= or), $\neg$ (= not), $\wedge\Rightarrow$ (= and then), $while$ (= while). From $atomic\ formulas$ p and q we build up $complex\ formulas$ $\alpha \wedge \beta$, $\alpha \vee \beta$, $\neg\alpha$, $\alpha \wedge\Rightarrow \beta$, and $\alpha\ while\ \beta$ in the usual way where we distinguish between $directives$ $\alpha!$ and $assertions$ α.

1.7.2 Representational Semantics

A theory of the meaning of speech acts is a theory of how the representations of the agent are updated by the communicative process. The propositional content of the speech act is given by a situation semantics in the style of [Barwise and Perry 1983]. Below we will assume that there is an interpretation function $Ref(p)$ whose value is the situation or event referred to by the atomic sentence p (see [Werner 1988a]). Ref gives the propositional content of basic sentences. Unlike Barwise and Perry, we use situation semantics to give a metadescription of the cognitive representations that the agent has of its world and not of the world itself.

The theory of how representational or cognitive states are transformed by messages is called the $pragmatics$ or $representational\ semantics$. Given a language L we define a pragmatic operator $Prag$, where for each sentence α in L, $Prag(\alpha)$ is a function from Rep into Rep. Thus $Prag$ takes a given subrepresentational state such as I in R and transforms it into a new substate $I' = Prag(\alpha)(I)$.

1.7.3 Pragmatic Interpretation of Assertions

For any formula $\alpha \in L$, $Prag(\alpha) : Rep \Rightarrow Rep$ is a function that distributes over the representational state $R \in Rep$ subject to the constraints that for all $I \in INF$, $S \in INT$, and $V \in VAL$, then $Prag(\alpha)(I) \in INF$, $Prag(\alpha)(S) \in INT$, and $Prag(\alpha)(V) \in VAL$, respectively. We assume $Holds(\alpha, H, \tau)$ is defined by induction where for atomic formulas $Holds(\alpha, H, \tau)$ if the situation referred to by α, i.e., $Ref(\alpha)$, is realized in H over time period τ. $Prag$ must additionally satisfy other conditions: for atomic assertions $Prag(\alpha)(I) = \{H^t : H^t \in I$ and $Ref(\alpha)$ is realized in $H\}$.

Let $Prag$ be defined for the formulas α and β. $Prag$ acts on information states as follows:

1. $Prag(\alpha \wedge \beta)(I) = Prag(\alpha)(I) \cap Prag(\beta)(I)$

2. $Prag(\alpha \vee \beta)(I) = Prag(\alpha)(I) \cup Prag(\beta)(I)$

3. $Prag(\neg \alpha)(I) = I - Prag(\alpha)(I)$

4. $Prag(\alpha \wedge\Rightarrow \beta)(I) = \{H^t : H^t \in I$ and $\exists$ time periods τ_0, $\tau' \in TP$ where $Holds(\alpha, H, \tau_0)$ and $Holds(\beta, H, \tau')$ and $\tau_0 < \tau'\}$

5. $Prag(\alpha \ while \ \beta)(I) = \{H^t : H^t \in I$ and $\forall \tau_0$, $\tau' \in TP$, if τ_0 contains τ' then if $Holds(\beta, H, \tau')$ then $Holds(\alpha, H, \tau_0)\}$

For example, the pragmatic interpretation of the sentence $\alpha =$ 'Jon opened the door' is arrived at as follows: α refers to the event of Jon opening the door. $Prag(\alpha)$ is an operator on the hearer's information state I such that $Prag(\alpha)I$ is the reduction of the set I to those histories where the event referred to by α occurred. The hearer A knows α if α holds in all the worlds in I. Thus, A comes to know that α as a result of receiving and interpreting the message α.

1.7.4 Pragmatic Interpretation of Directives

For atomic directives $Prag(\alpha!)(S) = \{\pi : \pi \in S$ and $\forall H \in \pi^*$, $Ref(\alpha!)$ is realized in $H\}$. Given $Prag$ is defined for directives $\alpha!$ and $\beta!$, then for complex formulas $Prag$ acts on the intentional substates as follows:

1. $Prag(\alpha! \wedge \beta!)(S) = Prag(\alpha!)(S) \cap Prag(\beta!)(S)$

2. $Prag(\alpha! \vee \beta!)(S) = Prag(\alpha!)(S) \cup Prag(\beta!)(S)$

16

3. $Prag(\neg\alpha!)(S) = S - Prag(\alpha!)(S)$

4. $Prag(\alpha! \quad \wedge\Rightarrow \beta!)(S) = \{\pi : \forall H \in \pi^* \text{ and } \exists \text{ time periods } \tau_0, \tau' \in TP \text{ where}$ $Holds(\alpha!, H, \tau_0) \text{ and } Holds(\beta!, H, \tau') \text{ and } \tau_0 < \tau'\}$

5. $Prag(\alpha! \ while \ \beta!)(S) = \{\pi : \forall H \in \pi^*, \exists \text{ time periods } \tau, \tau' \in TP \text{ such that}$ $Holds(\alpha!, H, \tau) \text{ and } Holds(\alpha!, H, \tau') \text{ and } \tau' \text{ contains } \tau\}$.

For example, if $\alpha! = $ 'Open the door', $\alpha!$ refers to the situation of the addressee A opening the door. $Prag(\alpha!)$ operates on A's intentional state S_A such that A opens the door. $Prag$ does this by removing all those possible plans of A that do not force $\alpha!$. And those are the plans π that have some world $H \in \pi^*$ where the situation referred to by $\alpha!$ is not realized in H. Viewed constructively, a plan is incrementally built up by the $Prag$ algorithm. The result is that the agent performs the directive in parallel with other goals he may have.

Note that $Prag$ describes the *pragmatic competence* of an ideal speaker and not the actual performance. He may for various reasons not accept the message. There is nothing in our account that would force the recipient of a command to automatically or mechanically obey that command. That will depend on the power relations and many other factors. Similarly, nothing in our account would force the recipient to believe an informative, and, without reflection, update the information state. But for him to understand the conventional meaning of the assertion or directive, the agent must know what the effect of the message is supposed to be if he were to accept it. Thus, a participant will have not just actual informational and intentional states I and S, but also hypothetical representational states III and HS that are used to compute the pragmatic effect of a given message. If the participant then accepts the message, III or HS becomes a part of the representational state $R = (I, S, V)$.

1.7.5 Pragmatic Operators

The interpretation of utterances is actually more complicated. Associated with a given formula α are several operators that give different kinds of information. Let $f_\alpha = Prag(\alpha)$ be the *interpretation* of α. To describe the *act of saying* α we introduce another operator, act_α, which is the operator giving the infomation that α was just said. $Time_\alpha$ is the *time operator* that shifts time according to how long it took to say α. Here we assume for simplicity that the act of uttering α takes one unit of time. We could of course relativize the time operator to α. Note, $Time_\alpha Time_\alpha \neq Time_\alpha$. Combining operators, $act_\alpha Time_\alpha$ is then the act of uttering α. Note, $act_\alpha Time_\alpha \neq Time_\alpha act_\alpha$. $f_\alpha act_\alpha Time_\alpha$ is the act of uttering and interpreting α . We are using the usual notation for operators where $f_\alpha act_\alpha Time_\alpha I_B = f_\alpha(act_\alpha(Time_\alpha(I_B)))$

We have several cases possible when A asserts the informative α to the audience B. The rightarrow "$\Rightarrow$" reads "is transformed into."

1. If B hears, understands, and accepts α then

   $I_B \Rightarrow f_\alpha act_\alpha Time_\alpha I_B$.

2. If B hears, but does not understand or accept α, but knows the syntactic string α and not some other string was uttered, then $I_B \Rightarrow act_\alpha Time_\alpha I_B$.

   Note that if α is a directive, then f_α acts on S_B and not on I_B. Yet it is known what was said. So here too, $I_B \Rightarrow act_\alpha Time_\alpha I_B$.

3. If B hears something was said and knows time has passed, but does not know what syntactic string was uttered, then $I_B \Rightarrow Time_\alpha I_B$.

4. More odd is the case where B does not hear α but gets the information of what was said subliminally and knows time passed. Then $I_B \Rightarrow f_\alpha Time_\alpha I_B$.

The full interpretation of α for the audience B depends on the force of α. Let $R_B = (I_B, S_B, V_B)$. Given that the message is accepted, some of the cases are as follows:

1. *Assertions*: $(I_B, S_B, V_B) \Rightarrow (f_\alpha act_\alpha Time_\alpha I_B, S_B, V_B)$

2. *Commands*: $(I_B, S_B, V_B) \Rightarrow (act_\alpha Time_\alpha I_B, f_\alpha S_B, V_B)$

3. *Statements of Intention*:

   $(I_B, S_B, V_B) \Rightarrow (act_\alpha Time_\alpha I_B, f_\alpha S_B^A, V_B)$

4. *Statements of Value*:

   $(I_B, S_B, V_B) \Rightarrow (act_\alpha Time_\alpha I_B, S_B, f_\alpha V_B^A)$

One can simplify matters by suppressing the action operator act_α as well as the time operator $Time_\alpha$ where the above cases indicate the form of a more complete description. Note too, that the discourse situation d can be viewed as yet another operator acting on the information state I_{agent} of the agents A, B. Since there are points of view, it is clear that the operator d is also a function of the agent and, more generally, of the role of the agent. Similarly, as we will see, the pragmatic operator is also a function of the role of the agent in question. For the extension of the above communication theory to the theory of speech acts see [Werner 1988b].

1.8   Social Cooperation and Communication

1.8.1   Overview

Social action is made possible by the communication of state information and process information. State information is relayed by informative speech acts. Process information is relayed by directive speech acts. The social act, abstractly viewed, results from the composition of the agents' strategies.

Intuitively, at the lowest level, the use of directives by an agent to control another can be viewed as a form of incremental plan passing. The plan is passed by messages that in effect are a coding for the construction of the plan or, more generally, a strategy. The recipient, if he understands the conventional meaning of the message, interprets the directive $\alpha!$ as a partial strategy. We can view the pragmatic effect of $\alpha!$ as either reducing the possible plans that guide actions of the agent, i.e., the set S or, equivalently, building up the intentional state of the agent.

Informatives are a way to pass state information and help to achieve a goal by either fulfilling the informational preconditions of an action required by a strategy, and, thereby, creating strategic abilities [Werner 1988d], or by acting as a form of indirect speech act [Allen 1979] where the sender gives information that the recipient uses to rationally deduce what the sender wants (see Section 1.3). Once interpreted, the indirect speech act pragmatically acts like a directive that sets up the intentional state of the recipient. We now present a slightly more formal account of cooperation.

1.8.2   Types of Communicative Cooperation

Social action demands different levels of communicational complexity and structure. The simplest case is a *master-slave relationship* with one-way communication. One agent A uses a directive $\alpha!$ to control the actions of the recipient B. It works because the message is given a pragmatic interpretation $Prag(\alpha!)$, which operates on the intentional state S_B in such a way that $Prag(\alpha!)S_B$ forces the desired goal, i.e., $Prag(\alpha!)S_B \parallel\Rightarrow g_A$. An intentional state S *forces a goal* g, $S \parallel\Rightarrow g$, iff $\forall \pi \in S$, π forces g, i.e., iff $\forall H \in \pi^*$, g is realized in H. A may also communicate state information β to B to fulfill informational preconditions required by a strategy or to perform an indirect speech act.

More complex is the case of *one-way cooperation* where A communicates $\alpha!$ to B so that $Prag(\alpha!)S_B + S_A \parallel\Rightarrow g_A$. By definition the composite $S + S'$ of two intentional states S, S' together *force* a goal g, in symbols, $S + S' \parallel\Rightarrow g$ iff $\forall \pi \in S$, $\pi_0 \in S'$, and $\forall H \in \pi^* \cap \pi_0^*$, g is realized in H. In other words, A sets up B's intentions so that when combined with A's intentions, their actions together achieve A's goal g_A.

Still more complex is the case of *mutual cooperation* where A and B have a mutual exchange of directives and informatives before proceeding to act. The mutual exchange results in a conversational history $h_\Theta = \Theta_1, \ldots, \Theta_n$ where each Θ is either a directive or an informative speech act that includes information about the speaker and addressee in the discourse situation d. The pragmatically interpreted conversation $Prag(h_\Theta) = Prag(\Theta_1) Prag(\Theta_2) \ldots Prag(\Theta_n)$ then results in the mutual goal $g_{A,B}$, i.e., $Prag(h_\Theta)R_B + Prag(h_\Theta)R_A \parallel \Rightarrow g_{A,B}$.

When there are inconsistencies between intentional states, the composition of intentional states requires a phase of conflict resolution. The resolution of the conflict may be intraagent or interagent. The process of interagent conflict resolution is called *negotiation*. Negotiation leads to intraagent conflict resolution in one or more of the agents. In *intraagent conflict resolution* a single agent resolves the conflict by readjusting his own intentions to fit those of the other agents. Prior intentions, the degree of cooperativity, the degree of commitment, and the evaluations are inputs to a rational decision making process that determines how that intraagent adjustment is made. If the relaxation of goals with replanning does not lead to consistent intentional states then a coopertive agent may give up goals below some threshold utility. The normatively contrained agent (see §9.9 below) will have additional restrictions placed on his cooperativity.

1.9   Social Roles and Structures

Communication has a cost. It takes time to build up the mutual intentional states of the agents through communicaton. This process of building up cooperative intentions has been called learning, training, and programming. All these processes are too costly to repeat anew whenever cooperation is required. Indeed, most complex social goals would be impossible to achieve. Efficient, sophisticated, and permanent societal cooperation is made possible by the formation of social structures.

1.9.1   Social Roles

As we will see, a *social structure* ΣT can be viewed as a set of social roles $\Sigma T = \{\text{rol}_1, \ldots, \text{rol}_n\}$. A *social role*, **rol**, is a description of an abstract agent $R_{\text{rol}} = < I_{\text{rol}}, S_{\text{rol}}, V_{\text{rol}} >$ that defines the state information, permissions, responsibilities, and values of that agent role. When an agent A assumes a role **rol** , he internalizes that role by constraining his representational state R_A to $R_A + R_{\text{rol}}$. Positively expressed, when an agent A assumes a role **rol**, he changes his representational state so that R_{rol} becomes part of R_A.

1.9.2   The Role of Agent

Note, being an *agent* is itself a role $\mathbf{rol}_{\mathbf{agent}}$ whose intentional and informational states must satisfy certain minimal constraints. The role of agent specifies that the agent has a cognitive structure $< I_{\mathbf{agent}}, S_{\mathbf{agent}}, V_{\mathbf{agent}} >$ and has the ability to perform actions in the environment Ω. Furthermore, the agent has a communicative competence, i.e., is able to speak and understand a semantically and pragmatically interpreted language L.

1.9.3   Roles and Plans

Without its informational and evaluational components, a role $\mathbf{rol}_A$ of an agent A is an *intentional substate* of the agent's overall intentional state S_A. Such an intentional substate can be formalized as a subset of possible strategies governing the agent's behavior. A set of such strategies S generates a *general partial strategy* $\Pi(S)$ where $\Pi(S)(I) = \cup_{\pi \in S} \pi(I)$ when S consists of pure strategies (see [Werner 1988d]). A role $\mathbf{rol}_A$ of an agent A then generates a general partial strategy $\Pi(\mathbf{rol}_A)$. Analogous to strategies, a role can force a goal; we can now refer to the potential of a role. The *potential* $\mathbf{rol}_A^*$ of a role consists of the possible histories that are compatible with that role.

　　Role relations: Role relations link roles. Significant types of role relations are *coupled to*, *depends on*, *dominates*, *subrole*, *specializes*, *conflicts with*, *compatible with*, and *generates*.

1.9.4   Properties of Roles

Since roles are a type of intentional state roles share all the properties of intentional states indicated above. Specifically, roles are compositional, dynamic, linguistically modifiable, partial, and govern behavior. Linguistic roles are also possible.

1.9.5   Communicative Roles

The types of communicative cooperation described above already presuppose the mutual acceptance of fundamental *communicative roles* $\mathbf{crol}_{agent}$ by the agents. As shown below in §12, in the *Master-Slave social structure* $\Sigma T_{Master-Slave} = < \mathbf{rol}_{Master}, \mathbf{rol}_{Slave} >$, the role of the master $\mathbf{rol}_{Master}$ contains the expectation that the master tells the slave what to do; thus, this expectation is a communicative subrole $\mathbf{crol}_{Master}$ of $\mathbf{rol}_{Master}$. The role of a slave $\mathbf{rol}_{Slave}$ carries the expectation that the slave follows the instructions of the master. Thus, the slave also has a communicative subrole $\mathbf{crol}_{Slave}$. Both the slave and master roles contain $\mathbf{rol}_{agent}$ as a subrole. The role of agent already contains a communicative subrole $\mathbf{crol}_{agent}$. The communicative roles $\mathbf{crol}_{Master}$ and $\mathbf{crol}_{Slave}$ are further specializations of $\mathbf{crol}_{agent}$. Thus the master is at least a communicative agent and the slave must be able to understand the instructions and execute them. The master and slave roles are tightly coupled in that each role depends on the other.

1.9.6 Roles as Rule Sets

We have defined intentional state as a set of strategies, and this set generates a partial strategy that governs the actions of the agent. A partial strategy is a partial function. Functions can be represented by a set of *if-then* rules. Hence, a strategy can be seen as a set of rules that determine the behavior of the agent. Therefore, an intentional state can be described by a set of rules. We can thus explicitly model various roles by rule sets.

In the case of linguistic roles, dialogue rule sets determine the linguistic strategies of the agent. A common core of rules describes the basic linguistic competence of an agent. In the case of one agent being a consultation system that is engaging in a consultation dialogue with a user-agent, the system can assume various dialogue specific roles by switching roles, i.e., dialogue rule sets. We envision systems that can adjust cooperatively, both linguistically and nonlinguistically, by assuming different roles in different situations. In fact, we integrated some of these ideas in the WISBER project [Bergmann and Gerlach 1987], [Werner 1989b].

1.9.7 Multiple Roles

Let *RoleCapacity(A)* be the set of possible roles that agent A can assume. Thus if rol_i is in *RoleCapacity*(A), then A is capable of doing the actions required by that role. *RoleCapacity*(A) is a time-dependent function since A may gain more role capabilities through learning and training. Also, A need not be capable of assuming all roles in *RoleCapacity*(A) simultaneously.

An agent normally assumes several roles $\text{rol}_A^1, \ldots, \text{rol}_A^k$, where these are part of *RoleCapacity*(A). Let *Roles*$(A) = \text{rol}_A^1, \ldots, \text{rol}_A^k$ be the set of roles agent A assumes. *Roles*$(A) \subseteq$ *RoleCapacity*(A). Since each role rol_A^i in *Roles*(A) generates a partial strategy $\Pi(\text{rol}_A^i)$, the set of *Roles*(A) itself generates a partial strategy $\Pi($*Roles*$(A))$ that describes the agent's overall intentional role state: it describes the agent's intentions as constrained by all his roles.

Given a group G of m agents $A = 1, \ldots, m$, a *role distribution* is the function *Roles* that assigns to each agent in G a set of roles *Roles*(A). The *group role GRol*$(G) = \{$*Roles*$(A) : A \in G\}$ is then the complete *multiagent intentional role state* of the social structure with the given role distribution.

1.9.8   Role Expectations, Projections, and Cooperation

Since agents have representations of not only their own roles but also partial representations of the roles of other agents, an agent has role expectations about another agent's behaviour. Roles may have associated sanctions imposed by the social structure if an agent does not fulfill his role. Formally, a *role expectation* is a role representation $\mathbf{rol}_B^A$ that an agent B has of another agent A's role $\mathbf{rol}_A$. We also say that B *projects* the role $\mathbf{rol}_B^A$ onto A. In so far as agent A's role $\mathbf{rol}_A$ has sanctions associated with it, these sanctions can be viewed as role expectations $\mathbf{sanction} - \mathbf{rol}_A^B(\mathbf{rol}_A)$ that A has of those other agents B. Here, A projects onto B the sanction role. Thus, roles with sanctions are strongly coupled to other sanction roles.

A may also have a representation of the role that B expects A to fulfill. This can be represented as $\mathbf{rol}_A^{BA}$. We call these A's *projected expectations*. If A has an active cooperative role $\mathbf{coop} - \mathbf{rol}$ with regard to B, $\mathbf{rol}_A^{BA}$ may become a demand or norm. The force of such projected expectations will depend on the degree and type of cooperativity required by the cooperative role.

Mutual role expectations, both positive and negative, and their accuracy make smooth, complex, permanent cooperative social activity possible. Put differently, there is a mutual representation of the other agents' roles as well as their own roles that, together with communication, allows the agents to achieve coordinated social action. Roles constrain the intentional states of the agents sufficiently so that communication does not have to bear all the weight of coordination.

1.9.9   The Normatively Constrained Agent

A social structure may have implicit and codified *laws* and *norms* that further define the intentional states of the agents as well as the roles of the social structure. These laws and norms have their effect by acting on the intentional states of the agents. The laws that apply to all persons define the role of $\mathbf{rol}_{legally\,responsible\,person}$, which defines the legal expectations the given society has of each of its members. Individuals with special roles are governed by additional laws and norms that further define those roles. Since roles are compositional, one can imagine constructing agents (such as cooperative systems or robots) that are locally cooperative with other agents, and at at the same time are sufficiently constrained by higher priority norms. The advantage is that global social interests are not endangered by excessive local cooperation between agents.

1.9.10   The Duality of Roles and Models of the Other

Since roles are just a constrained representational state, a role determines the strategic actions of an agent or serves as a model of the other agent. Thus the same mental structure can function in two distinct ways. For example, a child that observes the reactions of one of its parents builds up an intention-model of the strategies used by that parent in various situations. When the child internalizes that model by identifying with the parent, the childs intentional state incorporates the parent model. The new intentional state of the child then deals with those situations as the parent would have. Similarly, a robot may attain new roles by observing the reactions of other agents in situations, building up a model of the intentional substate of the other agents in those situations, and then modifying its own intentional state by identification and internalization of those intention-models or roles.

1.10   Social Structures and Social Groups

1.10.1   Static Social Groups

A *social structure* ΣT is defined to be a set of social roles $\Sigma T = \{\mathbf{rol_1}, ..., \mathbf{rol_n}\}$ in a given environment Ω relative to a language L.

A *social group* $\Sigma\Gamma = <L, G, \Sigma T, Roles, \Omega>$ consists of

1. A language L

2. A group of agents G that satisfy the agent role $\mathbf{rol}_{agent}$

3. A social structure ΣT

4. A distribution function of roles, *Roles*, on G with the restriction that: if $\mathbf{rol}_i \in Roles(A)$, then $\mathbf{rol}_i \in RoleCapacity(A) \cap \Sigma T$

5. An environment Ω.

A social group is a set of agents, each with a set of roles and a common language and environment. The roles are such that the composition of $Roles(Agent_i)$ for each $Agent_i$ in G forces the social goals.

1.10.2   Dynamic Social Groups

A *dynamic social structure* ΣT_t is defined to be a time dependent function ΣT whose value, $\Sigma T_t = \{\mathbf{rol_1}, \ldots, \mathbf{rol_n}\}$ is a set of roles for given time t, in a given environment Ω, and relative to a language L. Thus a social structure is a dynamic entity that can vary with time and situation.

A *dynamic social group* $\Sigma\Gamma_t = < L, G_t, \Sigma T_t, Roles_t, \Omega >$ consists of

1. A language L

2. A dynamic set of agents G_t , i.e., a function G from time instants in T to sets of agents who satisfy the agent role

3. A dynamic social structure ΣT_t

4. A distribution function of roles $Roles_t$ on G with the restriction

   if $\mathbf{rol}_i \in Roles_t(A)$, then $\mathbf{rol}_i \in RoleCapacity_t(A) \cap \Sigma T_t$

5. An environment Ω.

A social group $\Sigma\Gamma$ is a dynamic social group $\Sigma\Gamma_t$ when G, ΣT , and *Roles* are time dependent functions. At any instant t, the *state of the social group* is given by $\Sigma T_t = <$ $L, G_t, \Sigma T_t, Roles_t, \Omega >$ relative to $RoleCapacity_t$. G is a function from time instants to sets of agents, ΣT_t gives a set of roles for each time t. $Roles(A, t) = Roles_t(A)$ gives the set of roles of the agent A at time t.

Note that while $Roles(A, t)$ is a function that assigns roles to agents, this does not necessarily mean that role assignment is computed externally or globally. The agent's local representational state may determine what roles are active. An example of local role determination is the contract net protocol (see §11 below). Roles themselves may have preconditions that determine when they become active. And they may have termination conditions that specify when they become deactive.

It becomes apparent that the social group can vary along each of the following five dynamic dimensions: (1) The set of agents G in the group may vary. (2) The roles defining the social structure ΣT may vary. Thus the social structure may vary. (3) Since each agent, by definition, assumes the agent role, each of the agents has a time-dependent information and intentional state. (4) The other roles a given agent assumes may vary since the role distribution function may vary with time. The greater the role capacity of each of the agents the greater the flexibility of the group. If each agent can assume all group roles in ΣT , then there can be rapid role taking and switching as the situation demands. (5) The environment Ω consists of worlds that vary with time. The only time independent structure is the language L. But that is not an essential limitation.

1.10.3 Role Change

There are three forms of dynamism. First, role change is possible by *role switching*. The role distribution function may switch agents' roles in a social structure. Rapid role switching is possible if the agents can assume a variety of roles in ΣT. Second, the social structure may change within the limits of the agents' role capacities. Third, the *role capacity* of an agent may change, by (a) acquiring new roles and abilities through programming, learning, or observation (a costly, time consuming process); (b) modifying a given role by communication using the *Prag* operator; and (c) generating a role by a combination of role composition and subtraction with other roles, called *Rapid Role Prototyping*. Roles can be constructed rapidly if the agent has a repertoire of subroles and abilities. Once constructed they can be refined by programming and communication to meet particular needs. Rapid Prototyped Roles may exist temporarily or situationally, constructed as the need arises, or they may be added to the repertoire (RoleCapacity) and thus become habitual.

The *origin of a role* results from the communicative interchange between the agent and other agents. Learning a role is a complex communicative process that may involve training. Once a role is learned it becomes part of the agent's repertoire of possible intentional substates. If a role is part of the agent's role repertoire, then it can be used as a subrole in the formation of more complex roles. Once a role is accepted it becomes part of the permanent intentional state of the agent. In the case of a robot, learning a role may involve programming the role through a combination of high (task-level) and low level programs, communicative feedback, and guidance.

In some cases, agents in a DAI system may transfer roles to other agents the way other programs are transferred over a network. Then role transfer can be almost immediate. And, with such communicative possibilities, roles can be 'learned' as quickly as the communication channel allows. This special case assumes that at least one of the agents has the role in memory. If the communication is fast enough, then to the outside world the agents' will appear to all have the same role capacity even though only some of the agents actually have the role in memory at any given time.

We have not mentioned possible situations in defining the above functions. Yet it is clear that the roles a given agent assumes depends on the group situation. Situation based role taking makes agents flexible. Furthermore, once the robot has a basic repertoire of roles, more rapid development of complex roles is possible. This leads to the idea of a calculus of roles that can be combined creatively to form new roles as the situation demands.

1.11 The Contract Net as a Social Group

1.11.1 What is a Contract Net?

Described in terms of our theory, a *contract net* [Smith 1980], [Davis and Smith 1983] consists of a group of distributed agents called *nodes* that communicate (negotiate) to solve a problem jointly by task sharing. Every agent has the same communicative competence, i.e., every agent is capable of accepting and assigning tasks. Every agent has the same social competence; each agent can take on all possible roles. The agents can take on the role of *manager* (who announces contracts, evaluates and accepts bids, supervises task execution, and processes the result of the execution) or the role of *contractor* (who makes bids and executes tasks in contracts). These roles are taken up dynamically during the course of problem solving. A node may take on both roles simultaneously for distinct contracts.

The *agents* in a contract net have representational states. The information state I_{node} at a given time t is given by the agent's local database of facts at time t. The intentional state S_{node} of the agent is given by its procedures and their current processing state. The intentional state also contains the *roles* that are specified by the procedures. The evaluative state V_{node} is given by portions of procedures that evaluate task announcements, bids, and task awards. The strategies that constitute intentions can be implemented as procedures. The various types of conditional responses of a strategy are reflected in the conditional statements of the associated procedures.

The *protocol* is a metalevel description of the message types (speech acts), the communicative strategies, and the roles of the agents. The contract net protocol specification is a syntactic description of the possible messages allowed in the communication between nodes. By itself this is not very profound. What makes the contract net so interesting and novel is that the protocol specification is given an intuitive procedural semantic description. With each message is associated a set of procedures that interpret and generate the messages for a given node. Viewed from our theoretical perspective, the messages are given a pragmatic interpretation by indicating how they effect and are generated by the informational and intentional states of a node. The procedures interpreting the protocol messages are implicit descriptions of linguistic and task intentional states.

1.11.2 The Contract Net Social Group

A *Contract Net Social Group* is a social group
$$\Sigma\Gamma_{ContractNet} = <L_{CNet}, G, \Sigma T_{CNet}, Roles, \Omega_{CNet} > \text{ where the following holds:}$$

1. The *language* L_{CNet}

(a) *Syntax*: The language L_{CNet} consists of

   i. Task/Bid Specifications: $Task, Task_1, Task_2, \ldots, Task_n$

   ii. Speech act types: *Task-Announcement, Bid, Award*

   iii. Messages: If T is a task/bid specification and SA is a speech act type, then $SA(T)$ is a message of L_{CNet}. These are the only messages in L_{CNet}.

The language L_{CNet} contains the messages as specified by the contract net protocol specification in [Smith 1980, Figure 5, page 1111]. Specifcally, L_{CNet} contains messages of the following types: *Task-Announcement, Bid*, and *Announced-Award* (not in the basic implementation and not included here: *Directed-Award, Acceptance, Refusal, Request, Information, Termination, Node-Available, Interim-Report*, and *Final-Report*). These are speech act types that contain task and bid specifications. We simplify the example by identifying task and bid specifications, referring to them by *Task*. For example, a bid is of the form *Bid(Task)*, where *Bid* is the speech act type and *Task* is the bid/task specification.

(b) The *referential interpretation*: $Ref(Task) \subseteq Actions$. $Ref(Task)$ consists of the possible action-situations of doing the task. In [Smith 1980] this is done by a task processor, part of a node, that carries out the computation associated with user tasks.

(c) The *pragmatic interpretation*: Given information state $I_{Contractor}$,

   i. $Prag(Task - Announcement(Task))(LS_{Contractor}) =$
$LS'_{Contractor}$
The *Task-Announcement* message acts on the linguistic-cognitive intentional state $LS_{Contractor}$ of a potential contractor node. The new intentional state $LS'_{Contractor}$ is defined by the Announcement Ranking and Bid procedures.

   ii. $Prag(Bid(Task))(LS_{Manager}) = LS'_{Manager}$
When it receives a bid, the Manager node updates its intentional state $LS_{Manager}$ by activating the Bid Ranking and Award procedures.

   iii. $Prag(Bid(Task))LS^{Contractor}_{Manager} = LS'^{Contractor}_{Manager}$
On receiving the bid, Bid(*Task*) the manager knows that the contractor has the intention of doing the task if the contractor sends a contract award. While such nested representations of the intentions of other agents were not in Smith's original work, they may be useful for more complex cooperative tasks.

   iv. $Prag(Award(Task))(S_{Contractor}) = S'_{Contractor} = \{\pi : \pi \in S_{Contractor}$ and

$\forall H \in \pi^* \cap I^*_{Contractor}$, $\exists a \in Ref(Task)$ such that $Agent(a) = Contractor$, $Time(a) > Time(I_{Contractor})$ and a is realized in H}.

The award of the task is a command from the manager that directly modifies the intentions of the contractor node. It does so by activating the Execution procedure. Or, put in strategic terms, the *Prag* operator is such that it updates the intentional state of the Contractor $S_{Contractor}$ such that $Prag(Award(Task))S_{Contractor}$ is the reduction of $S_{Contractor}$ to those strategies $\pi \in S_{Contractor}$ where the Contractor carries out the task described by $Ref(Task)$.

v. $Prag(Award(Task))(S^{Contractor}_{Manager}) \supseteq$
$Prag(Award(Task))(S_{Contractor})$
Furthermore, $Prag(Award(Task))(S^{Contractor}_{Manager}) \parallel \Rightarrow Task$
The Manager expects that the Contractor intends to do the awarded task. Again, this is not explicitly represented by Smith.

2. The *set of agents* $G = \{n : n$ is a node $\}$ where the information state I of an agent is a local database of facts. The intentional state S is implicitly defined by procedures that interpret and react to messages. The evaluative state V is given by procedures that evaluate announcements and bids. Roles determine which of these procedures is active.

3. The *contract net social structure* $\Sigma T_{Manager-Contractor} =$
$< \mathbf{rol}_{Manager}, \mathbf{rol}_{Contractor} >$. Here, $\mathbf{rol}_{Manager}$ and $\mathbf{rol}_{Contractor}$ contain $\mathbf{crol}_{Manager}$ and $\mathbf{crol}_{Contractor}$ as communicative subroles. The roles $\mathbf{rol}_{Manager}$ and $\mathbf{rol}_{Contractor}$ are such that the Manager announces and awards tasks. The Contractor makes bids and carries out awarded tasks. The roles are implemented as procedures in CNET.

4. The *role distribution function Roles* is a time and situation dependent function defined on G: $Roles_{t,s}(node) = \mathbf{rol}_{Manager}$ or $\mathbf{rol}_{Contractor}$ depending on time t and situation s.

5. Ω_{CNet} is the *space of all possible histories* of the system.

1.11.3 Discussion: What is a Protocol?

Traditionally, a protocol specifies who can say what to whom and the possible reactions to what is said by the other party. Smith gives a formal syntactic specification of the contract net protocol by defining the possible types of messages that can be sent. Informally, he describes the semantics and pragmatics of the messages, as well as the linguistic role strategies, by describing the procedures that determine the reactions of an agent to any given message. These reactions may include generating a new message. Implicitly, the agents take on roles when they have unfulfilled goals or tasks. A protocol specification does more than just specifying possible messages. The explicit syntactic protocol specification is a small part of the overall description.

Hidden in a protocol specification is a global architectural specification of the distributed system. This global architecture of the distributed system is what we call a social group. What we have done by translating the contract net protocol description into that of a formal social group is to make explicit the cognitive structure of the agents, the semantics and the pragmatics of the message language, the communicative strategies behind a protocol, the social roles taken by the nodes, and the social structure.

1.12   An Example Language Game

Consider a simple example of a master slave group of two persons, Mason and Apprentice, who hold the roles of master and slave, respectively. The language contains only one command *Brick!*, which means *Bring me a brick!* We can represent this formally as follows:

A *Master-Slave Group*($L_{Brick!}$) is a social group

$\Sigma\Gamma_{Master-Slave} = <L_{Brick!}, G, \Sigma T_{Master-Slave}, Roles, \Omega_{Brick!} >$ where the following holds:

1. The *language* $L_{Brick!}$

   (a) *Syntax*: The language $L_{Brick!} = \{Brick!\}$. $L_{Brick!}$ contains the single command *Brick!*, which is to mean *Bring me a brick!*

   (b) The *referential interpretation*: *Ref*(*Brick!*) $\subseteq$ *Actions*. *Ref*(*Brick!*) consists of the possible action-situations of bringing a brick.

   (c) The *pragmatic interpretation*:
   Given information state $I_{Apprentice}$, $Prag(Brick!)S_{Apprentice} = \{\pi : \pi \in S_{Apprentice}$ and $\forall H \in \pi^* \cap I^*_{Apprentice}, \exists a \in Ref(Brick!)$ such that $Agent(a) = Apprentice$, $Time(a) > Time(I_{Apprentice})$ and a is realized in $H\}$.

   The *Prag* operator is such that it updates the intentional state of the apprentice $S_{Apprentice}$ such that $Prag(Brick!)S_{Apprentice}$ is the reduction of $S_{Apprentice}$ to those strategies where the Apprentice brings a brick from the pile.

2. The *set of agents* $G = \{Mason, Apprentice\}$, where R_{Mason} and $R_{Apprentice}$ each specialize the agent role $\mathbf{rol}_{agent}$.

3. The *social structure* $\Sigma T_{Master-Slave} = <\mathbf{rol}_{Master}, \mathbf{rol}_{Slave}>$. Here, $\mathbf{rol}_{Master}$ and $\mathbf{rol}_{Slave}$ contain $\mathbf{crol}_{Master}$ and $\mathbf{crol}_{Slave}$ as communicative subroles (see above). The roles $\mathbf{rol}_{Master}$ and $\mathbf{rol}_{Slave}$ are such that the Master gives the order to the Slave and the slave obeys. In effect, these roles update the communicative and cognitive intentions of the agents so that the Master gives and the Slave follows commands.

4. The *role distribution function Roles* is defined on G: $Roles(Mason) = \mathbf{rol}_{Master}$ and $Roles(Apprentice) = \mathbf{rol}_{Slave}$

5. $\Omega_{Brick!}$ is an *environment* where there is a pile of bricks a short distance from the Mason with the Apprentice being able to bring bricks to the Mason.

The agents Mason and Apprentice fulfill the additional roles $\mathbf{rol}_{Mason}$ and $\mathbf{rol}_{Apprentice}$. They are further specializations of the master and slave roles. Note that a formalization of the Wittgensteinian language game *Brick!* has been achieved (see [Wittgenstein 1953]). It is a simple but fascinating example, since it provides a view of the interrelated functioning of language, mind, and social structure as a totality.

The society generated by the social structure is able to function because its agents $G = \{A_1, \ldots, A_n\}$ take on the communicative and social roles that achieve the societal goals $g_{society}$. The roles and laws are such that $Roles(A_1) + \cdots + Roles(A_n) \parallel \Rightarrow g_{society}$.

1.13 Further Applications to Distributed Systems

The experience gained from the construction of actual and simulated distributed systems is an invaluable source of empirical data for constructing theories about the nature of communication, cooperation, and organization. The multiagent systems designed and implemented by [Smith 1980], [Davis and Smith 1983], [Corkill and Lesser 1983], [Durfee and Lesser 1987], and [Gasser and Rouquette 1988] are based on ideas that are similar to the ones that we are trying to formalize within a general theory.

Gasser describes a simulated system of agents cooperating in a game against another group of agents [Gasser and Rouquette 1988]. The notion of agents having roles is used to give the system an organization. The metaphor used by Gasser is very close to our ideas. In the context of distributed problem solving, [Corkill and Lesser 1983] also used the notion of roles to describe organizational structuring. According to them, an *organizational structure* provides each agent with a high-level view of problem solving in the network by specifying a set of responsibilities and interaction patterns available to each agent. When we look at the way the organizational structure is implemented it becomes apparent that Corkill and Lesser had intuitions quite close to our own when we developed the formal

31

definition of social structure based on social roles. There is a correspondence between their organizational structure and our formal definition of social structure. Furthermore, their set of node responsibilities and interaction patterns are instances of our more abstract formal definition of a social role.

However, in the implementation the roles are only implicitly given by the setting of thresholds and weight parameters associated with "interest areas." In a later work, [Durfee and Lesser 1987] generalize the idea of interest areas with the idea of partial global plans, node plans, and local plans of nodes. Local plans correspond roughly to the local strategies of an agent. Node plans are the way local plan information is communicated betwen nodes. Thus, node plans correspond, roughly, to our directive messages that give process information. Partial global plans ($PGP's$) combine local plans into a more global view. Thereby, $PGP's$ correspond, roughly, to our intentional superstates, the composition of agents' local intentions. However, no formal or systematic account of communication, intention, social organization, or cooperation is given by Durfee and Lesser.

Thus, while there are many points of similarity and contact between previous work in distributed systems and our theory, it should be emphasized that previous work in distributed systems did not have any explicit theory of intention, nor is there an explicit theory of communication and how that changes information and intentional states. There is also no explicit formal theory of social organization and cooperation. The combination of experience and expertise gained by distributed system builders, together with a more systematic theoretical foundation, should lead to future developments in distribued artificial intelligence.

1.14   Conclusion

We have developed a theory of linguistic communication as well as a theory of social structure that explains social cooperation. We did this by developing a formal account of the agent's knowledge states, specifically its intentional states. The pragmatic interpretation links the linguistic message with its effect on the planning process as defined by the intentional state. It becomes possible to build up intentional states of unlimited complexity. This allows us to give an account of social cooperative action, because the intentional states of the agents are mutually modified by a communicative exchange, i.e., a conversation or discourse. Intentional states are also central to our theory about the nature of social roles and social structures. The theory of intentional states makes possible our attempt to provide a unified theory of communication and social structure, because the intentional states are set up by communication in conjunction with social structures in such a way that the social goal is achievable. The theory of communication and social structure was applied to give a formal analysis of the contract net protocol and a Wittgensteinian language game.

We have provided a general theoretical framework for designing systems with a communicative and social competence. Our theory integrates situation semantics into a broader theory of pragmatic meaning, and fits well with planning models in robotics. It also fits well with discourse and speech act theories. Of more global significance is the fact that our theory of communication fits well with economic theory [von Neumann and Morgenstern 1947], [Myerson 1988]. We have attempted to provide a unified view of communication, cognitive states, and social structure in multiagent systems. This unified view will, hopefully, illuminate the complex relationship between language, mind, and society.

Acknowledgements

This work was in part supported by the BMFT and was part of the joint project WISBER. The WISBER partners include Nixdorf Computer AG, SCS GmbH, Siemens AG, Universitaet Hamburg, and Universitaet Saarbruecken. It was also in part supported by grants from Bowdoin College.

References

[Allen 1984] J. F. Allen, "Towards a General Theory of Action and Time," *Artificial Intelligence*, Vol. 23, 1984, pp. 123–154.

[Allen 1979] J. F. Allen, "A Plan-Based Approach to Speech Act Recognition," Ph.D. Thesis, Department of Computer Science, University of Toronto, 1979.

[Allen and Perrault 1980] J. F. Allen and C. R. Perrault, "Analyzing Intention in Utterances," *Artificial Intelligence*, Vol. 15, 1980, pp. 143–178.

[Appelt 1985] D. E. Appelt, *Planning English Sentences*, Cambridge University Press, New York, 1985.

[Barwise and Perry 1983] J. Barwise, and J. Perry, *Situations and Attitudes*, Bradford Books/MIT Press, 1983.

[Bergmann and Gerlach 1987] H. Bergmann and M. Gerlach, "Semantisch-pragmatische Verarbeitung von Ausserungen im natuerlichsprachlichen Beratungssystem WISBER," in: W. Brauer, W. Wahlster, eds., *Wissensbasierte Systeme, GI-Kongress 1987*, Springer Verlag, Berlin, 1987, pp. 318–327.

[Bratman 1987] M. Bratman, *Intention, Plans, and Practical Reason*, Harvard University Press, London 1987.

[Brooks 1982] R. A. Brooks, "Symbolic Error Analysis and Robot Planning," *International Journal of Robotics Research*, Vol. 1, No. 4, 1982, pp. 29–68.

[Brooks 1986] R. A. Brooks, "A Robust Layered Control System for a Mobile Robot," *IEEE Journal of Robotics and Automation*, Vol. RA-2, No. 1, 1986, pp. 14–23.

[Cohen 1978] P. R. Cohen, "On Knowing What to Say: Planning Speech Acts," Techn. Rep. 118, Department of Computer Science, University of Toronto, 1978.

[Cohen and Levesque 1987] P. R. Cohen, and H. Levesque, "Intention = Choice + Commitment," *Proceedings AAAI-87*, Seattle, WA, 1987, pp. 410–415.

[Cohen and Perrault 1979] P. R. Cohen, and C. R. Perrault, "Elements of a Plan-Based Theory of Speech Acts," *Cognitive Science*, Vol. 3, 1979, pp. 177–212.

[Corkill and Lesser 1983] D. D. Corkill, V. R. Lesser, "The Use of Meta-Level Control for Coordination in a Distributed Problem Solving Network," *Proc. 8th International Joint Conference on Artificial Intelligence*, Karlsruhe, Germany, 1983, pp. 748–756.

[Davis and Smith 1983] R. Davis, and R. G. Smith, "Negotiation as a Metaphor for Distributed Problem Solving," *Artificial Intelligence*, Vol. 20, 1983, pp. 63–109.

[Dijkstra 1968] E. W. Dijkstra, "Cooperating Sequential Processes," in F. Genuys, ed., *Programming Languages*, Academic Press, New York, 1968.

[Durfee and Lesser 1987] E. H. Durfee, and V. R. Lesser, "Using Partial Global Plans to Coordinate Distributed Problem Solvers," *Proceedings of the Tenth International Joint Conference on Artificial Intelligence*, 1987, pp. 875–883.

[Fagin *et al.* 1986] R. Fagin, J. Y. Halpern, and Y. V. Moshe, "What Can Machines Know? On the Epistemic Properties of Machines," *Proceedings AAAI-86*, Philadelphia, PA, 1986, pp. 428–434.

[Fikes and Nilsson 1971] R. E. Fikes, and N. J. Nilsson, "STRIPS: A New Approach to the Application of Theorem Proving to Problem Solving," *Artificial Intelligence*, Vol. 2, 1971, pp. 189–208.

[Galliers 1988] J. R. Galliers, "A Strategic Framework for Multi-Agent Cooperative Dialogue," *Proceedings 8th European Conference on Artificial Intelligence*, 1988, pp. 415–420.

[Gasser and Rouquette 1988] L. Gasser, and N. Rouquette, "Representing and Using Organizational Knowledge in Distributed AI Systems," USC Technical Report, *Proceedings Workshop on Distributed Artificial Intelligence*, Lake Arrowhead, California, May, 1988.

[Genesereth *et al.* 1986] M. R. Genesereth, M. L. Ginsberg, and J. S. Rosenchein, "Cooperation without Communication," *Proceedings AAAI-86*, 1986, pp. 561–567.

[Genesereth and Nilsson 1987] M. R. Genesereth, and N. J. Nilsson, *Logical Foundations of Artificial Intelligence*, Los Altos, CA, 1987.

[Georgeff 1983] M. Georgeff, "Communication and Interaction in Multi-agent Planning," *Proceedings AAAI-83*, 1983, pp. 125–129.

[Grosz 1985] B. J. Grosz, "The Structures of Discourse Structure," Technical Note 369, Artificial Intelligence Center, SRI International, Menlo Park, California, 1985.

[Grosz and Sidner, 1987] B. J. Grosz, C. L. Sidner, "Attention, Intentions, and the Structure of Discourse," *Computational Linguistics*, Vol. 12, No. 3, 1987, pp. 175–204.

[Halpern and Moses 1984] J. Y. Halpern, and Y. Moses, "Knowledge and Common Knowledge in a Distributed Environment," *Proceedings 3rd ACM Conference on Principles of Distributed Computing*, 1984, pp. 50–61.

[Halpern 1987] J. Halpern, "Using Reasoning About Knowledge to Analyze Distributed Systems," *Annual Reviews Computer Science*, 1987, pp. 37–68.

[Hewitt 1977] C. Hewitt, "Control Structures as Patterns of Passing Messages," *Artificial Intelligence*, Vol. 8, 1977, pp. 323–363.

[Hintikka 1962] J. Hintikka, *Knowledge and Belief*, Cornell University, Ithaca, New York, 1962.

[Hoare 1978] C. A. R. Hoare, "Communicating Sequential Processes," *Communications ACM*, Vol. 21, 1978, pp. 666–677.

[Lozano-Pérez 1983] T. Lozano-Pérez, "Robot Programming," *Proceedings IEEE*, Vol. 71, No. 7, 1983, pp. 821–841.

[Konolige 1980] K. Konolige, "A First-Order Formalization of Knowledge and Action for a Multiagent Planning System," Technical Note 232, Artificial Intelligence Center, SRI International, Menlo Park, California, 1980.

[Moore 1980] R. C. Moore, "Reasoning About Knowledge and Action," Technical Note 191, Artificial Intelligence Center, SRI International, Menlo Park, California, 1980.

[Myerson 1988] R. B. Myerson, "Credible Negotiation Statements and Coherent Plans," to appear in *Journal of Economic Theory*, 1988.

[Pednault 1985] E. P. D. Pednault, "Preliminary Report on a Theory of Plan Synthesis," Technical Note 358, Artificial Intelligence Center, SRI International, Menlo Park, California, 1985.

[Rosenschein 1986] J. S. Rosenschein, "Rational Interaction: Cooperation Among Intelligent Agents," Ph.D. Thesis, Stanford University, 1986.

[S. Rosenschein 1986] S. J. Rosenschein, "Formal Theories of Knowledge in AI and Robotics," Technical Note 362, Artificial Intelligence Center, SRI International, Menlo Park, California, 1986.

[Smith 1980] R. G. Smith, "The Contract Net Protocol: High-Level Communication and Control in a Distributed Problem Solver," *IEEE Transactions on Computers*, Vol. C-29, No. 12, 1980, pp. 1104–1113.

[Villain 1985] M. Villain, "The Restricted Language Architecture of a Hybrid Representation System," *Proceedings 9th International Joint Conference on Artificial Intelligence*, Los Angeles, CA, 1985, pp. 547–551.

[von Neumann and Morgenstern 1947] J. von Neumann and O. Morgenstern, *The Theory of Games and Economic Behavior*, Princeton University Press, Princeton, NJ, 1947.

[Werner 1988a] E. Werner, "Toward a Theory of Communication and Cooperation for Multiagent Planning," *Theoretical Aspects of Reasoning About Knowledge: Proceedings of the 2nd Conference*, Morgan Kaufman Publishers, 1988, pp. 129–142.

[Werner 1988b] E. Werner, "A Formal Computational Semantics and Pragmatics of Speech Acts," *COLING-88: Proceedings of the 12th International Conference on Computational Linguistics*, Budapest, Hungary, 1988.

[Werner 1988c] E. Werner, "Social Intentions," Panel on Interaction Among Intelligent Agents, *Proceedings of the 8th European Conference on Artificial Intelligence*, Munich, Germany, 1988, pp. 719–723.

[Werner 1988d] E. Werner, "Intention, Information and Ability: Outline of a Unified Theory," WISBER Report No. B37, University of Hamburg, West Germany, 1988.

[Werner 1989a] E. Werner, "The Modal Logic of Games," WISBER Report No. B48, University of Hamburg, West Germany, 1989.

[Werner 1989b] E. Werner, "Communication in WISBER," WISBER Report No. B51, University of Hamburg, West Germany, 1989.

[Werner 1989c] E. Werner, "Two Ways of Representing Knowledge," WISBER Report No. B44, University of Hamburg, West Germany, 1989.

[Wittgenstein 1953] L. Wittgenstein, *Philosophical Investigations*, Oxford, Basil Blackwell, 1953.

Eric Werner
Department of Computer Science
University of Hamburg
2000 Hamburg 50, West Germany
and
Department of Computer Science
Bowdoin College
Brunswick, Maine 04011

Chapter 2

The Structure of Ill-Structured Solutions: Boundary Objects and Heterogeneous Distributed Problem Solving

Susan Leigh Star

Abstract

The paper argues that the development of distributed artificial intelligence should be based on a social metaphor, rather than a psychological one. The Turing Test should be replaced by the "Durkheim Test," that is, systems should be tested with respect to their ability to meet community goals. Understanding community goals means analyzing the problem of due process in open systems. Due process means incorporating differing viewpoints for decision-making in a fair and flexible manner. It is the analog of the frame problem in artificial intelligence. From analyses of organizational problem solving in scientific communities, the paper derives the concept of boundary objects, and suggests that this concept would be an appropriate data structure for distributed artificial intelligence. Boundary objects are those objects that are plastic enough to be adaptable across multiple viewpoints, yet maintain continuity of identity. Four types of boundary object are identified: repositories, ideal types, terrain with coincident boundaries, and forms.

2.1 Introduction: Larger than Life and Twice as Natural

Artificial intelligence has long relied on natural and social metaphors in a variety of ways, ranging from a source of inspiration for design to attempts at modelling natural information processing.[1] Why?

The reasons have fallen roughly into two categories: attempts at intelligence and attempts at intelligibility. *Attempts at intelligence* have had as their long term goal the creation of a human or biological simulacrum—however that is defined—something that will pass the Turing Test. Metaphors have long been a way of bridging the enormous gap between the current capabilities of machines and the state of the art in computer science, and the complexity and sophistication of natural information processing systems. *Attempts at intelligibility* have had as their long term goal the production of something that will be usable and understandable by human intelligence. Metaphors used for these purposes point to the embeddedness of systems, user-friendliness, situated action, and so forth.

Yet in the metaphoric use of natural information processing, some important considerations become implicit. This especially includes understanding the relationship between the original source of metaphors and the final artifact. Some of the methodological debates in artificial intelligence reflect a deep uncertainty about the status of natural metaphors. Would a completely formal system allow them at all? If one is committed to a formal system, wherein does the fidelity to nature lie? Or do natural and artificial systems share formal properties to be discovered? ([Hall and Kibler 1985] review these issues.) Many of these concerns are being brought to light by research in distributed artificial intelligence. This is first because the original Turing goal could not be met by distributed work, and secondly because the social, not the psychological or the biological, appears to many researchers in the field both as an important metaphor and as part of the system.

2.2 From the Turing Test to the Durkheim Test

The original Turing Test [Turing 1950] involved a computer being able to mimic a woman well enough so that a human observer could not distinguish between a human male and a "female" computer. The test was predicated on a closed-universe model using "discrete state digital computers:"

---

[1]There are numerous descriptions of attempts to use such models; see e.g., [Ericsson and Simon 1979] for a review of sources of evidence on cognition.

"The prediction which we are considering [of all future states] is, however, rather nearer to practicability that that considered by Laplace. The system of the 'universe as a whole' is such that quite small errors in the initial conditions can have an overwhelming effect at a later time ... Even when we consider the actual physical machines instead of the idealized machines, reasonably accurate knowledge of the state at one moment yields reasonably accurate knowledge any number of steps later ... Provided it could be carried out sufficiently quickly the digital computer could mimic the behavior of any discrete-state machine. The imitation game could then be played with the machine in question and the mimicking digital computer and the interrogator would be unable to distinguish them. Of course the digital computer must have an adequate storage capacity as well as working sufficiently fast. Moreover, it must be programmed afresh for each new machine which it is desired to mimic ... This special property of digital computers ... is described by saying that they are *universal* machines."

Later in the article Turing reiterates that these computers can meet any new situation, as long as they have enough storage capacity.

Turing's model is more than a quaint, outdated vision of what computers can do. By going back to the original source, some fundamental values (and value conflicts) in the field of artificial intelligence are revealed, and therein some of the reasons for the ambivalence and confusion about metaphors. Turing's test world is closed, as already pointed out above. But it also has the following properties that are being hotly contested by distributed artificial intelligence at this time:

- testing is done by individuals, not communities. There is no doubt in the tester's mind about what constitutes a valid result (in this case, stereotyped female behavior);

- computers, because they are programmable, are universal. Once a situation can be formally analyzed, it becomes amenable to understanding through this universal language;

- the only restriction on intelligence is lack of storage capacity (or processing power).

Critiques of these propositions have been coming from distributed artificial intelligence for some time. For example, Hewitt's open systems model posits that all nontrivial real-world systems are open. They include properties of the real world, including distributed information processing, asynchronous updates, arms' length relationships between components, negotiation, and continual evolution [Hewitt and DeJong 1983], [Hewitt 1986],

[Hewitt 1988]. These systems are open in several senses: there is no global temporal or spatial closure, and there is an absence of a central authority. Thus, rigid *a priori* protocols that will homogenize data and decision-making both beg the question of openness and limit the problem-solving capacity of the system in the real world. Flexibility and evolution are the central concerns.

No amount of increased storage capacity can bypass the problems posed by open systems. The structure of the original Turing Test, relying solely on a fixed repertoire of rules in order to mimic a range of behaviors, cannot accommodate this type of distributed system. The reasons are the same as for Hewitt's original critique: it could not analyze conflicting viewpoints within the system, and the fundamentally open nature of real world systems inevitably gives rise to such conflicts.

The conceptual struggle in distributed artificial intelligence has been with the tensions implied by the idea of a universal formal language and the inconsistency which arises from the distributed, open nature of the system itself. For example, [Durfee and Lesser 1987] propose the idea of partial global plans that dynamically model and incorporate the findings from distributed nodes of a system, maintaining the openness of the system but achieving coherence across nodes. [Cammarata *et al.* 1983] state that

> "A main challenge to distributed problem solving is that the solutions which a distributed agent produces must not only be locally acceptable, achieving the assigned tasks, but also they must be interfaced correctly with the actions of other agents solving dependent tasks. The solutions must not only be reasonable with respect to the local task, they must be *globally coherent* and this global coherence must be achieved by *local computation alone.*"

In response to this challenge, the metaphors in this line of work have gone from single humans or human psychology[2] to organizations, interactions, negotiation, blackboards, networks and communities. For example, [Fox 1981] discusses the "technology transfer" possible between human organizations and artificial intelligence systems; [Gasser 1987] calls for cooperation between distributed artificial intelligence and other fields of study concerned with coordinated action and distributed problem solving. I propose that this change in metaphoric base be recognized by replacing the vision of the Turing Test with a test adequate to meet the challenges of distributed open systems: the Durkheim Test.

Emile Durkheim (1858–1917) was a French sociologist who attempted to demonstrate the irreducible nature of what he called "social facts." For example, you could not understand differential suicide rates in different locations by simply saying that each case was

---

[2]I include network models of cognition here; I mean that the metaphors have moved away from individualist, black boxed models of single actors.

40

pathological; something was happening at the "system level" that did not reduce to the terms of lower levels. Social facts, he said, are thus *sui generis* (or irreducible). He proposed the following law: "The determining case of a social fact should be sought among the social facts preceding it and not among the states of the individual consciousness," followed by the codicil: "The function of a social fact ought always to be sought in its relation to some social end" [Durkheim 1938].

The test of intelligence of a distributed open system is necessarily an ecological one. This means that it is *sui generis* at the social/system level, incorporating all parts of the system. Testing one node will not give reliable results; testing the whole open system is never possible (see e.g., [Lesser and Corkill 1981]. In the words of [Davis and Smith 1983], "When control is decentralized, no one node has a global view of all activities in the system; each node has a local view that includes information about only a subset of the tasks." Thus, the very concept of a test must change in order to deal with such systems. Following Durkheim, we can say that it would be communal, irreducible, distributed, and dynamic. It is also important to note that it cannot be applied solely after a design is complete. In order to understand the acceptance and use of a machine in and by a community, that community must be actively present as it evolves.

So the Durkheim test would be a real time design, acceptance, use and modification of a system by a community. Its intelligence would be the direct measure of usefulness applied to the work of the community; its ability to change and adapt, and to encompass multiple points of view while increasing communication across viewpoints or parts of an organization. Such a test also changes the position of metaphors with respect to design and use considerations. In an open, evolving system, the boundaries between design and use, between technology and user, between laboratory and workplace, necessarily blur. Neither is the organization of work something that can be added after the design process [Kling and Scacchi 1982]. [Chang 1987] develops a model of this he calls participant systems. Thus, social metaphors may remain sources of inspiration, or guidelines for human-computer interface. But if we are stringently to apply the principles of open systems to design, and account for differing viewpoints and evaluation criteria at every step of the way, social systems become deeply implicated at all times.

The futility of the Turing Test comes not from lack of storage capacity or processing power, but from a fundamental misunderstanding of the nature of computers and society as closed, centralized, and asocial. As that misunderstanding gets replaced by an open system, ecological, and political model of organizations, workplaces, and situations (which include both machines and human organization), the Turing Test will be replaced by different forms of evaluation. (For a discussion of this from both sociological and computer science

41

perspectives, see [Bendifallah *et al.* 1988].)

2.3 Due Process, the Frame Problem, and Scientific Communities

As noted above, the distributed and open nature of real systems gives rise to the existence of different viewpoints within the system. A viewpoint in this sense can occur at any level of organizational scale, from hardware to human organization. It can arise from, for example, asynchronous updates to a knowledge base, resulting in different ways of processing information at different nodes based on differences in a knowledge base. At higher levels, it can result from differences in the structure of tasks performed, different commitments, or different long or short term goals.

The simultaneous existence of multiple viewpoints and the need for solutions which are coherent across divergent viewpoints is a driving consideration in distributed artificial intelligence. [Hewitt 1986] and [Gerson 1987] have discussed aspects of this as the problem of *due process*: a legal phrase that refers to collecting evidence and following fair trial procedures. The due process problem in either a computer or human organization is this: in combining or collecting evidence from different viewpoints (or heterogeneous nodes), how do you decide that sufficient, reliable and fair amounts of evidence have been collected? Who, or what, does the reconciling, according to what set of rules?

[Davis 1980] notes that cooperation is necessary in order to resolve this class of problems, but that many researchers who came to distributed processing via attempts to synthesize networked machines see cooperation as a form of compromise "between potentially conflicting views and desires at the level of system design and configuration." The two motivations he suggests for cooperation are insolubility by a single node and compatibility (joining of forces).

The interdependence suggested by these motivations would seem to work against pluralism of viewpoints. How can two entities (or objects or nodes) with two different and irreconcilable epistemologies cooperate? If understanding is necessary for cooperation, as is widely stated in the distributed artificial intelligence literature, what is the nature of an understanding that can cooperate across viewpoints?

There is a fundamental similarity between these concerns about cooperation, i.e., the due process problem, and the frame problem in artificial intelligence. The frame problem, as [Hayes 1987] notes, "arises when the reasoner is thinking about a changing, dynamic world, one with actions and events in it ... it only becomes an annoyance when one tries to describe a world of the sort that people, animals and robots inhabit." It is a problem, he states, not in computation, but in representation; it occurs in the presence of spatial or temporal change.

Spatial or temporal change is significant in this regard because of the epistemological incompatibilities that such change may bring about. As an actor moves through time and space, new information or new axiomatic requirements evolve (or devolve, depending on viewpoint), thus shifting the assumptive frame. Which axioms to retain or change, depending on which things can be taken for granted (or not) is at the heart of the frame problem [Pylyshyn 1987].

From the viewpoint of open systems, the problems of due process and the frame problem are figure-ground to one another. In the problem of due process, viewpoints evolve and change with new information and new situational constraints. The concept of due process means evaluating and synthesizing potentially incompatible viewpoints in the decision-making process: adducing evidence. The problem is one of drawing on different evidentiary bases. It is the differences in situation and viewpoint that make for epistemological incompatibility. In open systems, the lack of a sovereign arbiter means that questions of due process must be solved by negotiation, rules and procedures, case precedents, etc. (see [Hewitt 1988]).

The frame problem arose in the context of dealing with moving actors, absorbing information in a fashion that threatens the stability of their axiomatic structure. A robot, moving through novel open space, must find a robust way to deal with that novelty without having to add so many new axioms that it becomes bogged down in a "combinatorial implosion." But the problem is *not* really one of moving *through* neutral territory: in fact, it is an interactional problem. *Environment* really means a series of interactions with other objects: actors, events, and new kinds of ordered actions. In other words, the moving robot is forced to evaluate a series of interactions by picking and choosing from the heterogeneous, evolving, potentially incompatible viewpoints of other actors outside its original closed world.

The reconciliation between multiple viewpoints in the frame problem has thus been mischaracterized as a single actor problem. In fact, viewed temporally, and taking the actual content of the changing environments into account, the frame problem can be seen as a reconciliation between old and new experience in the same actor through a series of actions in open, distributed space.[3] The content of this experience is interactional because environments are a set of new actors and events. Solving the frame problem means adjudicating decisions about which evidence is important for which circumstances, and

---

[3]Sociologists discuss this as the problem of continuity of identity. (See [Strauss 1969].) The problem of inertia is structurally similar to the track-record heuristic described by [Hewitt 1986] in his discussion of open systems.

which can be taken for granted. The continuity of the robot's actions relies on a set of metarules that are structurally identical to the due process problem: What data does it take from which viewpoint? What is kept and what is discarded (thus the many discussions of relevance and inertia in the frame problem literature)? How can a decision be reached that incorporates both novelty and sufficient closure for action?

Human actors routinely solve both the frame problem and the due process problem. They do so in a variety of ways, as noted both in the social science literature and in the frame problem literature, and in variably democratic ways. In the remainder of this paper I present one class of strategies employed by two scientific communities I have studied in some detail.

The studies began as an exploration of the scientific community metaphor in a long collaboration with Carl Hewitt. We analyzed issues that arose in the context of artificial intelligence research by looking at how human communities resolved them. These included issues such as due process [Gerson 1987], the resolution of conflict in a distributed community [Star 1989a], triangulation of evidence from domains with incompatible goals [Star 1986], resolution of local uncertainty into global certainty [Star 1985], local constraints on representing complex information [Star 1983], and the management of anomalous information [Star and Gerson 1987].

After some years, with the development of the open systems model and the evolution of our own social science work, the "metaphor gap" seems to be closing.[4] The status of the social/community metaphor in the face of real-world systems embedded in organizations has shifted as the boundaries of "computer," "system," and "actors" are perceived as being larger and wider than Turing's closed world model. Because advances in both artificial intelligence and social science call for the development of new *ecological units of analysis, methods, and concepts*, both the *content and role of metaphors have shifted*.

The concept of boundary objects as presented below thus is simultaneously metaphor, model, and high-level requirement for a distributed artificial intelligence system. The more seriously one takes the ecological unit of analysis in such studies, the more central human problem-solving organization becomes to design—not simply at the traditional level of human-computer interface, but at the level of understanding the limits and possibilities of a form of artificial intelligence [Star 1989b].

---

[4]Another factor may contribute to closing the gap. The metaphor, as a source of inspiration, models, or design specifications, works both ways: artificial intelligence is also a metaphor for sociological research (see [Star 1989a] for a discussion of this process)!

2.4 The Scientific Community and Open Systems

[Kornfeld and C. Hewitt 1981] proposed that the scientific community be taken as a good source of metaphors for open systems work. Because real world information systems are distributed and decentralized, they evolve continuously, embody different viewpoints, and have arms-length relationships between actors requiring negotiation. The internal consistency of an open system cannot be assured, due to its very character as open and evolving. The information in an open system is thus heterogeneous, that is, different locales have different knowledge sources, viewpoints, and means of accomplishing tasks based on local contingencies and constraints.

Scientific workplaces are open systems in Hewitt's sense of the term. New information is continually being added asynchronously to the situation. There is no central "broadcasting" station giving out information simultaneously to scientists. Rather, information is carried piecemeal from site to site (when it is carried at all), with lags of days, months, or even years.

Scientific work is distributed in this way. Thus, there is no guarantee that the same information reaches participants at any time, nor that people are working in the same way toward common goals. People's definitions of their situations are fluid and differ sharply by location; the boundaries of a locality or workplace are simultaneously permeable and fluid [Latour 1988]. Scientific theory-building is deeply heterogeneous: different viewpoints are constantly being adduced and reconciled.

Yet within what may sound like near chaos, scientists manage to produce robust findings. They are able to create smooth-working procedures and descriptions of nature that hold up well enough in various situations. Their ability to do so was what originally fascinated Hewitt and Kornfeld. In the absence of a central authority or standardized protocol, how is robustness of findings (and decision-making) achieved? The answer from the scientific community is complex and twofold: they create objects that are both plastic and coherent through a collective course of action.

Any scientific workplace can thus be described in two ways: by the set of actions that meets those local contingencies that constantly buffet investigators, or the set of actions that preserves continuity of information in spite of local contingencies (due process and the frame problem simultaneously). Understanding this requires a different appreciation of scientific theories than that traditionally put forward by philosophers. Scientific truth *as it is actually created* is not a point-by-point closed logical creation. Rather, in the words of ecologist Richard Levins, "our truth is the intersection of independent lies" (in [Wimsatt 1980]). Each actor, site, or node of a scientific community has a viewpoint, a partial truth consisting of beliefs, local practices, local constraints, and resources—none of which are fully verifiable across all sites. *The aggregation of those viewpoints is the source of the robustness of science.*

2.5   Heterogeneous Problem Solving and Boundary Objects

In the face of the heterogeneity produced by local constraints and divergent viewpoints, how do communities of scientists reconcile evidence from different sources? The problem is an old one in social science; indeed, one could say it reflects the core problem of sociology. One major concern of early sociologists, such as Robert Park and Georg Simmel, was to describe interaction between participants from groups (or worlds) with very different "definitions of the situation." This concern gave rise to a series of case studies of ethnicities, work groups, and subcultures now grouped loosely under the rubric "Chicago school sociology." Everett Hughes, a leader of this group, argued for an ecological approach to understanding the participation of heterogeneous groups within a workplace, neighborhood, or region. By this he meant that the different perspectives, or viewpoints, of the participants need to be understood in a *sui generis* fashion, not simply as a compilation of individual instances, and as situated action.

Some findings from our studies of scientists of potential interest to distributed artificial intelligence are that scientists

1. cooperate without having good models of each other's work;

2. successfully work together while employing different units of analysis, methods of aggregating data, and different abstractions of data;

3. cooperate while having different goals, time horizons, and audiences to satisfy.

They do so by creating objects that serve much the same function as a blackboard in a distributed artificial intelligence system. I call these *boundary objects*, and they are a major method of solving heterogeneous problems. Boundary objects are objects that are both plastic enough to adapt to local needs and constraints of the several parties employing them, yet robust enough to maintain a common identity across sites. They are weakly structured in common use, and become strongly structured in individual-site use.

Like the blackboard, a boundary object "sits in the middle" of a group of actors with divergent viewpoints. Crucially, however, *there are different types of boundary objects depending on the characteristics of the heterogeneous information being joined to create*

46

them. The combination of different time horizons produces one kind of boundary object; joining concrete and abstract representations of the same data produces another. Thus, this paper presents not just one blackboard, but a system of blackboards structured according to the dynamic, open-systems requirements of a community (including both machines and humans).

2.6   Types of Boundary Objects

In studying scientists, I identified heterogeneous subgroups within the scientific workplace. The analysis of boundary objects presented here draws on two case studies that incorporated radically different viewpoints in the conduct of work. First, I conducted a study of a community of neurophysiologists at the end of the nineteenth century in England. This group included both clinical and basic researchers, as well as hospital administrators, attendants, experimental animals, journalists and patients [Star 1989a]. Second, my colleagues and I conducted a study of a zoological museum from 1900–1940 at Berkeley [Star and Griesmer 1989], [Gerson 1987]. This group included professional biologists, amateur collectors, university administrators, animals, and local trappers, farmers, and conservationists.

What is interesting about these studies from the point of view of distributed artificial intelligence is that the structure and attributes of the information brought in from the different participants were distributed and heterogeneous, yet were successfully reconciled. Space prohibits a detailed discussion of all the differences in viewpoint, but two salient ones are summarized below.

First, in comparing clinical and basic research evidence, the following differences obtain: clinical research operates with a much shorter time horizon (cure the patient, not find the theoretical generalization) than basic research; the case is the unit of analysis for clinicians (an instance-based form of explanation), whereas for basic researchers it is analytic generalizations about classes of events. In clinical research, attention is directed toward concrete events such as symptoms, treatments and patient trajectories. Diagnosis draws on medical theory to validate concrete observations of this nature. In basic research, attention is directed toward analytic generalizations such as refinements to others' theories, statements about the applicability of an experiment to a larger body of knowledge. Work proceeds from the experimental situation and is directed outwards toward a body of knowledge. Finally, for the clinician, interruptions to work come in the form of complications, which are side effects to be dealt with locally and discarded from the evidentiary body (they never make their way into publication of the cases). Interruptions to work for the basic researcher come in the form of anomalies which must be accounted for in the body of evidence, either by controlling them or introducing them into the findings.

Second, in the world of the natural history museum, one primary source of comparison is between amateur and professional biologists. There are some similar differences as between clinicians and basic researchers. For the amateur collector of specimens, the specimen itself is the unit of analysis—a dead bird or a bone found in a specific location. Collecting, like clinical work, is the art of dealing on an instance-by-instance basis with examples and local contingencies. For the professional biologist, on the other hand, the specimens collected by amateurs form a part of an abstract generalization about ecology, evolution, or the distribution of species. The particular bug or beetle is not as important as what it represents. Furthermore, the work organization is highly distributed, ranging from the museum in Berkeley to various collecting expeditions throughout the state of California.

In analyzing these types of heterogeneity, I found four types of boundary objects created by the participants. The following is not an exhaustive list by any means. These are only analytic distinctions, in the sense that we are really dealing here with *systems* of boundary objects that are themselves heterogeneous.

2.6.1 Repositories

These are ordered piles of objects that are indexed in a standardized fashion. Repositories are built to deal with problems of heterogeneity caused by differences in unit of analysis. An example of a repository is a library or museum. They have the advantage of modularity.

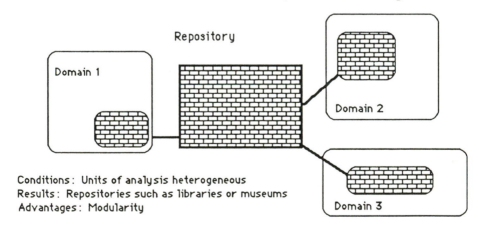

Figure 2.1: Boundary object: repositories

2.6.2 Ideal Type or Platonic Object

This is an object such as a map or atlas which in fact does not accurately describe the details of any one locality. It is abstracted from all domains, and may be fairly vague. However, it is adaptable to a local site precisely because it is fairly vague; it serves as a means of communicating and cooperating symbolically—a sufficient road map for all parties. Examples of platonic objects are the early atlases of the brain, which in fact described no brain, which incorporated both clinical and basic data, and which served as a means of communicating across both worlds. Platonic objects arise with differences in degree of abstraction such as those that obtain in the clinical/basic distinction. They result in the deletion of local contingencies from the common object, and have the advantage of adaptability.

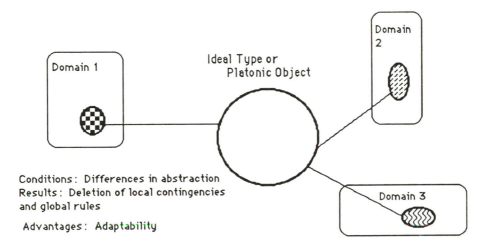

Figure 2.2: Boundary object: platonic object

2.6.3 Terrain with Coincident Boundaries

These are common objects which have the same boundaries but different internal contents.[5] They arise in the presence of different means of aggregating data and when work is distributed over a large-scale geographic area. The result of such an object is that work in each site can be conducted autonomously, but cooperating parties can work on the same area with the same referent. The advantage is the resolution of different goals. An example of coincident boundaries is the creation of the state of California itself as a boundary object for workers at the museum. The maps of California created by the amateur collectors

---

[5]See [Wimsatt 1980] for a fuller discussion of these issues.

and the conservationists resembled traditional roadmaps familiar to us all, and emphasized campsites, trails, and places to collect. The maps created by the professional biologists, however, shared the same outline of the state (with the same geopolitical boundaries), but were filled in with a highly abstract, ecologically-based series of shaded areas representing "life zones," an ecological concept.

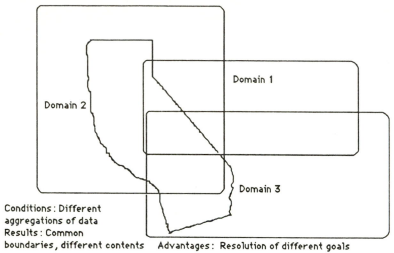

Figure 2.3: Boundary object: terrain with coincident boundaries

2.6.4   Forms and Labels

These are boundary objects devised as methods of common communication across dispersed work groups. Both in neurophysiology and in biology, work took place at highly distributed sites, conducted by a number of different people. When amateur collectors obtained an animal, they were provided with a standardized form to fill out. Similarly, in the hospital, night attendants were given forms on which to record data about patients' symptoms of epileptic fits in a standardized fashion; this information was later transmitted to a larger data base compiled by the clinical researchers attempting to create theories of brain and nervous system function. The results of this type of boundary object are standardized indexes and what Latour would call "immutable mobiles" (objects that can be transported over long distance and convey unchanging information). The advantages of such objects are that local uncertainties (for instance, in the collecting of animals or in the observation of epileptic seizures) are deleted. Labels and forms may or may not come to be part of repositories.

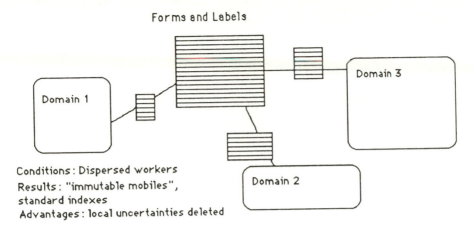

Figure 2.4: Boundary object: forms/labels

2.7   Summary and Conclusions

What are the implications for distributed artificial intelligence of understanding the creation of boundary objects by scientists? First, boundary objects provide a powerful abstraction of the sort called for by [Chandrasekaran 1981] to organize blackboards. They are, to use his terminology, neither committee nor hierarchy. They bypass the sort of problems of combinatorial implosion feared by Kornfeld and also bypass hierarchical delegation and representation. Unlike Turing's universal computer, the creation of boundary objects both respects local contingencies and allows for cross-site translation. Instead of a search for a logical Esperanto, already proved impossible in a distributed open systems context, we should search for an analysis of such objects. Problem-solving in the contexts described above produces workable solutions that are not, in Simon's terms, well-structured. Rather, they are ill-structured: they are inconsistent, ambiguous, and often illogical. Yet, they are functional and serve to solve many tough problems in distributed artificial intelligence.

The problems of instantiating descriptions in distributed systems [Pattison *et al.* 1987] require a device similar to the creation of boundary objects for accounting for shifting constraints and organizational structures. [Durfee *et al.* 1987] suggest a system that relies on cooperation and plan-based nodes that arrive at locally complete solutions for distributed problem solving. Again, the notion that systems of actors create common objects that inhabit different nodes in different fashions, and are thus locally complete but still common, should be useful here.

Future directions for research on these questions would include the following:

1. expanding the taxonomy of boundary objects and refining the conceptions of the types of information used in their construction;

2. examining the impact of combinations of boundary objects, and beginning to develop a notion of systems of such objects;

3. examining the problem of scaling up or applying an ecological, human/machine analysis to what is called multigrained systems in [Gasser *et al.* 1986].

The "Durkheim Test" referred to in the beginning of this paper is important in evaluating the construction and use of boundary objects. That is, the construction of such objects is a community phenomenon, requiring at least two sets of actors with different viewpoints. Analysis of the use of such an object at only one point in the system, or apart from its relationship to other nodes, will produce a systematic reductionist bias of the sort described by [Wimsatt 1980]. Heuristics used in such a fashion will reflect the neglect of the *sui generis* nature of the system. Furthermore, if the ecological unit of analysis recommended here and elsewhere in artificial intelligence is adopted, it should be noted that human designers, users, and modifiers of the computer systems involved will *make* boundary objects out of the information systems at every stage of the information processing trajectory.

Acknowledgements

Conversations with Geof Bowker, Lee Erman, Les Gasser, James Griesemer, Carl Hewitt, Rob Kling, Steve Saunders, Randy Trigg and Karen Wieckert were very helpful in formulating the ideas expressed here.

References

[Bendifallah *et al.* 1988] S. Bendifallah, F. Blanchard, A. Cambrosio, J. Fujimura, L. Gasser, E. M. Gerson, A. Henderson, C. Hewitt, W. Scacchi, S. L. Star, L. Suchman, and R. Trigg, "The Unnamable: A White Paper on Socio-Computational 'Systems,'" unpublished draft manuscript available from Les Gasser, Department of Computer Science, University of Southern California, Los Angeles, California, 1988.

[Cammarata *et al.* 1983] S. Cammarata, D. McArthur, and R. Steeb, Strategies of cooperation in distributed problem solving. *Proceedings IJCAI-83*, Karlsruhe, West Germany, August 1983, pp. 767–770.

[Chandrasekaran 1981] B. Chandrasekaran, "Natural and Social System Metaphors for Distributed Problem Solving: Introduction to the Issue," *IEEE Transactions on Systems, Man and Cybernetics*, Vol. SMC-11, No. 1, 1981, pp. 1–5.

[Chang 1987] E. Chang, "Participant Systems," in M. N. Huhns, ed., *Distributed Artificial Intelligence*, Morgan Kaufmann, Los Altos, CA, 1987, pp. 311-339.

[Davis 1980] R. Davis, "Report on the workshop on distributed artificial intelligence," *SIGART Newsletter*, 1980, p. 73.

[Davis and Smith 1983] R. Davis and R. G. Smith, "Negotiation as a Metaphor for Distributed Problem Solving," *Artificial Intelligence* Vol. 20, 1983, pp. 63–109.

[Durfee and Lesser 1987] E. Durfee and V. Lesser, "Using Partial Global Plans to Coordinate Distributed Problem Solvers," *Proceedings IJCAI-87*, Milan, Italy, August 1987, pp. 875–883.

[Durfee *et al.* 1987] E. Durfee, V. Lesser, and D. Corkill, "Cooperation through Communication in a Distributed Problem Solving Network," in M. N. Huhns, ed., *Distributed Artificial Intelligence*, Morgan Kaufmann, Los Altos, CA, 1987, pp. 29–58.

[Durkheim 1938] Emile Durkheim, *The Rules of Sociological Method*, Free Press, New York, 1938.

[Ericsson and Simon 1979] K. A. Ericsson and H. A. Simon, "Sources of evidence on cognition: An historical overview," C.I.P. Working Paper No. 406, Carnegie Mellon Dept. of Psychology, October 1979.

[Fox 1981] M. Fox, "An Organizational View of Distributed Systems," *IEEE Transactions on Systems, Man and Cybernetics*, Vol. SMC-11, No. 1, 1981, pp. 70–80.

[Gasser 1987] L. Gasser, "Distribution and Coordination of Tasks among Intelligent Agents," *First Scandinavian Conference on Artificial Intelligence*, Trumsoe, Norway, March, 1987.

[Gasser *et al.* 1986] L. Gasser, C. Braganza, and N. Herman, "MACE: A Flexible Testbed for Distributed AI Research," Technical Report CRI 87-01, Computer Research Institute, University of Southern California, 1986.

[Gerson 1987] E. M. Gerson, "Audiences and Allies: The Transformation of American Zoology, 1880–1930," *Society for the History, Philosophy and Sociology of Biology*, Blackburg, VA, 1987.

[Hall and Kibler 1985] R. P. Hall and D. F. Kibler, "Differing Methodological Perspectives in Artificial Intelligence Research," *The AI Magazine*, Fall 1985, pp. 166–178.

[Hayes 1987] P. J. Hayes, "What the frame problem is and isn't," in Z. W. Pylyshyn, ed., *The Robot's Dilemma: The Frame Problem in Artificial Intelligence*, Ablex, NY, 1987, pp. 123–137.

[Hewitt 1986] C. Hewitt, "Offices Are Open Systems," *ACM Trans. on Office Information Systems*, Vol. 4, 1986, pp. 271–287.

[Hewitt 1988] C. Hewitt, "Organizational Knowledge Processing," presented at *8th AAAI Conference on Distributed Artificial Intelligence*, Lake Arrowhead, California, May 1988.

[Hewitt and DeJong 1983] C. Hewitt and P. DeJong, "Analyzing the Roles of Descriptions and Actions in Open Systems," *Proceedings of the AAAI*, 1983, pp. 162–167.

[Kling and Scacchi 1982] R. Kling and W. Scacchi, "The Web of Computing: Computer Technology as Social Organization," *Advances in Computers*, Vol. 21, 1982, pp. 1–90.

[Kornfeld and C. Hewitt 1981] W. Kornfeld and C. Hewitt, "The Scientific Community Metaphor," *IEEE Transactions on Systems, Man and Cybernetics*, SMC-11, No. 1, 1981, pp. 24–33.

[Latour 1988] B. Latour, *Science in Action*, Harvard University Press, Cambridge, MA, 1988.

[Lesser and Corkill 1981] V. Lesser and D. Corkill, "Functionally Accurate, Cooperative Distributed Systems," *IEEE Transactions on Systems, Man and Cybernetics*, SMC-11, No. 1, 1981, pp. 81–96.

[Pattison *et al.* 1987] H. E. Pattison, D. Corkill and V. Lesser, "Instantiating Descriptions of Organizational Structures," in M. N. Huhns, ed., *Distributed Artificial Intelligence*, Morgan Kaufmann, Los Altos, CA, 1987, pp. 59–96.

[Pylyshyn 1987] Z. Pylyshyn, ed., *The Robot's Dilemma: The Frame Problem in Artifical Intelligence*, Ablex, Norwood, NJ, 1987.

[Star 1989a] S. L. Star, *Regions of the Mind: Brain Research and the Quest for Scientific Certainty*, Stanford Univeristy Press, Stanford, CA, 1989.

[Star 1989b] S. L. Star, "Human beings as material for artificial intelligence: Or, what computer science can't do," presented to *American Philosophical Association*, Berkeley, CA, March 1989.

[Star 1986] S. L. Star, "Triangulating Clinical and Basic Research: British Localizationists, 1870–1906," *History of Science*, Vol. 24, 1986, pp. 29–48.

[Star 1985] S. L. Star, "Scientific Work and Uncertainty," *Social Studies of Science*, Vol. 15, 1985, pp. 391–427.

[Star 1983] S. L. Star, "Simplification in Scientific Work: An Example from Neuroscience Research," *Social Studies of Science*, Vol. 13, 1983, pp. 205–228.

[Star and Gerson 1987] S. L. Star and E. Gerson, "The Management and Dynamics of Anomalies in Scientific Work," *Sociological Quarterly*, Vol. 28, 1987, pp. 147–169.

[Star and Griesmer 1989] S. L. Star and J. R. Griesmer, "Institutional Ecology, 'Translations,' and Coherence: Amateurs and Professionals in Berkeley's Museum of Vertebrate Zoology, 1907–1939," *Social Studies of Science*, August 1989.

[Strauss 1969] A. Strauss, *Mirrors and Masks: The Search for Identity*, The Sociology Press, San Francisco, 1969.

[Turing 1950] Alan Turing, "Computing Machinery and Intelligence," *Mind*, Vol. 59, 1950, pp. 433–460. Reprinted in E. Feigenbaum and J. Feldman, eds., McGraw-Hill, NY, 1963, pp. 11–35.

[Wimsatt 1980] W. C. Wimsatt, "Reductionist Research Strategies and Their Biases in the Units of Selection Controversy," in T. Nickles, ed., *Scientific Discoveries: Case Studies*, D. Reidel, Dordrecht, 1980.

Susan Leigh Star
Department of Information and Computer Science
University of California
Irvine, CA 92717

Chapter 3

Representing and Using Organizational Knowledge in Distributed AI Systems

Les Gasser, Nicholas F. Rouquette, Randall W. Hill, and John Lieb

Abstract

This paper reports on the state of our research toward a general coordination mechanism for distributed intelligent systems. In our view, a coordination framework or *organization* is a particular set of settled and unsettled questions about belief and action that agents have about other agents. Organizational change means opening and/or settling some different set of questions, giving individual agents new problems to solve and, more importantly, different assumptions about the beliefs and actions of other agents. To test these ideas we are developing a testbed called the Intelligent Coordination Experiment (ICE) in which we implement our coordination mechanisms.

3.1 Introduction

In the conduct of human enterprise, it is quite clear that many very large tasks are beyond the ability of individuals to achieve—their accomplishment requires many people working together in an organized fashion. The study of human organizations has a long and varied history (see, e.g., [March 1965], [Perrow 1979], [Weick 1979]). But, despite the clear need to comprehend how agents in distributed AI systems can be organized, there have been very few serious attempts to bring perspectives from the study of human organizations to bear (several related studies can be found in [Corkill 1982],

[Fox 1981], [Malone 1988], [Star 1989]). If we do take seriously calls for knowledge that will apply to multiagent aggregates in general, (i.e. including both people and machines) [Chandrasekaran 1981], [Lesser and Corkill 1983], [Wesson *et al.* 1981], we currently have little to go on. It is important that we begin to develop, as part of the science of DAI, a basis for the comparative analysis of human and machine approaches to collective action (cf. [Woolgar 1985]). This paper reports on our research toward a general coordination mechanism for distributed intelligent systems that we believe accounts for previous mechanisms, provides better flexibility than previous schemes, and is somewhat consistent with *symbolic interactionist* and *negotiated order* theories of organization and organized action (e.g., [Benson 1977], [Dalton 1959], [Gasser 1986], [Maines 1984], [Strauss *et al.* 1963], [Strauss 1978], [Strauss 1988]).

Intelligent agents that act together need to coordinate their actions to promote beneficial interactions, to avoid harmful interactions, and because individual decisions may have global impacts. We would like to have theories and mechanisms that allow us to understand, explain, and build adaptive systems of coordinated intelligent agents. To be both realistic and general, we must work toward theories that hold under the following assumptions (cf. [Hewitt 1986]):

- *No sharing.* It may be impossible to know whether two agents actually share any knowledge or common definitions, or what the meaning of "share" would actually be. In any case, it does not appear that "sharing" as commonly construed, is necessary for coordination or interaction[1].

- *No global viewpoint.* For reasons of resource limitation, if not also for the fact that is physically impossible for two agents to be in the same spacetime location, global knowledge is in general impossible. In DAI we commonly speak of the possibility of comprehensive global viewpoints, but we usually mean good and useful approximations. In the extreme, we need to consider open systems without this possibility.

- *No global control.* Clearly without a global viewpoint there can be no effective global control.

To be useful, any body of theory of the sort we seek must at least account for 1) reconfiguration in the face of change at several levels of abstraction, 2) resource limitations, 3) the intentions of agents, and 4) agents' *mutually constructed* definitions of and responses to their situation.

---

[1]Space does not permit a full articulation of this position; it is related to a pragmaticist approach to belief and action. For related ideas see [Bentley 1954], [Dewey 1916], [Dewey 1938], [Gasser 1989], [Peirce 1955].

3.2 Viewing Coordination Frameworks as Patterns of Settled and Unsettled Problems

In a multiagent system, the problem of *which agent does what, when* can be seen as the basic question of organization. This question is related to control—each agent's decision about what to do next—and it requires an answer that leads to activity that is better or worse along some dimension of evaluation, such as "coherence" or "coordination" [Bond and Gasser 1988b]. In any particular instance, this question may be answered using problem-solving activities (e.g., planning, negotiation, metalevel control) or on the basis of internalized conventions and *routines*. A routine is simply a set of actions that have been carried out (at some level of abstraction) according to an established pattern—a routine is action. In a sense, internalized conventions are the outcome of previously "solved problems" or "settled questions" that have been codified into routines. Conventions and routines are built in this way by repeated negotiation and problem solving.

In general, problem solving and routine action come bound together. Any coordination through problem solving depends on a context of previously settled routines and expectations (e.g., about interaction languages to use, or conventional problem-solving methods). An autonomous intelligent agent may have, at any moment, a wide array of choices about what to believe, what knowledge is relevant, and what actions to pursue. At any moment, some of these choices are settled, and some are open or unsettled [Dewey 1938]. Positions have been taken on the settled issues (by the agent itself or some other agent, or perhaps by a designer), and they can be taken for granted for further reasoning. However, it is important to remember that a settled question—in this case the solution to a coordination or control problem—may have to be unsettled in a new situation; the problem may have to be re-solved in a new way for the new situation. In Dewey's terms [Dewey 1916], certain tentative positions or reasoning perspectives of the agent will have to be given a "loan of certainty" so that the agent has a ground of belief on which to stand for the purpose of taking action. Some of this certainty may have been imparted by the designer of a system in establishing, for example, communication protocols or languages that cannot be revised by the agents themselves. Others (e.g. task allocation) may have been historically settled by problem solving and agreement among agents (cf. [Davis 1983]). If we consider which are the settled and unsettled questions regarding action and knowledge, and their relation to the question of *which agent does what, when*, i.e., to coordination and control, we can build a basis for reasoning about organization that is grounded in individual understanding of situations and local perspectives, and that requires no sharing.

We need organizational knowledge to understand and build systems of agents that can conserve resources by specializing, and reconfigure their functions and interactions as their context changes. Historically, DAI systems have very limited flexibility for adapting their organization, usually focusing on adapting a single aspect such as task allocation or problem-solving role [Cammarata *et al.* 1983], [Davis 1983], [Durfee *et al.* 87]. It is critical to develop a useful framework to make DAI systems more adaptable. This ought to be based on some basic concepts of organization and organizational change.

In our view, an organization is *a particular set of settled and unsettled questions about belief and action through which agents view other agents.* Said another way, we believe that an organization should *not* be conceived as a structural relationship among a collection of agents or as a set of externally-defined limitations to their activities. Instead, to achieve the simultaneous aims of decentralized control, no global viewpoints or sharing, and fidelity to observable human action, the way to define organization is to locate the concept of organization in the beliefs, expectations, and commitments of agents themselves. When agents experience "organization," they do not see global structures or fixed constraints on action—instead they see *interlocking webs of commitment* (e.g., to prior but changeable settlements of questions) and *patterns of action* (e.g., routines of others being played out).

Viewed from this perspective, organizational change means *opening and/or settling some different set of these questions in a different way*, giving individual agents new control problems to solve and, more importantly, a different context of assumptions about the beliefs and actions of other agents. This approach to the conception of organization and organizational change differs from less flexible structural perspectives based on nodes with particular responsibilities, authority relationships, action constraints and communication paths used in [Cammarata *et al.* 1983], [Pattison *et al.* 1987], [Durfee *et al.* 87]. It corresponds more closely to organization theories that are based on active, dialectical views of knowledge, on symbolic interactionism, on negotiated order theory, and in general on organizations seen as processes as opposed to structures [Dalton 1959], [Strauss *et al.* 1963], [Benson 1977], [Strauss 1978], [Maines 1984], [Gasser 1986], [Strauss 1988].

An agent's need to interact with others constrains its action choices *because of what it believes other agents expect it to do* (its commitments to others), *what it expects itself to do* (its commitment to its own future actions) and *because of what it expects of others* (its beliefs about the commitments of others). These expectations and commitments are interwoven into the agent's context of assumptive beliefs. In order to conserve resources, to act under time constraints, and to reduce uncertainty by being predictable, agents develop routines for action - standard or organized ways of behaving individually and collectively[2] [Gasser 1986].

---

[2]Our conception of routines differ from multiagent plans because they are taken for granted by all concerned - they are expectations, not explicit control. In addition, plans are unique and opportunistically generated.

A routine is not a data structure - it is a repeated pattern of action, which is the outcome of a particular set of beliefs, that is, settled questions. A routine can be represented abstractly as a case-based plan [Hammond 1986] or as a script [Schank and Abelson 1977], with the caveat that each agent may have a different representation of any routine, and that every representation of a routine is just an expectation—that is, a violable commitment to a future course of events. An agent can use its expectations of the routine actions of other agents as fixed points with which to reason. The more organized a group of agents, the more their action can be based on this expectation or default; *the expectations or defaults*[3] *are the organization.* Agents that participate in highly organized collectives have highly constrained actions, because most choices have already been made in the enactment of routines and encoded as default beliefs and the concomitant expectations of others' behavior. Routines also provide a basis for discovering and reasoning about failure because they provide expectations for how and why things happen, which may not be met.

To summarize, a collection of locally settled questions provides a set of default expectations and commitments that constrain an agent's actions and provide a set of fixed points or (when taken together across agents) routines, which can be used for coordination. The fixed points can be called an organization, or possibly a *coordination framework* for the agents. These are the mechanisms we will begin to elaborate below.

When other agents *don't* meet expectations, new problem solving is required to maintain coordination of action toward the agents' joint ends. The process of shifting from organized or routine behavior to reasoned problem solving behavior has several important features that impact the structures we design for implementing coordination mechanisms. First, an agent that participates in adaptive activities must have knowledge about the coordinated process in order to recognize, diagnose, and repair coordination failures, and to adapt to new situations for increased performance. Second, some previously settled questions (the default action expectations) must be reopened, and so there must be mechanisms for settling and unsettling questions. Third, decisionmaking is resource-limited, so an agent must be able to constrain the useful knowledge it considers to a particular context. Fourth, the agent must know how and when to shift focus from carrying out the actions that will achieve its current goals (and that are based upon previously settled assumptions of other agents' behaviors), to a metalevel of deciding when and how to re-coordinate. We need representations of action that allow an agent to flexibly shift its attention to appropriate metalevel settlements (the assumptions under which the actions were done). Finally, if we consider that a "single agent" in a multiagent system may actually be a distributed problem-solving (DPS) system, the settling, shifting, context-defining, adaptive, and representational mechanisms ought to

---

[3]I.e., the assumptive settled questions referred to above.

be both distributable and scalable to higher-order systems. These desiderata provide the specifications for the representational mechanisms we are building into our problem solvers in the ICE testbed.

3.3   A Multiagent Problem: ICE

To refine coordination mechanisms based on the framework above, we are developing a testbed called the *Intelligent Coordination Experiment* or *ICE*, based on a domain problem first presented by [Benda *et al.* 1986]. In this domain, two classes of agents, *red* and *blue*, may move in NSEW directions on a rectilinear *grid*. In a given instance, agents' degrees of movement freedom, speed, sensing range and period, etc., may be set to control the kind and complexity of knowledge required. Blue agents have the goal of blocking the path of any red agent. This problem is simple to solve (or to prove unsolvable) with assumptions of complete knowledge and global control. Because our goal is to investigate decentralized coordination mechanisms (not to find ways to block the red agent most efficiently), we make no such assumptions, and also require explicit knowledge for action.

Three features of this scenario generate coordination among agents. 1) When a red agent can move in several directions, several blue agents must act simultaneously to block it. Thus *unfilled quadrants* (see below) generate unsolved problems. 2) Each blue agent may try to minimize the energy expended by all blue agents for moving and communication. 3) When blue agents are in close proximity, they may block each other.

A solution to this problem has six phases, namely: *Problem recognition*—discovering a red agent is present; *Enlisting allies*—gathering blue partners with commitments to solve the problem; *Forming a coordination framework*—instantiating a set of behavioral expectations and commitments and a way of resolving disparities; *Midgame problem solving*—transforming the problem state into one with a known solution and assigned "roles;" *Endgame problem solving*—following a small set of rules in a known context (e.g., the *Lieb configuration*, below) to block the red agent; *Termination*—recognizing the final, blocked state (or the impossibility of reaching it). Each successive phase uses settled issues from the previously settled phase as context for current-level decisions and action. For example, without a recognized problem, no midgame problem solving makes sense. These six phases reflect solution stages in numerous types of multiagent problems.

By our definition above, different organizations exist at each phase or level. For example, at the outset, no blue agent knows which red movement it will block; even which blue agents will participate may be unsettled. But they may have some knowledge of what actions to take and what role to play to *form* a coordination framework (cf. [Cammarata *et al.* 1983],

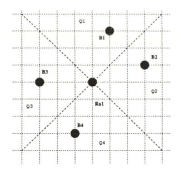 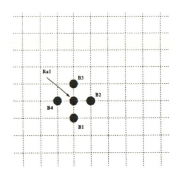

Figure 3.1: a. Blue agents in Lieb configuration   b. A final state

[Davis 1983]). Later, during the end-game, there must be well-assigned roles for which blue agent blocks which red agent path. Settling these organizational questions provides a context in which to settle other decisions of which precise, low-level moves to make, and roles to take in avoiding blue-agent blocks. The blue problem solvers may make several *organizational transitions* to track problem phases for a particular problem instance.

The Mid-game and End-game phases of ICE are of particular interest for this paper. When viewed as a search in a space of possible moves, the state space for this problem is huge (a branching factor on the order of 3125 between states!). We constrain this by noting that when agents reach the configuration shown in Figure 3.1a (which we call the *Lieb configuration*), blue agents may follow a set of simple rules (*Lieb rules*) and be guaranteed to block the red agent and reach a final state (Figure 3.1b). One agent's decision process for possible moves can be represented as a nondeterministic finite state automaton (NFSA). This NFSA includes states in which the agent is *in* its quadrant of the Lieb configuration, *out* of its Lieb configuration quadrant, on a *boundary* of its quadrant, or in a *final* state where the red agent is blocked. The NFSA decision points over time yield a high-level description of a space of possible actions. Solving the problem when represented this way means that each blue agent must find a way to remain in an *in* state until all blue agents reach a *final* state. This is not a certainty, since any *in* state contains possible transitions to the *boundary* state (an unfortunate move). These possible transitions reflect the blue agents' incomplete knowledge of the red agent; with complete predictive capability, it is possible always to choose moves that will keep the agent in an *in* state.

Unfortunately, this is not as easy as it seems. An agent must know *which* quadrant or boundary it is on at any moment (it changes with red-agent moves), which quadrant it *should* be on (relative to others), and how to achieve the *Lieb-configuration* originally. To remain *Lieb-configured*, each blue agent must have perfect knowledge of red agent moves. But when on a boundary or outside a quadrant, it must also know which other blue agents are "assigned" to which quadrants, to guarantee there is at least one per quadrant.

We can view a particular quadrant assignment made during the midgame as a particular organizational "form," indicating which agents have responsibility for which (red agent blocking) problems, and thus what issues to take for granted as settled context. Once these assignments have been settled, the agents are free to resolve End-game problems using move generation based on *Lieb* rules (Apply-LiebRules in Figure 3.4). However, this "form" may be only a *temporary* settlement of the quadrant-assignment problem. With uncertain knowledge the quadrant assignments may need to be resettled. This process amounts to an organizational transition, with partially new problem-solving expectations and commitments for some agents. This process is described in greater detail below.

3.3.1 Problem Complexes and Representation

Above, we have described organization using the concept of settled and unsettled problems or questions. We believe that problems don't exist individually, and we consider what is spoken of as *a problem* in conventional parlance to be a *problem complex* comprising numerous other problems. Some of these already have been settled, and some are unsettled. Said another way, a problem complex is a collection of some knowledge an agent thinks is already "fixed," combined with some things it doesn't know, arranged in some sort of relationship. The (settled and unsettled) problems making up the problem complex can be collected into those relating to *theory*, *method*, *representation* [Gerson and Gasser 1987], *interest*, and *action*. A *particular* problem complex can be seen as a boundary that has been drawn around a collection of other problems, and a framework for showing how they are related[4]. There are no primitive problems; all problems are complexes, i.e. relative to some context, and all are conceived as some set of settled and unsettled questions and a boundary.

Settling a problem (i.e., a problem complex) means settling the unsettled questions in the complex to some acceptable approximation. We never really consider a problem to be solved once and for all, but instead consider unsettled component questions to become *acceptably settled over some period*—no more work will be done on them now, because the settlements

---

[4]This definition is an attempt to make explicit the fact that *the actions of agents*, e.g., in drawing boundaries or establishing relevancy, defines problem complexes to be what they are. Which other problem complexes are included and which are excluded is a description and representation decision with important consequences. This definition is also intentionally both hierarchical and recursive. Drawing the boundaries of a problem complex is itself a problem, subject to temporary settlement and unsettlement. We will not consider the representational issues of the boundary problem in this paper. See [Kling 1987], [Star 1989].

```
(DotsPb ?Pb
    :Agents = ___                                              ; (instantiated)
        c: ∀B ∈: ?Pb.Agents, (BAgent-p B)
    :Potential-Solvers = ___
        c: ∀B ∈: ?Pb.Potential-Solvers, (Aligned [Self]?Pb [B]?pb)
        m: "Get solvers among the known Blue agents"
    :RedAgent = ___
        c: (= (Color ?Pb.RedAgent) 'Red)                       ; (instantiated)
    :Qᵢ-Blocker = ___
        c: in(?Pb.Qᵢ-Blocker,Qᵢ) ∧ Next-To(?Pb.Qᵢ-Blocker,?Pb.RedAgent)
        m: (Generate-and-Solve
            '(EndGame ?Eg
                    :Agent ?Pb.Qᵢ-Coord
                    :RedAgent ?Pb.RedAgent
                    :Quadrant ?Pb.Qᵢ
                    :Blocker.Report (Send :Where ?Pb.Qᵢ-Blocker
                                          :What ?Eg.Blocker.Value)))
    :Qᵢ-Coord = ___
        c: (BAgent-p ?Pb.Qᵢ-Coord) ∧ (Q-Coord-p ?Pb.Qᵢ-Coord)
        m: (Generate-and-Solve
                '(FindCoordinator ?Fc
                    :Agent ?Pb.Agents
                    :RedAgent ?Pb.RedAgent
                    :Quadrant ?Pb.Qᵢ
                    :Elected.Report (Send :Where ?Pb.Qᵢ-Coord
                                          :What ?Fc.Elected.Value))))
```

Figure 3.2: ICE problem description

are useful. This conception of problems does not completely capture the notion of intention, preference, or commitment in problem definition (cf. [Cohen and Levesque 1987]); We hope to integrate these, but the details are not worked out.

We represent the relationships among component problems in a problem complex using a *problem complex frame*. This representation draws on Lenat's representations of concepts as relatively more or less completely elaborated frames, and of problem solving as *concept elaboration* by generating and ranking tasks to elaborate underfilled slots [Lenat 1982], [Lenat 1983a], [Lenat 1983b]. Any problem, including a nonroutine problem, can be represented this way if we remember that the structure of the problem complex frame itself is a settled question, subject to reopening. Problems, after all, do get defined—before, during, or after problem solving. Several problem frames representing problem complexes in the ICE domain are shown in Figures 3.2–3.5.

Each problem frame is a flexible collection of slots, each of which describes one of the complex's component problems. (They are flexible, because a problem complex's bound-

```
(EndGame ?Eg
    :Coord = ___                              ; (instantiated)
    :RedAgent = ___                           ; (instantiated)
    :Quadrant = ___                           ; (instantiated)
    :Candidates = ___
        m: "Get a list from the acqaintances"
    :QFillers = ___
        c: ∀Qf ∈ ?Eg.QFillers, in(Qf,?Eg.Quadrant) ∧ ?Eg.QFillers ≠ ∅
        m: "Message from a blue agent" or "Ask coordinators for an agent"
    :Blocker = ___
        c: Next-To(?Eg.BLocker,?Eg.RedAgent)
        m: (dolist (c ?Eg.Candidates)
                (Generate-and-Solve
                    '(Follow-LiebRules ?Flr
                        :Agents c
                        :Quadrant ?Eg.Quadrant
                        :RedAgent ?Eg.RedAgent
                        :Blocker.report (Send :Whom (Coordinator :Quadrant ?Flr.Quadrant)
                                                    :Where EndGame.QFillers
                                                    :What ?Flr.Blocker)
                        :Blocked-Position.report (Send :Whom (Coordinator :Quadrant ?Flr.Quadrant)
                                                    :Where EndGame.Blocker
                                                    :What ?Flr.Blocker)))))
```

Figure 3.3: EndGame problem description

```
(Follow-Lieb-Rules ?Flr
    :Agent = ___                                    ; Coordinator (instantiated)
    :RedAgent = ___                                 ; (instantiated)
    :Quadrant = ___                                 ; (instantiated)
    :Blocker = ___
            c:  in(?Flr.Blocker,?Flr.Quadrant)
            m: (Generate-and-Solve
                    '(QFill ?Qf
                        :Agents ?Flr.Agents
                        :Quadrant ?Flr.Quadrant
                        :RedAgent ?Flr.RedAgent
                        :Filler.Report (Send :Where ?Flr.Blocker
                                             :What ?Qf.Filler)))
    :Blocked-Position = ___
            c:  Next-To(?Flr.Blocker,?Flr.RedAgent) ∧ in(?Flr.BLocker,?Flr.Quadrant)
            m: (Generate-and-Solve
                    '(Apply-LiebRules ?Alr
                        :Agent ?Flr.Agents
                        :Quadrant ?Flr.Quadrant
                        :RedAgent ?Flr.RedAgent
                        :Termination.Report (Send :Where ?Flr.Blocker
                                                  :What ?Alr.Agent)))
    :Termination = ___
            c:  (type ?Flr.Termination) = 'Termination-Msg
            m: (Generate-and-Solve
                    '(Find-Msg ?Msg
                        :From (Coord-name ?Flr.Quadrant)))))
```

Figure 3.4: Lieb strategy description

```
(QFill ?Qf
    :Agent = ___                                    ; (instantiated)
    :RedAgent = ___                                 ; (instantiated)
    :Quadrant = ___                                 ; (instantiated)
    :Filler = ___
            c:  in(?Qf.Filler,?Qf.Quadrant)
            m: (Generate-and-Solve
                    '(Move-To-Quadrant ?MtQ
                        :Agent ?Qf.Agent
                        :Quadrant ?Qf.Quadrant
                        :RedAgent ?Qf.RedAgent
                        :Termination.Report (Send :Where ?Qf.Filler
                                                  :What ?MtQ.Agent))))
```

Figure 3.5: Quadrant fill problem description

65

aries may change during the course of problem solving as the problem gets redefined.) Each slot comprises several facets, namely: Value (the value of the slot once settled), Type (a set of constraints describing acceptable values), Certainty (a certainty factor), Reason (a rationale for believing the value or its absence), Future (an indicator of a value to be supplied by another process in progress, Default (a default value that meets the type constraints), Methods (a set of ways of filling the slot acceptably), Report (a specification of what to report as results of the settlement and where to report it), and Description (documentation). Nested slots in frames are identified using familiar dot notation; variables are denoted with "?" before them.

The problem complexes shown in Figures 3.2–3.5 represent knowledge for solving the ICE problem. We divide the region surrounding a red agent RA_1 into four *quadrants*, in accord with the *Lieb* approach. Each quadrant is assigned a Quadrant Coordinator with a responsibility of getting some agent who will block RA_1 from that quadrant. (Coordinator responsibility may be carried out by one of the blue agents if there are only four.) There are two classes of unsettled issues at this level of description: who will be the Coordinator for each quadrant, and who will be the Blocker for each quadrant. Identifying a Coordinator requires settling another problem, the *Find-Coordinator* problem. Finding a blocker requires settling the *End-Game problem*, namely, getting someone directly next to RA_1. This in turn requires settling *Follow-Lieb-Rules* problems in each quadrant, which cannot be done until the quadrant has been filled by settling a *Qfill* problem for each quadrant. Of course, once a quadrant has been filled, the simple Lieb rules can be followed by the agent in that quadrant, irrespective of the settling of Qfill questions in other quadrants.

Generate-and-Solve (G&S) is the basic mechanism by which an agent can instantiate new problems. G&S may fail to instantiate a problem if the intended solver(s) (in these examples Agent(s) and Coord) does/do not agree to consider the problem. Once a problem has been instantiated, failure or success is determined by the degree to which slots are filled and partial/terminal reports will be sent (and possibly canceled) as specified at the time of problem instantiation.

Links among the problem complexes form a dynamic *problem solution graph* that represents how the results of solving some problems affect the knowledge needed to address other problems. A problem solution graph at the abstract, uninstantiated level is relatively static, and depends upon problem definition processes. Relationships among problem complex instances may be very dynamic, because they depend upon (actually, define) the current mix of settled and unsettled problems, and this mix may change. Both the static and dynamic aspects of problem unfolding are represented.

3.4   Settlement and Unsettlement

Open slots in problems are *settled* by executing methods that settle them. From an execution standpoint, methods are other problems, and may actually fail. If they succeed, they produce a tentative value that is inserted in the Value facet of their respective slot. (This value is always tentative because it may be revoked by a change in circumstances, as we shall illustrate below.) The value produced by a method must meet the constraints of the Type facet. Satisfaction of the constraints are checkable with respect to agent knowledge or world situations. For example, the Qfill.Filler.Type constraint in Figure 3.5 specifies that a Qfiller agent must be in the quadrant specified by Qfill.Quadrant, for the problem complex to be solved. Violation of this constraint could be resolved by changing either the quadrant in Qfill.Quadrant, or by changing the identity (and thus role) of the Qfill.Filler agent, or by generating and solving a Move-To-Quadrant problem complex, to put the agent into the correct quadrant. Some of this can be done opportunistically (see below).

Constraints that depend upon world situations (such as the quadrant in which an agent currently resides) can be sent to a *situation assessment* (SA) module, so as to direct its sensing and analysis. In the SA module, a network of constraints is established so that updating an observation about the world will lead to a check of appropriate constraints. In this example, problem solution graph forms a tree, and constraints can be checked from lower to higher, to prevent inconsistencies. The SA module has information linking constraints to problems so that their slots can be *unsettled* when constraint violations are detected. The SA's constraints are the assumptions of the blue agent at any moment. They are necessary for the further elaboration of a problem. These are the things to which certainty has been loaned, but which can be checked against the world. When new knowledge is received, it is checked against the relevant assumptions by the SA using a discrimination net.

New world situations or messages may cause constraint violations in settled slots. Constraint violations trigger the construction of new problem complexes—namely violation resolution problem complexes. For example, a new problem instance with an empty slot may violate a Type constraint saying that a slot may not be empty—this generates a new problem complex for filling the slot, which generates in turn a new problem instantiated from the description in the methods facet. Unsettlements of previously settled slots may be propagated to other problem-complexes using pointers in the reason, report, and methods facets, and may involve informing different agents. Since world knowledge and messages may have different interpretations in different contexts, unsettling a slot in one problem complex may not necessarily unsettle a similar slot in another problem-complex if the

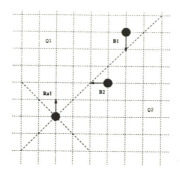

Figure 3.6: Initial configuration

underlying constraints are different.

Briefly, the basic control structure of Blue agents under this formulation is agenda-based, with separate, concurrent internal agents responsible for solving separate types of problems (e.g. planning, situation assessment (SA), metalevel control, execution, sensing, etc.). Each of these internal agents is a MACE agent [Gasser *et al.* 1987]. Each internal agent's *engine* comprises a *two level production lattice interpreter* (2LPLI). The 2LPLI uses a *production lattice* of tasks and assumptions (represented as problems settled at a metalevel) to interpret a dynamically changing set of domain-level tasks in its area of responsibility. The metalevel production lattice is generated by a planner, and comprises tasks described with links to possible contextualizing tasks and contextualizing assumptions. An example, taken from the production lattice of the (internal) execution agent, is shown in Figures 3.6–3.8.

3.5   Problem Shifts and Organizational Change in ICE

Figure 3.6 illustrates the initial configuration of two blue agents, B_1 and B_2, and Ra_1, the red agent. The two blue agents are operating in accordance with a set of settled questions about location, quadrant, and individual goals. Figure 3.7 shows the frames of the two quadrant coordinators C_{Q_1}, C_{Q_2} for Q_1 and Q_2 respectively.[5] Problem complex frames are identified by name, superscript, and subscript. The subscript refers to the agent or coordinator who spawned the instance, and the superscript uniquely identifies the frame instance. Eg^1_{Cq1} is the first frame generated by C_{Q_1}. Figure 3.8 shows the Flr^1_{Cq1} and Flr^1_{Cq2} frames that are respectively the problems that B_1 and B_2 try to solve to fill the `Blocker`

---

[5] B_1 could be the coordinator C_{Q_1}, and the indirect reference to the coordinator would still be "C_{Q_1}".

(EndGame Eg^1_{Cq1}
   :Coord $= C_{Q_1}$
   :RedAgent $= Ra_1$
   :Quadrant $= Q_1$
   :Candidates $= \{B_1, B_2, B_3, B_4\}$
   :QFillers $= \{B_1\}$
   :Blocker $=$ ___   ; B_1 is solving Flr^1_{Cq1}
        Future: Flr^1_{Cq1})

(EndGame Eg^1_{Cq2}
   :Coord $= C_{Q_2}$
   :RedAgent $= Ra_1$
   :Quadrant $= Q_2$
   :Candidates $= \{B_1, B_2, B_3, B_4\}$
   :QFillers $= \{B_2\}$
   :Blocker $=$ ___   ; B_2 is solving Flr^1_{Cq2}
        Future: Flr^1_{Cq2})

Figure 3.7: Coordinators' initial problems

(Follow-Lieb-Rules Flr^1_{Cq1}
   :Agent $= B_1$
   :RedAgent $= Ra_1$
   :Quadrant $= Q_1$
   :Blocker $= B_1$; Already solved by Qf^1_{B1}
        Constraint: $in(B_1, Q1)$
        Reason: (Derived-from-Applying-Method Qf^1_{B1})
   :Blocked-Position $=$ ___   ; Applying Lieb Rules in Alr^1_{B1}
        Future: $Alr^1_{B_1}$)
   :Termination $=$ ___)

(Follow-Lieb-Rules Flr^1_{Cq2}
   :Agent $= B_2$
   :RedAgent $= Ra_1$
   :Quadrant $= Q_2$
   :Blocker $= B_2$; Already solved by Qf^1_{B2}
        Constraint: $in(B_2, Q2)$
        Reason: (Derived-from-Applying-Method Qf^1_{B2})
   :Blocked-Position $=$ ___   ; Applying Lieb Rules in $Alr^1_{B_2}$
        Future: Alr^1_{B2})
   :Termination $=$ ___)

Figure 3.8: Agent problems

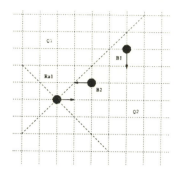

Figure 3.9: Configuration resulting from misprediction

slots of their respective coordinators (reports to Eg^1_{Cq1} and Eg^1_{Cq2}). Both B_1 and B_2 have filled their **Blocker** slots by successfully solving QFill problems (Qf^1_{B1} and QF^1_{B2}). They are now trying to get next to the Red agent (problems Alr^1_{B1} and Alr^1_{B2} respectively) by using *Apply-LiebRules* (see Figure 3.4 also).

To generate a proper move using the Lieb rules, each blue agent formulates a prediction about the direction it expects the red agent to move next. By default each blue agent assumes that the other blue agents will arrive at a correct prediction and will act in a rational manner, since the relevant problem complexes are already settled. In the example, we assume that B_1's prediction, while consistent with its own knowledge, is wrong.

Figure 3.9 shows the next situation where B_1 mispredicted Ra_1's moves and crossed the quadrant boundary. Each of the Flr problems have been instantiated with slot-report facets for **Blocked-Position** and **Blocker** filled, so B_1 knows to send a message to his quadrant coordinator concerning the crossing event. The coordinator in turn informs Q_2's coordinator that B_1 entered his region to keep knowledge current. (B_1 could have informed his own coordinator upon leaving the quadrant.) The two coordinators don't attempt any opportunistic change because it is cheaper for B_1 to try to go back to Q_1. The reasons for this concern metalevel heuristics for deciding how to resettle values when constraints are violated. The resulting updates are shown in Figures 3.10 and 3.11. Figure 3.11 shows how B_1 persists in his problem and does *not* change quadrant assignment (i.e., organizational role). The **Type** constraint of B_1's **Blocker** slot is $in(B_1, Q_1)$. This constraint is clearly violated. Planning to solve it, B_1 generated a new QFill problem complex in order to go back to Q_1. Since B_2 had no violated constraints, it didn't modify its frame at all. The two coordinators updated their endgame **QFiller** slots on the basis of B_1's quadrant-crossing message as shown in Figure 3.10.

70

(EndGame Eg^1_{Cq1}
    :Coord = C_{Q_1}
    :RedAgent = Ra_1
    :Quadrant = Q_1
    :Candidates = $\{B_1, B_2, B_3, B_4\}$
    :QFillers = $\emptyset$; B_1 moved away ...
    :Blocker = ___
        Future: Flr^1_{Cq1})   ; but woks on Flr^1_{Cq1}

(EndGame Eg^1_{Cq2}
    :Coord = C_{Q_2}
    :RedAgent = Ra_1
    :Quadrant = Q_2
    :Candidates = $\{B_1, B_2, B_3, B_4\}$
    :QFillers = $\{B_1, B_2\}$; B_1 moved in ...
    :Blocker = ___
        Future: Flr^1_{Cq2})   ; but doesn't work for me

Figure 3.10: Coordinator's problems after B_1's message

(Follow-Lieb-Rules Flr^1_{Cq1}
    :Agent = B_1
    :RedAgent = Ra_1
    :Quadrant = Q_2
    :Blocker = ___
        Constraint: $in(B_1, Q_1)$; Violated by $in(B_1, Q_2)$
        Future: Qf^2_{B1}   ; Re-resolve by new problem.
    :Blocked-Position = ___   ; Slot unsettled
    :Termination = ___)

(Follow-Lieb-Rules Flr^1_{Cq1} ; No change
    :Agent = B_2
    :RedAgent = Ra_1
    :Quadrant = Q_2
    :Blocker = B_2
        Constraint: $in(B_2, Q_2)$
        Reason: (Derived-from-Applying-Method Qf^1_{B2})
    :Blocked-Position = ___
        Future: Alr^1_{B2}
    :Termination = ___)

Figure 3.11: Agent problems after B_1's message

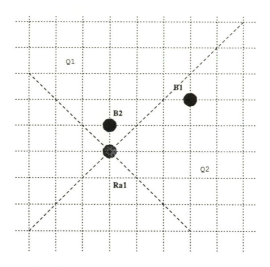

Figure 3.12: Opportunistic organizational change

(EndGame Eg^1_{Cq1}
    :Coord = C_{Q_1}
    :RedAgent = Ra_1
    :Quadrant = Q_1
    :Candidates = $\{B_1, B_2, B_3, B_4\}$
    :QFillers = $\{B_2\}$; B_2 moved in...
    :Blocker = ___
        Future: Flr^1_{Cq1})   ; but doesn't work for me.
(EndGame Eg^1_{Cq2}
    :Coord = C_{Q_2}
    :RedAgent = Ra_1
    :Quadrant = Q_2
    :Candidates = $\{B_1, B_2, B_3, B_4\}$
    :QFillers = $\{B_1\}$; B_2 moved away ...
    :Blocker = ___
        Future: Flr^1_{Cq2})   ; but works on Flr^1_{Cq2}

Figure 3.13: Coordinator's problems after B_2's message

(Follow-Lieb-Rules Flr^1_{Cq1} ; No change
   :Agent $= B_1$
   :RedAgent $= Ra_1$
   :Quadrant $= Q_2$
   :Blocker $= \_\_\_$
      Future: Qf^2_{B1}
   :Blocked-Position $= \_\_\_$
   :Termination $= \_\_$)

(Follow-Lieb-Rules Flr^1_{Cq2}
   :Agent $= B_2$
   :RedAgent $= Ra_1$
   :Quadrant $= Q_1$
   :Blocker $= \_\_\_$; Slot unsettled
      Constraint: $in(B_2, Q_2)$; Violated by $in(B_2, Q_1)$
      Future: Qf^2_{B2} ; Re-resolve by new problem.
   :Blocked-Position $= \_\_\_$; Slot unsettled
   :Termination $= \_\_$)

Figure 3.14: Agent problems after B_2's message

The next situation is depicted in Figure 3.12. In this case, B_2 has made a successive incorrect prediction that has caused it also to cross the quadrant boundary. His initial reaction is to update his problem as B_1 did (Figure 3.14). The coordinators first update their **QFiller** slots as shown in Figure 3.13. At this point, B_1 and B_2 (and their coordinators) have a choice:

- They can both re-resolve the current Follow-Lieb-Rules problem by generating and solving new QFill problems for Q_1 and Q_2 respectively (persistence).

- By opportunism, they can stay where they are. Aside from the issue of why a given agent intends to solve problems (which we assume they do), this problem concerns the reasons why an agent might change organizational roles and stay in the new quadrant. Support for alternatives in this choice may come from other problems that sit in the background and that emerge as interesting options under certain circumstances (here, unexpected change of quadrant by another agent). Under a paradigm whereby an agent updates information about problems that it solves and only those, mechanisms outside the agent are necessary for that agent to switch quadrant (organizational) roles, since quadrant responsibility problems are solved by the coordinator agents.

In this situation, C_{Q_1}, an opportunistic coordinator, can reason that B_2 can be next to the red agent faster than B_1. (See his **Blocker** constraint in Figure 3.3.) Thus, C_{Q_1} proposes

73

(Follow-Lieb-Rules Flr^2_{Cq1} ; $[C_{Q_1}$ proposes to $C_{Q_2}]$
   :Agent $= B_2$; Change of assigned coordinator.
   :RedAgent $= Ra_1$
   :Quadrant $= Q_1$; Change of assigned quadrant.
   :Blocker $= B_2$; Slot settled for free.
      Reason: (Input-from C_{Q_1}))
(Follow-Lieb-Rules Flr^2_{Cq2} ; $[C_{Q_2}$ proposes to $C_{Q_1}]$
   :Agent $= B_1$; Change of assigned coordinator.
   :RedAgent $= Ra_1$
   :Quadrant $= Q_2$; Change of assigned quadrant.
   :Blocker $= B_1$; Slot settled for free.
      Reason: (Input-from C_{Q_2}))

Figure 3.15: Plans exchanged between the coordinators

(EndGame Eg^1_{Cq1}
   :Coord $= C_{Q_1}$
   :RedAgent $= Ra_1$
   :Quadrant $= Q_1$
   :Candidates $= \{B_1, B_2, B_3, B_4\}$
   :QFillers $= \{B_2\}$; B_2 is still here ...
   :Blocker $= \underline{\quad}$
      Future: Flr^2_{Cq1})   ; but works for me now.
(EndGame Eg^1_{Cq2}
   :Coord $= C_{Q_2}$
   :RedAgent $= Ra_1$
   :Quadrant $= Q_2$
   :Candidates $= \{B_1, B_2, B_3, B_4\}$
   :QFillers $= \{B_1\}$; B_1 is still here ...
   :Blocker $= \underline{\quad}$
      Future: Flr^2_{Cq2})   ; but works for me now.

Figure 3.16: Coordinator problems after aligning their plans

(Follow-Lieb-Rules Flr^2_{Cq1}
    :Agent = B_2
    :RedAgent = Ra_1
    :Quadrant = Q_1
    :Blocker = B_2
        Reason: (Input-from C_{Q_1})
    :Blocked-Position = ___   ; Settle with new problem
        Future: Alr^2_{B1}
    :Termination = ___)
(Follow-Lieb-Rules Flr^2_{Cq2}
    :Agent = B_1
    :RedAgent = Ra_1
    :Quadrant = Q_2
    :Blocker = B_1
        Reason: (Input-from C_{Q_2})
    :Blocked-Position = ___   ; Settle with new problem
        Future: Alr^2_{B2}
    :Termination = ___)

Figure 3.17: Agent problems after coordinator plan agreement

to C_{Q_2} a modified plan (top of Figure 3.15). C_{Q_2} then tries to align this proposition with his problems. The alignment can be done by simply matching both problems descriptions, slot for slot, and looking for constraint violations. C_{Q_2}'s current problem doesn't provide a match (C_{Q_1}'s proposition uses B_2 as well as C_{Q_2}'s original problem). However, the alternative alignment method that generates a problem matching the proposition results in a compatible plan (bottom of Figure 3.15). Thus C_{Q_2} agrees to C_{Q_1} if its result is agreed on too. (cf. the *coordinated attack problem* [Halpern 1986]). The result of this negotiation by alignment is shown in Figure 3.16. Another negotiation is now engaged between C_{Q_1} and B_2 to verify that B_2 will agree to accept the new plan Flr^2_{Cq1}. Likewise, a similar negotiation occurs between C_{Q_2} and B_2. The outcome is shown in Figure 3.17 as far as the agents with blocking responsibility are concerned. Note that they further elaborate these problem complexes by filling in the `Blocked-Position` slots.

3.6   Conclusions

We have presented the beginnings of a framework for representing and revising organizational knowledge based on collections of settled and unsettled problem complexes. A simple multiagent ICE problem-solving system comprised of four blue agents, one red agent, and a grid simulation has been implemented on the MACE testbed. Each ICE agent comprises 6 MACE agents for different functions, and each incorporates a two-level production lattice interpreter as described briefly above. This system is being augmented with the representations described here, to test its possibilities for flexible reorganization. The aim of this research is to eventually employ automated discovery methods to uncover new coordination and control strategies for autonomous agents.

Acknowledgements

An earlier version of this paper was presented at the 1988 Workshop on Distributed Artificial Intelligence. We are grateful to participants of the workshop, and especially to Elihu M. Gerson, Carl Hewitt, and Leigh Star, for discussions and elaborations of these ideas. We also thank the referees for their helpful suggestions on earlier drafts. Finally, we acknowledge the generous support of Intel Scientific Computers, Inc., Sequent Computers, Inc. and the National Science Foundation under grant number CDA-8820847.

References

[Benda *et al.* 1986] M. Benda, R. Jagganathan, and R. Dodhiawalla, "On Optimal Cooperation of Knowledge Sources," Unpublished manuscript presented at the 1986 Workshop on Distributed Artificial Intelligence, Gloucester, MA, 1986. Available from Miroslav Benda, Boeing AI Center, Seattle, WA.

[Benson 1977] J. Kenneth Benson, ed., *Organizational Analysis: Critique and Innovation*, Sage Publications, Beverly Hills, CA, 1977.

[Bentley 1954] Arthur F. Bentley, *Inquiry Into Inquiries*, Sidney Ratner, ed., Boston: Beacon Press, 1954.

[Bond and Gasser 1988a] A. Bond and L. Gasser, *Readings in Distributed Artificial Intelligence*, San Mateo, CA: Morgan Kaufman, 1988.

[Bond and Gasser 1988b] A. Bond and L. Gasser, "An Analysis of Problems and Research in DAI," in [Bond and Gasser 1988a].

[Cammarata *et al.* 1983] S. Cammarata, D. McArthur, and R. Steeb, "Strategies of Cooperation in Distributed Problem Solving," *Proceedings IJCAI-83*, 1983, pp. 767–770.

[Chandrasekaran 1981] B. Chandrasekaran, "Natural and Social System Metaphors for Distributed Problem Solving," *IEEE Transactions on Systems, Man, and Cybernetics*, vol. SMC-11, January, 1981.

[Cohen and Levesque 1987] P. Cohen and H. Levesque, "Intention = Choice + Commitment," *Proc. AAAI-87*, Morgan Kaufman, 1987.

[Corkill 1982] Daniel D. Corkill, *A Framework for Organizational Self-Design in Distributed Problem Solving Networks*, Pd.D. Dissertation, Department of Computer and Information Science, University of Massachusetts, Amherst, 1982. (Also Technical Report COINS-TR-82-33, University of Massachusetts Department of Computer and Information Science, December, 1982.)

[Dalton 1959] Melville Dalton, *Men Who Manage*, New York: John Wiley, 1959.

[Davis 1983] Randall Davis, and Reid G. Smith, "Negotiation as a Metaphor for Distributed Problem Solving," *Artificial Intelligence*, vol. 20, 1983, pp. 63–109.

[Dewey 1916] J. Dewey, *Essays in Experimental Logic*, New York: Dover Publications, 1916.

[Dewey 1938] J. Dewey, *Logic: The Theory of Inquiry*, New York: Henry Holt and Company, 1938.

[Durfee *et al.* 87] E. Durfee, V. Lesser and D. Corkill, "Coherent Cooperation among Communicating Problem-Solvers." *IEEE Trans. on Computers*, vol. C-36, no. 11, November 1987, pp. 1275–1291.

[Fox 1981] M. Fox, "An Organizational View of Distributed Systems," *IEEE Transactions on Systems, Man, and Cybernetics*, vol. SMC-11, January 1981.

[Gasser 1986] L. Gasser, "The Integration of Computing and Routine Work," *ACM Transactions on Office Information Systems*, vol. 4, no. 3, July 1986.

[Gasser *et al.* 1987] L. Gasser, C. Braganza, and N. Herman, "MACE: A Flexible Testbed for Distributed Artificial Intelligence Research," in [Huhns 1987], 1987.

[Gasser 1989] L. Gasser, "No Sharing," USC DAI Group Research Note 51, Dept. of Computer Science, USC, June 1989 (in preparation).

[Gerson and Gasser 1987] Elihu M. Gerson and L. Gasser, "Notes on Problem Solving in Weak Systems," personal working papers, 1987.

[Goldstein 1975] I. Goldstein, "Bargaining Between Goals," *Proc. IJCAI-75*, 1975.

[Halpern 1986] Joseph Y. Halpern, "Reasoning About Knowledge: An Overview," *Proceedings of the 1986 Conference on Theoretical Aspects of Reasoning About Knowledge*, Morgan Kaufman Publishers, 1986, pp. 1–17.

[Hammond 1986] Kristian J. Hammond, "CHEF: A Model of Case-Based Planning," *Proceedings of the Fifth National Conference on Artificial Intelligence*, Philadelphia, PA, 1986.

[Hewitt 1986] C. Hewitt, "Offices are Open Systems," *ACM Transactions on Office Information Systems*, vol. 4, no. 3, July 1986.

[Huhns 1987] M. Huhns, ed., *Distributed Artificial Intelligence*, Pitman, 1987.

[Kling 1987] R. Kling, "Defining the Boundaries of Computing Across Complex Organizations" in R. Boland and R. Hirscheim, eds., *Critical Issues in Information Systems Research*, New York: John Wiley and Sons, 1987.

[Lenat 1982] D. Lenat, "AM: Discovery in Mathematics as Heuristic Search," in R. Davis and D. Lenat, *Knowledge Based Systems in Artificial Intelligence*, McGraw Hill, 1982.

[Lenat 1983a] D. Lenat, "Theory Formation by Heuristic Search," *Artificial Intelligence*, vol. 21, nos. 1,2, 1983, pp. 31–59.

[Lenat 1983b] D. Lenat, "EURISKO: A Program That Learns New Heuristics and Domain Concepts," *Artificial Intelligence*, vol. 21, nos. 1,2, 1983, pp. 61–98.

[Lesser and Corkill 1983] V. Lesser and D. Corkill, "The Distributed Vehicle Monitoring Testbed," *AI Magazine*, Fall, 1983.

[Maines 1984] David Maines, ed., *Urban Life*, Special issue on negotiated order theory, 1984.

[Malone 1988] Thomas W. Malone, "Organizing Information Processing Systems: Parallels Between Human Organizations and Computer Systems," in W. Zachary, S. Robertson and J. Black, eds., *Cognition, Cooperation and Computation*, Norwood, NJ: Ablex, 1988.

[March 1965] James G. March, ed., *The Handbook of Organizations*, Chicago, Rand-McNally, 1965.

[Pattison et al. 1987] E. Pattison, D. Corkill and V. Lesser, "Instantiating Descriptions of Organizational Structures," in [Huhns 1987], 1987.

[Peirce 1955] C. S. Peirce, "How to Make Our Ideas Clear," in Justus Buchler, ed., *Philosophical Writings of Peirce*, Dover, 1955.

[Perrow 1979] Charles Perrow, *Complex Organizations: A Critical Essay*, Glenview, IL: Scott, Foresman, and Co., 1979.

[Schank and Abelson 1977] R. Schank and R. Abelson, *Scripts, Plans, Goals, and Understanding*, Hillsdale, NJ: Lawrence Earlbaum, 1977.

[Star 1989] Susan Leigh Star, "The Structure of Ill-Structured Solutions: Boundary Objects and Heterogeneous Distributed Problem Solving," in L. Gasser and M.N. Huhns, eds., *Distributed Artificial Intelligence, Vol. II*, London: Pitman, 1989.

[Strauss et al. 1963] A. Strauss L. Schatzman, D. Ehrlich, R. Bucher, and M. Sabshin, "The Hospital and it Negotiated Order," in E. Friedson, ed., *The Hospital in Modern Society*, New York: The Free Press, 1963.

[Strauss 1978] A. Strauss, *Negotiations: Varieties, Processes, Contexts, and Social Order*, San Francisco: Jossey Bass, 1978.

[Strauss 1988] A. Strauss, "The Articulation of Project Work: An Organizational Process," *The Sociological Quarterly*, 1988.

[Weick 1979] Karl E. Weick, *The Social Psychology of Organizing*, Reading, MA: Addison Wesley, 1979.

[Wesson et al. 1981] R. Wesson, F. Hayes-Roth, J. W. Burge, C. Stasz, and C. A. Sunshine, "Network Structures for Distributed Situation Assessment," *IEEE Transactions on Systems, Man and Cybernetics*, SMC-11, January 1981.

[Woolgar 1985] S. Woolgar, "Why Not a Sociology of Machines? The Case of Sociology and Artificial Intelligence," *Sociology*, vol. 19:4, November 1985, pp. 557–572.

Les Gasser, Nicholas F. Rouquette, Randall W. Hill, and John Lieb
Distributed Artificial Intelligence Group
Computer Science Department
University of Southern California
Los Angeles, CA 90089-0782

Chapter 4

Dynamics of Computational Ecosystems: Implications for DAI

J. O. Kephart, T. Hogg, and B. A. Huberman

Abstract

Recently, Huberman and Hogg analyzed the dynamics of resource allocation in a model of computational ecosystems that incorporated many of the features endemic to most proposed DAI systems, including distributed control, asynchrony, resource contention, extensive communication among agents, and the concomitant problems of incomplete knowledge and delayed information. In this paper, we present computer simulations that verify quantitatively their theoretical predictions of complicated modes of behavior (such as persistent oscillations and chaos) for certain ranges of parameters. The simulations have also led to the discovery of new phenomena, including extremely long-lived metastable states and chaos induced by overly-clever local decision-making algorithms.

4.1 Introduction

In their seminal work on distributed problem solving, [Davis and Smith 1983] reiterated a question of central importance to distributed artificial intelligence: in the absence of global controls, how is the overall behavior of a group of cooperating agents related to that of the individual agents which comprise it? Some qualitative insight into this relationship has been provided by comparisons with various organizations in human society, including groups of human experts [Davis and Smith 1983], the scientific community [Kornfeld and Hewitt 1981], and economic markets [Miller and Drexler 1988], [Malone et al. 1988]. The Society of Mind [Minsky 1986] is another example of such an analogy. The essential features of most of these DAI models are a lack of central control, asynchrony, contention for resources, and extensive communication among agents, along with the concomitant problems of incomplete knowledge and delayed information.

Recently, [Huberman and Hogg 1988] have addressed the same question from a more quantitative perspective by analyzing the dynamical behavior of a computational ecosystem that incorporates the above-mentioned features. In this paper we compare the predictions of their theory to extensive computer simulations. We find that computational ecosystems can display a panoply of interesting behaviors, several of which are illustrated here. These include regimes that, depending on particular system parameters, are characterized by fixed points, oscillations, or even chaos. We demonstrate that imperfect knowledge suppresses oscillatory behavior at the expense of reducing performance. We show that enhancing the decision-making abilities of some of the individual components of the system can either improve or severely degrade the overall system performance. Finally, we show that systems can remain in nonoptimal metastable states for extremely long periods of time before escaping to the globally optimum state, in agreement with theoretical predictions [Ceccato and B. A. Huberman 1988].

4.2   Model of Computational Ecosystems

The basic model of a computational ecosystem considered in this paper, illustrated in Figure 4.1, is one in which A agents, engaging in various tasks, are free to choose among R resources according to their *perceived* (not necessarily correct) payoffs. In general, the payoff for using a particular resource depends upon the number of agents already using it. The information about resource usage that is available to the agents can be somewhat imperfect and delayed. Due to the absence of central control, the agents make their decisions asynchronously and independently of one another [Huberman and Hogg 1988].

Consider an agent that happens to be using a particular resource. At some randomly-determined time t, it reevaluates which resource it ought to use based upon the fraction of agents f_r which were using each resource r at time $t - \tau$, where τ is the time required for information to reach an agent. The agent uses this information to evaluate its perceived payoff for using each resource, which is supposed to reflect the benefit to be accrued to the agent for the completion of a task while using that resource. Unreliability in the information and mismatch between the perceived payoff and the actual payoff are modeled by adding a normally-distributed quantity with zero mean and standard deviation σ to each payoff. The agent then chooses the resource associated with the highest perceived payoff.

Using the complementary techniques of theoretical analysis [Huberman and Hogg 1988]

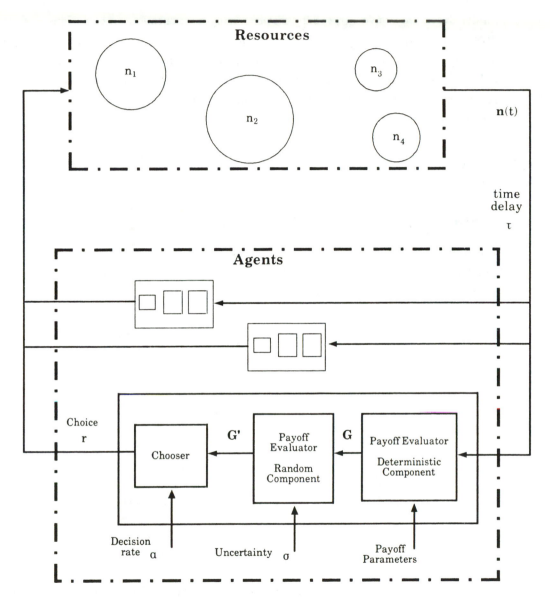

Figure 4.1: Model of a computational ecosystem with n_i agents using the ith resource. The circles denote computational resources, and the solid rectangles denote agents in the system, one of which is expanded to show how it computes which resource to use.

and simulation, we measure the fraction of agents using each resource as a function of time, from which we can calculate a number of quantities that reflect different aspects of the overall behavior of the system. The simulation is a straightforward implementation of the model described above. In order to study truly asynchronous interactions and to avoid artifacts associated with using the fixed time interval associated with a *clock*-driven simulation, we have chosen to use an *event*-driven simulation. After the simulation has proceeded up to some time t, the time at which the next choice is made by some agent is generated according to an exponential distribution with mean $(\alpha A)^{-1}$, where α is the decision rate per agent.

4.3 Dynamical Behavior of Computational Ecosystems

4.3.1 Stable Equilibria and Oscillations

Figure 4.2 illustrates two types of behavior that are typical of all of the computational ecosystems that we have studied. The payoffs are chosen so that the optimal use of resources is for 75% of the agents to use resource 1.

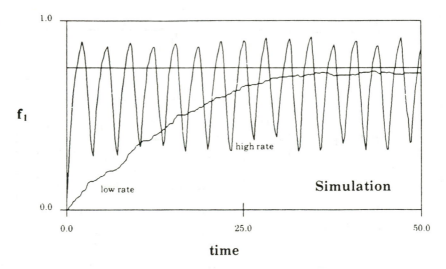

Figure 4.2: Fraction f_1 of agents using resource 1 in a simulation of 200 agents competing for two resources. Payoffs for resources 1 and 2 are $G_1 = -f_1$ and $G_2 = -3f_2$; the uncertainty is $\sigma = 0.125$. Lower curve: $\alpha = 0.04$. Upper curve: $\alpha = 1.0$. Straight line marks optimal value of $f_1 = 0.75$. Time is measured in units of the delay τ.

When only a few agents reevaluate their choice within one time delay interval, the sys-

82

tem relaxes to a stable equilibrium close to the optimal value of $f_1 = 0.75$, with small random fluctuations about this equilibrium. However, when many agents reevaluate their choice within one time delay, the system overshoots the equilibrium point, then overcompensates by overshooting too far in the other direction, resulting in persistent oscillations about an average value that is noticeably less optimal than for the stable equilibrium. In an intermediate range of the decision rate (not shown), the system overshoots the equilibrium point initially, but the oscillations about the equilibrium point eventually decay to the level of random fluctuations. Thus there are three distinct classes of behavior: nonoscillatory relaxation to equilibrium, damped oscillations about the equilibrium, and persistent oscillations.

The range of α in which each of these three classes of behavior occurs is shown in Figure 4.3. For extremely low decision rates (left side of region I), the system takes a very long time to relax to equilibrium. At moderately low decision rates (right side of region I), relaxation to equilibrium takes just a few delay times. In region II, the system exhibits damped oscillations which eventually relax to the equilibrium. Near the right-hand boundary of region II, the relaxation time increases substantially. Finally, in region III, the oscillations do not decay, and their amplitude increases with increasing α. In this regime, the correlation time does not represent relaxation to equilibrium; rather, it is the characteristic time during which the persistent oscillations of two different simulation runs remain in phase.

Two important conclusions can be drawn from Figure 4.3. First, the fact that the simulation involving 500 agents matches the theoretical curve most closely is consistent with the expectation that the mean-field theory is most accurate in the limit of an infinite number of agents. Second, the decision rate near the boundary of regions I and II is optimal because the system is both responsive (the relaxation time is short) and free of oscillations.

4.3.2 Chaotic Behavior

Slightly more complex systems can also exhibit period doubling and chaotic behavior. We present two examples of such systems in this section. In the first one, the payoffs are set so that the maximum payoff for using either resource occurs when other agents are using the same resource, i.e. the agents are to some extent cooperative. In the second example, the agents are strictly competitive (as in the previous section), but they can choose from among three resources.

Figure 4.4 summarizes the various types of behavior that can occur when cooperative agents choose between two resources. The payoffs and the uncertainty have been adjusted so that the boundaries between regions I and II and between regions II and III are the same

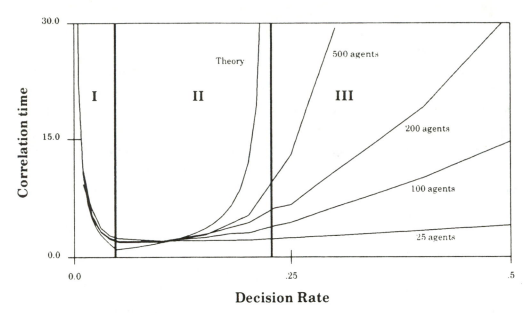

Figure 4.3: Correlation time as a function of decision rate α. Region I: stable equilibrium. Region II: damped oscillations. Region III: persistent oscillations.

as in the Figure 4.3. For large values of α, there are at least three additional behavioral regimes. In region IV, the oscillation period is doubled, and in region V, the system undergoes a period-doubling cascade containing oscillations of period 4, 8, 16, etc. Finally, region VI contains both periodic and chaotic behavior. In the latter case it is impossible to predict the future beyond a few delay times.

However, when we run a simulation with 200 agents for the same parameters that were assumed in Figure 4.4, we find no evidence of period doubling; instead, there is a direct transition from period-1 oscillation to chaos. This loss of the fine period-doubling structure in the route to chaos is typically observed in noisy systems [Crutchfield and Huberman 1980]. This suggests that many more agents are required to reduce the statistical fluctuations to the point where period doubling can be observed. However, by increasing the uncertainty parameter σ, we are able to observe period doubling, as illustrated in Figure 4.5. In Figure 4.6, the decision rate has been increased from that in Figure 4.5a, and the resultant behavior is chaotic.

Period doubling and chaos are also observed in systems of competitive agents choosing from among three resources, as illustrated in Figure 4.7. For the chosen parameters, the system follows a limit cycle with two loops, which indicates a doubled period. Figure 4.8 is a noisy simulacrum of Figure 4.7, which was obtained by running a simulation with 300 agents for the same parameters. The general shape and double-loop behavior of the

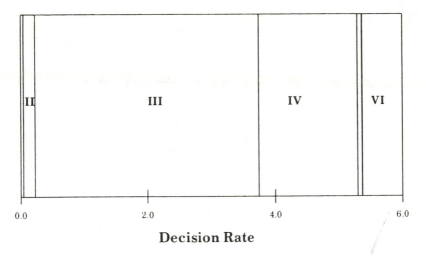

Figure 4.4: Behavioral regimes for cooperative agents and two resources (theoretical). Payoffs are $G_1 = 5.29 f_1 - 6.727 f_1^2$ and $G_2 = f_2 - f_2^2$; $\sigma = 0.125$. Regions I–III have the same behavior as in Figure 4.2. Region IV: oscillations with twice the period as in III, Region V: period-doubling cascade. Region VI: chaotic regime.

theoretical attractor in Figure 4.7 is still perceptible. By increasing the decision rate, the double-loop limit cycle is modified into the chaotic trajectory [Serra *et al.* 1986] illustrated in Figure 4.9, in which the evolution of any two initially nearby states is unpredictably different. In this case, the statistical fluctuations in a simulation would almost certainly obscure the chaotic nature of the trajectory unless the number of agents was drastically increased or the parameters were changed.

4.3.3 Oscillations and Suboptimality

One effective way to suppress coherent oscillations and chaotic behavior in a system is to intentionally increase the amount of randomness in the decision procedure. Let us return for a moment to the example of agents competing for two resources in Section 4.3.1. In Figure 4.3, the uncertainty parameter was fixed at $\sigma = 0.125$. Figure 4.10a illustrates how the onsets of damped and persistent oscillations increase with σ. If σ is sufficiently large, the threshold for persistent oscillations becomes infinite, completely curing the problem of persistent oscillations. However, increasing σ has the unfortunate side-effect of decreasing the equilibrium value of f_1, as illustrated in Figure 4.10b, and the system performance becomes noticeably suboptimal.

Figure 4.11 demonstrates that, for a fixed decision rate, the best possible performance of this system is obtained when the uncertainty is just enough to suppress persistent oscil-

a. Simulation

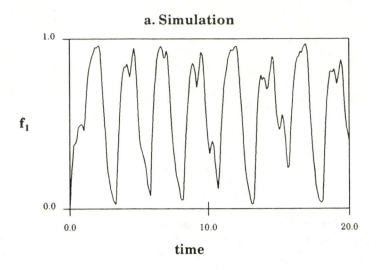

f₁

time

b. Theory

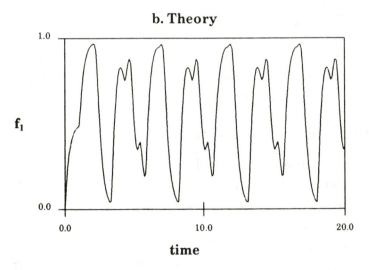

f₁

time

Figure 4.5: Oscillations in a system of cooperative agents with two resources after period doubling. Payoffs are the same as in Figure 4.4, but the uncertainty is increased to $\sigma = 0.25$. $\alpha = 3.5$. (a) Typical simulation run with 200 agents. (b) $f_1(t)$ predicted by mean-field theory.

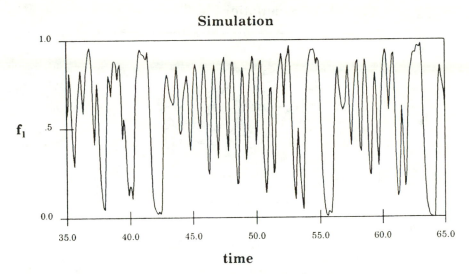

Simulation

f_1

time

Figure 4.6: Chaotic behavior in a cooperative system with two resources. All parameters are the same as in Figure 4.5, except that the decision rate has been increased to $\alpha = 6.0$.

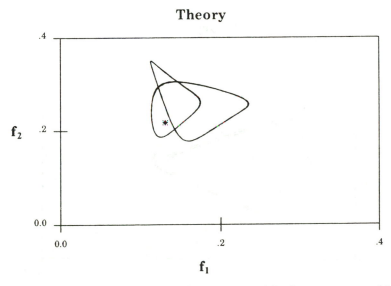

Theory

f_2

f_1

Figure 4.7: Period doubling in a competitive system with three resources (theory). In this phase-space plot, time has been eliminated by plotting $f_2(t)$ vs. $f_1(t)$ for $25\tau < t < 50\tau$. The payoffs are $G_1 = -10f_1$, $G_2 = -6f_2$, and $G_3 = -2f_3$. $\sigma = 0.125$ and $\alpha = 0.25$. The star indicates the optimal equilibrium point $(f_1, f_2) = (0.130, 0.217)$ to which the system would converge in the absence of delays and uncertainty (analogous to the $f_1 = 0.75$ line in Figure 4.2).

87

Simulation

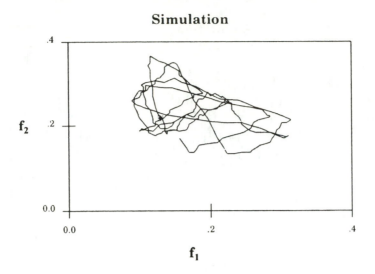

Figure 4.8: Noisy period-two limit cycle observed in simulated system of 300 competitive agents choosing among three resources. All parameters are the same as in Figure 4.7.

Theory

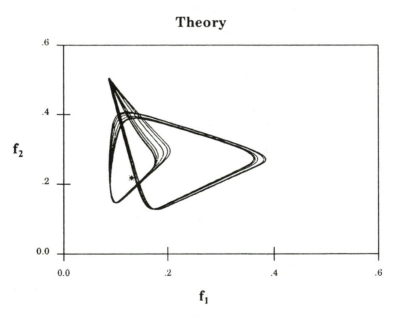

Figure 4.9: Chaotic attractor observed in competitive system with three resources (theory) under the same conditions as in Figure 4.7, except that the decision rate has been increased to $\alpha = 0.50$, and $100\tau < t < 150\tau$. $f_1(t)$ and $f_2(t)$ are chaotic.

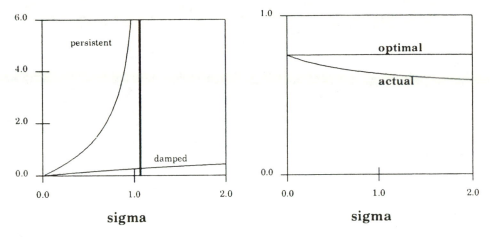

Figure 4.10: (a) Critical decision rates for damped and persistent oscillations as a function of uncertainty σ. (b) Equilibrium value of f_1 as a function of σ compared to the optimal value of $f_1 = 0.75$.

lations. For large decision rates, intentionally increasing σ can improve the system performance dramatically—from less than that for completely random decisions to just slightly less than that of a system with no uncertainty and no delays. From Figures 4.10a and 4.11, it can be shown that a system with an arbitrarily large decision rate can always be made to operate at greater than 76% of the optimal performance, provided that the intrinsic uncertainty is less than the critical value indicated by the vertical line in Figure 4.10a.

Similar effects occur in the more complex systems studied in Section 4.3.2. If the uncertainty used in the cooperative, two-resource system of Figure 4.6a is doubled, the system never progresses beyond period-2 oscillation even when α is made arbitrarily large, i.e., the chaotic regime is never reached at all. In the competitive, three-resource system illustrated in Figures 4.7–4.9, the equilibrium point drifts away from the optimal position indicated by the star, resulting in an optimality gap analogous to that illustrated in Figure 4.10b.

4.3.4 Smart Agents

A completely different approach to increasing the system performance by eradicating oscillations and chaos is to give some of the agents the ability to estimate the current resource utilization. For the simple system described in Sections 4.3.1 and 4.3.3, we introduce "smart" agents that continually monitor the oscillation period, estimating it as the time between successive maxima in $f_1(t)$. They intentionally increase their own time delay so as to match the perceived oscillation period, thereby obtaining (presumably) a better estimate of the current value of $f_1(t)$.

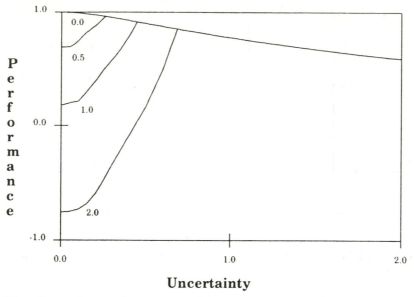

Uncertainty

Figure 4.11: Dependence of system performance upon randomness in decision procedure for various decision rates (indicated in figure.) Performance is calculated by adding time-averaged payoffs of all agents, normalized to 1 for no uncertainty or delays and 0 for random decisions (infinite uncertainty.)

As shown in Figure 4.12a, a system containing a mixture of 10% smart agents and 90% "normal" agents becomes somewhat more stable after the smart agents determine the oscillation period (which takes a few periods). A closer analysis reveals that the smart agents operate at a performance level of approximately 100% (as defined in Figure 4.11) and that the performance level of the normal agents doubles to nearly 50%—a sort of trickle-down effect. Encouraged by this success, one might be tempted to make all of the agents smart. However, as shown in Figure 4.12b, when all of the agents are smart, the system exhibits very large and complex oscillations, and the overall system performance is degraded substantially below that of a system consisting of all normal agents. For this particular system, it is best if approximately 20–50% of the agents are smart. Paradoxically, when the proportion of smart agents exceeds 80%, their performance can be substantially lower than that of the normal agents.

4.3.5 Punctuated Equilibria and Metastability

In all of the examples discussed so far, the behavior of the system after the transient has died out has been independent of the initial conditions. However, in both of the more complex systems discussed in Section 4.3.2 , it is possible to find certain ranges of parameters for

10% smart agents

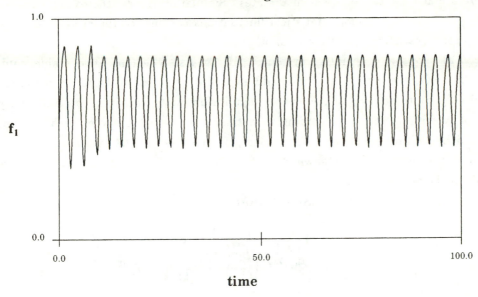

100% smart agents

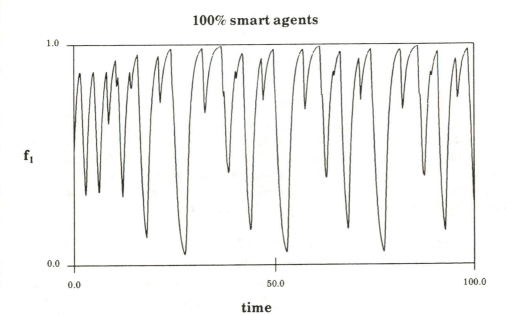

Figure 4.12: Fraction of agents using resource 1 as a function of time in a system with smart agents. All system parameters are the same as in Figure 4.2, and $\alpha = 1.0$. a) 10% smart agents. b) 100% smart agents.

which there are at least two different final states. Simulations reveal the existence of an interesting phenomenon: random statistical fluctuations can induce the system to jump almost instantaneously from one state to another.

Figure 4.13 shows a cooperative system of 10 agents, which has two stable equilibrium points. Contrary to what one would expect from mean-field theory, a system that is initially captured by the metastable equilibrium state can jump spontaneously to the globally optimal state. According to a theory of metastability in such systems [Ceccato and B. A. Huberman 1988], the amount of time spent in the metastable state is exponential in the number of agents, while the transition time from one state to another is logarithmic in the number of agents.

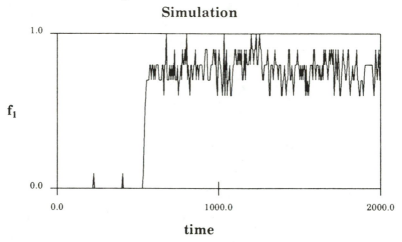

Simulation

time

Figure 4.13: Punctuated equilibria in a cooperative system of 10 agents. The payoffs are $G_1 = -1.65 + 10f_1 - 9f_1^2$ and $G_2 = 0$; $\sigma = 0.5$, $\alpha = 0.1$. There are two stable equilibrium points: one at $f_A = 0.02$ and another more optimal one at $f_B = 0.80$. After 530τ, a random statistical fluctuation induces the system to hop over the energy barrier at $f* = 0.05$, thereby escaping the metastable equilibrium f_A and settling into the globally optimal equilibrium f_B. The width of the transition region is less than 20τ.

Another example of this behavior is shown in Figure 4.14. In this case the system switches spontaneously between two period-1 limit cycles with different orientations in phase space. The metastability of nonoptimal choices and the suddenness of the transition between states is reminiscent of Darwinian evolutionary models of "punctuated equilibria" [Lande 1985, Newman *et al.* 1985].

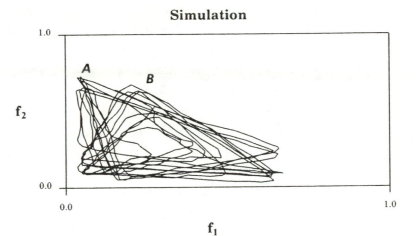

Simulation

Figure 4.14: Punctuated limit cycles in a competitive system of 300 agents choosing among three resources. All payoff parameters are the same as in Figure 4.7. $\sigma = 0.10$ and $\alpha = 1.0$. The system is quickly captured into a noisy version of limit cycle A, which it follows in a clockwise direction. Near $t = 172\tau$, there is a sudden transition taking less than 2τ to a noisy version of limit cycle B, which is followed counterclockwise. In this simulation run, which lasted for 1000τ, the system flipped its state three times.

4.4   Conclusion

Using both simulations and theoretical analysis, we have provided some quantitative answers to a fundamental question raised in [Davis and Smith 1983] about the conditions under which a system of cooperating agents can function acceptably well in the absence of central control. We have illustrated the complex behavior that can be exhibited by even the simplest computational ecosystems and investigated the dependence of this behavior upon delays and uncertainty in information and the degree of cooperation and competition among the agents. In general, the predictions of the theory of [Huberman and Hogg 1988] are validated by computer simulations, particularly in the limit of large numbers of agents. Simulations reveal that, in most cases, statistical fluctuations (neglected in the theory) do not shift the boundaries between various behavioral regimes; they merely blur those boundaries. One notable exception is the phenomenon of punctuated equilibria, which depends critically on the presence of fluctuations and thus can only be explained by theories which explicitly incorporate fluctuations [Ceccato and B. A. Huberman 1988, Lande 1985].

Designers of DAI systems must realize that complicated global behavior can arise from simple interactions among individual agents, and they must become aware of how they can tune various parameters of those interactions so as to avoid undesirable behavior. Given that slight complications introduced into the model in Section 4.3.2 yielded new behavioral phenomena, it is likely that real DAI systems would exhibit even more exotic behavior than that illustrated in this paper. Nevertheless, a number of system design principles can be deduced from our work. For example, delays have a strongly deleterious effect on system performance, but, as illustrated in Figure 4.11, a judicious increase in the randomness of the decision-making process of the individual agents can ameliorate the problem significantly. Another principle was mentioned near the end of Section 4.3.1: the system's responsiveness will be optimal if the decision rate is adjusted so that the system is on the threshold of persistent oscillations. As a final example, the smart-agent fable of Figure 4.12 cautions the system designer against blithely assuming that more locally-intelligent control algorithms will necessarily lead to better overall system performance.

Simple extensions of the analogy between computational ecosystems and biological ecosystems suggest several directions for future work. As do their biological counterparts, computational ecosystems can contain many different species of agents occupying different niches. Different species of agents may have different computational requirements and/or different strategies for obtaining the necessary resources. The work on smart agents is a first small step in the direction of understanding the effect of this differentiation. A second important feature of biological ecosystems is their ability to adapt to changing environments, which encourages us to seek feedback mechanisms that can give computational ecosystems the same evolutionary capability. As has been suggested by several authors [Davis and Smith 1983, Miller and Drexler 1988, Malone *et al.* 1988], the most successful DAI architectures might be founded upon economic rather than biological principles. By extending our model to include interactions in which the servers can participate in local control decisions on an equal footing with the clients, we might gain a good deal of insight into this issue.

References

[Ceccato and B. A. Huberman 1988] , H. A. Ceccato and B. A. Huberman, "Persistence of Non-Optimal Strategies," Xerox PARC Technical Report, 1988.

[Crutchfield and Huberman 1980] , J. P. Crutchfield and B. A. Huberman, "Fluctuations and the Onset of Chaos," *Phys. Lett.*, Vol. 77A, 1980, p. 407.

[Davis and Smith 1983] R. Davis and R. G. Smith, "Negotiation as a Metaphor for Distributed Problem Solving," *Artificial Intelligence*, Vol. 20, 1983, pp. 63–109.

[Huberman and Hogg 1988] , B. A. Huberman and T. Hogg, "The Behavior of Computational Ecologies," in B. A. Huberman, ed., *The Ecology of Computation*, North-Holland, Amsterdam, 1988, pp. 77–115.

[Kornfeld and Hewitt 1981] , W. A. Kornfeld and C. E. Hewitt, "The Scientific Community Metaphor," *IEEE Transactions on Systems, Man and Cybernetics*, Vol. SMC-11, 1981, pp. 24–33.

[Lande 1985] , R. Lande, "Expected time for random genetic drift of a population between stable phenotypic states," *Proc. Natl. Acad. Sci. USA*, Vol. 82, 1985, p. 7641.

[Malone *et al.* 1988] , T.W. Malone, R. E. Fikes, K. R. Grant, and M. T. Howard, "Enterprise: A Market-like Task Scheduler for Distributed Computing Environments," in B. A. Huberman, ed., *The Ecology of Computation*, North-Holland, Amsterdam, 1988, pp. 177–205.

[Miller and Drexler 1988] , M. S. Miller and K. E. Drexler, "Markets and Computation: Agoric Open Systems," in B. A. Huberman, ed., *The Ecology of Computation*, North-Holland, Amsterdam, 1988, pp. 133–176.

[Minsky 1986] , Marvin Minsky, *The Society of Mind*, Simon and Schuster, New York, 1986.

[Newman *et al.* 1985] , C. M. Newman, J. E. Cohen, and C. Kipnis, "Neo-darwinian evolution implies punctuated equilibria," *Nature*, Vol. 315, 1985, p. 400.

[Serra *et al.* 1986] , R. Serra, M. Andretta, M. Compiani, and G. Zanarini, *Introduction to the Physics of Complex Systems*, Pergamon Press, Oxford, 1986.

J. O. Kephart, T. Hogg, and B. A. Huberman
Dynamics of Computation Group
Xerox Palo Alto Research Center
Palo Alto, CA 94304

Part II

Cooperation by Negotiation

Chapter 5

Communication-Free Interactions among Rational Agents: A Probabilistic Approach

Jeffrey S. Rosenschein and John S. Breese

Abstract

Recent work on interactions among rational agents has put forward a computationally tractable, deduction-based scheme for automated agents to use in analyzing multiagent encounters. While the theory has defined irrational actions, it has underconstrained an agent's choices: there are many situations where an agent in the previous framework was faced with several potentially rational actions, and no way of choosing among them. This paper presents a probabilistic extension to the previous framework of Genesereth, Ginsberg, and Rosenschein [Genesereth *et al.* 1986] that provides agents with a mechanism for further refining their choice of rational moves. At the same time, it maintains the computational attractiveness of the previous approach.

The probabilistic extension is explicitly representing uncertainty about other players' moves. A three-level hierarchy of rationality is defined, corresponding to ordinal, stochastic, and utility dominance among alternative outcomes. The previous deduction-based formalism is recast in probabilistic terms and is seen to be a particular special case of a more encompassing dominance theory. A technique is presented for using the dominance ideas in interactions with other agents operating under various types of rationality.

5.1 Introduction

5.1.1 Interactions Among Rational Agents

Research on artificial intelligence has begun to concern itself with the design of an autonomous agent operating in real-world environments. Along one dimension, this requires that the agent be capable of dealing with dynamic and incompletely specified situations. It must be able to reason about change, recover from failures, and deal with uncertainty both in the state of the world and in the effects of its own actions.

An equally important capability is the ability to interact flexibly with other agents. There are, in fact, few scenarios where an agent could be expected to operate with *complete* autonomy; almost always there will be others with whom the agent must interact. This will be true whether the agent is operating on a factory floor, building outposts on Mars, or running errands to the corner store. These other agents will in general possess a wide range of reasoning capabilities and thus the agent should be capable of interacting flexibly with agents of different rationality "types."

There has been considerable work in recent years by AI researchers on formalisms for representing interagent beliefs [Konolige 1980], [Konolige 1984], [Appelt 1982], [Moore 1980], [Moore 1984], [Halpern and Moses 1984], an important component of the reasoning necessary for cooperation. Agents must reason about one another's beliefs to predict activity, provide information, and adapt their own behavior to others' expectations.

Another line of work has been considering the agent interactions themselves as objects about which to reason [Genesereth *et al.* 1984, Genesereth *et al.* 1986, Rosenschein 1986]. In this research, the agents have been defined as operating under the constraints of various *rationality axioms* that restrict their choices in interactions. The effects of various axioms and their relationships to one another have been analyzed.

The current paper continues along this latter line of research. The basic extension proposed is to recognize that reasoning about other agents' actions must deal with uncertainty and to incorporate an explicit mechanism for doing so. Uncertainty is inherent in encounters because of incomplete information about others' objectives, options, and reasoning processes. We address issues of uncertainty against a backdrop of increased interest in decision-theoretic concepts of probability and utility theory in AI research [Breese 1987, Horvitz *et al.* 1988]. At the same time, we exploit the fact that decision-theorists and game-theorists have been considering the use of Bayesian decision theory in situations of strategic interaction [Aumann 1987], [Kadane and Larkey 1982], [Wilson 1986], [Nau and McCardle 1988]. Though we are not proposing an extension to the concepts of equilibrium proposed by game-theorists, the work in this paper integrates previous studies of rational interaction based on a deductive framework with decision-theoretic ideas and is a first step towards operationalizing recent advances in game-theoretic solution concepts.

5.1.2 Perspectives on Multiagent Interactions

We examine reasoning about other agents from two different perspectives, the "prescriptive/descriptive" approach and the "jointly prescriptive" approach. Both perspectives have their place in the theory of rational interacting agents, though each leads us to ask different questions about how automated agents should be designed. This paper is focused on prescriptive/descriptive issues, though we make several observations and report results regarding jointly prescriptive methods.

Prescriptive/Descriptive

A "prescriptive/descriptive" approach requires two types of theories to fully capture a multiagent interaction [Kadane and Larkey 1983]. First, we need a normative theory of what our primary agent *should* do given its values and information. We have a prescriptive theory when we not only define these normative principles for rational behavior, but augment these with a prescription or method for identifying rational moves. This is precisely the approach we take in developing our notion of prescriptive rationality. Second, we require a descriptive theory of other agents. A descriptive theory is useful to the extent it can be used to predict the actions of other agents, and may be based on varying degrees of assumed "rationality" of others.

The "prescriptive/descriptive" approach is basically decision analytic: using our model of interaction, we prescribe a particular course of action for one agent based on the description it has of other agents. This was the approach taken in previous DAI work, where different information about others' rationality would cause an agent to act appropriately. This "prescriptive/descriptive" perspective is central in our design of an agent capable of interacting intelligently, particularly when we will have no control over (and limited information about) the design of the other agents.

Jointly Prescriptive

Of course, if our descriptive theory is the same as our prescriptive theory, i.e., if the best theory one has about other agents is based on introspection regarding one's own reasoning processes, this results in a "jointly prescriptive" approach. "Jointly prescriptive" concerns form the basis for much of modern game theory [Luce and Raiffa 1957]. These approaches, by and large, develop models of interaction that have certain globally desirable properties, given that all agents subscribe to the same fundamental solution strategies and have common knowledge regarding most aspects of the problem. The "jointly prescriptive" perspective is well-suited to closed systems where the interacting agents are all centrally designed. With total control over their methods of interaction (and hence the ability to engineer away uncertainty regarding others' decision-making strategies), the designer is looking for desirable properties, such as stability and pareto-optimality of solutions.

The jointly prescriptive perspective also has a role to play in competitive interactions. For example, some interaction strategies are known from the game theory literature to be "stable," i.e., if an agent uses this strategy, no opponent can benefit from playing any other strategy. A designer could feel safe in incorporating such a strategy into his agent—he need have no fear of the strategy's presence becoming known, since there is no effective counter-strategy. Thus the identification of stable strategies (which is a jointly prescriptive notion) can be important to any single agent's designer. Similarly, a demonstration of a strategy's stability *and* pareto-optimality might be an effective argument in getting many agents' designers to incorporate it:[1] the best that other agents can do is to "play along," and the overall final results have certain desirable characteristics.

5.1.3 Assumptions

This paper is concerned with single interactions among agents; though there is a mechanism for using the results of past encounters, there is no explicit concern about future interactions. Each agent is assumed capable of assigning some value to a hypothetical outcome, and (in this paper) we will assume that these assigned payoff values, for all agents, are common knowledge among them all.[2] In addition, once the interaction has been recognized, there is no further communication among the agents; each must decide on its action alone. This is the no-communication scenario used in [Genesereth *et al.* 1986].[3] The agents are assumed to be operating under certain axioms, to be discussed, that control their behavior.

---

[1]This was, for example, the argument made in [Ginsberg 1987].

[2]Uncertainty about payoffs can be incorporated into the framework, and is a topic for future research. Also, common knowledge is not always required; for a fuller discussion of how much knowledge is actually needed, see [Rosenschein 1988].

[3]While this scenario is a simplification of what might be found in real-world encounters, it is a useful starting point for an analysis of interactions. There are also a variety of instances when the assumption that no communication is possible is quite realistic, such as when agents designed in different countries or by different manufacturers unexpectedly encounter one another.

5.1.4 Overview

In Section 5.2 we introduce the formal notation for our analysis. In Section 5.3, various forms of dominance among alternatives are developed. The deduction-based formalism given in [Rosenschein 1986] is recast in probabilistic terms, and is seen to be a particular special case of a more encompassing dominance theory.

In Section 5.4 we consider questions relating to the design of an agent using the dominance relations, in the "prescriptive" portion of a "prescriptive/descriptive" approach. Axioms of behavior are given in Section 5.5 that might describe our agent's opponents,[4] and the ramifications these axioms have on the prescriptive dominance techniques are discussed. In Section 5.6 we briefly consider, from the "jointly prescriptive" perspective, the global properties of the methods we have outlined.

5.2 Notation

We will follow the convention of representing a game as a payoff matrix. Figure 5.1 is a representation of a two agent encounter.

K

	c	d
a	3 $\quad^1$	1 $\quad^2$
b	2 $\quad^5$	0 $\quad^1$

J

Figure 5.1: A payoff matrix

A game corresponds to a set P of players and, for each player $i \in P$, a set M_i of possible moves for i. For $S \subset P$, we denote $P - S$ by $\overline{S}$. We denote by m_S an element of M_S; this is a collective move (or a "joint" move) for the players in S. To $m_S \in M_S$ and $m_{\overline{S}} \in M_{\overline{S}}$ corresponds an element $\vec{m}$ of M_P. The payoff function for a game is a function

$$p : P \times M_P \rightarrow \mathbb{R}$$

whose value at $(i, \vec{m})$ is the payoff for player i if move $\vec{m}$ is made. The function p thus encodes the payoff matrix in function form.

---

[4]Throughout this paper, our use of the term "opponent" should not be taken in its colloquial sense. When our agent interacts with other agents, we will sometimes refer to them as its opponents, without intending that the agents are necessarily involved in conflict. There may be a convergence of interests among all parties.

We denote by $prob_i(m_{\bar{i}} \mid m_i, \xi)$ the probability distribution that agent i has over all the other players making move $m_{\bar{i}}$ (with ξ representing i's knowledge of the world, including his knowledge of other agents). The probability may depend, as seen from this expression, on i's own move m_i.

We could use dual matrices to represent an interaction between agents, with associated probability distributions on their moves. Consider the two matrices in Figure 5.2.

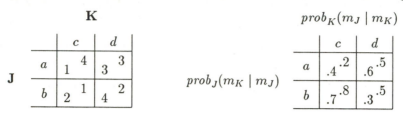

Figure 5.2: Payoff and probability matrix

The left matrix is to be interpreted in the same manner as it was above, namely as defining the payoffs each agent will receive from various outcomes. In addition, each agent is assumed to have a probability distribution on the other's moves, given a move of his own. The second matrix in Figure 5.2 displays these distributions. For example, if J considers that he will make move b, he considers that there is a .7 probability that K will make move c, and a .3 probability that K will make move d. Of course, in the probability matrix the columns sum to 1 for K, and the rows sum to 1 for J.

We define a secondary payoff function $pay(i, m_i)$, which gives us the *set* of possible payoffs to i of making move m_i:

$$pay(i, m_i) = \{p(i, \vec{m}) : prob_i(m_{\bar{i}} \mid m_i, \xi) > 0\}. \tag{5.1}$$

The expression $prob_i(m_{\bar{i}} \mid m_i, \xi) > 0$ denotes the set of responses "considered possible" to i's move m_i.[5] There are many potential moves that might be expected of other agents, depending on assumptions about them (and their assumptions about you), and similarly, many different subjective probability distributions that one might have over their potential moves. In Section 5.5 we list several alternate definitions and indicate how each affects the *pay* function or probabilities.

The final element of our notation that needs to be introduced is the notion of a "utility function" over payoffs. The utility function summarizes the agent's attitudes toward uncertain options, while payoffs summarize the agent's valuation under certainty of each possible joint move. The *utility of a joint move* for agent i in our notation is represented

---

[5]Careful readers will note that this expression subsumes the role of the *allowed* function in [Rosenschein 1986].

as $U_i(p(i, \vec{m}))$; it is a function from the real numbers to the real numbers. We then define the *expected utility* for agent i of a joint move as follows:

$$EU_i(\vec{m}) = \sum_{m_{\bar{i}} \in M_{\bar{i}}} U_i(p(i, \vec{m})) prob_i(m_{\bar{i}} \mid m_i, \xi).$$ (5.2)

More generally, the summation can be replaced by an integration. In their foundational work, [von Neumann and Morgenstern 1947] formalized rationality in terms of axioms that require an agent to behave as if maximizing expected utility.

5.3 Dominance

A concept essential to this work is *dominance*: when the payoffs resulting from one move are better than those resulting from some other move, for some precise definition of "better," the inferior move is said to be *dominated*. Previous treatments used only one kind of dominance, namely *ordinal dominance*, an "absolute" dominance between the members of two sets. In this paper we consider how two other kinds of dominance, *stochastic* and *utility* dominance, can be combined with the axiomatic approach.

5.3.1 Ordinal Dominance

Ordinal dominance is straightforward: for nonempty sets $\{\alpha_i\}$ and $\{\beta_j\}$, we say that $\{\alpha_i\}$ is ordinally dominated by $\{\beta_j\}$ (written $\{\alpha_i\} <_o \{\beta_j\}$) if $\alpha_i \leq \beta_j$ for all i, j, and at least one element of $\{\alpha_i\}$ is less than every element of $\{\beta_j\}$. For example, the set $\{5, 3\}$ ordinally dominates the set $\{3, 1\}$, since *every* member of the first is greater than or equal to every member of the second, and in at least one case the relationship is strictly greater than.

5.3.2 Stochastic Dominance

The Intuition

Before launching into the formal definition of stochastic dominance, we will present the intuitions behind its use. A *lottery* is defined to be a set of payoffs with associated probabilities. A lottery can be viewed as a state contingent payoff—in an interaction between agents, the payoff is contingent on the (uncertain) move of the opponent.

Stochastic dominance [Whitmore and Findlay 1978] between two alternative lotteries is commonly represented graphically as follows. Consider a graph whose x-axis represents various payoffs, and whose y-axis represents cumulative probabilities (i.e., runs from 0 to 1). For each agent's lotteries, we draw a curve onto this coordinate space whose y position at any x value represents the probability that the agent will receive *less than* that value from that lottery. Each curve begins at the point $(p,0)$ and increases to a maximum of $(q,1)$, where p and q are the minimum and maximum possible payoffs, respectively. If the first lottery's curve lies completely below and to the right of a second lottery's curve (with possible overlap—but no crossing—of the curves permitted), we say that the first lottery stochastically dominates the second. This means that for any given value, the player has a better chance of getting it or less from the second lottery than from the first.

For example, consider an agent that has two lotteries available to him. In the first, he has .2 chance of getting a payoff of 4, a .5 chance of getting a payoff of 6, and a .3 chance of getting a payoff of 7. We draw this lottery's curve as in Figure 5.3.[6] The curve rises by .2 at 4, rises an additional .5 at 6, and rises an additional .3 at 7.

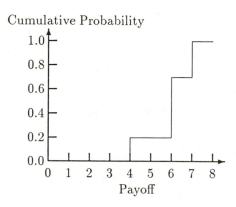

Figure 5.3: Agent's first lottery

Now imagine that there is a second lottery, where he has a .3 chance of getting a payoff of 3, a .2 chance of getting 5, and a .5 chance of getting 6. This second lottery's curve looks like that in Figure 5.4.

If we now combine these two curves, it is evident that at all points the second curve are above those of the first curve for a given payoff—thus, the second lottery has a higher probability of getting a particular value or less for all values and therefore the first lottery stochastically dominates the second (see Figure 5.5).

Stochastic dominance is relevant in evaluating an agent's choices in the extended payoff matrix below, where purely ordinal considerations leave the agent with an ambiguity. Assume that our agent J is faced with the interaction shown in Figure 5.6.

---

[6]The diagram in Figure 5.3 is typical of lotteries with discrete moves and payoffs—a step function. We could, just as easily, have a continuous set of payoffs, which would result in a smooth curve in the diagram with no vertical climbs.

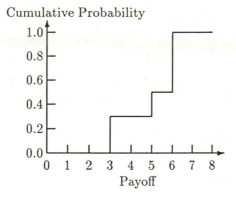

Figure 5.4: Agent's second lottery

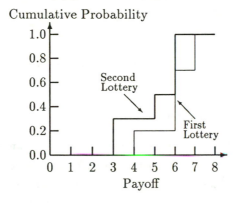

Figure 5.5: A comparison of the two lotteries

K

		c	d
J	a	1 4	3 3
	b	2 1	4 2

$prob_J(m_K \mid m_J)$

$prob_K(m_J \mid m_K)$

	c	d
a	.5 .4	.5 .4
b	.5 .6	.5 .6

Figure 5.6: An uncertain interaction

If J considers his own potential outcomes, given the probability distribution he assumes over K's moves, he will reason that he has a .5 chance of receiving the value from either column, given any choice of his moves. Thus, if he chooses move a, he faces a .5 chance of getting either 1 or 3; if he chooses move b, he faces a .5 chance of getting either 2 or 4. Although there is no ordinal dominance here, there is stochastic dominance between the two moves, seen as two separate lotteries (Figure 5.7). Thus, a player who was evaluating stochastic dominance would realize that move a was dominated.

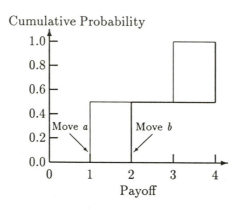

Figure 5.7: Stochastic dominance between two moves' outcomes

Formal Notation for Stochastic Dominance

Since there may be several outcomes with the same payoff to an agent, and since in the probability analysis that the agent performs these outcomes are identical, we would like to "collapse" these identical outcomes in our notation (e.g., combine *all* the chances of getting 3 into a single probability). Thus, we write agent i's subjective probability of getting a certain payoff value, given his choice of move m_i and all his knowledge of the world, as follows:

$$prob_i(v \mid m_i, \xi) = \sum_{\{m_{\bar{\imath}} \mid p(i, \bar{m}) = v\}} prob_i(m_{\bar{\imath}} \mid m_i, \xi).$$

We describe this as the payoff lottery for i given move m_i. When we have

$$\forall x \left(\int_{-\infty}^{x} prob_i(v \mid c_i, \xi) \, dv < \int_{-\infty}^{x} prob_i(v \mid d_i, \xi) \, dv \right)$$

we will say that the payoff lottery for i of move d_i is stochastically dominated by the payoff lottery for i of move c_i.[7]

---

[7]For the reader being newly introduced to stochastic dominance, it might seem odd that c_i's lottery, being everywhere *less than* d_i's lottery, dominates d_i. The curves for better lotteries rise further to the

5.3.3   Utility Dominance

As opposed to ordinal or stochastic dominance, *utility dominance* employs the aggregate measure of "expected utility," which introduces a total order (with equality) over payoff lotteries. The utility function encodes the agent's attitudes toward risky or uncertain payoffs. A utility function that is linear in payoffs will result in expected value decision making.

When the following situation holds,

$$\int_{-\infty}^{\infty} U(v) prob_i(v \mid d_i, \xi) \, dv < \int_{-\infty}^{\infty} U(v) prob_i(v \mid c_i, \xi) \, dv, \qquad (5.3)$$

we say that the expected utility for agent i of move c_i dominates the expected utility for agent i of move d_i. Note that the dominating move is on the larger side of the inequality, in contrast to the definition of stochastic dominance, where the dominating move is on the smaller side of the inequality.

5.4   Rational Moves—A Prescription for an Agent

In this section we describe a prescriptive theory for rational agents in interactions. The criteria for optimality is that the agent should choose the course of action that maximizes its expected utility. However, we propose a method that makes use of alternative means of screening moves by which an agent can reduce the number of, and data requirements for, expected utility calculations.

5.4.1   Rationality Using Ordinal Dominance

We will denote by $R_o(p, i)$ the ordinally rational moves for the agent i in the game p. An individual agent i is said to be exhibiting *ordinal rationality* if it makes moves solely from the set $R_o(p, i)$. The following axiom defines a criterion for eliminating a move from $R_o(p, i)$:

$$pay(i, d_i) <_o pay(i, c_i) \Rightarrow d_i \notin R_o(p, i). \qquad (5.4)$$

In other words, if d_i is ordinally dominated by c_i (every possible payoff to i of making move d_i is less than every possible payoff to i of making move c_i), then d_i is ordinally irrational for i. Note that this does not imply that c_i *is* ordinally rational, since there may be still better moves available.

---

right, and therefore their integrals are smaller up to any given point.

109

5.4.2 Rationality Using Stochastic Dominance

An individual agent i is said to be exhibiting *stochastic rationality* if it makes moves solely from the set $R_s(p, i)$. The following axiom defines a criterion for eliminating a move from $R_s(p, i)$:

$$\forall x \left(\int_{-\infty}^{x} prob_i(v \mid c_i, \xi)\, dv < \int_{-\infty}^{x} prob_i(v \mid d_i, \xi)\, dv \right) \Rightarrow d_i \notin R_s(p, i). \tag{5.5}$$

Thus, if d_i is stochastically dominated by any c_i, then d_i is stochastically irrational for agent i. Note again that this does not imply that c_i is stochastically rational—Equation 5.5 is a rule to exclude moves from R_s, not to prove that they are members.

5.4.3 Rationality Using Utility Dominance

An agent is utility rational if it seeks to maximize *expected utility*, as defined in Equation 5.2. The following axiom defines a criterion for eliminating a move from $R_u(p, i)$, the set of moves with maximal expected utility:

$$\int_{-\infty}^{\infty} U(v) prob_i(v \mid d_i, \xi)\, dv < \int_{-\infty}^{\infty} U(v) prob_i(v \mid c_i, \xi)\, dv \Rightarrow d_i \notin R_u(p, i). \tag{5.6}$$

Thus, if the expected utility of d_i is dominated by the expected utility of any c_i, then d_i is utility irrational for agent i. Note once again that this does not imply that c_i is utility rational. However, this definition of rationality differs from the previous ones in that we know there is a unique member of R_u, or a set of equivalent members (i.e., with the same expected utility). Thus this definition can actually be used to narrow the agent's choices to a single move, given the necessary computational resources to find it.

5.4.4 The Relationship Among Rationalities

The three definitions of rationality are related in the following ways:

$$d_i \notin R_o(p, i) \Rightarrow d_i \notin R_s(p, i) \wedge d_i \notin R_u(p, i) \tag{5.7}$$

$$d_i \notin R_s(p, i) \Rightarrow d_i \notin R_u(p, i) \tag{5.8}$$

$$R_u(p, i) \subseteq R_s(p, i) \subseteq R_o(p, i) \tag{5.9}$$

The fact that ordinal dominance between two moves implies stochastic dominance between the same two moves for any probability distribution is a simple consequence of their definitions. The fact that stochastic dominance implies utility dominance for any monotonic utility function is a well-known result from decision theory. Stochastic dominance is a robust measure of desirability for the agent, since moves can be eliminated no matter what the risk attitude of the agent as encoded in a utility function.

5.4.5 Using the Dominance Relations

We will exploit the hierarchy of rationalities (as defined in Equation 5.9) in our automated agent's activity. Ultimately, he would like to identify the set $R_u(p, i)$, but rather than directly trying to find the utility maximizing move, he can prune his search space by eliminating moves from R_o and R_s. Our agent therefore uses the three-level hierarchy of dominance relations, and their related rationality axioms, as follows:

1. Remove ordinally dominated moves. If a single move remains, select it and finish.

2. Assign and/or determine some properties of $prob_i(m_{\bar{\imath}} \mid m_i, \xi)$, the probabilities of opponents' moves given each of the agent's possible moves. We admit partial information regarding probabilities because this partial information may be sufficient to eliminate irrational moves in steps 3 and 5.

3. Remove stochastically dominated moves. If a single move remains, select it and finish.

4. Assess and apply a utility transformation to the lotteries defined by the remaining moves.

5. Remove utility dominated moves. All remaining moves will have identical expected utilities. Select one and finish.

Using this technique, our agent is able to maintain his commitment to being a utility maximizer, and still reduce the computational burden of computing expected utility. Information regarding the probability distributions of opponents' moves is used effectively. The search space can in many instances be radically pruned using this technique.

5.4.6 An Example

Consider an agent who is confronted with an encounter represented by the payoff matrix in Figure 5.8. Using ordinal dominance, he is immediately able to rule out moves c and d, leaving him with options a and b. While neither of these moves is ordinally dominated, he would still like to choose between them. He assesses the likelihood that his opponent will make any particular move as equiprobable (perhaps his opponent is only able to reason about ordinal dominance, and thus has no dominated moves; see below, Section 5.5.2). He is then able to conclude that move b is stochastically dominated by move a; move a is thus chosen. Had there been no stochastic dominance, he would have proceeded to compute the expected utility of moves a and b.

K

	e	f	g	h
a	5^1	6^2	5^1	7^2
b	4^2	5^1	6^2	7^1
c	4^1	3^2	4^1	3^2
d	0^2	1^1	2^2	3^1

J

Figure 5.8: Using ordinal and stochastic dominance

In general, however, the probability distributions over opponents' moves will not be readily available, and the computational burden of calculating or estimating these probabilities will overshadow the burden of calculating the best move *given* those probabilities. In the next section we describe various approaches where the axiomatic description of opponents allows the agent to deduce properties of the probability distribution for use in the framework described above.

5.5 Axioms of Rationality—Description

As described above, the second element of our prescriptive/descriptive approach is a descriptive theory of other agents. We will call the agent to whom we are endowing the prescriptive theory the "agent," and the other agents that we are describing as the "opponents." We describe a framework of rationality that allows us to express many levels of rationality that might be operating in opponents. The ultimate purpose of these axioms is to allow the agent to deduce $prob_i(m_{\bar{\imath}} \mid m_i, \xi)$ from more fundamental information.

In the remainder of this section, we describe various classes of rationality that this approach can address, and demonstrate how our three-tiered dominance analysis operates in each situation. Finally, we describe how to incorporate uncertainty about what axioms are present in other agents.

5.5.1 Minimal rationality

An assumption of minimal rationality corresponds to a situation where the agent has no information regarding the rationality of his opponents. This may include a recognition that other players are engaging in potentially irrational behavior (e. g. that the choices the opponents make are independent of their payoffs).

In this case we have

$$\{m_{\bar{\imath}} : prob_i(m_{\bar{\imath}} \mid m_i, \xi) > 0\} = M_{\bar{\imath}},$$

that is, any combined set of moves by the other agents is possible. One version of minimal rationality implies a commitment to equiprobable moves by the opponents:

$$prob_i(m_{\bar{\imath}} \mid \xi) = prob_i(m'_{\bar{\imath}} \mid \xi)$$

for all opponents' moves $m_{\bar{\imath}}$ and $m'_{\bar{\imath}}$. The effect of this is for the agent to assume that the others will be choosing their moves arbitrarily and ignoring any variation in payoffs.

Minimal rationality does not imply equiprobable assessments. Other information regarding tendencies and biases (aside from explicit consideration of payoffs) that opponents have displayed in the past can form the basis for assigning probabilities. The important point is that the assessment is not based on any explicit model of rationality of opponents. It therefore most closely resembles standard decision making under uncertainty, where uncertainty arises from lack of information and stochastic processes in the environment.

5.5.2   Separate rationality

In separate rationality the agent explicitly admits the possibility that each opponent is rational (to a greater or lesser degree) and has specific capabilities for reasoning about the moves others, including the agent, will take. Below, we examine several types of rationality that might conceivably be exhibited by opponents.

Ordinally Rational Opponents

If the agent assumes that his opponents are at most ordinally rational, then a successive winnowing process can be used to reduce the payoff matrix to a relevant set (this assumes, as well, that the opponents have knowledge of the agent's ordinal rationality; see [Rosenschein 1988]). Ordinally dominated moves, for both the agent and opponents, are repeatedly removed. The agent then restricts attention to a *reduced* matrix consisting of all ordinally undominated moves (along with opponents' responses). If the remaining set is a single entry, then there is a unique solution.

If there are multiple entries, then the opponents and the agent are left with an ambiguity— any of the moves not ordinally dominated are equally desirable. The agent can assume that the opponents will choose arbitrarily within the set of remaining moves—considering the

113

opponents minimally rational as in Section 5.5.1. The agent is permitted to make this inference because the opponents are only capable of reasoning about ordinal dominance; thus further reasoning about the agent by the opponents is impossible (this was the situation exhibited in the example of Section 5.4.6).

There is a potential subtlety in using the above method for ordinal dominance. Consider a situation where our agent has several ordinally dominated moves; does it matter which is "removed" first from the payoff matrix? As it turns out, the order of removal, both for the agent and his opponents, is irrelevant for ordinal dominance.

Stochastically and Utility Rational Opponents

Here we address the issue of opponents who, like the agent, are capable of engaging in probabilistic reasoning. Since both agent and opponents can reason probabilistically about each other, there is the potential for infinite regress: the agent's choice is dependent on what he believes his opponents will do, which depends on the opponents' beliefs about the agent, and so on.

One weak form of rationality that lends itself to probabilistic reasoning is due to Strait [Strait 1987]: if the agent prefers one payoff to another, then his opponent will assign a higher probability to the move with that payoff, and similarly for the agent's assessments of the opponents. One consequence of this principle is that the probability distribution over opponents' moves is dependent on the agent's move, i.e., the agent must consider $prob_i(m_{\bar{i}} \mid m_i, \xi)$. This dependence is not due to a causal linkage, since we are assuming simultaneous action, but rather results from the agent reasoning about the possibility of the opponents "outguessing" him given a particular move.

The foregoing principle results in a set of constraints on probabilities, given our assumption that the payoffs in the encounter are common knowledge and that all players have monotonic utility functions. There are various methods for dealing with constraints and/or bounds on probability in decision-making situations.

We can strengthen Strait's principle by adding an assumption that the opponents are Bayesian decision makers. We will restrict our attention to the case where there is a single opponent who is capable of screening moves based on both stochastic and utility dominance relationships. Furthermore, the opponents will be assumed to know that the agent is similarly an expected utility maximizer in making choices.[8]

The infinite regress of reasoning alluded to above is a real concern under these assumptions. One way of dealing with the regress is by explicitly modeling (by way of a probability

---

[8]This situation more closely resembles the jointly prescriptive theories of game theory.

114

distribution) the number of levels of regress that the agent believes an opponent will reason, and encoding the agent's perception of the opponent's uncertainty at each level. For example, the agent could reason that there is a fifty percent chance that the opponent will reason one level deep, a thirty percent chance two levels deep, a twenty percent chance three levels deep, and zero for all others. This is computationally complex, but is likely to be effective in a world inhabited by computationally limited reasoners.

5.5.3 Unique rationality

Under unique rationality, the agent assumes that the opponents' moves are fixed in advance, i.e.,

$$prob_i(m_{\bar{i}} \mid c, \xi) = prob_i(m_{\bar{i}} \mid d, \xi)$$

for all moves c and d to be made by agent i. This can also be expressed as the independence relation,

$$prob_i(m_{\bar{i}} \mid m_i, \xi) = prob_i(m_{\bar{i}} \mid \xi)$$

which states that the agent's probability distribution does not depend on the move the agent makes. Conceptually, the opponents are assumed to have sealed away their moves before the agent makes his choice. This is orthogonal to the question of *how* the opponents will make their choices; thus, unique rationality can be combined with the various forms of separate rationality presented above, or with minimal rationality. The crucial question here is not whether the opponents are *reasoning* about the agent, but whether their moves will actually be dependent on the move made by the agent (as they are in *informed rationality* below). In certain situations, the assumption of unique rationality allows a technique called case analysis to be applied when computing ordinal dominance (see [Rosenschein 1986]).

5.5.4 Informed rationality

Under informed rationality, the agent assumes that opponents have perfect information—they know precisely what move the agent is to take. Informed rationality eliminates uncertainty in the encounter when payoffs are common knowledge. The agent's task in this case is to make a choice that maximizes his benefit, given that his opponents will respond omnisciently to his move. This is the situation, for example, when there is a time-lag in the making of choices, and the opponents will be able to actually *respond* to our agent's move.

5.5.5 Uncertainty about Rationalities

In this section we have sketched various classes of rational opponent that our prescriptively designed agent might encounter, and presented some analysis of how each case is analyzed. In general, though, an agent may be uncertain about what class of opponent he faces in a given encounter. Probability theory provides a solution—assign a probability distribution to the types of agent that might be encountered and form a composite distribution over the opponents' moves based on analysis of each case.

5.6 The Jointly Prescriptive Issues

Ideally, a set of agents who all use the three-level hierarchy of ordinal, stochastic and utility rationality, with coherent probability distributions, will arrive at stable solutions. In general, however, this cannot be guaranteed. Aumann [Aumann 1987] has shown that a construct termed *correlated equilibria* is the result of interactions between utility-maximizing agents. The equilibrium is a probabilistic notion, a generalization of the mixed randomized strategies developed by game theorists. Each agent selects a definite alternative—the uncertainty in the equilibrium is due to the joint uncertainty of the agents about other agents' moves. The existence of correlated equilibria is based on the existence of a common knowledge prior probability distribution over some underlying state of nature. Differences in probability distributions by the agents are the result of differences in information. Though Aumann has provided a characterization of equilibria, they are inherently uncertain due to the uncertainty of the participants and may in fact admit a wide range of possible solutions. Recently Nau and McCardle [Nau and McCardle 1988] have shown that correlated equilibria are consistent with a notion of joint coherency in noncooperative games. This work, however, has not provided an operational procedure for deriving the equilibria based on a single agent's information.

5.7 Conclusion

The design of automated agents can benefit from the theoretical underpinnings of decision analysis, and game theory. Builders of autonomous agents will want to know that their creations are capable of adaptive behavior in the face of various opponents, and can use the "prescriptive/descriptive" aspects of decision analysis to guide their agents' design. The builders of full multiagent systems will want to ensure certain desirable global properties, and can use the "jointly prescriptive" aspects of game theory to choose the agents' built-in strategies.

We have presented a technique that exploits the relationship among ordinal, stochastic, and utility dominance. Combining it with logical axioms that describe opponents, it is particularly suitable for a deductive engine to use in deciding on a move in an interaction. The technique is based on computational considerations, pruning certain moves before performing computationally expensive operations (such as finding expected utility). We have also presented a sampling of rationality axioms that might be useful to an agent's designer, and given some ramifications of their use. This is basically a prescriptive analysis, discussing one way in which an interacting intelligent agent could be built.

References

[Appelt 1982] D. E. Appelt, "Planning Natural Language Utterances to Satisfy Multiple Goals," Tech Note 259, SRI International, Menlo Park, California, 1982.

[Aumann 1987] R. J. Aumann, "Correlated Equilibrium As an Expression of Bayesian Rationality," *Econometrica*, vol. 55, no. 1, January 1987, pp. 1–18.

[Breese 1987] J. S. Breese, *Knowledge Representation and Inference in Intelligent Decision Systems*, PhD thesis, Stanford University, 1987. Also published as Research Report 2, Rockwell International Science Center, Palo Alto Lab, Palo Alto, California, April 1987.

[Genesereth *et al.* 1984] M. R. Genesereth, M. L. Ginsberg, and J. S. Rosenschein, "Solving the Prisoner's Dilemma," Report no. STAN-CS-84-1032, Computer Science Department, Stanford University, November 1984.

[Genesereth *et al.* 1986] M. R. Genesereth, M. L. Ginsberg, and J. S. Rosenschein, "Cooperation without Communication," *Proceedings of The National Conference on Artificial Intelligence*, Philadelphia, PA, August 1986, pp. 51–57.

[Ginsberg 1987] M. L. Ginsberg, "Decision Procedures," in M. N. Huhns, editor, *Distributed Artificial Intelligence*, Morgan Kaufmann Publishers, Inc., Los Altos, California, 1987, pp. 3–28.

[Halpern and Moses 1984] J. Y. Halpern and Y. Moses, "Knowledge and Common Knowledge in a Distributed Environment," *Proceedings of the Third Annual ACM Conference on Principles of Distributed Computing*, Vancouver, British Columbia, Canada, 1984.

[Horvitz *et al.* 1988] E. J. Horvitz, J. S. Breese, and M. Henrion, "Decision Theory in Expert Systems and Artificial Intelligence," *International Journal of Approximate Reasoning*, vol. 2, 1988, pp. 247–302.

[Kadane and Larkey 1982] J. B. Kadane and P. D. Larkey, "Subjective Probability and the Theory of Games," *Management Science*, vol. 28, no. 2, February 1982, pp. 113–120.

[Kadane and Larkey 1983] J. B. Kadane and P. D. Larkey, "The Confusion of Is and Ought in Game Theoretic Contexts," *Management Science*, vol. 29, no. 12, December 1983, pp. 1365–1379.

[Konolige 1980] K. Konolige, *A First-Order Formalization of Knowledge and Action for a Multi-Agent Planning System*, Tech Note 232, SRI International, Menlo Park, California, December 1980.

[Konolige 1984] K. Konolige, *A Deduction Model of Belief and its Logics*, PhD thesis, Stanford University, 1984.

[Luce and Raiffa 1957] R. D. Luce and H. Raiffa, *Games and Decisions, Introduction and Critical Survey*, John Wiley and Sons, New York, 1957.

[Moore 1980] R. C. Moore, *Reasoning about Knowledge and Action*, Tech Note 191, SRI International, Menlo Park, California, 1980.

[Moore 1984] R. C. Moore, "A Formal Theory of Knowledge and Action," in J. R. Hobbs, and R. C. Moore, eds., *Formal Theories of the Commonsense World*, Ablex Publishing Co., 1985.

[Nau and McCardle 1988] R. F. Nau and K. F. McCardle, *Coherent Behavior in Noncooperative Games*, Working Paper 8701, The Fuqua School of Business, Duke University, Durham, North Carolina, 1988.

[Rosenschein 1986] J. S. Rosenschein, *Rational Interaction: Cooperation Among Intelligent Agents*, PhD thesis, Stanford University, 1986. Also published as STAN-CS-85-1081 (KSL-85-40), Department of Computer Science, Stanford University, October 1985.

[Rosenschein 1988] J. S. Rosenschein, "The Role of Knowledge in Logic-Based Rational Interaction," *Proceedings of The IEEE Phoenix Conference on Computers and Communication*, IEEE, Scottsdale, Arizona, March 1988, pp. 497–504.

[Strait 1987] R. S. Strait, *Decision Analysis of Strategic Interaction*, PhD thesis, Stanford University, 1987.

[von Neumann and Morgenstern 1947] J. von Neumann and O. Morgenstern, *Theory of Games and Economic Behavior*, Princeton University Press, Princeton, 1947.

[Whitmore and Findlay 1978] G. A. Whitmore and M. C. Findlay, eds., *Stochastic Dominance: An Approach to Decision Making Under Risk*, D. C. Heath and Company, Lexington, Massachusetts, 1978.

[Wilson 1986] J. Wilson, "Subjective Probability and the Prisoner's Dilemma, *Management Science*, vol. 22, no. 1, January 1986, pp. 45–55.

Jeffrey S. Rosenschein
Computer Science Department
Hebrew University
Jerusalem, Israel

John S. Breese
Rockwell Science Center, Palo Alto Laboratory
444 High Street
Palo Alto, CA 94301

118

Chapter 6

Multiagent Compromise via Negotiation

Katia Sycara

Abstract

Much of the work in DAI has dealt with agents that cooperate to achieve common high level goals. Our research deals with situations where cooperative behavior cannot be assumed and resolution of ensuing conflicts is necessary. Conflict resolution is achieved through direct negotiation among the interacting agents or through a third party, the mediator. We present a general negotiation model that handles multiagent, multiple-issue, single or repeated encounters based on integration of case-based reasoning and multiattribute utility theory. The negotiation model is implemented in a computer program, the PERSUADER, that resolves labor management disputes.

6.1 Introduction

A great deal of the work conducted in DAI has dealt with groups of agents pursuing a common high level goal [Durfee *et al.* 1985], [Lesser and Corkill 1983], [Cammarata *et al.* 1983]. Agents in such systems work as a team. Their interactions are guided by cooperation strategies meant to improve their common performance. In environments where each agent is pursuing his own set of goals, cooperative behavior cannot be assumed. The agents' behavior may result in conflicts that have to be resolved to assure progress in the problem solving effort. Conflict resolution is achieved through direct negotiations among the interacting agents or through a third party, the mediator.[1]

The negotiation process involves *identifying* potential interactions either through communication or by reasoning about the current states and intentions of other agents in the system and *modifying* the intentions of these agents so as to avoid harmful interactions or create cooperative situations.

Negotiation can be used to deal with several issues of concern in distributed problem solving:

- Network coherence

- Task and resource allocation among the intelligent agents

- Recognizing and resolving disparities in goals and viewpoints of agents

- Determining organizational structure.

To negotiate effectively, an agent must reason about the beliefs and intentions of others; therefore, the development of general negotiation models leads to techniques for

- Representing and maintaining belief models

- Reasoning about other agents' beliefs

- Influencing other agents' intentions and beliefs

Previous work in modeling interactions among noncooperative intelligent agents is the work of [Rosenschein 1985], who used a game-theoretic approach characterized by payoff matrices that contain the agents' payoffs for each possible outcome of an interaction. Although this research laid theoretical foundations for the study of nonbenevolent interactions, it has certain drawbacks. Most of the research assumes a single encounter: no consideration is given to any past or future interaction. No attempt is made to influence other agents' intentions. It is assumed that agents have *common knowledge* of the payoff matrix associated with the interaction, an assumption that may be unrealistic considering that the agents are nonbenevolent and loosely coupled. Another drawback of the approach is that, even if the payoff matrix were known, the matrix may quickly become intractable for large games involving many agents and outcomes.

Other work on negotiations is reported in [Sathi *et al.* 1986]. In this approach the agents negotiate by relaxing their conflicting constraints until a compromise is reached. No criterion is proposed, however, for selecting relaxations so as to achieve a compromise. In

---

[1]Mediation has proven its worth in difficult real-world conflicts where direct negotiations among the disputants have been unable to resolve the conflict.

120

the absence of such a criterion, the agents could get caught in an infinite loop of exchanging offers that do not converge. The constraints and their relaxations are statically known. No attempt is made to influence other agents' relaxations.

We present a general negotiation model that handles multiagent, multiple-issue, single or repeated encounters based on an integration of *case-based reasoning* and *multiattribute utility theory*. The model is able to generate a proposal, to generate a counterproposal that narrows the agents' differences, to take into consideration changing circumstances, to reason about other agents' beliefs, and to modify other agents' beliefs. The process of constructing a compromise solution is one of incremental modification of solution parts rather than a composition of partial solutions. The conflict resolution model we present parallels real-world negotiations. It was constructed and implemented with the help of two practicing labor mediators, one of whom primarily helped in the development phase and the other in the informal validation phase. It is implemented in a computer program called the PERSUADER that resolves adversarial conflicts in the domain of labor relations [Sycara 1987, Sycara 1988b].

The PERSUADER system consists of three agents: a company, its union, and the mediator whose task is to help the other two agents reach an acceptable compromise. The mediator is engaged in parallel negotiations with the union and company agents. The negotiation process consists of three main tasks: generation of a proposal, generation of a counterproposal based on feedback from a dissenting party, and persuasive argumentation. The mediator generates an initial compromise proposal and presents it to the union and company each of which evaluate the proposal from their perspectives and give the mediator their reaction. If both accept the proposal, then it is the final compromise. If one of the agents rejects it, the mediator decides whether to change the proposal or to attempt to change the disagreeing party's mind.

The messages that the negotiating agents exchange contain the following information:

- The proposed compromise.

- Persuasive arguments.

- Agreement or disagreement with the compromise or argument.

- Requests for additional information, such as with which issue in the proposed compromise the agent disagrees.

- Reason for disagreement.

- Utilities/preferences of the agents associated with disagreed upon issues.

The last two pieces of information are optional, since, in a noncooperative situation, the agents might not want to reveal their utilities or reasons.

6.2   Requirements for a Negotiation Planner

Negotiation is a process in which the parties iteratively propose compromises and argue with each other until a settlement is reached. A compromise solution is a "package" whose parts are strongly interconnected and interacting. Moreover, negotiations take place in a changing environment. These characteristics of negotiations define the requirements for a negotiation planner.

- A multiagent negotiation with multiple conflicting goals is a lengthy and iterative process. The parties start by having goals that are very far apart and whose distance has to be narrowed gradually to zero. Therefore, a planner for negotiation needs to plan in an *iterative* rather than a *one-shot* fashion since it is rare that all adversaries will agree to an initial proposal.

- After each round of proposals the adversaries communicate with a mediator or each other about which parts of a proposal they agree or disagree on. Hence a planner for negotiation needs to be able to receive *feedback* about the quality of its plan, evaluate it, and use it to modify the plan or construct a new plan.

- Negotiations take place in a dynamically changing world. During the course of negotiations, conditions in the world that affect the adversaries' behavior and goals might change. Besides expectation violations that arise from a changing world, a planner might have its expectations about the behavior of the agents violated (e.g., human irrationality). Therefore, a planner for negotiation needs to be able to take into consideration any changes in the planning context. In other words, it needs to have a *reactive component*.

- Since final agreement is reached through narrowing the difference in the demands of the adversaries, a planner for negotiation must have a way of *predicting and evaluating* whether each new proposal indeed narrows these differences.

- Reaching a compromise through negotiation entails that each of the adversaries must abandon partially or totally some of their goals. Since nobody does that willingly, the adversaries have to be convinced to do it. Hence, a planner for negotiation needs to have a component that generates *persuasive arguments*.

122

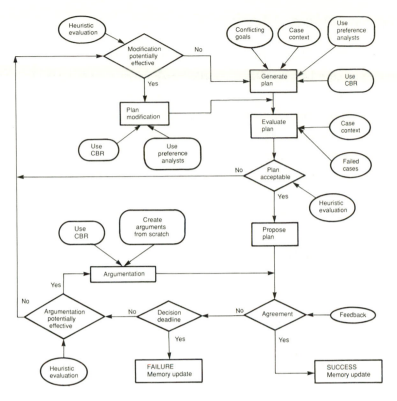

Figure 6.1: The negotiation process

The PERSUADER's agents incorporate all the above characteristics. The input is a set of conflicting goals of a company and union and the dispute context. The final output is either a single plan in the form of an agreed upon settlement or an indication of failure if the parties to the dispute did not reach agreement within a particular number of proposals (to simulate the inability of parties in the real world to reach agreement before a strike deadline). The final output is reached through iterations of the following tasks: (1) propose an initial compromise, (2) repair and improve a rejected compromise, and (3) change an adversary's view of the merits of a proposal. These tasks are performed using knowledge of past negotiations and settlements (cases), knowledge of the labor domain, and common-sense knowledge about human irrationality. Figure 6.1 presents an agent's actions in the negotiation process.

6.3 Negotiation Methods

Negotiation in the PERSUADER is performed through integration of case-based and analytic methods. The case-based method is called *case-based reasoning* [Kolodner *et al.* 1985, Sycara 1987] and the analytic is called *preference analysis*. These methods are employed in all negotiation tasks, namely in generation of an initial proposal, repair of a rejected proposal to formulate a counterproposal, and persuasive argumentation. The integration of heuristic and analytic methods makes the PERSUADER both robust and flexible. The problem solver does not break down when heuristic methods fail. In addition, the problem solver has the flexibility to use whichever method type is more natural to the particular problem-solving stage in which it is engaged.

6.3.1 Case-Based Reasoning (CBR)

Case-based reasoning involves choosing an appropriate previous case, identifying differences between that case and the current situation, and then using those differences to criticize and modify the previous solution to fit the current problem. Case-based negotiation uses a memory of past negotiation experiences as guides to present negotiations. Cases are organized hierarchically in memory around important domain concepts. In labor mediation such concepts include the industry to which the company belongs, the geographical location of the company, the international union to which the local union belongs, and the job classification of the union members. To perform case-based reasoning, cases need to be organized and retrieved in terms of conceptual similarity. The basic idea behind similarity between two concepts is that they have important common attributes. Similar concepts are organized in larger groupings based on their similarities and are contrasted from each other in terms of their differences. The high-level knowledge structure that the PERSUADER uses to organize similar concepts in memory is called a *generalized episode* [Kolodner 1984, Schank 1982]. Generalized episodes organize cases into a hierarchical network whose nodes are either another generalized episode or an individual case.

Cases in which conjunctive goals are totally or partially satisfied are stored in memory so that they can be reused in similar situations. The idea is that the tradeoffs and compromises that similar parties under similar circumstances were willing to make constitute a first approximation to the compromise being pursued. The PERSUADER also stores failed decisions (impasses) and their failure reason (if one can be found) as well as dependencies among decisions taken at different times in the negotiation. Failed resolutions can be recalled and thus used to warn the problem-solving agent of potential difficulties in future similar situations. Thus, the agent avoids repeating past mistakes.

Having a memory of past problem solving experiences (successes and failures) is important in distributed problem solving since

- Case-based inference minimizes the need for information exchange, thus minimizing communication overhead.

- Anticipating and avoiding problems through reasoning from past failures helps the agents minimize the exchange of proposals that will be rejected.

- If the repair of a past failure is also stored in memory, computation by each agent is minimized.

The above statements are tentative conclusions drawn from limited experimentation by running the PERSUADER with and without the case memory. When very similar cases were available, a compromise was quickly reached; when similar cases were not available, a greater number of proposals were exchanged in reaching the same quality of compromise (in the sense of avoiding a potential problem).

The process of case-based reasoning consists of the following steps: (1) retrieve appropriate precedent cases from memory, (2) select the most appropriate case from those retrieved, (3) construct an approximate solution, (4) evaluate the approximate solution for applicability to the current case, and (5) modify the approximate solution appropriately.

To retrieve a set of cases similar to the current one, the PERSUADER uses a set of salient domain features as indices. An evaluation function based on a prioritization of the index features is used to select the best (most similar) case. Knowledge is extracted from the solution part (the contract) of the selected case, and adjusted through standard adjustments to form the approximate solution. The values of the various issues in the precedent contract are checked to determine (1) whether the considered value violates any known applicability conditions and (2) whether the considered value has resulted in a past failure. If either condition is true, the value is further adjusted to the specifics of the current situation using both CBR and known heuristics [Sycara 1988c].

Before proposing the adapted compromise to the agents, the PERSUADER tries to *anticipate* potential difficulties with the contemplated compromise so that it can avoid them. This is done through *intentional reminding* [Schank 1982] of failed compromises where the conjunction of the solution's features are used as indices to retrieve failures that have the same features as the contemplated compromise. If an associated repair is stored along with a retrieved failure, the PERSUADER applies the repair to get a compromise that avoids the difficulty [Sycara 1988a]. If no repair is stored, the PERSUADER avoids suggesting the contemplated solution.

Finding an initial compromise through CBR: an example The PERSUADER in this example is trying to find an acceptable compromise for the Happy Gourmet Inc., a company that makes kitchenware, and its union. The union wants 13% increase in wages, 7% increase in health benefits, and strict seniority. The company wants no increase in wages, no increase in health benefits, and promotions and layoffs to be determined completely by company criteria. The PERSUADER searches memory to ascertain prevailing practice. The best contracts to reason from are contracts of competitors.

```
Searching memory with index KITCHEN-PRDS-INDUSTRY
4 cases found
Select case2 (Pots and Pans Inc.),
    since it has similar (degree 2) geographical area
Happy Gourmet Inc. is located in Philadelphia
Pots and Pans Inc. is located in Baltimore
Contract of Pots and Pans Inc. provides for 11% in wages,
    5% increase in health benefits, strict seniority
```

The PERSUADER uses known heuristic modifications, namely adjustments with respect to the competitor's position in industry and area wage differentials between Philadelphia and Baltimore, to make initial adjustments to the contract of Pots and Pans Inc. These adjustments result in a ballpark compromise with 9% increase in wages, 4% increase in health benefits, and strict seniority.

The PERSUADER now adapts the ballpark compromise to the current situation. Checking the finances of the company, it finds out that Happy Gourmet Inc. had suffered 4% losses in the past three years. It searches memory for similar cases, selects the most similar and applies the heuristic used in that case.

```
Searching memory with index KITCHEN-PRDS-INDUSTRY and CONTINUOUS-LOSS
2 cases found
Select case2 since it is same area, same company size
Apply heuristic used in that case
Decrease increases in wages by half percentage of losses
Increase in wages becomes 7%
```

Before proposing the updated compromise, the PERSUADER searches memory to discover potential problems with the contemplated seniority language. It retrieves a case in which the company had filed a grievance protesting that the strict seniority language obliged it to lay off junior key employees in times of slump. The arbitrator in that case

126

did not vindicate the company because no provision for key employees was written in the contract but proposed that the company get such a provision for its next contract.

```
Searching memory with index FAILURE, STRICT-SENIORITY
1 case found
Apply repair used in this case
Except key employees from layoffs in seniority language
```

6.3.2 Preference Analysis

When appropriate past cases are not available, the PERSUADER uses preference analysis [Sycara 1988d] as a "from scratch" planning method. Preference analysis is based on *multiattribute utility theory* [Keeney and Raiffa 1976]. Each agent has his utility curve for each issue involved in the negotiation. Combining these individual utility curves in an additive or multiplicative fashion results in an overall utility curve associated with a particular proposal that involves the negotiation issues.[2] This function maps the individual utility values associated with the many issues in a proposal to a single number, the payoff of the agent with the proposal. To make his choice, an agent selects the proposal that maximizes his payoff. The overall utility curve expresses the tradeoffs that an agent is willing to make among the various issues.

Preference analysis is particularly suited to problems involving multiple goals not all of which can be simultaneously and entirely satisfied. If an agent knows another agent's utilities, he can model the tradeoffs that the other agent is willing to make among the many issues and goals in the negotiation and predicts which compromise the second agent will be most willing to accept. If the adversary refuses a particular proposal, which happens if the proposal's payoff is unacceptably low, the problem solver can calculate the payoff of various possible counterproposals. Based on these calculations, it can predict which counterproposal represents an improvement (increasing the adversary's payoff) over the rejected one. Without an ability to predict which counterproposal has a chance of been accepted, the adversaries could blindly exchange offers that do not converge to an acceptable compromise. An agent needs to know the utilities of other agents only for the contemplated counterproposals and not for each possible outcome of the interaction. He makes inferences about these utilities based on his experiences with similar parties. Knowledge of utilities does not have to be accurate. Knowing the shape of the utility curves gives much inferential power compared to assuming statistical indifference. Moreover, the utilities are used

---

[2]Additive functions are the ones most frequently used in practice [Keeney and Raiffa 1976].

primarily to construct an initial solution, which gets modified in the course of the problem solving.

To obtain other agents' utilities, a problem solver can (1) follow an assessment procedure that elicits the decision maker's utilities,[3] (2) retrieve the utilities of similar parties, or (3) hypothesize the shape of the utility curves from knowledge of the agents' role (e.g., an agent is a union) and domain-specific factors (e.g., the industry to which the company belongs is in recession). The PERSUADER derives the agents' utilities by retrieving utilities of similar previously encountered decision makers. If such experiences are not available, it uses a set of domain specific heuristics to hypothesize the shape of the utility curves.

The compromise that the PERSUADER proposes is the one that *maximizes the joint payoff of the agents and minimizes the payoff difference*. This criterion combines maximal gains with equity. To arrive at this criterion, we run a few examples using either maximization of the joint payoff (Pareto optimal solution), or minimization of the payoff difference. Maximizing the joint payoff usually gave contracts with quite unequal utilities for the agents. The payoff of one party would be so low as to practically guarantee rejection of the settlement[4]. On the other hand minimizing the payoff difference cannot discriminate between two solutions, one of which gives both parties payoffs of 90 (on a 0 to 100 scale) and the other payoffs of 20. For details of the calculation and examples, see [Sycara 1987, Sycara 1988d].

6.4 Belief Modification through Persuasive Argumentation

Multiagent systems need the ability to reason about and change (1) the beliefs and intentions of others and (2) other agents' behavior. In multiagent negotiations, this ability constitutes a necessity. There exists a rich literature dealing with the logic of knowledge and belief [Appelt 1985, Genesereth and Nilsson 1987, Konolige 1983, Moore 1980, Halpern and Moses 1984]. Belief and belief modification in the PERSUADER is based on the conjunctive goals of the agents and their interactions. A belief in the PERSUADER involves the correspondence between a state (a possible settlement) and the other agents' actions. Group knowledge [Genesereth and Nilsson 1987] in the PERSUADER focuses on the facts of the case, such as proposals, counterproposals, negotiation and context. If agreement on a compromise were obtainable by inference from these facts, negotiation would be unnecessary. The goals, plans, and utilities of other agents are largely unknown. The

---

[3]Such procedures are well documented in the decision sciences literature.

[4]The nonsuitability of Pareto optimal solutions for negotiations has also been independently reported by [Kersten 1985].

negotiation process itself is a search of a dynamic problem space where an agent's beliefs about other agents' beliefs over the cycle of proposals continuously changes the space being searched. What was not a solution at one point becomes a solution at a later point.[5] The PERSUADER attempts to influence the process toward solution convergence by constructing sophisticated arguments to bring about belief states of the agents that are necessary in achieving compromise states.

The argumentation model in the PERSUADER system provides both for selecting and adapting previously used arguments through case-based reasoning [Sycara-Cyranski 1985b], and for constructing arguments from scratch [Sycara-Cyranski 1985a]. Regardless of which method an agent uses for argument generation, its reasoning is guided by argumentation goals and strategies. Argumentation goals (e.g., "change the importance that the persuadee attaches to a goal") are associated with the ways that a persuadee's beliefs and behavior can be affected by an argument. Since an agent rejects a compromise if it gives him low payoff, convincing him to change his evaluation of the rejected compromise is modeled as producing an argument to increase the payoff the compromise gives him. Hence, the task of a persuader can be viewed as finding the most effective argument that will increase the agent's payoff. Since an agent's payoff can be approximated as a linear combination of his utilities, his payoff can be increased by (1) changing the importance (coefficient) the agent attaches to an issue, and (2) by changing the utility value of an issue. These constitute a persuader's argumentation goals. Argumentation strategies (e.g., "indicate a change in the contribution of the present goal to a higher level goal of the persuadee") are used to achieve the argumentation goals.

A persuadee's *belief structure* involves his goals, the importance he attaches to them, and relations among them. Different arguments change different parts of the belief structure. The persuadee's beliefs are represented in a directed acyclic graph, which is searched during argument generation and updated according to the persuadee's reaction to the argument. The nodes represent goals with the associated importance and desired direction of change (increase, or decrease). The arcs represent the contribution of a goal to the achievement of its parent goal. Figure 6.2 presents a (partial and simplified) view of a company's belief structure.

The PERSUADER generates a variety of arguments based on different argumentation goals and strategies [Sycara 1987]. In the rest of this section and the next section, we illustrate the PERSUADER's argument generation process by presenting a threatening argument (in which the argumentation goal is to change the importance the persuadee at-

---

[5]In a labor negotiation, for example, it is unlikely that either party would accept their eventual compromise, if it were presented at the inception of negotiations.

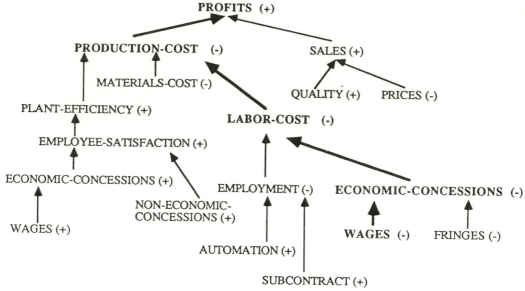

Figure 6.2: A company's partial belief structure

taches to an issue, and the strategy is to point out to the persuadee unpleasant consequences of its attitude toward a proposal).

Since an increase in wages contributes to (1) an increase in economic concessions, labor costs and production costs, and (2) a decrease in company profits, one of the company's goals is to decrease wages (Figure 6.2). The subgoal of decreasing employment contributes to a decrease in economic concessions, labor costs and production costs. Decreasing employment violates the goal of a union of increased employment. This can be checked by examining a union's belief structure. The argument, addressed to a union that has refused a proposed wage increase, "If the company is forced to grant higher wage increases, then it will decrease employment" is meant to decrease the importance the union attaches to wage increases by pointing out unpleasant consequences for the union of forcing an unwanted by the company wage increase.

To generate the above argument, the PERSUADER finds out which company goals are violated by the union's refusal. Then, it finds out what compensating actions the company might use in retaliation (for more details on the algorithm, see [Sycara-Cyranski 1985a]). To do this, the PERSUADER matches the wage goal in the company's belief graph. It propagates the wage increase that the union wants to force to the ancestors of the wage goal. Children of these ancestors might indicate subgoals that the company can fulfill to counteract the wage increase. Such a counteracting action, which violates a union goal more important than the wage increase, constitutes an argument for reducing the importance that the union attaches to wage increase.

The argument generating process may result in producing multiple, potential arguments. The most effective of the arguments produced must be chosen. The PERSUADER uses the strategy of presenting the "weakest" (less convincing) argument first, presenting "strong" arguments only when the weak ones have been rejected. We have developed a hierarchy of argument types according to their convincing power. The position of an argument type in this hierarchy is, in general, domain dependent. For the labor domain, the hierarchy (from weakest to strongest) is as follows: (1) appeal to universal principle, (2) appeal to a theme, (3) appeal to authority, (4) appeal to "status quo," (5) appeal to "minor standards," (6) appeal to "prevailing practice," (6) appeal to precedents as counterexamples, (7) appeal to self-interest, and (8) threaten.

6.4.1 Generating a persuasive argument: An example

In the Happy Gourmet Inc. negotiation, the PERSUADER suggests the compromise derived through CBR (Section 6.3.1). The company agrees saying that the increase in wages is the highest it can afford, but the union wants a higher increase. The PERSUADER's argumentation goal becomes to convince the union to accept the proposed increase. This can be accomplished by decreasing the importance the union attaches to wage increases (for details of this calculation, see [Sycara 1987]).

```
Importance of wage-goal1 is 6 for union1
Searching company1 goal-graph...
Increase in wage-goal1 by company1 will result in increase
    in economic-concessions1, labor-cost1, production-cost1
Increase in wage-goal1 by company1 will result in decrease in profits1
To compensate, company1 can decrease fringe-benefits1, decrease
    employment1, increase plant-efficiency1, increase sales1
Only decrease fringe-benefits1, decrease employment1
    violate goals of union1
Importance of fringe-benefits1 is 4 for union1
Importance of employment1 is 8 for union1
Since importance of employment1 > importance of wage-goal1
One possible argument found
```

6.5 Narrowing the Parties' Differences

When a proposed compromise is rejected, the PERSUADER uses persuasive argumentation to convince the rejecting party to change its mind rather than modify the rejected solution. This is an efficient strategy since the negotiation is successfully concluded if the rejecting party accepts the solution. Modifying the solution is less desirable since it might result in a compromise that is now unacceptable to the party that had previously agreed to the solution. If argumentation is unsuccessful, the PERSUADER engages in compromise modification.

To generate appropriate modifications, the PERSUADER uses both CBR and heuristics. It ascertains from the rejecting agent's feedback the objectionable issues, the reason for the rejection, and the importance the agent attaches to the issues. The issues and reason for rejection are used as indices in the case memory to select similar impasses, to select the best case out of those retrieved, and to access the associated modification. This modification is adapted and applied to the current impasse. It is then evaluated according to the criterion that it must increase the rejecting party's payoff by a greater amount than it (possibly) decreases the payoff of the parties that had agreed to the compromise. This criterion ensures narrowing of the parties' differences.

If the contemplated compromise conforms to the criterion, it is proposed. If it does not, modifications from other retrieved similar impasses are tried. If CBR fails to produce a suitable modification, or the rejecting party does not disclose the reason for rejection, the PERSUADER uses heuristics that it knows about.

6.5.1 Narrowing the Parties' Differences: An Example

In the Happy Gourmet Inc. negotiations, confronted with the union's refusal to accept an increase in wages less than 7%, the PERSUADER tries to augment increases in health benefits in the hope that the union will accept the new "package." It searches memory for impasses where health benefits needed to be increased, selects the best and accesses the associated modification.

```
Searching memory with index FAILURE, HEALTH-BENEFITS, TOO-LOW
5 impasses found
Select impasse1
    since it is same industry, same area, same job classification
Looking at modification "increase health benefits by
    additional 2%" from impasse1
Since majority of workers are older modification1 seems applicable
```

```
Apply improvement criterion
Success
Contract3 that resulted from applying modification1 will be proposed
```

6.6 Results

The PERSUADER has a representation component based on utilities but the richness of real world situations make the utility model only an approximation of actual behavior. It has been documented in the operations research literature [Kersten 1985] that the utility based approach by itself is incapable of capturing the complexity of real situations. The power behind the PERSUADER lies in the marshalling of CBR, models of beliefs and theories of argumentation to search regions adjacent to the "simplified" optimal solution to find solutions which are actually acceptable.

The experiments examined the efficiency of the program when features involved in guiding this search were disabled. Cases were defined by the parties' positions and case constraints which made their feasible solutions lie outside the mathematically optimal region. The deviations might be purely quantitative as in cases in which the parties' positions were too far apart to allow computable solutions. In other instances they involved aspects of a case such as attribution of blame which were not represented in the utility model. To reach a successful compromise both parties' payoffs had to be greater than 70% and the case constraints satisfied.

In the next paragraphs, we give a brief description of the our experiments. Each set of experiments was run using five different disputes drawn from a set of disputes the PERSUADER had previously resolved successfully. Communication overhead was defined as the number of proposals exchanged until agreement was reached.

1. *Running the system without memory.* The system hypothesizes the utilities of the agents from what it knows about the agent's role and the current context of the dispute. The system calculates the compromise that maximizes the joint payoff and minimizes the payoff difference. When one of the parties rejects the proposed solution, the system evaluates the rejected compromise and modifies it to increase the utility of the rejecting party. In the experiments, we used increments of 10% of the demanded value of the most important issue. So, for example, if the union has rejected a proposal that gives it a 12% wage increase, and wages were the most important of the union goals, then the wage increase is augmented by 1.2%. A calculation is done to check that this modification (1) increases the rejecting party's payoff, and (2) the modification's increase in utility for the rejecting party is greater than the decrease in utility of the party that had accepted the proposal.

The heuristic used was that the agents would reach agreement if both of their payoffs were greater than 70%. On one occasion, this could not be reached. On the remaining four, the number of proposals exchanged was on the average 30% more than the number of proposals exchanged when the system was run with the memory, so that proposal modifications were gotten from the memory. (No argumentation was used in this set of experiments).

2. *Experiments with and without argumentation.* When argumentation was used (1) the number of proposals exchanged until agreement was reached was smaller than the number of proposals exchanged without argumentation. (2) the number of proposals plus arguments were somewhat less (17 vs. 18 on the average) than without argumentation. However, with argumentation, the final agreement was better, in the sense of maximizing the joint payoff and minimizing the payoff difference.

3. *Experiments where no failure avoidance was used.* In about half the cases, the parties had objections that were avoided when the same cases were run with the failure avoidance mechanism (Section 6.3.1).

4. *Experiments where no preference analysis was used to evaluate proposals.* The criterion was to propose the best proposal that resulted using only CBR. The same heuristic (used also in the first set of experiments) of 10% increase of the most important issue's value for the rejecting party was used. There were no utilities associated with the proposals but only a rank-ordering in terms of importance. In two cases, this resulted in oscillatory behavior: party A rejects a proposal, the proposal is changed in party A's favor resulting in counterproposal1, party B rejects counterproposal1; counterproposal1 is changed in party B's favor, and the result is rejected by party A.

5. *Experiments where the parties did not give feedback as to the reason of proposal rejection.* The perturbation heuristic of 10% change in the most important issue of the rejecting party was used to create a counterproposal. Communication overhead increased by 23%.

6.7 Conclusion

The integration of case-based and utility-based negotiation constitutes a framework for the development of a general theory of negotiation in multiagent, multiple-goal situations. This theory defines the requirements of a negotiation planner as (1) iterative, (2) reactive, (3) having the ability to predict whether collective progress towards convergence to a compromise is being made and (4) having the ability to reason about and modify the beliefs of other agents.

The case-based and analytic methodologies support each other in various ways to make a problem solver both robust and flexible. First, the utility-based method provides a way to construct solutions "from scratch" when past cases are not available. Second, case-based inference can be used to shortcut tedious computations. Third, the utility-based method provides a way to evaluate case-based solutions. Fourth, the utility-based method provides information that guides memory retrieval. The synergy of the approaches results in robustness and flexibility of each agent. Moreover, it could contribute to the reliability of solving a problem in a distributed fashion by alleviating the difficulty of missing agents.

A current limitation of CBR is the storage requirements of the dynamic case memory and the speed of update to form the proper generalizations. Memory retrieval is fast. The search for improvements in the organization of the case memory is one of the outstanding research problems for CBR researchers.

From our research with the system, we draw the following conclusions:

- In situations that are not fully cooperative, agents select their actions so as to optimize their own utilities. Coherence in these situations is achieved through negotiation.

- An agent's ability to influence other agents' beliefs results in improved problem solving

- Communication overhead is minimized by

  - having good criteria to evaluate proposals. In our model, such criteria are provided through preference analysis.
  - avoiding bad proposals. In our model, this is done through case-based inference and preference analysis.
  - having models of other agents' beliefs. In our model, this is done through a memory for cases.

We are performing more extensive experimentation to refine these conclusions.

Acknowledgements

This research has been sponsored in part by the Army Research Office under contract No. DAAG 29-85-K0023 and in part by NSF Grant No. IST-8317711.

References

[Appelt 1985] D. Appelt, *Planning English Sentences*, PhD thesis, Stanford University, 1985.

[Cammarata *et al.* 1983] S. Cammarata, D. McArthur, and R. Steeb, "Strategies of Cooperation in Distributed Problem Solving," *Proceedings IJCAI-83*, Karlsruhe, West Germany, 1983, pp. 767–770.

[Durfee *et al.* 1985] E. Durfee, V. Lesser, and D. Corkill, "Coherent Cooperation Among Communicating Problem Solvers," Technical Report, Department of Computer Science and Information Science, University of Massachusetts, Amherst, Massachusetts, 1985.

[Genesereth and Nilsson 1987] M. R. Genesereth and N. J. Nilsson, *Logical Foundations of Artificial Intelligence*, Morgan Kaufmann, 1987.

[Halpern and Moses 1984] J. Halpern and Y. Moses, "Knowledge and Common Knowledge in a Distributed Environment," IBM RJ 4421, IBM Research Laboratory, San Jose, CA, October 1984.

[Keeney and Raiffa 1976] R. L. Keeney and H. Raiffa, *Decisions with Multiple Objectives*, John Wiley and Sons, New York, 1976.

[Kersten 1985] G. E. Kersten, "Nego - Group Decision Support System," *Information and Management*, Vol. 8, 1985, pp. 237–246.

[Kolodner 1984] J. L. Kolodner, *Retrieval and Organizational Strategies in Conceptual Memory: A Computer Model*, Lawrence Erlbaum Associates, Hillsdale, NJ, 1984.

[Kolodner *et al.* 1985] J. L. Kolodner, R. L. Simpson, and K. Sycara-Cyranski, "A Process Model of Case-Based Reasoning in Problem Solving," *Proceedings of IJCAI-85*, Los Angeles, CA, 1985, pp. 284–290.

[Konolige 1983] K. Konolige, "A Deductive Model of Belief," *Proceedings of IJCAI-83*, 1983, pp. 377–381.

[Lesser and Corkill 1983] V. R. Lesser and D. D. Corkill, "The Distributed Vehicle Monitoring Testbed: A tool for investigating distributed problem solving networks," *The AI Magazine*, Vol, 4, No. 3, Fall 1983, pp. 15–33.

[Moore 1980] R. Moore, "Reasoning about Knowledge and Action," Technical Note 191, SRI International, 1980.

[Rosenschein 1985] J. S. Rosenschein, *Rational Interaction: Cooperation Among Intelligent Agents*, PhD thesis, Stanford University, Palo Alto, CA, 1985.

[Sathi *et al.* 1986] A. Sathi, T. E. Morton, and S. Roth, "Callisto: An Intelligent Project Management System," *AI Magazine*, Vol. 7, 1986, pp. 34–57.

[Schank 1982] R. C. Schank, *Dynamic Memory*, Cambridge University Press, Cambridge, 1982.

[Sycara 1987] K. Sycara, *Resolving Adversarial Conflicts: An Approach Integrating Case-Based and Analytic Methods*, PhD thesis, School of Information and Computer Science, Georgia Institute of Technology, Atlanta, GA, 1987.

[Sycara 1988a] K. Sycara, "Patching Up Old Plans," *Proceedings of the Tenth Annual Conference of the Cognitive Science Society*, Montreal, Canada, 1988.

[Sycara 1988b] K. Sycara, "Resolving Goal Conflicts via Negotiation," *Proceedings of AAAI-88*, St. Paul, MN, 1988.

[Sycara 1988c] K. Sycara, "Using Case-Based Reasoning for Plan Adaptation and Repair," *Proceedings of the 1988 Case-Based Reasoning Workshop*, Clearwater, FL, 1988, pp. 425–434.

[Sycara 1988d] K. Sycara, "Utility Theory in Conflict Resolution," *Annals of Operations Research*, Vol. 12, 1988, pp. 65–84.

[Sycara-Cyranski 1985a] K. Sycara-Cyranski, "Arguments of Persuasion in Labor Mediation," *Proceedings of IJCAI-85*, Los Angeles, CA, 1985, pp. 294–296.

[Sycara-Cyranski 1985b] K. Sycara-Cyranski, "Persuasive Argumentation in Resolution of Collective Bargaining Impasses," *Proceedings of the Seventh Annual Conference of the Cognitive Science Society*, Irvine, CA, 1985, pp. 356–360.

Katia P. Sycara
The Robotics Institute
Carnegie-Mellon University
Pittsburgh, PA 15213

Chapter 7

Conflict-resolution Strategies for Nonhierarchical Distributed Agents

Mark R. Adler, Alvah B. Davis, Robert Weihmayer, and Ralph W. Worrest

Abstract

Conflict resolution is a critical capacity required for coordination in systems of intelligent, autonomous, interacting agents. We discuss methods of conflict detection and conflict resolution that we have examined in the domain of telephone network traffic control. Agents were given planning capabilities to increase the power of agent interaction without undue addition of single-agent domain knowledge. We discuss several conflict-resolution strategies and present initial performance results. We also suggest that negotiation is inextricably bound with planning, since each process needs information gained from the other to function efficiently and effectively.

7.1 Introduction

Distributed AI systems will be built or formed to meet the needs of complex problem-solving tasks. Distributed intelligent systems arise through

- integration of existing intelligent systems via the creation of a supervisory intelligent system to control the efforts of the team,

- chance encounters of intelligent systems capable of organizing themselves, and

- creation of a set of intelligent systems built to work together.

The first case does not require new technology, since building intelligent systems to use existing tools is done today, achieved most simply by designing a controlling and coordinating system that deals with the existing subsystems as a human would deal with them. The second is a good long-range goal, but more appropriate to applications such as autonomous land vehicles and remotely piloted aircraft, and may demand much larger and more general knowledge bases. We consider here means of supporting the third way of building distributed intelligent systems.

A major design goal of distributed systems is the minimization of potential conflict, since unresolved conflicts reduce system efficiency and resolution of conflicts adds overhead to the problem-solving process. Designers of intelligent systems need tools to select and implement communication and coordination mechanisms. Our work started with the addition of very simple communication rules to simple autonomous agents, which allowed them to avoid conflict at a very low level. Conflict detection and resolution form the focus of our current effort.

We are surveying a range of coordination strategies that work within the problem domain and looking for indications of problem-dependent and situation-dependent factors that will allow either system designers or, preferably, the agents themselves to choose the coordination strategy that best suits the tasks they collectively face. Our initial approach is an empirical one based on group performance against a simulated environment. We focus here on specific techniques useful in the design of systems that must occasionally overcome conflicts, even while avoiding many.

7.2   The Network Management Problem

Planning is the key to being able to coordinate activity effectively. Some past efforts (e.g., contract net and multistage negotiation) rely on the built-in domain-problem-solving skills of the agent, while some (e.g., information-distribution policies and partial global planning) rely on an added coordination mechanism. Our work is an extension of our "planner-less" cooperation studies in immediate conflict resolution [Sandell and Worrest 1985]. We explore the incremental additions needed in planning skill to achieve improvement in coordination among cooperating agents solving a set of interacting subproblems. The key issue is resolution of local plan conflicts, through either a policy of avoiding them from the start of problem-solving or a process of resolving them after they appear.

[Smith 1980] describes the contract net approach to task sharing. A contract net, while dynamic, is a hierarchical task-allocation mechanism relying on a single agent for coordination and integration for each subtask. "Negotiation" is the bid/award approach to subtask allocation. [Conry *et al.* 1986] describe a clever strategy for coordinating local plans through requests for action and the sharing of resource-conflict and goal-conflict information. Thus, the only global information about the system that each agent receives is the set of incompatible plans. Local plans are done of the basis of tentative commitments to a set of goals and their satisfaction. "Negotiation" is a process of exchange of conflict information and tentative commitments of resources to plans. [Steeb *et al.* 1984] also chose a dynamic and centralized approach to allocating work in their domain of distributed air-traffic control. They explore several organizational policies used to decide which agent should solve the problem. "Negotiation" in this system is the process by which an authoritative agent is selected.

[Genesereth and Rosenschein] developed models of rationality as part of common knowledge that would permit agents to coordinate their efforts, under certain circumstances, without explicit communication. This work is important because it prescribes what is the smallest amount and kind of information needed about a conflict to resolve it. It also gives an indication of when there is no good resolution mechanism. [Durfee and Lesser 1987] describe what can be accomplished with sophisticated planners (where planners plan their own activity and coordinate these activity plans with the rest of the group). Their Partial Global Planning framework unifies the planning styles of multiagent planning, contract net, and functionally-accurate, cooperative problem-solving. "Negotiation" is done through the exchange of problem-solving plans. They have experimented with various communication topologies and coordination mechanisms. Our planning is much simpler and the negotiation less integrated with the local problem-solving process.

The domain for our study is circuit-switched network traffic control (for example, the kind of routine activity that happens in a local telephone company). This domain has several interesting properties: sensor data is not available in real-time—it is presented in 5-minute summaries; control actions do not affect current traffic—controls affect new requests for service (since calls typically last for three minutes, there is a lag between installing a control change and seeing its full effect); demand for service is stochastic; controls have a fine-grained precision; there is always a solution to any problem—though the cost may be quite high; and, finally, overload problems tend to be fairly local and the communication costs of handling local problems from a centralized location tend to be heavy.

A centralized solution would suffer from these costs. A distributed solution would be able to take advantage of the fact that most problems are small and localized. The distributed solution would have greater reliability because no single component is responsible for the control of the entire system. The independence of each distributed component would also provide a system of checks and balances against the possibility of a bad decision by one of them in its present situation.

On the other hand, the problem is superlinear and so independent agents would have to coordinate very well in searching for a solution to larger problems. The partitioning in space of the traffic-management responsibilities will not always coincide with the location of traffic overloads: thus the need for intelligent cooperative problem-solving.

The basic problem that the agents are to solve is excessive demand for the resources in one part of the network (due either to an unusual number of calls or the failure of some part of the network itself). The first consequence of poor network control is that calls that might otherwise have been routed are blocked; the second is that, with continued poor control, a problem can build upon itself until the entire network fails. Therefore, there are two basic tasks: situation assessment (sometimes called diagnosis) and response generation (often called planning). In addition, the agents have the tasks of communicating with each other and the world and coordinating their activities—especially with respect to the actions they will take in the world (as opposed to the assessment or response-generation activities they perform internally). More specifically, agents have the tasks of

Evaluating plans to detect conflicts: An effective plan requires knowledge of the current traffic volumes, current controls in place, network configuration, and goal and subgoal requirements for other agents.

Forming a model of other agents: The minimum requirements are an approximation of traffic volume and network capacity, understanding of shared network components, and at least an approximation of the agents' overall goals and priorities.

Producing counter-proposal plans: This requires a reasonably deep understanding of the original proposal, its conflict with respect to the agent's own goals, and the generation either of an alternative plan to cover the conflicts or minimize their impact or of an argument that appeals to global considerations in order to abandon its own or other agents' subgoals.

Negotiating plans with other agents: This requires the establishment of a communication protocol, generation of plans and counter-proposal plans, mutual understanding of goals and subgoals, and evaluation of alternative plans.

Each agent in our study is an autonomous problem-solver, fully capable of handling the range of problems it faces. Agents employ blackboard-based reasoning [Englemore and Morgan 1988], with blackboards divided into "panels" that embody the problem-solving subtasks the agents face. The homogeneous group of agents has geographically divided responsibilities with no overlaps. They do not have access to sensor data outside their regions of control. They do not have topological information outside their regions of control, with two exceptions: (1) they know which nodes belong to each controller and (2) they know which nodes are at the other end of the links across their borders. There is a high-enough cost for communication that independent activity is preferred unless there is a direct indication that coordination could be helpful. The group is flat with no control nodes. They make minimal attempts to model each other, limiting their models to state rather than processing information.

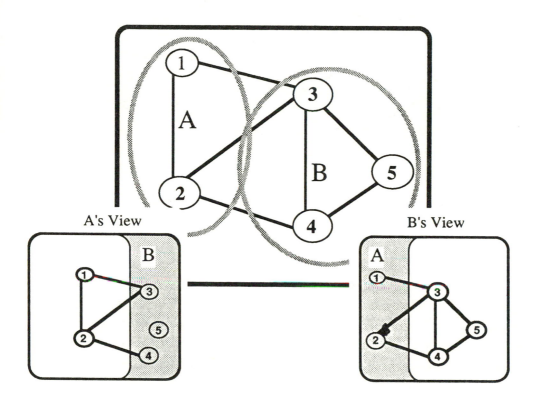

Figure 7.1: Agent views of the world

7.3 Example

We consider below an example of negotiation in which two agents discover a conflict after they have both completed their plans. They begin discussion at the level of effects of their plans on one another and move successively higher in their description of their goals, motivating the subgoals or actions that they developed until they reach the point at which each can find alternative goal expansions meeting their own needs while not interfering with, and perhaps assisting in, the realization of their neighbor's goals. The goal tree illustrated in the following figure shows some of the plan development relevant to this problem.

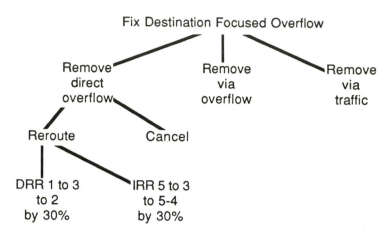

Figure 7.2: Partial goal tree for destination focused overload

The Problem

There is a Destination Focused Overload at node 3. Agent A's plan redirects 1 to 3 traffic to node 2 as a via node, which would increase the volume on links 1-2 and 2-3. Agent B's plan cancels a significant amount of 5 to 3 and 5 to 1 traffic, and redirects 4-3 traffic to node 2 as a via node, which would increase the volume on links 2-4 and 2- 3. Since there is not enough capacity on the 2-3 link to hold both the proposed increases, the two agents find themselves in conflict over the use of a resource.

The Dialogue

(Arbitrarily, A begins)

A: My increase on 2-3 is a result of a control to do a destination reroute on 3-bound, direct traffic off the overloaded 1-3 link we share, which is part of the Destination Focused Overload problem we have jointly recognized. This is the only reroute available for this traffic in my region. I have no other reroutes available for your traffic.

144

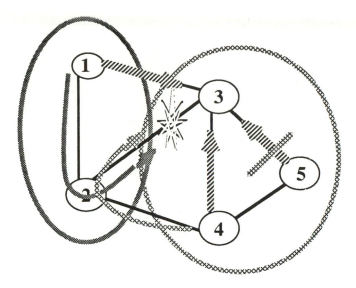

Figure 7.3: Conflict over control of destination focused overload

B: My increase on 2-3 is a result of a control to do a destination reroute on 3-bound, direct traffic off one of my overloaded links, which is part of the Destination Focused Overload problem we have jointly recognized. I have no reroutes available for this traffic in my region. I have no reroutes available in my region for your traffic to which you referred.

A: We cannot resolve this conflict at the resource level. The subgoal I was meeting was Reroute Direct Overflow for the traffic mentioned. My two possible expansions are Destination Reroute and Immediate Reroute. If I used the Immediate Reroute expansion instead, the effects on your region would not change. Therefore, I have no useful alternative expansions at this level.

B: The subgoal I was meeting was Reroute Direct Overflow for the traffic mentioned. My two possible expansions are Destination Reroute and Immediate Reroute. If I used the Immediate Reroute expansion instead, the effects on your region would not change. Therefore, I have no useful alternative expansions at this level.

A: We cannot resolve this conflict at this subgoal level. The subgoal at the next higher level I was meeting was Remove Direct Overflow. My two possible expansions are Reroute Direct Overflow and Cancel Direct Overflow. Using the latter choice would be extremely expensive to me.

B: The subgoal at the next higher level I was meeting was Remove Direct Overflow. My two possible expansions are Reroute Direct Overflow and Cancel Direct Overflow. Using the latter choice would be extremely expensive to me.

A: While we could resolve the conflict by imposing high costs on one or both of us by choosing alternative expansions, we still have higher levels of alternatives to consider. Let's talk about those first to try to find a better solution. The goal at the highest level I was meeting was Fix Destination Focused Overload. My three possible expansions are Remove Direct Overflow, Remove Via Overflow, and Remove Via Traffic. I could employ the Remove Via Traffic expansion at slight cost, with the result that 4-bound traffic on the 1-3 link we share would decrease by 30 calls and 4-bound traffic on the 2-4 link we share would increase by 30 calls. 3-bound traffic on the 1-3 link we share would increase by 30 calls and would decrease on the 2-3 link we share.

B: Your Remove Via Traffic expansion would allow me to decrease the 3- bound traffic I send you on the 2-4 link we share by 30 calls and would make no other changes in effects on you.

A: Your response to my suggested Remove Via Traffic expansion is satisfactory for me. Conflict is resolved.

In the preceding dialogue, we saw agents use the number of alternatives available to them, and the costs of those alternatives, to decide what to propose. If neither agent could find an acceptable alternative at the current level of discussion, they moved to the next higher level of their goal trees to search for alternatives. In this example, the agents had to go to the highest level before one of them could find an attractive alternative expansion that met the other agent's requirements.

7.4   Conflict-resolution Paradigms

Generally speaking, resources needed to solve a problem are the physical sources of conflict: there aren't enough or they are in the wrong place or they aren't the right kind. In the domain of telephone traffic management, conflict occurs when two or more agents want to use a given resource (typically, one of a set of lines between two switches) that cannot handle both their demands simultaneously (a resource-level conflict), or when one agent has goals that cannot be achieved if another agent's goals are to be realized (a goal-level conflict). In this domain, successful conflict resolution means that agents resolve conflict with an increased cost that is compensated for by an increase in overall network measures of performance.

Our work has focused on developing archetypes for cooperation that include conflict resolution and minimize the exchange of information among agents. In addition, we are seeking to find measures that permit the conflict-resolution strategy to be selected by the agents involved, based on the local information they have. Ideally, agents would find effective strategy-selection criteria for each conflicting subproblem, allowing arbitration on small points, for example, while another strategy is being used on the major conflicts.

Several conflict-resolution paradigms have arisen out of our examination of the traffic-management domain. These paradigms respond to problems agents could not solve as effectively without complete exchange of network information. However, they seem to be quite general. The most interesting of these are the negotiation styles we call **conflict-driven plan merging** and **shared plan development**.

In the course of negotiation, agents develop understandings of each other at the goal level, and thus can find complex solutions involving trade-offs and novel approaches to solving shared problems that neither could have recognized independently. Negotiation is a process of communication established between two conflicting agents in which they try to develop or refine their plans jointly so that the goals of each are satisfied. Agents exchange representations of their goals, look for conflicts in realizing them, develop understandings of the motivations behind those goals, and look for actions they can take jointly to meet their own goals while at the same time helping other agents achieve their goals. Negotiation is engaged when a conflict is obvious to the various parties and no predefined mechanism exists for resolving it.

In order to negotiate, agents need a language to exchange information about each other's condition and to express actions they can take themselves or wish each other to take. For a given style of negotiation, a protocol establishes when negotiation begins, how it continues, and when it is concluded. In the first style, illustrated in the example above, agents examine their independently developed plans for conflicts and negotiate by revising their goal trees at successively higher levels until they find an approach that eliminates the conflict. We call this style conflict-driven plan merging. In the second style, the agents perform a process we call shared plan development, beginning with top-level goals and arriving at ways of refining those goals at each level so that conflicts do not develop.

In **conflict-driven plan merging**, the language must be able to describe goals, plans, and abstract states of the world. The model of the other agent is a copy of its own structure, including state variables and explicit planning knowledge. What is not explicitly included in this process is the body of knowledge used to plan the negotiation—the gamesmanship of negotiation. "Gamesmanship" involves strategies for selecting moves in order to force the other agent into a move that is considered preferable. This is a large part of human negotiation, but only present in our approach in the sense that agents seek to provide the best justification possible for their suggested actions.

In **shared plan development**, the language the agents share must permit them to converse on abstract views of the world and their intentions. The language may need to involve explicit use of hypothetical-case description and differential analysis in order to talk about how one view of the world relates to another. Talking is now motivated by heuristics about the possible impact of one's local actions (in the abstract) on the rest of the network and on potential states the rest of the network may be experiencing (based on local observations). The model of the other agent is comparable to that of conflict-driven plan merging.

Negotiation styles vary along several axes. (See Figure 7.4.) One axis is the degree to which goals are expanded before negotiation begins. The negotiation process can be engaged after agents have developed plans and detected conflict, or it can be used throughout the plan-refinement process. A second parameter is the complexity of information exchanged between agents and the scope of the model each builds of the other. A third is the degree of control an agent has over the negotiating process itself, that is, whether the protocol for negotiation allows agents flexibility in conducting and concluding negotiations. The two styles discussed above vary only along the first axis.

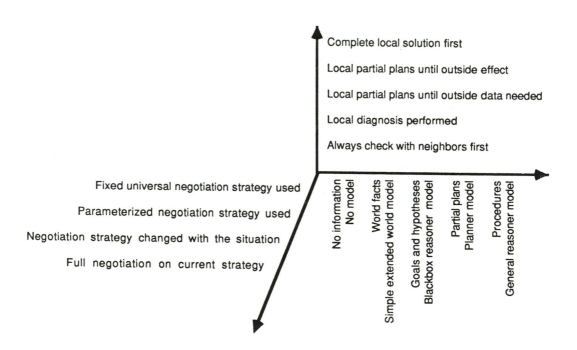

Figure 7.4: Dimensions of negotiation paradigms

In exploring the range of ways that agents could be built, we have identified a number of other cooperation paradigms. We call these paradigms independence, design, convention, arbitration, mutual accommodation, and centralization. These paradigms are distinguished by the information agents exchange, the degree to which one agent can directly enlist another's help, the degree to which two agents understand each other's goals, and the extent to which the technique commits the agents, a priori, to the outcome following its employment. Each is described briefly and a table summarizing their characteristics follows.

Independence: Conflicts may exist, but agents do no more to avoid them or deal with them than they do for any physical process in the world. Other agents are not treated as intelligent or willful. This leads to two problems: either an agent treats another as unchangeable and works harder than needed to avoid it, or it works to change the agent as it would any passive function and the other counters its efforts. Since they are independent, they need no special mechanisms for interacting. An agent can model other agents (as seen in [Genesereth and Rosenschein] and the POISE system [Croft *et al.* 1983]) by guessing their plans and goals based on observations of their behavior and common knowledge.

Design: Conflicts, though present in the environment, are avoided a priori by designing the system to distribute resources and allocate tasks in such a way that conflicts no longer exist in the working system. The problem with designed conflict avoidance is that it is not adaptable to the specific situation.

Convention: Conflicts exist in the domain, but a protocol for resolving them is built into each agent. For example, rules of the road (e.g., drive on the right on a two-lane road) represent just such a procedure. In divided-highway design, on the other hand, conflict of this sort is impossible because of the designed allocation of resources to each direction.

Arbitration: This is one form of conflict resolution by convention: it uses some procedure that conflicting agents agree on to settle resource or goal disputes. Generally, agents use arbitration when they have been unable jointly to negotiate a resolution under the current constraints (they have run out of time to make a decision, for example). Therefore, they need a mechanical method to resolve the conflict so that they can continue with other tasks at hand. Agents also use arbitration when they recognize that negotiation, with its attendant costs, is unlikely to yield a better solution. That recognition may come when agents find they are making little progress because they have little room to maneuver, or when they rediagnose a problem and discover it to be of a type defined as best solved by arbitration. Whether such rules can in fact be determined remains one of our open experimental questions.

Arbitration ranges from resolution procedures as simple as random choice to those using highly complex analysis to apportion resources or goals. We have developed one form of arbitration that is concerned not with problem solution, but rather with situation assessment. When agents view parts of problems that overlap agent boundaries, their lack

149

of complete knowledge sometimes leads them to incorrect diagnosis. To avoid complete exchange of diagnostic information, agents use an arbitration technique that defines a protocol for communication of diagnoses and a hierarchy of problem types. Arbitration defines the diagnosis to be whichever of the conflicting diagnoses occupies the highest position in the hierarchy.

Mutual Accommodation: Agents use this conflict-resolution process when they have wide latitude in problem-solving. In this paradigm, agents do not exchange goals or make explicit trade-offs with each other, but rather refine their plans to accommodate, as much as possible within their local performance requirements, the effects of one another's plans. Therefore, the language they share must describe partial world states (paralleling sensory data). They need no model of the other agent except to note that it is an agent. This technique is an iterative one, in which agents alternate in responding to each other's latest proposals accommodating one another. The process terminates when there is effectively no change needed for both to achieve their goals. The process fails when at least one of the agents has no further latitude to accommodate the other without compromising its own goals.

Our past experiments in a resource-allocation-game domain examined one style of mutual accommodation. An agent developed its next move and then communicated it to other agents; its actions were purely responsive to current conditions. Agents accommodated each other simply by choosing actions that did not interfere with the announced intentions of other agents.

Centralization: Conflicts exist, but many of the problems of synchronization and differing evaluation are reduced by selecting one agent to formulate a group plan that satisfies all relevant constraints. This involves selecting a decision maker and getting information to that agent.

We believe that negotiation will allow agents to develop joint solutions that are superior to those arrived at simply by responding to one another's latest effects without understanding the motivations behind them. Agents can detect potential trade-offs, which no agent alone could know about, and can develop a conception of overall network good, which is wholly lacking in the other paradigms. Table 7.1 summarizes these relationships.

7.5 Experimental Plan

Our initial hypothesis is that the latitude available to agents in taking actions that meet their local performance criteria, along with the complexity of the problem (roughly the number of interacting constraints to be dealt with), determine which paradigm should be

Table 7.1: Representational and Communication Requirements for Conflict-resolution Paradigms

Conflict-resolution Paradigm	Language	Communication	Model
Conflict-driven Plan Merging	Sensory data, common names, and plan trees with context tags. (Implicit requests possible)	To enable conflict detection, computed effects of local actions are broadcast whenever they will change. Conflicting pairs exchange plan subtrees justifying the declared effects.	Explicit model containing state and planning information.
Shared Plan Development	Sensory data, common names, plan trees with context tags, abstract data, and (perhaps) explicit requests.	To enable conflict detection, computed use of abstract resources are broadcast whenever they will change. Conflicting pairs exchange plans justifying the declared effects.	Explicit model containing state and planning information.
Independence, Design, and Convention	No shared language.	No explicit communication.	No model needed, though use of one may improve coordination.
Arbitration	Sensory data, (abstract) state information, and (perhaps) resource allocation.	However the conflict is detected, conflicting pairs give enough information to the arbiter to permit it to allocate the resources in conflict.	Implicit identification of other agent as an intelligent process.
Mutual Accommodation	Sensory data and common object names.	Computed effects of local actions are broadcast whenever they will change.	Implicit identification of other agent as an intelligent process.
Centralization	Sensory data, (abstract) state information, and (perhaps) resource allocation.	However the conflict is detected, conflicting pairs give enough information to the planner to permit it to solve the problem.	No model needed.

151

used. For example, when network conditions are extremely light, agents have wide latitude in problem solving: there are many possible reroutes for traffic and many alternate solutions to the problem. Measures of network routing efficiency are of little importance in such conditions (though blocking percentages remain significant), and so agents should use mutual accommodation, avoiding the high communication costs inherent in negotiation. When network conditions are very heavy, agents have few alternative routing strategies available, and arbitration is the quickest and cheapest means of preventing complete degradation of network performance. It is in moderate conditions that agents can best use negotiation to find solutions of higher quality than either mutual accommodation or arbitration could achieve. Communication costs will be justified by the quality of solution obtained, and yet will not be as high as when there is little room to maneuver.

To assess agent performance using these techniques, we need evaluation functions of two types: one to rate the achieved network performance, and another to judge the costs and progress of the conflict-resolution technique used. The functions we design for the first purpose will use such standard measures as network blocking, bandwidth and network utilization, efficiency of call transport and reachability of network destinations. Evaluation functions for agent performance in conflict resolution will weigh communication volume, number of interagent exchanges, and total processing time and elapsed time spent in conflict resolution.

Challenging the agent teams will be problem scenarios that, on a fixed network topology, use increases in the volume of traffic demand to decrease the latitude the agents have and increase the complexity of the problem they face. The scenarios we will be generating are 1) no problems, 2) one small problem completely contained in a single agent's region, 3) a local problem whose solution involves using resources of another agent, 4) a shared problem for which the locally generated plans are optimum, 5) a shared problem requiring coordination, and 6) a shared problem with no "good" solution.

The agent teams are chiefly characterized by the conflict-resolution strategy they employ. Providing benchmark information, two teams will consist of no agents and one agent. This gives us information to detect and compensate for less-than-perfect problem-solving knowledge. The remaining teams will consist of two agents utilizing one of the conflict-resolution protocols.

7.6   Experience and Results

To support our experiments, we have implemented a network simulator and a multipanel blackboard system in LOOPS on Xerox 1108 workstations. We have run experimental scenarios with a single agent and with two agents applying the mutual accommodation style of conflict resolution. We are in the process of completing our experiments using the negotiation strategies of conflict-driven plan merging and shared plan development.

We examine below our initial results for the mutual accommodation paradigm. We show results for the uncontrolled network, for the network controlled by a single agent, for the network controlled by two agents working independently, and for the network controlled by two agents using mutual accommodation for conflict resolution.

7.6.1 Scenario: Destination Focused Overload at City3 (City3 receives all via traffic)

A Destination Focused Overload at City3 results from an unusually high number of calls to City3 from City1, City4, and City5. There are milder increases from City3 to each of those three cities. The result of these increases on the network is that 40 calls (about 6%) fail, and that the standard deviation from average link utilization is 23%, meaning that the network has become fairly unbalanced. Calls are using about 1.17 links on average to reach their destinations, not much different from normal. The results are shown in Tables 7.2 and 7.3.

Table 7.2: Benchmarks: Uncontrolled and Single Agent

Network Parameter	No Agents	One Agent	
		Initial	Final
Network blocking percent	6.0	7.10	.87
Hops/call completed	1.17	1.17	1.17
Mean link utilization percent	74	78	86
Network balance (std. dev.)	23	7.20	4.94
Agent Costs	No Agents	One Agent	
Exchanges	0	0	
Number of KSs fired	0	41	

7.6.2 Interpretation of Results

We see from these results that the uncontrolled network shows the worst performance, although there are no agent costs incurred. Single-agent performance, as expected, achieves the best solution at the least cost, and serves as a reference against which multiagent performance in various paradigms can be compared. Two agents working locally achieve a better solution than the uncontrolled network, with 88 KSs fired. The mutual accommoda-

Table 7.3: Teams: Two Agents Working Locally or in Mutual Accomodation

Network Parameter	Agent A			Agent B		
	Initial	Local	M.A.	Init	Local	M.A.
Network blocking percent	5.14	0	0	7.53	.31	.31
Hops/call completed	1.01	1.06	1.05	1.18	1.18	1.14
Mean link utilization percent	69	80	84	82	90	85
Network balance (std. dev.)	4.70	2.69	3.60	6.78	4.08	4.62
	Local Merged			M.A. Merged		
Network blocking percent	2.74			.268		
Hops/call completed	1.27			1.23		
Mean link utilization percent	94.9			85.4		
Network balance (std. dev.)	5.06			4.62		
Agent Costs	Local Only			Mutual Accommodation		
Exchanges	0			13		
Number of KSs fired	88			176		

tion paradigm, with 176 KSs fired and 13 exchanges, shows a solution quality intermediate between that of the single-agent solution and the two-agent noncommunicating solution.

7.7 Planning Requirements and the Structure of Agent Knowledge

Our work so far has highlighted the limitations of sharing only the effects of plans, rather than the goals underlying the plan generation. Our future experiments (in negotiation via goal exchange) will enable us to quantify the differences in both the quality of the resulting plans and the costs in achieving them.

Effective negotiation requires an agent to have the ability to assess its alternatives. In order to do so, it must be able to understand the interrelations of actions so that it can find the entire range of alternatives. It should also be able to determine which of the various alternatives it prefers and for what reasons. Finally, it should predict as accurately as it can what reception another agent might grant its proposed alternatives. In other words, it must know about alternatives and their consequences, their likely costs to itself, and benefits to its negotiating partner. Similarly, it must be able to foresee not only the immediate effects of a partner's suggested action on its own region, but also any limitations its acceptance of a proposed action might impose on its own ability to act. Such an understanding cannot be arrived at without recourse to planning.

From the point of view of multiagent problem-solving, the function of a planning component is three-fold: to develop the best local plan with a view both to its effects on neighboring agents and to the help that other agents might provide in goal realization, to develop an array of alternatives for meeting the current goal or subgoal so that changes in a plan can be made to benefit goals independent of those used in plan expansion, and to assess the impact of and respond well to the actions of other agents.

We have implemented agent reasoning components in a multipanel blackboard system. Blackboard architectures were used effectively in HEARSAY-II [Lesser and L. Erman 1977] and in various efforts in DAI [Corkill and Lesser 1983]. Particularly relevant is the work by B. Hayes-Roth [Hayes-Roth 1985], which focuses on the control aspects of blackboard architectures. In our system we partition areas of domain knowledge as well as control. Each panel is itself a small blackboard, used as a focus of attention for processing information. The panels correspond to functions that are as independent from one another as possible. Our system also contains a separate control panel that determines the execution flow among the blackboard panels that contain the domain knowledge.

If we view each panel as a small expert system, then the interaction among the panels, especially the interaction between the subpanels and the control panel, can itself be viewed as cooperation among several expert systems to achieve a common goal. By studying the communication between these panels, we expect to further our understanding of the methods and requirements for combining expert systems of similar structure but differing content.

A multipanel approach has the following advantages:

Modularity Knowledge can be partitioned into more manageable chunks. The goal is to decompose the problem into loosely coupled subproblems, allowing independent efforts on the part of the project members. If the panels are organized correctly, then the knowledge sources that they contain should be more or less self-contained. The multipanel blackboard can be used as a building block for building the different agents.

Appropriate Level of Detail The facts pertaining to the low-level reasoning of interest to only one facet of the analysis do not obscure more generally important information. Each panel posts its conclusions in the central control area, where it is made available to all other panels within the agent. The details of the analysis are contained in the panel's own small blackboard.

Control By providing a central control module, the execution of the blackboard can be more easily monitored and debugged. The separation of knowledge and control offers

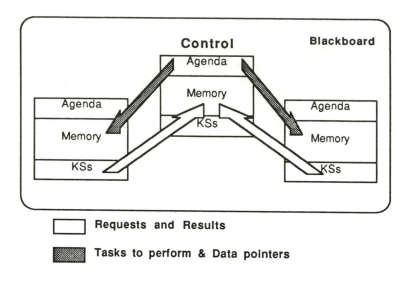

Figure 7.5: Interpanel communication

an opportunity to experiment with a variety of control strategies, using knowledge sources to guide the execution as well as the reasoning.

Development and Debugging Both the control flow and the data flow among the separate panels follow strict conventions. Control passes from the control panel to an appropriate subpanel and then returns. Likewise, data of general interest is posted to the control panel and from there is made available to the other panels. This modular approach has led to easier development and debugging. Both the control-flow and data-flow paths are easier to follow during execution of the system.

A multipanel approach also has the following disadvantages:

Modularity Partitioning the knowledge creates problems in other panels due to changes by independent developers that affect the interaction between the panels (which may be an indication that the panels should be merged).

Appropriate Level of Detail Partitioning the environment inhibits the broad interaction of KSs and the partial results typical of blackboard systems.

Control Control is allocated in large chunks. Metaknowledge sources must be provided to govern control.

As we pointed out above, one of the advantages of partitioning knowledge among blackboard panels is that it highlights the interactions between the separate panels. In our domain, we have separated the planning and negotiation functions. Our experiments have pointed out the close connection between these two groups of knowledge, which may benefit from being merged. The initial separation has led to our deeper understanding of the interrelationships between planning and negotiation.

7.8   Future Work

Our domain experience suggests that this work be extended in two dimensions: 1) addition of complexity to address the problems of larger network systems controlled by more than two agents and 2) investigation of systems of heterogeneous agents. The domain requires a deeper model of reasoning about conflicts and motivations, the development of agent models, and the promotion of a greater degree of knowledge-sharing through communication among the agents.

7.8.1   Larger Groups

In order to clarify the functional structure of a sophisticated traffic management agent that can plan, negotiate, and resolve conflicts with peer agents, we have until now focused our discussion on pair-wise agent interactions. An important question we intend to address is whether these techniques are applicable to simultaneous conflict among several or many agents. If all parties to a conflict must interact in pairs and in the same degree as that found in two-agent conflicts, then the amount of communication and processing time required will rise exponentially with the number of agents involved. Clearly, such an approach would be intractable for large numbers of problem-solving agents.

To a great extent, we can rely on the local nature of problems in our domain to restrict the number of controlled regions involved in solving any problem. However, we believe that the solution to this problem lies both in domain considerations and, more generally, in the roles that agents play in a group conflict. Specific goals and constraints of individual agents should cause them to restrict their interest to certain aspects of a conflict, so that interested parties would negotiate over the pieces of a conflict or its solution that impinge on them, while leaving other aspects of the conflict to be resolved by other agents. As an example, the main actors in destination-focused-overload conditions, involving interregional trunk facilities and correspondingly many agent regions, tend to be the agent with the focus nodes and the agents with residual capacity on trunks to the focus; other agents may not even need to negotiate with each other. Pieces of solutions would be joined together into a coherent global solution either grass roots-style, as special-interest groups develop their plans internally and then merge them with other special-interest groups, or by dispassionate agents, whose role it may be to serve as overseers of the negotiation process.

The manner in which people converse in groups serves as one model for multiagent interactions. Individuals may be heard sequentially, one speaker at a time with all others listening; accordingly to parliamentary rules, with a chair as arbiter; in small subcommittees that perform most of the work, with routine deference by other group members to subcommittee decisions and occasional use of prescribed procedures to overrule them; in formal organizations (often hierarchies) that limit conversations to a very small number, with designated arbiters for peer conflict resolution; and in markets, often with brokers, that perform preselection of interested people and limit conversation types and their parameters (e.g., the buy/sell conversation).

These methods all involve pair-wise conversations, but the number of conversations is generally constrained to fewer than the number of all possible pairs. Our initial work using two agents is a necessary first step toward solving problems with many agents. Our initial experiments should help to extract the essence of these protocols, which will then be used as the basis for developing group protocols.

An important goal in large groups of agents is to limit communication, yet to do so in such a way that proper coordination can still occur. [Conry et al. 1986] illustrated achievement of this goal with a very simple communication restriction and certain clever rules about what to send. Their approach also avoided the severe problems of loss of synchronization among agents and of agents cycling on competing solutions.

As an alternative approach to the large-group problem, our problem-solving strategy could be modified to adopt a centralization style in which, once the group identifies the problem, a single agent is given the ultimate responsibility for solving it and contracts out various subtasks for planning and/or implementing the response. Smith's contract net is a classic approach [Smith 1980]; the underlying paradigms could be extended for use by the traffic-management agents we have developed. Agents could broadcast their local congestion diagnosis to neighboring agents and establish a consensus for action by entering into manager/contractor relationships. In fact, the task-sharing and dynamic-control features of the contract net are clearly desirable in our context. Interestingly, the bidding process would amount to a selective pair-wise negotiation process, and if we assumed completeness of task allocation as well as a schedule implicit in the bidding process, there would need to be no more pair-wise negotiation and the process would terminate with the accomplishment of the planning tasks. In some of the work by [Steeb et al. 1984] on Distributed Air Traffic Control, good conflict-resolution performance was achieved, for example, by conferring privileged status on the most-knowledgeable and/or the least-constrained agent. The framework was a hierarchical organization. In our domain, a dynamically initialized team of agents is a more likely candidate organizational-structure-and-control paradigm. However, agents do acquire privileged status by virtue of their relationship to the congestion problem to be solved and leads to an implicit role-assignment process.

7.8.2 Heterogeneous Agents

As stated earlier, one of the main reasons for building multiagent expert systems is to use agents with diverse realms of expertise and experience to solve problems ill-suited to agents sharing a single perspective. Division of labor becomes more difficult in that there is an additional constraint on the allocation of task to agent and there is a greater need for analogical reasoning and explanation to permit the agents to work together.

The question to be resolved in heterogeneous systems is how the differences affect agents' abilities to work together. In human systems, it can be argued that the volume of information two humans share is far greater than their differences. In a simple model of a producer/consumer pair, the common knowledge can be limited to volumes, trade intentions and practices, and the commodity in question, and from this a reasonably effective barter over price can take place. However, a rich negotiation requires far more common experience and knowledge, such as the purposes to which the consumer puts the commodity and the means by which the producer acquires it. By this argument, in order to get the richest cooperation the "heterogeneous" agents would have to know everything known by each other.

To borrow again from human models, the factors that separate individuals tend to be experiential. Expertise is not rooted in knowledge of the laws of a domain, but rather in the everyday application of those laws to practice. Each agent is generally capable of solving problems, but merely lacks a few of the laws or the bulk of the practices that are used to solve common problems. Cooperation in the system is facilitated by this common experience and permits agents to describe problems and exchange ideas on solutions without each being able to generate good solutions efficiently.

Organizations exist to simplify the interactions that occur within a group of agents working on a recurring task. One of the more common organizations for humans is that of a control hierarchy. In this heterogeneous organization, there are at least two kinds of agents: supervisors and subordinates. Such an organization mirrors the present organization of the people doing network management. We will be investigating how to preserve the useful autonomy that individuals have in well-managed hierarchies, while adding control systems on top of fully functional, existing subsystems.

Further work is needed on the models agents have of each other and of the organizations involved, so that they can reason about conflicts, cooperation, and protocols for communication, and choose the best strategy to follow. As [Genesereth and Rosenschein] illustrated, the need for communication in any interaction can be reduced if there are models of the decision processes of the other agents. Each of our protocols could be examined and extended by giving each agent more explicit models of the other agents, along with the reasoning necessary to assess the possible states (and therefore needs and actions) of the other agents in the system.

7.8.3 Knowledge Sharing

The question of knowledge sharing as a mechanism of cooperation follows our current effort in a couple of natural ways. There are two kinds of knowledge: information about the world, and procedures for using information. The conflict-resolution paradigms discussed here used information sharing to communicate with each other. Since this is "static" information, there is no other way to share it than to give it away. The methods of giving it away can be streamlined given other information about agents:

- If an agent's model of others is rich enough, the agent can analyze other agents to offer them new information that will allow them to solve their problems.

- Agents may develop alliances and more formalized roles in their joint problem-solving (that is, they may form organizations).

Procedures, on the other hand, can be shared in a number of ways:

- If other agents describe their situations, an agent can solve problems for them using its own procedures.

- If other agents give an agent enough information, the agent can solve mutual problems (cf. the approach taken by [Durfee and Lesser 1987]).

- If agents can talk about goals and plans, then with a small addition to the language they can describe rules and procedures to each other. At that point, an agent can give another a rule that it can use to compute a better answer to its problem. (The risks of such an approach are significant, however).

In conclusion, this research has produced a rich testbed for ideas and a workable classification of conflict-resolution strategies that we believe will be useful to system designers as well as to the system itself in carrying out distributed problem-solving.

160

References

[Conry et al. 1986] S. Conry, R. Meyer, and V. Lesser, "Multistage Negotiation in Distributed Planning," COINS Technical Report 86-67, University of Massachusetts, 1986.

[Corkill and Lesser 1983] D. Corkill and V. Lesser, "The Use of Meta-level Control for Coordination in a Distributed Problem Solving Network," *Proceedings Eighth IJCAI*, 1983, pp. 748–756.

[Croft et al. 1983] B. Croft, L. Lefkowitz, and V. Lesser, "POISE: An Intelligent Assistant For Profession Based Systems," *Proceedings of the Conference on Artificial Intelligence*, Rochester, MI, 1983.

[Durfee and Lesser 1987] E. Durfee and V. Lesser, "Using Partial Global Plans to Coordinate Distributed Problem Solvers," *Proceedings Tenth IJCAI*, 1987, pp. 875–883.

[Englemore and Morgan 1988] R. Englemore and T. Morgan, eds., *Blackboard Systems*, Addison-Wesley Publishing Company, 1988.

[Genesereth and Rosenschein] M. Genesereth and J. Rosenschein, "Cooperation without Communication," Report #HPP-84-5, Stanford Heuristic Programming Project, 1984.

[Hayes-Roth 1985] B. Hayes-Roth, "A Blackboard Architecture for Control," *Artificial Intelligence*, Vol. 26, 1985, pp. 251–321.

[Lesser and L. Erman 1977] V. Lesser and L. Erman, "A Retrospective View of the HEARSAY-II Architecture," *Proceedings Fifth IJCAI*, Cambridge, MA, 1977, pp. 790–800.

[Sandell and Worrest 1985] H. Sandell and R. Worrest, "Cooperative Real-Time Planning: An Experimental Study," *Proceedings of NCSE'85 Technical Program*, 1985, pp. 79–84.

[Smith 1980] R. Smith, "The Contract Net Protocol: High-Level Communication and Control in a Distributed Problem Solver," *IEEE Transactions on Computers*, Vol. 29, No. 12, 1980, pp. 1104–1113.

[Steeb et al. 1984] R. Steeb, D. McArthur, S. Cammarata, S. Narain, and W. Giarla, "Distributed Problem Solving for Air Fleet Control: Framework and Implementations," Rand Note N-2139-ARPA, 1984.

Mark R. Adler, Alvah B. Davis, Robert Weihmayer, and Ralph W. Worrest
GTE Laboratories Incorporated
40 Sylvan Road
Waltham, MA 02254

Chapter 8

Constraint-Directed Negotiation of Resource Reallocations

Arvind Sathi and Mark S. Fox

Abstract

The resource reallocation problem requires multiagent choices under multiple-criteria, most of which are based on qualitative attributes. The conditional specification of a reallocation request (e.g., requiring a swap for one workstation with another) results in chains of reallocation transactions, which increase in complexity with the number of resources and agents. Also, the initial intentions for transactions may differ from the final transaction due to give-or-take on resource components. This work is motivated by human negotiation procedures, such as logrolling, bridging, and unlinking. We view the process of reallocation negotiations as being constraint based. Constraints can be used both for evaluation of existing alternatives as well as for creating new ones. We define a set of qualitative evaluation and relaxation (alternative generation) techniques based on human negotiation problem solving. The search uses several aspects of constraints, such as constraint importance, looseness, utility, and threshold levels. We evolve a mixed problem solving approach in which agents search individually in earlier stages and as a group in later stages. The constraint-directed negotiation approach is validated for the quality of solution in comparison to expert human negotiators on a variety of negotiation problems using a partial factorial design. The final version of the problem solver performs marginally better than the expert on experimental problems.

8.1 Introduction

Consider an engineering organization that is divided into a set of groups (agents) each possessing computing resources. As the projects each group works on change, the initial allocation of resources has to be adjusted to reflect any new requirements. Adjustment is performed through the buying and selling of resources, primarily between groups. The buying and selling process is often complex due to conditions placed upon them. For example, a group currently owning an Explorer and requiring a MicroVAX may wish to give up its explorer only if it can get a MicroVAX. As a result, a typical reallocation transaction specifies one or more buys and sells of resources among groups. A *simple transaction* involves selling of a resource from one group to another. A *trade* involves a two way exchange of workstations between two groups. A *cascade* involves an open or closed chain of buys and sells among more than two groups. Size and number of transaction chains increase rapidly with the number of resources and groups. In a typical resource negotiation, it is not uncommon to find cascade chains of 5 to 10 transactions. As each transaction involves at least two groups, it can be administered only if agreed upon by everyone involved. Finally, the initial intentions for transactions may differ from the final agreed upon transactions due to give-or-take on portions of resources to make the best out of partial matches.

There are a number of constraints and objectives faced by the groups as they buy or sell workstations. For example:

- Workstations carry maintenance cost. Unused workstations reduce profit margins.

- Workstations are required for program development. Absence of the workstation may imply reduced revenues.

- Maintenance and depreciation cost allocation for workstations ranges from $1,000 to $3,200. Groups prefer the most inexpensive workstations as long as they meet the other requirements.

- Workstations differ in development and debug environment. Engineers' productivity is higher for the workstations equipped with better development and debugging tools. Such workstations are also the most expensive. Often a trade-off is struck between cost and development environment.

- Different projects require different workstations due to the delivery software requirements which may specify the type of workstation, display mode (color or black & white), memory or disk space, etc.

- Workstations may be located anywhere in the building. They can be relocated, if needed, to bring them closer to the engineer's office. There is a cost associated with the relocation.

- Workstations can sometimes be shared by two groups. The accounting department recognizes (in terms of monthly allocation of maintenance) equal sharing of a workstation between two groups. In such a case, each group is charged for half of the share. Depending on the need, the workstations can be moved from wholly owned to shared status and vice-versa.

- Exchanges of resources may be conditional. Often the groups seek exchanges of less desirable workstations for more desirable ones. This is achieved by floating conditional bids where the sell bid is conditional on the buy bid. In the presence of conditional and nonconditional bids, sometimes the conditions can be unlinked from one bid and linked to another.

- Unnecessary changes to existing allocations are avoided. Any change involves unproductive engineering time in moving files and development environment from one workstation to another.

The goal for each group is to acquire the right mix of workstations to meet current workstation requirements while keeping the negotiation time to a minimum. Every time a change is sought by a group, fresh allocation (i.e., allocation from scratch without any regard to current allocations) can not be used as a problem solving technique. In most reallocation situations, a small percentage of resource allocations are changed. The groups would prefer not considering the rest of the workstations that are already allocated. At the same time, in otherwise unsolvable situations, some existing allocations could sometimes be changed.

We call this problem the *resource reallocation* problem. It is a subproblem of the more general distributed planning problem in that

- there are multiple agents each possessing resources at the outset.

- each agent has one or more activities to perform in parallel, where each activity requires resources.

- each agent may require either additional or fewer resources.

- activities do not have to be selected nor sequenced.

Though conceptually simpler, the resource reallocation problem is combinatorially complex, due to the number and size of cascades that need to be performed in order to maximize the number of satisfied bids. Also, there are significant information requirements due to what has to be known in order to construct cascades.

Negotiation is required to solve the reallocation problem. Negotiation is composed of two phases: a *communication* phase where information relevant to the negotiation is communicated to participating agents, and a *bargaining* phase where "deals" are made between individuals or in a group (also called "social choice" [Arrow 1951]. In resource reallocation, information about available bids has to be communicated minimally, while agents may individually or as a group make tradeoff decisions about how to satisfy requirements.

Prior research in negotiation has focused on protocols for supporting price system contracting [Smith 1980]. What to communicate about an agent's position has been investigated by [Genesereth *et al.* 1986]. In this case, the focus was on the communication of the payoff matrix for a single decision problem with an a priori enumeration of decisions. Bargaining was explored by [Sycara 1987] where multiple agents alter their positions on multiple issues during multiple encounters. Case-based reasoning and multiattribute utility analysis were used to alter an agent's position. Relative to this research, we are concerned less with the protocols of negotiation and more with what is to be communicated about an agent's bargaining position and how their positions are to be changed over time.

In contrast to these approaches, our methodology builds upon the concept of constraint-directed negotiation as outlined in [Sathi 1986]. Within this framework agents' objectives are represented via sets of constraints together with their utilities. When a conflict occurs, agents negotiate by modifying either the current solutions or the constraints until a compromise is reached. Thus, **joint solutions are generated through a process of negotiation, which configures or reconfigures individual offerings**. In this approach, the agents do not need to know the other agents' utilities for each possible outcome of the interaction, nor do they even need to be aware of all the possible outcomes. Rather they iteratively exchange offers until a compromise is found. Beliefs about the other agents' utilities are used merely to speed up the convergence to a mutually acceptable solution.

Negotiators use different strategies for converging to a solution depending on the search space and the topology of the constraint space. For example, in an extreme situation in which constraints affect only individual offerings (as in Game Theory), a distributed negotiation in the form of a market is sufficient. However, **if most of the constraints are conditional upon multiple offerings, mediator-driven cooperative negotiation is more appropriate**. Though much literature is available on the former situation [Marschak and Radner 1972], [Baiman 1982], the latter situation is more frequent and not so well understood. In this paper, we report the results of research that has focused on a subset of this problem. In particular, we investigate constraint satisfaction and relaxation processes in the reallocation of resources among agents in an engineering organization.

In the rest of this paper we describe the perspective humans use in performing negotiation: a constraint directed process. We then describe the representation of constraint knowledge and an agent's "bargaining" position. Finally, three negotiation algorithms are described. Each algorithm defines a different mode of communication and bargaining.

8.2 Approach

The negotiation process can be viewed as constraint directed search in a problem space. A state is defined by a set of transactions and cascades that are formed by pairing buy and sell bids. States are evaluated using constraints. Constraint-directed negotiation would simply reduce to heuristic search, if constraints were used only for evaluating negotiation positions. In constraint-directed negotiation we view constraints as fundamental in the generation of new negotiation positions. More complex transactions can be formed by the process of constraint satisfaction and relaxation. Our approach to constraint-directed negotiation defines a set of qualitative satisfaction and relaxation operators based on human negotiation problem solving [Pruitt 1981]. The three operators are

Composition: A grouping of buy and sell bids or transactions in order to satisfy a complex constraint. Composition takes as input a group of transactions, each of which is unacceptable on conditional constraints (see Section 8.3.2 for a definition), and creates a cascade (a new state) that is acceptable on the conditional constraints.

Reconfiguration: A change in resource attribute value in order to meet the requirements of a buyer. Workstation reconfiguration takes as input a set of workstation attribute definitions that are unacceptable on a set of requirement constraints and reconfigures them to create a new workstation (and thus a new state) that is acceptable on the requirement constraints.

Relaxation: Selective constraint violation on less important constraints in order to accept a transaction that is acceptable on more important constraints. Relaxation takes as input a set of preferences. If an alternative (transaction or cascade) is acceptable or dominant on more important constraints, it removes the low importance preferences if they prefer other alternatives.

In a typical scenario, a good solution cannot be found by means of simple pair-wise exchanges. It is only by composing and reconfiguring bids and transactions can the maximum number of bids be satisfied. The difficulty is the combinatorics of composition and reconfiguration.

Now that the problem space has been defined, including the operators for generating new states via composition, reconfiguration and relaxation, the problem remains to search the space in an efficient manner. In the rest of the paper, we describe the representation of knowledge in more detail, followed by the constraint-directed negotiation strategies.

8.3   Representation

This section addresses the constraint representation. It elaborates the contents of a constraint, their classification hierarchy and their evaluation process. In the resource reallocation problem, most of the constraints are qualitative. That is, their utilities and importances can not be expressed using numbers. In our definitions and evaluations, we describe how the qualitative utilities are combined without the use of arithmetic operations.

8.3.1   Environment

Negotiation is performed among a set of **agents**. Each agent owns a set of **resources** employed by the agent to fulfill resource **requirements**. If there is a difference between the resource requirement and the resources owned by an agent, changes in resource ownership are solicited through **buy** and **sell** bids. A **buy bid** expresses an intention to acquire a resource for a specified requirement. Similarly, a **sell bid** expresses an intention to sell a specified resource. Resources have a number of **attributes**. Each resource is described as a set of **attribute-value** pairs. A requirement contains a set of restrictions on the attribute values. A **transaction** is a pair of bids, one of which is a buy bid while the other is a sell bid. Together they express a joint intention between a buyer and a seller to change the ownership of resources from the seller to the buyer. A **cascade** is a set of two or more transactions that can be executed only together.

8.3.2   Constraints

Constraints are used to evaluate transactions and cascades[1]. They specify the cost or the restrictions in choosing a transaction or a cascade by an agent or a group of agents for an attribute or for the transaction as a whole. The constraint specifies preference for an alternative in the form of **utility**, minimally accepted or a **threshold** for a utility

---

[1]The representation is an extension of the constraint representation defined in [Fox 1983].

and a constraint **importance** relative to other constraints. Constraints, as well as their importance, utilities and thresholds may differ from one agent to another.

A **requirement constraint** measures the extent of match between a resource specified in a sell bid and a requirement specified in a buy bid. It takes at least two possible utilities: "acceptable" if the match is found and "unacceptable" if the match is not found. For example, a *workstation-type* constraint is a requirement constraint. It matches the value of the *workstation-type* attribute for the workstation with the value of the *workstation-type* attribute for the requirement. If the workstation value is a subset of the requirement value, the utility is acceptable, otherwise it is not. Thus, Symbolics 3640 is acceptable for a requirement for Symbolics (as Symbolics 3640 is a subset of Symbolics models), while MicroVAX is not.

In a **fixed requirement constraint**, the resource attribute value can not be changed and the requirement for the attribute value can not be waived. A **reconfigurable requirement constraint** measures the cost of changing an attribute value for a resource. For example, a workstation can be relocated from one location to another.

A **conditional constraint** measures the utility of a set of transactions as a group. It specifies whether the respective sell and buy bids should be executed conjunctively (AND) or disjunctively (OR). For example, an agent may own a Symbolics and may require an Explorer. He may specify the buy and sell bids as conditional, whereby the sell bid for the Symbolics workstation cannot be executed unless his buy bid for the explorer workstation is satisfied.

Each constraint specifies a **utility** that measures relative preference, limitation or cost for the chosen value compared to the other values and the constraint threshold. The utility itself is an attribute that can take either an ordinal or cardinal form depending on the chosen level of specification.

The constraint **threshold** measures the acceptable limit of the utility below which the constraint is considered violated. Threshold can be specified as an ordinal or cardinal attribute.

A **preference** specifies a utility without any threshold satisfaction level. Any transaction would score a satisfactory utility for a preference, though one transaction may be preferred over another. Such constraints are useful as tie-breakers among competing transactions or cascades that have equal utilities for the other constraints.

The utilities are measured as follows:

- For cardinal attributes (e.g., maintenance cost), the utility is specified as a direction (positive or negative) between the utility attribute and the attribute constrained. If the direction is positive, the objective is better satisfied with higher values of the attribute. For example, the direction is negative for the attribute maintenance cost because a lower value in maintenance cost is preferred over a high value. In addition, a transformation function can be specified that maps the attribute values to utility values. By default, the transformation function is identity (i.e., the utility value is the same as the attribute value).

- For ordinal attributes (e.g., workstation development and debugging environment), the utility is specified as a direction. A positive direction implies that the utility is in the same direction as the ordinal rank while a negative direction implies the utility opposes the direction for ordinal rank. For example, the utility direction is positive for workstation development environment as programmers prefer better development and debugging facilities. Utility specification for ordinal attributes can at best be ordinal.

- For nominal attributes (e.g., hardware platform requirement), the utility is specified for each value in comparison to the other values and the threshold. The preference is specified in the form of a "predicate" that either matches a value or does not match the value. The utility is specified for both "match" and "nonmatch" between the requirement and the chosen value. There may be as many relaxation specs as the possible values for the nominal attribute[2]. The match and nonmatch utilities specify the rank order among the utility of match, nonmatch, and threshold. For example, if the requirement demands a "Symbolics" workstation (a fixed requirement), the predicate would match a workstation of the type "Symbolics" and would not match for any other type of work-station. The match-utility is greater than the threshold while the nonmatch utility is less than the threshold (as the constraint is nonflexible).

The constraint **importance** specifies the priority order among the constraints for the agent. Importance can be specified using either ordinal or cardinal attributes. In our discussions, we will restrict ourselves to an ordinal definition of importance.

8.3.3   Negotiation Position

A **position matrix** is a set of transactions or cascades evaluated on a set of constraints. A row represents a single transaction and its utilities for each constraint. A position constraint is the aggregate utility for a transaction or cascade on all the constraints specified in the position matrix.

---

[2]The partial matches are currently ignored.

Table 8.1: Negotiation Position

Constraint	Constraint			
	C_1	C_2	C_3	C_4
Importance	I_1	I_2	I_3	I_4
Threshold	Th_1	Th_2	Th_3	Th_4
Transaction/Cascade	Utility			
T_1	U_{11}	U_{12}	U_{13}	U_{14}
T_2	U_{21}	U_{22}	U_{23}	U_{24}
T_3	U_{31}	U_{32}	U_{33}	U_{34}

For example, Table 8.1 shows a position matrix. T_1, T_2 and T_3 are transactions (i.e., sell/buy combinations). C_1, C_2, C_3 and C_4 are constraints with thresholds Th_i and importances I_i and U_{ij} is the utility of constraint C_i for transaction T_j.

Constraint utilities can be compared across alternatives transactions or cascades. The result of evaluation places the alternative in either of the following three categories:

- Unacceptable (the alternative is unacceptable on the constraint)

- Acceptable (the alternative is acceptable on the constraints)

- Dominant (the alternative is dominant over other alternatives on the constraint).

Having generated an evaluation on each constraint, how do we build an overall evaluation for the alternative that combines the evaluations on individual constraints? A number of combinational strategies are available through the researchers of behavioral decision theory [Tversky 1969], [Payne 1976], [Svenson 1979], [Johnson and Payne 1985]. Some of the well-known strategies are as follows:

- Additive utility: Given a set of utilities for constraints, the overall utility is the sum total of all the individual utilities. In order to execute this strategy, the utilities must be cardinal as it requires an arithmetic operation.

- Additive difference: This can be used to compare two transactions. To compute additive difference, first we compute the difference between utilities for the two alternatives on each constraint. These differences are then added. If the sum is positive, then the first alternative is better. Otherwise, the second alternative is better. Like additive utility, this method also requires cardinal utilities.

- Elimination by aspects: Given a threshold utility for the constraint, the utility for each constraint for a transaction/cascade is compared with the corresponding threshold or the utilities on other constraints. Transactions with low utilities on any constraint are eliminated from the consideration. This process continues till only one transaction remains. Unlike the above combination rules, elimination by aspect can be used if the utilities are ordinal as it requires no arithmetic operation. It can also be used for identifying an acceptable subset of transactions or cascades (by using constraint threshold as the comparison point).

- Lexicographic semiorder: It is similar to elimination by aspects. It examines the transactions on each constraint and eliminates those which have values less than the dominant alternative. The rule is applied first by using the most important constraint and then by using the second most important constraint, and so on. Like elimination by aspects, this rule requires only ordinal utilities and importances. It can be used for identifying the dominant set.

In a comparative study, Johnson and Payne found a remarkable reduction in the comparison effort for elimination by aspects and lexicographic semiorder. The accuracy of these rules depends on the distribution of importance and the emphasis placed on the noncompensatory nature of the domain. Thus, if the importances are too far apart, a combination of elimination by aspect and lexicographic semiorder are sufficient to identify the acceptable set and to select from within the acceptable set. These strategies can be used by individual agents to identify their favorite alternatives. They are not usable in consolidating the preferences across agents.

Now, how do we apply elimination-by-aspect and lexicographic semiorder to position evaluation by an agent? The positions themselves are viewed as constraints. They carry composite utility, which is an ordinal measure with the following categories:

No bid: There exists no bid in the position matrix.

No transactions: There exist only buy and sell bids but no transactions. Buy and sell bids alone are insufficient to make a transaction.

Unacceptable: The transaction or cascade evaluates to less than threshold for a constraint.

Acceptable: The transaction/cascade is above threshold on every constraint but does not dominant every other transaction/cascade.

Dominant: The transaction/cascade dominates every other transaction/cascade.

The above classification is also a ranking of alternatives (in ascending order).

The position constraints can be classified into the following categories:

172

1. Fixed requirement position (FP) measures the overall evaluation for a transaction on requirement constraints. Their utility is derived from the utility for the individual requirements using the following algebra:

   "Unacceptable-bid" + "Unacceptable-bid" = "Unacceptable-bid"

   "Unacceptable-bid" + "Acceptable-bid" = "Unacceptable-bid"

   "Acceptable-bid" + "Acceptable-bid" = "Acceptable-bid"

   In other words, if "unacceptable-bid" were assigned a rank of 1 and "Acceptable-bid" were assigned a rank of 2, the composite match takes the lowest of a set of utilities.

2. Transaction position (TP) measures the overall utility for a transaction. It follows the same algebra as described above.

3. Cascade position (CP) measures the overall utility on constraints applicable to cascades such as conditional constraints.

4. Agent position (AP) measures the overall utility of all of an individual agent's constraints.

5. Group position (GP) measures the overall satisfaction of all the negotiating parties. It combines all the agent positions.

Using elimination by aspects and dominance analysis, we can evaluate each of the above positions for a set of transactions into any of categories defined above (no bids, no transactions, unacceptable, acceptable and dominant). Using lexicographic semiorder and the preference constraints, we can further search among acceptable transaction for the dominant ones.

8.4 Negotiation Operators

Using the insight of human negotiations, we define, in this section, three constraint satisfaction and relaxation operators—composition, reconfiguration, and relaxation—that can be used for modifying transactions or cascades, for creating new cascades, or for changing the evaluation of transactions. The human negotiation literature refers to these strategies as bridging, unlinking and logrolling, respectively [Pruitt 1981].

8.4.1   Composition

Composition satisfies a constraint by means of composition. Composition occurs between two negotiators when a new option is developed by combining together two existing alternatives which satisfy both parties' most significant constraints. In the context of resource reallocation, composition is the act of grouping or combining buy and sell bids, transactions or cascades in order to meet conditional constraints. Suppose there exist two transactions $T_{i1,j1}$ and $T_{i2,j2}$ each of which are acceptable to the respective buyers on the nonrelaxable resource requirements. Also, suppose one of the negotiating parties specifies a conditional constraint $(S_{i2}\ B_{j1})$ that prohibits selling workstation in the sell bid S_{i2} without buying for requirement specified in B_{j1}. A cascade formed by combining the two transactions satisfies the conditional constraint.

Composition is typically used by resource reallocation negotiators as a strategy for building cascade solutions. Each agent has a set of conditional bids which need to be executed together. By bringing two transactions together, agents build cascade solutions that bridge on their most important needs.

8.4.2   Reconfiguration

Cooperative negotiations, in which both parties get all they were seeking, occasionally occur as a result of the discovery of a fortunate composition formula. But such agreements are not always available. It is usually necessary for one or both parties to make selective changes in the offerings to derive a mutually agreeable alternative. Reconfiguration is a process of regrouping the bundle of negotiated goods. Suppose there exist two buy bids for 0.5 workstation each and a single sell bid for a workstation. The two halves of the workstation can be unlinked from each other to provide viable sell alternatives for each buy bid. Regrouping may occur to define a new workstation configuration.

As an example of reconfiguration, agent m requires a Symbolics running the KC-3-2 tool suite. Agent n is offering a Symbolics running KC-3-1. The Symbolics offered by agent n can be reconfigured. Thus, the current tool suite will be removed from its disk and a new one loaded. The end result is what agent m desires. This requires several hours of an engineer's time to change the workstation configuration.

There are many reconfiguration possibilities in the workstation negotiations:

- Committed allocations of resources to requirements are reconfigurable. It is possible for an agent to enter new bids into the market place by breaking existing resource and requirements pairs, generating sell bids for the resources and the buy bids for the requirements. Thus, in a negotiation situation where the existing buy and sell bids are not matching with each other, additional bids can be introduced through reconfiguration, thereby increasing the number of options for each bid.

- Conditional bids can be reconfigured. Given a conditional bid (S_{k1}, B_{k2}) and an unconditional sell bid S_{k3} from the same agent, B_{k2} can be unlinked from the conditional bid and reconfigured with S_{k3}.

- Resource definitions are a way of packaging workstation components into a single package. Depending on the needs, resources can be reconfigured. The most obvious example is that of breaking the ownership of a single workstation into a shared ownership where the use of workstation in the morning is unlinked from the afternoon use. Similarly, two agents may swap memory boards, disk drives or displays separately from the workstation, or may move to the workstation from one location to another.

The focus of reconfiguration is a conceptual group $G = \{m_i\}$, where m_i are the group members. Similar to Simplex iterations on decision variables, reconfiguration searches for a group in which the value of holding the members together in the group is less than the value of breaking the group members apart and reorganizing the groups. The groups in the above example are existing resource allocations, conditional bids and resource configuration definitions. Our focus of attention in reconfiguration are those changes that result in strict or weak increase in utilities without trade-offs. Thus, the utility on each constraint should either increase or remain the same.

8.4.3 Relaxation

Relaxation is the process of ignoring constraints in case a chosen alternative is unacceptable on a specific constraint. When bargaining concerns a set of issues, it may be possible to arrange an exchange of concessions. One party concedes on issues A, B and C, and the other on issues D, E, and F. This exchange will be successful in reconciling interests to the extent that the parties have differing priorities across the set of issues—concessions on A, B and C being minimally costly to the first party but providing considerable benefit to the second, and concessions on D, E, F being minimally costly to the second party yet providing considerable benefit to the first. This process is called logrolling in human negotiations [Pruitt 1981].

Given a set of preferences for transactions, the agents need to find a common preference. The common preference is not easy to find. First of all, a single agent may find it difficult to aggregate preferences on different constraints. In addition, there is no easy mechanism for voting on preferences across agents. Relaxation provide an approximate technique for

| | Complexity | | |
	Small	Medium	Large
Small	No of Constraints Small	No of Constraints Medium	No of Constraints Large
Medium	No of Constraints Large	No of Constraints Small	No of Constraints Medium
Large	No of Constraints Medium	No of Constraints Large	No of Constraints Small

Size

Figure 8.1: Latin square design

selecting transactions or cascades that perform the best on the most important constraints for each individual.

Much as voting or weighting techniques can be used to identify only near dominance, but not marginal dominance, the relaxation technique suffers from the same weakness. In a decision between two alternatives, if one is almost dominant, then it can be spotted. If there are close runners, then one may use random assignment or more exact methods for finding a solution. Relaxation does not always result in unambiguous conflict resolution but sometimes it can be used for breaking ties. Under the assumption of ordinal information for the importances and utilities, this may be the best we could do.

8.5 The Negotiation Process and Experimental Results

Table 8.2: Cell Statistics

Conditions	Latin Square Cell								
	1-1	1-2	1-3	2-1	2-2	2-3	3-1	3-2	3-3
Size	Low	Low	Low	Med	Med	Med	High	High	High
Complexity	Low	Med	High	Low	Med	High	Low	Med	High
No. of constraints	Low	Med	High	Med	High	Low	High	Low	Med
Managers	3	3	3	6	6	6	9	9	9
Workstations	9	8	7	36	25	27	61	81	75
Requirements	9	9	9	36	28	21	61	72	59
Sell-bids	1	3	2	7	8	14	10	30	36
Buy-bids	1	4	4	7	11	8	10	21	20
Fixed reqs.	1	7	6	14	28	8	30	15	20
Relaxable attrb.	1	5	4	14	22	4	30	15	19
Total trans.	1	12	8	49	88	112	100	630	720
Conditionals	0	1	1	0	1	5	5	15	17

Three search strategies have been investigated for the efficient generation of negotiated reallocations. To test their performance, a double-blind experiment[3] was performed over a latin square of nine classes of problems (see Figure 8.1 and Table 8.2). The latin square rows differentiate the test cases on size. Thus, each cell in the first row has three agents and on an average nine workstations-requirements pairs. Each cell in the second row has six agents and up to thirty-six workstations-requirement pairs. Each cell in the third row has nine agents and up to eighty-one workstations-requirement pairs. The columns differentiate on the complexity. Thus, each cell in the first column has no workstation/requirements imbalance, has each requirement fully specified using workstation parameters, and only 20% of the population has reallocation bids. Each cell in the second column has an average of 10% imbalance, only 75% of the workstation attributes are specified in the requirements and 30% of the population is being reallocated. Each cell in the third column has 20% imbalance, only 50% of the workstation attributes are specified for requirements and 40% of the population is being reallocated. The superimposed third dimension differentiates in terms of number of constraints (3, 6, or 9).

8.5.1 CDN I

The CDN I algorithm investigated the use of the composition operator in a completely distributed, nonnegotiated, greedy approach to reallocating resources. At the outset, each agent possesses a set of resources, buy bids, sell bids, and constraints on both bids and

---

[3]The same 9 problems were given to the program and to an expert. Their performance were rated by another expert without knowledge of who generated the solutions.

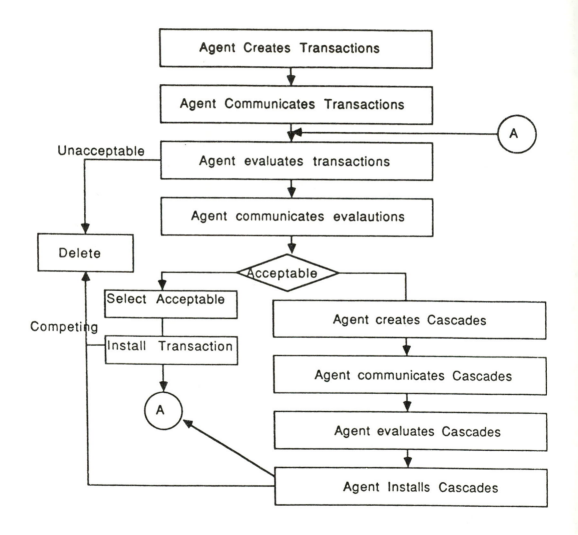

Figure 8.2: CDN I algorithm

resources. In the first step, each agent communicates its sell bids to all other agents. Consequently, each agent has only a partial model of the potential set of transactions. Each agent creates a position matrix containing its buy bids and all known sell bids in order to identify potential transactions. Each buy-sell pair is combined into a potential transaction if it satisfies the agent's own fixed requirement constraints. Potential transactions along with the position constraints (i.e., aggregate evaluation of the known constraints for each potential transaction) are communicated to all agents. If an agent's buy bid participates in more than one potential transaction, a deadlock constraint, specifying that the installation of a transaction cannot be performed without agreement of the other participating agent, is created and communicated to the other agent. If any transaction is acceptable as it is (i.e., without any relaxations on the conditional constraints, or deadlock constraints), then it is installed by the buying agent. Installation of a transaction by an agent is communicated immediately to other agents so that it can be removed from further consideration.

Once all the transactions are exhausted, the focus moves to the creation of cascades by using the composition operator to construct conditionally constrained transactions. If the resulting cascades are acceptable on conditional requirement constraints, they are installed and communicated. Competing cascades generated by a single agent are differentiated among using preference constraints. If different agents have competing cascades, preference is given to the agent which generated its cascade first. Figure 8.2 flow charts the decision process.

Experiment 1 evaluated the performance of CDN I over 90 randomly generated situations. The performance of CDN I was poor:

- All the bids with acceptable transactions on fixed requirements were not installed. In the most complex transactions (size-high complexity-medium and size-medium complexity-high), the system failed to install transactions though they were identified during relaxation of fixed requirements This is because many acceptable transactions compete with each other at both transaction and cascade levels. Choice of one of the competing cascade results in the removal of competing transactions and cascades. If the corresponding buy or sell bid has no other transactions, the bid remains unresolved. See Figure 8.3.

- The CPU time increased rapidly as the cases became more complex. To focus on the causes, we plotted the CPU time/bid as the number of bids were also increasing rapidly (which increases the complexity of the problem exponentially). Both the number of bids and the CPU time/transaction increases nonlinearly with the increase in the size. A careful examination revealed that most of the increase in CPU time

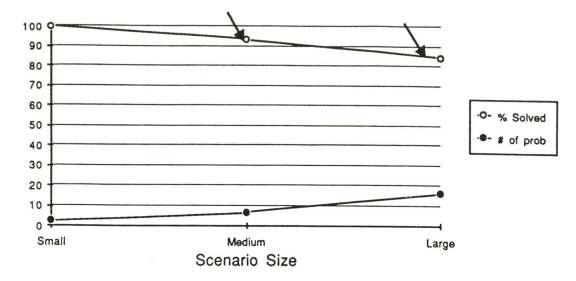

Figure 8.3: CDN I performance—missing transactions

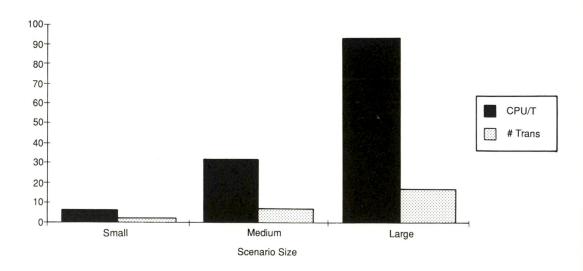

Figure 8.4: CDN I performance—CPU Time by Size

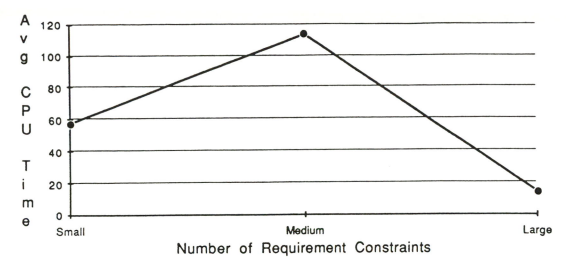

Figure 8.5: CDN I performance—CPU Time by Number of Constraints

comes from the need for maintaining consistency among local knowledge-bases (one for each agent). In the version of algorithm used for this experiment, no thought was given on whether a piece of information should be kept in a local or shared memory. Thus, there are trade-offs to be considered. Keeping information in common memory would slow down access and require task synchronization. Keeping information in local memory increases number of messages in order to maintain consistency of data. See Figure 8.4.

• The CPU time per transaction increased with the number of constraints from low to medium but then it decreased from medium to high. This was an interesting behavior. Initially the CPU time increases as the effort increases, but then after a point adding more constraints builds tighter and fewer matches, thereby reducing the total time for comparisons. See Figure 8.5.

8.5.2 CDN II

The problem of not be able to satisfy all bids in the CDN I algorithm was due largely to the combination of each agent's myopic view in constructing compositions and being too opportunistic in its selection of transactions to install. Since each agent knew only

181

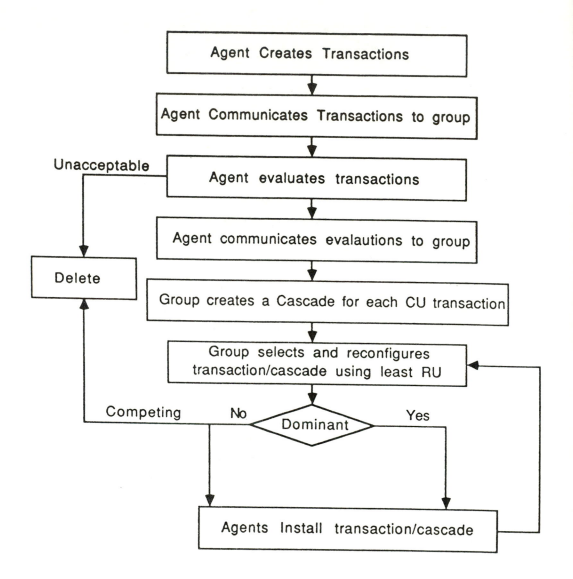

Figure 8.6: CDN II algorithm

182

of their own buy bids, they installed immediately transactions that were of only local value. If an agent had delayed in installing transactions and waited to find out about the transactions constructed by other agents, then it could have (1) constructed cascades that satisfied the conditional constraints and (2) chosen alternative transactions to maximize the remaining bids. Accordingly, we refined the algorithm into CDN II that delays the selection of transactions until after cascades have been formed.

To obtain a more global view, each agent must communicate all potential transactions, position evaluations, and cascades. An agent's constraints are not communicated. Rather than have each agent construct its own transactions and cascades, CDN II algorithm uses a central mediator to perform this task. The purpose of the mediator is to compose cascades that maximize the number of bids satisfied. All transaction and cascade evaluations are done individually by each agent, while composition, reconfiguration, and relaxation are performed by the mediator.

In CDN II, the reconfiguration and relaxation operators are introduced. The evaluation of reconfigurable requirements results in either acceptable or unacceptable utility. If a transaction is unacceptable on reconfigurable requirements, then it can still be selected, though incurring a cost of reconfiguration. This selection minimizes the number of reconfigurations[4].

The CDN II reallocation process is described as follows (also see Figure 8.6):

1. For each buy and sell bid pair, the group create a transaction in common memory.

2. Each agent evaluates the transactions associated with his buy bids on requirement constraints.

3. Each agent deletes all the transactions which are unacceptable on fixed requirement constraints. All the remaining transactions are acceptable to the respective buyers.

4. The group uses transaction composition to create an acceptable cascade for each acceptable transaction. If the transaction carries no conditional bids, it is acceptable, otherwise the transactions are grouped with other transactions using the conditional constraint evaluations located in individual agents' memory and position evaluations stored in the group memory.

5. If there exists an acceptable cascade that does not require reconfigurations and does not compete with any other cascade (i.e., does not have any buy or sell bids in common with any other cascade), then the group selects it and installs the changes

---

[4]Note that a count of reconfigurable requirement violations is still an ordinal operation on the utilities.

proposed by the buy and sell bids. If there are no transactions or cascades, then the algorithm stops.

6. If there exist a set of acceptable cascades that do not require reconfigurations and compete with each other on buy or sell bids, the group chooses a cascade with the maximum number of bids (using relaxation operator to break ties). Each affected agent installs the chosen cascade and deletes all the competing cascades. Steps 5 and 6 are repeated for each acceptable cascade.

7. If there exists a set of acceptable cascades that require reconfigurations, then the group selects one with the least number of reconfigurations (using relaxation to break ties) and applies the reconfiguration operator to derive the acceptable cascade. Each agent installs the chosen cascade and deletes all the competing cascades. Steps 5 to 7 are repeated for each cascade requiring reconfiguration.

The above algorithm essentially carries each transaction through a number of levels shown in Table 8.3. No commitment is made unless all the transactions pass through levels 1, 2, 3, and 5.[5] Level 1 carries all the new buy and sell bids. At this level, buy and sell bids are paired to form transactions. Each such transaction is moved to level 2 where it is evaluated around requirement constraints. All the unacceptable transactions are dropped to level -1 where they get deleted; the rest are moved to the cascade evaluation level (level 2) where they are evaluated around the conditional constraints and moved to level 3. At level 3, all the evaluations from individual agents are combined to build group evaluations. On the basis of the group evaluation, each transaction is moved to any of the above four levels. All the transactions that are already dominant (i.e., they do not compete with other transactions on any bid and are acceptable on all the fixed and conditional constraints) are moved to level 4, where they are selected for installation. All the transactions that require composition as they currently violate conditional constraints are moved to level 5, where transaction composition is applied to generate new cascades that no longer violate conditional constraints. The acceptable transactions are moved to level 6 where relaxation is applied to select among competing transactions. Level 7 gets all the transactions that currently violate reconfigurable requirement constraints and unlinks the transactions to create new definitions for workstations and sell bids. Levels are executed in the order, smallest first. Thus, if there are any dominant transactions, then they are executed before those waiting to be bridged.

The selection criterion for level 5 is acceptability on reconfigurable requirement constraints. Level 6 selects transaction or cascade with the largest number of bids first and

---

[5]The only exceptions are the unique dominant bids, i.e., those without deadlock constraints.

Table 8.3: Search Levels in CDN II	
Level 7:	Transactions requiring Unlinking
Level 6:	Transactions requiring Relaxation
Level 5:	Transactions requiring Composition
Level 4:	Dominant Transactions
Level 3:	Group Evaluation Level
Level 2:	Conditional Evaluation Level
Level 1:	Transaction Evaluation Level
Level 0:	New Bids
Level -1:	Unacceptable Transactions

breaks ties using preferences. Level 7 selects the transaction or cascade with the largest number of bids first and breaks ties using the number of reconfiguration changes.

The algorithm produced good results and was placed in competition with the expert (experiment 2) using the Latin Square design described earlier. The results are summarized in Table 8.4. The expert outperformed CDN II for both very small and very large problems, whereas differences were only marginal for the rest of the problems. The results are somewhat contrary to expectation, especially in the large cases. The computer program considers many more alternatives than the expert does, but still loses on the quality of results. How did the expert outperform the computer program, specially in large cases? Verbal traces of the expert's problem solving process show the following patterns of search:

- Emphasis on conditionals: In each experiment, the expert started the problem solving by grouping all the bids into three categories—single buys, single sells, and conditionals. The expert worked on the conditionals first and used the conditionals themselves for forming the chain as far as possible. The computer program did resolve the conditionals first but did not give any extra weight to forming chains within the conditionals only. As a result, the first cascade from the expert is typically bigger than the first cascade from the computer program. The average chain length is 2.3 for the first chain made by the expert while that of the computer program is a mere 1.1.

- Emphasis on rare bids: The expert used opportunistic selection when encountering a less populous workstation type or a requirement with too many attributes. No such intelligence was built into the selection mechanism of the computer program.

8.5.3 CDN III

There were two major differences between CDN II and the expert. The expert gave higher emphasis to the conditional bids in the early stages of search, thereby generating cascades

185

with bigger chains. She also used her knowledge of the less populous workstations to select rarer buy bids opportunistically. This extra knowledge was enough to offset the extra effort in identifying larger number of cascades by the computer program. Our first reaction was to explore the possibility of searching for bigger chains during composition.

Unfortunately, search for bigger chains during composition was not feasible under the current algorithm. CDN II resolves all composition alternatives before moving to commitments. Any extra search during composition produces exponential growth in the CPU time. When we tried to apply a refined version of CDN II that searched for bigger chains, the system showed limits to CPU time (for experiment cell 3-2, the algorithm ran overnight just generating cascade chains).

One solution is to use domain-specific information for selecting transactions for composition. The search can easily be modified using the findings of the verbal protocols by specifying domain-specific heuristics (e.g., "Search for a Sun workstation"), but the intelligence incorporated will not work if the environment changes. It is important to study the root cause for the difference in performance and build measures that use the structure of problem space rather than the surface-level domain-specific heuristics. This section analyzes the structure of the problem space and builds a modified algorithm that takes advantage of the structure in selecting candidates during relaxation.

In an earlier section, we discussed a number of attributes related to constraints. The first is constraint importance. Fixed requirements are considered more important than the conditional constraints. We also discussed the relaxation utility. Given that the utility for preference is higher than the threshold even if the preference is not met, the relaxation operator associated with the preferences is applied last. None of these attributes captured the structure of the problem space. Often in job shop scheduling, a bottleneck resource is given preference in the early stages of the search. Presumably, the problem space is smaller around the bottleneck (less in the number of alternatives) and hence can be opportunistically attacked first. The question is how to map the problem space and identify areas that are "narrower" than others?

The above insight can be formalized into the concept of **looseness**. The looseness of a constraint measures the number of relaxations (alternatives) per constraint. Thus, for requirement constraints, looseness is the number of transactions that can meet a requirement. Since, each transaction has only one buy bid, looseness for the transaction is the same as looseness for its buy bid. An inverse function can be used to measure how many constraints are affected by a relaxation.

Looseness can be used for prioritizing the relaxation process. Thus, looseness for requirement constraint can be used for prioritizing composition candidates. Similarly, loose-

186

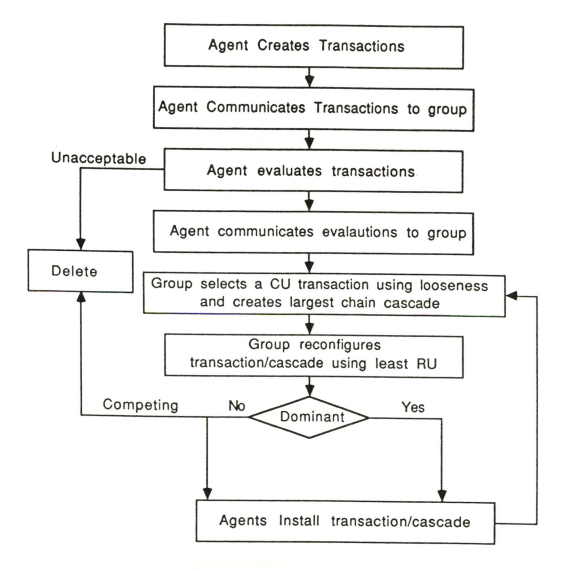

Figure 8.7: CDN III algorithm

ness in conditional constraints can be used for prioritizing reconfiguration, and so on. As discussed above, if we look for larger chains during composition, we need to have good starting points. Such a starting point would have a low value for looseness on requirement constraints. While the CDN II algorithm tried to generate a better solution through more exhaustive search, the CDN III algorithm uses a more intelligent selection during composition.

The modified algorithm refers to the solution levels in Table 8.3 and is as follows (also see Figure 8.7):

1. For each buy and sell bid pair, create a transaction and move the transaction to level 1.

2. Evaluate the transaction on fixed (nonrelaxable) requirement constraints.

3. Move all the transactions which are unacceptable on fixed requirement constraints to level -1, move the rest to level 2.

4. Evaluate transactions on conditional constraints in level 2 and move to level 3.

5. At level 3, group transaction evaluations from agents and move the transaction to one of level 4, 5, 6, or 7.

6. At level 4, if there exists an acceptable cascade that does not require reconfigurations and does not compete with any other cascade (i.e., does not have any buy or sell bids in common with any other cascade), select it and install the changes proposed by the buy and sell bids. If there are no acceptable cascades, stop.

7. At level 5, use looseness values to sort the transactions requiring composition. Start with the smallest value of looseness and find a cascade that is acceptable on conditional constraints. If there is more than one choice, select the one with the largest chain. Move to level 6,7, or 4 depending on whether competing cascades are found and evaluation on reconfigurable requirement constraints.

8. At level 6, if there exist a set of acceptable cascades that does not require reconfigurations and compete with each other on buy or sell bids, then choose a cascade with the maximum number of bids (use relaxation operator to break ties). Install the chosen cascade and delete all the competing cascades.

9. At level 7, if there exists a set of acceptable cascades which require reconfigurations, select one with the least number of reconfigurations (use relaxation operator to break

Table 8.4: Experiment 2, 3 Results

Conditions	Latin Square Cell								
	1-1	1-2	1-3	2-1	2-2	2-3	3-1	3-2	3-3
Size	Low	Low	Low	Med	Med	Med	High	High	High
Complexity	Low	Med	High	Low	Med	High	Low	Med	High
No. of constraints	Low	Med	High	Med	High	Low	High	Low	Med
Scores									
Expert	2	2	1	2	1	1	1	3	0
CDNIII	2	2	3	2	3	3	3	1	4
Constraint Violation: unresolved buy									
Expert	0	1	2	0	3	0	2	0	0
CDNII	0	1	2	0	3	0	0	3	6
CDNIII	0	1	2	0	3	0	1	0	0
Constraint Violation: unresolved sell									
Expert	0	0	0	0	0	6	2	9	16
CDNII	0	0	0	0	0	6	0	12	22
CDNIII	0	0	0	0	0	6	1	9	16
Constraint Violation: reconfigurations									
Expert	0	0	0	0	1	2	8	6	8
CDNII	0	1	1	0	0	2	0	4	7
CDNIII	0	0	0	0	0	1	7	9	3
Constraint Violation: broken conditionals									
Expert	0	0	1	0	0	0	0	1	4
CDNII	0	0	0	0	0	1	0	2	4
CDNIII	0	0	0	0	0	0	0	2	0
Total Constraint Violations									
Expert	0	1	3	0	4	8	12	16	28
CDNII	0	2	3	0	3	9	0	21	39
CDNIII	0	1	2	0	3	7	9	20	19

Variation in Number of Constraint Violations				
Conditions	System	Variation		
		Low	Med	High
Size	Expert	4	12	56
	CDNII	5	12	60
	CDNIII	3	10	48
Complexity	Expert	12	21	39
	CDNII	0	26	51
	CDNIII	9	24	28
Constraints	Expert	24	29	19
	CDNII	30	41	6
	CDNIII	27	20	14

ties) and apply unlink algorithm (see [Sathi 88]) to derive the acceptable cascade. Install the chosen cascade and delete all the competing cascades.

The steps are repeated based on which levels are nonempty. Levels are prioritized—if a lower level has any accumulated bids or transactions, then it gets executed first. The only exception is after a cascade is found at level 5.

The quality of results generated by CDN III exceeds those of CDN II and the expert (see Table 8.4). The expert violated 72 constraints, CDN II violated 77 constraints and CDN III violated 61 constraints. CDN III consistently performed better than the expert except for one case involving medium complexity and small number of constraints where the expert performed marginally better.

There are many deficiencies yet to be resolved that offer a potential for future research:

1. We discovered some interactions between constraint importance and looseness in our experiments. Search strategies need to take such interactions into account while deciding upon how to select states and operators. This is an area which requires further experiments to understand how these two constraint attributes interact with each other. For example, CDN II excels in experiment cell 3-1. This cell had the most uniform looseness and the highest number of constraints per bid.

2. We did not deal with situations which required a mix of qualitative and quantitative reasoning. In a number of situations, qualitative reasoning is used to identify one or two good alternatives and then quantitative reasoning is used to fine tune or select one of the alternatives. For example, in the workstation negotiations, quantitative reasoning can be used in the final stage of the negotiation to bargain the sharing of reconfiguration costs for selecting among the competing alternatives. Due to this deficiency, CDN algorithms cannot be used in situations involving bargaining.

3. We did not study the impact of knowledge sharing on the evaluation of constraint relaxation processes. In a distributed situation, not only the constraint evaluations but also alternatives or new ways of relaxation may be shared across the negotiators. This would form an interesting extension towards a truly distributed negotiation solution.

4. Real systems are often created in decision support mode. CDN can be extended into a decision support system where the problem solver can be used for most of the time consuming pattern matching and search processes and the human decision-maker can create new forms of relaxation or decide which constraints to logroll. CDN has a lot

more potential as a decision-support than as an automated problem solver. How the mixed mode problem solving will actually work is the subject for another research.

8.6 Conclusions

Our goal is to explore the concept of constraint-directed negotiation as a means to achieve plan synchronization and resource allocation. Our approach has been to solve a narrow version of this problem on real data in order to understand the complexity of the decision process and the associated search processes. A number of important insights have come out this research:

- In order to maximize the number of satisfied resource buys and sells, it is necessary to generate solutions via composition to satisfy conditional constraints, decomposition of configurations to satisfy reconfiguration constraints and relaxation of requirements to satisfy portions of constraints.

- Maximization can occur only when multiple agents cooperatively negotiate, thereby creating complex cascades of transactions.

- The choice of cascades can be viewed as an opportunistic process in which looseness is the metric of choice.

- The participation of more than two agents in the cascading process is best achieved in a mediated, group problem-solving mode.

The last point is somewhat surprising. In situations involving conditionality between the decisions of three or more agents, mediated solutions appear to be better than totally distributed negotiations, where agents conduct their own negotiations.

References

[Axelrod 1984] Robert Axelrod, *The Evolution of Cooperation*, Basic Books, 1984.

[Arrow 1951] K. J. Arrow, *Social Choice and Individual Values*, Wiley, New York, 1951.

[Baiman 1982] S. Baiman, "Agency Research in Managerial Accounting: A Survey," *Journal of Accounting Literature*, Vol. 1, 1982, pp. 154–213.

[Baykan and Fox 1987] C. Baykan and M. Fox Opportunistic Constraint Directed Search in Space Planning *Proceedings of the International Joint Conference on Artificial Intelligence*, Milano, Italy, 1987.

[Cammarata *et al.* 1983] S. Cammarata, D. McArthur, and R. Steeb, "Strategies of Cooperation in Distributed Problem Solving," Tech Report N-2031-ARPA, The Rand Corporation, 1983.

[Durfee *et al.* 1985] E. H. Durfee, V. R. Lesser, and D. D. Corkill, "Coherent Cooperation Among Communicating Problem Solvers," Technical Report, Department of Computer and Information Science, University of Massachusetts, Amherst, Massachusetts, September 1985.

[Fox 1983] M. Fox, *Constraint-Directed Search: A Case Study of Job-Shop Scheduling*, Ph.D. Thesis, Department of Computer Science, Carnegie-Mellon University, 1983.

[Fox 1986] M. Fox, "Observations on the Role of Constraints in Problem Solving," *Proceedings of the Canadian Society for Computational Intelligence*, 1986.

[Genesereth *et al.* 1986] M. Genesereth, M. Ginsberg, and J. Rosenschein, "Cooperation Without Communication," *Proceedings of the Fifth National Conference on Artificial Intelligence*, 1986, pp. 51–57.

[Johnson and Payne 1985] E. J. Johnson and J. W. Payne, "Effort and Accuracy in Choice," *Management Science*, Vol. 31, No. 4, April 1985, pp. 395–414.

[Lesser and Corkill 1983] V. R. Lesser and D. D. Corkill, "The Distributed Vehicle Monitoring Testbed: A tool for investigating distributed problem solving networks," *The AI Magazine*, Vol. 4, No. 3, Fall 1983, pp. 15–33.

[Marschak and Radner 1972] J. Marschak and R. Radner, "Economic Theory of Games," *Cowles Foundation Monograph 22*, Yale University Press, 1972.

[Parunak 1987] H. Van Dyke Parunak, "Manufacturing Experience with the Contract Net," in M. N. Huhns, ed., *Distributed Artificial Intelligence*, Chapter 10, Pitman Publishing and Morgan Kaufmann Publishers, 1987, pp. 285–310.

[Payne 1976] J. W. Payne, "Task Complexity and Contingent Processing in Decision Making: An Information Search and Protocol Analysis," *Organization Behavior and Human Performance*, Vol. 16, 1976, pp. 366–386.

[Pruitt 1981] D. G. Pruitt, *Negotiation Behavior*, Academic Press, New York, 1981.

[Sadeh *et al.* 1988] N. Sadeh, K. Sycara, M. Fox, J. Hynynen, and A. Wittmann, "Trends in Coarse-Grained Distributed AI," Working Paper, Intelligent Systems Laboratory, The Robotics Institute, Carnegie Mellon University, Pittsburgh, PA, 1988.

[Sathi 1986] A. Sathi, T. E. Morton, and S. F. Roth, "Callisto: An Intelligent Project Management System," *The AI Magazine*, Vol. 7, No. 5, Winter 1986, pp. 34–52.

[Sathi 1988] A. Sathi, *Cooperation Through Constraint Directed Negotiation: Study of Resource Reallocation Problems*, Ph.D. Thesis, Graduate School of Industrial Administration, Carnegie-Mellon University, 1988.

[Shaw and Whinston 1983] Jeng-Ping Shaw and A. B. Whinston, "Distributed Planning in Cellular Flexible Manufacturing Systems," Technical Report, Management Information Research Center, Krannert Graduate School of Management, Purdue University, West Lafayette, Indiana, 1983.

[Smith 1980] R. G. Smith, "The Contract Net Protocol: High-Level Communication and Control in a Distributed Problem Solver," *IEEE Transactions on Computers*, 1980.

[Smith 1983] S. P. Smith, "Exploiting Temporal Knowledge to Organize Constraints," CMU-RI-TR-83-12, Intelligent Systems Laboratory, The Robotics Institute, Carnegie Mellon University, 1983.

[Steeb *et al.* 1981] R. Steeb, S. Cammarata, F. Hayes-Roth, P. Thorndyke, and P. Wesson, "Distributed Intelligence for Air Fleet Control," Tech Report R-2728-ARPA, The Rand Corporation, 1981.

[Svenson 1979] O. Svenson, "Process Descriptions of Decision Making," *Organization Behavior and Human Performance*, Vol. 23, pp. 86–112, 1979.

[Sycara 1987] E. P. Sycara, *Resolving Adversarial Conflicts: An Approach Integrating Case-Based and Analytical Methods*, Ph.D. Thesis, School of Information and Computer Science, Georgia Institute of Technology, 1987.

[Tversky 1969] A. Tversky, "Intransitivity of Preferences," *Psychological Review*, Vol. 76, 1969, pp. 31–48.

Arvind Sathi and Mark S. Fox
Center For Integrated Manufacturing Decision Systems
The Robotics Institute
Carnegie Mellon University
Pittsburgh, PA 15213

Part III

Cooperation by Planning

Chapter 9

Plans for Multiple Agents

Matthew J. Katz and Jeffrey S. Rosenschein

Abstract

Research in distributed artificial intelligence has historically focused on two distinct classes of problems. One paradigm, "planning for multiple agents," considers issues inherent in centrally directed multiagent execution (Smith's Contract Net [Smith 1978], [Smith 1980] falls into this category, as does other DAI work such as [Rosenschein 1982],[Pednault 1987]). In the second paradigm, "distributed planning," multiple agents participate more autonomously in deciding upon and coordinating their own actions [Corkill 1982], [Rosenschein and Genesereth 1985], [Durfee *et al.* 1987].

The work described in this paper is in the first category, planning for multiple agents. Taking the STRIPS representation of actions [Fikes and Nilsson 1971], and directed acyclic graphs (DAGs) as plan representations particularly well-suited to parallel execution, we formally analyze the following three issues: 1) How can a DAG plan be verified (i.e., how can we be sure such a plan will be correct, given our uncertainty about exactly when actions will be performed)? 2) How can DAG plans be generated? 3) What is an efficient algorithm to be used by a supervisor directing the execution of a DAG plan by multiple agents?

9.1 Introduction

9.1.1 Previous Work

Research on planning for multiple agents has gone in various directions. One of these proceeds from the idea that each of several agents has a task of his own that he performs by carrying out an appropriate sequential plan. This research then attempts to synthesize multiagent plans from simpler single agent plans [Georgeff 1983], [Georgeff 1984], [Stuart 1985], focusing primarily on problems of synchronization through conflict avoidance and, sometimes, of cooperation among agents. Another approach has the central objective of saving time and engendering cooperation by means of 'parallel' plans such as those that may be represented by DAGs [Smith 1978], [Corkill 1979], [Pednault 1987].

Parallel plans—or nonlinear plans—appear in research on single agents as well, in an effort to overcome the difficulties inherent in trying to achieve several goals simultaneously and to reduce the computational complexity of the planning process [Sacerdoti 1975], [Allen and Koomen 1983]. However, it is assumed that what is ultimately executed is a sequence of operations.

With respect to the representation of action, it is commonly argued that classical frameworks (e.g., STRIPS) are not adequate for reasoning about multiagent domains [Lansky 1987], [Georgeff 1986]. Some research, however, remains within the classical framework [Pednault 1987], as does the present paper.

9.1.2   Assumptions

Every plan is a binary acyclic relation over a set of operations, that is, a binary relation whose transitive closure is a partial order. Equivalently, a plan is a directed acyclic graph (DAG). Of course, not every binary acyclic relation is a valid plan since, for example, not every sequence of operations is legal. Therefore, we will call a binary acyclic relation a *plan-like relation*.

Our domain of actions is represented by employing the STRIPS method (i.e., each operation is represented by a precondition set, a delete set, and an add set). There are two or more agents such that any one of them can execute any of the operations in the domain. Any change that is observed is an effect of the agents' actions; that is, the domain is static.

Our basic premise is that the agents will execute operations only when told to do so by a *supervisor*, who directs the execution of the plan. Agents always obey the supervisor's commands and do not fail unless another agent who is executing another operation interferes (or, of course, if they have been incorrectly directed to carry out a task, i.e., the necessary preconditions are not present when a task is attempted). An especially significant assumption in this work is the 'Uncertainty Assumption,' which states that we cannot know in advance the duration of any operation's execution. However, we do assume that all operations are inherently finite, i.e., if they were to be carried out in isolation with their preconditions satisfied, they would eventually terminate.

9.1.3 Overview

Section 9.2 presents the underlying domain and its representation in more detail, and defines when a plan-like relation is considered a valid plan for given initial and goal states. In particular, it defines when an empty relation is considered a plan, that is, when it is possible to execute a set of operations in parallel.

Informally, a plan-like relation is a valid plan if it is guaranteed to work. Of course, this definition does not offer a practical method for determining whether a plan-like relation is a valid plan, and in particular it does not offer a method for determining whether it is possible to execute a set of operations in parallel. In Section 9.2 we provide a necessary condition for it to be possible to execute a set of operations in parallel. Subsequently, however, we assume that it can be independently determined (by the supervisor) whether a set of operations can be executed in parallel from a given state. This may, in general, rely on information specific to the domain.

A special type of plan-like relation that will be called a *levels relation* plays an important role, and will be introduced in Section 9.3. Informally, a levels relation is a sequence of sets of operations such that the execution of an operation at any level may not begin before all of the operations at the previous level have been executed.

Section 9.3 offers a method for verifying that a given plan-like relation is a valid plan. This method does not recognize all plans, but the plans not recognized are 'awkward,' and an example is given. We call the class of plans recognized by this method *strict plans*. While the verification method remains exponential, it still turns out to be considerably better than other alternatives.

In Section 9.4, we present a method for generating all the best strict plans over a given set of operations (in our case, the set of operations of a sequential plan for the given initial and goal states).

Section 9.5 treats the plan execution phase, focusing on the execution of plans that are levels relations. More precisely, it provides an algorithm that allows the supervisor, under certain conditions, to send a command before it is enabled.

9.2 The Underlying Domain, Its Representation, and Execution in Parallel

9.2.1 The Underlying Domain and Representation

Our environment will be represented in the following way:

1. A (suitable) collection of relation names is chosen; every chosen n-ary relation name has a set of n-tuples attached to it. For example, in the blocks world, 'on' is a chosen binary relation name and the set attached to it is the set of pairs of blocks.

2. A possible state, S, is represented by the following set:

$$\left\{ t(a) \;\middle|\; \begin{array}{l} t \text{ is a chosen relation name,} \\ a \text{ is an element in the set attached to } t, \text{ and} \\ \text{the truth value of } t(a) \text{ in } S \text{ is 'true'} \end{array} \right\}$$

3. Every operation is represented by three sets as in STRIPS: a precondition set, a delete set, and an add set. The elements in each set are of the form $t(a)$, where t is a chosen relation name and a is an element in the set attached to it. It is possible to execute an operation from a state, S, if and only if its precondition set is contained in S. The state of the world at the moment when an operation execution ends, S_e, is determined in the standard STRIPS fashion, by deleting the delete set from S_b and adding the add set to S_b. We require that *for every operation, its add and delete sets are disjoint*, so the order in which propositions are deleted and added is irrelevant.

Sequential Plans

- A set, T, of elements of the form $t(a)$, where t is a chosen relation name and a is an element in the set attached to t, is a *partial state* if there is a state, S, such that $T \subseteq S$.

- If it is possible to execute an operation, o, from a state, S, then *the result of executing o from S, $r(o, S)$*, is the state $(S - DEL) \cup ADD$, where DEL and ADD are o's delete and add sets respectively.

- An operation sequence, $o_1 \ldots o_n$, $n \geq 1$, is *possible from a state, S*, if it is possible to execute o_1 from S, it is possible to execute o_2 from $r(o_1, S)$, it is possible to execute o_3 from $r(o_2, r(o_1, S))$, ...

- If $o_1 \ldots o_n$ is possible from S, then *the result of $o_1 \ldots o_n$ from S, $r(o_1 \ldots o_n, S)$*, is $r(o_n, \ldots, r(o_1, s) \ldots)$.

- An operation sequence, $o_1 \ldots o_n$, $n \geq 1$, is a *sequential plan for* (T_I, T_G), where T_I and T_G are partial states, if for every state, S, such that $T_I \subseteq S$,

   1. $o_1 \ldots o_n$ is possible from S, and

   2. $T_G \subseteq r(o_1 \ldots o_n, S)$

The supervisor, after sending an agent an instruction, must wait until he receives a 'finished' message from that agent before he may send him another instruction.

Uncertainty Assumption   We cannot make any assumptions concerning the time interval that begins with the receipt of an instruction by an agent and that ends with the release of the appropriate 'finished' message, except that the interval is finite. For example, it is possible that the agent will delay the actual beginning of the execution, will pause somewhere during the execution, will delay the release of the 'finished' message, will slow down or speed up the execution in various segments. In short, we are in the dark until the agent reports 'finished.'

9.2.2   Execution in Parallel

Now suppose that there are two or more agents available. We wish to exploit this fact in order to achieve our goals faster.

Definition 1 Let $o_1, \ldots, o_k$, $k \geq 1$, be operations and let S be a state. Let O be the set of *symbols* whose elements are $o_1, \ldots, o_k$.

- We say that *it is possible to execute $o_1, \ldots, o_k$ in parallel from S (O is possible from S)* if whenever the supervisor gives instructions from S to k agents to execute these operations, every agent proceeds without interference and does the work indicated by the operation, and the states attained in this way are identical.

- If it is possible to execute $o_1, \ldots, o_k$ in parallel from S (O is possible from S), then *the result of executing $o_1, \ldots, o_k$ in parallel from S, $r(o_1, \ldots, o_k, S)$, (the result of O from S, $r(O, S)$)* is this common state.

We take O to be the set of symbols and not the set of operations, because it is possible that two different symbols stand for the same operation.

From the Uncertainty Assumption we get the following result:

Result   If it is possible to execute $o_1, \ldots, o_k$ in parallel from S, then every permutation of $\{o_1, \ldots, o_k\}$ is a sequential plan for $(S, r(o_1, \ldots, o_k, S))$.

Actually, this result is not dependent on the Uncertainty Assumption, because, before sending the next instruction, the supervisor can await the 'finished' message from the agent who received the previous instruction. The following theorem provides a necessary condition for it to be possible to execute $o_1, \ldots, o_k$ in parallel from S. It follows from the result above.

Theorem 1 If it is possible to execute $o_1, \ldots, o_k$ in parallel from S, then

a. $PRE_i \subseteq S, 1 \leq i \leq k$.

b. $DEL_i \cap PRE_j = \emptyset, 1 \leq i, j \leq k, i \neq j$.

c. $DEL_i \cap ADD_j = \emptyset, 1 \leq i, j \leq k, i \neq j$.

Proof: For this proof and subsequent ones, see [Katz 1988].

Result If it is possible to execute $o_1, \ldots, o_k$ in parallel from S, then $r(o_1, \ldots, o_k, S) = (S - (\cup_{i=1}^{k} DEL_i)) \cup (\cup_{i=1}^{k} ADD_i)$.

Inertia Assumption In any execution of $o_1, \ldots, o_k$ in parallel from S, at the moment an execution of an operation ends and at any following moment, the elements of the add set are present and the elements of the delete set are absent.

The only way in which the Inertia Assumption would not be valid is if it were possible to simultaneously add and delete some proposition over the domain.

Definition 2 Let $o_1, \ldots, o_k$, $k \geq 1$, be operations and let O be the set of symbols whose elements are $o_1, \ldots, o_k$. We say that *it is possible to execute $o_1, \ldots, o_k$ in parallel (O is possible)* if there is a state such that for each i, PRE_i is contained in it, and for each such state, S, it is possible to execute $o_1, \ldots, o_k$ in parallel from S (O is possible from S).

9.2.3 Plan-Like Relations

A plan-like relation is an acyclic binary relation over the set of symbols whose elements are $o_1, \ldots, o_n$, $n \geq 1$, where every symbol stands for some operation (we treat the pair (o_i, o_i), $1 \leq i \leq n$, as a cycle). In other words, a plan-like relation is a binary relation over $\{o_1, \ldots, o_n\}$, $n \geq 1$, such that its transitive closure is a partial order (i.e., a directed acyclic graph [DAG] whose set of vertices is $\{o_1, \ldots, o_n\}$).

Of course, not every plan-like relation is a plan for some pair of states. Below, we will define when a plan-like relation is considered a plan for given initial and goal states. Informally, a plan-like relation is considered a plan if it is guaranteed to work.

When a plan, D, is passed to the supervisor, he sends the agents the appropriate instructions according to the following rule:

Sending Rule The supervisor may send the instruction o_j, $1 \leq j \leq n$, to an agent, x, if

a. For each o_i, $1 \leq i \leq n$, such that $(o_i, o_j) \in D$, the supervisor already sent the instruction o_i and received the appropriate 'finished' message.

b. x is free, that is, the supervisor didn't send x an instruction since he last received a 'finished' message from x.

Definition 3 Let D be a plan-like relation and let S be a state.

- An *itinerary of D* is a time-stamped description of a potential execution of the operations $o_1, \ldots, o_n$ moment-by-moment, beginning at the moment of the onset of activity (time 0) and ending at the moment after which there is no further activity, all this subject to D (that is, for each o_i, o_j, if $(o_i, o_j) \in D$, then the execution of o_j begins after the execution of o_i ends). In other words, an itinerary of D consists of the juxtaposition of possible descriptions of the executions of these operations, where every operation is executed in isolation, without regard to potential interference among actions.

Let α be an itinerary of D.

- We say that α *is possible from S* if it is realistic from S; that is, if it can be carried out from S by means of n agents without 'getting stuck' for whatever reason.

- If α is possible from S, then *the result of α from S*, $r(\alpha, S)$, is the state attained when it is carried out from S.

- We say that D *is possible from S* if every itinerary of D is possible from S, and for each two itineraries, α, β, of D, $r(\alpha, S) = r(\beta, S)$.

- If D is possible from S, then *the result of D from S*, $r(D, S)$, is $r(\alpha, S)$, where α is any itinerary of D.

- We say that D *is a plan for (T_I, T_G)*, where T_I and T_G are partial states, if for every state, S, such that $T_I \subseteq S$, D is possible from S and $T_G \subseteq r(D, S)$.

It is clear that if we pass to the supervisor a plan-like relation, D, that is possible from the current state, S_c, and the supervisor obeys the sending rule, then the state attained is $r(D, S_c)$, and in the light of the Uncertainty Assumption, any one of the itineraries of D may be the description of what took place. In particular, the empty relation over $\{o_1, \ldots, o_n\}$, $n \geq 1$, is possible from some state, S, if and only if it is possible to execute $o_1, \ldots, o_n$ in parallel from S ($\{o_1, \ldots, o_n\}$ is possible from S).

From now on, we will assume that we have a (possibly domain-specific) method for determining whether it is possible to execute $o_1, \ldots, o_k$ in parallel from S, where $o_1, \ldots, o_k$ are operations and S is a state. We are interested in a method to determine whether a plan-like relation is possible from a given state. The definitions don't offer such a method; a plan-like relation has an infinite number of itineraries. In the next section we present such a method.

9.3 Plan Verification

In this section we develop a practical method for determining whether a plan-like relation is a plan for given initial and goal states. We introduce the term *levels relation*, fit to each plan-like relation a *set* of levels relations, and present the Verification Theorem, which states that a plan-like relation is a plan if its set of levels relations fulfills a particular condition. We then offer a shortcut to the method inherent in the Verification Theorem for determining whether a plan-like relation is a plan.

9.3.1 Levels Relations

Definition 4 A *levels relation* is a relation, L, over the set of symbols whose elements are $o_1, \ldots, o_n$, $n \geq 1$ (where every symbol stands for some operation) that has the following property:

It is possible to divide $\{o_1, \ldots, o_n\}$ into h, $h \geq 1$, sets, $O_1, \ldots, O_h$, such that

a. For each h', $1 \leq h' \leq h - 1$, for each $o_i \in O_{h'}$ and $o_j \in O_{h'+1}$, $(o_i, o_j) \in L$.

b. For each o_i, o_j, if $(o_i, o_j) \in L$, then there is h', $1 \leq h' \leq h - 1$, such that $o_i \in O_{h'}$ and $o_j \in O_{h'+1}$.

In other words, a levels relation is a relation over $\{o_1, \ldots, o_n\}$, $n \geq 1$, that has the form shown in Figure 9.1, where $k_h = n$ and $\{i_1, \ldots, i_n\} = \{1, \ldots, n\}$. We will represent a levels relation by the sequence whose h'th element is the h'th level, that is, by $(O_1, \ldots, O_h)$.[1]

It is clear that a levels relation, L, is a plan-like relation and therefore we may ask whether L is possible from a given state.

Definition 5 Let L be a levels relation, $L = (O_1, \ldots, O_h)$, and let S be a state. We say that L is *possible from S* if O_1 is possible from S, O_2 is possible from $r(O_1, S)$, O_3 is possible from $r(O_2, r(O_1, S))$, ...

---

[1] We will say that "level 1 is lower than level 2" though graphically it is higher.

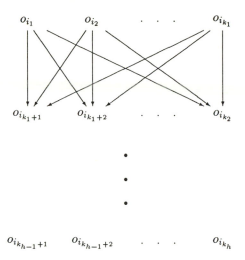

Figure 9.1: A levels relation

Notice that if L is *possible from S, then L is possible from S, because any itinerary of L is a sequence of h itineraries such that the h'th itinerary in the sequence is an itinerary of the empty relation over $O_{h'}$. The converse is not always true; there are levels relations that are possible from S, but not *possible from S.

Example Assume that A is some object, and that the agents are capable of executing the operations $spray\_blue(A)$ and $spray\_white(A)$ (possibly simultaneously). The operation $spray\_blue(A)$ is represented by the sets $PRE = \{A$ is hanging properly$\}$, $DEL = \{$white$(A)\}$, and $ADD = \{$blue$(A)\}$, and $spray\_white(A)$ is represented similarly. Moreover, assume that A is hanging properly in the current state, S. Then the levels relation

$$\bigl(\{spray\_blue(A), spray\_white(A)\}, \{spray\_blue(A)\}\bigr)$$

is possible from S, but not *possible from S. The final state (namely blue(A)) is guaranteed, regardless of A's color after the first level, so the levels relation is possible from S. However, since the state after the first level is uncertain, the levels relation is not *possible from S.

It follows that if L is *possible from S, then we may talk about the result of L from S; it is $r(O_h, \ldots, r(O_1, S) \ldots)$.

To each plan-like relation, D, we will fit a *set* of levels relations, $LEVELS_D$:

$$LEVELS_D \overset{\text{def}}{=} \left\{ L \;\middle|\; \begin{array}{l} L \text{ is a levels relation over } D\text{'s base, and} \\ \text{for each } o_i, o_j, \\ (o_i, o_j) \in D \implies o_i \text{ is in a level lower than } o_j\text{'s} \end{array} \right\}$$

205

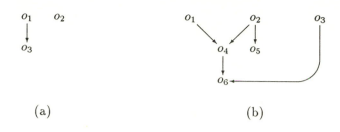

(a)   (b)

Figure 9.2: Two plan-like relations

Example If D is the plan-like relation of Figure 9.2(a), then

$$LEVELS_D = \{(\{o_1\}, \{o_2\}, \{o_3\}), (\{o_1\}, \{o_3\}, \{o_2\}), (\{o_2\}, \{o_1\}, \{o_3\}),$$
$$(\{o_1, o_2\}, \{o_3\}), (\{o_1\}, \{o_2, o_3\})\}.$$

9.3.2 The Verification Theorem

It is simple to determine whether any particular levels relation is *possible from a given state. We will employ levels relations, therefore, to make manageable the case in which a general plan-like relation is being verified.

Definition 6 Let D be a plan-like relation and let S be a state. We say that D *is strictly possible from S* if for each $L \in LEVELS_D$, L is *possible from S.

Lemma 1 If D is strictly possible from S, then for each $L_1, L_2 \in LEVELS_D$, $r(L_1, S) = r(L_2, S)$.

Theorem 2 Let D be a plan-like relation and let S be a state. If D is strictly possible from S, then D is possible from S, and $r(D, S) = r(L, S)$, where L is any element in $LEVELS_D$.

As shown in the example above (with *spray_blue* and *spray_white*), a plan-like relation may be possible from a given state without being strictly possible from that state. Intuitively, however, the awkwardness of such plans should be clear; the first level in our example is completely superfluous, and doesn't contribute to the goal state.

If we were to assume that the execution of an operation, in itself, doesn't take any time, the theorem would be trivial, since there would be an obvious mapping (many to one) from the collection of itineraries of D to $LEVELS_D$. But, in fact, it is possible that an execution of an operation will overlap both of two others that may not overlap each other, and thus there is no such clear mapping.

206

9.3.3 The Verification Method

When a plan-like relation, D, and a state, S, are given and we want to determine whether D is strictly possible from S, must we follow the method suggested by Definition 6, or are there shortcuts that we can take? The latter is the case, and in this section we will present such a shortcut.

Induced Sets

Definition 7 Let *LEVELS* be a set of levels relations over $\{o_1, \ldots, o_n\}$, $n \geq 1$.

- *The set induced by LEVELS, $I(LEVELS)$, is*

$$\bigcup_{L \in LEVELS} I(L) \ ,$$

  where $I(L)$, *the set induced by L, is* $LEVELS_L$.

- It is clear that $LEVELS \subseteq I(LEVELS)$. We say that $LEVELS$ is *complete* if $LEVELS = I(LEVELS)$.

Let L be a levels relation, $L = (O_1, \ldots, O_h)$. Notice that $I(L)$ (that is, $LEVELS_L$) is identical to

$$\left\{ L' \ \middle| \ \begin{array}{l} L' \text{ is a levels relation over } L\text{'s base, } L' = (O'_1, \ldots, O'_{h'}), \text{ and} \\ \text{there are } i_1, \ldots, i_{h-1}, 1 \leq i_1 < i_2 < \cdots < i_{h-1} \leq h' - 1, \text{ such that} \\ O'_1 \cup \cdots \cup O'_{i_1} = O_1 \text{ and } O'_{i_1+1} \cup \cdots \cup O'_{i_2} = O_2 \text{ and } \ldots \text{ and} \\ O'_{i_{h-1}+1} \cup \cdots \cup O'_{h'} = O_h \end{array} \right\}$$

Informally, $I(L)$ is the set whose elements are those levels relations that are obtained from L by 'stretching' it.

The next lemma follows immediately from the definition of $LEVELS_D$, where D is a plan-like relation.

Lemma 2 For each plan-like relation, D, $LEVELS_D$ is complete.

Lemma 3 Let L be a levels relation and let S be a state. If L is $*$possible from S, then for each $L' \in I(L)$, L' is $*$possible from S and $r(L', S) = r(L, S)$.

Theorem 3 Let D be a plan-like relation and let S be a state. Let $LEVELS$ be a set of levels relations over D's base such that $I(LEVELS) \supseteq LEVELS_D$. If for each $L \in LEVELS$, L is $*$possible from S, then D is strictly possible from S and $r(D, S) = r(L', S)$, where L' is any element in $LEVELS_D$.

Example Let D be the plan-like relation

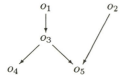

Let $LEVELS$ be the set of levels relations

$$\{(\{o_1, o_2, o_3\}, \{o_4, o_5\}), (\{o_1, o_3\}, \{o_2, o_4\}, \{o_5\})\},$$

and assume that $LEVELS$ satisfies the condition of Theorem 3. It follows from Theorem 3 that D is strictly possible from S, because $I(LEVELS) \supseteq LEVELS_D$. ($|LEVELS_D| = 17$.)

If a plan-like relation, D, and a state, S, are given and all we know is that there exists a set of levels relations over D's base, $LEVELS$, whose induced set *strictly contains* $LEVELS_D$, and it ($LEVELS$) doesn't satisfy the condition of Theorem 3, then we may not conclude automatically that D is not strictly possible from S.

But, if a plan-like relation, D, and a state, S, are given and we know that there exists a set of levels relations over D's base, $LEVELS$, whose induced set is *equal to* $LEVELS_D$, and it ($LEVELS$) doesn't satisfy the condition of Theorem 3, then we may conclude that D isn't strictly possible from S. This is so because $LEVELS \subseteq LEVELS_D$ ($LEVELS \subseteq I(LEVELS)$ and $I(LEVELS) = LEVELS_D$) and therefore, if D were strictly possible from S, then $LEVELS$ would satisfy the condition of Theorem 3.

Example (continues the previous example)
If $LEVELS$ doesn't satisfy the condition of Theorem 3, then we may not conclude automatically that D is not strictly possible from S. This is because D does not allow the executions of o_1 and o_3 to overlap each other, while the elements of $LEVELS$ do, that is, $I(LEVELS) \supset LEVELS_D$. But if we had taken $LEVELS$ to be the set

$$\{(\{o_1, o_2\}, \{o_3\}, \{o_4, o_5\}), (\{o_1\}, \{o_2, o_3\}, \{o_4, o_5\}), (\{o_1\}, \{o_3\}, \{o_2, o_4\}, \{o_5\})\},$$

then we would have had

D is strictly possible from S if and only if $LEVELS$ satisfies the condition of Theorem 3.

This is because in this case $I(LEVELS) = LEVELS_D$.

Compressed Sets

Let D be a plan-like relation. Obviously, we would like to be able to go directly to a minimal set of levels relations over D's base whose induced set is equal to $LEVELS_D$. We saw that such a set is necessarily contained in $LEVELS_D$. To each plan-like relation, D, we will fit a set that is contained in $LEVELS_D$, $C(LEVELS_D)$ (the C stands for $COMPRESSED$):

$$C(LEVELS_D) \stackrel{\text{def}}{=} \left\{ L \left| \begin{array}{l} L \in LEVELS_D,\ L = (O_1, \ldots, O_h),\ \text{and} \\ \text{there is no } h',\ 1 \leq h' \leq h-1,\ \text{such that} \\ \text{for each } o_i \in O_{h'} \text{ and } o_j \in O_{h'+1}, \\ o_i \text{ and } o_j \text{ are incomparable in } D \end{array} \right. \right\}$$

Example   If D is the plan-like relation of Figure 9.2(a), then

$$C(LEVELS_D) = \{(\{o_1, o_2\}, \{o_3\}), (\{o_1\}, \{o_2, o_3\})\}.$$

If D is the plan-like relation of Figure 9.2(b), then $|C(LEVELS_D)| = 7$, while $|LEVELS_D| = 123$.

Theorem 4 Let D be a plan-like relation.

a. $I(C(LEVELS_D)) = LEVELS_D$

b. $C(LEVELS_D)$ is the smallest set among the collection of sets of levels relations over D's base whose induced set is equal to $LEVELS_D$.

In [Katz 1988] an algorithm is presented for generating $C(LEVELS_D)$, along with a detailed example of its use. When the algorithm is used, $C(LEVELS_D)$ is generated in a direct way, and not, for example, by marking it out of $LEVELS_D$. Verification then proceeds by checking that each element in $C(LEVELS_D)$ is *possible from S.

9.4   Plan Generation

In this section we will develop an algorithm for generating the best strict plans for (S_I, S_G) in X, where S_I and S_G are states and X is an appropriate search space. We will close in on the set of best strict plans in three stages. In the first two stages, temporary sets U and V are constructed. Both have the property that for each best strict plan there is a single element in the set, from which the plan is obtained by adding zero or more arcs. In the third stage, the set of best strict plans is generated from V. To lay the foundation for this stage, we treat the general issue of generating a plan-like relation from a given set of levels relations (Section 9.4.3). Use of the algorithm presented in this section may be costly; therefore, Section 9.4.6 describes a relatively inexpensive way to generate a specific class of best strict plans.

Best Strict Plans in X

A strict plan (for (S_I, S_G)) in X is a best strict plan in X if there is no other strict plan in X that is contained in it.[2] Of course, this definition may allow multiple best strict plans. Nevertheless, we define a best strict plan in X in this way because, in general, our model doesn't enable us to choose, with full confidence, the better between two different strict plans in X that are incomparable in terms of $\subset$. For example, consider the following two plans over $\{o_1, o_2, o_3, o_4\}$: $\{(o_1, o_2), (o_1, o_3), (o_1, o_4)\}$ and $\{(o_2, o_3), (o_3, o_4), (o_2, o_4)\}$. Though the height of the first plan is only two while the height of the second is three, the execution of the latter may terminate earlier if, say, the execution of o_1 takes three or more times longer than the execution of any other of the operations.

Of course, eventually only one of the best strict plans in X will be passed to the supervisor, so we must have a heuristic rule for picking this plan. We won't state such heuristic rules, because in any real setting that corresponds to our model, the Uncertainty Assumption (Section 9.2.1) is not completely valid; we may have, for example, some information about the expected duration of operation executions, and therefore a heuristic rule that is based on the extra information can be used. Nevertheless, the algorithm to be developed is still useful, because in any real setting it can serve as the basis for a local algorithm that incorporates the appropriate heuristic rules.

As was said, we are going to develop an algorithm for generating the best strict plans in X, where X is an appropriate search space. What is an appropriate search space, and why do we restrict ourselves to such a space? If $o_1 \ldots o_n$, $n \geq 1$, is a sequential plan for (S_I, S_G), then the set of partial orders over $\{o_1, \ldots, o_n\}$ is one appropriate search space. By restricting ourselves to such a space, we make the problem more tractable while assuring that there exists a strict plan in the space. Even if we were to begin with the totally unrestricted space, the plans found would fall within such X spaces.

Additional Assumptions

The algorithm is based on two additional assumptions. In their absence, the algorithm remains applicable, but the strict plans that are generated may not be the best ones. The two assumptions follow.

State Independence Assumption   Let $o_1, \ldots, o_k$, $k \geq 1$, be operations. Exactly one of the following two possibilities is correct:

---

[2]As was mentioned above, a plan-like relation can be thought of as a set of pairs of operation symbols. Therefore, the usual set interpretation should be given to the phrase 'contained in it.'

- It is possible to execute $o_1, \ldots, o_k$ in parallel; that is, there is a state that contains $PRE_1 \cup \cdots \cup PRE_k$, and for each such state, S, it is possible to execute $o_1, \ldots, o_k$ in parallel from S.

- For each state, S, that contains $PRE_1 \cup \cdots \cup PRE_k$, it is *not* possible to execute $o_1, \ldots, o_k$ in parallel from S. (Therefore, by Theorem 1, it is not possible to execute $o_1, \ldots, o_k$ in parallel from any state.)

D-disjoint, A-disjoint Assumption   Let o and o' be operations and let S be a state. If it is possible to execute o, o' in parallel from S, then $DEL \cap DEL' = \emptyset$ and $ADD \cap ADD' = \emptyset$.

The State Independence Assumption eliminates the possibility that there are $o_1, \ldots, o_k$, $k \geq 1$, and S_1, S_2 that contain $PRE_1 \cup \cdots \cup PRE_k$, such that it is possible to execute $o_1, \ldots, o_k$ in parallel from S_1 and it is not possible to execute $o_1, \ldots, o_k$ in parallel from S_2. In other words, the State Independence Assumption asserts that the question whether it is possible to execute $o_1, \ldots, o_k$ in parallel from a state S that contains $PRE_1 \cup \cdots \cup PRE_k$ is independent of S; it is a property of $\{o_1, \ldots, o_k\}$.

The assumption is intuitively familiar, because it is often said that $o_1, \ldots, o_k$ can be executed in parallel without referring to a specific state. Sometimes, the validity of the assumption can be guaranteed by choosing carefully the relation names for representing the domain.

The D-disjoint, A-disjoint Assumption is also commonly used (for example, Georgeff's [Georgeff 1986] *direct effects formulas*).

9.4.1   Stage One — Constructing U

Let S_I and S_G be states and assume that a sequential plan, $o_1 \ldots o_n$, $n \geq 1$, for (S_I, S_G) is given. Let X be the set of partial orders over $\{o_1, \ldots, o_n\}$. Notice that if D is an element in X such that D is a plan for (S_I, S_G) and L is an element in $LEVELS_D$, then surely L is a plan for (S_I, S_G), that is, L is possible from S and $r(L, S) = S_G$, but L might not be *possible from S.

Let Y be
$$\left\{ D \,\middle|\, \begin{array}{l} D \in X \text{ and} \\ D \text{ is a strict plan for } (S_I, S_G) \end{array} \right\}$$

Let Z be
$$\left\{ D \,\middle|\, \begin{array}{l} D \in Y \text{ and} \\ \text{there is no } D' \in Y \text{ such that} \\ D \text{ is obtained from } D' \text{ by adding arcs} \end{array} \right\}$$

In other words, Z is the set whose elements are the minimal elements of Y; that is, Z is the set of best strict plans in X. Our overall goal is to develop an algorithm for generating Z.

Lemma 4 Let $D \in Y$. If it is *not* possible to execute $o_i, o_j, i \neq j$, in parallel, then exactly one of the following two possibilities is correct:

- $(o_i, o_j) \in D$; that is, the arc that leaves o_i and enters o_j belongs to D.
- $(o_j, o_i) \in D$; that is, the arc that leaves o_j and enters o_i belongs to D.

Let DEL_ADD denote the set $(DEL_1 \cup ADD_1) \cup \cdots \cup (DEL_n \cup ADD_n)$. To each $p \in DEL\_ADD$ we will fit a set, B_p, that is contained in $\{o_1, \ldots, o_n\}$:

$$B_p \overset{\text{def}}{=} \{o_i \mid o_i \in \{o_1, \ldots, o_n\} \text{ and } p \in DEL_i \cup ADD_i\}$$

Result   Let $D \in Y$ and $p \in DEL\_ADD$. Then $D|_{B_p}$ (D restricted to B_p) is a total order over B_p.

Lemma 5 Let $D \in Y$ and $p \in DEL\_ADD$.

a. If $p \in S_G$ ($p \notin S_G$), then p belongs to the add set (delete set) of the last element in $D|_{B_p}$.

b. For each $o_i \in B_p$ such that $p \in PRE_i$, o_i comes in $D|_{B_p}$ immediately after an element that adds p, unless $p \in S_I$. In the latter case o_i may also come first.

Lemma 4 and Lemma 5 form the basis on which we characterize the set U. The construction of U is the first stage in closing in on Z.

Let U be the set of relations over $\{o_1, \ldots, o_n\}$ that satisfy the following conditions:[3]

a. For each o_i, o_j, $i \neq j$, if it is possible to execute o_i, o_j in parallel, then neither of the arcs $(o_i, o_j), (o_j, o_i)$ belongs to the relation, and if it is not, then exactly one of them belongs to it.

b. The relation is cycle free.

c. For each $p \in DEL\_ADD$, (a) and (b) of Lemma 5 are true for the relation.

---

[3]See [Katz 1988] for a more efficient way of constructing U than the one implied here.

Notice that condition (b) (together with condition (a) of course) assures that for each $p \in DEL\_ADD$, the relation restricted to B_p is a total order over B_p, and therefore condition (c) makes sense.

From what we have seen so far, it follows that for each $D \in Y$ there is a single $D' \in U$ such that D is obtained from D' by adding zero or more arcs, and therefore, since $Y \subseteq X$, for each $D \in Y$ there is a single $D' \in \overline{U}$ such that D is obtained from D' by adding zero or more arcs, where $\overline{U}$'s elements are U's elements closed under transitivity.

9.4.2 Stage Two — Constructing V

Now that we have constructed $\overline{U}$, we note the following characteristic of its elements.

Lemma 6 Let $D' \in \overline{U}$. For each $p \in DEL\_ADD$ and $o_i \in \{o_1, \ldots, o_n\} - B_p$ such that $p \in PRE_i$, exactly one of four possibilities is correct, as illustrated in Figure 9.3. Whereas possibility (a) has no arc between o_i and B_p, possibilities (b),(c), and (d) have such arcs. The arcs in (b) leave B_p; the arcs in (c) leave o_i; and the arcs in (d) leave both B_p and o_i. In (a), *the lower (upper) limit of o_i in regard to p is S_I (S_G); in (b), it is o_l (S_G); in (c), it is S_I (o_u); and in (d), it is o_l (o_u). The section of $D'|_{B_p}$ that corresponds to o_i is the one* that rests on the angle described by the dashed lines; the dashed lines are omitted if it is empty.

Notice that for each o_j in the section of $D'|_{B_p}$ that corresponds to o_i, o_j adds p.

Lemma 7 Let $D' \in \overline{U}$ such that there is a plan in Y that is obtained from D' by adding zero or more arcs, and let D be such a plan. For each $p \in DEL\_ADD$ and $o_i \in \{o_1, \ldots, o_n\} - B_p$ such that $p \in PRE_i$,

- If, in D', the lower limit of o_i in regard to p is S_I and $p \notin S_I$, then the arc that leaves the first element in $D'|_{B_p}$ and enters o_i belongs to D.

- If the lower limit of o_i in regard to p is o_l and o_l doesn't add p, then o_l is not the last element in $D'|_{B_p}$, and the arc that leaves the element of B_p that comes immediately after o_l and enters o_i belongs to D.

We will now give the rules for constructing the set V; its construction is the second stage in closing in on Z. The rules are based on Lemma 6 and Lemma 7.

Let V be the set that is obtained from $\overline{U}$ by applying to each $D' \in \overline{U}$ the following sequence of instructions:

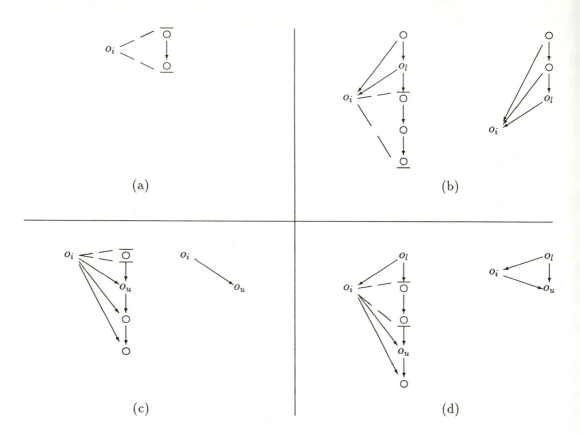

(a)

(b)

(c)

(d)

Note: we have omitted the 'transitive' arcs of $D'|_{B_p}$.

Figure 9.3: The four possibilities

1. If there are p and o_i as above such that the lower limit of o_i in regard to p is the last element in $D'|_{B_p}$ and it doesn't add p, then return; we will not use D' in constructing V.

2. $A \leftarrow \emptyset$.

   For each p and o_i as above:

   - If the lower limit of o_i in regard to p is S_I and $p \notin S_I$, then add to A the arc that leaves the first element in $D'|_{B_p}$ and enters o_i.

   - If the lower limit of o_i in regard to p is o_l and o_l doesn't add p, then add to A the arc that leaves the element of B_p that comes immediately after o_l and enters o_i.

3. If the relation $D' \cup A$ is cycle free, then add it to V.

It follows from Lemma 7 that for each $D \in Y$ there is a single $D' \in V$ such that D is obtained from D' by adding zero or more arcs, and therefore, since $Y \subseteq X$, for each $D \in Y$ there is a single $D' \in \overline{V}$ such that D is obtained from D' by adding zero or more arcs, where $\overline{V}$'s elements are V's elements closed under transitivity.

9.4.3   From Sets of Levels Relations to Plan-Like Relations

We now need to take a short detour to lay the foundation for the third and last stage of our algorithm. In this section we will treat the issue of generating a plan-like relation from a given set of levels relations. This is the converse of the issue dealt with in Section 9.3.1.

Lemma 8 The function that associates $LEVELS_D$ to D, where $D \in X$, is one-to-one.

It follows from Lemma 8 together with Theorem 4 (part a) that

Result   The function that associates $C(LEVELS_D)$ to D, where $D \in X$, is one-to-one.

Lemma 9 Let $D, D' \in X$.
$LEVELS_{D'} \subset LEVELS_D \iff D'$ is obtained from D by adding arcs, that is, $D' \supset D$.

To each set of levels relations over $\{o_1, \ldots, o_n\}$, $LEVELS$, we will fit an element in X, $Dag(LEVELS)$, such that if $LEVELS$ is the set of levels relations of some plan-like relation, D, then $Dag(LEVELS) = D$:

$$Dag(LEVELS) \stackrel{\text{def}}{=} \left\{ (o_i, o_j) \; \middle| \; \begin{array}{l} 1 \leq i,j \leq n, i \neq j, \text{ and} \\ \text{there is } L \in LEVELS \\ \text{such that } o_i \text{ does not} \\ \text{come before } o_j \text{ in } L \end{array} \right\} \cup \left\{ (o_i, o_i) \; \middle| \; 1 \leq i \leq n \right\}$$

215

where the bar means take the complementary set.

Informally, to construct $Dag(LEVELS)$, we start with the set $\{(o_i, o_j)|1 \leq i, j \leq n\}$. We then discard the reflexive pairs as well as the pairs (o_i, o_j), where o_i comes in one of the levels relations after or together with o_j.

Example If $LEVELS$ is the set

$$\{(\{o_1, o_2\}, \{o_3\}), (\{o_1\}, \{o_3\}, \{o_2\})\},$$

then $Dag(LEVELS)$ is the plan-like relation of Figure 9.2 (a).

The following two lemmas will confirm that $Dag(LEVELS)$ has the desired properties.

Lemma 10 Let $LEVELS$ be a set of levels relations over $\{o_1, \ldots, o_n\}$. Then $LEVELS_{Dag(LEVELS)} \supseteq LEVELS$.

Result Let $LEVELS$ be a set of levels relations over $\{o_1, \ldots, o_n\}$. Then $LEVELS_{Dag(LEVELS)} \supseteq I(LEVELS)$.

Notice that it is possible that $LEVELS_{Dag(LEVELS)} \supset I(LEVELS)$. For example, in the last example, the levels relation $(\{o_1\}, \{o_2, o_3\})$ is in $LEVELS_{Dag(LEVELS)}$, but not in $I(LEVELS)$.

Lemma 11 Let $LEVELS$ be a set of levels relations over $\{o_1, \ldots, o_n\}$. Then for each $D \in X$ such that $LEVELS_D \supseteq LEVELS$, $Dag(LEVELS)$ is obtained from D by adding zero or more arcs, that is, $Dag(LEVELS) \supseteq D$ (that is, $LEVELS_{Dag(LEVELS)} \subseteq LEVELS_D$).

Result Let D be a plan-like relation. Then $Dag(LEVELS_D) = D$.

Lemma 12 Let $LEVELS_i$ be a set of levels relations over $\{o_1, \ldots, o_n\}$, $i = 1, 2$. If $I(LEVELS_1) = I(LEVELS_2)$, then $Dag(LEVELS_1) = Dag(LEVELS_2)$.

We now return to developing the plan-generation algorithm.

9.4.4 Stage Three — Constructing Z

To each $D' \in \overline{V}$ we will fit two sets, $Y_{D'}$ and $Z_{D'}$, that are contained in Y and Z respectively:

$$Y_{D'} \stackrel{\text{def}}{=} \left\{ D \,\middle|\, \begin{array}{l} D \in Y \text{ and} \\ D \text{ is obtained from } D' \text{ by adding zero or more arcs} \end{array} \right\}$$

216

$$Z_{D'} \stackrel{\text{def}}{=} \left\{ D \,\middle|\, \begin{array}{l} D \in Z \text{ and} \\ D \text{ is obtained from } D' \text{ by adding zero or more arcs} \end{array} \right\}$$

Then it follows from the conclusion at the end of Section 9.4.2 that for each $D'_1, D'_2 \in \overline{V}$, $D'_1 \neq D'_2$, it holds that $Y_{D'_1} \cap Y_{D'_2} = \emptyset$ and $\cup_{D' \in \overline{V}} Y_{D'} = Y$.

It also follows from that conclusion that for each $D \in Z$ there is a single $D' \in \overline{V}$ such that D is obtained from D' by adding zero or more arcs (because $Z \subseteq Y$). Therefore, for each $D'_1, D'_2 \in \overline{V}$, $D'_1 \neq D'_2$, it holds that $Z_{D'_1} \cap Z_{D'_2} = \emptyset$ and $\cup_{D' \in \overline{V}} Z_{D'} = Z$.

It is clear that $Z_{D'} \subseteq Y_{D'}$, where $D' \in \overline{V}$. Moreover, it is clear that

$$Z_{D'} \subseteq \left\{ D \,\middle|\, \begin{array}{l} D \in Y_{D'} \text{ and} \\ \text{there is no } D_0 \in Y_{D'} \text{ such that} \\ D \text{ is obtained from } D_0 \text{ by adding arcs} \end{array} \right\}$$

that is, $Z_{D'}$ is contained in the set whose elements are the minimal elements of $Y_{D'}$. But it is also clear that $Z_{D'}$ contains the set on the right, because if D is an element in the set on the right, and $D \notin Z_{D'}$, then D is obtained from more than one element of $\overline{V}$. This, as we have seen, is impossible. Thus we obtain

$$Z_{D'} = \left\{ D \,\middle|\, \begin{array}{l} D \in Y_{D'} \text{ and} \\ \text{there is no } D_0 \in Y_{D'} \text{ such that} \\ D \text{ is obtained from } D_0 \text{ by adding arcs} \end{array} \right\} \qquad (9.1)$$

The following lemma assures that for each $D' \in \overline{V}$, $Z_{D'} \neq \emptyset$. The lemma follows from the way in which V was constructed.

Lemma 13 Let $D' \in \overline{V}$. (Then $D' \in X$ and therefore $LEVELS_{D'}$ is defined.) Let $L \in LEVELS_{D'}$, $L = (O_1, ..., O_h)$.

1_a. For each $o_i, o_j \in O_1$, $i \neq j$, it is possible to execute o_i, o_j in parallel.

1_b. For each $o_i \in O_1$, $PRE_i \subseteq S_I$.

2_a. For each $o_i, o_j \in O_2$, $i \neq j$, it is possible to execute o_i, o_j in parallel.

2_b. For each $o_i \in O_2$, $PRE_i \subseteq (S_I - (\cup_{o_j \in O_1} DEL_j)) \cup (\cup_{o_j \in O_1} ADD_j)$.

$\vdots$

h_a. For each $o_i, o_j \in O_h$, $i \neq j$, it is possible to execute o_i, o_j in parallel.

h_b. For each $o_i \in O_h$, $PRE_i \subseteq ((\ldots((S_I - (\cup_{o_j \in O_1} DEL_j)) \cup (\cup_{o_j \in O_1} ADD_j))\ldots) - (\cup_{o_j \in O_{h-1}} DEL_j)) \cup (\cup_{o_j \in O_{h-1}} ADD_j)$.

$h+1$. $((\ldots((S_I-(\cup_{o_j \in O_1} DEL_j))\cup(\cup_{o_j \in O_1} ADD_j))\ldots)-(\cup_{o_j \in O_h} DEL_j))\cup(\cup_{o_j \in O_h} ADD_j) = S_G$.

Notice that under the State Independence Assumption, if L is a levels relation over $\{o_1, \ldots, o_n\}$, $L = (O_1, \ldots, O_h)$, then L is *possible from $S_I \iff O_1$ is possible, and for each $o_i \in O_1$, $PRE_i \subseteq S_I$, and O_2 is possible, and for each $o_i \in O_2$, $PRE_i \subseteq r(O_1, S_I)$, and $\ldots$

Result   Let $D' \in \overline{V}$ and let $L \in LEVELS_{D'}$.

a. L is *possible from $S_I \iff$ every level of L is possible.

b. If L is *possible from S_I, then $r(L, S_I) = S_G$.

c. For each $L' \in LEVELS_{D'}$ such that every level of L' has no more than two elements, L' is *possible from S_I.

d. If L is *possible from S_I, then $\overline{L}$, the transitive closure of L, is in $Y_{D'}$.

Theorem 5 Under the following assumption $\overline{V} = Z$.

Pairwise Assumption   Let $o_1, \ldots, o_k$, $k \geq 1$, be operations and let S be a state. If for each o_i, o_j, $i \neq j$, it is possible to execute o_i, o_j in parallel from S, then it is possible to execute $o_1, \ldots, o_k$ in parallel from S.

Notice that together with the State Independence Assumption, the Pairwise Assumption can be restated as follows: Let $o_1, \ldots, o_k$, $k \geq 1$, be operations. If there is a state that contains $PRE_1 \cup \cdots \cup PRE_k$ and for each o_i, o_j, $i \neq j$, it is possible to execute o_i, o_j in parallel, then it is possible to execute $o_1, \ldots, o_k$ in parallel.

We will proceed without the Pairwise Assumption.

Let $D' \in \overline{V}$ and let $G(LEVELS_{D'})$ be the set

$$\left\{ L \,\middle|\, \begin{array}{l} L \in LEVELS_{D'} \text{ and} \\ L \text{ is 'good'; that is, } L \text{ is *possible from } S_I \end{array} \right\}$$

Let $LEVELS$ be a set of levels relations over $\{o_1, \ldots, o_n\}$ such that $I(LEVELS) = G(LEVELS_{D'})$. Notice that by Lemma 2 and Lemma 3 $G(LEVELS_{D'})$ is complete, and therefore there is such a set (for example, $G(LEVELS_{D'})$ is such a set). The set $LEVELS$ may be found by generating $C(LEVELS_{D'})$ and applying the ideas in Section 9.3.3.

If $LEVELS_{Dag(LEVELS)} = I(LEVELS)$ (that is, $LEVELS_{Dag(G(LEVELS_{D'}))} = G(LEVELS_{D'})$), then $Z_{D'} = \{Dag(LEVELS)\}$ and we are done. But it is more likely that $LEVELS_{Dag(LEVELS)} \supset I(LEVELS)$ and, if so, we must continue.

It is easy to see that

$$Y_{D'} = \{D \mid D \in X \text{ and } LEVELS_D \subseteq G(LEVELS_{D'})\}$$

because if D is an element in X such that $LEVELS_D \subseteq G(LEVELS_{D'})$, then for each $L \in LEVELS_D$, L is *possible from S_I and $r(L, S) = S_G$, and therefore $D \in Y$. Now, by Lemma 9, D is obtained from D' by adding zero or more arcs, and therefore $D \in Y_{D'}$. If D is an element in $Y_{D'}$, then by Lemma 9, $LEVELS_D \subseteq LEVELS_{D'}$. Since $D \in Y$, for each $L \in LEVELS_D$, L is *possible from S_I, and therefore $LEVELS_D \subseteq G(LEVELS_{D'})$.

As a result from the above equation and Lemma 9, we get that for each $D \in Y_{D'}$, D is obtained from $Dag(LEVELS)$ by adding zero or more arcs. From this point forward, no shortcut is available and $Z_{D'}$ is found on the basis of this result, Equation 9.1, and methods already presented.

9.4.5 An Example

We augment the 'standard' blocks world by adding to it a new operation type: $label(x)$ (stick a label on the upper face of block x). $label(x)$ is represented by the sets $PRE = \{\text{clear}(x)\}$, $DEL = \emptyset$, and $ADD = \{\text{labeled}(x)\}$. Let S_I be the state

$$\{ \text{ ontable(A), on(B,A), clear(B), ontable(C), clear(C),}$$
$$\text{ontable(D), on(E,D), clear(E), ontable(F), clear(F),}$$
$$\text{labeled(A) }\},$$

and let S_G be the state

$$\{ \text{ ontable(B), on(A,B), clear(A),}$$
$$\text{ontable(D), on(C,D), on(E,C), clear(E),}$$
$$\text{ontable(F), clear(F),}$$
$$\text{labeled(A), labeled(E), labeled(F) }\}.$$

S_I and S_G are depicted in Figure 9.4 (a). A sequential plan for (S_I, S_G) is shown in Figure 9.4 (b). Our overall goal is to generate the best strict plans in X, the set of partial orders over $\{o_1, \ldots, o_{12}\}$.

Applying the first two stages of the algorithm yields the set V that is shown in Figure 9.5. Since the Pairwise Assumption is valid in our augmented blocks world, $Z = V$.

9.4.6 A Specific Class of Best Strict Plans

For a specific element in U, we know in advance that there is a best strict plan that is obtained from it by adding zero or more arcs; that is, we know that it will turn into an element of V when the instructions (1),(2), and (3) in Section 9.4.2 are applied to its transitive closure. This knowledge enables us to skip the tedious search for an element of V, when a single best strict plan is required.

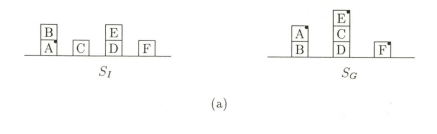

S_I $\qquad\qquad\qquad\qquad$ S_G

(a)

o_1: $\quad unstack(\text{B,A})$ $\quad o_2$: $\quad putdown(\text{B})$ $\quad o_3$: $\quad pickup(\text{A})$ $\quad o_4$: $\quad stack(\text{A,B})$
o_5: $\quad unstack(\text{E,D})$ $\quad o_6$: $\quad stack(\text{E,F})$ $\quad o_7$: $\quad pickup(\text{C})$ $\quad o_8$: $\quad stack(\text{C,D})$
o_9: $\quad unstack(\text{E,F})$ $\quad o_{10}$: $stack(\text{E,C})$ $\quad o_{11}$: $\quad label(\text{E})$ $\quad o_{12}$: $\quad label(\text{F})$

(b)

Figure 9.4: A sequential plan for (S_I, S_G)

The element referred to is the element in U that is implied by the given sequential plan, that is, the element in U that is obtained (from the empty relation) in the following way:

For each o_i, o_j, $i < j$,
if it is not possible to execute o_i, o_j in parallel, then add the arc (o_i, o_j).

Pednault [Pednault 1987] sees this way as a method for generating a best strict plan. This is correct only under the strong implicit assumptions which he makes such as the Pairwise Assumption; we, however, do not make some of these assumptions.

It is clear that the relation obtained in this way, D_0', is really an element in U, that is, it satisfies the conditions (a), (b), and (c) in Section 9.4.1. (D_0' satisfies (c) because the given sequential plan does.) It is also clear that an element of V is produced when the instructions (1),(2), and (3) in Section 9.4.2 are applied to the transitive closure of D_0', because it (the transitive closure) is not rejected in the first decision point, and the relation obtained, D_1', is not rejected in the second decision point, since the given sequential plan that is obtained from it by adding zero or more arcs is cycle free.

By Lemma 13, $Z_{D_1'} \neq \emptyset$; its elements are the best strict plans, D, with the following property:

For each o_i, o_j, $i < j$,
it is not possible to execute o_i, o_j in parallel $\implies (o_i, o_j) \in D$.

$Z_{D_1'}$ can be generated according to the description in Section 9.4.4.

220

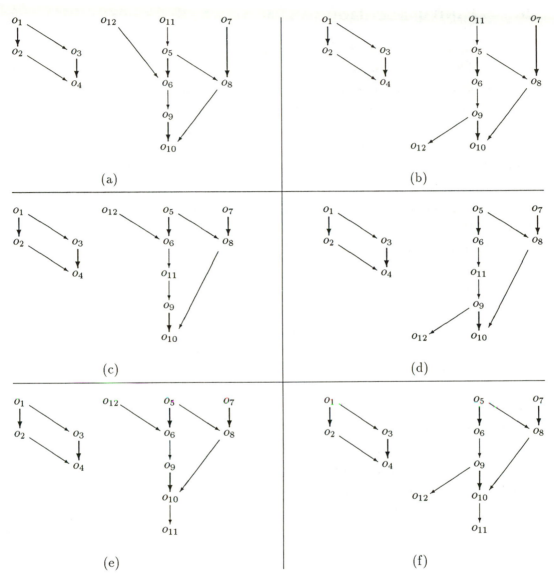

Figure 9.5: The set V

Example Continuing the example presented in Section 9.4.5, this class of best strict plans consists of the single relation shown in Figure 9.5 (f).

9.5 Plan Execution

Assume that the strict levels plan[4] $\{(o_1, o_3), (o_2, o_3)\}$ is passed to the supervisor. A possible scenario of its execution is: The supervisor sends the instructions o_1 and o_2 to two agents. Now, he must wait for both 'finished' messages before he may send o_3. The 'finished' message from the agent who got o_1 arrives almost immediately, but the one from the agent who got o_2 arrives after a relatively long wait. After both 'finished' messages arrive, the supervisor sends the instruction o_3. The final 'finished' message arrives again after a long wait. Now assume that this scenario fits the actual execution, and that $\{(o_1, o_3)\}$ (over $\{o_1, o_2, o_3\}$) is also a strict plan for achieving the requested goal. Then, if $\{(o_1, o_3)\}$ were passed to the supervisor instead of $\{(o_1, o_3), (o_2, o_3)\}$, the execution would take much less time.

In this example, if the supervisor, after receiving the first 'finished' message, were able to conclude (correctly) that he may send o_3 without having to wait for the second 'finished' message, then the unnecessary wait in the execution of the levels plan would be avoided.

We will present an algorithm that can replace the sending rule when a strict levels plan is passed to the supervisor. Under certain conditions, this algorithm enables the supervisor to send an instruction earlier than the plan allows. For instance, it enables the supervisor to reach the conclusion just mentioned. Thus when the algorithm is used, the risk in terminating the search for a plan upon discovering a best strict levels plan that is not a best strict plan is reduced.

Sometimes, the combination of a strict levels plan and the algorithm may even be superior to an ostensibly better strict 'general' plan. For example, assume that each pair from $\{o_1, o_2, o_3\}$ is possible from the initial state, but $\{o_1, o_2, o_3\}$ is not. Then the relation $\{(o_1, o_3)\}$ over $\{o_1, o_2, o_3\}$ is a best strict plan for $(S_I, (S_I - (\cup_{i=1}^3 DEL_i)) \cup (\cup_{i=1}^3 ADD_i))$. Now assume that the strict levels plan $\{(o_1, o_3), (o_2, o_3)\}$ is passed to the supervisor. Then the supervisor, guided by the algorithm, will realize, after receiving the first 'finished' message, that he may send the instruction o_3 even if the 'finished' message was from the agent who got o_2. That is, the actual execution of the levels plan is at least as fast as the execution of the best strict plan.

---

[4]As expected, a levels plan is a levels relation that is a plan. Note that a strict levels plan is actually a levels relation that is *possible from the initial state and its result from that state is the goal state.

9.5.1   The Algorithm

Assume that there are k, $k \geq 2$, agents (every agent has an ID number which is a number between 1 and k), and that a strict levels plan, L, $L = (O_1, \ldots, O_h)$, for (S_I, S_G) was passed to the supervisor (L is a relation over $\{o_1, \ldots, o_n\}$). We now offer an algorithm that can replace the sending rule in guiding the supervisor's action. Subsequently, we will fine-tune the algorithm so that the resulting execution is faster than the execution that would be obtained under the sending rule. In order to avoid complex notations, we assume that for each $o_i, o_j \in \{o_1, \ldots, o_n\}$, $i \neq j$, o_i and o_j stand for different operations.

Impatient Supervisor Algorithm

The variables that will be used and their initial values are as follows:

- S, the current state, is initially S_I.

- $BUSY\_AGENTS$, the set whose elements are the ID numbers (together with additional information) of the agents that are currently busy, is initially empty.

- O_i^w, the instructions from O_i that were not sent yet (are waiting to be sent), is initially O_i.

- O_i^{ex}, the instructions from O_i that are being executed, is initially empty.

- l, the current level, is initially 1.

While there is an operation in $\{o_1, \ldots, o_n\}$ that was not sent yet, that is, while $O_1^w \cup \cdots \cup O_h^w \neq \emptyset$, do

1. Find an operation in $O_1^w \cup \cdots \cup O_h^w$ that is 'good' according to the goodness test below (Procedure 1). In the pursuit of a 'good' operation, you may:

   a. Check whether a 'finished' message from the agent whose ID number is i, $1 \leq i \leq k$, was received, that is, check whether the i'th box contains a 'finished' message. If it does, carry out Procedure 3.

   b. Retest an operation that was previously 'no good.'

   c. Stop a test in the middle in order to check whether 'finished' messages were received, but in such a case you may not use the information gathered during the part of the test that was already carried out.

2. Send the operation you have found to a free agent, that is, carry out Procedure 2.

Notice that it is permitted to check whether 'finished' messages were received after finding a 'good' operation in $O_l^w \cup \cdots \cup O_h^w$ and before sending it.

Procedure 1

A goodness test of an operation, o_i, that is from level l'

$t \longleftarrow l' - l$

$t = 0$: o_i is 'good'

$t \neq 0$:   if

1. $\{o_i\} \cup O_l^{ex} \cup O_{l+1}^{ex} \cup \cdots \cup O_h^{ex} \cup O_l^w$ is possible from S

2. $\{o_i\} \cup O_{l+1}^{ex} \cup O_{l+2}^{ex} \cup \cdots \cup O_h^{ex} \cup O_{l+1}^w$ is possible from $r(O_l^{ex} \cup O_l^w, S)$

3. $\{o_i\} \cup O_{l+2}^{ex} \cup O_{l+3}^{ex} \cup \cdots \cup O_h^{ex} \cup O_{l+2}^w$ is possible from $r(O_{l+1}^{ex} \cup O_{l+1}^w, r(O_l^{ex} \cup O_l^w, S))$

$\quad\vdots$

t. $\ldots$

then o_i is 'good'

else o_i is 'no good'

Procedure 2

Sending an operation, o_i, that is from level l' to the agent x

1. Send o_i to the agent whose ID is x

2. $BUSY\_AGENTS \longleftarrow BUSY\_AGENTS \cup \{(x, o_i, l')\}$

3. $O_{l'}^w \longleftarrow O_{l'}^w - \{o_i\}$

4. $O_{l'}^{ex} \longleftarrow O_{l'}^{ex} \cup \{o_i\}$

Procedure 3

Treating a 'finished' message that was received from the agent x

1. Remove the message from the box (the x'th box)

2. Delete from $BUSY\_AGENTS$ the threesome whose first element is x, (x, o_i, l')

224

3. $O_{l'i'}^{ex} \longleftarrow O_{l'i'}^{ex} - \{o_i\}$

4. $S \longleftarrow (S - DEL_i) \cup ADD_i$

5. If $l' = l$ and $O_l^w = \emptyset$ and $O_l^{ex} = \emptyset$, then $l \longleftarrow \bar{l}$,

    where $\bar{l}$ is the first level above l in which $O_{\bar{l}}^w \cup O_{\bar{l}}^{ex} \neq \emptyset$. If there is no such level, then $\bar{l}$ is h.

Of course, the actual implementation of the algorithm would be more efficient: it would allow the supervisor to exploit information from previous tests (including stopped tests). This point (exploiting information from previous tests) is ignored in the algorithm, because it would interfere in conveying the main point of the algorithm.

Lemma 14 If the supervisor obeys the algorithm, the execution will proceed smoothly and the final state will be the requested state, S_G. That is, every agent, upon receiving an instruction, will proceed without interference to do the work indicated by the instruction, the supervisor won't reach a dead end (he will send all the instructions), and the final state will be S_G.

Notice that the supervisor's image of the situation doesn't necessarily coincide with reality; for example, it may occur that the execution of an operation has terminated, while the supervisor continues to act as if it has not. This lack of congruence between the supervisor's perception and the actual facts, however, doesn't affect the correctness of the algorithm.

9.5.2 Fine-Tuning the Algorithm

The algorithm gives the supervisor full freedom in picking the next operation to be tested, thus enabling the supervisor to act unwisely. The supervisor might pick an operation that is less likely to be 'good' and that requires a longer test than others, though there are free agents that are waiting for instructions. In particular, the supervisor might overlook the operations in the current level (that is, the operations in O_l^w), when there are such.

Therefore, we fine-tune the algorithm so that it will be reasonable to expect that the execution will end earlier if the supervisor obeys it rather than the sending rule. We fine-tune it by changing the first instruction in the loop's body to:

Find an operation in $O_l^w \cup \cdots \cup O_h^w$ that is 'good' and whose level is *minimal*. That is, test the operations in O_l^w first, the ones in O_{l+1}^w second, and so on, until you encounter a 'good' one. But if, while still searching, you turn to treat incoming messages, you must go back to the starting point, that is, to O_l^w.

It is clear that Lemma 14 remains correct. Of course, the actual implementation of the algorithm would be more efficient; it would give the supervisor criteria for determining whether he must actually return to the starting point, or whether some later point is acceptable.

Notice that now, whenever $O_l^w \neq \emptyset$, the operation that will be sent will be from O_l^w and it will be found immediately. Only if $O_l^w = \emptyset$, will the supervisor search for a 'good' operation in higher levels. Therefore, it is reasonable to expect that the agents will be exploited more if the algorithm is used instead of the sending rule. That is, it is reasonable to expect that the execution of a strict levels plan will end earlier if the algorithm is used.

Remark Testing whether an operation from a higher level than l is 'good' is time-consuming. Under the 'Pairwise Assumption' (Section 9.4.4), such a test is performed significantly faster, because what actually is performed is the following:

$t \longleftarrow l' - l$

$t = 0$: o_i is 'good'

$t \neq 0$: if

1. for each $o_j \in O_l^{ex} \cup O_{l+1}^{ex} \cup \cdots \cup O_h^{ex} \cup O_l^w$, it is possible to execute o_i, o_j in parallel from S

2. for each $o_j \in O_{l+1}^w$, it is possible to execute o_i, o_j in parallel from $r(O_l^{ex} \cup O_l^w, S)$

3. for each $o_j \in O_{l+2}^w$, it is possible to execute o_i, o_j in parallel from $r(O_{l+1}^{ex} \cup O_{l+1}^w, r(O_l^{ex} \cup O_l^w, S))$

$\vdots$

t. ...

then o_i is 'good'

else o_i is 'no good'

9.6   Conclusion

Methods have been presented for the verification, generation, and execution of plans for multiple agents represented as DAGs. The method of verification, which is based on 'levels relations,' makes it possible to determine efficiently whether a DAG is a plan, despite its potentially infinite number of itineraries. This method of verification is exploited in a method for generating the best strict plans over a search space, spanned by the operations of a sequential plan for the given initial and goal states. Equipped with a strict levels plan, the method of execution enables the supervisor to speed the execution phase by sending 'early' instructions.

Acknowledgements

The authors would like to thank the Palo Alto Laboratory of the Rockwell Science Center for providing partial support for this work.

References

[Allen and Koomen 1983] J. F. Allen and J. A. Koomen, "Planning Using a Temporal World Model," *Proceedings of the Eighth International Joint Conference on Artificial Intelligence*, Karlsruhe, West Germany, August 1983, pp. 741–747.

[Corkill 1979] D. D. Corkill, "Hierarchical Planning in a Distributed Environment," *Proceedings of the Sixth International Joint Conference on Artificial Intelligence*, Tokyo, Japan, August 1979, pp. 168–175.

[Corkill 1982] D. D. Corkill, *A Framework for Organizational Self-Design in Distributed Problem-Solving Networks*, PhD thesis, University of Massachusetts, Amherst, Massachusetts, 1982.

[Durfee *et al.* 1987] E. H. Durfee, V. R. Lesser, and D. D. Corkill, "Cooperation through Communication in a Distributed Problem Solving Network," in M. N. Huhns, ed., *Distributed Artificial Intelligence*, Morgan Kaufmann Publishers, Inc., Los Altos, California, 1987, pp. 29–58.

[Fikes and Nilsson 1971] R. E. Fikes and N. J. Nilsson, "STRIPS: A New Approach to the Application of Theorem Proving to Problem Solving," *Artificial Intelligence*, Vol. 2, No. 3/4, 1971, pp. 189–208.

[Georgeff 1983] M. P. Georgeff, "Communication and Interaction in Multi-agent Planning," *Proceedings of the National Conference on Artificial Intelligence*, Washington, D.C., August 1983, pp. 125–129.

[Georgeff 1984] M. P. Georgeff, "A Theory of Action for Multi-agent Planning," *Proceedings of the National Conference on Artificial Intelligence*, Austin, Texas, August 1984, pp. 121–125.

[Georgeff 1986] M. P. Georgeff, "The Representation of Events in Multiagent Domains," *Proceedings of the National Conference on Artificial Intelligence*, Philadelphia, Pennsylvania, August 1986, pp. 70–75.

[Katz 1988] M. J. Katz, *Plans for Multiple Agents*. Master's thesis, Hebrew University, Jerusalem, Israel, 1988.

[Lansky 1987] A. L. Lansky, "A Representation of Parallel Activity Based on Events, Structure, and Causality," in M. P. Georgeff and A. L. Lansky, eds., *Reasoning About Actions & Plans*, Morgan Kaufmann Publishers, Inc., Los Altos, California, 1987, pp. 123–159.

[Pednault 1987] E. P. D. Pednault, "Formulating Multiagent, Dynamic-World Problems in the Classical Planning Framework," in M. P. Georgeff and A. L. Lansky, eds., *Reasoning About Actions & Plans*, Morgan Kaufmann Publishers, Inc., Los Altos, California, 1987, pp. 47–82.

[Rosenschein 1982] J. S. Rosenschein, "Synchronization of Multi-agent Plans," *Proceedings of The National Conference on Artificial Intelligence*, Pittsburgh, Pennsylvania, August 1982, pp. 115–119.

[Rosenschein and Genesereth 1985] J. S. Rosenschein and M. R. Genesereth, "Deals among Rational Agents," *Proceedings of the Ninth International Joint Conference on Artificial Intelligence*, Los Angeles, California, August 1985, pp. 91–99.

[Sacerdoti 1975] E. D. Sacerdoti, "The Nonlinear Nature of Plans," *Advance Papers of the Fourth International Joint Conference on Artificial Intelligence*, Tbilisi, Georgia, USSR, September 1975, pp. 206–214.

[Smith 1980] R. G. Smith, "The Contract Net Protocol: High-Level Communication and Control in a Distributed Problem Solver," *IEEE Transactions on Computers*, Vol. C-29, No. 12, December 1980, pp. 1104–1113.

[Smith 1978] R. G. Smith, *A Framework for Problem Solving in a Distributed Processing Environment*, PhD thesis, Stanford University, 1978.

[Stuart 1985] C. Stuart, "An Implementation of a Multi-agent Plan Synchronizer," *Proceedings of the Ninth International Joint Conference on Artificial Intelligence*, Los Angeles, California, August 1985, pp. 1031–1033.

Matthew J. Katz and Jeffrey S. Rosenschein
Computer Science Department
Hebrew University
Jerusalem, Israel

Chapter 10

Negotiating Task Decomposition and Allocation Using Partial Global Planning

Edmund H. Durfee and Victor R. Lesser

Abstract

To coordinate as an effective team, cooperating problem solvers must **negotiate** over their use of local resources, information, and expertise. Sometimes they negotiate to decide which *local* problem-solving tasks to pursue, while at other times they negotiate over the decomposition and distribution of tasks. They might negotiate by sharing all of their information, or by exchanging proposals and counterproposals, or by working through an "arbitrator." In general, negotiation is a complex process of *improving agreement on common viewpoints or plans through the structured exchange of relevant information.* In this paper, we describe how **partial global planning** provides a versatile framework for negotiating in different ways for different reasons, and we examine in detail its utility for negotiating over whether and how problem solvers should decompose and transfer tasks to improve group performance. Finally, we propose how our approach can be extended to capture even more fully the complexity, flexibility, and power of negotiation as a tool for coordinating distributed problem solvers.

10.1 Introduction

A central focus of distributed problem-solving research is coordination—the problem-solving **nodes** in a network should coordinate their use of distributed resources. These resources

229

might be physical (such as computing capacity or communication capabilities) or informational (such as information about the problem(s) being solved or problem-solving expertise). Finding an appropriate technique for coordinating a network depends on the distribution of these resources in the current situation faced by that network, and on the local autonomy of the nodes. Autonomous nodes have their own possibly disparate goals, knowledge, and decisionmaking criteria. Nonetheless, they should still find ways to agree on how to coordinate when coordination could help them achieve their goals better.

Negotiation is the term used in distributed problem-solving research to denote the process by which autonomous nodes coordinate their views of the world and act and interact to achieve their goals. A number of very different techniques with varying behavior, but all embodying aspects of negotiation, have been developed by drawing on the rich diversity in how humans negotiate in different contexts [Conry *et al.* 1986], [Davis and Smith 1983], [Lander and Lesser 1988], [Rosenschein and Genesereth 1987], [Sycara 1988]. This has led to confusion and misunderstanding among researchers who are studying different aspects of the same phenomenon.

For example, the groundbreaking work by Smith and Davis identified **contracting** as a form of negotiation where a node decomposes a large problem into subproblems, announces the subproblems to the network, collects bids from nodes, and awards the subproblems to the most suitable bidders [Davis and Smith 1983, Smith 1980]. In turn, the bidders might subcontract their subproblems. Contracting solves the **connection problem**: nodes match problems to solve with nodes having the resources (expertise, data, computing power) to solve them. However, nodes must often negotiate for other reasons. For example, to solve the **decomposition problem**, nodes should negotiate over decomposing their problems in the first place. Or when subproblems are inherently distributed, nodes must solve the **association problem** by communicating to discover which nodes are working on associated subproblems, and negotiating over how, when, and where to form complete solutions by sharing results. Moreover, negotiation is often an iterative exchange of **counterproposals** leading to **compromise**. Contracting, therefore, is just a rudimentary form of negotiation because it solves only the connection problem using a single round of information exchange.

One general definition of negotiation is: *the process of improving agreement (reducing inconsistency and uncertainty) on common viewpoints or plans through the structured exchange of relevant information.* That is, negotiation leads nodes toward shared plans (where they know of each other's planned actions) or consistent viewpoints (so they are likely to make compatible decisions about local actions). Although they might exchange information of different kinds and in various forms, they begin with some common knowledge about what they might attempt to achieve and how to express themselves. Their negotiation has both protocol and purpose. To negotiate in a wide variety of contexts, nodes need a rich vocabulary, reasoning methods to exploit all the uses of this vocabulary, planning mechanisms to predict and work toward likely future events and interactions, and decisionmaking criteria to choose how to negotiate given the current and possible future situations.

In this paper, we describe how partial global planning embodies a more complete approach to negotiation that allows nodes to solve the connection, decomposition, and association problems using diverse methods such as compromise, appealing to an arbitrator, and trading counterproposals. We use experiments to show how the greater variety of information that nodes exchange, and their ability to plan and predict, lead to more effective cooperation decisions. Finally, we outline future research directions that we hope will lead to even more general techniques for negotiation.

10.2   Partial Global Planning

Partial global planning is a flexible approach to coordination that does not assume any particular distribution of subproblems, expertise, or other resources, but instead lets nodes coordinate in response to the current situation [Durfee 1988, Durfee and Lesser 1987]. Each node can represent and reason about the actions and interactions for groups of nodes and how they affect local activities. These representations are called **partial global plans** (PGPs) because they specify how different *parts* of the network *plan* to achieve more *global* goals. Each node maintains its own set of PGPs that it may use independently and asynchronously to coordinate its activities.

A PGP is a frame-like structure that nodes use as a common representation for exchanging information about their objectives and plans. The PGP's **objective** contains information about *why* the PGP exists, including its eventual goal (the larger solution being formed) and its importance (a priority rating or reasons for pursuing it). Its **plan-activity-map** represents *what* the nodes are doing, including the major plan steps being taken concurrently, their costs and expected results, and why they are being taken in a particular order. Its **solution-construction-graph** contains information about *how* the nodes should interact, including specifications about what partial results to exchange and when to exchange them. Finally, a PGP's **status** contains bookkeeping information, including pointers to relevant information received from other nodes and when it was received. A PGP is thus a general structure for representing coordinated activity in terms of goals, actions, interactions and relationships.

Besides their common PGP representation, nodes also need at least some common

231

knowledge about how and when they should use PGPs to negotiate. This common knowledge is called the **organization**, and is broken into two parts. The **domain-level organization** specifies the general, long-term problem-solving roles and capabilities of the nodes. Given its local goals and plans and the domain-level organization, a node can locally hypothesize potential interactions with other nodes and identify relevant PGP information. It then uses the **metalevel organization**, which indicates the coordination roles of the nodes, to decide where and when to exchange PGPs during negotiation. For example, if organized one way, the nodes might negotiate through a single coordinator that forms and distributes coordinated PGPs for the network, while if organized differently, the nodes might negotiate by broadcasting relevant information and individually forming more complete PGPs.

Given their common representation for PGPs and their shared organizational knowledge, nodes form, exchange, manipulate, and react to PGPs. In some task domains, the set of possible PGPs might be enumerable, so that once the nodes have classified their current situation they invoke the proper PGP. In other task domains, nodes might need to construct PGPs from their local goals, plans, and information. Our partial global planning approach allows a node to encode a local plan in a special PGP called a **node-plan** (because it corresponds to a single node). Guided by the metalevel organization, nodes can then exchange their node-plans and PGPs to build models of each other. A node uses its models of itself and others to identify when nodes have PGPs whose objectives could be part of some larger network objective, called a **partial global goal**, and combines the related PGPs into a single, larger PGP to achieve it. Given the more complete view of group activity represented in the larger PGP, the node can revise the PGP to represent a more coordinated set of group actions and interactions and a more efficient use of network resources. Finally, the node updates its local plans based on this improved view of group problem solving.

10.3 Implementation

We have implemented the partial global planning framework in the Distributed Vehicle Monitoring Testbed (DVMT), which simulates a network of vehicle monitoring nodes that track vehicles moving through an acoustically sensed area [Lesser and Corkill 1983]. The acoustic sensors and problem-solving nodes are geographically distributed, so that each node receives signals from a local subset of sensors. Nodes track vehicles through their own sensed areas and then exchange partial tracks to converge on a complete map of vehicle movements. A node applies signal processing knowledge to correlate its sensor data, eliminating errorful sensor data as it integrates correct data into an answer map. Each node has a blackboard-based problem-solving architecture, with knowledge sources and levels of abstraction appropriate for vehicle monitoring.

Nodes must coordinate to use their resources effectively as they solve the inherently distributed problem of tracking vehicles through the overall area. They must communicate to identify possible overall solutions to work toward, and then decide which subproblems to pursue individually and where to send local results. They should coordinate to avoid duplicating effort in tracking vehicles through overlapping sensed areas and to share partial tracks that might help other nodes resolve uncertainty about their own information. Nodes should consider their local expertise (knowledge sources) when deciding which local subproblems to solve and which subproblems to transfer to more suitable nodes if possible. In short, because subproblems, expertise, and other resources may be inherently but possibly unevenly distributed, nodes must be able to solve the association, decomposition, and connection problems.

The details of how local and partial global planning have been implemented in the DVMT have been given in [Durfee 1988], [Durfee and Lesser 1988b], [Durfee and Lesser 1988a], [Durfee and Lesser 1987], so we will only outline the relevant aspects here. The local planner develops a plan at multiple levels of detail, including a representation of major plan steps. In the DVMT, a major plan step corresponds extending a partial track into a new time frame (such as extending the track derived from data d_i–d_j into d_{j+1}, where d_k is data sensed at time k). This step might take several processing actions to analyze the new data, filter out noise, and integrate the correct data into the track. For each major plan step, the local planner roughly estimates what partial results will be formed and when. By representing and coordinating their major plan steps, nodes cooperate effectively without reasoning about details that are frequently revised and quickly outdated.

Each node has a partial global planner (PGPlanner) as an integral part of its control activities. The PGPlanner builds a node-plan from each local plan, where a node-plan's objective indicates the possible track(s) being developed and its plan-activity-map is a sequence of plan-activities. Each **plan-activity** represents a major plan step, and has an expected begin time, end time, and partial result, derived from the local planner's estimates. Guided by the metalevel organization, nodes exchange PGPs and node-plans so that one or more of them develops more encompassing PGPs. When combining PGPs into a single, larger PGP, a node merges the smaller PGP's plan-activity-maps to represent the concurrent activities of all participating nodes, and can reorder the plan-activities to improve coordination. It also builds a solution-construction-graph to indicate which partial tracks formed by the plan-activities should be exchanged to share useful information and construct the complete solution. The PGPlanner then revises local plans based on the PGP. Details of how domain-dependent information and decision-making criteria are encoded and incorporated in the partial global planning framework are given elsewhere [Durfee 1988, Durfee and Lesser 1987].

10.4 Negotiation and Task Passing

PGPs represent *expectations* about how nodes could coordinate their actions and inter-actions, along with the context (individual objectives, plans, and relationships) that led to those expectations. Negotiation involves exchanging PGP information so that different nodes generate increasingly similar expectations (PGPs). In fact, in stable environments where nodes' plans do not change because of new data, failed actions, or unexpected effects of their actions, nodes can converge on identical PGPs. More generally, however, nodes work in dynamic domains where data, network, and problem-solving characteristics change and communication channels have delay and limited capacity. In these cases, nodes nego-tiate to *improve* agreement on PGPs; partial global planning allows effective cooperation despite such incomplete agreement.

Partial global planning provides a framework for negotiation that can solve many dif-ferent coordination problems. For example, when coordinating their pursuit of inherently distributed subproblems, nodes negotiate to solve the association problem by selectively ex-changing PGPs to recognize larger network goals and coordinate how they form and share partial results. When nodes have different PGPs (expectations) for working together on the same larger goal, they negotiate by exchanging PGPs to form a compromised PGP that uses the "best" (most up-to-date) information from each of their PGPs. Alternatively, they can negotiate through a third "arbitrator" node (which is assigned that role in the met-alevel organization) that forms and distributes a common PGP. The specific mechanisms in the DVMT for this type of negotiation are described elsewhere [Durfee 1988].

In our framework, nodes also can negotiate to solve the decomposition and connection problems by representing proposed problem decompositions and subproblem assignments in PGPs. A node sends such a proposal to possible contracting nodes, which can agree to or reject it, or generate a counterproposal indicating an alternative decomposition, subproblem assignment, or both. By exchanging PGPs, nodes negotiate over both decompositions and contracts. Because a PGP includes information about the larger problem being solved and the participating nodes' activities, a node has more context for accepting, rejecting, or countering a proposal than in a typical contracting protocol, as we now describe in detail.

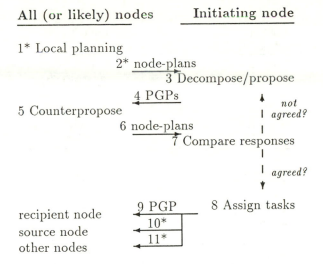

The major steps in task passing are shown. Steps marked with a * are optional.

Figure 10.1: Task passing steps

Before it can transfer tasks, a node must solve the decomposition problem. In some applications, a node might use only local knowledge such as static procedures for how to *always* decompose certain types of tasks. More generally, however, a node cannot intelligently decompose a task without knowledge about other nodes, so that it can decide whether to pursue the task (it might be unimportant relative to other nodes' tasks) and, if so, which nodes might be able to assist it. Before task passing begins, therefore, nodes could share local views. In our framework, nodes form and exchange node-plans so that some nodes develop more global views. These activities are shown graphically in Figure 10.1, steps 1 and 2. Note that these steps are optional, but they help a node make better decisions about decomposing and announcing tasks.

In step 3 (Figure 10.1), a node examines its PGPs, which can represent local activities or activities of several nodes if steps 1 and 2 were taken. The node's PGPlanner checks the solution-construction-graph to detect a *bottleneck* node that expects to complete its partial result much later than other nodes working on the PGP (a node working alone is always a bottleneck). For example, in Figure 10.2a, node 2 is a bottleneck because it expects to finish its activities (to process data d_5–d_{13}) much later than node 1. If it finds a bottleneck node, the node initiates task passing if it is responsible for coordinating the bottleneck node, based on the metalevel organization. Thus, in a network with a central coordinating

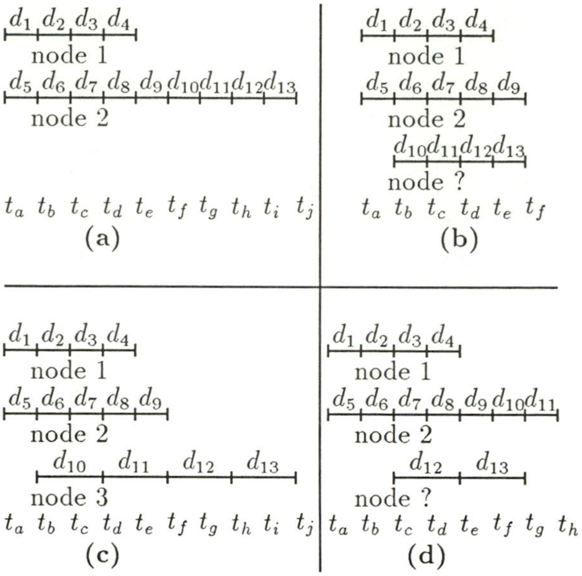

d_1 d_2 d_3 d_4
node 1
d_5 d_6 d_7 d_8 d_9 d_{10} d_{11} d_{12} d_{13}
node 2

t_a t_b t_c t_d t_e t_f t_g t_h t_i t_j
(a)

d_1 d_2 d_3 d_4
node 1
d_5 d_6 d_7 d_8 d_9
node 2
d_{10} d_{11} d_{12} d_{13}
node ?
t_a t_b t_c t_d t_e t_f
(b)

d_1 d_2 d_3 d_4
node 1
d_5 d_6 d_7 d_8 d_9
node 2
d_{10} d_{11} d_{12} d_{13}
node 3
t_a t_b t_c t_d t_e t_f t_g t_h t_i t_j
(c)

d_1 d_2 d_3 d_4
node 1
d_5 d_6 d_7 d_8 d_9 d_{10} d_{11}
node 2
d_{12} d_{13}
node ?
t_a t_b t_c t_d t_e t_f t_g t_h
(d)

Graphic depictions of how a plan-activity-map represents possible task decompositions and assignments. In (a) node 2 is a bottleneck node, and (b) indicates a possible transfer of tasks to an unknown node. Node 3 provides the counterproposal in (c), and this triggers the new proposal in (d).

Figure 10.2: Task passing example

node, that node initiates task passing, while in a broadcast organization where each node has equal responsibility, the bottleneck node itself initiates task passing. Unlike protocols where only nodes with tasks can initiate task passing, our framework permits a node to have an "agent" negotiate for it.

The initiating node's PGPlanner forms a task to pass, where the task is to generate some piece of the bottleneck node's partial result. The task is represented as a sequence of plan-activities. Before deciding on a decomposition, the PGPlanner scans its models of nodes to identify underutilized nodes that might perform this task. A node is underutilized if it participates only in lowly-rated PGPs or is idle, where a node without any local plans can transmit an **idle node-plan** to explicitly indicate its availability. When the PGPlanner finds underutilized nodes, or when the metalevel organization specifies that nodes should attempt to pass tasks despite incomplete network views, then the PGPlanner forms a task to pass from the bottleneck node's activities. For the situation in Figure 10.2a, the PGPlanner decides to reduce the bottleneck by assigning plan-activities for data d_{10}–d_{13} elsewhere (Figure 10.2b).

236

From its subproblems, a node could predict related subproblems that might arise later. In the DVMT, the PGPlanner extrapolates vehicle tracks to predict whether a possible recipient node might receive sensor data in the future, and builds a **future node-plan** to represent processing this data. The PGPlanner estimates when the earliest future node-plan will begin and whether the recipient node could complete the passed task before this time. If not, the PGPlanner avoids interfering with the future local tasks by removing the node from consideration. If, later on, the future tasks fail to arrive or are unimportant, the PGPlanner can reinitiate task passing.

When it has a task to send and potential recipients, the PGPlanner copies the task's plan-activities and modifies these copies by altering their begin and end times based on estimates of when a recipient node could pursue them (considering communication delays). It also changes the name of the node performing these plan-activities to a special *unassigned* marker. These new plan-activities are inserted in the PGP's plan-activity-map. For example, in Figure 10.2b, an unknown node is expected to start the transferred task at time t_b (because of communication delays). The modified PGP is sent to the potential task recipients or broadcast if specified in the metalevel organization (Figure 10.1 step 4).

When it gets the PGP (Figure 10.1 step 5), a recipient node's PGPlanner extracts the unassigned plan-activities from the plan-activity-map and builds a node-plan from them with this node's name replacing the special marker. The PGPlanner then examines its current set of PGPs and node-plans to determine the earliest that it could begin working on the plan-activities. During this computation, it also uses its own information to form future node-plans since it might have information the initiating node lacks. The PGPlanner modifies the plan-activities to avoid interfering with any actual or expected commitments. It also modifies them if it has or lacks expertise that may affect the time it needs to complete them. In Figure 10.2c, for example, node 3 expects to take twice as much time for each plan-activity because it lacks expertise.

Having modified the new node-plan (if necessary), the recipient node sends it to the initiating node as a counterproposal (Figure 10.1 step 6). As it receives node-plan messages, the initiating node stores them with the PGP. When it has waited long enough (depending on communication delays), the PGPlanner scans the responses (Figure 10.1 step 7) to find which nodes could complete the task earliest, and if any could complete the task sooner than the node currently with the task can, then the PGPlanner decides to transfer the task (possibly to several nodes to increase reliability). Otherwise, the initiating node might give up on passing the task, or it might further negotiate over problem decomposition. To negotiate, the initiating node modifies and sends a PGP proposing that nodes do fewer or different plan-activities (in Figure 10.1, it returns to step 3). In Figure 10.2d, for example, the PGPlanner might propose to transfer a smaller task covering data d_{12}–d_{13} (note that the extra round of negotiation further delays the task's expected starting time). Because PGPs contain information about why and how nodes could cooperate, nodes need not simply accept or reject tasks, but instead can engage in multistage negotiation [Conry *et al.* 1986]. Alternatively, the larger task could be passed, and node 3 could then subcontract out parts of it to other nodes.

Once an assignment has been negotiated, the initiating node updates the PGP to represent the assignment (Figure 10.1 step 8). It sends this PGP to the chosen node(s) (Figure 10.1 step 9), and either sends the task (subproblem to solve) if it has it, or sends the PGP to the **source** node (that has the task) so it will send it (Figure 10.1 step 10). The node that sends the task also keeps a copy in case communication errors, node failures, or poor coordination cause a need to reassign the task.

The initiating node might also send the PGP to unchosen nodes, depending on the metalevel organization. Whether they explicitly receive the PGP (Figure 10.1 step 11), or they learn that they were not chosen because the task does not arrive when expected, the unchosen nodes remove the future node-plan they formed and adjust other future node-plans. For example, if it had responded to several PGPs and had modified plan-activities based on possibly receiving tasks, then once a task is awarded elsewhere the PGPlanner may modify and transmit other future node-plans to indicate that it could pursue tasks earlier. This way, nodes can respond to multiple requests and update their responses when tasks are assigned, although because of communication delays the updated information may not reach an initiating node before the task is assigned and a less than optimal assignment might be made. In a network with communication delays, potentially errorful channels, and asynchronous activities at the different nodes, such incoherence is unavoidable.

10.5   Results

Our experiments focus on simple task passing negotiations; more detailed discussions and experiments with larger networks are provided elsewhere, along with results showing partial global planning's ability to coordinate nodes with inherently distributed subproblems and its overhead costs [Durfee 1988, Durfee and Lesser 1987]. We use two simple two-node environments (Figure 10.3). In the first (A), a vehicle moves through node 1's sensed area and then turns, missing the area sensed by node 2, while in the second (B) the vehicle is detected by node 2. In each case, we simulate data d_i arriving at time i. A knowledge source takes 1 time unit to execute, and the communication delay between nodes is also 1 time unit. These environments explore negotiation for task passing and the role of prediction

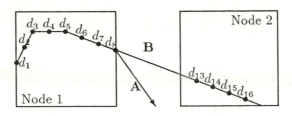

Node 1 senses data in both environments, while node 2 only senses data in B.

Figure 10.3: Task passing environments

in deciding whether to accept a task. Environment A is a case where task passing will improve network performance by using node 2's resources in parallel with node 1's, while environment B is a case where prediction allows nodes to avoid passing tasks that the recipient will be unable to complete.

The experimental results are summarized in Table 10.1. Beginning with environment A, experiment E1 uses a noncooperative metalevel organization: node 1 working alone needs 44 time units to generate the solution. In a broadcast organization without prediction (E2), the nodes exchange node-plans (node 2 has an idle node-plan) and each forms its own PGPs. Node 1 passes d_5–d_8 to node 2 early on and they cooperatively form the overall solution sooner than in E1. A centralized organization with node 2 as coordinator (E3) is even faster since node 2's proposed task passing is to itself and it accepts the proposal without delay. When nodes can build predictions, they expect node 2 to get its own tasks. With the broadcast organization (E4), nodes delay task passing until after the expected tasks fail to arrive, at which point they only pass d_6–d_8. The delay causes them to form the overall solution later, and the same thing occurs in the centralized organization (E5). Thus, nodes can recover from incorrect predictions, but they may degrade performance.

With environment B, however, the predictions are correct. When noncooperative (E6), the nodes individually form their own solutions. In a broadcast organization without prediction (E7), node 1 sends d_5–d_8 to node 2 because it expects node 2 to be available. Node 2 ignores the task until it forms its own result, and then only works on d_7–d_8 (node 1 kept copies of d_5–d_6 which it completes locally). Thus, node 2 does help node 1, but failure to predict future tasks causes unnecessary communication overhead from exchanging too much information. In the centralized organization (E8), the task d_5–d_8 passed by node 1 is adopted earlier by node 2 (because node 2 proposes and accepts at the same time), and node 2 prefers it to its own task. Consequently, the nodes form d_1–d_8 together first as if node 2 had no tasks of its own (as in E3), and then they pass tasks and work together on d_{13}–d_{16}. This cooperation on both tasks involves substantial communication.

239

Exp	Env	MLO	Pred	Pass	Done	STime
E1	A	loc	-	-	-	44
E2	A	bc	none	d_5-d_8(12)	d_5-d_8	33
E3	A	cn(2)	none	d_5-d_8(11)	d_5-d_8	32
E4	A	bc	all	d_6-d_8(19)	d_6-d_8	35
E5	A	cn(2)	all	d_6-d_8(18)	d_6-d_8	34
E6	B	loc	-	-	-	44/32
E7	B	bc	none	d_5-d_8(12)	d_7-d_8	39/32
E8	B	cn(2)	none	d_5-d_8(11) d_{15}-d_{16}(27)	d_5-d_8 d_{15}-d_{16}	32/42
E9	B	bc	all	d_8(35)	d_8	42/32
E10	B	cn(2)	all	d_8(34)	d_8	42/32
E11	B	cn(1)	local	d_8(35)	d_8	42/32

Abbreviations

Env:	The problem-solving environment
MLO:	Metalevel organization: loc=local, bc=broadcast, cn(n)=centralized with node n coordinator.
Pred:	Nodes a node can predict future tasks for.
Pass:	Tasks passed in network (and time passed).
Done:	Passed tasks that are actually by recipient.
STime:	The time to find solution(s); if more than one, earliest time for each is given (d_1-d_8/d_{13}-d_{16}).

When they can predict future tasks, nodes avoid premature task passing. In both a broadcast (E9) and centralized (E10) organization, they recognize that they will both be busy, and do not pass tasks until after node 2 completes its result, at which time node 1 sends d_8 to node 2. By waiting until after node 2's local tasks are complete, they incur much less communication overhead because they send only what node 2 can process in time. However, by waiting until node 2 is completely done before negotiating, they waste time transferring tasks while node 2 is idle. That is why E7 found the solution sooner—it had received (too many) tasks ahead of time. We hope to improve our mechanisms to negotiate over passed tasks *as* a node is completing its local tasks. We also plan on studying the tradeoffs in making and reacting to predictions. Specifically, we want to develop mechanisms that will decide how and when to make predictions given knowledge about the current situation, including the probability of making correct predictions and the costs of missed or incorrect predictions.

Finally, in E11 we minimize overhead spent in reasoning about others by allowing nodes to hypothesize only their own future node-plans. We use environment B with a centralized organization, but where node 1 is the coordinator. Unable to predict node 2's future plan, node 1 sends a PGP proposing task passing to node 2 early on. Node 2 uses that PGP to hypothesize its future node-plan, and responds to node 1 that it could not perform the task until much later. Thus, nodes negotiate despite incomplete local views to arrive at appropriate task passing decisions, and use information in the PGP that is not transmitted in typical contracting protocols.

10.6 Discussion

Partial global planning provides a more general framework for negotiation in distributed problem-solving networks than contracting because nodes can communicate more information (encoded in PGPs), can structure their coordination activities (encoded in the metalevel organization), can plan for and predict possible future events that affect negotiated decisions, and can use these mechanisms flexibly to negotiate over whatever coordination problems (association, connection, decomposition) they face in their current situation. Through implementing and evaluating our framework in the DVMT, we have examined its costs and benefits, and shown how it integrates planning, prediction, and negotiation. Moreover, although the low-level representations of objectives and actions and the criteria for ordering them are domain-dependent, the high-level PGP structures and the methods for forming, exchanging, manipulating, and revising them provide a generic foundation that should be applicable in a variety of domains such as air-traffic control, job scheduling, and multiple-robot environments.

Ours is not a completely general framework for negotiation, however, because of one important limitation. Although it flexibly allows nodes to negotiate over their plans at a specific level of detail, it does not allow negotiation at other levels. For example, to supply the context needed to agree on a plan, nodes might need to exchange more detailed information about their current situation, such as what data they are working with. Or nodes might need to negotiate at a higher level, because although they might have common views of each other's goals and plans, they might have different views on how to compare, rank, or combine this information. That is, nodes might need to negotiate not only over what they should do (such as what actions to take), but also over the criteria to use when deciding what they should do (such as why some actions are preferable to others). And then given the ability to negotiate at several levels, how should nodes decide at what level to negotiate at any given time?

Clearly, many questions remain regarding negotiation in distributed problem-solving networks, and much work needs to be done. We are optimistic that these questions will eventually be answered, however, based on our experience with partial global planning. There, by moving to a new representation for plans and interactions, we discovered that negotiation for sharing partial results and for assigning tasks, which have traditionally been treated separately, are really just two sides of the same coin. We hope that applying partial global planning in other domains will help us to develop similar insights that will lead to an even more complete framework for negotiation.

Acknowledgements

This research was sponsored, in part, by the National Science Foundation under CER Grant DCR-8500332, and by the Office of Naval Research under University Research Initiative Grant Contract N00014-86-K-0764, and under Contract N00014-79-C-0439.

References

[Conry *et al.* 1986] S. E. Conry, R. A. Meyer, and V. R. Lesser, "Multistage Negotiation in Distributed Planning," in A. Bond and L. Gasser, editors, *Readings in Distributed Artificial Intelligence*, Morgan Kaufmann Publishers, 1988.

[Davis and Smith 1983] R. Davis and R. G. Smith, "Negotiation As a Metaphor for Distributed Problem Solving," *Artificial Intelligence*, Vol. 20, 1983, pp. 63–109.

[Durfee 1988] E. H. Durfee, *Coordination of Distributed Problem Solvers*, Kluwer Academic Publishers, 1988.

[Durfee and Lesser 1988b] E. H. Durfee and V. R. Lesser, "Incremental Planning to Control a Time-Constrained, Blackboard-Based Problem Solver," *IEEE Transactions on Aerospace and Electronics Systems*, Vol. 24, No. 5, September 1988, pp. 647–662.

[Durfee and Lesser 1988a] E. H. Durfee and V. R. Lesser, "Predictability Versus Responsiveness: Coordinating Problem Solvers in Dynamic Domains," *Proceedings of the Seventh National Conference on Artificial Intelligence*, August 1988.

[Durfee and Lesser 1987] E. H. Durfee and V. R. Lesser, "Using Partial Global Plans to Coordinate Distributed Problem Solvers," *Proceedings of the Tenth International Joint Conference on Artificial Intelligence*, August 1987, pp. 875–883.

[Lander and Lesser 1988] S. Lander and V. R. Lesser, "Negotiation among Cooperating Experts," *Proceedings of the 1988 Workshop on Distributed Artificial Intelligence*, May 1988.

[Lesser and Corkill 1983] V. R. Lesser and D. D. Corkill, The Distributed Vehicle Monitoring Testbed: A Tool for Investigating Distributed Problem Solving Networks," *AI Magazine*, Vol. 4, No. 3, Fall 1983, pp. 15–33.

[Rosenschein and Genesereth 1987] J. S. Rosenschein and M. R. Genesereth, "Communication and Cooperation among Logic-Based Agents," *Proceedings of the Sixth Phoenix Conference on Computers and Communications*, February 1987, pp. 594–600.

[Smith 1980] R. G. Smith, "The Contract-Net Protocol: High-level Communication and Control in a Distributed Problem Solver," *IEEE Transactions on Computers*, Vol. C-29, No. 12, December 1980, pp. 1104–1113.

[Sycara 1988] K. Sycara, "Resolving Goal Conflicts Via Negotiation," *Proceedings of the Seventh National Conference on Artificial Intelligence*, August 1988, pp. 245–250.

Edmund H. Durfee
Department of Electrical Engineering and Computer Science
The University of Michigan
Ann Arbor, MI 48109

Victor R. Lesser
Department of Computer and Information Science
University of Massachusetts
Amherst, Massachusetts 01003

Chapter 11

Mechanisms for Assessing Nonlocal Impact of Local Decisions in Distributed Planning

S. E. Conry, R. A. Meyer, and R. P. Pope

Abstract

The ability to reason about the nonlocal impact of local decisions is crucial in distributed problem solving systems. When agents in such a system have a limited view of the global system state, decisions are necessarily made from a local perspective. It is often the case, however, that nonlocal constraints may affect the viability of such a local decision. In this paper, we describe mechanisms whereby an agent in a distributed problem solving system can assess and reason about the nonlocal impact of local actions. These mechanisms have been devised for use as part of a process involving multistage negotiation in distributed planning and are illustrated in the context of a multistage negotiation protocol.

11.1 Introduction

In this paper we present a formalism that allows an agent in a distributed planning system to reason about the interaction between consequences of its local decisions and constraints existing elsewhere in the system. We also show how this formalism provides a natural mechanism by which agents incrementally expand knowledge about the nonlocal impact of their local decisions *without* constructing a complete global view.

We view distributed problem solving as a process that is carried out by a group of semiautonomous agents, each of which has a limited view of the global system state and

245

control over only a subset of the resources required to determine a problem solution. Multistage negotiation [Conry *et al.* 1988] has been developed as a means by which an agent can acquire enough knowledge to reason about the impact of local activity on nonlocal state and modify its behavior accordingly. This protocol can be viewed as a generalization of the contract net protocol [Smith 1980, Smith and Davis 1981, Davis and Smith 1983]. It produces a cooperation strategy that is similar in character to the Functionally Accurate, Cooperative (FA/C) paradigm [Lesser and Corkill 1981], in which nodes iteratively exchange tentative and high level partial results of their local subtasks.

Subtask or subgoal interaction problems are of critical importance in problem solving systems. Since our work has largely been focused on distributed planning, we have been particularly concerned with determining the nature of subgoal interactions and devising a way of reasoning about these interactions in a distributed environment.

In many domains, planning can be viewed as a form of distributed resource allocation problem in which actions require resources in order to satisfy system goals. The resources available generally have three significant characteristics: resources are indivisible (not consisting of component resources), the supply of resources is limited, and use of these resources cannot be time shared for concurrent satisfaction of multiple goals. Our model of planning differs from many others in that both control over resources and knowledge about these resources are distributed among problem solving agents. Some of the resources are under the direct control of a single agent, while control over others is *shared* by two agents. Utilization of a shared resource requires coordination between the agents that share its control.

In this kind of environment, global goals may arise concurrently in multiple agents. The system objective is one of finding a set of resource allocations that satisfies as many of the global goals as possible, subject to constraints. We view distributed planning as a process that proceeds in two phases: plan generation and negotiation.

For each global goal, plan generation determines a set of plans each of which is feasible, taken in isolation. Each of these plans consists of a collection of *plan fragments*, one resident in each participating agent. Plan fragments which collectively form a (global) plan must embody a consistent choice of resource allocations. This consistency is reflected in the presence of constraints that enforce a coordinated allocation of resources that are shared among agents. It is important to note that when a resource r is shared by two agents (agent A1 and agent A2), allocation of r for use in satisfying a goal must occur in *both* agent A1 and agent A2. To motivate this assumption, suppose that r is a conveyor belt and the system goal is one of solving a set of product distribution problems. Agent A1 and agent A2 must make a coordinated decision to allocate r in a plan for solution of some system problem, as there is only *one* copy of this resource in the system. When we assume that

246

Table 11.1: Simple Example Scenario

Agent A1					Agent A2			
goal	plan frag	r1	r2		goal	plan frag	r1	r4
resource count		1	1		resource count		1	1
g1	pf1	1	1		g1	pf4	1	1
g2	pf2	1			g3	pf5		1
	pf3		1					

there may be several goals the system is attempting to satisfy concurrently, it becomes clear that it may not be possible to satisfy *all* of the global goals because of resource allocation conflicts. Negotiation is necessary to select a set of plans that satisfies as many global goals as possible.

In the sections that follow, we describe a formalism that has been developed for abstracting and propagating information about nonlocal impact of decisions made locally. Our work provides mechanisms for determining impact at three levels: locally on the level of plan fragments, locally on the level of goals, and nonlocally. We first present formal definitions that characterize this impact and demonstrate the construction of sets that reflect various levels of impact. We then illustrate the utility of these definitions in the context of a more complex example that embodies a richer set of conflicts than the simple one used to illustrate the definitions. Finally, we indicate ways in which a distributed planning system can make use of this formalism in arriving at an acceptable solution.

11.2   Reasoning about Constraints and Conflicts

For the purposes of illustrating our definitions, we consider a simple scenario in which there are two agents (agents A1 and A2) in a distributed planning system. In this example scenario, each of these agents has knowledge concerning certain resources. This local knowledge is indicated in Table 11.1. If the entry on the *resource count* line for resource r in agent i is k, then the system has k copies of resource r to utilize in problem solving. The shared resources are evident, as they are known to more than one agent. Notice that $r1$ is a shared resource. There is only one copy of $r1$ in the system and its allocation must be jointly controlled by A1 and A2.

This scenario assumes that the system is attempting to simultaneously satisfy three global goals: g1, g2, and g3. During plan generation, global plans have been determined for each of these goals. These plans and the resource requirements associated with each

Table 11.2: Composition of Global Plans

plan	goal	plan frags	r1	r2	r4
resource count			1	1	1
p1	g1	pf1, pf4	1	1	1
p2	g2	pf2	1		
p3	g2	pf3		1	
p4	g3	pf5			1

are shown in Table 11.2. It should be noted that Table 11.2 shows the global plans from a *global* perspective. No single agent in a distributed problem solving system has complete knowledge concerning any of these plans. Indeed, unless some system goal can be satisfied by a single agent using its own local resources, no single agent is even aware of the total number of alternative plans that have been generated.

From Table 11.2, it is evident that global plans are composed of collections of local *plan fragments*. For instance, global plan p1 is composed of plan fragments pf1 and pf4, while global plan p4 consists of pf5. This example scenario is extremely simple. It is intended only to provide a means for illustrating the definitions and does not have sufficient complexity to demonstrate the nature of interactions in more complex situations.

To enable an agent to efficiently exchange knowledge concerning the nonlocal impact of local decisions, we determine a *conflict set* for each plan fragment. We then use the conflict set to construct an *exclusion set* for each plan fragment that reflects the potential impact on an agent's ability to participate in satisfying other goals, assuming that plan fragment x is executed. At the highest level of abstraction, we use exclusion sets to form *infeasibility sets*. Knowledge summarized in its infeasibility set allows an agent to reason about the way in which its decision to satisfy one goal may affect its ability to satisfy other goals. Finally, we propagate these local concepts to other agents with the construction of induced exclusion sets.

Before formalizing these concepts, we introduce our notational conventions.

Notation:

- We define maximal and minimal subsets of sets whose elements are sets in the standard way. Given a set of sets $S = \{S_1, \ldots, S_n\}$ with a partial order $\subseteq$ (set containment) defined on the elements of S, we say that S_i is **maximal** if $\not\exists S_j \ni S_i \subseteq S_j$. Furthermore, S_i is **minimal** if $\not\exists S_j \ni S_j \subseteq S_i$.

- $P_A = \{$ all plan fragments known to agent A $\}$.

- If $pf_x \in P_A$, then pf_x is associated with satisfaction of some goal $g(pf_x)$.

- The set of goals known to agent A is
$$G_A = \{g \mid g = g(pf_x) \text{ for some plan fragment } pf_x \in P_A\}.$$

- For each goal g in G_A, there is an associated set of plan fragments
$$P_g = \{x \mid x \in P_A \text{ and } g = g(x)\}.$$

- $copies(r_i)$ denotes the number of copies of resource r_i available for use by agent A.

- R_x denotes the resources required to execute plan fragment pf_x.

- $r_i(pf_x)$ denotes the number of copies of resource r_i needed by plan fragment pf_x.

- A set of plan fragments in Agent A, $Q = \{pf_1, \ldots, pf_n\} \subseteq P_A$, is said to be **compatible** if $\sum_{k=1}^{n} r_i(pf_k) \leq copies(r_i)$ for all i and if, for all pf_x in Q, $g(pf_i) \neq g(pf_j)$ for $j \neq i$.

- A **maximal compatible set of plan fragments in A relative to pf$_x$** is a maximal subset, M, of $S_x = \{Q \mid Q \text{ is a compatible set of plan fragments and } pf_x \in Q\}$.

The conflict set for plan fragment pf_x indicates the minimal impact (locally) of a choice to execute pf_x. The conflict set for pf_x can be constructed by considering each maximal set M of mutually feasible plan fragments (*including pf_x*) known to an agent. For each such set, M, the complement of M relative to P_A is an element of the conflict set for pf_x.

More formally, the **Conflict Set** for plan fragment pf_x is constructed as follows: Let $X = (P_A - P_g) \cup \{pf_x\}$, where $g = g(pf_x)$. For each maximal compatible subset M of plan fragments in A relative to pf_x, the set $X - M$ is a member of the conflict set for pf_x. Thus, $CS_{pf_x} = \{c \mid c = X - M$, where M is a maximal compatible subset of plan fragments in A relative to $pf_x \}$.

To illustrate this formalism, we compute the conflict set for pf1 in our simple scenario. There is only one maximal compatible subset of plan fragments in A for pf1, namely $\{pf1\}$. $X = (\{pf1, pf2, pf3\} - \{pf1\}) \cup \{pf1\} = \{pf1, pf2, pf3\}$, so that $CS_{pf1} = \{(\{pf1, pf2, pf3\} - \{pf1\})\} = \{\{pf2, pf3\}\}$.

We are concerned with the conflict set because the conflict set for a plan fragment gives information as to the negative impact of executing that plan fragment. The maximal compatible subsets, on the other hand, indicate maximal sets of feasible choices that are available. There is no reason to believe that an agent should choose some one of these maximal subsets for execution. Indeed, a given agent might never participate in system satisfaction of some of the global goals. Though the view of the conflict set as being formed using the complements of maximal feasible sets (with respect to the set of all plan fragments known to the agent) is intuitively appealing, it is often more computationally attractive to treat the conflict set of pf_x in its dual form: as the collection of minimal mutually infeasible sets of plan fragments, given that plan fragment pf_x is to be executed.

Three significant observations can be made concerning the conflict set of plan fragment pf_x. First, the complement of each element of the conflict set is indeed a maximal feasible set. Secondly, the agent will be *compelled* to forego execution of all plan fragments in *some* element of the conflict set if it chooses to execute plan fragment pf_x. The local impact of a decision can thus be related to the size of elements in the conflict set. Finally, representation of impact in the form of a conflict set seems to provide a substantially more compact form of representation that can be more efficiently used in reasoning than many others.

The conflict set for a plan fragment reflects the impact of executing that plan fragment *at the level of mutually infeasible sets of plan fragments*. It is often necessary to reason about the impact that executing a particular plan fragment would have on the potential satisfaction of other goals.

The **Exclusion Set** for a plan fragment, pf_x, is a collection of sets of goals, at least one of which must be abandoned if pf_x is selected for execution. Thus, if the agent selects plan fragment pf_x then one of the elements of the exclusion set is a set of goals that *cannot* be satisfied through action on the part of this agent. The exclusion set is defined as follows:

For each $S \in CS_{pf_x}$, we define $G_S = \{g \mid P_g \subseteq S\}$. Thus G_S, for an element S of the conflict set, is the set of goals that that cannot be satisfied locally if plan fragments in S are eliminated from consideration. We let $H = \{G_S \mid S \in CS_{pf_x}\}$ and define the **exclusion set for plan fragment pf$_x$**, ES_{pf_x}, as the collection of the minimal subsets of H.

Returning to our example, we compute the exclusion set for pf1. The conflict set for pf1 has one element, $CS_{pf1} = \{\{pf2, pf3\}\}$. Using the definition of G_S, $G_{\{pf2,pf3\}} = \{g2\}$. Thus, $H = \{\{g2\}\}$ and $ES_{pf1} = \{\{g2\}\}$.

The exclusion set exposes relationships between plan fragments and goals. It is often desirable to detect and reason about mutually infeasible goals. The relationship of infeasibility is a very strong one. Goal g1 is (locally) infeasible with goal g2 if each of the (local) plan fragments for g1 has g2 in every element of its exclusion set (and conversely). When two goals are (locally) mutually infeasible, an agent knows that it cannot act to satisfy both goals, due to local constraints. Once exclusion sets have been determined, infeasibility is not difficult to detect. In our example scenario, g1 and g2 are mutually infeasible in agent A1.

The three types of relationships we have discussed are all rooted in local constraints. Conflict, exclusion, and infeasibility are essentially concepts that would not be particularly significant were it not for the constraints on joint execution of plan fragments that exist locally. Although the concept of conflict does not appear to propagate in a meaningful manner, exclusion does. The key element in this propagation lies in the observation (which we have made before) that a choice on the part of one agent to satisfy a goal through execution of a specific plan fragment constrains the set of remaining choices that are available to other agents for satisfaction of that goal.

As we have seen, the construction of exclusion sets allows us to assess the impact of executing of a plan fragment that is due to local conflict. In addition, we would like to know how the conflict associated (locally) with execution of a plan fragment affects the ability of other agents to satisfy their goals. The **Induced Exclusion Set** is our mechanism that provides a vehicle for propagating this information by capturing the essence of the impact that local decisions have nonlocally.

In the discussion that follows, we assume that in a distributed environment one agent does not have knowledge concerning another agent's internal state. It specifically does not have any knowledge about resources over which it has no control. The agent must therefore gain knowledge about the impact its choice has on other agents *from those agents*, directly or indirectly.

The **Induced Exclusion Set** for a plan fragment, pf_x, in Agent A, is a collection of sets of goals, one of which must be abandoned by one or more nonlocal agents if Agent A executes pf_x. The induced exclusion set for pf_x, IE_{pfx}, is defined as follows:

Let $X_{pfx} = \{pfi \mid pfx \in P_A, pfi \notin P_A, R_x \cap R_i \neq \phi, \text{ and } g(pfx) = g(pfi) \}$. Thus, each individual plan fragment in X_{pfx} is a nonlocal plan fragment that may connect directly with pfx (via a shared resource) in some global plan.

For each agent, K, with plan fragments in X_{pfx} we must determine the contribution to the induced exclusion set for pfx due to constraints known by agent K. For each plan fragment $p \in X_{pfx} \cap P_K$, we therefore let

$$e_p = \{e \mid e = es \cup ie \text{ for } es \in ES_p \text{ and } ie \in IE_p\}$$

Notice that each e_p is a set of sets, each of whose members reflects potential conflict that could arise if plan fragment p is selected by agent K. In this construction, each es represents a contribution to e_p that reflects constraints local to agent K, while each ie denotes a contribution that agent K has received from other agents relative to plan fragment p. For this reason, it is necessary to combine these contributions into a single element, $E_{K,pfx}$, that may be propagated to Agent A. $E_{K,pfx}$ is defined as the collection of minimal subsets of $\bigcup e_p$ for $p \in X_{pfx} \cap P_K$.

Continuing the definition, the **induced exclusion set for plan fragment pfx**, IE_{pfx}

is the collection of the maximal subsets of $E = \bigcup E_{K,pfx}$. This definition of IE_{pfx} permits incremental construction of induced exclusion sets under the assumption that initially $IE_{pfx} = \phi$ for all plan fragments.

Once again, returning to our example, we can now compute the induced exclusion set for pf1. $X_{pf1} = \{pf4\}$. Since, $ES_{pf4} = \{\{g3\}\}$ and initially, $IE_{pf4} = \{\phi\}$, $e_{pf4} = \{\{g3\}\}$. Thus, $E_{A2,pf1} = \{\{g3\}\}$ so that $IE_{pf1} = \{\{g3\}\}$.

The induced exclusion set is incrementally built during negotiation. When one agent (agent A) requests information about the impact of executing plan fragment pf_x on another agent (agent B), agent B attempts to summarize all the knowledge it has about that impact. This knowledge is initially found in the exclusion sets of each of its plan fragments which coordinate with plan fragment pf_x. As has been mentioned, the induced exclusion set in agent A for plan fragment pf_x is empty initially. As nonlocal knowledge becomes available, this set is augmented in the obvious way. Given sufficient time, an agent can acquire knowledge about the system wide impact of executing each of its plan fragments. It does so, however, *without* the exchange of detailed information concerning resource availability in the system.

11.3   Reasoning about Nonlocal Conflict

The formalism described in the previous section has been devised as a reasoning mechanism for use in a distributed planning system with the following characteristics:

- System goals arise in a distributed fashion.

- The same system goal may be generated at more than one agent, independently.

- Due to limited interagent bandwidth for coordination, it is not feasible to exchange a complete set of relevant constraints.

- Nonlocal constraints exist among plans being developed (independently) at agents in the system.

- The global problem being addressed is, in general, overconstrained. A choice to satisfy some goals may make it impossible to satisfy others. Choice heuristics are necessary.

- No single agent has a complete global view of overall system status. There is no single locus of control.

An example of an application that exhibits these characteristics is that of service restoral in communications systems [Conry *et al.* 1988].

The objective of a distributed planning system in this type of environment is the determination of a set of plans satisfying as many of the global goals as possible, given the set of locally applicable constraints. Since no agent has a global view and there is no central locus of control, it is necessary to arrive at a satisfactory solution in a distributed fashion through multiple stages of negotiation. The purpose of negotiation is twofold. Negotiation enables agents to gain enough knowledge about the impact of their own proposed actions relative to achievement of the system objective to make an informed local decision. It also enables agents to come to an agreement with other agents when arbitration among equally attractive alternatives is necessary.

The formalism presented in the previous section plays a central role in enabling agents to assess the extent of nonlocal impact of their local decisions. It does so because negotiation involves the incremental interchange of information in the form of induced exclusion sets among the agents. The construction of induced exclusion sets and the way in which these reasoning mechanisms bring a distributed planning system to a convergent view are best illustrated with the aid of a more complex example. In this section, we consider a scenario involving four agents cooperatively attempting concurrent satisfaction of four goals. A number of global plans have been constructed during plan generation, as indicated in Table 11.3. These global plans are related to their constituent plan fragments in Table 11.3 and local knowledge about plan fragments is shown in Table 11.4. It is important to note that each agent has *only* the local knowledge about plan fragments shown in Table 11.4. This means, for example, that agent A is aware that plan fragment A-b for goal g1 coordinates with some plan fragment known to agent B as a component in some global plan or plans in satisfaction of g1. Agent A knows this because resource $r11$ is shared between agents A and B. Agent A *does not know* anything about plan fragments that are local to agent B.

As has been observed, this set of formalisms has been devised for use as a reasoning mechanism in a system that employs *Multistage Negotiation* [Conry *et al.* 1988]. This cooperation paradigm assumes that each agent's goals are either primary goals or secondary goals. An agent's primary goals are important because they represent system tasks that cannot be performed unless this agent participates. An agent with a primary goal p knows that an acceptable plan for satisfying p has been determined when the negotiation protocol reflects that this is the case.

Suppose that during negotiation, agent C proposes to satisfy g1 through execution of C-a. Due to the coordination required because plan fragment C-a uses a resource it shares with agent D, goal g1 cannot be satisfied in this way unless agent D also participates. Agent C's proposed action means that agent D must choose either D-a or D-b.

plan	plan fragments	r1	r2	r3	r4	r5	r6	r7	r8	r9	r10	r11
g1p1	A-a B-a C-a D-a	1	1			1	1			1		
g1p2	A-a C-a D-b	1	1			1		1	1			
g1p3	A-a C-c	1	1		1							
g1p4	A-b B-b C-b	1				1					1	1
g1p5	D-c						1		1			
g2p1	A-c C-d	1	1	1	1							
g2p2	A-d B-c D-d	1						1		1		1
g2p3	C-e D-e			1	1	1	1		1			
g3p1	A-e C-f D-f	1	1	1		1		1				
g3p2	A-e C-f D-g	1	1	1		1	1					
g3p3	C-f D-f				1	1		1				
g3p4	C-g D-g				1	1	1					
g4p1	A-f B-d	1										1
g4p2	A-f B-e C-i	1		1	1						1	1
g4p3	A-g C-h D-h		1			1						
g4p4	A-g C-h D-i		1			1						
g4p5	C-j D-h				1	1		1				
g4p6	C-j D-i				1	1	1					

The conflict set (in D) for D-a is:

$$\{ \quad \{D\text{-}d, D\text{-}f, D\text{-}g, D\text{-}h, D\text{-}i\}, \quad \{D\text{-}d, D\text{-}e, D\text{-}g, D\text{-}h, D\text{-}i\},$$
$$\{D\text{-}d, D\text{-}e, D\text{-}f, D\text{-}h, D\text{-}i\}, \quad \{D\text{-}d, D\text{-}e, D\text{-}f, D\text{-}g, D\text{-}i\},$$
$$\{D\text{-}d, D\text{-}e, D\text{-}f, D\text{-}g, D\text{-}h\} \quad \}$$

(This corresponds to the set of maximal compatibles $\{\{D\text{-}a, D\text{-}e\}, \{D\text{-}a, D\text{-}f\}, \{D\text{-}a, D\text{-}g\}, \{D\text{-}a, D\text{-}h\}, \{D\text{-}a, D\text{-}i\}\}$.) Thus the exclusion set for D-a is

$$\{\{g3, g4\}, \{g2, g4\}, \{g2, g3\}\}.$$

The other alternative available to agent D (given that it knows it must coordinate with agent C's proposed action) involves selection of D-b for execution. The conflict set for D-b is

$$\{ \quad \{D\text{-}d, D\text{-}f, D\text{-}g, D\text{-}h, D\text{-}i\}, \quad \{D\text{-}d, D\text{-}e, D\text{-}f, D\text{-}h, D\text{-}i\},$$
$$\{D\text{-}d, D\text{-}e, D\text{-}f, D\text{-}g, D\text{-}h\} \quad \}$$

corresponding to the maximal compatible set $\{\{D\text{-}b, D\text{-}e\}, \{D\text{-}b, D\text{-}g\}, \{D\text{-}b, D\text{-}i\}\}$, so the exclusion set for D-b is also

$$\{\{g3, g4\}, \{g2, g4\}, \{g2, g3\}\}.$$

Table 11.4: Local Knowledge About Plan Fragments

Agent A

goal	plan frag	r1	r2	r11
	resource count	3	2	2
g1	A-a	1	1	
	A-b	1		1
g2	A-c	1	1	
	A-d	1		1
g3	A-e	1	1	
g4	A-f	1		1
	A-g		1	

Agent C

goal	plan frag	r2	r3	r4	r5	r10
	resource count	2	3	2	2	1
g1	C-a	1			1	
	C-b			1		1
	C-c	1		1		
g2	C-d	1	1	1		
	C-e		1	1	1	
g3	C-f	1	1		1	
	C-g			1	1	
g4	C-h	1			1	
	C-i		1	1		1
	C-j			1	1	

Agent B

goal	plan frag	r9	r10	r11
	resource count	1	1	2
g1	B-a	1		
	B-b		1	1
g2	B-c	1		1
g4	B-d			1
	B-e		1	1

Agent D

goal	plan frag	r5	r6	r7	r8	r9
	resource count	2	2	1	3	1
g1	D-a	1	1			1
	D-b	1		1	1	
	D-c		1		1	
g2	D-d				1	1
	D-e	1	1		1	
g3	D-f	1		1		
	D-g	1	1			
g4	D-h	1		1		
	D-i	1	1			

Notice that a choice by agent D to execute plan fragment D-a compels agent D to forego local satisfaction of two of the other three global goals about which it has local knowledge. *Which* two of the three should be abandoned is dependent on decisions made elsewhere.

To see this, observe that a choice by agent D to (locally) satisfy g1 with D-a and also to locally satisfy g2 involves execution of D-e because D-d is not jointly feasible with D-a (due to contention over r9). Furthermore, a choice to execute both D-a and D-e would preclude agent D's participation in satisfaction of both g3 and g4, as all plan fragments in D relative to g3 and g4 require r5. Similar arguments reveal that if agent D elects to execute D-a and also to participate in satisfying g3, it cannot also participate in satisfying g2 and g4. Likewise, a choice to execute D-a and satisfy g4 in agent D requires that g2 and g3 be (locally) abandoned. This reasoning has been abstracted and embodied in formation of the exclusion set for D-a.

Regardless of the alternative chosen by agent D, assuming that agent C insists on executing plan fragment C-a, agent D can (locally) participate in satisfaction of only one global goal *other than* g1. In response to a request for impact information (during negotiation) from agent C relative to its proposed execution of plan fragment C-a, agent D transmits the information that {{g3, g4}, {g2, g4}, {g2, g3}} should be added to the induced exclusion set for C-a. Through this transaction, agent C learns that its choice to satisfy g1 through executing C-a forces some agent elsewhere in the system (in this case agent D) to abandon two of the remaining three goals. It does *not*, however, mean that satisfaction of all four goals is not jointly feasible. They are simply not jointly feasible using agent D's participation, providing agent C elects to execute C-a.

Through negotiation, it is possible to determine that a solution permitting satisfaction of all four global goals is feasible. Indeed, it is easily verified that all four goals can be jointly satisfied through choice of global plans g1p3, g2p3, g3p1 and g4p1. To see how this happens, suppose (for the sake of discussion) that using local criteria early in negotiation, agents propose that the following plan fragments in partial satisfaction of system goals: agent A proposes A-a for g1, agent B selects B-d for g4, agent C chooses C-e for g2, and agent D proposes D-f for g3. Typical local criteria could be based on heuristics that utilize factors associated with the local exclusion set as well as an agent's perception of a goal's priority or importance.

As a result of these local decisions, subsequent exchange of information during negotiation reveals that the induced exclusion sets for the associated plan fragments are: for A-a, {{g2},{g3},{g4}}; for B-d, {{g1},{g2},{g3}}; for C-e, {{g1},{g3},{g4}}, and for D-f, {{g1},{g2},{g4}}. In addition, knowledge is gained in agent A that proposed satisfaction of g3 and g4 requires A-e and A-f, in agent C that proposed satisfaction of g1 and g3 makes use of C-c and C-f, and in agent D that other agents propose to satisfy g2 in ways that require use of D-e. Each agent can now examine its own local exclusion sets and its induced exclusion sets to learn that these choices are compatible in the sense that no local constraints on resource availability will be violated by the proposed actions. Thus, a globally consistent set of plans has been determined.

It is certainly possible (and even probable) that agents will not arrive at a globally consistent choice of plans on a first attempt. Any choice resulting in a perceived unavoidable violation of constraints in any agent can be detected through examination of exclusion sets and induced exclusion sets. Indeed, the interested reader can find an example of a case in which an overconstrained problem is handled and a satisficing solution found through multistage negotiation using these reasoning mechanisms in reference [Conry *et al.* 1988]. The discussion in that paper is primarily focused on the negotiation process and its example is illustrated on the level of interagent transactions during negotiation.

11.4   Status and Concluding Remarks

In this paper, we have presented mechanisms whereby an agent in a distributed planning system whose agents are myopic can assess and reason about the nonlocal impact of local decisions. A process of multistage negotiation involving an iterative exchange of nonlocal impact information in the form of induced exclusion sets results in a monotonic aggregation of nonlocal knowledge that leads the agents to a convergent view.

Algorithms for determining the conflict, exclusion, and infeasibility sets associated with a plan fragment have been developed and implemented. In addition, mechanisms for transitive propagation have been devised, allowing an agent to incorporate the knowledge it acquires in its local data structures and reason using that new knowledge. A system utilizing these mechanisms in distributed planning for service restoral in communication systems has been implemented in our distributed simulation facility [Conry *et al.* 1988], [MacIntosh and Conry 1987].

Acknowledgements

This work was supported, in part, by the Air Force Systems Command, Rome Air Development Center, Griffiss Air Force Base, New York 13441-5700, and the Air Force Office of Scientific Research, Bolling AFB, DC 20332 under Contract No. F30602-85-C-0008. This contract supports the Northeast Artificial Intelligence Consortium (NAIC).

References

[Conry *et al.* 1988] S. E. Conry, R. A. Meyer, and V. R. Lesser, "Multistage Negotiation in Distributed Planning," in A. Bond and L. Gasser, eds., *Readings in Distributed Artificial Intelligence*, Morgan Kaufman, August 1988.

[Davis and Smith 1983] R. Davis and R. G. Smith, "Negotiation as a Metaphor for Distributed Problem Solving," *Artificial Intelligence*, vol. 20, no. 1, January 1983, pp. 63–109.

[Lesser and Corkill 1981] V. R. Lesser and D. D. Corkill, "Functionally Accurate, Cooperative Distributed Systems," *IEEE Transactions on Systems, Man, and Cybernetics*, vol. SMC-11, no. 1, January 1981, pp. 81–96.

[MacIntosh and Conry 1987] D. J. MacIntosh and S. E. Conry, "SIMULACT: A Generic Tool for Simulating Distributed Systems," *Proceedings of the Eastern Simulation Conference*, April 1987.

[Smith 1980] R. G. Smith, "The Contract Net Protocol: High Level Communication and Control in a Distributed Problem Solver," *IEEE Transactions on Systems, Man, and Cybernetics*, vol. SMC-10, No. 12, December 1980.

[Smith and Davis 1981] R. G. Smith and R. Davis, "Frameworks for Cooperation in Distributed Problem Solving," *IEEE Transactions on Systems, Man, and Cybernetics*, vol. SMC-11, no. 1, January 1981, pp. 61–70.

S. E. Conry, R. A. Meyer, and R. P. Pope
Clarkson University
Potsdam, NY 13676

Chapter 12

An Object-oriented Multiple Agent Planning System

M. Kamel and A. Syed

Abstract

This chapter describes an object-oriented solution to the problem of generating coordinated, concurrent, actions involving multiple agents, such as robots, to transform an initial state of a given world into a desired goal state. The solution views the agents as subplanners, each of which generates a plan to solve a subproblem of the given planning problem. The partitioning into subproblems is performed by applying an "object-oriented decomposition" concept. In this concept, the decomposition of the problem is based on assigning each agent specific objects to act on.

This chapter also describes the structure of a multiagent planning system based on the proposed approach. This structure contains five modules: User Interface, Problem Decomposition, Subplanners, Constraint Analyzer, and Scheduler. These modules are supported by a knowledge base that includes knowledge about the objects, agents, relationships between objects, and agents' capabilities. The functionality of each of these modules and the overall control structure of the system are discussed. The potential application of the proposed planning system is illustrated by an example.[1]

---

[1]Part of this work was presented at the *2nd International Conference on Expert Systems and the Leading Edge in Production Planning and Control*, South Carolina, 1988.

12.1 Introduction

Planning in artificial intelligence refers to the process of generating a sequence of actions to achieve a given goal. Earlier planners have mainly produced plans that are executable by a single agent, such as a robot arm. These planners, referred to as single agent planning systems, have been applied to a wide variety of application domains. Applications tackled by these systems include job shop scheduling for turbine production using ISIS II [Fox 1982], electronic circuit design using NASL [McDermott 1978], mechanical engineers apprentice supervision by NOAH [Sacerdoti 1977], and aircraft carrier mission planning by AIRPLAN [Masui 1983].

There has been a growing interest in the field of Distributed Artificial Intelligence (DAI). DAI is concerned with the application of artificial intelligence to coordinate the activities of multiple distributed agents, such as robots in Flexible Manufacturing Systems (FMS), in order to achieve a common task or a goal. Planning in DAI, typically referred to as Multiple Agent Planning (MAP), involves generating *synchronized, concurrent* plans for agents to achieve a given goal.

MAP is particularly significant in manufacturing, where it plays a critical role in the integration of product design and fabrication. Planning of manufacturing processes, called *process planning*, involves translating the engineering design information, regarding certain products, into a process plan containing an appropriate sequence of operations for agents (robots and/or machines) to manufacture these products.

Increased efficiency is desirable in two aspects of process planning: plan generation and plan execution. Generation of a process plan by conventional methods requires a significant amount of time and experience. Attempts to increase the efficiency have resulted in a number of automated process planning methodologies, including CAM-I [Link 1983], GENPLAN [Hegland 1981], and CADCAM [Chang and Wysk 1981]. The automation of process planning is viewed as a means of bridging the gap between computer aided design (CAD) and computer aided manufacturing (CAM), and increasing the efficiency of the overall system [Rosenbaum 1983].

Automated process planners have thus far examined primarily the means for increasing the efficiency with which the plans are generated. The next step in further increasing the efficiency of the system is to generate coordinated plans that can be executed concurrently by multiple agents. This paper presents an object-oriented approach for multiple agent planning to produce *synchronized, concurrent* plans for agents to achieve a given goal. Part of this work has been discussed in [Kamel and Syed 1988].

12.2   Related Work

Among the important research issues concerning MAP are the decomposition of the main task or the goal into subtasks for individual agents (*problem decomposition*) and the actual process of generating the sequence of actions for each agent (*plan generation*).

In the area of problem decomposition, [Lansky and Fogelsong 1987] have proposed a strategy that *partitions* the planning domain based on the notion of locality. In this strategy, the domain properties and constraints are localized into independent regions of activity, in order to achieve fewer, manageable, and easily identifiable interactions between these regions. Such a partitioning method depends very much on the explicit knowledge of the underlying interactions in the domain, and it is mainly suited for environments that require containment of these interactions. Moreover, it is inappropriate when a large number of interactions, which cannot be readily identified prior to the planning process, may exist in the domain.

[Smith and Davis 1981] have proposed the concept of *negotiation* as a means for assigning decomposed subtasks to agents. In this concept, the agents (potential contractors) submit their bids on subtasks, for which they are suited, to an agent (manager) with subtasks to be solved. The manager awards the contract for solving these subtasks to the most appropriate agents based on their bids. The main limitation of this concept is that it assumes that one can partition the main task into appropriate subtasks prior to their assignment to individual agents through the process of negotiation.

[Lesser and Erman 1980] have proposed a model for distributed problem solving in connection with their experimentation with the HEARSAY-II speech interpretation system [Erman 1980]. Their distributed model consists of a network of systems (nodes), each of which is capable of performing significant local processing in a self-directed way. The problem is decomposed with the goal of minimizing the internode communication relative to intranode processing. The information available to each node may be incomplete or inconsistent with respect to the information of other nodes. The strength of their model lies in its emphasis on handling the uncertainty resulting from the distribution as an integral part of the network problem solving process. The HEARSAY-II architecture and the application area appears to be suitable for the decomposition required by this model. Issues related to control distribution and selection of an appropriate network configuration need to be resolved before the applicability of this approach can be generalized.

In the context of generalizing single agent planning to a distributed environment, [Corkill 1979] distributed the hierarchical planning approach of NOAH [Sacerdoti 1977]. Corkill assumed a problem decomposition based on allocating conjunctive subgoals to different processors. In his paper, he noted that this approach may not guarantee a close correlation between the spatial distribution of the planning process and the spatial distribution of environmental information and of effectors required during plan execution. In generating the plan, distributed NOAH makes use of send and receive messages to communicate changes and effects resulting from actions. This can contribute significantly to the complexity of generating the plan due to the fact that messages have to be generated for each assertion and deletion that occur in the world model.

Most of the work related to *plan generation* has been in the area of knowledge representation and plan synchronization. [Georgeff 1986] examined the knowledge representation of events in a multiagent domain. He constructed a model of atomic actions and events to help in determining whether or not two or more actions in the plan can be performed simultaneously. [Stuart 1985] and [Georgeff 1983] addressed the synchronization aspects of multiagent planning with the assumption that the original goal has been decomposed into subtasks for agents and their separate plans have been generated to solve these subtasks. To synchronize these plans, they have described a mechanism that avoids generation of all possible interleavings of operations, based solely on the analysis of the conditions specified in the actions. However, as the agents' actions are assumed to be largely independent of one another, the need for modification or regeneration of the plans to accommodate the effects of other agents' actions was not considered.

To a large extent, the *problem decomposition* and the *plan generation* aspects of multiagent planning have been examined in isolation from one another. The object-oriented multiagent planning approach, presented in this paper, is an attempt at integrating both the *problem decomposition* and the *plan generation* aspects into a single framework, thereby relating planning decomposition to execution decomposition. The approach allows an arbitrary number of implicit interactions to exist between agents. Unlike most other approaches [Georgeff 1983, Stuart 1985] that attempt to synchronize the plans of agents after they have been generated independently for each agent and do not allow modifications to the generated plans, our approach incorporates synchronization during the plan generation process and allows modifications of the plans as needed to accommodate the effects of agents' actions on one another.

One of the main advantages of our approach is that it can be used as a *testbed* to facilitate the analysis and comparison of different planning configurations based on the capabilities of the agents, characteristics of the multiagent domain, and assignment of the subtasks to the agents.

262

12.3 An Object-oriented Approach to Multiagent Planning

The main objective of the object-oriented approach is to exploit the concurrency between agents. This approach is similar to the data parallel approach in parallel processing [Hillis and Steele 1986]. In this approach, the aim is to extract the parallelism that exists in a program at the data level; the computations (operations) are performed simultaneously across sets of data. Similarly, the object-oriented approach to multiagent planning treats the objects in the domain as data and generates the parallel operations to be performed by the agents in the domain.

By viewing the world as a set of objects and agents to manipulate the objects, the planning problem becomes the problem of finding the sequence of concurrent actions by the agents to transform the initial state (an instantiation of objects, agents, and their relationship) of the world into the desired goal state. The agents in the world are viewed as subplanners that generate plans to solve subproblems. The subproblems are produced by applying a partitioning concept called the *"object-oriented problem decomposition."* The decomposition of the problem is based on assigning each agent specific objects to act on. The subproblems are defined in terms of the initial and goal substates involving the objects assigned to subplanners. Thus, $subplan_j$ consists of a sequence of actions (operations) on objects, assigned to $agent_j$, to achieve the final state of these objects. Figure 12.1 conceptualizes the relationships between objects, agents, and operations.

The approach allows each subplanner to generate a subplan for its agents involving only those actions that manipulate its objects and pose actions that affect other objects as constraints to their corresponding subplanners. While the subplanner needs to satisfy the constraints for its objects from other subplanners, it considers the constraints it generates to be the responsibility of other subplanners. Thus, each subplan has to accommodate the constraints generated by other subplanners as part of its plan to solve the assigned subproblem. The overall plan is a sequence of concurrent actions of all subplans. The constraints represent the coordination points among the agents.

12.4 System Structure

A planning system, named OMAPS (Object-oriented Multiple Agent Planning System), has been designed based on the approach described above. It consists of five modules: User Interface, Problem Decomposition, Subplanners, Constraint Analyzer, and Scheduler. The modules are supported by a knowledge base that contains knowledge of the objects, agents

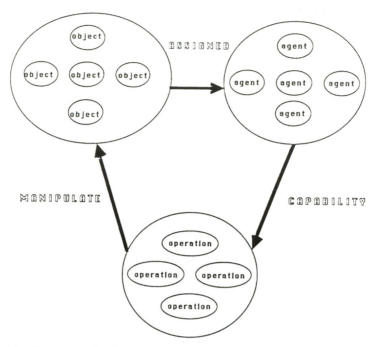

Figure 12.1: Conceptual relationship between objects, agents, and operations

and their capabilities, relationships between objects, and available actions (operations) for each agent. The system structure is shown in Figure 12.2. In the following sections, we describe the functionality of each module.

12.4.1   User Interface

The User Interface (UI) module is designed to allow the user to define the multiagent environment and present to the user the generated multiagent plan. The UI guides the user in building the domain knowledge (objects, relations, operators and agents) and specifying the problem definition (initial state and desired final state of the world). UI achieves this using two main functions called *Define-Domain* and *Define-Problem*.

To build the domain knowledge, the *Define-Domain* function allows the user to define knowledge structures called *Object-Class*, *Object*, *Relation*, *Agent*, and *Operator* that capture the specific knowledge about the types of objects, relations between objects, types of agents, and types of operations agents can perform in the multiagent domain. These structures are represented in the knowledge base to be used by the Problem Decomposition

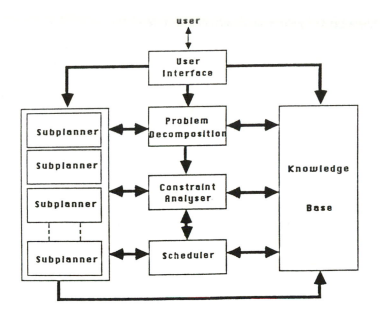

Figure 12.2: Multiagent planning system structure

module, the Subplanners module, and the Constraint Analyzer module.

The *Object-Class* knowledge structure is useful in grouping objects with similar attributes. It describes the name given to the class, relationships and operators (as defined by the user) that apply to the objects belonging to this class, the attributes that are common to all members of the class, and default attributes that are expected to be valid in the absence of information. For example, we may group objects, such as nails, screws, and bolts, into a class called *FASTENER*, defined as

OBJECT CLASS   *{ Example of an Object Class }*

1. *NAME*: FASTENER

2. *OPERATORS*: (Pickup, Insert)

3. *RELATIONS*: (on, heldby)

4. *CLASS − ATTRIBUTES*: (length, radius)

5. *CLASS − DEFAULTS*: (content: steel)

As specified by the relations in the class, an object belonging to this class can be on the table or held by an agent. According to the operators in the structure, an agent can pick up this object or insert it into another object. The shape of the objects in this class are defined by the length and radius dimensions. By default the objects in this class are made up of steel.

The specific objects in the domain are instantiated using the knowledge structure, called *Object*, which includes the name of the object, the name of the class the object belongs to, the allowable relationships it may have with other objects and agents, and the attributes that are specific to this object. An example of an object called BOLT that belongs to the class *FASTENER* is represented as

OBJECT   { *Example of an Object Instance* }

1. *NAME*: BOLT

2. *CLASS*: FASTENER

3. *RELATIONS*: (inside, on, heldby)

4. *OBJECT − ATTRIBUTES*: (length 1) (radius 0.25) (threaded)

In addition to the relations specified in the class, the object *Bolt* includes the relation *inside* that states that it can be inside another object. Similarly, the attribute list of the object contains the specific attribute *threaded*, as well as the specific information about the attributes, length and radius, defined by its class.

Relationships between objects are represented using a structure that includes the name of the relation and the attributes of the relation. The attributes of a relation may be used to provide more specific information about the relationship between two objects. For instance, to describe a relationship such as object1 is attached to object2 at some predefined coordinate position (x1,y2), we may use the following relation:

RELATION   { *Example of a Relation* }

1. *NAME*: attachedto

2. *ATTRIBUTES*: (x1,y1)

An operation (action) is applied by an agent to manipulate its objects. However, when the agent applies the action, it can affect objects belonging to other agents. For instance, an agent's action may require certain relationships to hold on objects belonging to another agent, before the action can be applied. Similarly, execution of an agent's action, may change the relationships on objects assigned to other agents.

In order to adequately capture the affects of an agent's actions, a knowledge structure called *Operator* represents the action using a combination of declarative and procedural knowledge. The *Operator* structure contains the name of the action, a list of preconditions that must be satisfied before the action can be applied, add and delete lists that state

266

the assertions that are to be added and deleted once the action is applied, and a call to a procedure, named *Generate_Constraint* to generate the constraints for other agents affected by the action. The *Generate_Constraint* procedure requires as its argument the name of the operator that calls this procedure.

For example, the operation of inserting object X inside object Y can be represented as

OPERATOR   { *Insert object X inside object Y* }

1. *NAME*: INSERT(X Y)

2. *PRECONDITIONS*: *forall Z* (NOT (Z inside Y)) AND (X heldby Robot)

3. *DELETELIST*: (X heldby Robot)

4. *ADDLIST*: (X inside Y)

5. *CONSTRAINT – PROC*: Generate_Constraint(INSERT(X Y))

The knowledge about the agents present in the domain is represented by a knowledge structure, called *Agent*. This structure includes the name of the agent, its Communication Capability (CC), and its Operational Capabilities (OC). The CC subfield of the structure maintains the list of names of those agents that have the ability to directly communicate with this agent. Communications with agents, whose name is not on this list, are performed indirectly through agents on the list. Operational capabilities of the agent are those actions that an agent is capable of performing on the objects in the domain and are expressed as a list of operators. The following is an example of an agent, named Robot_I, that can communicate with Robot_II and can pick up an object:

AGENT   { *Example of an Agent* }

1. *NAME*: Robot_I

2. *CC*: (Robot_II)

3. *OC*: (Pickup)

The problem definition function of the UI allows the user to specify initial and desired final states of the world in terms of the objects, agents, and their relationships. Each state is defined by selecting instantiated *Object* and *Agent* structures corresponding to the objects and agents in the state and by mapping among them the relationships they hold in the state.

12.4.2   Problem Decomposition Module

The Problem Decomposition (PD) module interacts with the UI and Subplanners modules. This module incorporates the object-oriented problem decomposition strategy that specifies the assignment of objects to subplanners.

267

This module permits the user to test a variety of scenarios (planning configurations) based on the information provided to the UI module in the form of domain knowledge and problem definition. The planning configurations are defined in terms of the number of agents available to execute the plan, the assignment of objects to each agent, and capabilities of agents. The PD module uses this information to generate subproblem definitions and subdomain knowledge to be passed to the subplanners. The subproblem definition for a subplanner consists of the initial and final substates (objects and their relationships) of the objects assigned to its agent.

The PD module is also responsible for creating subplanners for the agents specified in the configuration. It assigns operators to the created subplanners based on the capabilities of the corresponding agents.

Selection of Planning Configuration

The performance of the multiagent plan for a given configuration depends to a large extent on how the objects are assigned to the agents. Generally, it is difficult to accurately predict the performance of multiagent plans solely from the assignment of objects to agents before the plans are generated. Certainly for some problems, it will be infeasible to generate and compare multiagent plans using all possible assignment of objects to agents, especially when the number of objects is large.

One possibility is to seek the user's assistance in prescribing a set of configurations. The user may have some knowledge about physical or logical constraints that may help in selecting the planning configuration. Developing automated techniques for assigning the objects to agents and selecting the best configuration(s) is an interesting research problem on its own and is currently being investigated by the authors. For the purpose of the current work we explain a simple and preliminary technique in which objects are assigned to agents according to the following two principles:

- Divide and share the task equally among the agents: The objective of this principle is to utilize each agent equally in order to improve the concurrency in multiagent plans. We divide the task equally among the agents by assigning approximately the same number of objects to all agents. This division of tasks is based on the assumption that the number of actions required to achieve the goal is well distributed over the objects.

- Avoid situations in which objects are assigned to different agents when a linearity (order) of the actions to be performed on the objects is apparent. Thus, actions on one object cannot be performed until certain actions on another object are completed.

268

One can predict such information from the relationships between objects given in the initial and final states. For example, in the relationship (A on B) (C on D), an agent cannot pick up object B until object A is picked up by an agent since A is on top of B. However, C and A, which do not hold any relationships, can be picked up by two different agents, concurrently. Thus, in this example, we may wish to assign A and B to the same agent and assign C to a different agent.

Based on the above mentioned principles, one can obtain possible assignments for each agent by applying a simple graph partitioning algorithm. The algorithm uses a graph to represent the initial and final states. The nodes in the graph denote the objects in the domain and the edges between two objects represent the relationship that exists between these objects in the initial or the final state. The graph is partitioned into subgraphs, each of which is associated with a unique agent in the domain. The algorithm partitions the graph such that the subgraphs contain approximately the same number of objects or nodes and that the number of edges that connect one subgraph to another are minimized. The objects in each subgraph are assigned to the agent associated with that subgraph. It should be noted that the above method may not be suitable for problems where the number of objects in the domain is small and/or the goals require a long sequence of actions on some objects and not on the others.

12.4.3   Subplanners Module

The Subplanners module consists of a number of subplanners that are created by the PD module. Each subplanner is associated with an agent in the domain, and it receives subproblem definition (initial and final substates) along with the necessary subdomain information for its agent from the PD module. The initial and final (goal) substates for a subplanner consist of objects assigned to its agent and their relationships in the initial and final states. In addition, it may receive *Interagent Constraints* (actions of other subplanners) from the Constraint Analyzer during the planning process.

The main function of each subplanner is to produce a subplan to achieve the subgoals (subproblem) involving the objects assigned to its agent. The subplan, generated by each subplanner, must lead to the desired final state and, at the same time, satisfy any of the *Interagent Constraints* imposed on the subplanner by other subplanners.

Interagent Interactions

Each subplanner may have *Interagent Constraints* to be satisfied by those subplanners that are affected by the actions in its subplan. The *Interagent Constraints* are generated by the actions in the subplan using the constraint procedure *Generate_Constraints*, indicated in the definition of the operator. The constraint procedure requires the name of the operator (using this procedure) as its argument. The argument allows the constraint procedure to access the preconditions, delete and add conditions of the operator, and determine the objects involved. Based on the objects' assignment to agents, the constraint procedure generates *Interagent Constraints* for those subplanners whose objects are affected by the operation. The Constraint Analyzer module manages the constraints and monitors their satisfaction by the subplanners.

An interagent constraint is represented as the instantiated action of the subplan that affects other agents. By posing the action that affects another agent as interagent constraint, the subplanner receiving the interagent constraint is able to determine not only how it affects its agent's objects from the add and delete conditions of the action, but also what the action *demands* from it by examining the preconditions of the action which involve the objects assigned to its agent. Consider a simple scenario with two robots, RI and RII, and two objects, A and B. Objects A and B are assigned to RI and RII, respectively. Assume that RI is holding A and it decides to insert object A into object B using the operator INSERT(X Y), described in section 4.1. In this case, the interagent constraint posed by the subplanner of RI to the subplanner of RII is the same instantiated action, INSERT(A B). The demand for subplanner of RII consists of the precondition, *forall* Z (NOT (Z inside B)), and its effect on RII is described by the addlist, (A inside B); the deletelist does not affect the subplanner of RII since it does not involve the object assigned to RII.

In order to satisfy an interagent constraint, the affected subplanner includes it within its subplan along with its own actions as an action of the agent, generating the constraint, To include an interagent constraint in the subplan, the subplanner must satisfy the *demands* of the interagent constraint. If for instance the subplanner is unable to satisfy the demands in the current situation (substate of the subplanner), it will attempt to include some actions of its own agent or other constraints in the subplan that may help to satisfy these demands. When the demands of the interagent constraint are satisfied, the subplanner updates the current substate using the add and delete conditions of the constraint that involve the objects belonging to this subplanner. Since a satisfied interagent constraint is treated as an action, it can also generate constraints for other agents. The constraint procedure ensures that these new interagent constraints are not generated for the original subplanner.

While, the interagent constraints that are satisfied by the subplan are not executed by its agent, they serve as synchronization points between the agent that generated the constraint and the agent whose subplan satisfies these constraints. Nonblocking *send* and blocking *wait* primitives are used to synchronize the multiagent plan. When an agent encounters a satisfied interagent constraint during the execution of its subplan it sends a message, consisting of the satisfied constraint operator, to the agent that generated this constraint. Similarly, when the agent encounters the action that generated the interagent constraint during the execution of the subplan, it must wait until the corresponding *send* messages from the agents that are affected by this action are received indicating that the constraint is satisfied.

Our representation of interaction differs from other multiagent approaches. In distributed NOAH [Corkill 1979], the interactions between processors occur for each and every assertion and deletion of facts in the world model, which may introduce a significant complexity in dealing with interactions, particularly when there are large number of actions involved in the multiagent plans. In contrast, we represent interactions as interagent constraints which are actions of agents that affect other agents. This representation of interaction allows for greater degree of cooperation between agents than most other approaches [Georgeff 1983, Stuart 1985], since one agent is able to demand from other agents certain conditions to hold on some objects which only these agents can satisfy by manipulating their objects. By posing actions as interagent interactions, our representation avoids generating multiple interactions for each and every assertion or deletion that are caused by the same action. Moreover, it limits the number of such interactions to those actions that affect objects of other agents.

Subplan Generation

The world model is distributed among the subplanners as substates. Each substate for a subplanner represents its agent, the assigned objects, the relationships that these objects hold with its agent and objects assinged to other agents, at a particular instant. Each subplanner is responsible for maintaining and updating its own substates to reflect the effect of actions on its objects. The synchronization among the substates of various subplanners is carried out solely through interagent constraints.

The subplanner for an $agent_j$ employs a tree search algorithm to generate the subplan. Each $node_i$ in the tree carries the following information:

- $action_i$: action which leads to $node_i$. It can either be an operator of $agent_j$ or a constraint, operator of another agent affecting objects of $agent_j$. Actions represent the edges in the tree leading to the nodes.

- $type_i$: indicates the type of $action_i$ with a value of (*send*, *agent_name*), (*wait*, *agents_name*) or *execute*. A type (*send*, *agent_name*) implies that $action_i$ is a constraint from the agent specified by *agent_name*, and a send message must be sent to

271

that agent. An action type (*wait, agents_name*) means that $action_i$ affects objects assigned to agents specified in *agents_name*, and, hence, $agent_j$ must wait for a send message from the affected agents before executing the action or sending a message if the action is a constraint from another agent. As only one constraint, $constraint_i$, can be generated by $action_i$ for another agent, the $constraint_i$ itself is used as the message. A type *execute* is used when $action_i$ is $agent_j$'s own operator that does not affect objects of other agents. In this case, action can be executed without any interactions from other agents.

- $substate_i$: a description of substate, in terms of relationships involving $agent_j$ and its objects, which results from applying $action_i$ to the substate at the parent node of $node_i$.

- $InConstraints_i$: operators of other agents, affecting $agent_j$ that have to be satisfied in the path from $node_i$ to the goal node.

- $SatisfiedInConstraints_i$: constraints that have been satisfied thus far in the path from the root node to $node_i$.

- $OutConstraints_i$: list of constraints generated by $action_i$ for other agents.

- $distance_i$: measure of the distance of $node_i$ from goal node, computed as number of remaining unsatisfied constraints in $InConstraints_i$ + the number of differences in the relationships that objects of $agent_j$ hold in $substate_i$ and the goal substate.

- $parent_i$: parent node of $node_i$.

The root node contains the initial substate, the constraints from other agents, if any, and its distance value from the goal node. A path in the tree leading from the root node to a node with a distance of zero is considered to be the subplan. This path not only achieves the goal substate but satisfies the constraints from other agents, as well. Constraints are satisfied by treating them as operators of other agents and including them in the subplan.

Starting by the root node, the following algorithm generates a subplan by repeatedly expanding the best node, $node_i$, where best refers to the minimum distance from the goal node, in an attempt to find a node with a zero distance from the goal node:

Algorithm Generate-Subplan

- $node_i$ = root node in the tree

- While (There are nodes in the tree that have not been selected previously for expansion) and ($distance_i > 0$) do

  1. For each $constraint_k \in InConstraints_i$ do
     - If (TestCPrecond($constraint_k$, $node_i$) == successful) then
       (a) $node_k$ = ExpandNode($constraint_k$, $node_i$)
       (b) $OutConstraints_k$ = list of constraints generated by invoking the procedure specified in the definition of $constraint_k$.
       (c) If $OutConstraints_k \neq$ empty then
           $type_k = (wait$, name of the agents affected by the $constraint_k)$
           else
           $type_k = (send$, name of the agent that generated $constraint_k)$

  2. For each $operator_k \in agent_j$'s operators do
     - If (TestPrecond($operator_k$, $node_i$) == successful) then
       (a) $node_k$ = ExpandNode($operator_k$, $node_i$)
       (b) $OutConstraints_k$ = list of constraints generated by invoking the procedure specified in the definition of $operator_k$.
       (c) If $OutConstraints_k \neq$ empty then
           $type_k = (wait$, name of the agents affected by the $operator_k)$
           else
           $type_k = execute$

  3. $node_i$ = node with the smallest distance in the tree and has not yet been considered for expansion (Choose the oldest node to break the tie).

- End While

- If $distance_i = 0$ then

  $subplan$ = sequence of actions and their types extracted from the nodes in the path leading from the root node to the current node, $node_i$

  SubplanOutConstraints = list of constraints, from the subplan, extracted from $OutConstraints$ field of each node in the path leading from the root node to $node_i$.

  else report that a solution cannot be found

End of Generate-Subplan

During each iteration, the algorithm examines, separately, each of the constraint operators in $InConstraints_i$ and each of the operators for $agent_j$ as possible candidates for expanding the current node, $node_i$. The procedure $TestCPrecond$ tests the preconditions of constraint operators, while the procedure $TestPrecond$ checks the preconditions of $agent_j$'s operators. In both of these cases, if the preconditions are successful, $node_i$ is expanded into a new node and added to the tree. The iterations end either when a path from the root node to the goal node is found or when no more nodes can be expanded. If a path to the goal node is found, the algorithm ends by extracting the subplan and its constraints, $SubplanConstraints$, for other agents, from this path; otherwise, it notifies that a solution is not found.

Procedure $TestCPrecond$ tests only those preconditions of $constraint_k$ that involve $agent_j$'s objects, while ignoring the rest of the preconditions. Procedure $TestPrecond$ tests the validity of each of the preconditions of $operator_k$ in $substate_i$. However, the test for a given precondition is similar in both procedures. In the event that a precondition does not hold in $substate_i$, two specific cases are analyzed by each procedure regarding the assignment of the objects in the relationship involved. Suppose that the relation used in the precondition is between $object_m$ and $object_n$, i.e., ($object_m$ $relation$ $object_n$), then the two cases are:

- $object_m$ is assigned to $agent_j$: In this case, because $object_m$ can only be manipulated by $agent_j$, the action cannot be applied until $agent_j$ satisfies the precondition. The procedure returns a message indicating that the preconditions of $action_k$ at $node_i$ is not satisfied.

- $object_m$ is assigned to $agent_l$, where $l \neq j$: In this case, $agent_l$ is assumed responsible for satisfying this condition. The precondition is ignored provided that it meets the following two conditions concerning the harmful and helpful interactions between $agent_j$ and $agent_l$:

    - The precondition does not harm $agent_l$ by forcing it to undo the affect of its earlier actions. This condition is tested by examining the add and delete list of satisfied constraint operators in $SatisfiedInConstraints_i$ list. The procedure returns a failure message if it finds a precondition that delineates an earlier action of $agent_l$.

    - There are no unsatisfied constraints from $agent_l$ that satisfy this precondition. This condition ensures that the action, whose precondition is being tested, occurs in the subplan after those actions of $agent_l$ that help to satisfy its precondition. This condition is tested by examining the add and delete lists of unsatisfied constraint operators in $InConstraints_i$ list.

Both TestCPrecond and TestPrecond procedures return a *successful* message if no failure conditions exist for each of the tested preconditions.

The procedure ExpandNode expands $node_i$ into another node, $node_k$, by applying $action_k$. The algorithm for ExpandNode is as follows:

Algorithm ExpandNode $(action_k, node_i)$

- create a new node, $node_k$

- $substate_k = \text{ApplyOperation}(substate_i, action_k)$

- $InConstraints_k = InConstraints_i$

- $SatisfiedInConstraints_k = SatisfiedInConstraints_i$

- If $action_k$ is a constraint from $InConstraints_k$ then remove it from $InConstraints_k$ and add it to $SatisfiedInConstraints_k$

- $distance_k =$ number of constraints in $InConstraints_k$ + number of differences in the relationships that objects of $agent_j$ hold in $substate_k$ and the goal substate.

- $parent_k = node_i$

- return($node_k$)

End of ExpandNode

The ApplyOperation algorithm returns a new substate, $substate_k$, by applying add and delete conditions of $action_k$ to $substate_i$. The new substate reflects the effect of $action_k$ on $agent_j$'s objects in $substate_i$. The algorithm first sets the $substate_k$ to the same assertions as in $substate_i$. It then adds only those conditions from the add list to $substate_k$ that affect the objects assigned to $agent_j$. Next, it deletes from $substate_k$ only those conditions of the delete list that involve the objects assigned to $agent_j$.

12.4.4 Constraint Analyzer

The task of the Constraint Analyzer (CA) module is to ensure that all of the *Interagent Constraints* resulting from generated subplans are satisfied by those subplanners that are affected by them. Thus, one of the function of the CA module is to gather the *Interagent Constraints* from the subplans produced in the most recent execution cycle of the subplanners. The gathered constraints are stored in a *Constraint Table* whose columns indicate the names of the subplanners generating the constraints and the rows represent the subplanners affected by the constraints. A new execution cycle will be initiated if new constraints are generated. If a subplanner fails to satisfy any of the constraints in its column entries and no new constraints have been generated after the current cycle, the CA module reports to the user that a solution cannot be reached.

275

12.4.5   Scheduler

The primary function of the scheduler is to supervise the execution of the Subplanners. From the operational point of view, the Scheduler considers the Subplanners as autonomous processes that can be in one of the two conditions, *ready* or *idle*. A *ready* status implies that the subplanner has been assigned either a subgoal (by the PD module) or a new set of *Interagent Constraints* (by the CA module), and, thus, it is executed by the Scheduler. Each execution of the subplanner generates a subplan that achieves its goal and satisfies the assigned constraints. At the end of each execution, the status of the subplanner is changed to *idle*.

12.5   Control Structure

The control structure of OMAPS involves the coordination between the five modules. To generate the multiagent plan, the user first interacts with the UI module to provide adequate domain knowledge and problem definition. Next, the control is passed to the PD module, where the user formulates a specific planning configuration. The planning configuration includes number of agents involved in the multiagent plan, objects assigned to each agent and agent's capability. The PD module, then, creates subplanners corresponding to the agents in the planning configuration, and generates the subproblem definitions (initial and final substates) for each subplanner using the assignment of objects to their agents and the problem definition (initial and final states). The initial and final substates for a subplanner consist of only its objects and their relationships in the initial and final states. The PD sets the status of each subplanner to *ready*, so they can be executed by the Scheduler.

Once the problem is decomposed by the PD module, the control is passed to the scheduler. The subplans for the subproblems are obtained through the execution of *ready* subplanners. Execution of a subplanner results in a subplan containing sequence of actions on objects assigned to its agent. A number of iterations may be required (depending on the generated interactions) before reaching the final plan. In each iteration, the Scheduler executes the current set of ready subplanners. The generated subplan attempts to satisfy both the goal state, starting from the initial state, and the assigned *Interagent Constraints*. At the end of each iteration, the status of the subplanners returns to *idle*.

After each iteration, the CA module is invoked to determine whether or not a new iteration of subplanning is necessary based on the constraints gathered in the *Constraint Table*. It assigns the new constraints to subplanners that are affected by them and sets their execution status to *ready*. A *ready* status of one or more subplanners signals the Scheduler to begin a new iteration of planning and execute the subplanners with *ready*

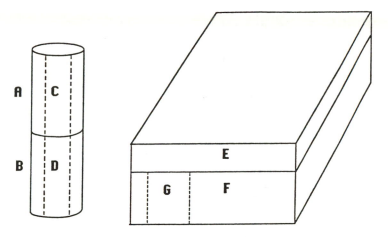

Figure 12.3: The raw material represented in terms of objects

status. The iterations end, when no new constraints can be generated. End of iterations is detected by having all of the subplanners in the *idle* state. A solution is obtained if, at the end of the iterations, the subplanners satisfy the constraints assigned to them and achieve their goal substates. The control is then passed to the UI module. The UI module then reports the results and in case of success displays to the user the multiagent plan consisting of subplans generated from the final iteration. The subplans are specified as sequences of agents' actions that contain the necessary synchronization points.

12.6 Example

To illustrate the potential application of OMAPS' methodology to the manufacturing domain, we consider the metal cutting problem of producing a desired part from raw material, as shown in Figures 12.3 and 12.4. We assume the availability of three agents (Robot I, II, and III), each of which is capable of performing the actions defined in Figure 12.5. These operations are high level specifications of detailed machine operations on objects. For example, the high level operation *REMOVE (X Y)* may be translated into two specific sequences of machine operations, such as *DRILL* and *BORE*.

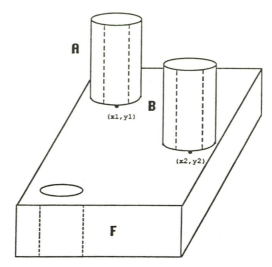

Figure 12.4: The desired part represented in terms of objects

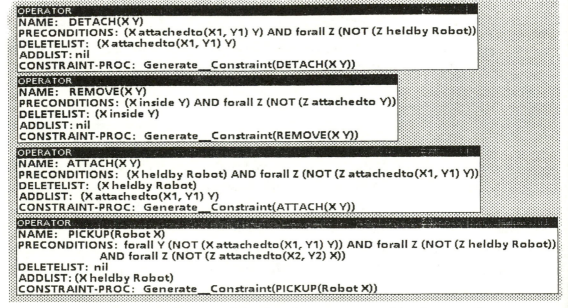

```
OPERATOR
NAME:  DETACH(X Y)
PRECONDITIONS: (X attachedto(X1, Y1) Y) AND forall Z (NOT (Z heldby Robot))
DELETELIST:  (X attachedto(X1, Y1) Y)
ADDLIST: nil
CONSTRAINT-PROC:  Generate__Constraint(DETACH(X Y))

OPERATOR
NAME:  REMOVE(X Y)
PRECONDITIONS: (X inside Y) AND forall Z (NOT (Z attachedto Y))
DELETELIST:  (X inside Y)
ADDLIST: nil
CONSTRAINT-PROC:  Generate__Constraint(REMOVE(X Y))

OPERATOR
NAME:  ATTACH(X Y)
PRECONDITIONS:  (X heldby Robot) AND forall Z (NOT (Z attachedto(X1, Y1) Y))
DELETELIST:  (X heldby Robot)
ADDLIST:  (X attachedto(X1, Y1) Y)
CONSTRAINT-PROC:  Generate__Constraint(ATTACH(X Y))

OPERATOR
NAME:  PICKUP(Robot X)
PRECONDITIONS:  forall Y (NOT (X attachedto(X1, Y1) Y)) AND forall Z (NOT (Z heldby Robot))
              AND forall Z (NOT (Z attachedto(X2, Y2) X))
DELETELIST: nil
ADDLIST: (X heldby Robot)
CONSTRAINT-PROC:  Generate__Constraint(PICKUP(Robot X))
```

Figure 12.5: Definitions of the domain operators used in the example

The Object classes in the example domain are based on the general structural similarities of possible objects (see [Bandyopadhyay 1986]). We define two special classes to be used here, corresponding to the shapes of the cylinder and the rectangle-prism, using the *object class* structures shown below. **OBJECT_CLASS** { *cylinder class* }

1. *NAME*: cylinder

2. *OPERATORS*: (Detach, Attach, Pickup, Remove)

3. *RELATIONS*: (inside, heldby, attachedto)

4. *CLASS − ATTRIBUTES*: (diameter, length)

5. *CLASS − DEFAULTS*: (nil)

OBJECT_CLASS { *rectangle-prism class* }

1. *NAME*: rectangle-prism

2. *OPERATORS*: (Detach, Attach, Pickup, Remove)

3. *RELATIONS*: (inside, heldby, attachedto)

4. *CLASS − ATTRIBUTES*: (length, base, height)

5. *CLASS − DEFAULTS*: (nil)

Each class describes the allowable relations and operations on the objects, belonging to the class, and the structural attributes of the class. For simplicity, we ignore the class defaults.

The specific instances of objects to be manipulated in the example domain are extracted from the description of the raw material and the required product by the user. The raw material and the part to be manufactured are conceptually viewed as set of objects, defined by the classes, that hold certain relationships. The objects have to be defined such that the agents are able to achieve the relationships these objects hold in the required part by manipulating them and their relationships in the initial material.

For the purpose of this example we may assume three relations: *heldby*, *inside*, and *attachedto*. The relation *heldby* is used when an object is held by a robot. The relation *inside* is used to describe an object being inside another object and the relation *attachedto(xcoordinate, ycoordinate)* is used to indicate that an object is attached to another object at the given coordinate (default coordinates are assumed in the absence of the attributes).

Figures 12.3 and 12.4 show the breakdown of the raw material and the part in terms of objects. Objects named A, B, C, D, and G are specific instances of the class defined above as *cylinder*, and objects called E and F belong to the class called *rectangle-prism*.

279

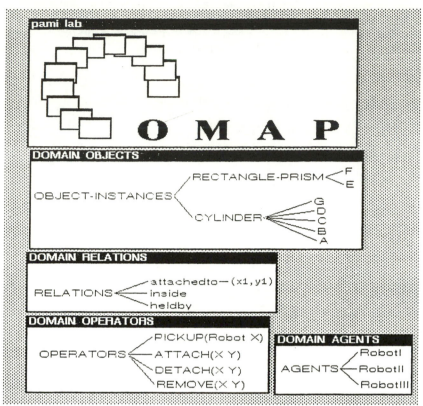

Figure 12.6: Domain objects, their classes, relations, operators and agents used in the example

Objects C, D, E, and G are not shown in Figure 12.4 since they are not part of the final product and their final destination is not significant, i.e., they may be considered waste. Figure 12.6 summarizes the domain knowledge used in this example. The initial and the final states, stated in terms of the objects and their relationships in the initial raw material and the desired part are listed in Table 12.1.

Once, the domain knowledge is acquired by the UI, we need to decompose the planning problem using the Problem Decomposition module. The assignment of objects to agents is based on the graph partitioning heuristic method suggested in section 12.4.2. Figure 12.7 combines the relationships in the initial and final substates in the form of a graph. The graph is partitioned into three subgraphs corresponding to the three agents. The maximum number of edges that connect any one subgraph to another is 1, and the sum of all edges connecting the subgraphs is 3. If we associate the subgraph I, II, and III, with the agents RI, RII, and RIII, we can assign objects A and C to Robot I, objects B and D to Robot II,

Table 12.1: Problem Definition for the Example

Initial State	Final State
(A attachedto B) (C inside A)	(A attachedto(x1,y1) F)
(D inside B) (E attachedto F)	(B attachedto(x2,y2) F)
(G inside F)	

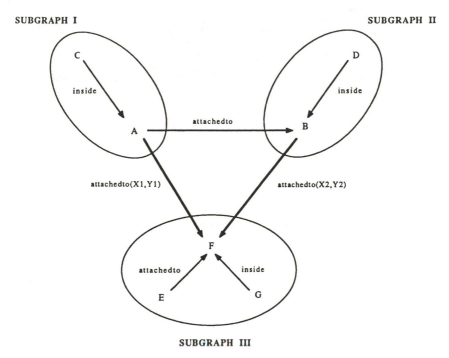

Figure 12.7: An example of partitioning the object relationship graph into subgraphs for agents

and objects E, F and G to Robot III. The assignment of objects to agents is summarized in Figure 12.8. Based on this assignment, PD module distributes the appropriate initial and final substates to the subplanners associated with Robot I, II, and III.

The subplan generated by each subplanner in the first iteration, based on the above assignment of objects, are listed in Tables 12.2, 12.3, and 12.4. The first column entries of each table show the sequence of actions in the subplan. The second column entries provide the type information about each action, the third column contain the objects of other agents affected by the action, and the third column shows relationships in the substates resulting from the execution of each action. The action type *execute* implies that the corresponding action can be executed as soon as the preceding action in the subplan is

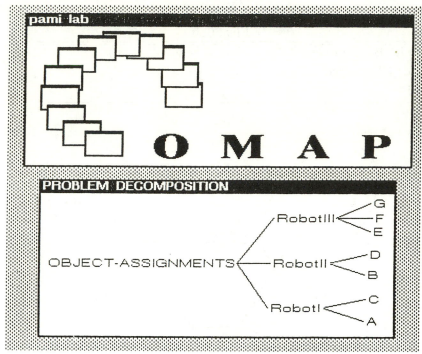

Figure 12.8: Assignment of domain objects to agents

completed. Actions with type *wait agent_name* are constraints for the agent, specified by *agent_name*, and, therefore, must wait for a corresponding *send* message from that agent before it can be executed. An action with type *send agent_name* is a constraint from the agent, specified by *agent_name*, and it indicates that the constraints have been satisfied.

A partial trace of the search tree generated by the subplanner of Robot I is illustrated in Figure 12.9. For simplicity, at each node we only show information about the *action*, its *type*, *substate*, $InConstraints$ (INC), $SatisfiedInConstraints$ (SINC), and *distance*. We also show only those immediate childrens of a node that have the minimum distance to the

Table 12.2: Subplan for Robot I (RI) Generated in the First Iteration

ACTIONS	TYPE	AFFECTED OBJECTS	SUBSTATE RELATIONSHIPS
			(A attachedto B) (C inside A)
Detach(A B)	wait RII	B	(C inside A)
Remove(C A)	execute		
Pickup(RI A)	execute		(A heldby RI)
Attach(A F)	wait RIII	F	(A attachedto(x1,y1) F)

282

Table 12.3: Subplan for Robot II (RII) Generated in the First Iteration

ACTIONS	TYPE	AFFECTED OBJECTS	SUBSTATE RELATIONSHIPS
			(A attachedto B) (D inside B)
Remove(D B)	wait RI	A	(A attachedto B)
Pickup(RII B)	execute		(B heldby RII)
Attach(B F)	wait RIII	F	(B attachedto(x2,y2) F)

Table 12.4: Subplan for Robot III (RIII) Generated in the First Iteration

ACTIONS	TYPE	AFFECTED OBJECTS	SUBSTATE RELATIONSHIPS
			(E attachedto F) (G inside F)
Detach(E F)	execute		(G inside F)
Remove(G F)	execute		

goal. The nodes are numbered according to their order of expansion. The path from the initial node to the node satisfying the goal for the subplanner consists of Node 1, Node 2, Node 4, Node 5, and Node 9, with Node 2 and Node 9 representing interagent constraints (indicated by type wait) for RII and RIII, respectively.

Table 12.5, summarizes the constraints generated by the subplans from the first iteration. The agents generating the constraints and agents affected by the constraints are shown by row and column entries, respectively.

In the second iteration, subplanners whose agents are affected by the constraints (listed in Table 12.5) generate new subplans to solve their subproblems as well as satisfying the constraints affecting them. The subplans generated in the second iteration are shown in Tables 12.6, 12.7, and 12.8. The constraints satisfied by the subplan are shown in italic.

A partial trace of the search tree generated by the subplanner of RI in second iteration is illustrated in Figure 12.10. The root node contains the Interagent Constraint operator, *Remove(D B)*, generated in the first iteration by subplanner of RII for RI's subplanner. The effect of this unsatisfied constraint is reflected in the distance value of the root node from

Table 12.5: Constraint Table for First Iteration

	Robot I	Robot II	Robot III
Robot I		Detach(A B)	Attach(A F)
Robot II	Remove(D B)		Attach(B F)
Robot III			

283

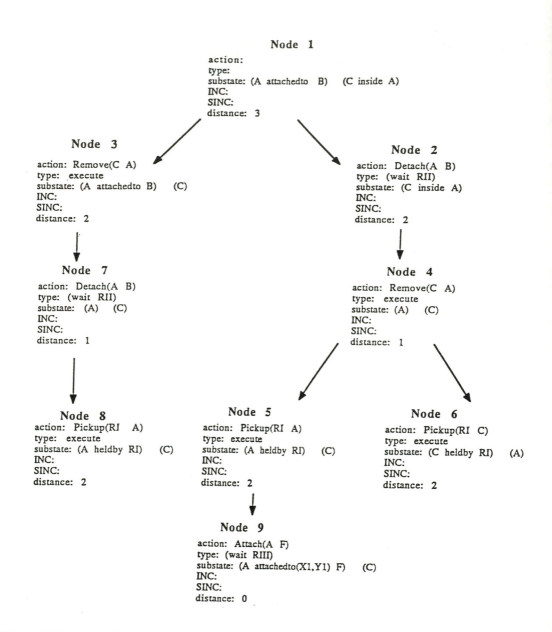

Figure 12.9: A partial trace of the search tree used in the first iteration by the subplanner of RI

Table 12.6: Subplan for Robot I (RI) Generated in the Second Iteration

ACTIONS	TYPE	AFFECTED OBJECTS	SUBSTATE RELATIONSHIPS
			(A attachedto B) (C inside A)
Detach(A B)	wait RII	B	(C inside A)
Remove(D B)	send RII		(C inside A)
Remove(C A)	execute		
Pickup(RI A)	execute		(A heldby RI)
Attach(A F)	wait RIII	F	(A attachedto(x1,y1) F)

Table 12.7: Subplan for Robot II (RII) Generated in the Second Iteration

ACTIONS	TYPE	AFFECTED OBJECTS	SUBSTATE RELATIONSHIPS
			(A attachedto B) (D inside B)
Detach(A B)	send RI		(D inside B)
Remove(D B)	wait RI	A	
Pickup(RII B)	execute		(B heldby RII)
Attach(B F)	wait RIII	F	(B attachedto(x2,y2) F)

Table 12.8: Subplan for Robot III (RIII) Generated in the Second Iteration

ACTIONS	TYPE	AFFECTED OBJECTS	SUBSTATE RELATIONSHIPS
			(E attachedto F) (G inside F)
Detach(E F)	execute		(G inside F)
Attach(A F)	send RI		(G inside F) (A attachedto(x1,y1) F)
Attach(B F)	send RII		(G inside F) (A attachedto(x1,y1) F) (B attachedto(x2,y2) F)
Remove(G F)	execute		(A attachedto(x1,y1) F) (B attachedto(x2,y2) F)

Table 12.9: Final Multiagent Plan

Time	Robot I (RI)	Robot II (RII)	Robot III (RIII)
t1	Detach(A B)	waiting for RI	Detach(E F)
t2	Remove(C A)	Remove(D B)	Remove(G F)
t3	Pickup(RI A)	Pickup(RII B)	idle
t4	Attach(A F)	Attach(B F)	idle

the goal. The demands of this constraint are satisfied in Node 4 (indicated by type send) which includes it as an action of RII. As a result, the *SatisfiedInConstraints* (SINC) field of Node 4 and all its successors contain the interagent constraint to indicate that it has been satisfied from the path starting from the root node to this node. The path from the initial node to the node satisfying the goal consists of Node 1, Node 2, Node 4, Node 5, Node 6, and Node 8.

The subplans from the second iteration, combined together and coordinated using the communication regarding the constraints, form the final multiagent plan (see Table 12.9). Assuming that each action in the multiagent plan requires one time unit and the overhead for send and receive primitives is negligible, the entire plan can be executed concurrently in 4 units of time. This is in contrast to 9 units, if the same plan is executed by one agent.

12.7   Conclusions

In this paper, we have presented a new approach to solve the multiagent planning problem. The approach employs an *object-oriented problem decomposition* concept that permits the formulation of different planning configurations in terms of objects, agents available in the domain, and the strategy of assigning objects to agents. An important concept that has been introduced by the approach is the interagent constraint that plays the role of coordinating between the concurrent actions of the multiagents and their interactions. Treating interactions as constraint actions provides efficient and concise representation of these interactions. Our representation avoids generating multiple interactions for each and every assertion or deletion that is caused by the same action. Moreover, it limits the number of such interactions to those actions that explicitly involve the objects assigned to other agents.

The structure of a multiagent planning system based on the proposed approach has been discussed. The structure is characterized by its utilization of a knowledge base that includes knowledge about the domain, the planning configuration, and the problem to be solved. A number of knowledge structures have been introduced to capture the different

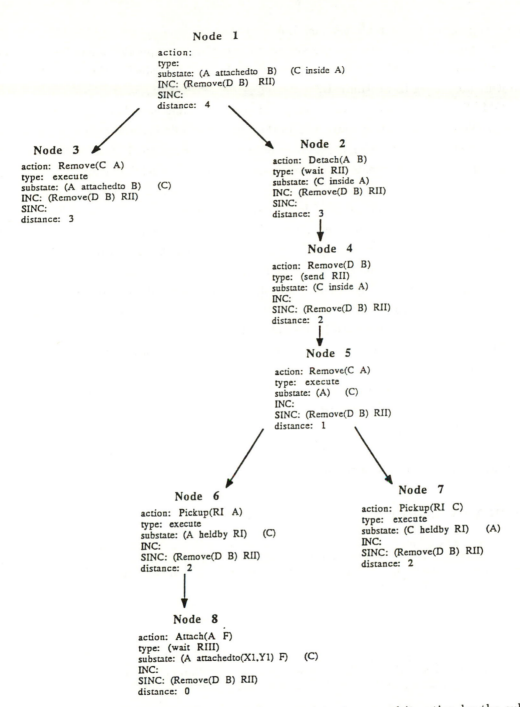

Node 1

action:
type:
substate: (A attachedto B)   (C inside A)
INC: (Remove(D B) RII)
SINC:
distance: 4

Node 3

action: Remove(C A)
type: execute
substate: (A attachedto B)   (C)
INC: (Remove(D B) RII)
SINC:
distance: 3

Node 2

action: Detach(A B)
type: (wait RII)
substate: (C inside A)
INC: (Remove(D B) RII)
SINC:
distance: 3

Node 4

action: Remove(D B)
type: (send RII)
substate: (C inside A)
INC:
SINC: (Remove(D B) RII)
distance: 2

Node 5

action: Remove(C A)
type: execute
substate: (A)   (C)
INC:
SINC: (Remove(D B) RII)
distance: 1

Node 6

action: Pickup(RI A)
type: execute
substate: (A heldby RI)   (C)
INC:
SINC: (Remove(D B) RII)
distance: 2

Node 7

action: Pickup(RI C)
type: execute
substate: (C heldby RI)   (A)
INC:
SINC: (Remove(D B) RII)
distance: 2

Node 8

action: Attach(A F)
type: (wait RIII)
substate: (A attachedto(X1,Y1) F)   (C)
INC:
SINC: (Remove(D B) RII)
distance: 0

Figure 12.10: A partial trace of the search tree used in the second iteration by the sub-planner of RI

287

knowledge types of the multiagent environment.

The potential application of the system to manufacturing problems has been demonstrated with an example. The planning system (OMAPS) described in this paper has been implemented using INTERLISP-D.

OMAPS can be used to test and experiment with different planning configurations and problem decomposition strategies. In this structure, different multiagent plans can be generated simply by changing the number of agents and assignment of objects to agents.

Besides the object oriented problem decomposition, the modularity and versatility of the structure allows it to support other types of strategies, as well. To this end, the authors have developed a *functional problem decomposition* strategy that is more suitable for agents with disparate capabilities [Kamel and Syed]. Under this scheme, the capability of each agent in the domain is represented by a set of operators that the agent can apply to change the relationships between objects in the domain. The PD module decomposes the planning problem into subproblems by assigning specific relations in the domain to agents based on their capabilities. A particular relation is assigned to the agent if it has an operator to realize the relationship described by the relation.

The issue of obtaining optimal assignments of objects or relations to agents is an important issue that deserves more research. We have explained an intuitive method that is suitable for situations when the required actions are expected to be well distributed over the objects. Another important issue that we have not addressed is detecting and avoiding deadlocks in the generated concurrent plans. Our future work will include solution to these problems and integration of the system with multirobot arms in order to investigate execution and monitoring of the generated concurrent plans.

Acknowledgements

This work was supported by MRCO (Manufacturing Research Corporation of Ontario), an Ontario center of excellence, Grant no. 0798685. The authors would like to thank the anonymous reviewers for their constructive comments which have been helpful in improving the presentation of the paper.

References

[Bandyopadhyay 1986] S. Bandyopadhyay, S. P. Dutta, D. Meloche, and S. P. Rana, "Component Description for Knowledge Based Process Planning," *Int. Journal of Advanced Manufacturing Technology*, Vol. 1, No. 3, May 1986, pp. 55–73.

[Chang and Wysk 1981] T. C. Chang and R. A. Wysk, "Interfacing CAD/Automated Process Planning," *AIIE Transactions*, September 1981.

[Corkill 1979] D. D. Corkill, "Hierarchical Planning in a Distributed Environment," *Proc. IJCAI*, 1979, pp. 168–175.

[Erman 1980] L. D. Erman, F. Hayes-Roth, and D. R. Reddy, "The Hearsay-II Speech-understanding System: Integrating Knowledge to Resolve Uncertainty," *Computing Surveys*, Vol. 12, June 1980, pp. 213–253.

[Fox 1982] M. S. Fox, B. Allen, and G. Strohm, "Job Shop Scheduling: An Investigation in Constraint-Directed Reasoning," *Proc. AAAI*, 1982, pp. 155–158.

[Georgeff 1986] M. P. Georgeff, "The Representation of Events in Multiagent Domains," *Proc. AAAI*, 1986, pp. 70–75.

[Georgeff 1983] M. P. Georgeff, "Communication and Interaction in Multiagent Planning," *Proc. AAAI*, 1983, pp. 115–119.

[Hegland 1981] D. E. Hegland, "Out in Front with CADCAM at Lockheed-Georgia," *Production Engineering*, November 1981.

[Hillis and Steele 1986] W. D. Hillis and G. L. Steele Jr., "Data Parallel Algorithms," *Communications of the ACM*, Vol. 29, December 1986, pp. 1170–1183.

[Kamel and Syed 1988] M. Kamel and A. Syed, "An Automated Multiagent Planning System," *Proc. the 2nd International Conference on Expert Systems and the Leading Edge in Production Planning and Control*, North-Holland, New York, May 1988, pp. 367–384.

[Kamel and Syed] M. Kamel and A. Syed, "A Multiagent Planning Method for Agents with Disparate Capabilities," submitted for publication.

[Lansky and Fogelsong 1987] A. L. Lansky and D. S. Fogelsong, "Localized Representation and Planning Methods for Parallel Domains," *Proc. AAAI*, 1987, pp. 240–245.

[Lesser and Erman 1980] V. R. Lesser and L. D. Erman, "Distributed Interpretation: A Model and Experiment," *IEEE Trans. on Computers*, Vol. C-29, No. 12., December 1980, pp. 1144–1163.

[Link 1983] Link, C. H., "CAM-I Automated Process Planning System," *SME*, paper no. MS78-213, 1983.

[Masui 1983] S. Masui, J. McDermott, and A. Sobel, "Decision-Making in Time Critical Situations," *IJCAI-83*, Karlsruhe, West Germany, August 1983, pp. 233–235.

[McDermott 1978] D. V. McDermott, "Planning and Acting," *Cognitive Science*, Vol. 2, 1978, pp. 71–109.

[Rosenbaum 1983] J. D. Rosenbaum, "A Propitious Marriage: CAD and Manufacturing," *IEEE Spectrum*, May 1983, pp. 49–52.

[Sacerdoti 1977] E. D. Sacerdoti, *A Structure for Plans and Behaviour*, Elsevier-North Holland, 1977.

[Smith and Davis 1981] R. G. Smith and R. Davis, "Frameworks for Cooperation in Distributed Problem Solving," *IEEE Trans. on Systems, Man, and Cybernetics*, Vol. SMC-11, No. 1, January 1981, pp. 61–70.

[Stuart 1985] C. Stuart, "An Implementation of a Multiagent Plan Synchronizer," *Proc. IJCAI*, 1985, pp. 1031–1033.

[Vogel and Adlard 1981] S. A. Vogel and E. J. Adlard, "The AUTOPLAN Process Planning System," *Proc. 18th Numerical Control Society Annual Meeting and Technical Conference*, May 1981, pp. 422–429.

M. Kamel and A. Syed
Pattern Analysis and Machine Intelligence Group
Department of Systems Design Engineering
University of Waterloo
Waterloo, Ontario, N2L 3G1
Canada

Part IV

Architectures for DAI

Chapter 13

DATMS: A Framework for Distributed Assumption Based Reasoning

Cindy L. Mason and Rowland R. Johnson

Abstract

The Distributed ATMS, DATMS, is a problem solving framework for multiagent assumption based reasoning. It is based on the problem solving paradigm of result sharing rule-based expert systems using assumption based truth maintenance systems. We are implementing and experimenting with the DATMS under MATE, a Multi-Agent Test Environment, using C and Common Lisp on a network of Sun workstations. This framework was motivated by the problem of seismic interpretation for Comprehensive or Low-Yield Test Ban Treaty verification, where a widespread network of seismic sensor stations are required to monitor treaty compliance, and seismologists use assumption based reasoning in a collaborative fashion to interpret the seismic data. The DATMS framework differs from other previously designed problem solving organizations in (1) its method of reasoning, (2) its ability to support an explanation facility, and (3) its addressing of the problem of culpability.

13.1 Introduction

Research on assumption based reasoning can generally be classified into two camps, the logicians and the practitioners [Hanks and McDermott 1987b]. Formal approaches to characterizing default reasoning include McDermott and Doyle's nonmonotonic logic [McDermott and Doyle 1980], McCarthy's circumscription [McCarthy 1980], and Reiter's default logic [Reiter 1980]. This paper is concerned with the practical aspects of building a system of cooperating assumption based reasoners.

In order to implement this kind of reasoning, inference systems require belief revision mechanisms. The most notable efforts in this field for single agent problem solvers are the truth maintenance systems (TMS) of Doyle (single context) [Doyle 1979] and de Kleer (multiple context) [deKleer 1986]. The DATMS (Distributed Assumption-based Truth Maintenance System) framework supports assumption based reasoning in a multiagent problem solver. The philosophy of this work is that assumption based reasoning can be achieved rather naturally in a multiagent problem solver using a belief revision system based on multiple contexts, i.e., an assumption-based TMS (ATMS). Single-context TMSs require an agent to maintain a single consistent set of facts, while ATMSs provide a mechanism to represent multiple, possibly inconsistent, sets of facts.

This chapter describes the DATMS framework. First we motivate the development of the framework, introducing the problem of seismic verification, and briefly review the notions of assumption based reasoning and truth maintenance. Following this we describe a model of problem solving for distributed assumption based reasoning. We then discuss some of the issues in distributed assumption based reasoning and present a problem solving framework, the DATMS framework, to address these issues. Finally, we describe some of our implementation experiences and some of the assumption based reasoning mechanisms that may be used for network coordination and control.

13.2 Background

13.2.1 Problem Domain

Many of the motivations for this research come from the problem of automating seismic monitoring for Comprehensive or Low-Yield Nuclear Test Ban Treaty verification. In the event a treaty is ratified, in-country monitoring networks will be required and tens of thousands of events must be analyzed. The ultimate goal of verification data processing research is to understand the issues of building a system to interpret and classify (discriminate) each event. Here we focus on the seismic interpretation problem. It is the authors' intent to build a data processing system that reasons and forms interpretations much like the seismologists. A single agent system that interprets data from a seismic array in Norway has been implemented and is undergoing extensive testing [Mason 1988].

The seismologists' interpretation network consists of a number of individuals who interpret data for a particular geological region or sensor site. Each seismologist reasons about the data using assumptions and guesses as constraints and knowledge particular to a geological region and sensor technology.

To form an accurate interpretation of their sensor data, seismologists can exchange partial or full interpretations and verify what they have seen, or give pointers to other seismologists as to what they should be seeing. In no case does a seismologist conclude the presence or absence of an event unless it is evidenced by his/her own sensor data. This aspect of the network solution comes from the fact that seismologists may be viewing different seismic events. This is particularly important in the seismic treaty verification problem, where multiple artificially induced seismic events, jamming, or other evasion scenarios might be used to evade treaty provisions. A single uncompromised station may be the only witness to a clandestine event.

A DAI solution to the seismic interpretation problem occurs naturally, emphasizing the following aspects of the human interpretation network we are trying to model.

Decomposition: Problem decomposition is static. Each agent is assigned the problem of interpreting data from a single sensor site or geological region.

Granularity: Each agent is a full scale expert system, possessing complete interpretation knowledge for its sensor site.

Cooperation: The problem easily falls into the result-sharing cooperating experts paradigm. However, an agent's decision to believe an event has occurred is not decided merely by counting the number of stations that have or have not witnessed the event, but in the relative convincing force of its own evidence. This perspective on belief updating has caused us to revise some ideas presented in Smith and Davis' original model of problem solving activity in a result sharing network.

Network Solution: Individual agents are not required to come to a consensus, as in distributed sensor networks [Lesser and Corkill 1983]. The network solution currently consists of a report collating event interpretations from each station. This report is then analyzed for discrimination purposes. We anticipate an interaction between seismic experts and discrimination experts in a later version of the system.

13.2.2 Assumption Based Reasoning and Truth Maintenance

Assumption based reasoning is a style of reasoning in which the problem solver makes inferences based on assumptions or plausible guesses. A classic example of this type of reasoning (modernized in [Ginsberg 1987]) is the following: if we know that most birds fly and that Opus is a bird, then we may reasonably conclude that Opus can fly. Furthermore, we can conclude that when Bill shoves Opus over the edge of the Grand Canyon, Opus lives, because he can fly.

The general idea of assumption based reasoning is that we can use an assumption (or default conclusion) and the inferences it entails as long as there is no information to indicate these beliefs are wrong.[1] As formulated by [Reiter 1980], "in the absence of any information to the contrary, assume ... " A reasoning agent may use its assumption and consequent deductions as long as they are consistent with what is currently known or believed. This consistency based approach to nonmonotonic reasoning is presented well in [Reiter 1988] and [Ginsberg 1987]. The role of assumption based reasoning in AI systems includes (but is not limited to) diagnosis and interpretation, and is generally useful when dealing with prototypical information.

The difficulty in implementing assumption based reasoning is that default assumptions and their consequents are tentative conclusions. If we find out later that Opus is a penguin, the original assumption and subsequent inferences must be revised. The fact that Opus can fly must be withdrawn because penguins cannot fly. The fact that Opus lives after he was shoved into the canyon must be withdrawn as well, since it depends on the fact that Opus could fly.

In order to implement this kind of reasoning in a program, we must keep records of dependencies among facts; then when a revision is necessary, we can update our set of currently believed facts (beliefs). We need

1. A record of the assumption dependencies and inference history of each fact

2. A mechanism to maintain inference histories and keep track of which facts are valid or invalid

3. A way to specify what constitutes an inconsistency and when it occurs.

The program components concerned with these belief maintenance items are separated from the domain components in what is known as a truth maintenance system.[2] As a result, we view the problem solver as composed of an inference engine subsystem and a truth maintenance subsystem, as shown in Figure 13.1. Then we can separate the domain issues from the consistency issues.

---

[1] This type of reasoning can be traced to the THNOT operator in MICRO-PLANNER [Sussman 1970].
[2] Also referred to as a reason maintenance or belief revision system.

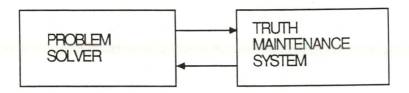

Figure 13.1: Conceptually, the truth maintenance system is separated from the problem solver

13.3   Problem Solving Model

The DATMS framework is based on the paradigm of result-sharing cooperating experts [Smith and Davis 1981], where the experts use assumption based reasoning to derive solutions. In this mode of cooperation, problem decomposition and task assignment are static and occur prior to problem solving (e.g., in a distributed sensor network application, each expert interprets data from its sensing station). In general, individual subproblems cannot be solved by the expert independently, so experts rely on the exchange of results in forming a solution, as shown in Figure 13.2.

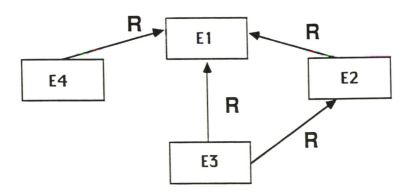

Figure 13.2: Result-sharing model of cooperation

As depicted in the original result-sharing model of Davis and Smith, agents transmit subproblem results when the result is judged to be relevant to another expert's problem solving. A transmitted result can be used in several ways: 1) it can be integrated with partial results to produce a more complete local hypothesis, which may then be communicated to other experts 2) it may be used to confirm or deny local solutions, and 3) it can help direct the search for a local solution.

We argue that this model of result-sharing problem solving activity leads to a situation where experts can lose their individual perspective, by revising their own beliefs without self-supporting evidence. Although the experts may come to a consensus, it may be the wrong consensus, since agents can update their beliefs with faulty information and then pass it on and contaminate other agent's beliefs.

13.3.1 The Problem of Belief Revision

The problem solving scenario of Smith and Davis presumes mutual credibility and trust among the agents. When expert E1 uses expert E2's results to confirm or deny its own result, E1 presupposes E2's results are indeed credible and may revise the confidence in its own results based on what E2 says. And what E3 says and E4 says and so on. So that E1's results eventually have a confidence rating reflecting the inputs from every agent E1 listened to, regardless of whether those agents started with bad data (e.g., sensor errors), were somehow compromised by a third party, or are intentionally lying about their results.

The problem is even sharper in an assumption-based reasoner where a fact is either believed or not. Suppose expert E1 believes fact f. E2 tells E1 it does not believe f. If E1 trusts E2, E1 may revise its own belief in f. Now suppose E3 tells E1 it believes f. Does E1 change its belief status again?

This difficulty is particularly visible in applications such as seismic treaty verification, where there is reason to believe experts may be compromised, but it also relates to the more general problem of how to determine which agents are better informed in updating beliefs.

There are at least two basic problems here:

1. How do we ensure all agents' views are consistent?[3]

2. How do we determine when an agent's beliefs should be revised?

In addressing these questions, we argue that in an assumption based reasoning network it is unreasonable and intuitively wrong to try and ensure all agents views are consistent. It is better to have a "hung jury" and let agents stand by their beliefs based on their own view of the evidence. This view of assumption based reasoning permits the possibility that a single agent may be the only one to have uncompromised evidence or information.

---

[3]By consistent here, we do not refer to the problem of updating databases with consistent copies of results, but to the problem of requiring agents' to drive the system towards a unanimous network solution.

298

Although this perspective is drawn from the practical aspects of an application, it can be seen as extending Reiter's philosophy of default reasoning [Reiter 1980][4] to the multiagent case. Each agent reasons with sets of beliefs that are internally consistent with respect to assumptions it currently holds (in Reiter's terms, its *extensions*), although the union of any two agent's assumptive contexts (extensions) may be inconsistent.

Our case for a liberal belief revision policy is further supported by the following observations:

1. We can find no satisfactory answer to the question, "How do we determine which agent is right?" We could consider that domain specific information might let us decide which agents are more credible (e.g., a vision system in a tower has a better perspective than one on the ground and an agent with an array of sensors has more information gathering power than one using a simple sensor). But these solutions still do not address the problem of how to deal with result sharing agents whose information may be faulty (intentionally or otherwise).

2. It may be theoretically impossible to achieve consistency anyway. Konolige's observation about belief systems is relevant here: "Agents can draw conclusions from an initial set of beliefs, but they do not necessarily derive all the logically possible ones" [Konolige 1986]. This statement refers to the observation that the inferences an agent makes may be limited due to the constraints of time and space. Although Konolige's observations deal with the general problem of what facts an agent may deduce from its inference rules and base set of beliefs, it is easy to see how this observation extends to the problem of detecting inconsistencies.

13.3.2   A New View of Problem Solving Activity

To support this belief updating philosophy, Smith and Davis' [Smith and Davis 1981] basic method for result sharing is modified for assumption based reasoners as follows:

1. An individual agent will not transmit results or hypotheses that it cannot wholly substantiate based on its own data, problem perspective and knowledge. Results may be aggregated for the purpose of determining how an agent's findings fare with others, but the aggregate is not to be transmitted.

2. An agent will not revise its beliefs according to whether they are confirmed or denied by externally generated results. It may use confirmation or denial to guide its search

---

[4]For an alternative and more conservative view of single agent default reasoning, see [Hanks and McDermott 1987a].

299

for a solution, but an agent will not adopt the views of its fellow experts unless the views or results can be substantiated by its own findings.

In assumption-based result sharing networks, results may be viewed as both inconsistency findings and problem solving hypotheses, since transmitted results can subsequently be shown to be inconsistent. The agent's final solutions are the consistent sets of facts comprising its hypotheses.

It should noted that this belief revision philosophy demands a two-tiered result synthesis process. The first level involves the synthesis of the individual agent's solutions. A second level is required to create possible interpretations or explanations for the collection of interpretations as a whole. For example, the fact that three individual stations did not see seismic events (but *should* have seen them) and reported noise may be indicative of a sensor jamming scenario.

13.4 Issues

13.4.1 Contradiction Knowledge

Typically ATMSs work best where there are a number of solutions and all must be found [deKleer 1986]. The dependency records (TMS nodes) of the ATMS allow facts from multiple contexts (assumptions) to be simultaneously maintained in the problem solvers database—this reduces the cost of context switching. However, this introduces control problems. In a multiagent assumption based reasoner, the number of contexts an agent considers can be dangerously high, since each fact it receives from other agents may involve yet another context. In quantitative reasoners, confidence rankings may be used to help focus the search. In an assumption based reasoner we rely on the application of contradiction knowledge to reject inconsistent theories and limit the number of partial hypotheses. As a result, contradiction knowledge plays a key role in limiting control and communication problems in a multiagent assumption based reasoning system.

13.4.2 Culpability

Culpability is the extent to which results derived by a system may be traced back to each cooperating individual. Culpability plays a role in three areas of a multiagent assumption based reasoning system:

1. Creating new facts by making deductions

2. Propagating effects of a contradiction

3. Creating an explanation facility

Dependency records are a good general purpose mechanism for maintaining inference histories in systems dealing with assumptions. However, consider the general form of a deduction,

$$a_1 \wedge a_2 \wedge \cdots \wedge a_n \rightarrow c$$

The information used to create the data dependency record for c comes from the data dependency records generated for the antecedents, $a_1 \cdots a_n$. Communicated antecedents have no local dependency records since they were deduced externally. Within the context of the reasoning agent, the dependency information needed for c is unavailable.

13.4.3 Identifiers

A fact identifier is a symbol designating or referencing a fact or datum that is used by the assumption based reasoner for pattern matching and building justifications and assumption sets. An identification scheme for a multiagent assumption based reasoner must provide unique identification within the global context of a system of agents in order to allow for

- Building assumption sets and justifications from a mixture of internally deduced and communicated facts

- Including communicated facts within assumption sets and justifications

- Sharing facts

- Transmitting inconsistency findings

- Determining culpability.

13.4.4 Truth Maintenance Communication Policy

Since facts involved in contradictions may depend on communicated facts a belief revision strategy must include specifications on how the other agents are to be informed—whether or not they will inform every agent of the network about the inconsistency or just the agents directly involved, etc. Three kinds of inconsistencies will arise, those involving only internally deduced facts, those involving a mixture of internally and externally deduced facts, and those involving only externally deduced facts. In general, an agent will not possess the knowledge to detect inconsistencies involving only external inconsistencies, so the latter situation may be dismissed. From an anthropomorphic perspective, we might say, the agents are well behaved and do not "nose into" other agents' business.

13.4.5 Trust

There are many different degrees of trust (or distrust) that must be considered in order to decide how an agent will deal with an incoming fact or inconsistency message. In essence, each problem solving system must embrace a model of trust upon which agent interaction and belief revision are based. The degree of trust can be viewed as a spectrum ranging from tautologists to liars. In between, there are possible liars, possible but unlikely liars, agents who are unknowingly compromised, knowingly compromised, and so on.

For the problem of seismic monitoring, we view the agents as being benevolent, since they are under our own control, and we trust the integrity of the agents, although the information one agent sends may not reflect a world or reality that is shared by other agents. That is, the agents do not lie, but communicated hypotheses must be weighed against local data, since the sender may be unknowingly compromised. An agent receiving a fact cannot adopt it as the ultimate truth. Instead, the agent considers its consistency against its set of possible worlds (assumptive contexts).

13.5 DATMS

13.5.1 The Assumption Based Reasoning Agent

As shown in Figure 13.3, each agent has the sophistication of a rule-based expert system. Further, each agent is equipped with inference rules, communication rules, a facts data base, a network interface (message passing software), and an assumption-based truth maintenance system (ATMS). The ATMS is composed of truth maintenance rules and an assumptions data base.

The basic formula for implementing assumption based (default) reasoning here is to allow agents to make assumptions and work with their consequents until contradictory information is found. The idea of performing a complete consistency check on assumptions before using them is ineffective, especially in a multiagent environment, where databases are updated with asynchronously arriving results. The only practical approach to implementing nonmonotonic reasoning in rule-based systems is to perform incremental consistency checks with each inference cycle. This is achieved through the use of antecedent demons and rules that define inconsistency conditions.

The assumption based reasoning techniques presented here build upon concepts found in [Stallman and Sussman 1971] and [deKleer 1986]. Each fact is tagged with a justification indicating the rule and antecedent facts used to create it and the assumptions under which the fact is believed. This information is useful in providing an explanation facility as well

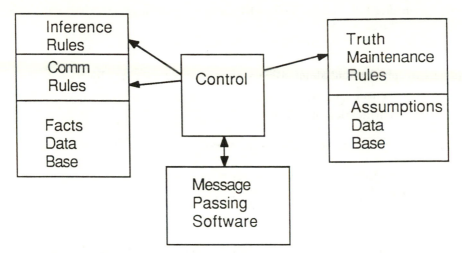

Figure 13.3: Architecture of the assumption based reasoning agent

as a trace of rule operation for debugging and understanding the system's behavior. This same information is also used to determine the current set of beliefs and to implement dependency-directed backtracking.

13.5.2   The Truth Maintenance System

The DATMS creates and maintains inference histories using a data structure known as a TMS "node" [Doyle 1979, deKleer 1986] and an assumptions data base. Contradiction knowledge is expressed in terms of a special class of rules called TMS rules. As a result, the detection of contradictory conditions occurs during pattern matching.

The TMS Node

The TMS node acts as a referent to the inference history and assumptions supporting each fact or datum asserted by the problem solver and is used by the truth maintenance system in determining the fact's belief status. In the DATMS, a TMS node links the identity of the corresponding fact with an assumption set and justification. An individual TMS-node has the form

< Fact-ID, Justification, Assumption-Set-ID >

where Fact-ID is a unique identifier, Justification is the inference history for the fact, and Assumption-Set-ID is the index of the assumption set, which must be consistent for the corresponding fact to be believed. The Fact-ID is a complex entity comprised of a locally unique fact identifier followed by the identity of the agent originating the data item.

$$\text{Fact-ID} = <\text{identifier} : \text{agent}>$$

Contrary to the distributed operating system goals of viewing objects independently of their hosts, this identifier is explicitly associated with the agent responsible for deriving the result. The identification of a datum

- provides unique identification within the global context of the system of agents.

- gives uniform identification for internally and externally generated results for the purpose of building assumption sets and justifications from a mixture of internally deduced and communicated facts.

- provides a way to trace data items back to each individual agent, supporting global belief revision and an explanation facility.

- allows an agent to integrate the beliefs of other agents while keeping its own results distinct from those developed from a different perspective.

The Justification for a fact is the set of data items that directly deduce the fact. Communicated facts have Justification "EXTERNAL" since the antecedents reside in an external agent. The Assumption-Set-ID is an index into the assumptions data base where the assumption set for the fact is maintained. The concepts of justifications and assumption sets are discussed and illustrated by an example in the following section.

The Assumptions Data Base

The assumptions data base contains an assumption set and a status label for each fact inferred or communicated into the agent's facts data base. The assumption set for a fact indicates the assumptions upon which its belief ultimately depends (i.e., a fact is believed if its assumption set is believed). More formally, an assumption set is defined to be a subset of the known facts. The set of all possible assumption sets is the power set of the known facts. Let

$$F = \{f_1, f_2, \ldots, f_n\}$$

be the set of known facts. Then $\{f_1\}, \{f_2\}, \ldots, \{f_i, f_j\}, \ldots, \{f_1, f_2, \ldots, f_n\}$, are all potential assumption sets. In general, for any assumption set A, $A \subset F$ and $A \in F^*$.

An assumption set A is labeled either CONSISTENT or INCONSISTENT. CONSISTENT means that facts of A are consistent with one another, i.e., they can all be believed at the same time. INCONSISTENT means that the facts of A are inconsistent, i.e., they

304

cannot all be believed at the same time. Let A and B be assumption sets with $A \subset B$. If A is INCONSISTENT then B must also be INCONSISTENT, since the subset of facts of A that cause it to be INCONSISTENT will also be in B.

Each fact f has an assumption set $A(f)$ associated with it. In essence, f is *believed* if $A(f)$ is CONSISTENT and is *disbelieved* if $A(f)$ is INCONSISTENT. The manner in which assumption sets are assigned to facts, their labels and possible subsequent relabeling provides the mechanism by which assumption based reasoning or assumption based truth maintenance is realized. When the rule

$$a_1 \wedge a_2 \wedge \ldots \wedge a_n \rightarrow c_1 \ldots c_m$$

fires, there is the set of antecedent facts $a_1, \ldots, a_n$ and the consequent facts $c_1 \ldots c_m$. Each consequent fact, c_i, can be created by one of four actions, each of which produce a different value for $A(c_i)$. The actions and the values for $A(c)$ (consequent subscripts have been dropped for simplicity) are

Given (c): $A(c) = c$; c is used as a premise. C is inferred with no antecedents and holds universally in local environments.

Assumed (c): $A(c) = \bigcup\limits_{j=1}^{n} A(a_j) + c$; c is a data item that is a reasoned assumption. C is dependent on itself as well as the assumptions of the antecedent facts.

Asserted (c): $A(c) = \bigcup\limits_{j=1}^{n} A(a_j)$; c is a data item that depends solely upon the assumption sets of its antecedent facts.

Communicated (c): $A(c) = \hat{A}(\hat{c})$, c is a data item which depends upon the communicated assumption set for the external data item, $\hat{c}$.

References to external items are denoted by $\hat{h}\hat{a}\hat{t}\hat{s}$.

The following example demonstrates some of these ideas. Suppose we have the following set of inferences in Agent Opus:

$$\top \quad \rightarrow \quad GIVEN(p), GIVEN(q), COMM(\hat{c}) \qquad (13.1)$$
$$p \wedge q \quad \rightarrow \quad ASSUME(r) \qquad (13.2)$$
$$r \wedge \hat{c} \quad \rightarrow \quad ASSERT(s) \qquad (13.3)$$

This gives rise to <fact, assumption set> pairs, as follows:

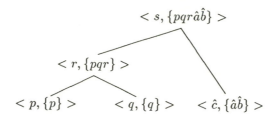

In rule (1), facts p and q are created using the GIVEN operator, hence have assumption sets $\{p\}$ and $\{q\}$, respectively. Fact $\hat{c}$ is communicated and is associated with the communicated assumption set, $\{\hat{a}\hat{b}\}$. Facts p and q then act as antecedent facts in rule (2), giving rise to fact, r, using the ASSUME operator. Assumption set $A(r)$ is the union of the assumption sets on the left hand side, plus r; $A(r) = A(p) \cup A(q) + r = \{pqr\}$. Finally, fact s is ASSERTed from antecedents r and $\hat{c}$ in rule (3). S has assumption set $A(s) = A(r) \cup A(\hat{c}) = \{pqr\hat{a}\hat{b}\}$.

Assigning fact IDs 1 - 5 to these facts in Agent Opus's data base yields the corresponding TMS nodes, Assumption Data Base, and Facts DataBase.

TMS Nodes			
Node–ID	Fact-ID	Justification	Ass. Set Index
99	1:Opus	(Rule-1 ())	11
100	2:Opus	(Rule-1 ())	12
101	3:Opus	EXTERNAL	13
102	4:Opus	(Rule-2 $(p\ q)$)	14
103	5:Opus	(Rule-3 $(r\ \hat{c})$)	15

Opus's Facts DataBase

Fact	DataBase-ID	Status
p	1:Opus	Believed
q	2:Opus	Believed
$\hat{c}$	3:Opus	Believed
r	4:Opus	Believed
s	5:Opus	Believed

Opus's Assumptions DataBase

Index	Assumption Set	Status
11	{1:Opus}	Consistent
12	{2:Opus}	Consistent
13	{21:Bill 22:Bill}	Consistent
14	{1:Opus 2:Opus 4:Opus}	Consistent
15	{1:Opus 2:Opus 4:Opus 21:Bill 22:Bill }	Consistent

Bill's Facts DataBase		
Fact	DataBase-ID	Status
a	21:Bill	Believed
b	22:Bill	Believed
c	23:Bill	Believed

Bill's Assumptions DataBase		
Index	Assumption Set	Status
.	{21:Bill}	Consistent
.	{22:Bill}	Consistent
.	{21:Bill 22:Bill}	Consistent

Truth Maintenance Rules

The right hand side actions thus far have been concerned with creating facts. The system is monotonic in that facts are never deleted. Nonmonotonic reasoning is achieved by changing the label value of an assumption set. This is accomplished through a special class of rules called TMS rules. TMS rules having the following general form:

```
(TMSRULE  NAME

          PATTERN

          (CONTRADICT <(Comm Policy) | (Agent-List)> (Fact-List)))
```

In a TMS rule, PATTERN names a group of believed facts which constitute an inconsistency. If the antecedent pattern successfully matches against the facts data base, an inconsistency among facts has occurred and the action CONTRADICT is invoked to repair the Assumptions Data Base. For example, if the generic TMS rule

$$a_1 \wedge a_2 \wedge \ldots \wedge a_n \rightarrow CONTRADICT(a_j \ldots a_k)$$

executes, then the assumption set $\cup_{i=j}^{k} A(a_j)$ and any other assumption sets containing it are marked INCONSISTENT. These assumptions sets are considered to be "NOGOOD"s and are cached in a "NOGOOD" data base.

It should be noted that the CONTRADICT predicate allows the specification of a list of antecedent facts. As a result of detecting an inconsistency, an agent's current set of *believed* facts is updated. Because the current set of beliefs is consulted during pattern matching, there is a direct effect on problem solving and communication behavior of the agent. The applications designer must be able to control belief revision and choice of a new context using domain knowledge. As a result, the syntax of the CONTRADICT predicate allows

307

the rule-writer to specify a list of antecedent facts or culprits to be used in building the INCONSISTENT or "NOGOOD" assumption set. This approach differs from the domain independent belief revision strategies employed in [Doyle 1979] and [deKleer 1986].

As shown by the TMS rule syntax, the CONTRADICT predicate also takes an argument that directs how the inconsistency finding should be propagated among the other agents. CONTRADICT transmits the inconsistency finding according to either a TMS communications policy, Comm Policy, or an explicit list of agents, Agent-List, to determine which agents (if any) should be contacted with a TMS message containing the NOGOOD assumption set. This idea is illustrated in Figure 13.4. The TMS communications policy is a data structure containing either declarative or procedural knowledge to compute the set of agents to whom inconsistency findings should be transmitted. The applications designer can create any number of communications policies and then refer to them by name in a TMS rule.

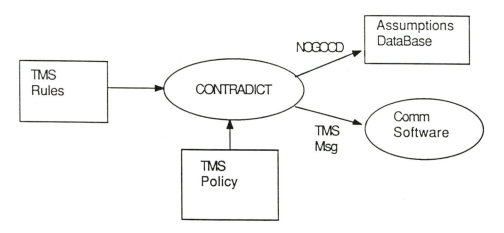

Figure 13.4: Truth maintenance rules invoke the CONTRADICT function to perform belief revision, possibly transmitting TMS messages

Upon receiving a TMS message, the transmitted NOGOOD set is treated as though it were locally derived and entered into a NOGOODS database; any assumption sets containing it are entered into the NOGOODS database as well. In accordance with the problem solving model, the transmitted NOGOOD contains only facts about data from the originating agent, so it will not affect beliefs founded only on local evidence. It may, however, cause work on beliefs based on a combination of local and external facts (the aggregated hypotheses) to halt.

In the previous example, if Agent Opus receives a TMS message from Bill containing the NOGOOD $\{\hat{a}\hat{b}\}$, then the assumption set $\{\hat{a}\hat{b}\}$ as well as $\{pqr\hat{a}\hat{b}\}$ is marked as INCONSISTENT and entered into the NOGOOD database. The corresponding facts $\hat{c}$ and s are now disbelieved by Agent Opus.

Opus's Facts DataBase

Fact	DataBase-ID	Status
p	1:Opus	Believed
q	2:Opus	Believed
$\hat{c}$	3:Opus	Disbelieved
r	4:Opus	Believed
s	5:Opus	Disbelieved

Opus's Assumptions DataBase

Index	Assumption Set	Status
11	{1:Opus}	Consistent
12	{2:Opus}	Consistent
13	{21:Bill 22:Bill}	Inconsistent
14	{1:Opus 2:Opus 4:Opus}	Consistent
15	{1:Opus 2:Opus 4:Opus 21:Bill 22:Bill }	Inconsistent

Opus's NOGOODS DataBase

{21:Bill 22:Bill}
{1:Opus 2:Opus 4:Opus 21:Bill 22:Bill}

Bill's Assumptions DataBase

Index	Assumption Set	Status
.	{21:Bill}	Consistent
.	{22:Bill}	Consistent
.	{21:Bill 22:Bill}	Inconsistent

13.5.3 Result Sharing Mechanisms

This section describes the mechanisms for transmitting and receiving facts. Two features are used to construct and implement a transmitting communications strategy—communication rules, and a communications policy data structure. Communication rules specify which facts should be transmitted and when they should be sent. They also define the set of agents to whom the facts should be sent by referencing either an explicit agent list, or a communications policy that defines or computes an agent list.

The communications policy data structure contains either declarative or procedural knowledge to compute the set of agents to whom facts should be transmitted. This structure is created by the applications designer and then be referenced in a communication rule. The construction of a collection of communication rules and policy structures defines a strategy for communicating within a particular problem domain.

309

Communication rules having the following general form:

```
(COMMRULE  NAME
           PATTERN
           (SEND <(Comm Policy) | (Agent-List)> (Fact-List)))
```

PATTERN specifies the conditions under which the facts on the right hand side should be sent. The right hand side action, SEND, transmits (Fact-List) according to either the communication policy or the specified agent list. This idea is illustrated in Figure 13.5.

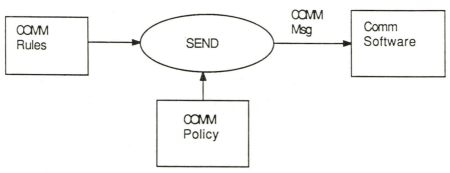

Figure 13.5: Result sharing is accomplished through communication rules. Rule writers may specify a procedure to calculate a list of agents or may explicitly name a set of agents.

For example, in the seismic domain, a rule to transmit the location of a seismic event looks like

```
(COMMRULE  send-location
      (BELIEVE   ((EVENT instance   $E1)
                 ($E1   has-loc     $L1)
                 ($E1   begin-time $BEG1)
                 ($E1   end-time    $END1)
                 ($E1   azimuth     $AZ)))
      (SEND  USE-LOC-POLICY
                 ((EVENT instance   $E1)
                 ($E1   has-loc     $L1)
                 ($E1   begin-time $BEG1)
                 ($E1   end-time    $END1)
```

```
                    ($E1    azimuth    $AZ))))
```

where USE-LOC-POLICY is a communication policy that uses domain knowledge including sensor type and location, and procedures which use geological zone, and earth velocity models to determine the list of agents to whom the message should be transmitted. If the left hand side pattern is matched successfully, the SEND action transmits the facts describing a seismic event.

What remains to be described are the mechanisms for defining a policy of receiving facts. The declarative

```
                (FOBJECT Object-Type)
```

specifies the type of information (facts) an agent will receive and store in its local database. During each inference cycle the agent checks for incoming messages. Any facts received that have not been declared in this fashion will be ignored.

This declaration also defines the class of foreign facts or foreign objects that will be created in an agent's database. The assumption based reasoning agents thus can distinguish externally deduced facts from internally deduced facts in working memory. This enables a rule writer to separate the agent's own perspectives from those of other agents. For example, if we have the declarative

```
                (FOBJECT FEVENT)
```

an agent containing the following seismic rule can use incoming information about seismic events witnessed by other agents to help search for a seismic event in its own data.

```
(INF-RULE LOOK-FOR-EVENT
        ((UNKNOWN (EVENT  instance   $E1)
                  ($E1    has-loc    $L1))
         (BELIEVE (FEVENT instance   $E2)
                  ($E2    has-loc    $L2)
                  ($E2    begin-time $B2)
                  ($E2    end-time   $END2)
                  ($E2    origin     $Agent)
                  ($Agent sensor-type 'Array)))
         (ASSUME  (make-event (begin-time $B2)
                              (end-time $END2)))))
```

The rule indicates the condition that there is a seismic event (EVENT) for which the agent has no location. The agent tries to use information about an event (FEVENT), seen by another agent using an array of sensors, to find enough data to create its own interpretation of an event. Using the begin and end times as assumptions, the agent may then fire rules that apply signal processing procedures to seismic data bracketed by the begin and end times, eventually driving up enough evidence to support an interpretation of the event.

The designer could also use the FOBJECT construct to define problem solving duties, since the kind of information an agent may access, in effect, determines the kind of activities it can perform.

13.5.4 Messages

The format of a message is shown in Figure 13.6. Each message contains the message type, either TMS or RESULT. TMS messages contain a NOGOOD assumption set. RESULT messages contain a list of $< fact, assumptionset >$ pairs, i.e., a set of facts comprising a hypothesis. Each message also has a TO slot indicating the list of agents to whom it is sent and a FROM slot indicating the originator of the message.

Msg Type	To	From	NOGOODS or FACTS

Figure 13.6: DATMS message format

13.5.5 Inference Engine Cycle

The basic inference engine cycle for assumption based reasoning agent, *Opus*, is the following (refer to Figure 13.7)

Inferencing

1. Check current set of beliefs against all rules. Decide which inference rule to fire.

2. Execute the inference rule. Record the inference as a justification and record the resulting new TMS node (assumption set) for the newly deduced fact.

Belief Updating and Result Sharing

312

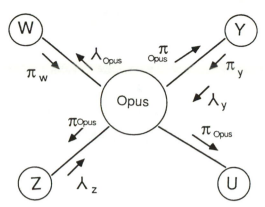

Figure 13.7: Assumption based reasoner Opus passes TMS messages and result messages. π_{Opus} represent TMS messages. λ_{Opus} represent messages containing facts

3. Execute all instantiated truth maintenance rules.

4. If an inconsistency is detected, record any new NOGOODS and propagate the effects of the contradiction. Communicate TMS messages to each agent designated by the truth maintenance communication policy.

5. Execute all instantiated communication rules. Accept any incoming messages.

6. Using any truth maintenance messages received, update NOGOODS data base with incoming NOGOODS.

7. Using any result messages received, update working memory and assumptions database with incoming facts (e.g., contained in messages from agents Y and Z, $\lambda_y, \lambda_z, etc.$)

13.6   Implementation Experiences with DATMS

We have implemented the DATMS framework on Sun workstations (see Figure 13.8) and are currently investigating communication and control strategies for distributed assumption based reasoning organizations. The Multi-Agent Test Environment (MATE) program, shown in Figure 13.9, provides a test bed for building a distributed assumption based reasoner and enables us to measure message traffic and vary the number of expert systems or agents. Development and testing is taking place in the classic "animal identification" domain [Winston 1984] and in the domain of seismic interpretation, using the four station Deployable Seismic Verification System testbed in the Nevada Test Site area.

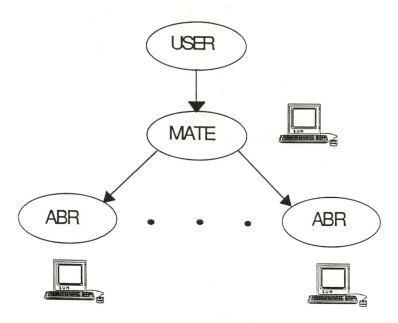

Figure 13.8: The MATE test program and assumption based reasoning lisp processes each execute on a Sun workstation

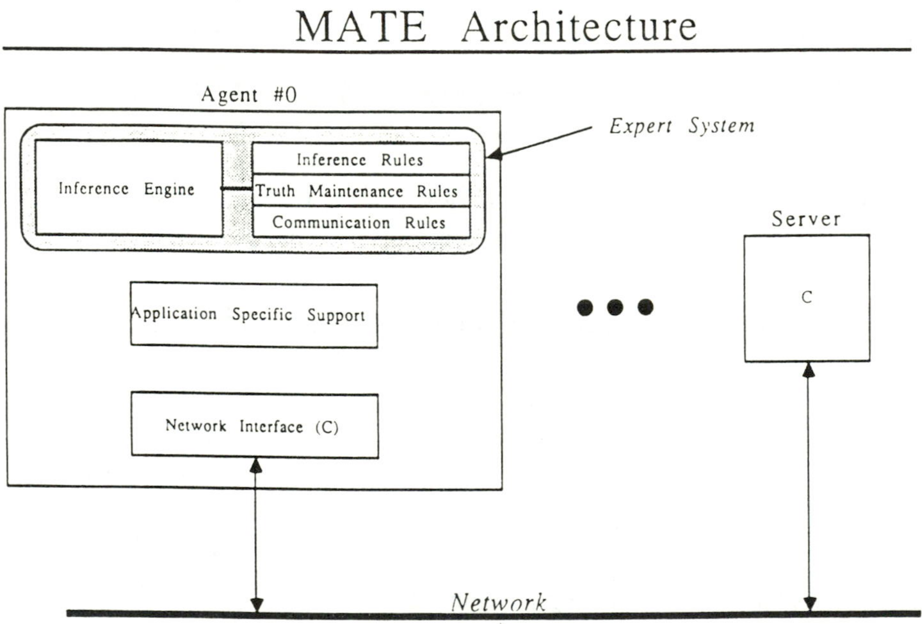

MATE Architecture

Agent #0

Expert System

Inference Engine

Inference Rules
Truth Maintenance Rules
Communication Rules

Application Specific Support

Network Interface (C)

Server

C

Network

Figure 13.9: The MATE environment provides a communication server and supports any number of communicating expert system configurations

13.6.1   Control

In building our seismic problem solver, we use the distinctive features of an assumption based reasoning system to focus control. For example, assumption sets provide a ready means to select among competing rule instantiations and it is easy to perform set operations on assumption sets. We may focus on hypotheses whose context (assumption set) has the most impact or overlap with the rest of the instantiations. The assumption set can also be used to separate the instantiations according to the amount of foreign evidence they contain.

Another way to deal with control in a multiagent assumption based reasoner is to use the number of inferences behind each fact in the left hand side to rank instantiations. Although inferences may vary in discrimination power, in general, the more inferences made without encountering a contradiction the more credible the hypothesis becomes. The total number of inferences made on an interpretation may be a measure of the interpretation's credibility. This ranking can also be used to limit the transmission of results.

13.6.2 . Communication

The communication activities of an individual seismologist are to a great extent driven by the relative location of an event and his or her ability to predict the group of seismologists that should have seen it. Hence, no particular domain independent communications strategy (such as nearest neighbor) can provide a reasonable approach to limiting the communications of the seismic agents over an unpredictable pattern of event locations. We have instead focused on the use of domain specific knowledge in the COMM rules to determine the sphere of relevant agents on a per event basis.

13.6.3   On Performance

Although TMSs by their very nature are domain independent, there is a growing body of evidence which supports the theory that their performance is highly task-specific [Provan 1987]. In essence, the strategy of an agent in evaluating a partial hypothesis is to make all possible inferences about the partial hypothesis to try to find a reason to discard it. In general, the ability to apply discriminatory contradiction knowledge early in problem solving may be a feature of the domain. As a result, the performance of any TMS will be highly dependent upon the nature of the task at hand. This property of TMSs is amplified in the multiagent case, where early detection of contradictions can affect the number of transmissions that take place during problem solving.

13.7 Summary

This chapter has described a problem solving organization for distributed assumption based reasoning, the DATMS framework. The organization is being used to develop a distributed artificial intelligence system to interpret data from a seismic sensor network for nuclear test ban treaty verification. Each agent interprets data from a sensor site or geologic region and relies on its communications to guide its search for an interpretation of its own data.

Key features of the DATMS framework are

- It provides a problem solving organization for qualitative distributed artificial intelligence systems

- It uses familiar rule-based expert systems technology. Each DATMS agent is an expert system where contradiction knowledge, communication knowledge and domain knowledge are expressed as rules.

- It supports a liberal belief revision policy that allows agents to consider multiple alternative perspectives at once.

- It accomplishes belief revision using a distributed multiple context truth maintenance system.

- It provides the information necessary to build an explanation facility that traces inference histories across the network of agents.

Acknowledgements

The author gratefully acknowledges the support of a University of California Student-Employee Fellowship at Lawrence Livermore National Laboratory.

References

[deKleer 1986] J. deKleer, "An Assumption Based TMS," *Artificial Intelligence*, vol. 28, 1986.

[Doyle 1979] J. Doyle, "A Truth Maintenance System," *Artificial Intelligence*, vol. 12, 1979, pp. 495–516.

[Ginsberg 1987] M. Ginsberg, in *Readings in Non-Monotonic Reasoning*, M. Ginsberg (editor), Morgan-Kaufmann, 1987, p. 15.

[Hanks and McDermott 1987a] S. Hanks and D. McDermott, "Nonmonotonic Logic and Temporal Projection," *Artificial Intelligence*, vol. 33, 1987, pp. 495–516.

[Hanks and McDermott 1987b] S. Hanks and D. McDermott, "Default Reasoning, Non-monotonic Logics, and the Frame Problem," in *Readings in Non-Monotonic Reasoning*, M.Ginsberg (editor), Morgan-Kaufmann, 1987, pp. 390–395.

[Lesser and Corkill 1983] V. R. Lesser and D. D. Corkill, "The Distributed Vehicle Monitoring Testbed: A Tool for Investigating Distributed Problem Solving Networks," *The AI Magazine*, Fall 1983, pp. 15–33.

[Konolige 1986] K. Konolige, *A Deductive Model of Belief*, Morgan Kaufmann Publishers, Inc, Los Altos, CA, 1986.

[Mason 1988] C. Mason, R. Johnson, R. Searfus, D. Lager, and T. Canales, "A Seismic Event Analyzer for Nuclear Test Ban Treaty Verification," *Proc. Third International Conference on Applications of Artificial Intelligence in Engineering*, August 1988.

[McCarthy 1980] J. McCarthy, "Circumscription - A Form of Non-monotonic Reasoning," *Artificial Intelligence*, vol. 13, April 1980, pp. 27–39.

[McDermott and Doyle 1980] D. McDermott and J. Doyle, "Non-Monotonic Logic I," *Artificial Intelligence*, vol. 13, April 1980, pp. 41–72.

[Provan 1987] G. Provan, "Efficiency Analysis of Multiple-Context TMSs in Scene Representation," *Proc. Sixth National Conference on Artificial Intelligence*, vol. 1, 1987.

[Reiter 1988] R. Reiter, "Nonmonotonic Reasoning," in *Exploring Artificial Intelligence*, H. E. Shrobe and the American Association for Artificial Intelligence (editors), Morgan-Kaufmann, 1988, pp. 453–457.

[Reiter 1980] R. Reiter, "A Logic for Default Reasoning," *Artificial Intelligence*, vol. 13, April 1980, pp. 81–132.

[Smith and Davis 1981] R. G. Smith and R. Davis, "Frameworks for Cooperation in Distributed Problem Solving," *IEEE Trans. on Systems, Man, and Cybernetics*, vol. SMC-11, no. 1, January 1981, pp. 61–70.

[Sussman 1970] G. Sussman, T. Winograd and E. Charniak, "Micro-Planner Reference Manual," AIM-203, MIT, Cambridge, MA, 1970.

[Stallman and Sussman 1971] R. Stallman, and G. Sussman. "Forward Reasoning and Dependency-Directed-Backtracking In a System For Computer Aided Circuit Analysis," *Artificial Intelligence*, vol. 9, no. 2, pp. 135–196.

[Winston 1984] P. H. Winston, *Artificial Intelligence*, Second Edition, Addison-Wesley Publishing Company, Reading, MA, 1984, pp. 182–191.

Cindy L. Mason and Roland R. Johnson
University of California
Lawrence Livermore National Laboratory
P.O. Box 808
Livermore, CA 94550

Chapter 14

Experiments on Cage and Poligon: Measuring the Performance of Parallel Blackboard Systems

H. Penny Nii, Nelleke Aiello, and James Rice

Abstract

Some ways in which blackboard systems can be made to operate in a multiprocessor environment are described in this paper. Cage and Poligon are two concurrent problem solving systems based on the blackboard model. The factors that motivate and constrain the design of parallel systems in general and parallel problem-solving systems in particular are discussed. Experiments performed on these two software architectures are described and their results and implications enumerated and explained.

14.1 Introduction

In this paper we introduce two software systems, Cage [Aiello 1986] and Poligon [Rice 1986]. Cage and Poligon are two blackboard systems designed to exploit multiprocessor hardware with the intent of achieving computational speed-up. Blackboard systems, although architecturally well suited for problems requiring the interpretation of multiple streams of signal and symbolic data, are often computationally too expensive to perform reasonably in a real-time environment. Cage and Poligon, the results of two subprojects of the Advanced Architectures project at the Knowledge Systems Laboratory of Stanford University, are attempts to produce high performance parallel blackboard systems.

The Cage system is a conservative attempt to introduce parallelism into the existing, serial blackboard architecture AGE. The Cage architecture represents an experiment into

what could reasonably be achieved given the current state of commercially available multiprocessors, most of which are shared-memory machines with from several to a few tens
of processors. An example of such a machine might be the BBN Butterfly^{TM} machine[1].

Poligon, which makes a radical shift from conventional blackboard systems, anticipates
future developments in parallel hardware architectures. It is designed to work on the next
generation of distributed-memory machines using hundreds or thousands of processors.

A general background and the general motivations for the development of Cage and
Poligon are discussed in Sections 14.2 and 14.3. The rationales for the design of Cage and
Poligon are discussed in Sections 14.4 and 14.5 respectively. Since both systems run on
simulated machines, the simulation system, CARE, is discussed briefly in Section 14.6.

Experiments have been performed on these two systems, some of which are described
in Section 14.8 together with their results. The application problem, Elint, which drove
the experiments, is described in Section 14.7. Since Cage and Poligon are very different
systems, both from the standpoint of software design and hardware requirements, it is
difficult to compare the performance of the two systems. In addition, since the research
goals for the two system architectures are different, the set of experiments performed on
them are different. To facilitate some form of comparison between the two types of system,
however, one particular experiment was designed to be performed, as closely as reasonably
possible, on both systems. The relative performance of the two systems is discussed in
Section 14.9 in the context of these particular experimental results.

14.2   Background

A *Concurrent Problem Solving System* is a network of autonomous, or semiautonomous,
computing agents that solve a single problem. In building concurrent problem solvers, our
objectives are twofold: (1) to evolve or invent models of problem solving in a multiagent
environment and (2) to gain significant performance improvement by the use of multiprocessor machines [Smith 1981]. One of the important practical concerns of using many
computers in parallel is to gain computational speed-up[2]. Centralized control is useful in
a serial (single) problem solver for obtaining a valid solution and coherent problem-solving
behavior, but it is not compatible with performance gain in a multiagent environment.
Cage and Poligon attempt to find a balance; to achieve adequate coherence with minimal
global control and to gain performance with the use of multiple processors.

---

[1]Butterfly is a registered trade mark of Bolt Beranek and Newman Corporation.

[2]Although multiple computers can be used because of the need for redundancy, a mix of specialized
hardware or a need for physical separation, and so on.

14.2.1 Problem Solving and Concurrency

Those problems that have been successfully solved in parallel, such as partial differential equations and finite element analysis, share common characteristics. They frequently use vectors and arrays; solutions to the problems are very regular, using well understood algorithms; and the computational demands, for example, for matrix inversion, are relatively easy to compute. In contrast, the class of applications we are addressing (and AI problems in general) are ill-structured or ill-defined. There is often more than one possible solution. Paths to a solution cannot be predefined and must be dynamically generated and tried, and generally, data cannot be encoded in a regular manner in array-like structures. The data structures for the solution states are often graph structures that must be dynamically created, precluding static allocation and optimization. These differences indicate that to run problem solving programs in parallel, current techniques for parallel programs must be augmented or new ones invented. It is worth reviewing some of the key points to be addressed in building concurrent, problem-solving programs.

14.2.1.1 Problem Solving Issues

Problem solving has traditionally meant a process of searching a tree of alternative solutions to a problem. Within each generate-and-test cycle, alternatives are generated at a node of a tree and promising ones selected for further processing. Knowledge is used to prune the tree of alternatives or to select promising paths through the tree. It is an axiom that the more knowledge there is, the less generation and testing has to be done. In most expert systems pieces of knowledge recognize intermediate solutions and solution paths, thereby eliminating search. These two types of problem-solving techniques have been labeled *search* and *recognition* [McDermott and Newell 1983]. In the search technique the majority of computing time is taken up in generating and testing alternative solutions; in the recognition technique the time is taken up in *matching*, a process of finding the right piece of knowledge to apply. Most applications use a combination of search and recognition techniques. A concurrent problem solving framework must be able to accommodate both styles of problem solving.

In serial systems, metaknowledge (control knowledge) is often used to reduce computational costs [Corkill and Lesser 1983]. One common approach decomposes a problem into hierarchically organized subproblems, and a control component selects an efficient order in which to solve these subproblems. This approach enhances the performance of search and recognition problem solving by reducing the number of alternatives to search or the amount of knowledge to match. In concurrent systems metaknowledge and controllers become fan-in points, or hot-spots. A *hot-spot* is a physical location in the hardware where a shared resource is competed for, forcing an unintended serialization. Does this mean that problem solving systems that rely on centralized control are doomed to failure in a concurrent environment? Can control be distributed? If so, to what extent? If more knowledge results in less search, can a similar trade-off be made between knowledge and control? That is, in concurrent systems where control, especially global control, is a serializing process, can knowledge be brought to bear to alleviate the need for control? These are some of the basic questions that studies in concurrent problem solving need to address.

14.2.1.2 Concurrency Issues

The biggest problem in concurrent processing was first described in [Amdahl 1967]. Simply stated, it is as follows: the length of time it takes to complete a run with parallel processes is the length of time it takes to run the longest serial process plus some overhead associated with running things in parallel. Take a problem that can be decomposed into a collection of independent subproblems that can run concurrently, but which internally must run serially. If all of these components are run concurrently, then the run-time for the whole problem will be equal to the run-time for the longest running component, plus any overhead needed to execute the subproblems in parallel. Thus, if the longest process takes 10% of the total run time if the processes were run end-to-end (serially), then the maximum speed-up possible is a factor of 10. Even if only one percent of the processing must be done sequentially this limits the maximum speed-up to one hundred, however hard one tries and however many processors are used. This is a very depressing result, since it means that many orders of magnitude of speed-up are only available in very special circumstances.

This raises the issue of *granularity*, the size of the components to be run in parallel. Amdahl's argument indicates the need for as small a granularity as possible. But, if the overhead cost of process creation and process switching is expensive, we want to do as much computation as possible once a process is running, that is, favor a larger granularity. In addition, in a multicomputer architecture a balance must be achieved between the load on the communication network and on the processors. It is often the case that as process granularity decreases, the processes become more tightly coupled, that is, there is a need for more communication between them. The communication cost is, of course, a function of the hardware-level architecture, including bandwidth, distance, topology, and so on. Finding an optimal grain size at the problem solving level is a multifaceted problem.

Even if one is able to find an optimal granularity, there are forces that inhibit the processes from running arbitrarily fast in parallel. Some of the more common problems are

- *Hot-Spots* and *Bottlenecks*: It is frequently the case that a piece of data must be shared. Multiple, simultaneous requests to access the same piece of data cause memory contention. A number of processes competing for a shared resource—memory or processors — causes a degradation in performance. These processor and memory hotspots restrict the flow of data and reduce parallelism.

- *Communications*: Multicomputer machines do not have a shared address space in which to have memory bottlenecks of the kind mentioned above. However, the communications network over which the processing elements communicate represents a shared resource which can be overloaded. It has a finite bandwidth. Similarly, multiple, asynchronous messages to a single processing element will cause that element to become a hot-spot.

- *Process Creation*: Execution of the subproblems, into which the overall problem is divided, requires that they run as processes. The cost of the creation and management of such processes is nontrivial. There is a process grain size at which it is faster to run many subprocesses sequentially than to execute them in parallel.

Some issues and constraints associated with parallelizing programs were introduced above. We now introduce some concepts that are important in writing concurrent programs, an understanding of which is useful to subsequent discussions.

- *Atomic operation*: This refers to a piece of code which is executed without interruption. In order to have consistent results (data) it is important to define appropriate atomic operations. For instance, an update to a slot in an object might be defined to be atomic. Primitive atomic actions are usually defined at the system level.

- *Critical sections*: Critical sections are usually programmer-defined and refer to those parts of the program which are uninterruptible, that is, atomic. The term is usually used to describe large, complex operations that must be performed without interruption.

- *Synchronization*: This term is used to describe that event which brings asynchronous, parallel processes together synchronously. Synchronization primitives are used to enforce serialization.

- *Locks*: Locks are mechanisms for the implementation of critical sections. Under some computational models, a process that executes a critical section must acquire a lock. If another process has the lock, then it must wait until that lock is released.

323

- *Pipeline*: A pipeline is a series of distinct operations which can be executed in parallel but which are sequentially dependent; for instance, an automobile assembly line. The speed-up that can be gained from a pipeline is proportional to the number of pipeline stages, assuming that each stage takes the same amount of time. Such a pipe is well balanced. Because reasoning consists of sequentially dependent inference steps, pipeline parallelism is a very important source of parallelism in problem solving programs.

14.2.1.3 Background Motivation

In experiments conducted at CMU [Gupta 1986], Gupta showed that applications written in OPS [Forgy and McDermott 1977] achieved speed-up in the range of eight to ten, the best case being about a factor of twenty. The experiments ran rules in parallel, with pipelining between the condition evaluation, conflict resolution, and action executions. The overhead for rule matching was reduced with the use of a parallelized Rete algorithm. (In programs written in OPS, roughly 90% of the time is spent in the match phase.) The speed-up factors seem to reflect the amount of relevant knowledge chunks (rules) available for processing a given problem solving state, and this number appears to be rather small. Although the applications were not written specifically for a parallel architecture, the results are closely tied to the nature of the OPS system itself, which uses a monolithic and homogeneous rule set and an unstructured working memory to represent problem solving states.

The premise underlying the design of Cage and Poligon is that this discouraging result can be overcome by dividing and conquering. It is hoped that by partitioning an application into loosely-coupled subproblems (thus partitioning the rule set into many subsets of rules) and by keeping multiple states (for the different subproblems), multiplicative speed-up, with respect to Gupta's experimental results, can be achieved. If, for example, a factor of seven speed-up can be achieved for each subproblem by the simultaneous execution of its rules, it is possible to obtain an overall speed-up of seven times the number of subproblems. The challenge, of course, is to coordinate the resulting asynchronous, concurrent, problem-solving processes toward a meaningful solution with minimal overheads. The focus of Cage and Poligon has been on the methods and techniques required to obtain coherent solutions from many independent subproblem solvers.

14.2.2 The Blackboard Model and Concurrency

The foundation for most knowledge-based systems is the problem-solving framework in which an application is formulated. The problem-solving framework implements a computational model of problem solving and provides a language in which an application problem can be expressed. We begin with the Blackboard Model [Nii 1986a], [Nii 1986b], which is a problem-solving framework for partitioning problems into many loosely coupled sub-problems. Both Cage and Poligon have their roots in the blackboard model of problem solving. The blackboard approach seems, at first glance, to admit the natural exploitation of concurrency, such as

- Knowledge parallelism, in which the knowledge sources and rules within each knowledge source can run concurrently;

- Pipeline parallelism, in which transfer of information from one level to another (one method of implementing a reasoning chain) forms pipelines; and

- Data parallelism, in which the blackboard is partitioned into solution components that can be operated on concurrently.

In addition, the dynamic and flexible control component can be extended to control the parallel execution of different components of the system.

These characteristics of blackboard systems have prompted investigators, for example [Lesser and Corkill 1983] and [Ensor and Gabbe 1985], to build distributed and-or parallel blackboard systems. The study of parallelism in blackboard systems goes back to Hearsay-II [Fennell and Lesser 1977].

The blackboard problem-solving metaphor is very simple: A collection of intelligent agents gather around a blackboard, look at pieces of information written on it, think about them, and add their conclusions as they come to them. This is shown in Figure 14.1.

There are some basic assumptions made in this model, an understanding of the implications of which is vital to an understanding of the difficulties of achieving parallelism in blackboard systems.

- All of the agents can see all of the blackboard all of the time, and what they see represents the current state of the solution.

- Any agent can write his conclusions on the blackboard at any time without getting in anyone else's way.

- The act of an agent writing on the blackboard will not confuse any of the other agents as they work.

These assumptions imply that a single problem is being solved asynchronously and in parallel. However, the problem solving behavior, if it were to be emulated in a computer, would

Figure 14.1: Blackboard metaphor

result in very inefficient computation. For example, for every agent to "see" everything simultaneously requires stopping everything until every agent has looked at everything.

Existing, serial blackboard systems make a number of modifications to this blackboard metaphor in order to make a reasonable implementation on conventional, serial hardware. In effect, the blackboard metaphor is modified so that it *cannot* be executed in parallel. Some of these modifications, also shown in Figure 14.2, are

- Agents are represented as *knowledge sources*. These knowledge sources are schedulable entities and only one can be running at any time. It will be shown later that one of the possible sizes for computational grains is the knowledge source.

- To coordinate the execution of knowledge sources, a scheduler, or some other central control mechanism, is implemented. In many ways, this is an efficiency gaining mechanism in which control knowledge selects only the most productive knowledge source at any given moment to work on the problem.

- The blackboard is not "globally visible" in the sense prescribed by the blackboard metaphor. Instead, the blackboard is implemented as a data structure, which is sufficiently interconnected to enable a knowledge source to find its way from one data item to a related one easily. Knowledge sources generally work on a limited area of the blackboard, known as the knowledge source's context. Often knowledge sources and their contexts are treated as self-contained subproblems.

326

- An implicit assumption is made that a knowledge source operates within a valid, or *consistent context*. That is, the values of the different properties of an objects on the blackboard are consistent with respect to each other, and are the same everywhere they are mentioned. To assure this, for example, a knowledge source is never interrupted while it is making changes to the blackboard.

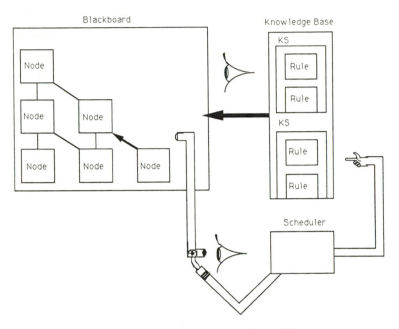

Figure 14.2: Serial blackboard model

Trying to parallelize serial blackboard systems characterized above directly has certain limitations. First, the granularity of the central scheduler that decides what knowledge sources to run in parallel is one of the main factors that limit speed-up. The results of a Cage experiment described later indicates that the main reason for its modest speed-up was the scheduler. To attain significant speed-up, the notion of centralized control must be abandoned. Second, one of the most difficult problems in parallel computation is to maintain consistent data values and to achieve a coherent solution state. In concurrent blackboard systems, consistency and coherence problems occur in three different contexts: (1) on the entire blackboard—maintaining relationships that make sense among the objects (global coherence of the solution); (2) in the contents of the nodes—assuring that all slot values are from the same problem solving state (mutual data consistency); and (3) in the slots—keeping the value being evaluated from changing before the evaluation is completed (data consistency).

14.3 The Advanced Architectures Project

Cage and Poligon, two frameworks for concurrent problem solving, are being developed within the Advanced Architectures Project (AAP) [Rice 1989] at the Knowledge Systems Laboratory of Stanford University. The objective of the AAP is the development of broad system architectures that exploit parallelism at different levels of a system's hierarchical construction. To exploit concurrency one must begin by looking for parallelism at the application level and be able to formulate, express, and utilize that parallelism within a problem-solving framework. A framework must, in turn, be supported by an appropriate language and a software-hardware system. The system levels chosen and some issues for study are

- Application level: How can concurrency be recognized and exploited?

- Problem solving level: Is there a need for a new problem-solving metaphor to deal with concurrency? What is the best process and data granularity? What is the trade-off between knowledge and control?

- Programming language level: What is the best process and data granularity at this level? What are the implications of choices at the language level for the hardware and system architecture?

- System-hardware level: Should the address spaces be common or disjoint? What should the processor and memory characteristics and granularity be? What is the best communication topology and mechanisms? What should the memory-processor organization be?

At each system level one or more specific methods and approaches have been implemented in an attempt to address the problems at that level. These programs are then vertically integrated to form a family of experimental systems—an application is implemented using a problem-solving framework using a particular knowledge representation method, all of which use a specific programming language, which in turn runs on a specific architecture simulated in detail on the Lisp-based CARE simulator [Delagi 1986] (see Section 14.6). Each family of experiments is designed to evaluate, for example, the system's performance with respect to the number of processors, the effects of different computational granularity on the quality of solution and on execution speed-up, ease of programming, and so on. The results of one such family of experiments have been reported in [Brown *et al.* 1986] and [Schoen 1986].

Within the context of this AAP organization, Cage and Poligon are two frameworks (or shells) implemented to study the problem-solving level. Both Cage and Poligon use frames and condition-action rules to represent knowledge. The target system architecture for Cage is shared-memory multiprocessors; the target architecture for Poligon is distributed-memory multiprocessors, or multicomputers.

Both Cage and Poligon aim to solve a particular, but broad, class of applications: the interpretation of continuous streams of errorful data, using many diverse sources of knowledge. Each source of knowledge contributes pieces of a solution which are integrated into a meaningful description of the situation. Applications in this class include a variety of signal understanding, information fusion, and situation assessment problems. The utility of blackboard formulations has been successfully demonstrated by programs written to solve problems in our target application class [Brown *et al.* 1982], [McCune and Drazovich 1983], [Nii *et al.* 1982], [Shafer *et al.* 1986], [Spain 1983], [Williams *et al.* 1984].

Most of the systems in this class use the recognition style of problem solving with knowledge bases of facts and heuristics; numerical algorithms are also included as a part of the knowledge. Some search methods are employed, but they are generally confined to a few of the knowledge sources. An example problem in this class, called Elint (described in Section 14.7), was implemented in both Cage and Poligon.

In designing a concurrent blackboard system for the AAP, two distinct approaches seemed possible; one, to extend a serial blackboard system, and the other, to devise a new architecture to exploit the event-driven nature of blackboard systems. Each has its advantages and problems; they are described in the following sections.

14.4 Extending the Serial System: Cage

In this section we discuss the Cage system, its origins, and its architecture [Aiello 1986]. In order to put this into a proper perspective, we first give a brief description of the (serial) AGE system [Nii and Aiello 1979], upon which Cage (Concurrent AGE) is closely modeled. The AGE and Cage systems are functionally identical other than that Cage allows parts of the system to be executed in parallel.

14.4.1 The AGE system

The AGE system is one implementation of the blackboard problem-solving model [Nii 1986a] and [Nii 1986b] mentioned in Section 14.2.2. The knowledge in an AGE application is expressed both in the structure of the blackboard—the declaration of the blackboard *levels*—and in the knowledge base itself. An AGE knowledge base is composed of a number of *knowledge sources*, each of which contains a number of *rules*. Rules are condition-action pairs, as is the case in most blackboard systems.

Knowledge sources are invoked by the scheduler, which is user programmable. The selection of applicable knowledge sources is performed by the use of *events*.

An event is a symbolic token that is posted by AGE after a knowledge source makes a significant modification to the blackboard. For instance, a chess playing blackboard system might, after placing the opponent in check, post an event indicating that the opponent is in check. This event is recorded by the system on a global event queue along with information about the posting agent and the cause of the event. This allows the system to focus its attention on the parts of the blackboard which are active and provides the appropriate context in which to invoke any appropriate knowledge sources. The event tokens are defined by the user and posted automatically by the AGE system any time a node on the blackboard is changed.

The knowledge sources are labeled with the event tokens in which they are interested. This allows the user-specified scheduling mechanism to invoke only those knowledge sources whose label matches the event token. The label on the knowledge source is referred to as the knowledge source *precondition*.

Within the knowledge sources rules can be invoked in two ways:

- The condition parts of the rules are evaluated until a match is found. This search for an applicable rule is performed serially in the lexical order of the rules. This mechanism is referred to as *Single-Hit*.

- The condition parts of all of the rules are evaluated and all rules that match are executed. The execution of the action parts of the matched rules is performed serially in the lexical order of the rules. This mechanism is referred to as *Multiple-Hit*.

These rule invocation strategies are peculiar to the AGE system and its derivatives.

14.4.2 The Cage Architecture

The basic components of the Cage system are as follows:

- A global data store (the blackboard) on which emerging solutions are posted as object, attribute, and value triples. Objects on the blackboard are organized into levels of abstraction.

- Globally accessible lists on which control information is posted (for example, a list of events, a list of expectations, and so on).

330

- An arbitrary number of knowledge sources, each consisting of an arbitrary number of rules.

- Control information that can help to determine at any given point in the problem-solving process which blackboard node is to be in focus and which knowledge sources are to be executed.

- Declarations that specify which components are to be executed in parallel and at what points synchronization is to occur. The components for potential concurrency are knowledge sources, rules, condition parts of rules, and action parts of rules.

The user can run Cage serially (at which point Cage behavior is identical to that of AGE), or with prespecified components running concurrently. In the serial mode, the basic control cycle begins with the selection and execution of a knowledge source. Cage uses a global list structure, called the *event list*, to record the changes to the blackboard. The scheduler selects one of the events (the user can specify how the event is to be selected, such as FIFO, LIFO, or any user-defined best-first method). The resulting event in focus is then matched against the knowledge source preconditions. The knowledge sources, whose preconditions match the focus event, are then executed in some predetermined order. The condition parts of the rules within each knowledge source are evaluated, and the action parts of the rules, whose conditions are satisfied, are executed. Each action part may cause one or more changes on the blackboard which are recorded on the event list. Figure 14.3 shows the Cage control cycle in the serial mode.

By selecting one of the concurrency control options, the user can alter the simple, serial execution of knowledge sources and their parts to execute in parallel. The various concurrency options shown in Figure 14.4 are summarized below.

Knowledge Source Control

Serial:

Pick an event and execute the associated knowledge sources.

Parallel:

As each event is generated execute the associated knowledge sources in parallel, *OR*

Wait until all the active knowledge sources complete execution and invoke the knowledge sources relevant to all the resulting events concurrently.

Within Each Knowledge Source

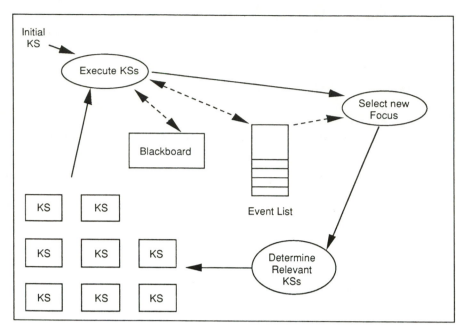

Figure 14.3: Cage serial control cycle

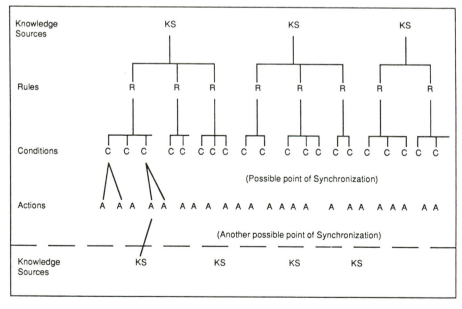

Figure 14.4: Parallel components of Cage

332

Serial:

> Perform context evaluation and then
>
> Evaluate the condition parts, then execute the action part of the first rule whose condition side matched (Single-Hit), *OR*
>
> Evaluate all the condition parts then execute serially all the action parts of those rules whose conditions side matched (Multiple-Hit).

Parallel:

> Perform context evaluation in parallel.
>
> Evaluate all condition parts in parallel, and then
>
> Synchronize (that is, wait for all the condition side evaluations to complete) and choose one action part, *OR*
>
> Synchronize and execute the actions serially (in lexical order), *OR*
>
> Execute the actions in parallel as the condition parts match.

Within Rules

Serial:

> Evaluate predicate in the condition part, then execute each action.

Parallel:

> Evaluate the predicates in the condition parts in parallel, then execute the actions in the action part in parallel.

14.4.3   Discussion of the Concurrent Components

We described the mechanisms for concurrency in Cage. We now discuss where and how these mechanisms can be used to gain speed-up.

14.4.3.1   Knowledge Source Concurrency

Knowledge sources are logically independent partitions of the domain knowledge. A knowledge source is selected and executed when changes made to the blackboard are relevant to that knowledge source. Theoretically, many different knowledge sources can be executing at the same time. But, knowledge sources are often serially dependent, reflecting the reasoning process.

In the class of applications under consideration, the solution is built up in a pipeline-like fashion up the blackboard hierarchy. That is, the knowledge source dependencies form a chain from the knowledge sources working on the most detailed level of the blackboard to those working on the most abstract level. The implication is that knowledge sources can run in parallel along pipes formed by the blackboard data. (When the program is model-driven, this pipeline works in the reverse direction.)

There are two potential ways for knowledge sources to run in parallel: (1) knowledge sources working on different regions of the blackboard asynchronously (working on sub-problems in parallel) and (2) knowledge sources working in a pipelined fashion exploiting the flow of information up, or down, the data hierarchy (pipeline the reasoning). Both sources of parallelism are possible due to data parallelism inherent in the application.

14.4.3.2 Rule Concurrency

Each knowledge source is composed of a number of rules. The condition parts of these rules are evaluated for a match with the current state of the solution, and the action parts of those rules that match the state are executed. The condition parts of all the rules in a knowledge source, being side-effect-free by design, can be evaluated concurrently without fear of unpleasant interactions. In cases where all the matched rules are to be executed (Multiple-Hit), the action parts can be executed as soon as the condition part is matched successfully. If only one of the rules is to be selected for execution (Single-Hit), the system must wait until all the condition parts are evaluated, and one rule, whose action part is to be executed, must be chosen[3]. The situation in which all of the rules are evaluated and executed concurrently potentially has the most parallelism. However, if the rules access the same blackboard data item, memory contention becomes a hidden point of serialization.

The asynchronous firing of rules is associated with two types of problem: timeliness and coherence. First, the state which triggered the rule may be modified by the time the action part is executed. The question is then: is the action still relevant and correct? Second, if a rule accesses attributes from different blackboard objects, there is no guarantee that the values from the objects are consistent with respect to one another.

Condition-part concurrency: Each condition part of a rule may consist of a number of predicates to be evaluated. These predicates can often be evaluated concurrently. In the chosen class of applications these predicates frequently involve relatively large numeric computations, making parallel evaluation worthwhile. However, as discussed above, if the clauses refer to the same data item, memory contention would force a serialization, nullifying the apparent benefits of concurrent execution.

Action-part concurrency: Often, when a condition part matches, more than one potentially independent action is called for, and these can be executed in parallel.

The problem of data consistency occurs both in Cage and in Poligon. It can be partially alleviated by defining an atomic operation that includes both read and write on an object.

---

[3]Refer to [Gupta 1986] for the results of running OPS rules in parallel.

This ensures that between the time that an item of data is read, processed, and the result stored, there is no change in the state of the object[4]. For this to be possible there are two requirements : (1) all the data needed by the knowledge source is stored in an object and (2) a commitment is made about the granularity of the critical section—for example, *read the data for the condition part of a rule and execute the action part*. However, for most applications a knowledge source needs data stored in more than one node; and given the goal of the research, it is undesirable to commit to any particular process grain size. In order to enable experimentation with granularity, atomic actions in Cage are kept small and locks, block reads, and block writes are provided. Although an atomic block-read or -write operation does not solve the problems of timeliness or global coherence, it does ensure that the data within each node is consistent. And, although locks have a potential for causing deadlocks, they are provided for the user to construct larger critical sections, for example, the object creation process is made atomic using locks.

14.4.3.3 Concurrency Control

The action parts of rules generate events, and knowledge sources are activated by the occurrences of these events. In the (serial) AGE system events are posted on a global event list and, based on the type of these events, a scheduler invokes one or more knowledge sources. In order to eliminate this serial control scheme, a mechanism to activate the relevant knowledge sources immediately upon event generation is needed. This immediate activation of knowledge sources still requires a scheduler in Cage, but it is very small, and, from a problem solving perspective, effectively eliminates global control. In some cases this is acceptable, but for those cases where a more elaborate control is needed a centralized scheduler-control mechanism is provided. For instance, one mechanism allows the accumulation of events, after which all knowledge sources relevant to a subset of the events can be invoked in parallel.

Some answers to the many questions raised about concurrent problem solving are embedded in Cage's architecture. However, much of the burden is passed on to the applications programmer. Some useful programming techniques that were discovered are discussed below.

14.4.4 Programming with Cage

There are a number of problems that crop up in concurrent systems that do not appear in serial ones. The solutions to some of these problems involve reformulating the application

---

[4]In Lamina [Delagi *et al.* 1986], another programming framework developed for the AAP project, the comparable atomic action is read-process-write.

problem; some involve the use of programming techniques not commonly used in serial systems. The techniques discussed below fall into the second category.

14.4.5   Pitfalls, Problems, and Solutions

A need for the following programming techniques arose while implementing Elint (see Section 14.7) in Cage.

- When the only things to run in parallel are the knowledge sources, it is possible to read all the attributes of an object that are referenced in a knowledge source by locking the object once and reading all of the attributes. This is in contrast to locking the object every time an attribute is read by the rules. In other words, all necessary blackboard data is collected into local variables in the knowledge source's activation context before any rules are evaluated. This ensures that all the rules are looking at data from the same time.

- In a serial blackboard system one precondition may serve to describe several changes to the blackboard adequately. For example, suppose the firing of one rule causes three changes to be made serially. The last change, or event, is generally a sufficient precondition for the selection of the next knowledge source. In a concurrent system, however, all three events must be included in a knowledge source's precondition to ensure that all three changes have actually occurred before the knowledge source is executed.

- In general, a simple precondition consisting of an event token is not sufficient as it would be in a serial system. A detailed specification of the activation requirements of the knowledge sources must be available, either in their preconditions or in the global scheduler.

- It is important for the programmer, when writing the condition parts of rules, to keep in mind the possibility of running the predicates concurrently. This involves keeping predicates from accessing the same data.

- Occasionally two knowledge sources running in parallel may attempt to change an attribute at almost the same time. It is possible that the first change would invalidate the later changes. To overcome this race condition, a conditional action—an action which checks the value of a slot before making a change—was added. An alternative solution to the race condition is to lock a node for an entire knowledge source execution, which would seriously limit parallelism.

336

14.5 Pursuing a Daemon-driven Blackboard System: Poligon

Control in the blackboard model can be summarized as follows: *knowledge sources respond opportunistically to changes in the blackboard.* As discussed earlier, in reality, and especially in serial systems, the blackboard changes are recorded and a control component decides which change to pursue next. In other words, the knowledge sources do not respond directly to changes on the blackboard. A central scheduler generally dictates the problem-solving behavior. This is a serial process.

The basic question that led to the design of Poligon is *What happens if you get rid of the scheduler?* Instead of waiting until a scheduler activates a knowledge source, why not execute the knowledge source immediately as the relevant data is changed by attaching the knowledge source to the data? A blackboard change can then serve as a direct trigger for knowledge source activations. To accomplish this, assign a processor-memory pair for each blackboard object (called a *node* in Poligon), and have the knowledge sources (now on the blackboard processing element) communicate changes to other nodes by passing messages via a communication network. (See Figure 14.5.)

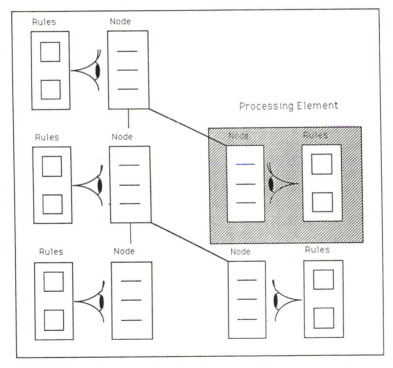

Figure 14.5: Organization of Poligon

Because a knowledge source is now activated directly by a blackboard change, and because a knowledge source is a collections of rules, one can view the rules as also being activated by that change. As a further refinement, a rule can be activated by a change to a particular slot (an attribute) of a blackboard node. If a change is made to a slot to which rules are attached, the condition parts of the triggered rules are evaluated; changes to other slots do not initiate any processing. Rule activation under these conditions are reminiscent of active values in object-oriented programming.

Poligon was designed from the start to exploit medium-grained parallelism; medium grain here referring to parts of rules, but not to small expressions. It is generally thought that in a shared-memory architecture performance gain levels off rather quickly as a result of physical limits in the bandwidths of the busses and switches connecting the processors and the memory. Thus, Poligon was designed from the start to be run on a form of distributed-memory multiprocessor. Because Poligon was designed for this form of hardware architecture, it differs considerably from existing serial implementations of blackboard systems.

14.5.1 The Structure of Poligon

In this section we describe the key features of Poligon. Instead of a detailed description of the implementation, a number of points that are central to Poligon's computational model are highlighted and contrasted with conventional blackboard implementations.

It should be noted that the user's cognitive model of the Poligon system and the system's implementation model are not necessarily closely connected. For instance, the Poligon system is implemented on an object-oriented substrate that uses message passing to invoke methods. No sign of this message-passing behavior is visible to the user, who views the Poligon system very much like a conventional blackboard system.

As stated above, Poligon is designed to run on distributed-memory machines—hardware that provides message-passing primitives as the mechanism for communication between processing elements. It is important to note that the way in which information flows on the blackboard can be viewed, at an implementation level, as a message-passing process. This allows a tight coupling between the implementation of a system such as Poligon and the underlying hardware. It also allows the development of a computational model that views a blackboard node as a process, responsible for its own housekeeping and for processing messages.

- *Poligon has no centralized scheduler.* This was motivated by a desire to remove any bottlenecks that might be caused by multiple, asynchronous processes trying to put events onto a single scheduler queue. (This problem is clearly manifested in Cage.) The elimination of a central scheduler requires a new knowledge invocation mechanism. *Poligon's rules are triggered as daemons by updates to slots in nodes.* The association between rules and the slots that trigger their invocation is made at compile-time, allowing efficient, concurrent invocation of all eligible rules after a blackboard event.

- When the centralized scheduler is eliminated, it also eliminates all global synchronization and any mechanism for focus of attention. This means that different parts of a Poligon program will run at different speeds, and each part will have a different idea of how the solution is progressing. The application writer is required not to make any assumptions concerning the global coherence or state of the solution.

- Having eliminated the scheduler, there is clearly no need for the separation of the knowledge sources from the blackboard. The Poligon programmer, therefore, specifies at compile-time the types of blackboard node with which a particular piece of knowledge is to be associated. At compile-time and at system initialization time, *knowledge is associated directly with the nodes on the blackboard that might invoke it.* In fact, when Poligon is running in its most optimized state the knowledge base is block-compiled and the rules are wired directly to the slots of the nodes, in which they are interested, eliminating all knowledge search.

- In conventional blackboard systems, knowledge sources are units of scheduling. If a system attempts to execute only its knowledge sources in parallel a great deal of potential parallelism will be lost by the failure to exploit parallelism at a finer grain. In Poligon, therefore, knowledge sources are simply collections of smaller pieces of knowledge in the form of rules. *All of the rules in a knowledge source can be executed in parallel.* Indeed, knowledge sources are compiled out by the Poligon compiler.

- Serial blackboard systems generally don't have a significant problem with the creation of new blackboard nodes. This is because of the atomic execution of knowledge sources. Such systems can usually be confident that, when a new node is created, no other node has been created that represents the same object. In parallel systems multiple, asynchronous attempts can be made to create nodes which are really intended to represent the same real-world object. Poligon provides mechanisms to allow the user to prevent this from happening.

- It is occasionally necessary to share data between a number of nodes. Since Poligon allows no global variables, it is necessary to find a way to define sharable, mutable

339

data, while still trying to reduce the bottlenecks that can be caused by shared data structures. Poligon, like many frame systems, has a generalized class hierarchy with the classes themselves being represented as user defined blackboard nodes. One way to view this is that the level structure on the blackboard is replaced by a class structure. The nodes belonging to a level are instances of a class. In addition, the classes nodes are active, serving as managers that create instance nodes. This level manager also stores data shared between all of the instances to support operations which apply to all members of a class. Shared data can therefore be implemented in a distributed manner by using slots on the level-manager (class) nodes.

- Most blackboard systems represent the slots of nodes simply as lists of values associated with the name of the slots. Because knowledge source executions are atomic in serial systems, programs can assume that no modification will have happened to the value list since it was read. In Poligon, because a large number of asynchronously running rules can be attempting to perform operations on the same slot simultaneously, a mechanism is needed to assure data consistency without slowing down the access to slots (a large critical section would reduce parallelism). *Poligon provides "smart" slots.* They are smart in the sense that they can have associated with them user defined behavior which can make sure that operations performed on the data leave the data consistent.

The problem of data consistency within a slot is reduced by the slot being able to determine cheaply and locally whether a modification is reasonable. Global solution coherence can be enhanced by the same process—slots can evaluate whether a modification will lead to a more precise solution. This causes a sort of distributed hill-climbing which helps the system evolve towards a coherent solution.

14.5.2   Shifting the Metaphor

Poligon's design looks very much like a frame-based program specialized for a particular implementation of the blackboard model. The expected behavior of the system is much closer to the blackboard problem-solving metaphor than serial systems, in one respect: the knowledge sources respond to changes in the blackboard *directly*[5]. There are two major sources of concurrency in this scheme, which are similar to those in Cage:

---

[5] As an historical note, this takes us back to Selfridge's Pandemonium [Selfridge 1959], which influenced Newell's ideas of blackboard-like programs [Newell 1962]. It also has some of the flavor of the actor formalism [Hewitt *et al.* 1973].

340

- Each blackboard node can be active simultaneously to reflect data parallelism—the more blackboard nodes, the more potential parallelism.

- Rules attached to a node can be running on many different processing elements simultaneously providing knowledge parallelism.

This daemon-driven system with a facility for exploiting both data and knowledge parallelism poses some serious problems, however. First, it is easy to keep the processors and communication network busy; the trick is to keep them busy converging toward a solution by doing useful work. Second, solutions to a problem will be nondeterministic, that is, each run will most likely produce different answers. Worse, a solution is not guaranteed since individual nodes cannot determine if the system is on the right path to an overall solution. That is, there is no global control to steer the problem solving. Within the AI field where we look for satisficing answers, nondeterminism *per se* is not a cause for alarm. However, nonconvergence to a solution or an incorrect solution is not acceptable.

One remedy to these problems is to introduce some global control mechanisms. Another solution is to develop a problem-solving scheme that can operate without a global view or global control. We have focussed our efforts in Poligon on the latter approach.

14.5.2.1   Distributed, Hierarchical Control

In Poligon, an hierarchical control mechanism is introduced that exploits the structure of the blackboard data. The level structure, in the AGE sense, of the blackboard are, as mentioned earlier, organized as a class hierarchy. Each level is a class and a blackboard object is an instance of that class. Class nodes, or level managers, contain information about their instances (number of instances, their addresses, and so on), and knowledges sources can be attached to level managers to control their instance nodes. Similarly, a super-manager node can control the level managers.

Within Poligon, the potential for control is located

1. Within each node, where action parts of the rules can be, though are generally not, executed serially. This is the only point at which the user can explicitly request serialization.

2. In the level manager which can, for example, be used to monitor the activities of its nodes. Since the level manager is the only agent that knows about the nodes on its level, a message that is to be sent to all the nodes on that level must be routed through their manager node. The level manager also controls the creation and garbage collection of the nodes, and it attaches the relevant rules to newly created nodes.

3. In the super-manager, whose span of control includes the creation of level managers and their activities, and indirectly their offspring.

The introduction of these control mechanisms solves some of the difficulties, but it also introduces bottlenecks at points of control, for example, at the level manager nodes. One solution to this type of bottleneck is to replicate the nodes, that is, create many copies of the manager nodes. The CAOS experiments, mentioned earlier, took this approach [Brown *et al.* 1986]. Although Poligon supports this strategy, our research is leading us to try a different tactic.

14.5.2.2 A New Role for Expectation-driven Reasoning

It was initially conjectured that model-driven and expectation-driven processing would not play a significant role in concurrent systems, at least not from the standpoint of helping with speed-up. One view of top-down processing in serial systems is as a means of gaining efficiency in the following way: In the class of applications under consideration, the interpretation of data proceeds from the input data up an abstraction hierarchy. The amount of information being processed is reduced as it goes up the hierarchy. Expectations, posted from a higher level to a lower level, indicate data needed to support an existing hypothesis, data expected from predictions, and so on. Thus, when an expected event does occur, the bottomup analysis need not continue up—the higher level node is merely notified of the event, and it does the necessary processing, for example, increases the confidence in its hypothesis. When the analysis involves a large search space, this expectation-driven approach can save a substantial amount of processing time in serial systems.

In Poligon hot-spots often occur at a node to which many lower level nodes communicate their results (a fan-in). The upward message traffic can be reduced by posting expectations on the lower level nodes and having them report back only when *unexpected* events occur. This approach, currently under investigation, is one way for a node to distribute parts of the work to lower level nodes, and hopefully relieves the type of bottlenecks caused by fan-ins at a node without resorting to node replication (which has its own management problems). This top-down expectation driven approach may turn out to be useful in relieving hot-spots. It is generally expected that within the abstraction hierarchy of the blackboard, information volume is reduced as one goes up the hierarchy. This translates into the following desideratum for concurrent systems: For an arbitrary node to avoid being a hot-spot, there must be a decrease in the rate of communication proportional to the number of nodes communicating with it. That is, the wider the fan, the less communication is allowable from each node to the fan-in point. It was found while reimplementing the serial

Elint application in Poligon, that the highest level nodes had to be updated for every new data item. Such a formulation of the problem, while posing no problem in serial systems, produces hot-spots and reduces parallelism in concurrent problem solvers.

14.5.2.3 A New Form of Rules

If, for any given data item, there are many rules that check its state, then the system must ensure that this data item does not change until all the rules have checked it. A typical example is as follows: Suppose there are two rules that are mutually exclusive, one performs some action if a data value is *on* and the other performs some other action if the value is *off*. How can we ensure that between the time the first rule accesses the data and the second does so, there is no other action that changes the data? It was found in Poligon (and also in Cage) that these mutually exclusive rules need to be written in the form of case-like conditionals (with the condition checking being atomic) to ensure data consistency. In these rules, at most one of the selectable action parts will be executed. Since the need for process creation and its maintenance is reduced by combining rules, this form of rule also helps to speed up overall rule execution. It does mean, however, that the grain size of the rules is generally bigger, at least at the source code level, and the programmers must think differently about rules than they do in current expert systems.

14.5.2.4 Agents with Objectives

At any given point in the computation, the data at different nodes can be mutually inconsistent or out of date. There are many causes for this, but one cause is that blackboard changes are communicated by messages and the message transit time is unpredictable. In the applications under consideration, where there are one or more streams of continuous input data, the problem appears as scrambled data arrival—the data may be out of temporal sequence or there may be holes in the data. Waiting for earlier data does not help, since there is no way to predict when that data might appear. Instead, the node must do the best it can with the information it has. At the same time, it must avoid propagating changes to other nodes if it has a low confidence in its output data or in its inferences.

Put another way, *each node must be able to compute with incomplete or incorrect data, and it must "know" its objectives to enable it to evaluate the resulting computation. A result is passed on only if it is known to be an improvement over a past result.* This represents a change from the problemsolving strategies generally employed in blackboard systems where the controller-scheduler evaluates and directs the problem solving. With no global controller to evaluate the overall solution state and with asynchronous problem-solving nodes, a

343

reasonable alternative is to make each node evaluate its own local state. Of course, there is no guarantee that the sum total of local correctness will yield global correctness. However, the organizations of blackboard applications seem to help in this matter. Blackboard systems are generally organized into subproblems, and each blackboard level represents a class of intermediate solutions. The knowledge sources are functionally independent, and their span of knowledge is limited to a few levels. This type of problem decomposition creates subproblem nodes (with relevant knowledge sources) which can have local objectives and a capability for self-evaluation[6]. The "smart" slots mentioned in Section 14.5.1 are used to implement this strategy.

The design of Poligon poses an interesting question—is it still a blackboard system? There is a substantial shift in the problem-solving behavior and in the way the knowledge sources need to be formulated. The structure of the solution is not globally accessible. There is no control mechanism to guide the problem solving at run time. The metaphor shifts to one in which each blackboard node is assigned a narrow objective to achieve, doing the best it can with the data passed to it, and passing on information only when the new solution is better than the last one. The collective action of the "smart" agents results in a satisficing solution to a problem[7].

Although there is a substantial shift away from the conventional implementation of the blackboard metaphor, Poligon evolved out of the mechanisms that were present in AGE. Most of the same opportunities for userdefined concurrency available in Cage are built into the system in Poligon. The Poligon language forces the user to think in terms of blackboard levels and knowledge sources. But the underlying system has no global data. Whether the divergence between the problem solving model (in the form of the Poligon language) and the computational model (in the form of its implementation in a particular form of hardware) makes the job of constructing concurrent, knowledge-based systems easier or more difficult for the knowledge engineer still remains to be seen. A difficulty might arise because the semantics of the Poligon language, that is, the mapping of the blackboard model to the underlying software and hardware architecture, is hidden from the user. For example, there is no notion of message-passing or of a distributed blackboard reflected in the Poligon language. In contrast, the choice of what, and how, to run concurrently is

---

[6]It is interesting to note that the need for local goals does not seem to change with process granularity. Although the methods used to generate the goals are very different, Lesser's group has found that each node in its distributed system needs to have local goals [Durfee *et al.* 1985]. In this system each node contains a complete blackboard system; each system (node) monitors the activities in a region of a geographic area which is monitored collectively by the system as a whole.

[7]In retrospect, these characteristics for concurrent problem solving seem obvious. When a group of humans solve a problem collectively by subdividing a task, we assume each person has the ability to evaluate his or her own performance relative to the assigned task. When there are uncaring people, the overall performance is bad, both in terms of speed and solution quality.

completely under user control in Cage.

14.6 The CARE Simulation System and Machine Architecture

CARE [Delagi 1986] is the name given both to the simulator used on the Advanced Architectures Project and to the hardware designs being developed on that simulator. The CARE software system consists of a kit of components with which the user can construct simulated multiprocessors. The processor components and their behavior and interconnection topology are easily defined and specialized by the user. CARE allows experimentation with a large number of simulated machines each with a differing numbers of processors. In addition, a number of system parameters can be used to investigate the performance of different hardware variants. For the purposes of the Cage and Poligon experiments, system parameters were held constant while the number of processors was varied for each experiment.

One of the most important features of the CARE system is the instrumentation that it provides (see Figure 14.6). The user can plug simulated probes onto the simulated multiprocessor. These probes take various measurements and are connected to instruments that display the different system characteristics. The instrumentation toolkit allows the user to watch the behavior of the system both from the point of view of hardware performance and the application program. This, for instance, allows the identification of bottlenecks and hot-spots during system execution. An example of a CARE instrument is shown in Figure 14.7.

The CARE machine architecture is not discussed in any detail in this paper, but some elucidation at this point should allow better understanding of the references made in later sections to the underlying hardware.

Each processing element in the CARE machine is made up of two processors; the *Operator*, whose purpose is to execute operating system functions and to perform the task of interprocessor communication, and the *Evaluator*, whose task is the execution of user code (see Figure 14.8). This design allows the user application to continue with its work, while communication is taking place.

The communication behavior of the simulated hardware used by Poligon and that used by Cage are different. In the Poligon system the CARE simulator is used to simulate an array of the processing elements, connected in a toroidal manner, such that each processing element can talk to its eight neighbors (up, down, left, right, and diagonal).

The Cage system uses an array wired in a similar manner, but in this case half of the pro-

Figure 14.6: CARE system's instrument toolkit. Collections of circuit components are wired to make multiprocessors. A variety of probes and instruments allows the flexible monitoring of both system and application.

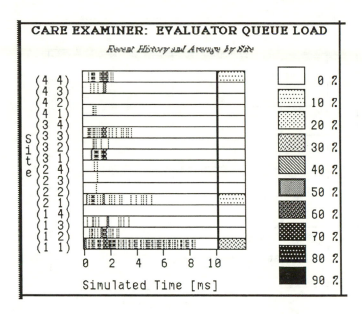

Figure 14.7: One of the instruments provided by the CARE system. This one shows the lengths of the Evaluator's process queue over time for each processing element (site).

cessing elements in the array are specialized to act solely as memory controllers or servers, that is the Evaluators are not used. This scheme combined with the dynamic, cut-through routing communication protocol [Byrd *et al.* 1987] used by CARE ensures that each of the processors executing user code has equal access to the memory-only processing elements. In this way Cage uses the distributed CARE architecture to simulate a sharedmemory machine.

14.7 The Elint Application

The Elint Application is a situation understanding application used in our experiments. It is, in fact, part of a larger signal understanding system called Tricero [Williams *et al.* 1984]. It was selected as an application, not only because is was in the problem domain in which we were interested, but also because it is a system of moderate complexity. It is complex enough to stress our software architectures and to give us a reasonable understanding of the problems of implementing real concurrent blackboard applications, yet simple enough that we could concentrate on the development of Cage and Poligon, rather than the application itself.

347

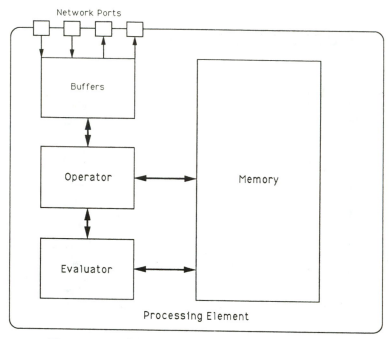

Figure 14.8: CARE machine processing element

The Elint task is to integrate reports from multiple, geographically distributed, passive radar collection sites in order to develop an understanding of the position and intentions of aircraft travelling through the monitored airspace (see Figure 14.9). As the aircraft travel, they use a number of different radar systems for such tasks as ground tracking-altimetry and target acquisition and tracking. The passive radar receivers in the Elint application are able to detect the bearing of the radar emissions (the position of the emitter must be deduced from more than one radar system, since these are passive devices) and the type of radar system which is making the emissions.

The application takes the multiple streams of reports from the collection sites, abstracts them into hypothetical radar emitters (perhaps aircraft), and tracks them as they travel through the monitored airspace. These emitters are themselves abstracted into clusters (perhaps formations of aircraft or single aircraft using multiple radar systems), which are themselves tracked (see Figure 14.10). Sometimes an aircraft in a cluster would split off, forcing the splitting of the representation of the cluster and rationalization of the supporting evidence. The nature of the radar emissions from the aircraft are also used to determine the intentions and degree of threat of each of the clusters.

The Elint application has a number of significant characteristics.

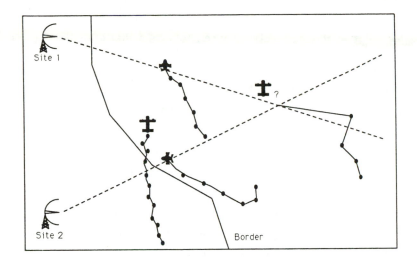

Figure 14.9: Elint problem. The radar collection sites must track the aircraft using the bearings of the received emissions. In this case the system must distinguish between the real positions of the aircraft and positions that are impossible.

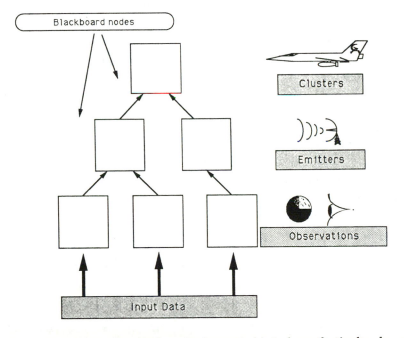

Figure 14.10: Elint application. Sensor data is abstracted into hypothetical radar emitters, which are tracked as clusters of emitters.

- The system must be able to deal with a continuous input data stream, and there is a need for real-time processing. (The Elint application on both Cage and Poligon is a *soft* real-time application, processing continuous input data as fast as possible. It is not a *hard* real-time application, since it does not guarantee any specific response time.)

- The application domain is potentially very data parallel. The ability to reason about a large number of aircraft simultaneously is very important.

- The aircraft themselves, as objects in the solution space, are loosely coupled.

An artifact of the application, which should be well understood, is the idea of an input data sampling interval. Since the Elint application is, in some sense, a simulation of the real world, it has a clock of its own which ticks at a constant rate with respect to the time in the real world. The data that comes into the system is timestamped. When the application's clock has reached a time which is the same as the timestamp on the input data record, the data is introduced into the system. The simulated time between two of these ticks can in certain circumstances be used to provide a measure of the throughput of the system. Thus, the tick interval is a parameter that can be varied to measure the system's potential throughput. For any given experiment the input data that was being used defines the number of radar emissions detected in that timeslice. From here on in this paper, therefore, we will use the term *timeslice* to indicate a period whose length is equal to one domain clock tick and *input data sampling interval* or *sampling interval*, for short, as the length of one timeslice in simulated time. The sampling interval will typically be quoted in simulated milliseconds or microseconds[8].

14.8   Experiments and Results

In this section we describe the experiments performed on the Poligon and Cage systems using the Elint application described in the previous section. We explain the reasons for performing the experiments, present the results of the experiments in detail, and draw conclusions from them.

It should be noted that the experiments mentioned here do not represent all of the experiments performed, but are simply those which we performed after learning from earlier ones. The earlier experiments taught us how better to perform the experiments and helped

---

[8]This is one aspect in which the Elint application is not realistic. In the real world, reports arrive at Elint data collection sites at a rate of one every few seconds. In order to stress our systems we had to turn up this rate until reports were arriving, in the case of Poligon, every 300 microseconds.

us to find numerous infelicities in both the Poligon and Cage systems and their respective Elint implementations.

14.8.1 Understanding the Graphs

In the following sections a large number of graphs will be shown, most of which will have the same format. The graphs plot either speed-up or both speed-up and input data sampling interval against the number of processors on which the experiment was performed. When both sampling interval and speed-up are plotted on the same graph, the sampling interval will always be labelled on the left Y-axis and the speed-up on the right Y-axis. A typical speed-up graph is shown in Figure 14.11.

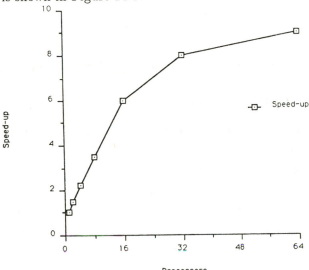

Figure 14.11: Example of speed-up *vs.* number of processors

In the best of all possible worlds, linear speed-up would result; that is, for each new processor that was added, the speed-up would increase linearly. The plot would be a straight line. In practice, however, the amount of realizable speed-up often tails off as the number of processors increases, giving the characteristic shape for the curve in Figure 14.11.

For the sake of completeness, the sampling interval will often be shown along with the speed-up. The speed-up is, in fact, simply calculated by dividing the sampling interval for the uniprocessor case by that for the N processor case. The display of the sampling interval shows how the system's throughput is affected by the number of processors. This is typically a decreasing curve as is shown in Figure 14.12—the system speeding up as the sampling interval is going down.

351

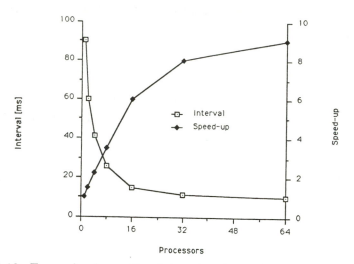

Figure 14.12: Example of sampling interval and speedup *vs.* number of processors

14.8.2   Experimental Method

An important part of these experiments is the method used to derive the measurements. Extensive experimentation was conducted before a method evolved, which could both define and measure the speed-up of these systems.

A simplistic method for measuring the speed-up of a parallel system would be to take the run-time for the application on a uniprocessor and then divide it by the run-time measured for different numbers of processors. This approach works well for systems whose behavior is not affected by the speed of the computation. In a real-time system with continuous streams of input data, however, the behavior of the system changes according to the degree to which the system is loaded. For example if more processors are added to a system it can become data starved, failing to deliver the speed-up of which it is capable.

To counter this phenomenon a different methodology was devised. A series of experiments is performed, during which the input data sampling interval is established such that on the largest processor network size the system is never data starved. The speed-up is measured using this sampling interval for other processor configurations, knowing that the delivered speedup for the large multiprocessor configuration would not be data starved. We found, however, that with all system parameters held constant (except for the number of processors) the application program was still behaving differently for the different experiments. This was because for small numbers of processors the system was getting backed up, and it was spending a significant amount of time queue-thrashing. That is, it was trying to keep data in order which, if the system had not been so overloaded, would not have got

352

out of order in the first place. This had the effect of making the application seem to run slower on smaller numbers of processors, thus giving an artificially high apparent speed-up.

What was needed, therefore, was a method for measuring the system's speed-up, while making sure that the system was always operating under the same load conditions. To accomplish this, the speed of the application on any particular processor configuration is defined as the lowest sampling interval (*i.e.*, highest throughput) that still gives nonincreasing latencies in the results. The latency measure is defined to be the time between the data coming into the system and the system emitting any reports concluded from the data.

Examples of increasing and constant latencies are shown in Figures 14.13 and 14.14. If the system can keep up with the sampling interval specified, the latency value should be largely constant, otherwise latencies increase over time as the system backs up.

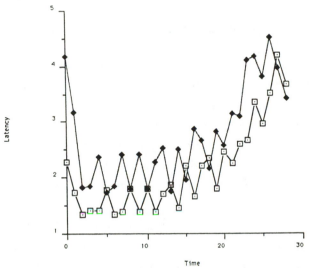

Figure 14.13: Increase of measured latency in domain time

In summary, the following method is used to measure the system's speed: for any given number of processors, the application is run with different sampling intervals until one is found that produces nonincreasing latencies. This sampling interval defines the processing speed for a given processor configuration. For a speed-up experiment, the above process is repeated for different processor configurations until the speed-up curve levels off.

14.8.3 Data Sets

An important aspect of the experiments on the Elint application is the scenario used to drive the experiment. A scenario represents the simulated radar information that an actual

353

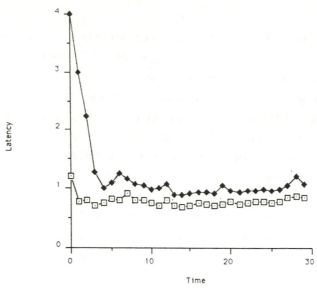

Figure 14.14: Constant measured latency over domain time

system would have received. In a real system, one would expect that the number of received radar emissions would vary over time. Although realistic, this sort of scenario is very hard to perform experiments on, since there are bound to be times when the system is either data starved or overloaded. Because of this, two of the data sets used for the experiments have the particular property that they have a constant density of input data over time.

The important characteristics of these data sets, therefore, are the number of radar emissions detected in each time unit, the number of radar emitters, and the number of clusters (see Section 14.7).

It should be noted that these data sets are used to measure the overall peak system performance for a given data set having the characteristics mentioned below. The system's response to transients in the amount of input data in a timeslice was not measured, nor was its performance for input data with less typical characteristics; for instance, a small number of aircraft, each using a large number of radar systems, or a large number of aircraft, each using very few radar systems. For convenience in describing the experiments, these data sets are referred to by the names *Thin, Fat,* or *Lumpy.* Their characteristics are listed below.

Fat. 240 Observations, 4 Emitters, 2 Clusters, 8 Observations per time-slice, 30 time-slices, 2 Observations per Emitter per time slice.

Thin. 60 Observations, 1 Emitters, 1 Clusters, 2 Observations per time-slice, 30 time-slices, 2 Observations per Emitter per time slice.

Lumpy. 186 Observations, 12 Emitters, 1 Cluster (which splits), 2 inconsistent observations, 1 ID error, variable number of Observations per time-slice, 30 time-slices.

14.8.4 Experiments with the Cage System

Seven separate sets of experiments, labeled C-1 to C-7, were run using the Elint application on Cage. The objectives of the first two sets of experiments were to compare Cage with Poligon, and to evaluate the efficiency and efficacy of the blackboard model for parallel execution. The third experiment compared different process granularity within Cage. The last four experiments were attempts to improve the performance of C-3 with different resource allocation schemes, more available processors, and a more efficient and accurate underlying simulator.

Cage is simulated on CARE as described in Section 14.6. In addition, Cage uses Qlisp [Gabriel and McCarthy 1984], a queue-based multiprocessing Lisp, which provides parallel evaluation of Let expressions and Lambda closures (see Figure 14.15). Each processor in the simulation is a multiprocess machine. Processes are assigned to available processors by a simple, nonpreemptive round-robin scheme.

Application
Cage
Qlisp
Care

Figure 14.15: System structure

14.8.4.1 Experiment C-1: Basic Speed-up

Description Experiment C-1 simply measures the speed-up attainable for a varying numbers of processors. For this experiment the scheduler started many knowledge source executions in parallel, waiting until they were done before selecting another set to run in parallel. Using a mixed data set with clusters, splits, inconsistencies, and id errors (the *Lumpy* data set) this experiment exercised all the problem solving capabilities in the Elint application. Experiment C-1 was run serially on one processor and on multiprocessors ranging from 2 to 16 processors. By comparing the time required to run the data set on one processor with the time required to run with the multiprocessors, a measure of speed-up was obtained. This is the simplistic speed-up measurement described in Section 14.8.2.

Purpose The main purpose of this first experiment is to get a base-line speed-up measurement for a simple concurrency configuration. The concurrency options used were concurrent knowledge source execution with synchronization control. This measurement can be used as a basis for comparing the performance of the system using more complex concurrency configurations.

Results The results of this first experiment are shown in Table 14.1 and Figure 14.16.

Table 14.1: Results of Experiment C-1

Processors	Speed-up at 20 ms Sampling Interval	Speed-up at 20 ms Sampling Interval
1	1.0	1.00
2	0.9	1.50
4	1.7	1.80
8	2.4	1.96
16	—	2.03

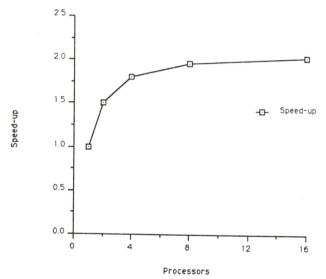

Figure 14.16: Speed-up derived in Experiment C-1

Interpretation The basic speed-up began to level off with 4 processors and reached a factor of 2 with 8 processors. To explain why only a factor of two speed-up was achieved, we need to look at the control cycle of a serial case. In the serial case, Figure 14.17, the scheduler selects one knowledge source to execute from among all the knowledge sources applicable at that time. In Experiment C-1 all the pending knowledge sources are executed in parallel, as seen in Figure 14.18.

Figure 14.17: Basic control cycle for serial execution

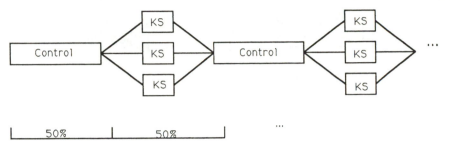

Figure 14.18: Basic cycle with serial control and parallel knowledge sources

Although the knowledge sources were run in parallel, "Amdahl's limit" restricts the speed-up to the longest serial component, in this case the scheduler plus the longest knowledge source. When all component parts of the execution were individually timed, it was found that slightly less than half of the total execution cycle time was being spent in the serial, synchronizing scheduler.

Experiment C-1 demonstrates that when knowledge source invocation is synchronized, speed-up gains are limited by the combined grain size of the scheduler and the largest knowledge source, no matter how many knowledge sources are run in parallel. It should be noted, however, that the grain size of the knowledge sources, as well as that of the scheduler, is very application dependent. In the following experiment knowledge sources were executed in parallel without synchronization, but knowledge sources were still invoked by a central scheduler.

14.8.4.2 Experiment C-2: Speed-up Measurement using a Smooth Data Set

Description The second experiment also measured speed-up, but in a manner that was felt to be more fair than the basic speed-up experiment, as explained in Section 14.8.2. Experiment C-2 was run with 1, 4, and 8 processors. In Experiment C-2 the knowledge sources were executed without synchronization, reducing the time spent waiting within the scheduler. As each knowledge source completed, the scheduler immediately invoked successor knowledge sources without waiting for any other knowledge sources to finish.

Purpose The purpose of this experiment was to see if eliminating synchronization results in improved speed-up. Experiment C-2 also provides standardized measurements of

357

speed-up and throughput to compare with results from Poligon, as was mentioned in the Introduction. This and subsequent experiments used the *Fat* data set.

Results The results of experiment are presented in Table 14.19 and Figure 14.20.

Figure 14.19: Results of Experiment C-2

Processors	Sampling Interval (ms)	Speed-up
1	700	1.00
4	225	3.11
8	180	3.89

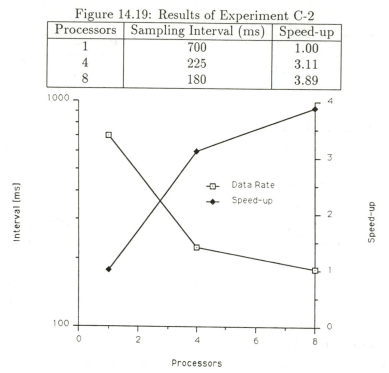

Figure 14.20: Results of Experiment C-2

Interpretation The Cage implementation of Elint has six different knowledge sources. During run-time, many copies of the knowledge sources can be running concurrently. Theoretically, if the pipelines formed between the levels on the blackboard are well-balanced, no overhead for process creation or process switching is incurred, and the scheduler takes zero time (all of which are impossible), a speed-up of $1 + P \times N$ should be possible with knowledge source concurrency, where P is the number of pipes and N is the number of knowledge sources in each pipeline. The *Fat* data set allows the creation of four pipes, so the maximum speed-up that is theoretically possible in this case is a factor of 25.

The speed-up obtained by running knowledge sources concurrently without synchronizing was slightly less than 4. This is almost double the speed-up obtained with synchronization, though some of this difference will have been caused by the smoother data set

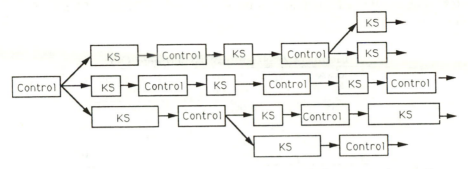

Figure 14.21: Logical view of unsynchronized knowledge source invocation

used. The time spent in the scheduler was reduced by almost half of that in Experiment C-1. However, it should be noted that the central scheduler is still a bottleneck. (See Figure 14.21.) Given the architecture of blackboard systems, the time spent in the scheduler can be reduced, but not eliminated, without a major shift in the way we view blackboard systems. Poligon is one such shift.

One important result of Experiment C-2 was to confirm the ease with which different concurrency options (see Section 14.4.2) could be used in Cage. Once the Elint application was running with parallel knowledge sources and synchronization, only one minor change to one rule was required to make it execute parallel knowledge sources without synchronization correctly. No change to Cage itself is required when changing the concurrency specifications.

14.8.4.3 Experiment C-3: Asynchronous Rules

Description In Experiment C-2 all possible concurrency at the knowledge source level was exploited. Experiment C-3 attempted to increase the speed-up by exploiting parallelism at a finer granularity. We hoped to gain an increase in the overall speed-up for each knowledge source by executing the rules of each knowledge source in parallel. There are several options in Cage for executing rules in parallel and we selected those that we expected to yield the most speed-up. The rules were executed with both condition and action parts running concurrently and without synchronizing between the condition and action parts. Otherwise the experimental variables of Experiment C-3 are identical to those of Experiment C-2—the same data set, sampling intervals, and number of processors.

Purpose The purpose of Experiment C-3 was to measure speed-up with process granularity at the level of rules.

Results The results of Experiment C-3 are presented in Table 14.22 and Figures 14.23 and 14.24.

Figure 14.22: Results of Experiment C-3

Processors	Speed-up over Experiment C-2	Total Speed-up
1	0.0%	1.00
4	-6.0%	2.92
8	5.8%	4.12
16	—	5.60

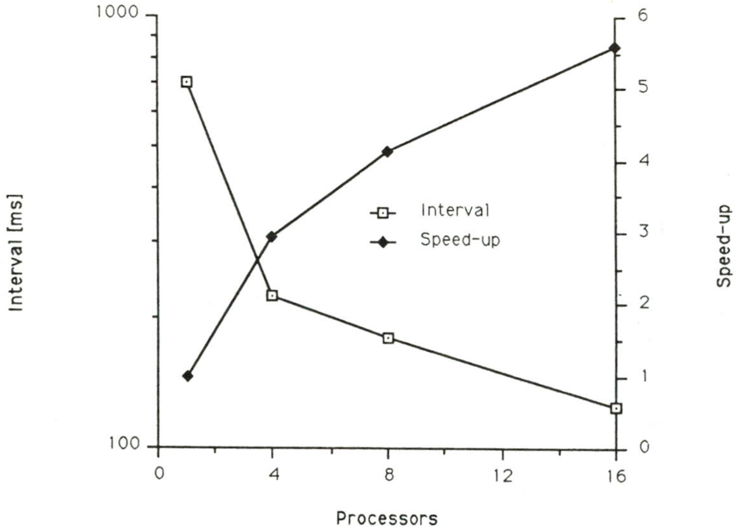

Figure 14.23: Experiment C-3

Interpretation The results of Experiment C-3 (see Table 14.2) were disappointing. For 8 processors only a 5.5% speed-up over Experiment C-2 was attained, for a total speed-up of 4.12. For 4 processors there was no speed-up at all over Experiment C-2. The overhead of spawning processes offset any gains from more parallelism.

There are several reasons for the small improvement in speed-up. In the Cage implementation of Elint, there are an average of 3.5 rules per knowledge source. Thus the maximum speed-up possible in Experiment C-3 is limited to 3.5 of the time spent executing knowledge sources in Experiment C-2. A detailed time trace revealed that in Experiment C-2 only 26% of the execution time of a knowledge source was expended on actually running the rules. A factor of 3.5 speed-up of only 26% of the total execution time, can result in at most a total gain of 7.4% over the knowledge source execution time.

360

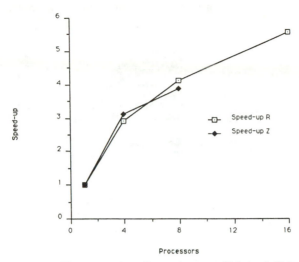

Figure 14.24: Experiments C-2 and C-3

Table 14.2: Speed-up change of Experiment C-3 over C-2

No. of Processors	4	8
Change in Speed-up	-6.0%	5.5%

These results are all for 8 processors. For 4 processors the gain was negated by the overhead cost of process spawning and resource allocation. The cost of spawning a rule was approximately the same as that for spawning a knowledge source.

As a result of these disappointing results, we ran Experiment C-3 on a 16 processor system in hopes of alleviating the congestion on the smaller grids. This resulted in slightly better results, a total speed-up of 5.6. This extra speed-up is due to the greater availability of free processors to handle the greater number of processes with rule level granularity.

14.8.4.4 Where Time is Being Spent in Cage

Throughout the Cage experiments with Elint, we had been troubled that the throughput Cage could achieve was low relative to Poligon. The best sampling intervals for Cage up to this point were around 120ms, while Poligon showed best sampling intervals in the order of a few milliseconds. In this section we explore the causes for the poor throughput.

During the experiments all the component parts of Cage were timed. In addition, timings for various parts of Qlisp were also taken. Figure 14.25 shows the average times taken for the basic components of the Cage system to process one data point in one time interval. As expected, most of the time was being spent setting-up and executing knowledge sources. Table 14.3 shows a breakdown of the time spent within a knowledge source. The times are averages for an entire simulation of the *Fat* data set, with 16 processors for Experiment C-3.

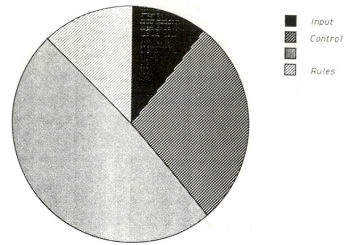

Figure 14.25: Average system usage per input data point

Table 14.3: Time Distribution for Typical Knowledge Source Execution

Knowledge Source	Average (ms)	High (ms)	Low (ms)
Wait and start-up time	2.48	71.84	0.45
Instantiation	0.62	8.94	0.12
Definitions	27.52	184.92	0.90
Creation	17.56	123.90	0.95
Node create	1.97	2.97	1.06
Match existing nodes	2.29	7.96	0.16
Qlisp	15.23	120.67	0.95
Slot reads	0.97	11.37	0.06
Rule wait and start-up	4.39	79.58	0.51
Rule execution	3.22	82.88	0*
Total execution time	28.45	186.09	1.19

*The lowest time for rule execution was too short to register accurately on Care's clock, which has an error margin of 30 ms.

14.8.4.5   Experiment C-4: Process Allocation

While the averages in the table in Table 14.3 are interesting, pointing out obvious places that need to be remedied, they do not tell the entire story. The first trace files showed timings that were very spiky. For example, while the average time for a knowledge source instantiation is 0.62ms, there were times when instantiation took as long as 8.94ms and other times when it only took 0.12ms. An initial explanation was that the spikes were caused by blocked and descheduled processes[9]. This is an indication of problems in resource allocation.

If the spikiness is due to competition between processes for processors, then we should see an increase in speed-up and a decrease in the spikiness by increasing the number of processors available to run the processes. An earlier C-3 experiment did show a significant improvement in speed-up between 8 to 16 processors and a reduction in spikiness. To prevent processes from being descheduled when they block, a variation on Experiment C-3 was run. Certain processes were preallocated to specific processors which were made unavailable for other processes; that is, some processors became special purpose processors. The preallocated processes were the input handler, the node creation-match handler, and the scheduler—all of which are large and used often. This experiment was run only on a 16-processor system, the minimum amount of hardware deemed necessary for this configuration. The results of this experiment were not conclusive.

The increase in speed-up of 3% (see Table 14.4) falls within the margin of error for these experiments and is not significant. However, while speed-up was not significant there was a reduction in the spikiness observed in the traces. The highs in Table 14.3 were reduced in every case, with an average decrease of 5.4ms, or 8%. However, the queue lengths for knowledge sources and node creation-match increased, indicating that (1) insufficient numbers of processors were available for the knowledge sources because of the three preallocated processors and (2) the node creation-match handler probably needed two or more processors to handle its load.

Table 14.4: Experiment C-3 Results Using Process Allocation

Number of processors	16
Speed-up for C-3	5.6
Speed-up with allocation	5.7
Increase	3%

14.8.4.6 Experiment C-5: Process Allocation

A second experiment involving specialized processor allocation was more successful. In this case only one processor, the input-handler, was used to execute the entire input procedure. Previously the creation of new input nodes (objects on the observation level), one for each

---

[9]Qlisp will deschedule a blocked process by placing the blocked process on the local processor queue and running the next process on that queue if there are other processes waiting on that queue. The blocked process must then wait for the new process to finish before the blocked process can resume.

input data item, had been handled by a separate creation handler. By eliminating the cost of spawning the separate creation process, and with it the possibility of blocking the input process while waiting for the creation to complete, the input node creation time was decreased by 59%. Also, spikiness in the creation measurement almost disappeared. These results are summarized in Table 14.5.

Table 14.5: Results of Experiment C-5

Experiment	Average	High	Low
Input node creation on different processor (C-3)	15.39	91.54	5.05
Input node creation on input processor	4.87	6.78	4.23

Although tuning the application by preallocating some processors for special purposes does gain some speed-up, an easier solution may be to use more processors. The last two experiments test this hypothesis by using an additional 16 processors, 32 in all.

14.8.4.7 Experiment C-6: Multiple Node Creators

In this and the final experiment the number of available processors was increased to determine if an insufficient number of processors was limiting the throughput. In this experiment the number of node creation process handlers was also increased from 1 to 4 in an attempt to break-up the node creation bottleneck. A major disadvantage of using more than one processor for creation is the possibility of two processors creating the same node at the same time. In order to bypass this problem, we dedicated a processor for each level of the blackboard to create its nodes. By tying the creation processes to individual blackboard levels, we avoided the problem of duplicate nodes. In preliminary runs of experiment C-6 we found that the addition of 16 processors, without specialized allocation of those processors, resulted in a negligible improvement in throughput. However, the allocation of some of those new processors specifically for node creation handling resulted in a 22% improvement in throughput over the best results of Experiment C-5, as shown in Table 14.6.

Table 14.6: Throughput Results of Experiments C-5, C-6, and C-7

Experiment	ms	Increase over C-5
C-5: Single creation processor	40	0%
C-6: Multiple creation processors	31	22%
C-7: Local creation	25	37%

14.8.4.8 Experiment C-7: Local Node Creation

In the final experiment we tried to eliminate the node creation bottleneck completely by doing all creation on the local processor, instead of on one or more specially allocated processors. To prevent the creation of duplicate nodes, the blackboard level node was locked by the knowledge source or the rule requesting the creation, until either a new node was created or an existing one was found. The use of local creation (on the same processor as the knowledge source or the rule requesting the node creation) improved throughput to 25ms, or a 37% improvement over Experiment C-5 (see Table 14.6).

14.8.4.9 Summary Discussion

There are two important measurements that can be considered the cumulative results of the Cage experiments. These are the maximum relative speed-up—comparing uniprocessor runs with multiprocessor runs, and the minimum sampling interval—measuring the total throughput.

Speed-up   Speed-up is a relative measure, comparing the uniprocessor speed with multiprocessor speed, using the methodology discussed in Section 14.8. The maximum speed-up achieved by Cage was 5.9 using a 32 processor grid with knowledge sources and rules running concurrently without synchronization. The factors limiting speed-up to 5.9 include

- Existence of central scheduler.

- Serial definition section of knowledge sources.

- Inefficient allocation of processes to processors.

- The high overhead of closures within knowledge sources which caused the copying of large amounts of local data combined with slow communication between the processors and memories.

Serial Definitions: In Cage each knowledge source consists of a set of local bindings, which we call *definitions*, and a set of condition-action rules which can reference the local definitions. The definitions include references to blackboard nodes, calculations with values retrieved from those nodes, and the creation of new nodes. The definitions are the only part of the knowledge sources executed serially during the Cage experiments. By executing the definitions for each knowledge source in parallel we could theoretically expect as much as a 40% increase in speed-up because there are an average of 11.5 definitions per knowledge source and definitions account for about 89% of the total knowledge source cost.

Executing the definitions in parallel is an option in Cage. The speed of the definitions would then be limited by the longest definition. A side-effect of a definition can be the creation of a new node. From Table 14.3 we can see that creation of a new node or matching for an existing node costs 63% of the total definition time. However, these definitions, as specified by the Elint application, are likely to have a number of implicit points of serialization because of data dependencies and do not all make equal computational demands. Thus the achievable improvement, in practice would be much less than the 63% quoted above.

Resource Allocation: The second way to gain speed-up is to improve the resource allocation. However, in most AI programs it is not possible to prespecify optimal allocations because of the dynamic nature of the programs. Given an application in Cage, a good resource allocation scheme can be evolved through experimentation, as was seen in Experiments C-4 , C-5, and C-6.

For Experiments C-1 to C-3 the identical allocation scheme was used regardless of the number of processors used, statically assigning some processes (input handler, for example) to specific processors but allowing them to be used by other processes. For example, in Experiment C-5 data input time was reduced from 15ms to 6.5ms with hand crafted processor allocations. Likewise, in Experiment C-6, which assigned separate processors to each blackboard level for node creation, throughput improved by 22% over Experiment C-5, which used a single creation process. This general scheme could be used for specific applications and specific numbers of processors.

Qlisp: The final factor limiting speed-up for Cage is the high overhead costs of the use of the Qlisp implementation, particularly Qlisp process closures. A Qlisp process closure is expensive for Cage, because Cage requires the copying of the context (the local definitions of a knowledge source) from the spawning processor to the executing processor. This overhead accounts for approximately 2/3 of the total node creation time.

Throughput Throughput is an absolute measure, measuring the rate at which input data can be processed, or the sampling interval, as discussed in Section 7. When the throughput that Cage can achieve is compared with that of Poligon, it is relatively low. The minimum sampling interval for Cage is about 10 times that of Poligon for the same number of processors. Cage was limited to a best sampling interval of about 25ms. The general reasons that limit speed-up also apply to the relatively poor throughput. First, a more efficient use of Qlisp, eliminating one unnecessary call, led to a 22% reduction in the sampling interval. Second, the latest test runs show a reduction in the sampling interval of 43% with the use of the latest CARE simulator. Third, as seen in Experiment C-6, the sampling interval was reduced to 31ms with 32 processors with some simple resource allocation optimization.

To summarize, Cage can execute multiple sets of rules, in the form of knowledge sources, concurrently. If the rule parallelism within each knowledge source could provide a certain speed-up, and if many knowledge sources could be run concurrently without getting in each other's way, it was hoped that we would get a multiplicative speed-up. The extra parallelism coming from working on many parts of the blackboard, in other words, by solving subproblems in parallel. It was found, however, that the use of a central scheduler to determine which knowledge sources to run in parallel drastically limits speed-up, no matter how many knowledge sources are executed in parallel. This is primarily a function of the granularity of the serial components. Nonetheless, a trade-off must be made between the high cost of process creation and switching, and granularity. We were able to get a speed-up factor of 4 by running knowledge sources in parallel. However, we were not able to get any significant speed-up by running the rules within each knowledge source in parallel, due in part to: (1) the large chunk of serial definitions in each knowledge source; (2) the fact that there is only an average of 4.5 rules in each knowledge source, and (3) the high overhead cost of process creation and switching. With more efficient definitions, additional rules, and faster process switching we may be able to get better relative speed-up and a higher throughput.

14.8.5   Experiments with the Poligon system

The following sections detail a number of experiments performed on the Poligon system using the Elint application. The purpose of these experiments was

- To measure the benefits of pipeline and data parallelism in the application.

- To determine the ability of the system to exploit rule parallelism.

- To estimate the costs of running the system without system optimizations, which reduce the ability of the programmer to debug applications.

- To determine whether some changes to the timing of the system were valid.

- To measure the costs of many of the primitive operations in Poligon so as to be able to estimate the granularity of a Poligon program.

14.8.5.1 Experiment P-1: Thin Data Set

Description This experiment simply used the experimental method elucidated in Section 14.8.2. Nothing special was done to the system in order to perform it. The data set was run on 1, 2, 4, 8, 16, 32, 64 and 128 processor systems. In order to determine each experimental data point, the input data sampling interval was adjusted until the latencies for the reports generated were nonincreasing.

Purpose The purpose of this experiment was threefold. First, it was to measure the performance of the system by deriving both speed-up and minimum sampling interval measures. Second, the experiment was intended to provide a base-line for comparison with subsequent experiments. Third it was intended, to evaluate the speed-up provided by the Elint application as a result of pipeline parallelism. This latter can be done using this data set because the data set results in the creation of only one pipe in the solution, unlike subsequent experiments using the *Fat* data set.

Results The results derived from this experiment are shown in Table 14.7 and are also shown in Figure 14.26. The minimum sampling interval is 2.5ms with 64 processors.

Table 14.7: Results of Experiment P-1

Processors	Sampling Interval (ms)	Speed-up
1	9.0	1.0
2	5.5	1.6
4	4.5	2.0
8	4.0	2.3
16	3.1	2.9
32	2.6	3.5
64	2.5	3.6
128	2.5	3.6

Interpretation From this experiment we can see that the Poligon system has produced a speed-up of 3.6 as a result of pipeline parallelism. This is a fairly encouraging result, since it shows that a certain amount of parallelism is being achieved due to parallel rule execution. We can conclude this because the pipes formed by the Elint application have only three stages resulting in a maximum speed-up of three for a simple pipe (see Figure 14.27).

368

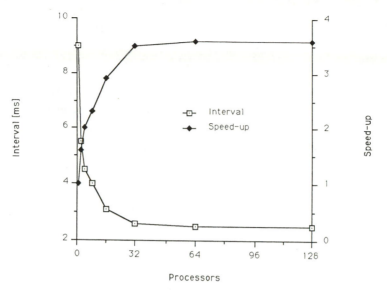

Figure 14.26: Results of Experiment P-1

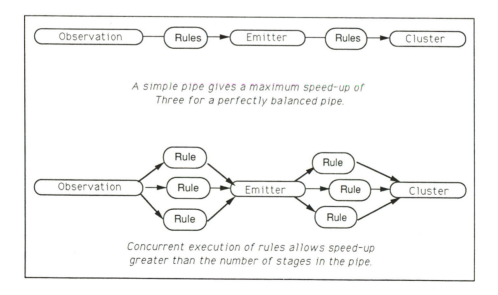

Figure 14.27: Rule parallelism in Poligon

14.8.5.2 Experiment P-2: Fat Data Set

Description This experiment was exactly the same as Experiment P-1, except for the data set used, which was the *Fat* data set.

Purpose The purpose of this experiment was twofold. First, it was to provide a baseline by which the Poligon system's performance could be compared with the implementations of the Elint application using the Lamina[10] and Cage systems. Second, it was intended to give a measure of the ability of the Poligon system to exploit parallelism in the data. This could not be determined from the previous experiment because the data set only allowed the creation of a single pipe during the execution of the program. In the *Fat* data set there were multiple emitters and clusters, which caused, quite intentionally, the creation of multiple pipes during the solution of the problem. In the *Fat* data set one would expect four pipes to be created. However, this does not mean that one would necessarily expect the speed-up to be four times greater than that delivered by a data set only one quarter the size (the *Thin* data set), although one might hope that it would be.

Results The results derived from this experiment are shown in Table 14.8 and in Figure 14.28. The minimum sampling interval is 2.7ms with 128 processors.

Table 14.8: Results of Experiment P-2

Processors	Sampling Interval (ms)	Speed-up
1	31.0	1.0
2	18.0	1.7
4	15.0	2.1
8	16.0	1.9
16	10.0	3.1
32	4.0	7.8
64	2.9	10.7
128	2.7	11.5

Interpretation The minimum sampling interval shown above is a measure of the application's ability to process data. This figure is compared to the best sampling intervals of the implementations of Elint using the Cage and Lamina systems in Table 14.9.

There are a number of reasons why the Poligon implementation of the Elint system was not as fast as that using Lamina. These fall into two main groups, those due to the

---

[10]For more information on these experiments, please see [Delagi and Saraiya 1988].

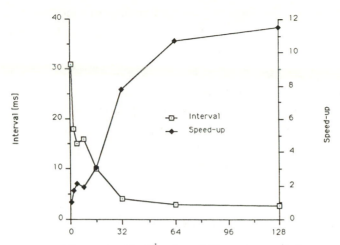

Figure 14.28: Results of Experiment P-2

Table 14.9: Peak Throughputs of Elint Implementations

System	Best Sampling Interval (ms)
Lamina	0.5
Poligon	2.7
Cage	25.0

encoding of the application and those due to the framework itself.

Application: The Elint application in Poligon was intentionally not tuned. That is to say, the application was an attempt to make an implementation of the original, serial implementation of Elint done using AGE. As a result of this, the application was coarser grained than the Lamina implementation (for example Lamina used seven-stage pipes). It was also not redesigned so as to improve its efficiency, whereas the Lamina implementation went through a number of different designs, so as to improve its efficiency and the balance of its pipes. Similarly, the Lamina implementation of Elint used a carefully crafted resource allocation strategy, while Poligon used a simple, random allocation strategy. Although effectively the only tuning done to the Poligon implementation of Elint was the addition of type declarations, this should not be taken as an indication that this is the sort of performance that one might expect from an application written by a naive user. The implementor of the application was, in fact, also the implementor of the Poligon system.

Framework: It is clear that there are significant costs associated with maintaining the abstraction model and mechanisms supported by Poligon. This has a substantial effect upon the minimum grain size that the system is able to achieve. The granularity of the Poligon system will be discussed below in greater detail. In short, the costs incurred by

371

the Poligon framework over those incurred by the Lamina implementation of Elint are: (1) the cost of rule invocation, (2) the cost of reading slots (due to the complex behavior of slots) and the cost of writing slots (due to the smart-slot protocol), and (3) the costs of communication.

The second conclusion that can be drawn from this experiment concerns Poligon's ability to exploit data parallelism. The minimum sampling interval for this experiment was not statistically different from that in Experiment P-1 (see Table 14.10). We can conclude, therefore, that almost linear speed-up results from increasing the width of the input data stream.

Table 14.10: Peak Throughput of Poligon Elint Application

Experiment	Data Set	Best Sampling Interval (ms)
P-1	*Thin*	2.5
P-2	*Fat*	2.7

14.8.5.3   Experiment P-3: Multiple Rules

Description   This experiment was performed using the *Thin* data set. All data points were measured on a 128 processor network. The Poligon system was modified so that whenever a rule was triggered to fire it would actually fire N rules, where N was a user definable parameter. Of these rules all but one were specialized so that they performed all of their operations except for executing their action parts. This can be done because of the guaranteed sideeffect free semantics of rule condition parts.

Purpose   The reason for performing this experiment was to try to find some measure of the ability of the Poligon system to exploit rule parallelism, that is, achieve speed-up through the concurrent activation of rules. Unfortunately, the Elint application was very sparse in knowledge and it is very hard to determine whether a system with different amounts of knowledge is solving qualitatively the same problem, so adding more knowledge would not give a good measure. It was decided, therefore, to invoke dummy rules to simulate, as closely as possible, the costs of rule invocation without actually executing the action parts of the rules. This guarantees that the system still performs as it should. If the Poligon system is able to exploit rule parallelism, then one would expect that the minimum input data sampling interval would remain constant, irrespective of the number of dummy rules fired. The slow-down experienced by the application should, therefore, give a rough measure of the usefulness of Poligon's architecture to exploit multiple, simultaneous rule activations.

372

Results The results of Experiment P-3 are shown in Table 14.11 and Figure 14.29.

Table 14.11: Results of Experiment P-3

Number of rules fired (including nondummy rule)	Sampling Interval (ms)	Slow-down
1	2.5	1.0
2	4.0	1.6
3	5.0	2.0
4	5.5	2.2

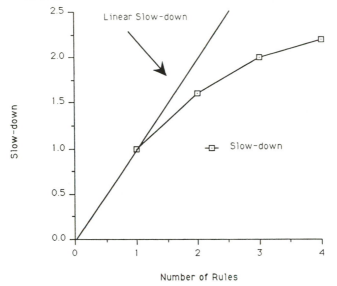

Figure 14.29: Slow-down due to invoking dummy rules in the Elint application. Values below the *Linear Slow-down* line indicate the exploitation of useful parallelism

Interpretation First, it should be noted that this experiment was performed on a fixed processor network size to eliminate one more variable factor. However, as the number of dummy rules activated increases, one would expect that the resources would become more scarce, reducing the performance of the system. This should be kept in mind when considering these results.

If one assumes that the amount of work performed by a dummy rule activation is approximately equivalent to the amount of work done by a nondummy rule, then we can conclude that the system slowed down by only a factor of 2.2, while doing four times as much work. This is by no means a perfect result, but it shows that the Poligon system can scale to cope with a knowledge base at least four times as large as that used by the Elint system and not clog up completely. In this case *large* is taken to mean the average number of applicable rules for any given set of slot updates. Untriggered rules cost nothing in terms of rule invocation overhead. The slowing down of the system was due to the following:

- The serial execution of the code that invokes rules.

- Resource contention.

- Communication overhead.

14.8.5.4 Experiment P-4: Make-Instance

Description In this experiment the 64 processor data point of Experiment P-2 was rerun with the Poligon system modified so as to charge for the time taken during the creation of Poligon nodes.

Purpose During all of the other experiments reported here the creation of the actual Lisp machine *Flavors* instance, which represents a Poligon node, is taken to take zero time. The reason for this is that Poligon nodes are implemented as *Flavors* instances and each of their slots are also *Flavors* instances. In a real system one could, with suitable compilation, implement these nodes simply as arrays. Even when the system does not charge for this instantiation the simulation still charges for the initialization of the node, which does not happen at *Flavors* instance creation time, since this occurs after the system's call to Make-Instance. In a real system, therefore, the creation of a node could be accomplished simply by allocating the memory and BLTing[11] a template into it. This could be done in a time which would be very small relative to the other times for operations in the system. Thus, it was decided not to charge for this instantiation in the simulation, because *Flavors* instance creation is very expensive due to its initialization protocol. This experiment, therefore, was a reality check to determine how much the experimental results were being affected by not charging for the creation of instances.

Results The minimum sampling interval achieved is 3.4ms.

Interpretation When the Elint system charged for the instantiation of *Flavors* instances the fastest sampling interval that the system could handle slowed down by some seventeen percent. From this one can conclude both that the experiments were not vastly affected by not charging for instance creation and that in a real system one would want to design the system so as to avoid this extra cost which, although not vast, is still significant.

---

[11]BLT instructions are fast Block Transfer instructions.

14.8.5.5 Experiment P-5: Optimization

Description This experiment was performed by rerunning the 64 processor data point taken for the experiment on the *Fat* data set. But, before this was done the Poligon system and the application were recompiled so as to be running in Poligon's development mode, with all of the Poligon system's optimizations turned off and source code debugging switched on.

Purpose This experiment was designed to show the relative performances of applications running in Poligon's development mode and in Poligon's production mode. A data point of this nature would allow one to make an estimate of the best case performance of one's system while still in the development phase.

Results The minimum sampling interval achieved is 9.0ms.

Interpretation This experiment showed that the benefit in application performance of the optimizations provided by Poligon over the development, unoptimized case is about a factor of three.

14.8.5.6 Experiment P-6: Granularity

Description This series of experiments was performed on the Poligon system without it running under the CARE simulator. Experiments were performed which timed a large number of the following:

- Slot reads.

- Slot writes.

- Slot writes, including the execution of rule invocation code up to but excluding the actual triggering of the rule.

- Slot writes, including the execution of rule invocation code including the creation of the rule invocation context, but excluding the execution of the *When*[12] part of the rules.

- Slot writes, which caused the triggering and evaluation of the *When* parts of rules.

---

[12] The *When* part of a rule is a sort of locally evaluated precondition.

Each component was run by finding a useful set of arguments for the relevant calls. It should be noted that this experiment ignored the cost of communication. This was taken as a fixed characteristic of the system.

Purpose   These experiments were designed to measure the cost of the fundamental operations in the Poligon system. This should allow the development of empirically derived formulae, which would allow the estimation of the computational grain size of a Poligon program.

Rule activation in Poligon goes through a number of stages, each of which will have associated costs. First there is the slot update, which causes the rule activation. The cost of slot updates will vary according to whether there were any attached rules or not. Second there is the context creation. This is the point at which the system creates the environment in which the rule will execute. It includes the copying of a template for the state information used during rule activation. Finally there is the evaluation of the *When* part of the rule. This is a piece of user code, which can clearly take an arbitrary amount of time. For this experiment, therefore, a representative *When* part was taken from the Elint application.

The minutiae of these experiments is not given here. Instead, the results are shown in a manner that allows the reader to see the granularity of the different measured components of the Poligon framework, without having to wade through a full explanation of the experiments themselves. As a result of these experiments, empirically derived formulae are shown, which denote either the real performance or a normal case measure taken from the Elint system.

Results and Interpretation   The time taken to read a slot was found to be independent of the length of the slot's value list and linearly related to the number of slots read. Corrected for the processor speed of a CARE machine, the formula for the calculation of the cost in microseconds of slot reads in Poligon is $1.36 + 0.94n$, where n = the number of slots being read.

The cost shown for slot reads is very low. Of course, this only gives a measure of the cost of local reads in Poligon and the measurement does not account for the cost of communication at all. However, because of the nature of blackboard systems, where rules tend to deal with data locally available and then pass their conclusions on to other nodes, most read operations that happen are, in fact, local. Making this operation fast is one of the main causes for the difference in performance between Poligon and Cage. In Cage all slot accesses have equal cost, but that cost is much higher than Poligon's local slot accesses because of having to make a read to shared memory.

Like slot read operations, the cost of writing slots is linearly related to the number of slots being written. The formula for the cost in microseconds for invoking nonrule slot updates, corrected for the speed of the processor, is $18 + 53.7n$, where n is the number of slot updates.

Because the user can supply arbitrarily complex code, which is executed at slot update time, it should be noted that this figure only reveals the lower bound for the cost of slot updates.

An expression was derived, by experiment, for the cost of rule invocation in Poligon. Some of the values in the expression are bound to be case dependent, but this expression should, nevertheless, be representative of the normal behavior of the system.

The cost of rule invocation is, therefore, given by the sum of the costs of the following operations:

- Slot writes for a slot with an attached rule.

- Creation of the rule activation context object.

- Copying of the definition template for the context object.

- Execution of a typical *When* part.

All but the first of these are application dependent characteristics. The results actually measured, therefore, are taken from a representative part of the Elint application. Substituting in measured values for the categories above, we have the cost of rule invocation being $128 + 160 + 370 + 400 = 1058$ microseconds.

This expression should not be taken as a final figure describing the potential performance of the Poligon architecture, but rather a measure of the performance that could be achieved without a major rewrite of the system and without spending a great deal of effort on the optimization of the system. It should be easy to eliminate most of the time due to instance creation and due to definition template copying in a production quality system. With sundry other optimizations a figure better than half of the one millisecond quoted above should be readily deliverable.

14.9   Discussion

In this paper we discuss the relationship between the blackboard model, its existing serial implementations, and the degree to which the parallelism intuitively thought to be inherent in the blackboard problem solving model is really present. Cage and Poligon, two implementations of the blackboard model designed to operate on two different parallel hardware architectures, are described, both in terms of their structure and the motivation behind their design.

Our framework (or shell) developments, application implementations on these frameworks, and performance experiments to date have taught us that (1) it is difficult to write real-time, data interpretation programs in a multiprocessor environment, and (2) performance gains are sensitive to the ways in which applications are formulated and programmed. In this class of application, performance is also sensitive to data characteristics.

The obvious sources of parallelism in the blackboard model, such as the concurrent processing of knowledge sources, do not provide much gain in speed-up if control remains centralized. On the other hand, decentralizing the control, or removing the control entirely, creates a computational environment in which it is very difficult to control the problem-solving behavior and to obtain a reasonable solution to a problem. As granularity is decreased, to obtain more potential parallel components, the interdependence among the computational units tends to increase, making it more difficult to obtain a coherent solution *and* to achieve a performance gain at the same time. We described some of the methods employed to overcome these difficulties.

In the application class under investigation, much of the parallelism came from from pipelining the blackboard hierarchy and from data parallelism; both from the temporal data sequence and from multiple objects (aircraft, for example). The Elint application was unfortunately knowledge poor, so that we were unable to explore knowledge parallelism extensively, except as a by-product of data and pipeline parallelism and in the somewhat artificial form described in Section 14.8.5.3. Elint has been implemented in both Cage and Poligon, and a number of experiments have been performed. The experiments were designed to measure and to compare performance by varying different parameters: process granularity, number of processors, sampling interval, data arrival characteristics, and so on.

Cage can execute multiple sets of rules, in the form of knowledge sources, concurrently. If the rule parallelism within each knowledge source can provide a speed-up in the neighborhood cited by Gupta, and if many knowledge sources can run concurrently without getting in each other's way, we can hope to get a speed up in the tens. Extra parallelism comes from working on many parts of the blackboard, in other words, by solving many subproblems in parallel. Unfortunately, experiments to date have not yet shown this (see Section 14.8.4).

It was found that the use of a central controller to determine which knowledge sources to run in parallel drastically limits speed-up, no matter how many knowledge sources are executed in parallel. Amdahl's limit and synchronization come strongly into play. The implication for Cage is that knowledge-source invocation should be distributed, without synchronization. This will eliminate two major bottlenecks; a data-hot spot at the event list, and waiting for the slowest process to finish during synchronization. One solution to this is to distribute the blackboard, which is one of the main characteristics of Poligon.

The performance of the Poligon system is limited by a different set of constraints. Although a Poligon programmer can, in principle, pick any desired size for the data grain size of the application's blackboard nodes, there will be some optimal grain size for a given application. If the blackboard nodes are small, then there will be more of them and the rules in the system will be more distributed. This should result in more potential parallelism and more communication.

Poligon tries to shield the user from the system cost associated with larger data grain sizes by allowing the concurrent execution of all the rules that may be interested in a given blackboard change. However, because of the nontrivial cost of rule invocation, and because resources are always scarce in the real world, it may be better to commit to a larger grain size and avoid the extra cost of communication and process management. Finding the optimum grain size for a program is still an unsolved problem. The development of a system that can take a specification of the user's program requirements and compile it into the best grain size is an important topic for research as more multiprocessor systems become available and programmers strive for higher productivity.

It is clear that much more research is needed in this area before a combination of a computational and problem-solving model can be developed that is easy to use, that produces valid solutions reliably, and that can consistently increase speed-up by a significant amount without undue programmer effort.

14.10 Conclusions

We have described the Cage and Poligon projects at Stanford University. Cage and Poligon are two different types of concurrent blackboard system. The same application, called Elint, has been mounted on each of these frameworks and experiments have been performed. The experiments, the experimental method, and the results have been enumerated and discussed. A summary of the results follows.

Cage: A peak speed-up factor of 5.7 was achieved for 16 processors, and improved to 5.9 for 32 processors. The throughput of the system was limited by four main factors: an inherent serialization due to the centralized scheduler, the unoptimized Cage system, the overheads due to the Qlisp concurrent Lisp language, and the overheads due to using a simulator for a distributed-memory multiprocessor as a simulator for a shared-memory machine. The fastest input sampling interval achieved by Cage with minimal optimization and 32 processors was 25ms.

Poligon: A peak speed-up factor of 11.5 was achieved with a best input data sampling interval of 2.7ms. Pipeline parallelism contributed about a factor of 3 of this improvement. The remaining speed-up was due to parallelism extracted from the data being processed. At least within the bounds of the experiments described, near linear speed-up has been shown for increasing complexity of the input data. It seems likely, therefore, that given more data the system would be able to achieve better results. It has been shown that as the knowledge base size increases, the Poligon system should deliver significantly better than linear slow-down, given sufficient resources.

Comparing the two systems, Poligon outperforms Cage by approximately a factor of 10. (Note that the speed-up factor of 5.9 for Cage and 11.5 for Poligon are not comparable, since the measurements are relative measures within the same framework between uniprocessor and multiprocessors. They indicate different abilities to exploit parallelism.) This is no great surprise, since the Poligon system takes a significantly more aggressive stance with respect to performance.

It is not clear whether the speed-up factors we obtained would apply to other problems. As mentioned throughout, the possible opportunities for concurrency and granularity are very application dependent, and thus it is very difficult to generalize from the results of one application. Nonetheless, in both Cage and Poligon the speed-up for our application came from: (1) data parallelism present in Elint, (2) pipelining of reasoning steps, (3) parallel matching for relevant rules, and (4) knowledge parallelism where more than one piece of knowledge was applicable for a given state. These sources of parallelism are fairly general and can be exploited by most applications.

Writing a real-time applications for Cage and Poligon was by no means simple. Many problems arose regarding timing measures, data consistency and coherence, and test scenarios that would not have arisen in other types of problems. Nonetheless, by attempting to solve a difficult problem, we were able to develop techniques and methodologies that will be useful for other applications in this class as well as in broader classes of problems. Much of what we learned has become a part of the frameworks; others were described in Section 14.4.4 for Cage and Section 14.5.2 for Poligon. It is our belief that both architectures represent viable ways of constructing concurrent blackboard systems.

Acknowledgements

The authors gratefully acknowledge the support of the following funding agencies for this project; DARPA/RADC, under contract F30602-85-C-0012; NASA, under contract number NCC 2-220; Boeing Computer Services, under contract number W-266875.

References

[Aiello 1986] Nelleke Aiello, "User-Directed Control of Parallelism: The Cage System," Technical Report KSL-86-31, Knowledge Systems Laboratory, Computer Science Department, Stanford University, April 1986.

[Amdahl 1967] Gene M. Amdahl, "Validity of a Single Processor Approach to Achieving Large Scale Computing Capabilities," *Proceedings of AFIPS Computing Conference 30*, 1967.

[Brown *et al.* 1982] Harold Brown, Jack Buckman, *et al.*, "Final Report on Hannibal," Technical Report (Internal Document), ESL, Inc., 1982.

[Brown *et al.* 1986] Harold D. Brown, Eric Schoen, and Bruce Delagi, "An Experiment in Knowledge-based Signal Understanding Using Parallel Architectures," Technical Report KSL-86-69, Knowledge Systems Laboratory, Computer Science Department, Stanford University, October 1986.

[Byrd *et al.* 1987] Gregory T. Byrd, Russel Nakano, and Bruce A. Delagi, "A Dynamic, Cut-Through Communications Protocol with Multicast," Technical Report STAN-CS-87-1178, Computer Science Department, Stanford University, 1987.

[Corkill and Lesser 1983] Daniel D. Corkill and Victor R. Lesser, "The Use of Meta Level Control for Coordination in Distributed Problem Solving," *Proceedings of the 7th International Conference on Artificial Intelligence*, 1983, pp. 748–755.

[Delagi 1986] Bruce Delagi, "CARE Users Manual," Technical Report KSL-86-36, Knowledge Systems Laboratory, Computer Science Department, Stanford University, 1986.

[Delagi *et al.* 1986] Bruce A Delagi, Nakul P. Saraiya, and Gregory T. Byrd, "LAMINA: CARE Applications Interface," Technical Report KSL-86-76, Knowledge Systems Laboratory, Computer Science Department, Stanford University, 1986.

[Delagi and Saraiya 1988] Bruce A. Delagi and Nakul P. Saraiya, "ELINT in LAMINA: Application of a Concurrent Object Language," Technical Report KSL-88-33, Heuristic Programming Project, Computer Science Department, Stanford University, 1988.

[Durfee *et al.* 1985] Edmund Durfee, Victor Lesser, and Daniel Corkill, "Coherent Cooperation Among Communicating Problem Solvers," Technical Report, Department of Computer and Information Sciences, September, 1985.

[Ensor and Gabbe 1985] J. Robert Ensor and John D. Gabbe, "Transactional Blackboards," *Proceedings of the 9th International Joint Conference on Artificial Intelligence*, 1985, pp. 340–344.

[Fennell and Lesser 1977] Richard D. Fennell and Victor R. Lesser, "Parallelism in AI Problem Solving: A case Study of Hearsay-II," *IEEE Transactions on Computers*, February 1977, pp. 98–111.

[Forgy and McDermott 1977] Charles Forgy and John McDermott, "OPS, A Domain-Independent Production System Language," *Proceedings of the 5th International Joint Conference on Artificial Intelligence*, 1977, pp. 933–939.

[Gabriel and McCarthy 1984] Richard P. Gabriel and John McCarthy, "Queue-based Multi-processing Lisp," *Proceedings of the ACM Symposium on Lisp and Functional Programming*, August 1984, pp. 25–44.

[Gupta 1986] Anoop Gupta, "Parallelism in Productions Systems," Technical Report, Computer Science Department, Carnegie-Mellon University, March, 1986.

[Hewitt *et al.* 1973] Carl Hewitt, P. Bishop, and R. Steiger, "A Universal, Modular Actor Formalism for Artificial Intelligence," *Proceedings of the 3rd International Joint Conference on Artificial Intelligence*, 1973, pp. 235–245.

[Lesser and Corkill 1983] Victor R. Lesser and Daniel D. Corkill, "The Distributed Vehicle Monitoring Testbed: A Tool for the Investigation of Distributed Problem Solving Networks," *AI Magazine*, Fall 1983, pp. 15–33.

[McCune and Drazovich 1983] Brian P. McCune and Robert J. Drazovich, "Radar with Sight and Knowledge," *Defense Electronics*, August 1983.

[McDermott and Newell 1983] John McDermott and Allen Newell, "Estimating the Computational Requirements for Future Expert Systems," Technical Report, Internal Memo, Computer Science Department, Carnegie-Mellon University, 1983.

[Newell 1962] Allen Newell, "Some Problems of Basic Organization in Problem-Solving Programs," in M. C. Yovits, G. T. Jacobi and G. D. Goldstein (eds.), *Conference on SelfOrganizing Systems*, Spartan Books, Washington, D.C., 1962, pp. 393–423.

[Nii and Aiello 1979] H. Penny Nii and Nelleke Aiello, "AGE: A Knowledgebased Program for Building Knowledge-based Programs," *Proceedings of the 6th International Joint Conference on Artificial Intelligence*, 1979, pp. 645–655.

[Nii *et al.* 1982] H. Penny Nii, Edward A. Feigenbaum, J. J. Anton, and A. J. Rockmore, "Signal-to-Symbol Transformation: HASP/SIAP Case Study," *AI Magazine*, Vol. 3, No. 2, 1982, pp. 23–35.

[Nii 1986a] H. Penny Nii, "Blackboard Systems: The Blackboard Model of Problem Solving and the Evolution of Blackboard Architectures," *AI Magazine*, Summer 1986, pp. 38–53.

[Nii 1986b] H. Penny Nii, "Blackboard Systems: The Blackboard Application Systems, Blackboard Systems from a Knowledge Engineering Perspective," *AI Magazine*, August 1986, pp. 82–106.

[Rice 1986] James Rice, "Poligon: A System for Parallel Problem Solving," Technical Report KSL-86-19, Knowledge Systems Laboratory, Computer Science Department, Stanford University, April, 1986.

[Rice 1989] James Rice, "The Advanced Architectures Project," Technical Report KSL-88-71, Knowledge Systems Laboratory, Computer Science Department, Stanford University, January 1989.

[Schoen 1986] Eric Schoen, "The CAOS System," Technical Report KSL86-22, Knowledge Systems Laboratory, Computer Science Department, Stanford University, April 1986.

[Selfridge 1959] Oliver G. Selfridge, "Pandemonium: A Paradigm for Learning," *Proceedings of the Symposium on the Mechanization of Thought Processes*, 1959, pp. 511–529.

[Shafer *et al.* 1986] Steven A. Shafer, Anthony Stentz, and Charles Thorpe, "An Architecture for Sensor Fusion in a Mobile Robot," *Proceedings of the IEEE International Conference on Robotics and Automation*, 1986.

[Smith 1981] B. J. Smith, "Architecture and Applications of the HEP Multiprocessor Computer System," *Proceedings of the International Society for Optical Engineering*, San Diego, California, August 1981.

[Spain 1983] David S. Spain, "Application of Artificial Intelligence to Tactical Situation Assessment," *Proceedings of the 16th EASCON83*, September 1983, pp. 457–464.

[Williams *et al.* 1984] Mark Williams, Harold Brown, and Terry Barnes, "TRICERO Design Description," Technical Report ESLNS539, ESL, Inc., May 1984.

H. Penny Nii, Nelleke Aiello, and James Rice
Knowledge Systems Laboratory
Stanford University
701 Welch Road
Palo Alto, California 94304

Chapter 15

Distributing Intelligence within an Individual

Barbara Hayes-Roth, Micheal Hewett, Richard Washington, Rattikorn Hewett, and Adam Seiver

Abstract

Distributed artificial intelligence (DAI) refers to systems in which decentralized, cooperative agents work synergistically to perform a task. Alternative DAI models resemble particular biological or social systems, such as teams, contract nets, or societies. Our DAI model resembles a single individual, characterized by adaptability, versatility, and coherence. The proposed DAI architecture comprises a hierarchy of loosely coupled agents for specific perception, action, and reasoning functions, all operating under the supervision of a top-level control agent. We demonstrate the proposed architecture in the Guardian system for intensive-care monitoring.

15.1   A Metaphor for DAI: The Intelligent Individual

Distributed artificial intelligence refers generally to systems in which decentralized, cooperative agents work synergistically to perform a task [Huhns 1987], [Bond and Gasser 1988]. Within this general description, however, there is considerable variability in the operational definitions of terms. "Agents" may refer to arbitrary numbers of more or less sophisticated computatational entities. "Decentralized" may refer to the distribution of knowledge, data, control, or computational resources among different agents. "Cooperative" may refer to a purely discretionary exchange of a small subset of available information or, at the other extreme, to an inevitable sharing of most information.

385

These alternative definitions of terms entail a space of DAI models, many of which bear metaphorical resemblances to biological or social systems, such as neural networks [Fahlman 1982], [Shastri 1987], complex problem solvers [Hayes-Roth et al. 1979], [Erman et al. 1980], [Hayes-Roth et al. 1986], [Nii 1988], [Wesson et al. 1988], [Steeb 1988], teams [Cammarata et al. 1983], [Lesser 1983], [Durfee et al. 1987], contract nets [Smith 1978], [Davis and Smith 1983], organizations [Fox 1988], and societies [Hewitt 1977], [Rosenschein 1985], [Kornfield and Hewitt 1988]. None of these models is "correct" or "incorrect." Rather, they capture different, complementary kinds of intelligence, with each model supporting different design objectives and task requirements.

Our DAI model metaphorically resembles a single intelligent individual characterized by adaptability, versatility, and coherence:

Adaptatability. An intelligent individual interacts with—influences and is influenced by—other dynamic entities in the external environment. It selectively perceives asynchronously sensed data from the environment. It reasons about perceived data to construct an interpretation of the environment. Given its interpretation, it decides to perform particular actions in order to affect external entities and to achieve its goals. In order to keep pace with external events and avoid missing important demands and opportunities for action, the individual performs these functions asynchronously and concurrently.

Versatility. An intelligent individual has many goals and engages in a corresponding variety of reasoning tasks, such as: interpretation of perceived events, diagnosis of exceptional situations, reactive response to urgent situations, model-based interpretation, action planning. Moreover, the individual can bring different reasoning methods to bear on a given task. For example, it may have both "quick and dirty" and more complete methods for diagnosis. The individual may perform multiple instances of several different tasks concurrently.

Coherence. An intelligent individual is and acts as a single entity. It attempts to construct a consistent interpretation of the world, acquire information relevant to its ongoing activities, notice important unanticipated events, and take actions that advance its goals. It establishes and modifies its own goals and dynamically allocates its limited resources among competing activities in accordance with its current goals and its current interpretation of the environment.

We are working on a hierarchical DAI architecture to support intelligent individuals as characterized above. The architecture may be summarized as follows. To support adaptability, the architecture provides locally controlled *perception/action agents* that perform low-level interpretation, abstraction, and filtering of sensed data and action programs. To support versatility, the architecture provides locally controlled *reasoning agents* that perform instances of generic reasoning tasks in various situational contexts. To support coherence, the architecture provides a top-level *control agent* that integrates the conclusions of subordinate agents into a dynamic global situation assessment and constructs a dynamic global control plan to guide the behavior of subordinate agents.

In the remainder of this paper, we explore the intelligent individual model and the proposed DAI architecture in more detail. Section 15.2 illustrates the concept of an intelligent individual in the context of an intensive-care monitoring task. Section 15.3 describes the proposed architecture and its instantiation in the Guardian system for intensive-care monitoring. Section 15.4 illustrates Guardian's performance in a typical monitoring scenario. Section 15.5 discusses conclusions.

15.2   Guardian's Task: Monitoring SICU Patients

The sickest surgical patients in the hospital are cared for in the surgical intensive care unit (SICU). Most of these patients have failure of one or more organ systems—usually lung or heart. Organ system failure is treated with life-support devices that assume the fundamental functions of the ailing system until it can heal. For example, the ventilator (see Figure 15.1) is an artificial breathing machine that augments the patient's own respiration. Life-support devices are adjusted based upon frequent patient observations. Some of these observations are made continually by automatic measuring machines, for example, measurements of air pressures and air flows in the patient-ventilator system. Some of the observations are made intermittently. Chest X-rays, for example, are usually taken once or twice a day. The short-term goal of SICU monitoring is to keep the patient comfortable and progressing toward therapeutic objectives. The long-term goal is to withdraw life-support devices gradually so that the patient eventually can function autonomously.

Current SICU monitoring practice instantiates the team model of distributed intelligence. Lead by the surgeon, different experts on the critical care team cooperate to interpret and synthesize large amounts of patient data. The surgeon, who performs the operation and is legally responsible for the patient, has the best grasp of the cause of the patient's problem, the surgical management of the disease, and the overall patient care strategy. Nurses, who are present at the bedside, have continuous access to automatically measured patient data and the best grasp of minute-to-minute details of the patient's condition. Other consultants have the best understanding of particular aspects of the patient's condition within their specialty. For example, respirator therapists have detailed knowedge

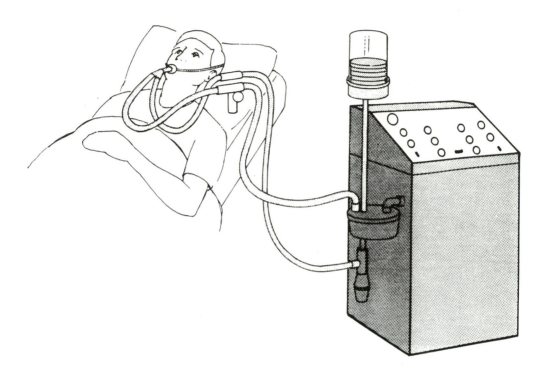

Figure 15.1: Patient supported by a ventilator

of the functioning and use of the respirator. Radiologists are expert at reading chest X-rays. High-quality patient monitoring requires cooperation among critical care team members to continuously interpret patient data and determine therapeutic actions.

The team model of SICU monitoring reflects both organizational and economic considerations. As medical knowledge has grown, the profession has distributed that knowledge among increasingly specialized practitioners. Each of these specialists is exceptionally well prepared to handle a part of the SICU monitoring task, but none is adequately prepared to handle the entire task. In addition, physician specialists are too valuable to take responsibility for the routine 80% of SICU monitoring activities. Nonetheless, the team model of SICU monitoring has serious limitations. Given the distribution of knowledge and skills among different experts with multiple responsibilities, these experts are rarely present in the SICU at precisely the moment their expertise is required. As a result, the following kinds of problems can occur:

Scenario 1: It is 3 a.m. Mr. Stone returned from the operating room 12 hours ago following an emergency replacement of the major blood vessel in his abdomen, the aorta. Now his urine output is 15 cc per hour. Since it has remained constant for the past 3 hours, the nurse has not given that number much attention. He is covering another patient who is much more unstable and consequently is a much higher priority. It is now 6 a.m. and the surgeon has returned for morning rounds. When she reviews the chart, she notices that the urine output has been 15 cc per hour since midnight. Anything less than 60 cc is a significant problem! She is quite distressed that the nurse had not called her when it first developed. Now the patient has a significant chance of developing renal failure with a 90 percent mortality. If the nurse had recognized the abnormal urine output, the crisis could have been completely avoided.

Scenario 2: It is 8 a.m. Dr. Payne, the radiologist, is trying to read the chest film on Mr. Jones. All that the X-ray requisition says is "Post-op chest." This provides very little contextual information. Dr. Payne needs to know how high the filling pressures are to differentiate pulmonary edema from adult respiratory distress syndrome. Although he is in the SICU, he does not have the time to go through the patient chart to find the necessary data. He is inexperienced with intensive care bedside practice and always has a difficult time finding the relevant information. Because he does not have a good background summary on Mr. Jones he cannot give a definitive reading and therefore has to "hedge."

In fact, Dr. William Knaus, a noted intensive care researcher, concluded from a study of over 5000 patients in thirteen medical centers that the likelihood of patient survival was related more to the exchange of information among SICU team members than to other factors, such as the amount of specialized treatment used [Knaus et al.]. Thus, the team model appears to be a suboptimal approach to the distribution of expertise for intensive-care monitoring. Although the team possesses the necessary knowledge and expertise, physical distribution of the knowledge among team members who have competing obligations means that all necessary knowledge may not be available at the time and place it is needed.

Of course, a DAI instantiation of the team model could guarantee continuous logical availability of all relevant expertise. However, the problem of coordinating team members that have competing obligations remains. Particularly in dynamic task environments, such as SICU monitoring, which require continuous problem identification and refocusing of attention, there is ample opportunity for divergence among independent team members. Finally, as previous work has shown [Bond and Gasser 1988], [Huhns 1987], there is an inherent conflict between the need to inform independent team members of one another's conclusions in case one of them requires response and the need to protect team members against distraction by one another's insignificant and erroneous conclusions. Accordingly, we hypothesize that intensive care monitoring would benefit from the capabilities associated above with the intelligent individual:

Adaptatability. An intensive care monitor must interact with an SICU patient whose complex biological functions are unstable and dependent upon the continuous aid of life-support devices. It also must interact with other medical staff and facilities both to obtain and provide patient-related information. The monitor must selectively perceive asynchronously sensed patient data and construct an interpretation of the patient's dynamic condition. Given its interpretation, the monitor must decide to perform particular therapeutic or communications actions in order to achieve therapeutic objectives for the patient and provide exchange information with medical staff. In order to keep pace with external events, the monitor must perform these functions asynchronously and in parallel.

Versatility. An intensive care monitor must engage in a variety of loosely-coupled patient monitoring activities. For example, it must interpret asynchronously perceived patient data, model the patient's dynamic condition based on these data, diagnose observed or inferred signs and symptoms, respond immediately to urgent situations, and plan courses of therapeutic action to manage evolving situations. In performing these tasks, it must employ a range of reasoning methods and strategies. It must use contextual information to focus its search among plausible conclusions. It must use "quick and dirty" reasoning methods when more precise methods are unavailable or exceed the available time. It must fall back on first principles when faced with problems that fall outside of its clinical knowledge. Ordinarily, it must perform multiple instances of these tasks concurrently. For example, it must continue to interpret newly perceived patient data while diagnosing previously perceived signs and symptoms. It must incorporate any relevant new data into its ongoing diagnostic reasoning. Throughout, it must remain poised to react to any urgent problems that arise.

Coherence. An intensive care monitor must act as a single entity. It must attend selectively to the available patient data so as to construct a consistent interpretation of the patient's dynamic condition, to acquire information relevant to its current monitoring activities, and to notice unanticipated signs and symptoms that may require interpretation or action. It must establish and modify local goals aimed at achieving its high-level therapeutic objectives. It must dynamically allocate its limited computational resources among competing monitoring activities in accordance with its current goals and model of the patient's condition.

15.3 Architecture for an Intelligent Individual

15.3.1 Overview of the Proposed Architecture

To support the capabilities discussed above, we propose a DAI architecture based on the blackboard control architecture [Hayes-Roth 1985, 1987a, 1987b, 1988], [Hayes-Roth 1987a], [Hayes-Roth 1987b], [Hayes-Roth 1988]. We illustrate the architecture with the Guardian system for intensive care monitoring [Hayes-Roth *et al.* 1989]. As indicated in the text, some of the proposed features are already implemented and distributed either logically or physically, while others are in earlier design stages.

The proposed architecture provides three general categories of function: (1) perception to acquire information from the environment; (2) action to affect entities in the environment; and (3) cognition to interpret perceived information, solve problems, make decisions, and plan actions. As illustrated in Figure 15.2, the architecture distributes the intelligence underlying these functions among locally controlled *perception/action agents* and *reasoning agents*, under the supervision of a single *control agent*. Each of these different agent types, in turn, comprises multiple subordinate agents. The following sections discuss each agent type and its communications with other agents in more detail.

15.3.2 The Control Agent

The top-level *control agent* has two responsibilities. First, it maintains a global situation assessment, integrating the conclusions of all subordinate agents. For example, Guardian's

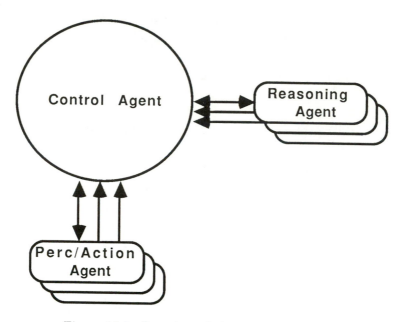

Figure 15.2: Overview of the proposed architecture

control agent integrates patient observations produced by perception agents with associated interpretations, diagnoses, predictions, and therapy plans produced by reasoning agents. Second, the control agent constructs dynamic high-level plans to guide the behavior of all subordinate agents. For example, Guardian's control agent decides which observations require response, what kinds of response are required, and what constraints should govern the response.

Framed within the BB1 blackboard control architecture and illustrated in Figure 15.3, the control agent comprises three logically distinct component agents currently implemented to run sequentially on a single processor: (1) an *agenda manager* identifies possible reasoning operations triggered by recent events; (2) a *scheduler* chooses the identified operation that best matches the current control plan; (3) an *executor* executes the chosen operation, making changes to the global situation assessment.

Executed operations fall into three categories. First, some operations change the global control plan that determines future scheduling decisions. The plan can be very abstract and ordinarily does not specify particular reasoning operations or reasoning agents. For example, Guardian's control agent might decide to diagnose an observed increase in the patient's peak inspiratory pressure (PIP) as quickly as possible. Given several pending reasoning agent activities, Guardian would prefer those that match all three features of its control decision (task=diagnose, object=increased PIP, manner=quickly) over those

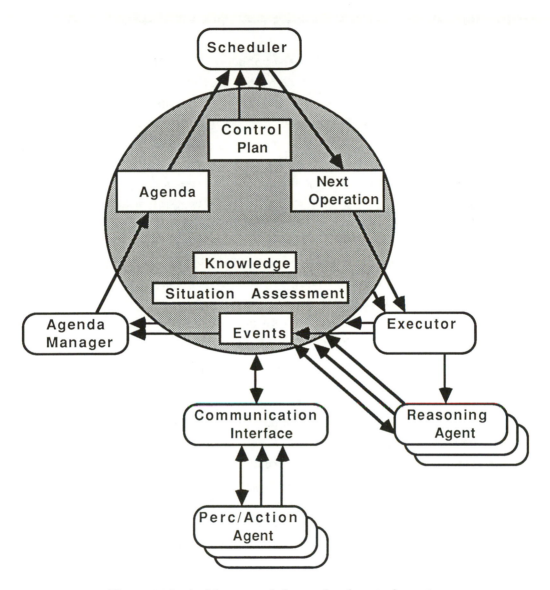

Figure 15.3: Architecture of the top-level control agent

that match fewer than three features. In addition, its perception agents would monitor PIP and related patient data variables more closely, while reducing attention to other variables. Finally, Guardian would favor actions to communicate and explain its diagnosis of the increased PIP to medical personnel over alternative possible actions. Thus, the global control plan enables an intelligent individual to dynamically allocate its distributed computational resources to particular classes of perception, action, and reasoning tasks in accordance with its goals and the evolving monitoring situation.

Second, some operations invoke distributed reasoning agents by recording an appropriate local control decision. For example, given the above decision to diagnose the increased PIP quickly, Guardian might perform an operation that invokes its relatively efficient associative diagnosis agent, Assoc, by recording an appropriate decision on the Assoc control plan. After elaborating its own strategy and performing reasoning operations that produce a diagnosis, Assoc would incorporate its conclusion in the global situation assessment. In the meantime, Guardian's control agent might invoke other reasoning agents, as suggested by its global control plan. Thus, BB1 permits an intelligent individual to perform multiple reasoning tasks concurrently, under the coordination of a global control plan, while maintaining a globally accessible situation assessment through the traditional blackboard mechanism [Engelmore and Morgan 1988].

Third, some operations manage I/O with perception/action agents. Some agents retrieve information previously placed in input buffers by perception agents and incorporate it in the global situation assessment. Others place information in output buffers for relay to appropriate remote agents, including new abstraction or filtering instructions for perception agents and new action programs for action agents (discussed below). The *communication interface*, an independent agent running on a separate processor, relays information between perception/action agents and BB1's I/O buffers [Hewett 1989]. It continuously monitors physical input ports from all perception agents, sorting input data into appropriate logical input buffers in BB1's global knowledge base. Conversely, it continuously monitors BB1's output buffers, sending information it finds to appropriate physical output ports. Thus, the communication interface shields the control agent from both the details of device-specific communication protocols and, more importantly, from I/O interference in its own performance. It similarly shields perception/action agents from the details of BB1 data structures.

We are working on two related changes to the BB1 control cycle. First, we plan to replace the optimizing agents described above with "satisficing agents:" (1) a *heuristic agenda manager* will identify promising (according to the current control plan) reasoning operations triggered by recent perceptual or cognitive events; (2) a *satisficing scheduler* will choose the first identified operation that satisfactorily matches the current control plan; (3) an *interruptable executor* will direct execution the chosen operation and make associated changes to the blackboard. Second, we plan to distribute these agents among continuously operating concurrent processes. Thus, the heuristic agenda manager will continuously identify promising operations as new events occur. The scheduler will choose satisfactory operations for execution whenever the agenda manager identifies them. The executor will direct execution of chosen operations until normal termination or interruption for a subsequently identified preferable operation. Distributing these three agents among concurrent processes offers the obvious advantage of improving the overall speed of the individual. In addition, we hypothesize that the two changes together will allow an individual to bound the latency of its own reasoning cycle in accordance with dynamic resource availability and time requirements [Hayes-Roth 1987a], [Hayes-Roth 1987b].

15.3.3 Reasoning Agents

Within the proposed architecture, each task-level reasoning agent constitutes a set of component reasoning operations that can be instantiated in a particular context and organized strategically to solve a problem or achieve an objective. For example, one of Guardian's reasoning agents, ICE [Hayes-Roth *et al.* 1988], generates alternative hypothetical diagnoses of observed signs and symptoms by tracing causal links in structure/function models of biological systems. Its component reasoning operations include: matching an observed sign to a model, tracing a causal link to a hypothesized fault type, and instantiating the hypothesized fault type in the context. Because this is a combinatorially explosive reasoning process, ICE needs to use information about the patient's history and current condition to decide which causal paths to follow.

In addition to ICE, Guardian has the following reasoning agents. *Classify* classifies new input data as instances of known categories of normal/abnormal parameter values and parses them into temporal episodes of stable values. *Assoc* uses belief networks to diagnose commonly observed signs and symptoms. *React* uses association networks to generate standard treatments for commonly diagnosed faults. *Backlog* establishes dynamic filters for use by Guardian's perceptual preprocessor as discussed below.

As illustrated in Figure 15.4, we implement each reasoning agent as a blackboard system within the BB1 architecture described above. Thus, each reasoning agent comprises: (1) a set of knowledge sources that instantiate relevant reasoning operations, given appropriate triggering events; (2) a solution blackboard on which executed knowledge sources construct an evolving solution to the task at hand; (3) a set of control knowledge sources that dynamically construct a control plan for the task at hand; and (4) a control blackboard on

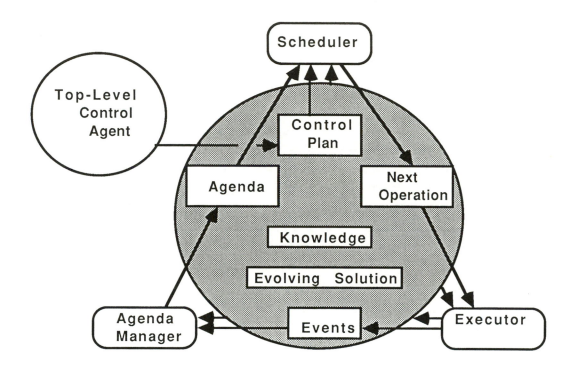

Figure 15.4: Architecture for a reasoning agent

which control knowledge sources construct their plan.

In the current implementation, Guardian's several reasoning tasks compete for cycles on a single processor. Thus, we have a hierarchy of control plans. The top-level control agent establishes a global control plan that favors particular reasoning tasks applied to particular data types. For example, Guardian's global control plan might favor responding to the patient's increased PIP quickly. In the context of this plan, individual reasoning agents establish their own local control plans favoring particular reasoning operations applied to particular intermediate results. For example, given the global control decision to diagnose the increased PIP, Assoc might decide to diagnose the increased PIP, but not to diagnose other observed signs and symptoms. A more sophisticated version of Assoc, which we are currently developing, might decide to interrupt its successive refinement of diagnostic hypotheses in time to meet a deadline corresponding to the constraint "quickly." With a less stringent time constraint, the ICE agent might decide to diagnose the increased PIP as well, pruning its search for plausible diagnoses in accordance with the time available. As soon as a reliable diagnosis appeared, Guardian's ReAct agent might decide to recommend an action to correct the underlying problem. On each cycle, the BB1 scheduler integrates both levels of control decisions to choose the next operation, thereby interleaving the component operations of multiple reasoning agents.

The logical distribution of reasoning skills among Guardian's several reasoning agents suggests that they can be distributed among distinct processes and run concurrently. For example, Guardian would benefit from being able to monitor newly perceived patient data, incorporate them into its evolving situation assessment, and make associated control decisions in an uninterrupted fashion. Any diagnostic reasoning undertaken could proceed concurrently. In fact, in some situations, Guardian would benefit from being able to invoke multiple diagnostic agents. Its Assoc agent would guarantee a quick diagnosis, while its ICE agent would attempt to produce a more complete and more precise diagnosis in the time available.

Because Guardian's different agents do not rely upon one another's intermediate results, they can run in parallel from a given initial state without producing inconsistencies. Thus, Guardian's top-level control agent might decide that it needs a quick diagnosis of the patient's increased PIP. Given this decision, Guardian's Assoc agent would perform the diagnostic reasoning, establishing its own control strategy within the goal and resource constraints set by the control agent, and recording its conclusions in the global situation assessment. Assoc's intermediate results during this reasoning task would not bear on other parallel efforts to diagnose the increased PIP or on other reasoning tasks, such as predicting the consequences of the increased PIP.

On the other hand, because Guardian's task environment is dynamic, its agents need to be aware of one another's asynchronously produced conclusions. For example, if Guardian decided that ICE should simultaneously perform its own model-based diagnosis of the increased PIP, Assoc's quick diagnosis might provide useful information in ICE's efforts to prune its search of plausible diagnoses. The global situation assessment provides this information and task-level reasoning agents can strongly localize regions of interest within it.

By contrast, although component operations within a task are modular and functionally independent, they have a much greater and less well defined potential for interaction. At the same time, control of reasoning is critical to achieving a coherent solution. For example, ICE needs to produce sequential chains of causal effects to explain how possible faults might have produced an observed irregularity in function. For these reasons, we do not anticipate distributing component reasoning operations within a task among concurrent agents at this time. (See also [Nii 1988] and [Rosenschein 1985].)

15.3.4 Perception/Action Agents

Hierarchically organized perception/action agents manage interactions between the individual and its environment. In the case of perception, *preprocessors* monitor peripheral sensors, translate and filter sensed data according to instructions from the top-level control agent, and send the results to the control agent for incorporation in the global situation assessment. The current version of Guardian has a single preprocessor, which manages patient data from approximately twenty sensors on the respirator, as well as lab reports and user interactions. (For development purposes, we replace the actual patient and respirator, as well as laboratory processes, etc., with simulations.) Under dynamic instructions from the control agent, the preprocessor abstracts sensed data (e.g., computes running averages, trends), filters the abstracted data (e.g., sends only abstracted values that differ from their predecessors by a specified amount), and sends the filtered data to the control agent. For example, Guardian's Backlog agent, monitors Guardian's cognitive load, its focus of attention, and sensed data rates. When these parameters change significantly, Backlog sends the preprocessor new abstraction and filtering instructions to insure that it sends appropriate abstractions of important patient data for the current situation and that it does not send unecessary information about currently irrelevant patient data. Thus, perceptual preprocessors enable the individual to attend selectively to sensed data so as to monitor currently important aspects of the environment, avoid perceptual overload, and minimize interference with other reasoning activities [Washington and Hayes-Roth 1989].

In the case of action, *drivers* receive action descriptions and performance constraints from the top-level control agent and manage action execution by peripheral effectors accordingly. The current version of Guardian has a set of display drivers, which interact with the user to communicate Guardian's observations, inferences, recommendations, and explanations. Thus, action drivers enable an individual to control execution of complex action programs, while minimizing interference with reasoning activities.

Figure 15.5 illustrates a more advanced model of perception/action agents. A perceptual preprocessor manages input data from multiple sensors and a driver manages action execution for multiple effectors. A superordinate agent, the mediator, integrates the two kinds of information to control perception/action programs without engaging the reasoning system. With this kind of agent, for example, Guardian could conduct an extended interaction with the user to review and explain a prior interval of SICU events, without interrupting its ongoing monitoring activities.

15.4 Guardian's Performance on a Typical SICU Scenario

15.4.1 Monitoring a Stable Ventilator-Assisted Patient

The scenario begins with a stable ventilator-assisted patient. As illustrated in Figure 15.6, the ventilator delivers a prescribed volume of air to the patient's two lungs on each breath. Two important measured parameters are the peak pressure applied by the ventilator and the tidal volume of air actually received by the patient on each breath. In the normal situation, these two parameters vary normally about the prescribed values.

As illustrated in Figure 15.7, Guardian's preprocessor receives every sensed data point for peak pressure and tidal volume. It applies "threshold filters" specified by Backlog and relays only data points that differ from their predecessors by the specified percentages. These data points are marked by vertical bars in Figure 15.7. The communications interface receives relayed data points and inserts them into appropriate logical input buffers, as illustrated in Figure 15.8, where they are available to Guardian's reasoning agents. Thus, Guardian's sensors, perceptual preprocessor, and communications interface function in parallel to provide selective perception—abstraction and filtering—of asynchronously sensed patient data.

Each new input data point triggers Guardian's Classify agent. Its constituent operations assign data points to value categories and to old or new temporal episodes of those value categories. Given its definition of threshold filters, Guardian interpolates between perceived data points of a given value category to model continuous temporal episodes (see Figure 15.9). Thus, Guardian incrementally builds a history of asynchronously perceived patient

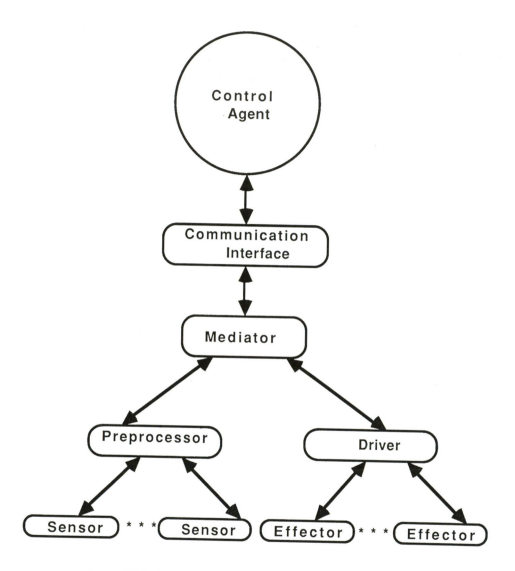

Figure 15.5: Illustrative hierarchical perception/action agent

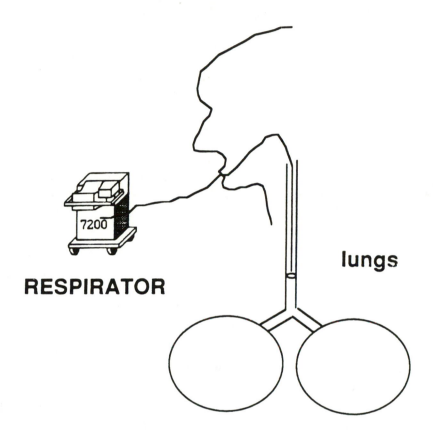

RESPIRATOR

lungs

Figure 15.6: Stable ventilator-assisted patient

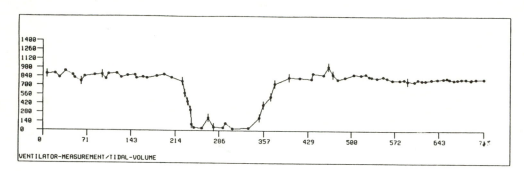

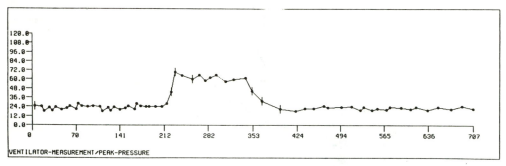

Figure 15.7: Sensed data as filtered by the preprocessor

data.

While classifying newly perceived input data, Guardian continues to perceive new data and monitor its input data rates. If new data of a given type arrive too quickly, they will overflow the input buffer and Guardian will build an incomplete patient history. If new data arrive too slowly, Guardian will build the patient history at an unecessarily low precision. In an effort to perceive sensed data at the maximum rate Guardian can handle, the Backlog agent monitors activity in all input buffers and adjusts the filter thresholds used by the preprocessor as necessary. The right side of Figure 15.8 graphically represents the current filter threshold for each input buffer, as established by Backlog.

Guardian's Classify and Backlog agents operate concurrently. As illustrated on the left side of Figure 15.10, the control agent makes separate decisions to perform tasks covered by these two agents and Guardian interleaves component operations for the two tasks on successive BB1 reasoning cycles. It is an artifact of the current implementation that Guardian has only one agent for classifying patient data and one for managing perceptual backlog. In general, its control decisions invoke whatever agents are capable of performing the designated tasks.

402

	add	drop	filter	
ICU-DATA-STREAM-0		[L] N H	[N] H		VENTILATOR-MEASUREMENT/TIDAL-VOLUME
ICU-DATA-STREAM-1		L [N] H	[N] H		VENTILATOR-MEASUREMENT/PEAK-PRESSURE
ICU-DATA-STREAM-2		L [N] H	[N] H		VENTILATOR-SETTING/RATE
ICU-DATA-STREAM-3		L [N] H	[N] H		VENTILATOR-SETTING/TIDAL-VOLUME
ICU-DATA-STREAM-4		L [N] H	[N] H		LABA/PACO2
ICU-DATA-STREAM-5		L [N] H	[N] H		LABA/PAO2
ICU-DATA-STREAM-6		L [N] H	[N] H		LABA/PH
ICU-DATA-STREAM-7		L [N] H	[N] H		OXIMETERA/SAO2
ICU-DATA-STREAM-8		L [N] H	[N] H		OXIMETERV/SVO2
ICU-DATA-STREAM-9		L [N] H	[N] H		SIEMENS/RADIAL-SYST
ICU-DATA-STREAM-10		L [N] H	[N] H		SIEMENS/RADIAL-DIAS
ICU-DATA-STREAM-11		L [N] H	[N] H		SIEMENS/RADIAL-MAP
ICU-DATA-STREAM-12		L [N] H	[N] H		SIEMENS/PULMONARY-SYST
ICU-DATA-STREAM-13		L [N] H	[N] H		SIEMENS/PULMONARY-DIAS
ICU-DATA-STREAM-14		L [N] H	[N] H		SIEMENS/PULMONARY-MAP
ICU-DATA-STREAM-15		L [N] H	[N] H		SIEMENS/WEDGE
ICU-DATA-STREAM-16		L [N] H	[N] H		SIEMENS/CVP
ICU-DATA-STREAM-17		L [N] H	[N] H		SIEMENS/CARDIAC-OUTPUT
ICU-DATA-STREAM-18		L [N] H	[N] H		SIEMENS/TEMPERATURE
ICU-DATA-STREAM-19		L [N] H	[N] H		SIEMENS/HEART-RATE
ICU-DATA-STREAM-20		L [N] H	[N] H		SIEMENS/ETCO2
ICU-DATA-STREAM-21		L [N] H	[N] H		URINE/OUTPUT
ICU-STATUS-STREAM-0		L [N] H	[N] H		
ICU-MESSAGE-STREAM-0		L [N] H	[N] H		

Figure 15.8: Input buffers and associated filters managed by backlog

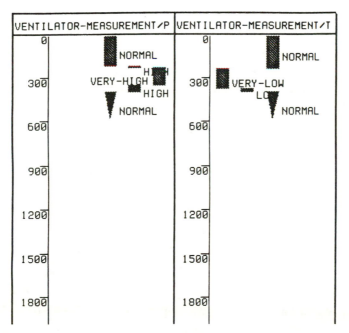

Figure 15.9: History of patient data constructed by classify

403

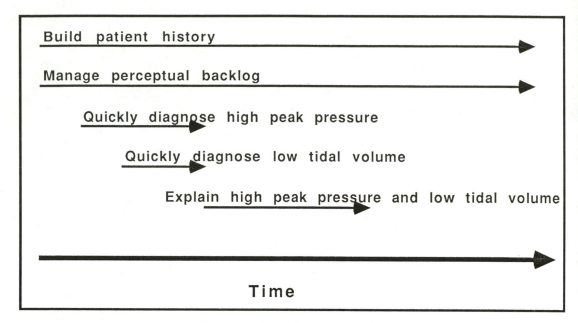

Figure 15.10: Global control plan

15.4.2 Diagnosing and Explaining Time-Varying Signs and Symptoms

After a period of monitoring a stable patient, Guardian notices that something has gone wrong. Classify notices abnormally high values for the parameter peak pressure (see the right side of Figure 15.9), triggering both Assoc and ICE. Guardian's control agent decides to diagnose this sign quickly, thereby favoring Assoc's relatively efficient associative reasoning but not ICE's computationally expensive model-based reasoning. Under less stringent time constraints, Guardian's control agent might allow both agents to diagnose a single problem.

Assoc diagnoses "one-sided intubation." As illustrated in Figure 15.11, when the respirator tube slips into one of the patient's bronchi, the ventilator delivers the prescribed volume of air to only one lung, causing peak pressure to rise. This triggers Guardian's ReAct agent, which would suggest a corrective action if executed.

However, because SICU monitoring is a dynamic situation, Guardian's control agent specifies concurrent performance of its backlog monitoring, classification, and diagnosis tasks, as illustrated in Figure 15.10. In fact, Guardian must be prepared to revise its diagnosis in light of new patient data. It so happens that, while Assoc is diagnosing "one-sided intubation," Classify records a new sign, low tidal volume. This new sign triggers both Assoc and ICE and, again, Guardian decides to diagnose it quickly, thereby favoring only Assoc.

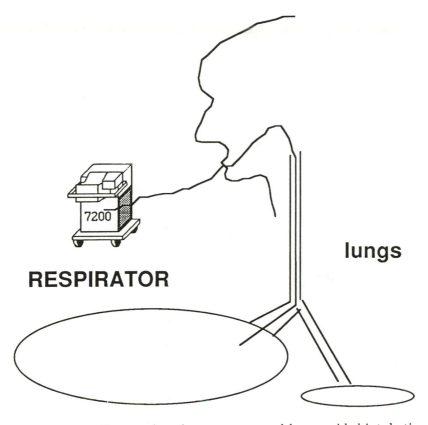

Figure 15.11: Increased peak pressure caused by one-sided intubation

Taking into account the new sign, Assoc revises its diagnosis in favor of "kinked tube." As illustrated in Figure 15.12, a kinked tube prevents the ventilator from delivering air past the point of the kink. As a result, peak pressure rises dramatically and tidal volume drops to zero. This diagnosis triggers Guardian's ReAct agent, which would suggest a corrective action if executed.

15.4.3 Falling Back on First Principles

Having hypothesized "kinked tube" with a stable, high probability, Guardian now learns (presumably from the nurse) that, in fact, there is no kink in the respirator tube. Without additional relevant patient data, Assoc cannot suggest alternative diagnoses. It certainly is not appropriate for ReAct to suggest any corrective actions. Therefore, Guardian's

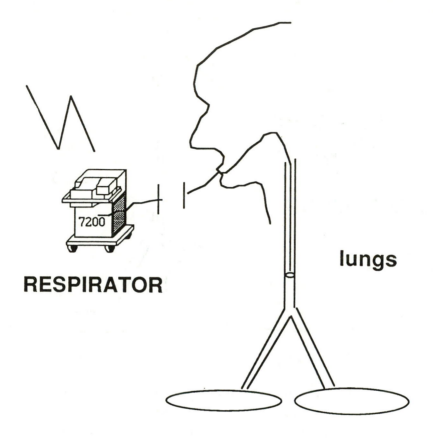

Figure 15.12: Increased peak pressure and decreased tidal volume caused by a kinked tube

control agent decides to explore possible faults to explain the observed patient data. This decision favors the previously invoked ICE agent, which uses its knowledge of potential faults in generic flow systems, along with its knowledge of the anatomy and physiology of the respiratory system, to hypothesize plausible problems underlying the observed high pressure and low tidal volume.

As illustrated in Figure 15.10, Guardian performs the ICE task concurrently with other tasks. Classify continues to integrate new input data into the patient model and Backlog continues to monitor input data rates. In addition, Backlog notices the decision to perform an ICE task, anticipates ICE's high demand for computational resources, and instructs the preprocessor to increase its filtering threshold to conserve resources. Figure 15.13 illustrates ICE's hypotheses regarding the observed decrease in tidal volume.

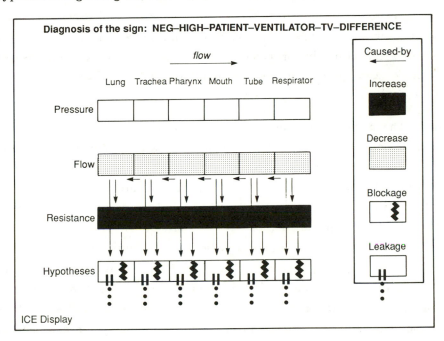

Figure 15.13: ICE hypothesizes plausible problems underlying the decrease in tidal volume

15.5   Conclusions

Let us recapitulate the proposed DAI architecture with respect to the characteristics of an intelligent individual:

Adaptability. The proposed architecture provides locally controlled agents for perception, action, and reasoning. Perception agents, which may constitute hierarchies of component agents, perform interpretation and filtering functions that provide the individual with highly relevant information in a compact form. Action agents, which also may constitute hierarchies of component agents, perform interpretation and control of potentially complex action programs. Reasoning agents, which constitute locally controlled blackboard systems, perform all knowledge-based reasoning functions. By distributing these functions among multiple agents, the architecture allows an intelligent individual to perceive, act, and reason quickly, asynchronously, and concurrently. Of course, the distribution of basic functions for sensing, acting, and reasoning among locally controlled agents is not a new concept. It appears throughout the literature on robotics and more conventional embedded systems. And many of these systems have some capabilities for modulation of sensor behavior. However, we believe that enabling reasoning agents to (re)program preprocessors and drivers continuously in accordance with a dynamic global control plan introduces a new source of power into the basic architecture. In particular, it enables the overall system to focus its perceptual processes on producing the most useful abstractions of the most useful sensed data for its current reasoning activities.

Versatility. The proposed architecture provides locally controlled agents for different generic reasoning tasks. Thus, it is specifically aimed at systems that integrate multiple reasoning tasks in the service of a global objective. In this regard it differs from most previous DAI models, which tend to fall into one of two paradigms. In the first paradigm, the problem is partitioned and the problem solver replicated for each partition. This paradigm is particularly well suited to problems that are spatially distributed, such as monitoring the activities of mobile entities in an external environment [Durfee *et al.* 1987], [Lesser 1983], [Steeb 1988], [Wesson *et al.* 1988]. Research in this paradigm focuses on the efficient and reliable exchange of data and hypotheses among agents so as to insure consistency of results, while protecting agents from excessive communications demands and distraction by unreliable information. In the second paradigm, the problem solver is partitioned and each part is applied to appropriate aspects of a shared problem. This approach is particularly well suited to problems that require the application of multiple distinct types of knowledge, such as speech understanding and other forms of signal interpretation [Fennell and Lesser 1988], [Lesser 1975], [Lesser 1979], [Nii 1988], [Rosenschein 1985]. Research in this paradigm focuses on getting a coherent solution from multiple problem solvers acting independently. By aiming at distribution of high-level reasoning tasks within a multitask system, the present approach addresses a new class of applications. The proposed architecture exploits natural boundaries between loosely-coupled reasoning tasks within these applications. It avoids the need for subordinate agents to communicate directly with one another and substantially limits their need to communicate indirectly via the global situation assessment. Thus, the ratio of intraagent computation to interagent communication is relatively high and the communicated information is highly constrained.

Coherence. Perhaps the most important feature of the DAI individual is its emphasis on central coordination of subordinate reasoning and perception/action agents. The top-level control agent performs this function by integrating all subordinate agents' conclusions in a dynamic global situation assessment and, based on that assessment, constructing a dynamic control plan to guide subordinate agents' behavior. The control plan influences what problems individual agents tackle and constrains their internal strategic control decisions. Nonetheless, subordinate agents retain considerable discretion over the actual strategies they adopt within the general guidelines of the global control plan. We view the proposed architecture as an intermediate position on the continuum between purely sequential and massively parallel architectures. As such, it aims to preserve the orderliness and explainability of sequential reasoning systems, while exploiting the speed-ups afforded by distributing component tasks whose order is not critical. For real-time, multitask applications such as Guardian, both properties are essential.

Acknowledgements

This research was supported by DARPA contract N00039-83-C-0136 and NIH contract 5P41-RR-00785 and by gifts from Rockwell International, Inc. and FMC Corporation, Inc. The Palo Alto VAMC supports Dr. Seiver's participation in the project. Mr. Adnan Darwiche and Mr. Luc Boureau recently joined the project. Mr. Reed Hastings and Mr. Nicholas Parlante worked on an earlier version of Guardian. We have had many fruitful discussions of the intensive care monitoring task with our colleague, Dr. Lawrence Fagan, and his students. We thank Professor Edward Feigenbaum for sponsoring the work at the Knowledge Systems Laboratory.

References

[Bond and Gasser 1988] A. H. Bond, and L. Gasser, eds., *Readings in Distributed Artificial Intelligence*, Morgan Kaufmann, 1988.

[Cammarata *et al.* 1983] S. Cammarata, D. McArther, and R. Steeb, "Strategies of Cooperation in Distributed Problem Solving," *Proceedings of the Eighth International Joint Conference on Artificial Intelligence*, 1983.

[Corkill *et al.* 1982] D. D. Corkill, V. R. Lesser, and E. Hudlicka, "Unifying data-directed and goal-directed control: An example and experiments," *Proceedings of the National*

Conference on Artificial Intelligence, 143–147, 1982.

[Davis and Smith 1983] R. Davis and R. G. Smith, "Negotiation as a Metaphor for Distributed Problem Solving," *Artificial Intelligence*, Vol. 20, 1983, pp. 63–109.

[Durfee *et al.* 1987] E. H. Durfee, D. D. Corkill, and V. R. Lesser, "Cooperation through communication in a distributed problem solving network," in M. N. Huhns, ed., *Distributed Artificial Intelligence*, London, Pitman, 1987.

[Engelmore and Morgan 1988] R. S. Engelmore and T. Morgan, eds., *Blackboard Systems*, Addison-Wesley Publishing Company, 1988.

[Erman *et al.* 1980] L. D. Erman, F. Hayes-Roth, V. R. Lesser, and D. R. Reddy, "The Hearsay-II Speech-Understanding System: Integrating Knowledge to Resolve Uncertainty," *Computing Surveys*, Vol. 12, 1980, pp. 213–253.

[Fahlman 1982] S. E. Fahlman, "Three Flavors of Parallelism," Technical Report, Carnegie-Mellon University, 1982.

[Fennell and Lesser 1988] R. D. Fennell and V. R. Lesser, "Parallelism in Artificial Intelligence Problem Solving: A Case Study of Hearsay II," in A. H. Bond and L. Gasser, eds., *Readings in Distributed Artificial Intelligence*, Morgan Kaufmann, 1988.

[Fox 1988] M. Fox, "An Organizational View of Distributed Systems," in A. H. Bond and L. Gasser, eds., *Readings in Distributed Artificial Intelligence*, Morgan Kaufmann, 1988.

[Hayes-Roth *et al.* 1979] B. Hayes-Roth, F. Hayes-Roth, S. Rosenschein, and S. Cammarata, "Modelling Planning as an Incremental, Opportunistic Process," *Proceedings of the Sixth International Joint Conference on Artificial Intelligence*, Vol. 6, 1979, pp. 375–383.

[Hayes-Roth 1985] B. Hayes-Roth, "A Blackboard Architecture for Control," *Artificial Intelligence*, Vol. 26, 1985, pp. 251–321.

[Hayes-Roth *et al.* 1986] B. Hayes-Roth, B. G. Buchanan, O. Lichtarge, M. Hewett, R. Altman, J. Brinkley, C. Cornelius, B. Duncan, and O. Jardetzky, "Protean: Deriving Protein Structure from Constraints," *Proceedings of the National Conference on Artificial Intelligence*, 1986.

[Hayes-Roth 1987a] B. Hayes-Roth, "A Multi-Processor Interrupt-Driven Architecture for Adaptive Intelligent Systems," Technical Report KSL-87-31, Stanford University, 1987.

[Hayes-Roth 1987b] B. Hayes-Roth, "Dynamic Control Planning in Adaptive Intelligent Systems," *Proceedings of DARPA Knowledge-Based Planning Workshop*, 1987.

[Hayes-Roth 1988] B. Hayes-Roth, "Making Intelligent Systems Adaptive," in K. VanLehn ed., *Architectures for Intelligence*, Lawrence Erlbaum, 1988.

[Hayes-Roth and Hewett 1988] B. Hayes-Roth and M. Hewett, "Building Systems in the BB1 Architecture," in R. Engelmore and A. Morgan, eds., *Blackboard Systems*, Addison-Wesley, London, 1988.

[Hayes-Roth *et al.* 1988] B. Hayes-Roth, R. Hewett, and A. Seiver, "Diagnostic Explanation Using Generic Models," Stanford University Technical Report KSL-88-20, 1988.

[Hayes-Roth *et al.* 1989] B. Hayes-Roth, R. Washington, R. Hewett, M. Hewett, and A. Seiver, "Intelligent Real-Time Monitoring and Control," *Proceedings of the Eleventh International Joint Conference on Artificial Intelligence*, 1989.

[Hewett 1989] M. Hewett and B. Hayes-Roth, "Real-Time I/O in Knowledge-Based Systems," in V. Jagannathan and R. T. Dodhiawala, eds., *Current Trends in Blackboard Systems*, Morgan Kaufmann, 1989.

[Hewitt 1977] C. Hewitt, "Viewing Control Structures as Patterns of Passing Messages," *Artificial Intelligence*, 1977, pp. 323–364.

[Huhns 1987] Michael N. Huhns, ed., *Distributed Artificial Intelligence*, Morgan Kaufmann, 1987.

[Knaus et al.] W. A. Knaus, E. A. Draper, D. P. Wagner, and J. E. Zimmerman, "An Evaluation of Outcome from Intensive Care in Major Medical Centers," private communication.

[Kornfield and Hewitt 1988] W. A. Kornfield, and C. E. Hewitt, "The Scientific Community Metaphor," in A. H. Bond and L. Gasser, eds., *Readings in Distributed Artificial Intelligence*, Morgan Kaufmann, 1988.

[Lesser 1975] V. R. Lesser, "Parallel Processing in Speech Understanding Systems: A Survey of Design Problems," in D. R. Reddy, ed., *Speech Recognition: Invited Papers Presented at the 1974 IEEE Symposium*, Academic Press, 1975.

[Lesser 1979] V. R. Lesser and L. D. Erman, "An Experiment in Distributed Interpretation," *Proceedings of the First International Cnference on Distributed Computing Systems*, 1979.

[Lesser 1983] V. R. Lesser, and D. D. Corkill, "The Distributed Vehicle Monitoring Testbed: A Tool for Investigating Distributed Problem Solving Networks," *AI Magazine*, Vol. 4, 1983, pp. 15–33.

[Nii 1988] H. P. Nii, N. Aiello, and J. Rice, "Frameworks for Concurrent Problem Solving: A Report on CAGE and POLIGON," in R. S. Engelmore and T. Morgan, eds., *Blackboard Systems*, Addison-Wesley Publishing Company, 1988.

[Rosenschein 1985] J. S. Rosenschein and M. R. Genesereth, "Deals Among Rational Agents," *Proceedings of the Ninth International Joint Conference on Artificial Intelligence*, 1985.

[Shastri 1987] L. Shastri, "A Connectionist Encoding of Semantic Networks," in M. N. Huhns, ed., *Distributed Artificial Intelligence*, Morgan Kaufmann, 1987.

[Smith 1978] R. G. Smith and R. Davis, "Distributed Problem Solving: The Contract Net Approach," Technical Report HPP-78-7, Stanford University, 1978.

[Steeb 1988] R. Steeb, S. Cammarata, F. Hayes-Roth, P. Thorndyke, and R. Wesson, "Architectures for Distributed Air-Traffic Control," in A. H. Bond and L. Gasser, eds., *Readings in Distributed Artificial Intelligence*, Morgan Kaufmann, 1988.

[Washington and Hayes-Roth 1989] R. Washington and B. Hayes-Roth, "Managing Input Data in Real-Time AI Systems," *Proceedings of the Eleventh International Joint Conference in Artificial Intelligence*, 1989.

411

[Wesson *et al.* 1988] R. Wesson, F. Hayes-Roth, J. W. Burge, C. Stasz, and C. Sunshine, "Network Structures for Distributed Situation Assessment," in A. H. Bond and L. Gasser, eds., *Readings in Distributed Artificial Intelligence*, Morgan Kaufmann, 1988.

Barbara Hayes-Roth, Micheal Hewett, Richard Washington and Rattikorn Hewett
Knowledge Systems Laboratory
Stanford University

Adam Seiver
Palo Alto Veterans Administration Medical Center
Palo Alto, CA 94305

Chapter 16

Learning and Adaptation In Distributed Artificial Intelligence Systems

Michael J. Shaw and Andrew B. Whinston

Abstract

The objectives of this paper are threefold: (1) to describe the learning processes existing in DAI systems, (2) to present the architecture and a methodology for incorporating machine-learning capabilities in DAI systems, and (3) to illustrate the proposed learning method for DAI by an intelligent manufacturing example.

16.1 Introduction

Learning denotes changes in the system that are adaptive in the sense that they enable the system to do the same tasks, or tasks drawn from the same population, more efficiently and more effectively the next time [Simon 1983]. Since the ability to learn is essential for any intelligent system, it should be a key element to consider in the design and construction of distributed artificial intelligence (DAI) systems.

Although barely discussed in the DAI literature, the consideration of making DAI systems able to learn can have significant impacts on developing distributed problem solving strategies. Most of the current efforts focus on enticing the agents to cooperate (e.g., [Durfee *et al.* 1987, Rosenchein and Genesereth 1984, Shaw 1989]), so that the problem-solving activities of the agents can proceed in a well concerted manner. The overall performance, however, is still hinged on the capabilities (i.e., the knowledge base) of the set of agents no matter how cooperative they are. Research on learning in DAI systems should start to be concerned with developing ways to improve the agents' knowledge and skill, so that not only can the individual agents be better at their tasks, but the whole DAI system can also keep improving its performance as a result. This research represents a step toward that goal.

To develop learning methods for DAI systems, two questions need to be answered: "What to learn?" and "How to learn?" The theses of this paper are that the DAI system should let the agents compete with each other and that the DAI system should adapt and evolve like natural systems do. From the problem-solving standpoint, introducing an element of competition will make any feature that the agents learn apparent; incorporating an evolution mechanism will give the agents a way to systematically, and progressively, improve themselves. From the computational standpoint, the market mechanism, which we use to make the agents compete, and the genetic transformation scheme, which we use to make the system adaptive, have been proven to be computationally efficient [Simon 1982, Holland 1975].

This paper describes a method treating distributed artificial intelligence (DAI) systems as adaptive organizations with the ability to improve by learning from past experience. The method is composed of two processes; (1) a bidding process, such as the one used in the contract-net framework [Smith 1980], for introducing an element of competition and for recording an agent's performance; and (2) a genetic transformation process, for searching for more efficient solutions.

The bidding process has been shown to be an effective coordination mechanism for multiagent problem solving [Davis and Smith 1983], [Shaw and Whinston 1985], [Gasser et al. 1987]. Based on the contract-net framework, each agent in the loosely coupled system bids for announced tasks and the best bidder is selected to be the contractor for task sharing. Our method extends this framework in the following manner: as a task is awarded to the best bidder, a hypothetical payment equivalent to the bid is paid, which in turn will affect the *strength* of the agents involved. The strength possessed by an agent reflects its ability to bid for tasks in the future.

Furthermore, the DAI system is viewed as an adaptive system capable of learning to improve its performance. The learning process is carried out by a genetic algorithm [Holland 1986]. It uses the strengths as the indication of fitness to discover desirable characteristics of those agents who have been successful; weaker agents will then be replaced by new agents inheriting these desirable characteristics, so that the overall performance can be improved. This competitive learning process would help the DAI system to adapt to its environment by the familiar "reproduction according to fitness" evolution. To illustrate the learning approach, this method is applied to the scheduling problems for flexible

414

manufacturing systems (FMS), which have been treated as DAI systems in our previous work [Shaw and Whinston 1985], [Shaw and Whinston 1988], [Shaw and Whinston 1989], [Shaw 1987a], [Shaw 1988].

The remainder of the paper is organized as follows: Section 16.2 details the different types of learning that can exist in DAI systems. Section 16.3 presents an organization for classifier systems and a distributed architecture that can be used to incorporate learning in DAI systems. Based on this architecture, Section 16.4 describes the bidding process based on a genetic representation and a message-passing formalism. Finally, Section 16.5 focuses on the generation of reproductive plans based on genetic transformations.

16.2 Learning in AI Systems

16.2.1 Machine Learning

The ability to learn is essential for any intelligent system. Interestingly, there has not been much work dealing with learning in the DAI literature. Learning in the multiagent setting has been discussed in the context of organization learning [Herriott *et al.* 1985], group induction [Laughlin 1988], adaptive control [Narendra and Thathachar 1974, DeJong 1980], and neural networks [Amari 1982, Gallant 1988]. Holland's work on the genetic algorithms and inductive learning, although incorporating a great deal of parallelism, is still concerned with the learning performed by a single agent. [Huhns *et al.* 1987] incorporated a learning component in a distributed knowledge-based system for adjusting heuristics and learning users' preferences.

The recent research in neural networks also concerns the learning process in a network of nodes. However, the neural-net model for learning differs from the method described in this paper in that a neural-net system learns by adjusting the weights of the interconnection links among the nodes. By contrast, a multiagent system should learn by assessing hypotheses and discovering new hypotheses, eventually reaching a hypothesis strong enough to be the learned concept. In other words, an agent in DAI systems usually has a richer set of knowledge than the mere weights used in a neural-net node.

Learning processes existing in a single agent include the acquisition of new declarative knowledge, the development of problem-solving skills through instruction or practice, the organization of knowledge into general, effective representations, and the discovery of new facts and theories through observation and experimentation. Machine learning methods have been developed for using computer models and algorithms to achieve these learning processes.

Machine learning methods developed for single agents have used a variety of models: rote learning, learning from instruction, learning by induction, learning by analogy, learning by competition, and learning from observation and discovery. (For more detailed surveys on machine learning, please refer to [Michalski *et al.* 1983, Michalski *et al.* 1986, Shaw 1987b]). To apply these methods to DAI systems, one needs to consider the structure of the systems.

16.2.2   Learning in DAI Systems

The learning processes in a DAI system are more complex than those in a single agent. To apply learning, the agents in the DAI system need to adjust, adapt, and learn from working with other agents in problem solving. More importantly, in a DAI system, the overall system is capable of achieving more tasks than the sum of tasks which can be individually achieved by the agents. This phenomenon is referred to as emerging intelligence. It is this emerging intelligence of DAI systems, that the group of agents collectively can offer something not available in the individuals, that makes DAI a potentially powerful problem-solving tool. The learning processes that go on among the agents may be the key factor resulting in emerging intelligence.

Another impact of learning on DAI is the process of group discovery, in which the agents of the systems will be engaged in collecting evidence, generating hypotheses, and evaluating hypotheses in order to discover new concepts collectively. For each individual agent, it surveys the environment, forms hypotheses based on the observations, and keeps searching for new evidence. As pointed out in [Lenat 1983], heuristics play a key role in this discovery process. By applying the right heuristics, evidence may confirm or disconfirm hypotheses, thus strengthening or weakening the agents' beliefs. This process continues until new concepts are derived that are supported by the observations and the agents' belief. In a DAI system, since the agents can share their beliefs, hypotheses, heuristics, and partial solutions, this sharing of information and knowledge may facilitate the discovery of new concepts. The key research issues are the information exchange scheme and the coordination strategies employed in the DAI system to achieve effective learning.

In a DAI system, two types of learning may occur: the agents can learn as a group, while at the same time, each agent can also learn on its own by adjusting its views and actions. As a group, learning takes effect in a DAI system in the form of (1) better coordination or (2) more efficient task and resource allocation. The improved coordination can be achieved by information sharing, knowledge sharing, or more efficient signalling among the agents. On the other hand, the task and resource allocation process can be improved by learning the specialization of agents (e.g., agent B is always good at task k), by learning the group characteristics (e.g., agents E and F work well as a team), by learning the patterns of tasks (e.g., for a given type of problem, it may be easier to break the problem into two tasks, C and D, and do D first), and finally, by learning such environmental characteristics as user preference or machine reliability.

For the individual agents, there are also two types of learning activities. An agent can (1) learn to improve its problem-solving skills or (2) learn by observing how the other agents solve problems. The first type of learning is similar to the learning in a single agent setting, including the improvement of heuristics, the revision of beliefs, and the use of more relevant common-sense knowledge [Huhns *et al.* 1988]. In addition, because of the presence of other agents in the system, the problem-solving skills of an agent can be further improved by absorbing the experience of other agents through explanation- based learning [Shaw *et al.* 1988], or it can simply ask for help in solving a given type of problem. In this aspect, it may be important for each agent to learn to cooperate with other agents. From the game-theoretic standpoint, cooperation is to form coalition that can lead to improved overall payoffs for the self interested agents. To learn to cooperate, each agent can adjust its beliefs, preference, and strategies. Cooperation also includes migrating and exchanging knowledge and heuristics, which is a form of knowledge acquisition in DAI systems.

16.3 A Framework for Incorporating Learning in DAI Systems

16.3.1 Classifier Systems

Classifier systems are a class of message passing, rule-based systems [Holland 1986, Rumelhart and Zipser 1987]. A classifier system consists of (1) a finite population of fixed length condition-action *rules* called classifiers, (2) a message list, (3) an input interface receiving messages from the environment, and (4) an output interface for affecting the environment.

A large number of rules in the classifier system can be active simultaneously. All rules are described in the form of *conditions* → *action* according to the structure

$$t_1 \wedge t_2 \wedge \ldots \wedge t_r \rightarrow a.$$

The LHS is a conjunction of r conditions, each of which specifies the set of messages satisfying it. The action, a, is the message sent when the condition part is satisfied. Each condition is a string of length L on the alphabet $\{1, 0, \#\}$. The LHS is satisfied if and only if every t_i matches some messages currently on the message list. An individual t_i matches a message if and only if for every 1 or 0 in t_i the same value occurs at the corresponding position in the message; "#" functions as a "don't care" symbol in a condition and matches unconditionally.

The basic execution cycle consists of the following steps:

1. Place all messages from the input interface on the current message list.

2. Compare all messages to all rule conditions and form the match set $\mathcal{M}$ of rules with satisfied LHSs.

3. Compute the bid of each rule in $\mathcal{M}$.

4. Select the rule, R, with the highest bid $b(R)$.

5. Reduce R's strength by $b(R)$.

6. Determine the set of rules that sent the messages that match with R's conditions, and increase their strength by the amount $b(r)/|\mathcal{M}|$, where $|\mathcal{M}|$ is the number of rules in $\mathcal{M}$.

7. Generate a new message from the action part of R for the message list.

8. Process the new message list through the output interface to produce system output.

9. If payoff is received from the environment, allocate it among the rules contributing to generating the messages.

10. Return to 1.

This rule-based inference process is characterized by (1) the *parallelism* in the way rules are selected, (2) the use of *competition* to resolve conflicts, and (3) all internal control information and external communication reside in the same data structure for *message passing*. It is precisely these characteristics that make the scheme extendable to distributed AI systems.

In addition, a genetic algorithm is employed to discover new rules. The idea is that the concept of strength is used as a basis for selecting highly useful rules as progenitors for new rules entering the competition. The genetic algorithm can be described as the following:

1. Select pairs from the set of highest-strength rules.

2. Apply genetic operators to the pairs, creating "offspring".

3. Replace the weakest rules with the offspring.

The purpose of this process is to explore "building blocks" for generating new rules. The genetic algorithm has been proven to be a highly efficient search process. The population of the rules may be thought of as a set of *hypotheses* representing the system's current estimate of the best means of obtaining payoff. The objective of the genetic algorithm is to generate new, possibly better rules by recombining building blocks from existing high strength rules and inserting the new rules into the population to compete for payoff.

16.3.2   Competitive Learning among Agents

Problem solving in DAI systems is a dynamic process and the actions of the agents must be coordinated to achieve globally good solutions. The communications medium, however, limits the amount of interactions among agents. Thus, the *coordination* among agents is always an important consideration in designing DAI systems. The flow of information and other activities of an agent must be efficiently directed and timed in concert with those of the other agents to achieve globally consistent and coherent solutions [Decker 1987, Yang 1985]. Most problem-solving processes handled in DAI systems consist of four phases, as follows:

1. The decomposition of the problem into subproblem tasks;

2. The allocation of the subproblem tasks among the agents;

3. The solving of the subproblem tasks by the assigned agents; and

4. The integration of the solutions, obtained in Phase 3, to obtain the global solution.

Using this "task sharing" strategy for distributed problem solving, the learning process can be deployed in a manner parallel to the induction process in the classifier system [Holland 1986]. That is, each agent has a genetic representation of its characteristics and capabilities; the agents would bid for tasks (i.e., solving subproblems) and, as a result of the bidding, the strength of the agents exchanging tasks would be affected by the bid. Periodically, agents that have poor performance would go through a genetic transformation to incorporate the characteristics and capabilities of those agents that have done well.

The bidding mechanism is especially suitable for task or resource allocation because of the combination of its efficient use of communications activities and being able to attain good global performance by distributed control. This has been pointed out by researchers in information economics [Harris and Raviv 1981] and DAI [Davis and Smith 1983]. Furthermore, our scheme treats the subproblem tasks as commodities traded between agents; through bidding, an agent can reassign a task to another agent or vice versa. The tasks are traded with payment equivalent to the bid, and the strengths of the buyer and seller (i.e., the manager and the contractor of the task) are updated accordingly. The idea of using the bidding scheme as a feedback mechanism to rate each agent is a new concept in the DAI literature and is used as a basis for learning and adaptation in our method.

To implement genetic algorithms for learning in DAI systems, a crucial design aspect is to represent the characteristics of each agent in the form of chromosomes. Using the aforementioned formalism, a chromosome can be represented by an L-string of symbols from the alphabet $\{0, 1, \#\}$. In general DAI systems, this can be interpreted as the capabilities, specializations, or characteristics of the agents. This interpretation is applicable to a variety of intelligent systems composed of networked "agents." For example, in flexible manufacturing systems [Shaw and Whinston 1988], each agent is a flexible manufacturing cell and its chromosome represents the type of operations the cell is set up for. In computer networks where each workstation is treated as an intelligent agent, the chromosome indicates the information resources the workstation is equipped with for handling different types of computation tasks. Yet a third example can be found in networks of expert systems, where the chromosome of an agent represents the specialization of the expert system in terms of the content of its knowledge base.

The inherent parallelism in the rule selection and the message passing mechanisms makes the organization for classifier systems particularly applicable to DAI. More importantly, in the classifier system all external communication is carried out by sending messages to the message list; therefore, the internal control signal and external communication reside in the same message structure.

In a classifier system, a message list is used to collect input information from the environment or from the actions of executed rules. For the distributed version of classifier systems, there is an additional source of incoming messages: the messages sent by other agents through the network. The architecture of such a DAI system with a message passing mechanism is shown in Figure 16.1. [Harms 1988] describes a simulation study on learning and problem solving in such a system.

From the control theory standpoint, the strength of an agent is treated as the state variable, the bid submitted as the control variable, and the bidding process essentially provides the feed-back mechanism that, triggered by the output (i.e., the outcome of the bidding process), would change the state value and adjust the subsequent control. The method uses the bid (control variable) as the coordination between agents and the strength (state variable) as the belief of a cell on its own ability and usefulness. In an effort to improve performance, learning occurs when the agents modify their beliefs and adaptation occurs when changes are made in the control variable. As a result, the better agents that have been successfully completing more tasks would increasingly be favored by the bidding

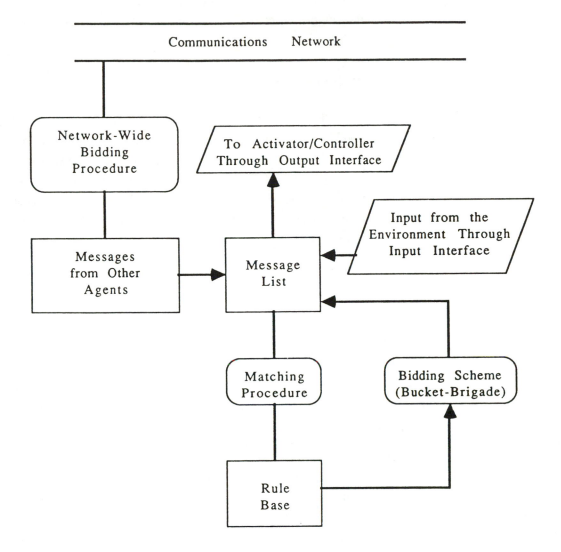

Figure 16.1: A distributed classifier system

process, thus accelerating the subsequent selection decision. The less useful agents, on the other hand, are forced to adapt and change their configuration by mimicking some of the features of the successful agents. Accordingly, two learning mechanisms are needed: one to determine the apportionment of credit to indicate each agent's past usefulness, the other to discover desirable features in agents and incorporate them in weaker agents. The tenet of this learning scheme is that the competition caused by bidding forces the agents to learn, adapt, and evolve.

16.4 The Bidding Process

In the following two sections we shall use intelligent manufacturing as an example of DAI systems to illustrate the proposed method integrating bidding and genetic transformation. The environment under study is a flexible manufacturing system (FMS) consisting of a network of flexible cells [Shaw 1987a]. In an FMS, the qualified cells would submit bids to earn the right of performing the incoming jobs—the lower the bid made by a cell, the more likely it is to be selected to get the job. The following three parameters jointly determine the size of the bid made by a cell c at time t:

1. Strength $(S(c,t))$: an indication of the past usefulness of c—higher S translates into higher productivity;

2. Specialization of the cell for the given job J, $(m(c,J))$: a parameter indicating how specialized c is to process J, depending on whether the set-up is especially designed for J (e.g., a gear cell is highly specialized for making gears); and

3. Readiness of the cell c in processing J, $(r(c,J))$: a parameter reflecting c's state of readiness for doing J, as influenced by its queue, operating conditions, and the availability of supporting equipment.

The strength of each cell is used as the capital that can be traded for service. Whenever a cell successfully wins a job contract through bidding, its level of strength increases by the amount of the bid. As a result, the subsequent bid made by the same cell will further increase its appeal because of the higher strength. Thus, the profitability of a cell depends on its ability to successfully perform jobs as much as possible. The amount of the bid is determined by the product of the three parameters:

$$B(c,J,t) = -W \times S(c,J) \times m(c,J) \times r(c,J)$$

where $m(c,J)$ and $r(c,J)$ are normalized to the range of [0,1]. W is a constant with usually a small value, such as 1/8 or 1/16.

The bidding process is carried out by the announce-bid-award cycle. Let k be the total number of operations possible in the FMS. The operation requirements announced for a job J is specified by a message of k-tuples as follows: $< O_1, O_2, \ldots, O_k >$, $O_j \in 1, 0, \#$, where $O_j = 1$ when the jth operation is required, $O_j = 0$ when the jth operation is not required, and $O_j = \#$ indicates that the capability of doing operation O_j is optional.

The capability of a cell, on the other hand, is represented by a similar type of k-tuples: $< t_1, \ldots, t_k >$, $t_j \in \{1, 0\}$, where $t_j = 1$ indicates that the cell is capable of performing the jth operation; and $t_j = 0$ indicates that the cell is not capable of performing the jth operation. The k-tuple used for representing the capabilities of each cell is treated as the chromosome of the cell. In an FMS, the cell's chromosome corresponds to the setup of the cell, which will be subject to reconfiguration as a result of learning and adaptation.

When a winning cell accepts the job, its strength is increased by the amount of the bid, that is, $S(c, t + l) = S(c, t) + B(c, J, t)$. At the same time, the cell c' that announced the job would reduce its strength by the same amount, $S(c', t + l) = S(c', t) - B(c, J, t)$. This exchange between cells c and c' can be interpreted as c' paid c for its service. For the system, the purpose of strengthening c is to reward the cell for being able to provide needed operations more efficiently than others. The more bids a cell wins, the greater is its strength. This scheme essentially encourages the cells to be utilized as much as possible.

16.5   Adaptation through Genetic Transformation

We view a DAI system as a cognitive system capable of adapting to the environment and improving its performance. This process of adaptation can be modeled after that of natural evolution. The goal is to abstract from natural systems the mechanisms of adaptation that can be incorporated in DAI systems, so that they can be of comparable sophistication. In evolution, the problem each species faces is one of searching for beneficial adaptations to a complicated and changing environment. The knowledge that each species has learned is embodied in the makeup of the chromosomes of its members. In general DAI systems, this learning process will change the knowledge distribution among the agents. For the cellular FMS system, this learning process amounts to a sequence of reconfigurations to increase the productivity of the system. This process can be based on models drawn from natural evolution and can computationally be achieved by the genetic algorithm described in Section 16.3.1.

The genetic algorithm was originally inspired by biological genetics, but was adapted by Holland to be a general problem solving technique. Here we use the idea of genetic transformation to improve the performance of a DAI system by searching for the most appropriate configuration. A class of genetic-based strategies for carrying out such search processes is called reproductive plans. As discussed previously, the ability of each agent (e.g., an expert system or a flexible cell) is represented by a chromosome. For a given DAI configuration, the bidding mechanism is used to coordinate the solution process among the agents; the strength of each agent is kept up to date to indicate its performance or fitness.

In general, a performance function F is used to define the concept of fitness of the DAI system. At any particular point in time, a reproductive plan maintains a population $A(t)$ which represents the current configuration of the agents being evaluated for fitness. A new generation $A(t+1)$ of agent configuration is constructed by simulating the dynamics of population development. That is, a selection probability is defined for each agent of generation t, $P(A_{it})$. which is proportional to the performance (i.e., fitness) of that agent. The next generation $A(t+1)$ is produced by choosing agents based on the selection probability; the new configuration of the agents is generated by applying genetic operators to the selected agents. Such a reproduction plan based on genetic transformation is shown in Figure 16.2.

Genetic operators are employed to exploit the selection process by producing new configuration for the agents that have high performance expectations. The choice of operators is motivated by the evolution mechanisms of natural system: crossover and mutation are the two basic genetic operators. Since each generation $A(t)$ is defined as the configuration of DAI agents, each agent's specialization is represented by a string of length L. The crossover operation works as follows: whenever a pair of agents a_i and a_j are selected from the current population $A(t)$ to undergo reproduction, their offspring a_k is produced by concatenating an initial segment of a_i with a final segment of a_j, based on a given crossover position that breaks the two strings into two segments. For example, let L be 7, a_i =< 0100100 >, a_j =< 1100110 >, and the crossover occur between the third and fourth positions, then a_k =< 0100110 > as a result of crossover.

A feature of the crossover operation is that it will produce offsprings with specializations that already exist in the current population [DeJong 1980]. For example, if every agent has a 0 in the first gene position, the crossover operation would not be able to produce an offspring with a 1 in that position. The second operation, mutation, can resolve this problem. The mutation operator generates a new agent by modifying one or more of the gene values of an existing agent. For example, a mutation occurring in agent a_j =< 1101001 > at the fifth position would produce a_k =< 1101101 >. With the mutation operator, the reproduction plan of a DAI system can guarantee that the probability of having a particular specialization in the agent configuration will never be zero, thus enabling a more complete coverage of the search space in the plan to find the best configuration.

For example, the machining capabilities embedded in an FMS cell can be viewed as its

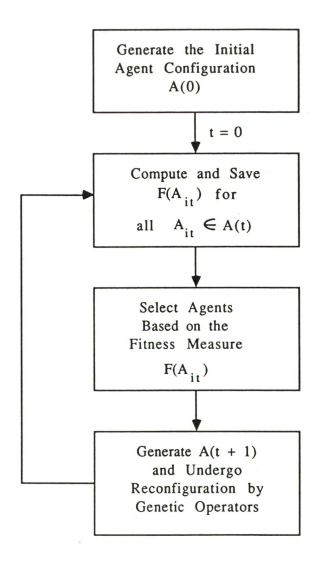

Figure 16.2: The reproduction plan for reconfiguring DAI agents

genetic material, using the same L-tuple representation described in the preceding section for representing the cell's capability list and the messages announced. Periodically, the FMS faces the need of reconfiguration due to the unbalanced utilization of the high-performance cells and the weaker cells.

The process of reconfiguring new cells hinges on the ability to discover and exploit good building blocks (i.e., good genes) based on experience. The building blocks are components of the cells that can be decomposed and recombined easily. The genetic algorithm uses the strengths as the indication of fitnesses to discover good building blocks. The knowledge representation of such a building block is a subset of the L-tuple called the schema. Reconfiguration then is the process of discovering schemata and combining them to form a new one, which in turn provides the new configuration of the cell. Interestingly, this idea of considering a block of operations in manufacturing cells fits very well with the concept of group technology of computer integrated manufacturing. The genetic algorithm proves to be an efficient technique for searching without exhaustive enumeration. Currently we are developing a heuristic procedure for carrying out such a learning process and testing it in simulated DAI systems.

16.6   Conclusions

In this paper we have shown an adaptive organization for DAI systems. The methodology presented has the following features: (1) it treats the DAI system as a market where each agent is analogous to a middle-man; (2) the agents use a strength parameter as the hypothetical capital for granting contracts or charging services; (3) the bidding process serves as a mechanism to determine task assignments and, at the same time, update the strength of the agents involved; (4) the bidding mechanism introduces an element of competition, since the strength would affect an agent's ability to bid; and (5) a genetic transformation scheme is used to recombine the genetic characteristics of well performing agents to produce new agents in place of weak ones. We have shown a distributed architecture, based on message passing, for incorporating the learning method in DAI systems. Also shown is the application of this methodology to the scheduling of flexible manufacturing systems.

Successful learning methods for DAI systems can have significant impacts on the development of distributed problem solving. This paper shows two mechanisms of adaptation abstracted from human organizations (a market) and natural systems (evolution) in the hope of achieving DAI systems with comparable performance and sophistication. In addition, we have pointed out the different types of learning processes that can occur in DAI systems and discussed the impacts of these processes on problem solving in DAI systems. Since learning in a sense can be viewed as problem solving [Langley *et al.* 1987, Shaw 1987b], it is possible that a DAI model can be developed that unifies problem solving and learning, resulting in truly intelligent systems.

References

[Amari 1982] S. Amari and M. Arbib, eds., *Competition and Cooperation in Neural Nets*, Lecture Notes Biomathematics, Vol. 45, Springer-Verlag, New York, 1982.

[Davis and Smith 1983] R. Davis and R. Smith, "Negotiation as a Metaphor for Distributed Problem Solving," *Artificial Intelligence*, Vol. 20, 1983, pp. 63–109.

[Decker 1987] K. S. Decker, "Distributed Problem Solving Techniques: A Survey," *IEEE Transactions on Systems, Man, and Cybernetics*, Vol. SMC-17, No. 5, 1987, pp. 729–740.

[DeJong 1980] K. DeJong, "Adaptive System Design: A Genetic Approach," *IEEE Transactions on Systems, Man, and Cybernetics*, Vol. 10, No. 9, 1980, pp. 566–574.

[Durfee *et al.* 1987] E. H. Durfee, V. R. Lesser, and D. D. Corkill, "Cooperation Through Communication in a Distributed Problem Solving Network," in *Distributed Artificial Intelligence*, M. N. Huhns, ed., Pitman, London, 1987, pp. 29–58.

[Gallant 1988] S. Gallant, "Connectionist Expert Systems," *Communications of ACM*, Vol. 31, 1988, pp. 152–168.

[Gasser *et al.* 1987] L. Gasser, C. Braganza, and N. Herman, "MACE: A Flexible Testbed for Distributed AI Research," in *Distributed Artificial Intelligence*, M. N. Huhns, ed., Pitman, London, 1987, pp. 119–152.

[Harms 1988] G. Harms, "A Simulation Study of Problem Solving Behavior in a Distributed Classifier System—The Genetic Approach," M.S. Thesis, Dept. of Electrical and Computer Engineering, University of Illinois at Urbana-Champaign, 1988.

[Harris and Raviv 1981] 9] M. Harris and A. Raviv, "Allocation Mechanisms and the Design of Auctions," *Econometrica*, Vol. 49, 1981, pp. 1477–1499.

[Herriott *et al.* 1985] S. R. Herriott, D. Levinthal, and J. March, "Learning from Experience in Organizations," *American Economic Review*, Vol. 75, 1985, pp. 298–302.

[Holland 1975] J. H. Holland, *Adaptation in Natural and Artificial Systems*, The University of Michigan Press, Ann Arbor, MI, 1975.

[Holland 1986] J. H. Holland, "Escaping Brittleness: The Possibilities of General Purpose Learning Algorithms Applied to Parallel Rule-Based Systems," in *Machine Learning: An Artificial Intelligence Approach*, Vol. 2, R. S. Michalski, J. G. Carbonell, and T. M. Mitchell, eds., Morgan Kaufmann, Los Altos, CA, 1986.

[Huhns *et al.* 1988] M. N. Huhns, L. M. Stephens, and D. B. Lenat, "Cooperation of DAI through Common-Sense Knowledge," *Proceedings of the 1988 workshop on Distributed Artificial Intelligence*, L. Gasser, ed., Lake Arrowhead, CA, 1988.

[Huhns *et al.* 1987] Huhns, M. N., Mukhopadhyay, U., Stephens, L. M., and Bonnell, R. D., "DAI for Document Retrieval: The MINDS Project," in *Distributed Artificial Intelligence*, M. N. Huhns, ed., Pitman, London, 1987, pp. 249–284.

[Langley *et al.* 1987] P. Langley, H. Simon, G. Bradshaw, and J. Zytkow, *Scientific Discovery: Computational Explorations of the Creative Processes*, MIT Press, Cambridge, MA, 1987.

[Laughlin 1988] P. R. Laughlin, "Collective Induction: Group Performance, Social Combination Processes, and Mutual Majority and Minority Influence," *Journal of Personality and Social Psychology*, Vol. 54, No. 2, 1988, pp. 254–267.

[Lenat 1983] D. B. Lenat, "The Role of Heuristics in Learning by Discovery: Three Case Studies," in *Machine Learning: An Artificial Intelligence Approach*, Vol. 1, R. S. Michalski, J. G. Carbonell, and T. M. Mitchell, eds., Tioga, Palo Alto, CA, 1983.

[Michalski *et al.* 1983] R. S. Michalski, J. G. Carbonell, and T. M. Mitchell, eds., *Machine Learning: An Artificial Intelligence Approach*, Vol. 1, Tioga, Palo Alto, CA, 1983.

[Michalski *et al.* 1986] R. S. Michalski, J. G. Carbonell, and T. M. Mitchell, eds., *Machine Learning: An Artificial Intelligence Approach*, Vol. 2, Morgan Kaufmann, Los Altos, CA, 1986.

[Narendra and Thathachar 1974] K. Narendra and M. Thathachar, "Learning Automata— A Survey," *IEEE Transactions on Systems, Man, and Cybernetics*, 1974, p. 44.

[Parunak 1987] H. Parunak, "Manufacturing Experience with the Contract Net," in *Distributed Artificial Intelligence*, M. N. Huhns, ed., Pitman Publishing, London, 1987.

[Rosenchein and Genesereth 1984] J. S. Rosenchein and M. R. Genesereth, "Communication and Cooperation," Technical Report HPP-84-5, Computer Science Department, Stanford University, Palo Alto, CA, 1984.

[Rumelhart and Zipser 1987] D. E. Rumelhart and D. Zipser, "Feature Discovery by Competitive Learning," in *Parallel Distributed Processing*, Vol. I, D. E. Rumelhart and McClelland, eds., MIT Press, Cambridge, MA, 1987.

[Shaw 1987a] M. Shaw, "Distributed Scheduling in Computer Integrated Manufacturing: The Use of Local Area Network," *International Journal of Production Research*, Vol. 25, No. 9, 1987, pp. 1285–1303.

[Shaw 1987b] M. Shaw, "Applying Inductive Learning to Enhance Knowledge-Based Expert Systems," *Decision Support Systems*, Vol. 3, 1987, pp. 319–322.

[Shaw 1988] M. Shaw, "Dynamic Scheduling in Cellular Manufacturing Systems: A Framework for Networked Decision Making," *Journal of Manufacturing Systems*, Vol. 7, No. 2, 1988, pp. 83–94.

[Shaw 1989] M. Shaw, "FMS Scheduling as Cooperative Problem Solving," *Annals of Operations Research*, Vol. 17, 1989, pp. 323–346.

[Shaw and Whinston 1985] M. Shaw and A. B. Whinston, "Task Bidding and Distributed Planning for Flexible Manufacturing," *Proceedings IEEE Conference on Artificial Intelligence Applications*, Miami, FL, 1985.

[Shaw and Whinston 1988] M. Shaw and A. B. Whinston, "A Distributed Knowledge-Based Approach to Flexible Automation: The Contract-Net Framework," *International Journal of Flexible Manufacturing Systems*, Vol. 1, No. 1, 1988, pp. 85–104.

[Shaw and Whinston 1989] M. Shaw and A. B. Whinston, "Applying Distributed Artificial Intelligence to Flexible Manufacturing," in *Advanced Information Technologies for Industrial Material Flow Systems*, Moody and Nof, eds., Springer-Verlag, New York, 1989, pp. 81–93.

[Shaw *et al.* 1988] M. Shaw, U. Menon, and S. Park, "An Explanation-Based Learning Approach to Computer-aided Process Planning," *Expert Systems for Manufacturing Design*, A. Kusiak, ed., Society of Manufacturing Engineer Press, MI, 1988, pp. 111–147.

[Simon 1983] H. A. Simon, "Why Should Machines Learn?" in *Machine Learning: An Artificial Intelligence Approach*, Vol. 1, R. S. Michalski, J. G. Carbonell, and T. M. Mitchell, eds., Tioga, Palo Alto, CA, 1983.

[Simon 1982] H. A. Simon, *The Sciences of the Artificial*, MIT Press, Cambridge, MA, 1982.

[Smith 1980] R. Smith, "The Contract-Net Protocol: High-Level Communication and Control in A Distributed Problem Solver," *IEEE Transactions on Computers*, Vol. C-29, No. 12, 1980, pp. 1104–1113.

[Yang 1985] J. D. Yang, M. N. Huhns, and L. M. Stephens, "An Architecture for Control and Communications in Distributed Artificial Intelligence Systems," *IEEE Transactions on Systems, Man, and Cybernetics*, Vol. 15, No. 3, 1985, pp. 316–326.

Michael J. Shaw
Department of Business Administration and The Beckman Institute of Advanced Science and Technology
University of Illinois at Urbana-Champaign
Champaign, IL 61820

Andrew B. Whinston
Departments of Information Systems, Computer Science, and Economics
Graduate School of Business and IC2 Institute
University of Texas at Austin
Austin, TX 78712-1175

Part V

Applications for DAI

Chapter 17

A Distributed Problem Solving Architecture for Knowledge Based Vision

D. M. Lane, M. J. Chantler, E. W. Robertson, and A. G. Mc-Fadzean

Abstract

This paper reports ongoing work investigating the use of a hybrid distributed problem solving (DPS) approach to a knowledge based vision task. A hierarchical architecture is employed using a number of interconnected processing agents termed rational cells. Different levels in the hierarchy are arranged to correspond to different levels of processing in the vision pyramid. It is argued that the approach differs from other hierarchical architectures for computer vision because of the way that mutually inconsistent and incorrect hypotheses can be represented throughout the architecture (so called functionally accurate processing), and the way these hypotheses are exchanged when cells interact. Horizontal interaction between cells at a given level in the hierarchy should be cooperative, involving the exchange of inconsistent and possibly incorrect partial hypotheses to resolve uncertainty resulting from disagreement and lack of information. Vertical interaction, however, need not be cooperative, because the vision pyramid contains distinct levels (i.e., is horizontally stratified). Nearly autonomous interaction is sufficient, involving the exchange of locally complete solutions (i.e., complete and correct from an individual cell's point of view). Although solutions passed vertically may be inconsistent when combined at the new level, cooperative interaction at the new level can resolve this. The application focus for the work is the automatic detection and classification of objects and shadows contained in image data derived from an active sector scanning sonar system. This knowledge based vision application is part of a much larger system with distributed problem solving tasks, involving an unmanned, free-swimming submersible vehicle currently being implemented for offshore energy exploration and production activities. After some introduction, the paper discusses the internal structure of the rational cell, the hybrid DPS architecture for knowledge based vision, and some preliminary results investigating processor loading and communication bandwidth for a distributed implementation of a sonar interpretation knowledge base.

17.1   Introduction

Despite its comparatively recent inception, the area of distributed problem solving (DPS) has started to become a more mature field in artificial intelligence research. From early work [Fennell and Lesser 1977], [Lesser and Erman 1980], [Lesser and Corkill 1981] building on the experience of the Hearsay blackboard architecture [Erman *et al.* 1980], theoretical issues have evolved, e.g., [Smith and Davis 1981], [Kornfeld and Hewitt 1981], [Fox 1981], [Davis and Smith 1983], [Genesereth *et al.* 1986], leading to the first signs of practical implementations of distributed AI (DAI) systems [Davis 1982], [Davis 1980], [Fehling and Erman 1983], [Hewitt and Lieberman 1984], [Huhns 1987], [Lesser and Corkill 1983], [Yang *et al.* 1985]. Eventually one can expect the appearance of commercially available products employing DPS ideas, completing the transition from theoretical research issue through first implementation and working prototype to properly engineered product.

This paper presents ongoing work that aims to take one more step towards the practical implementation of some DPS ideas. To this end, the long term application focus is the integration of information processing subsystems on an unmanned, free-swimming submersible vehicle. Equipped with sensors, actuators, and low bandwidth communication equipment, such vehicles are expected to form part of the next generation of technological tools used to carry out a range of survey, inspection and maintenance tasks during offshore energy exploration and production activities. They are a perceived need (both technological and commercial) as drilling progresses under ice and into deep water away from continental shelf depths [Submersible Symposium 1981].

Although DPS ideas could be applied in numerous ways to the complete vehicle, we have chosen to concentrate on one subsystem, in the expectation that this experience will form the foundation for future work. The subsystem in question involves a sector scanning sonar mounted on the front of the vehicle and used as one means of deriving up to date information about the surrounding environment for subsequent decision making activities, such as obstacle avoidance and mission planning. The requirement, therefore, is to detect objects (e.g., pipelines, wellheads, submerged cliffs, divers, and shipwrecks) in the vicinity of the vehicle according to the echoes they cause and the acoustic shadows they cast in the resulting sonar image. This so called interpretation task is also a requirement in geophysical data analysis of sidescan and subbottom sonar images, making the application relevant to a broader community [Eaves-Walton and Shippey 1987].

The paper consists of six parts. Section 17.2 briefly discusses knowledge based vision and introduces the motivations and some important concepts associated with distributing vision processing across a number of processing agents. Section 17.3 then introduces the rational cell and its implementation BOFFIN, which is the DPS agent at the heart of this distributed architecture work. Section 17.4 presents the hybrid FA/C, FA/NA architecture we are proposing for this computer vision problem, distinguishing between the virtual and physical system architecture and hence the difference between a cell and a processing node. A more detailed consideration of some architectural issues is also presented. Section 17.5 describes the sonar interpretation problem in more detail and Section 17.6 briefly discusses some other possible applications of the hybrid architecture. Results are presented showing object and shadow segmentations from a knowledge base executing in a single cell and some processor loading and communication bandwidth figures for the same knowledge base operating in the FA/NA architecture used for the first distribution trials. Sections 17.7 and 17.8 conclude by summing up and describing future work.

17.2 Distributing the Knowledge Based Vision Pyramid

Conventional thinking on computer vision represents different levels of processing as layers in a pyramid [Ballard and Brown 1982], [Marr 1982], [Hanson and Riseman 1978a] such that image processing occurs at the base, and processing of more abstract representations (feature vectors, symbolic classifications) occurs at higher levels. The use of a knowledge based approach to segmentation and classification tasks within the pyramid allows uncertainty to be represented and manipulated, and enables both rule based and algorithmic processing techniques to be used together to reason about the 3D world or to select parameters and image processing tools [Lane 1986].

Previous implementations of such KB vision pyramids have employed the blackboard style of architecture to structure the interactions between levels and between diverse types of processes, to provide a framework for manipulating the uncertainty, and to represent agreement and disagreement in knowledge source (KS) contributions [Hanson and Riseman 1978a] [Hanson and Riseman 1978b]. In the sonar domain, some success at image interpretation has been reported using this approach [Lane 1986], [Russell and Lane 1986]. However, because KS execute serially with no capability for preemption, the blackboard is effectively paralyzed while KS calculate their contributions. If some KS are computationally costly (e.g., image processing) and therefore time consuming, a bottleneck occurs and KS can queue for long periods of time in relation to the rate of data acquisition.

To be practical, therefore, for such real-time applications an alternative architecture that still possesses the strengths of the blackboard approach (diverse knowledge representations, structured KS interaction, modular construction, representation and manipulation of uncertainty etc.) is required. By distributing the processing necessary for image interpretation across a number of processing agents, sufficient speed up for real-time operation should be achievable. Thus, a suitable architecture may be derived by distributing the blackboard in some way [Fennell and Lesser 1977], [Lesser and Erman 1980], [Durfee *et al.* 1987], and including features traditionally found in real-time systems (e.g., reaction to interrupts, preemptive scheduling, and guaranteed response time). The architecture should do more than simply run KS in parallel because asynchronous updates to the blackboard occurring while other KS are executing can lead to inconsistency in the causal chains which link dependent hypotheses. Previous attempts to avoid this by locking those sections of the blackboard from which currently executing KS have triggered resulted in a blackboard bottleneck with more than 8 KS executing [Fennell and Lesser 1977].

For the vision application, we have chosen to distribute the blackboard such that boundaries are introduced to place parts of the single blackboard reasoning space and corresponding knowledge sources within different processing agents. Boundaries can be either vertical or horizontal, and therefore correspond to planes in the vision pyramid (Figure 17.1).

Knowledge sources that are active in a particular blackboard region are then allocated to separate processing agents, along with that portion of the blackboard. Communication between agents therefore forms the means of conceptually reuniting these portions. Because of the horizontally stratified nature of processing within the vision pyramid, a vertical partition will lead to reasonably well load-balanced agents, but with a high communication bandwidth. In contrast, a horizontal partition may lead to load imbalance (because image processing is more computationally costly than symbol manipulation) and a reduced communication bandwidth.

For the sonar interpretation application, the task is to identify a DPS strategy that distributes the blackboard architecture so as to minimise communication bandwidth with an even load balance across agents, whilst maintaining the necessary and useful features of

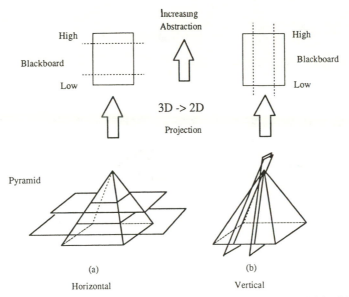

Figure 17.1: Partitioning boundaries for a vision pyramid and blackboard

a conventional blackboard. We believe a distributed problem solving approach is required because hypotheses derived from image data are uncertain and because partially formed results must be communicated between agents containing different parts of the vision pyramid [Decker 1987].

17.3   The Rational Cell

Before discussing the hybrid DPS architecture in more detail, this section first describes the processing agent at the heart of this DPS work. Termed the rational cell, it has its roots in blackboard based architectures such as Hearsay II [Erman *et al.* 1980] or HASP/SIAP [Nii *et al.* 1982], but implements some additional features that make it suitable for inclusion as an agent within a distributed architecture.

17.3.1   Concepts

The motivations for a cellular approach have stemmed from the desire for a set of basic components from which heterogeneous DAI networks can easily be constructed, and which allows investigation of both network and cell level research issues. To this end the cell has been defined in two parts, a cell interface specification called the *Global Network Language* (GNL), and the internal mechanisms of a cell called the *Cell Framework* [Robertson 1988] (Figure 17.2).

GNL's function is to provide a common format for the communication between cells of uncertain goals, information, and sensor data, which is independent of any internal

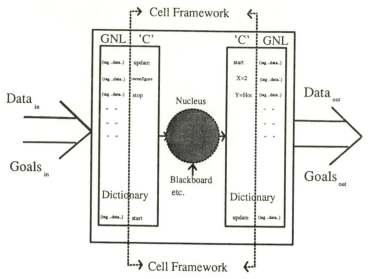

Figure 17.2: The rational cell

mechanisms. The basis of a cell's internal structure, comprising active and passive knowledge representation and an inference mechanism, may be selected from one of a number of standard cell frameworks, which may include logic, production rule, or blackboard based systems. Thus the cell, with its standard interface specification and variety of internal structures, facilitates the construction of networks of *heterogeneous* intelligent agents.

Currently, three types of blackboard based cell framework have been defined ranging from the simple type 1, suitable for man-machine interfaces and sensor data acquisition, to a type 3 cell that has been defined to have a learning capability [Lane 1986]. Type 2 cells have been the workhorses of most applications to date and are described in the following section.

17.3.2 Cell Framework—Current Design

Existing implementations of a cell framework [Lane 1986], [Robertson 1988], [Berry 1987] are blackboard based systems that manipulate a variety of numerical and symbolic data types using knowledge ranging from complex image processing algorithms to more abstract rule based expertise. The main components of a cell's framework are its inference mechanism, its knowledge representation, and its mechanism for handling uncertainty.

Inference Mechanism

The design supports both forward and backward chaining and the focus of attention of the system is controlled by metalevel knowledge sources which have access to a reasoning space known as the *knowledge source notice board*. The metalevel knowledge sources control an *agenda* according to a conflict resolution scheme that currently takes into account knowledge source and hypothesis time stamps, the level of abstraction of the knowledge sources, and priority levels. Metalevel KS also implement the GNL interface and perform housekeeping tasks, such as detecting stagnation on the problem domain blackboard. A primitive belief revision system has been implemented that removes chains of support for hypotheses when the underpinning data changes or becomes invalid, without forcing KS to be resorted into the agenda.

Knowledge Representation

Each cell contains a structured reasoning space or blackboard that is partitioned into a number of segments corresponding to the various levels of abstraction used by problem domain KS. Uncertain information, sensor data, and goals are stored on the blackboard as hypothesis frames and may represent images, feature characteristics, numerical measurements, symbols, and propositions. A limited history of each frame is kept to provide for reference to previous values, for the calculation of trends, and for observing changes in hypotheses at all levels of abstraction. Slots are provided within frames for such items as time stamps, certainty values, indications of supporting KS, and to represent agreeing and disagreeing versions of the hypothesis derived from different KS.

Active knowledge, consisting of problem domain and metalevel knowledge sources, comprises initialization, trigger and contribution fields. Hypotheses specified within the trigger field are those that are used when the KS is fired and the contribution field is executed. The contribution field may contain rule based, 2D signal processing, or conventional algorithmic expertise.

Uncertainty

Uncertainty within a cell may originate from a number of sources, including sensor noise, incomplete evidence and incomplete knowledge, and it may also be explicitly encoded into the knowledge base. Methods that allow uncertainty to be adequately expressed and propagated and which are soundly based have proved a difficult issue [Kanal and Lemmer 1986].

Current implementations of cells use an ad hoc approach to the representation and propagation of uncertainty. Knowledge source contributions to a hypothesis must include a confidence attribute, implemented as a certainty value ranging from 0% (don't know) to 100% (full confidence). Disbelief or negative confidence is not explicitly encoded and is therefore expressed as support for a competing version of a hypothesis, or not at all. A

439

hypothesis frame records a version of the hypothesis and associated certainty value for each knowledge source that contributes to that hypothesis. Support from knowledge sources may therefore agree or disagree.

Uncertainty propagates within a cell in two ways. The certainty values associated with agreeing and disagreeing versions of a hypothesis are combined to derive the current best version of the hypothesis and an associated certainty value. Also, the overall certainty value associated with hypotheses triggering a KS are combined to obtain the level of support the KS has for its conclusions. Thus far, ad hoc mechanisms have been implemented, propagating the most strongly supported of the differing hypothesis versions, but using the least well supported triggering hypothesis to derive overall KS support (i.e., a chain is as strong as its weakest link).

In addition, a primitive belief revision mechanism is employed to maintain consistency of causal chains of hypotheses when KS alter their contributions. Confidence in the credibility of a hypothesis is reduced to zero in the event that any hypothesis upon which it depends (perhaps through several other hypotheses) is altered. During subsequent inference cycles the contributing KS will retrigger and update either the belief or the actual contribution. Changes in hypotheses can thus cause large ripples across the blackboard as other hypotheses are made invalid.

17.4   Cell Organization for Knowledge Based Vision

This section overviews the hybrid distributed problem solving architecture employing a network of rational cells that is the focus of our current implementation effort. Some initial discussion on approaches to distributed problem solving is followed by a description of the architecture as applied to KB vision and a more detailed consideration of some design issues.

17.4.1   Approaches To Distributed Problem Solving

The design of a distributed problem solving system can be classified according to the nature of processing within a cell and the style of interaction that occurs (Figure 17.3).

A system that can manipulate uncertain data, which need not be consistent or correct, is referred to as Functionally Accurate (FA) [Lesser and Corkill 1981]. This is in contrast to Completely Accurate (CA) systems which manipulate certain data that must be consistent and correct. Similarly, a system where processing nodes operate primarily in isolation, and infrequently communicate solutions which are complete, are referred to as Nearly Autonomous (NA). Where there is a much tighter coupling between nodes, with many

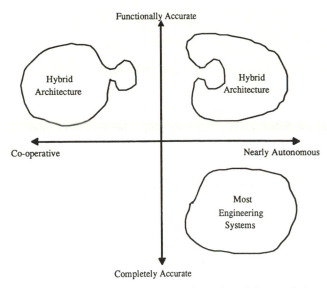

Figure 17.3: Approaches to distributed problem solving

more interactions of solutions that are only partially complete, the system is referred to as Cooperative (C).

Using this classification, most existing examples of distributed systems are of the Completely Accurate/Nearly Autonomous (CA/NA) type, relying instead upon a classification such as Flynn's to distinguish them (e.g., Single Instruction Multiple Data, SIMD, and Multiple Instruction Multiple Data, MIMD). In these systems computation within a node does not involve uncertain data, results are always entirely consistent and correct, and each node can complete its processing to produce a complete result with little external interaction. [Lesser and Corkill 1981] have discussed their approach to a Functionally Accurate/Cooperative (FA/C) system, where partial solutions comprising uncertain data that can be incorrect and inconsistent are exchanged between nodes in order to resolve ambiguity and iterate to a mutually agreeable solution. Hybrids of these two approaches (i.e., FA/NA and CA/C) are possible but have not been reported. In an FA/NA system, data is allowed to be uncertain, inconsistent, and incorrect, but internode coupling is loose and each node operates primarily in isolation, communicating only solutions that it regards as complete. There is therefore no cooperative mechanism to resolve ambiguity. In a CA/C system, there is no uncertainty and data must be consistent and correct. However partial solutions are allowed and, hence, nodes may iterate their processing in order to arrive at a solution.

An alternative and overlapping classification of distributed problem solving has been reported in [Smith and Davis 1981]. Systems are regarded as being either task sharing or result sharing in nature. In the former, tasks that form part of the problem decomposition are shared among available processors in a static (i.e., fixed a priori) or dynamic (i.e., changes on line) way. Dynamic task sharing is potentially a very powerful method as it

441

provides a mechanism for maintaining a balanced load across processors and for coping with node failure. The contract net is a good example of a task sharing system [Smith 1980]. A result sharing system is one where nodes cannot independently solve subproblems and must communicate partial results to arrive at a solution. It is therefore very similar to the Cooperative classification above.

17.4.2 Organizational Structure

This section describes a DPS architecture for KB vision, and discusses our implementation approach that distinguishes between the physical and virtual system architecture.

KB Vision Architecture

Thus far we have identified the need to communicate uncertain and partial results between cells implementing parts of the vision pyramid (Section 17.2), and have discussed some DPS architectures that may support this (Section 17.4.1). We have also shown that partitioning the pyramid vertically leads to a high communication bandwidth between cells but a good load balance across cells. Horizontal partitioning leads to a lower communication bandwidth and poor load balancing (Section 17.2).

Because there are distinct levels in the vision pyramid corresponding to segmentation, feature extraction, and classification (i.e., the pyramid is horizontally *stratified*), a cooperative approach to vertical interactions between cells seems inappropriate. It should suffice to communicate solutions from one level to another, which are *locally complete* (i.e., complete from an individual cell's point of view). However, the solutions will be uncertain and because they are local within a level, they may also be inconsistent and incorrect. Such inconsistencies may have to be resolved at a higher (or lower) level. Thus horizontal interactions within a level must be able to resolve ambiguity caused by uncertain, inconsistent, and possibly incorrect hypotheses. We can therefore say that *all cells must be capable of operating in a functionally accurate fashion, but that vertical communication can be nearly autonomous, and horizontal communication cooperative.* Hence the architecture should be a hybrid FA/C, FA/NA combination. This ties in well with the concept of communication bandwidth and the horizontal and vertical partitioning options. Horizontal, cooperative interaction between cells (i.e across vertical partitions) is relatively high bandwidth. Conversely, vertical, nearly autonomous interaction between cells (i.e., across horizontal partitions) is relatively low bandwidth. To implement this hybrid system, we are employing a hierarchical architecture (Figure 17.4), corresponding to these vertical and horizontal partitions.

442

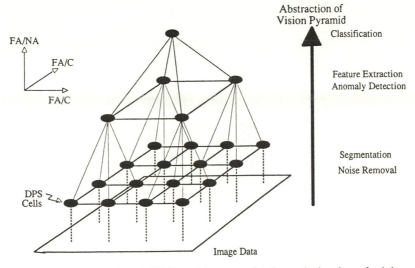

Figure 17.4: Hierarchical DPS architecture for knowledge based vision

Cells at the lowest level in the hierarchy are primarily concerned with image processing tasks to remove unwanted sensor noise at the pixel level and to produce appropriate segmentations of image regions. Cells at the highest level are concerned with abstract activities, such as symbolic inference to construct a world model. Cells at intermediate levels are concerned with tasks such as producing feature vectors to describe segmented regions of an image or the analysis of these features using a priori information about the sensing device and the surrounding environment to classify them as identifiable bona fide objects or just noise. Within a level, therefore, the knowledge bases contained within each cell are identical and appropriate to the level of processing within the vision pyramid. Furthermore, an implicit assumption is made that all cells are benevolent and there are no antagonisms arising through conflicting goals [Rosenschien and Genesereth 1985].

To distribute the image processing activity, cells at the base of the pyramid are allocated NxN pixel regions in the image (termed blocks) as a starting point for their data driven activity. Providing the hierarchy with a broad base reflects the fact that image processing activities are the most computationally demanding, and hence there are more cells allocated to it. Moving up the hierarchy to consider processing at higher levels in the vision pyramid, where feature extraction and classification take place, more abstracted information is required, which generally results in a lower computational load and, therefore, requires less distribution. Hence, the complete hierarchy has a pyramidal shape.

Many very basic image processing techniques involve the use of 3x3, 5x5, etc. kernel that is convolved with the image in some sense. Thus, pixels from adjacent image blocks must be made available to each cell by overlapping block boundaries (Figure 17.5).

This can be handled in two ways. Either,

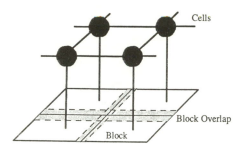

Figure 17.5: Overlapping block boundaries in the image at the base of the vision pyramid

1. pixel information is communicated by cooperative interaction between adjacent cells, or

2. cells are presented at startup with pixel information from a (N+k-1) by (N+k-1) image block. The blocksize, N, is dictated by the number of cells at the base of the pyramid and the image resolution. k is the maximum size of kernel which can be convolved.

We currently expect to use a hybrid of both, where raw image pixels from overlapping blocks are presented to each cell at startup. To allow kernels to be convolved with other images derived from the original, pixel information from the derived image is then exchanged between adjacent cells.

Because we wish to employ a KB vision approach, it is important that all cells are able to carry out some kind of abstract reasoning. At the base of the pyramid, for instance, this would involve simple reasoning to select an image processing tool or parameter. Thus all cells are endowed with a knowledge based processing capability. However, that ability is focused onto the processing required by the appropriate pyramid level when the cell's knowledge base is installed. It is therefore important to distinguish between levels of data abstraction used in the vision pyramid, and levels of abstraction used within a cell in order to carry out KB activities.

Physical and Virtual System Architectures

An important implementation concept that affects the reliability and load balancing aspects of the system performance is the distinction between a virtual system architecture, as perceived above when considering the distributed problem solving strategy, and the physical system architecture, as realised on a network of processor nodes that are physically interconnected (cf. [Hillis 1985]). We regard the hybrid FA/C, FA/NA hierarchical cellular decomposition as a virtual architecture, which may be implemented on a network of processors with a completely different interconnection topology (e.g., hypercube or token ring). There is thus a mapping function from *cells* in the virtual architecture to *nodes* in the physical architecture, and this need not stay constant.

Although this approach introduces additional implementation complexity, it also brings advantages. Specifically, if the physical to virtual mapping can be dynamically changed, then cells can be reallocated to other processing nodes if a node fails, or alternatively messages can be rerouted via other nodes. Thus, the complete hierarchy remains, but takes longer to carry out its processing and is therefore less able to respond to externally generated goals. Furthermore, if the physical architecture is perceived to have a load imbalance, then cells can be reallocated to improve throughput.

Currently it is difficult to estimate the overhead associated with this approach, either in processing time or man hours of development effort. Using commercially available software in implementation we hope to reduce the development effort (Section 17.4.4). The cost in processing time remains to be seen.

17.4.3   Architectural Issues

With the above general description in mind, there are a number of more detailed issues that are relevant to the hybrid architecture implementation.

Intercell Communication

As part of the specification of the FA/C and FA/NA modes of interaction, a communication protocol has been defined and implemented [Robertson 1988], providing a language that can be understood by all cells irrespective of their internal structure and that uses an asynchronous (i.e., no handshaking) mode of operation. A dictionary look up scheme is used to translate messages from this Global Network Language (Section 17.3.1) into the cell's internal knowledge representation. The GNL representation typically contains the hypothesis in question (image, numerical value, symbol, proposition), and overall confidence attribute and identification information such as the transmitting cell and the type of hypothesis.

Support information indicating agreement and disagreement for a hypothesis is not transmitted, because this has little meaning if cells in a network are allowed to be heterogenous in their internal design. However, this makes truth maintenance across the network difficult because the support structure is required by the truth maintenance system. To circumvent this it is proposed to retransmit hypotheses which have previously been passed if they change. Using the existing belief revision mechanism within the currently implemented cell will enable changes to propagate across internally located blackboards (Section 17.3.2).

For a distributed KB vision application, horizontal communication at the base of the pyramid comprises uncertain goals and information that may be strategic (metalevel) [Durfee 1987], or related more directly to the pixel information being processed. Because cells can be heterogeneous in terms of their internal structure (Section 17.3.1), the strategic information passed should be independent of the cell construction. Thus, there is no requirement for a cell to know the internal structure of its neighbour, provided the GNL message passing format is employed. An example of strategic horizontal communication would be a cell's current goals, the priorities attached to each, and some indication of the focus of activity within the cell. Examples of problem domain horizontal Cooperative communication at the base of the hierarchy would be hypotheses concerning the parameters used by the image processing (e.g., threshold selection), pixel and feature vector information relating to detected objects that overlap a block boundary, or goals enquiring about objects detected in adjacent blocks. At higher levels in the pyramid, horizontal communication remains Cooperative, but mainly transmits feature vector and symbolic information, appropriate to the feature extraction and classification stages in the vision processing.

Vertical communications, corresponding to an FA/NA mode, comprise locally complete hypotheses (goals or information) with an overall uncertainty value to be resolved at the next highest level. Examples are artifacts detected within an image block, classifications derived from feature vectors, perception goals, parts of the 3D world model, and operating parameters (e.g., blocksize). At the metalevel, response times for goals transmitted downwards enable a suitable focus of attention mechanism within each cell to decide the level of response.

Dimensions of the Hierarchical Structure

One of the motivations for investigating this hybrid DPS architecture is as a means of speeding up the KB vision processing by introducing parallelism (Section 17.2). However, it is not true to say that introducing additional cells ad infinitum will continually increase processing speed. Some consideration should therefore be given to the dimension and aspect ratio of the virtual system hierarchy that implements the vision pyramid. Figure 17.6 shows three trends that affect this.

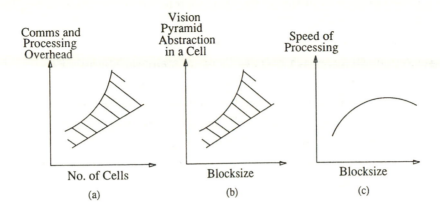

Figure 17.6: Trends influencing the optimum dimensions of the hybrid architecture

Clearly, as the number of cells increases, a greater processing overhead is incurred in coping with extra communication, increased numbers of goals placed on a cell's blackboard, and with metalevel reasoning influenced by a cell's other activities (Figure 17.6(a)). The exact nature of this relationship may be linear or otherwise, lying somewhere in the shaded region of the diagram. [Durfee *et al.* 1987] have indicated that exchanging metalevel hypotheses improves the efficiency and reliability of the cooperative problem solving process. Our inclination, however, is that with large numbers of cells the additional overheads associated with this may also slow the system down.

The spatial resolution of the image(s) being processed and the number of processors at the lowest level in the pyramid are two factors that dictate the blocksize to be used. Within each block, a cell has autonomy to carry out KB image processing the way it sees fit. From this, the higher level abstractions in the vision pyramid are obtained. The vertical extent of the hierarchy dictates the level(s) of the vision pyramid that are acceptable in a cell (e.g., in a completely flat structure, all levels from the pyramid must be present in each cell). Clearly, with a small blocksize it makes little sense to try and classify objects, and so the trend of Figure 17.6(b) is apparent. The vertical extent of the hierarchy is therefore dictated by the blocksize, such that it must be large if small image blocks are to be used.

With a very small blocksize (and therefore many cells) the overlap at the pixel level between adjacent image blocks will lead to much duplication of image processing effort. With a very large blocksize, therefore, there may be insufficient parallelism to achieve a significant speed increase over the single cell approach. This leads to the trend of Figure 17.6(c) where an optimum speed of processing could be expected with a given blocksize, dictated by the degree of overlap, which in turn is dictated by the kernel size, and hence the size of expected objects in the image. This therefore dictates the horizontal extent of the hierarchy.

Although the above trends are apparent, any decision on the optimum hierarchy dimensions is still very much a research issue, as there are many variables that have an influence and the relationships are difficult to analyse. In our initial implementation, therefore, we are constructing a pyramid with a 2x2 cell base and a single cell above (hence 4 connections per cell). Subsequent implementation will use a 4x4 base, with a 2x2 level above and a single cell at the top (hence up to 7 connections per cell). It is our expectation that from this exercise we will gain sufficient experience to comment in a more quantitative fashion on the optimum pyramid dimensions.

Temporal and Spatial Consistency

Inconsistency in the hierarchy may arise because of delays in updated versions of hypotheses propagating through the network (temporal) and because in a multisensor system (Section 17.6) different sensors will produce different versions of a hypothesis (spatial). These are in addition to the more conventional sources, such as sensor noise, incomplete information, or a lack of active knowledge (Section 17.3.2).

By employing an FA/C approach to horizontal communication we explicitly recognise that temporal and spatial inconsistencies can occur. By structuring each cell's knowledge base to operate in a cooperative way, we expect to be able to reduce this uncertainty by iterating to a mutually agreeable solution [Lesser and Corkill 1981]. Integral parts of this are the mechanisms for combining agreement and disagreement in KS support [Lane 1986] and for truth maintenance [Doyle 1982] within each cell. However, because of the iterative nature of cooperation, there are issues associated with convergence and stability of hypotheses that have yet to be resolved [Lane 1989].

Although vertical interactions are nearly autonomous, temporal and spatial inconsistencies from one level can propagate to the level above (or below). However, vertical communication should only occur when cooperation within a level has iterated to solutions that are satisfactory and are therefore regarded as locally complete. Uncertainty is still an integral part of this vertical communication, therefore, because of sensor noise, incomplete information, and lack of active knowledge.

An issue associated with consistency is that of coherent operation of cells within a level (i.e., they all progress at approximately the same rate). Using an asynchronous communication strategy (Section 17.4.3) allows cell activity to progress independent of other cells in the network. There is therefore no implicit mechanism that maintains coherency. Although incoherent operation implies inefficiency (i.e., not maximally exploiting parallelism through poor load balancing) we do not believe this presents a fundamental problem because of the mechanisms for belief revision within a cell. It is, however, a desirable property.

Representation and Location of 3D World Model

Model based processing is a powerful tool in vision applications where uncertainty is generated through sensor noise or through a shortage of available information. A priori knowledge of sensed structures, combined with recent measurements, serves to produce a world model that can be represented using a number of techniques (polygons, parametric equations, voxels, feature vectors, symbolic propositions) appropriate to positions in the vision pyramid. Because processing is distributed in a DPS architecture, it is entirely appropriate that any 3D world model be distributed also. Cells at each level are homogeneous in the knowledge they each possess. Thus they all require access to the complete model using a variety of representation schemes.

In the initial implementation, the 3D world model employed in [Lane 1986] is being used comprising symbolic and numerical representations distributed through the architecture, such that all cells have access to, or represent internally, the parts of the model they require. Previous work has shown that access to high level symbolic representations can have an important and beneficial effect when selecting image processing tools and parameters [Lane 1986]. Similarly, resolving ambiguity in the model at the most abstract level can benefit from access to low level numerical information (e.g., feature vector values). Although alterations to the model will occur during the natural course of events, this should be accommodated through the FA/C, FA/NA interaction strategies rather than by resorting to some globally accessible blackboard. The effectiveness of this approach is very much a research issue, however.

Problem Decomposition and Task Allocation

The allocation of tasks within a DPS may be either dynamic or static, corresponding to the task sharing or result sharing nature of the architecture [Smith and Davis 1981]. In general, FA/C systems employ a static task allocation because they use a result sharing approach. CA/NA systems, however, could potentially be task sharing in nature.

For the vision application as discussed here, the virtual system architecture is result sharing in nature and employs static task allocation and problem decomposition. Levels of the vision processing pyramid are uniquely mapped onto levels in the architecture hierarchy and regions of an image are similarly mapped to cells at the base. Active knowledge is therefore uniquely allocated to cells, such that cells at each level have an identical knowledge base. However, for the physical architecture (Section 17.4.2), cells need not be uniquely allocated to a processor, making the physical system architecture more of a task sharing organization. If this task sharing is dynamic in nature, then both reliability and load balancing are enhanced by allowing on line reconfiguration of the virtual-to-physical architecture mapping.

17.4.4   Implementation

To implement the physical system architecture upon which the virtual hierarchy resides, we are employing an array of Transputer processors [Homewood *et al.* 1987] connected to a SUN III workstation host. The Transputer is a RISC architecture specifically designed to implement embedded parallel systems. Although its native language OCCAM is not well suited to KBS programming, 'C' compilers with appropriate software support have become available. Such RISC architectures have been recognised as having potential for implementing distributed production systems [Forgy *et al.* 1984]. In this instance a commercially available operating system TROLLIUS (originating from Cornell University Department of Computer Science, but commercially available in much altered form from Transtech Devices in the UK) is being employed on the Transputers to provide basic mechanisms for multiple users, message passing between processors, (automatic routing through the network, asynchronous reception, UNIX like interfaces) and for developing and symbolic debugging of code. It effectively alleviates the programmer from some of the 'low level' distributed system implementation issues, and has provided the software interface to decouple the physical and virtual cell architectures. At the time of writing it provides the best software support available.

17.5   Application to Sonar Interpretation

This section considers the most developed application of this distributed problem solving work. A brief discussion of the sonar interpretation problem and a single cell knowledge base capable of segmenting objects and shadows from sonar images is followed by a description of the initial experiments carried out to validate GNL and to evaluate communication overheads and processor loading caused by using a horizontal partitioning of the vision pyramid and FA/NA interaction.

17.5.1   The Sonar Interpretation Problem

Sonar interpretation is the task of automatically analysing sonar data in order to extract information concerning the marine environment surrounding the sensing device. For the submersible application, this will typically involve detecting and describing man made objects such as pipelines, wellheads, divers, and other vehicles. For geophysical work it may equally involve analysing image textures to describe different geological layers such as sand, rock, shingle or oil. The task is nontrivial because the sonar data is typically corrupted by both the anomalous behaviour of the acoustic transmission medium (e.g., unwanted boundary and volume reverberation and varying propagation speeds throughout the medium) and by the nature of the sonar device itself (e.g., secondary sidelobe scanning and multipath and multipulse reflections). This creates various kinds of uncertainty in the data being processed, such as noise throughout the image, seabed clutter, ghost objects that do not correspond to real objects (so called anomalies), and inaccurate estimation of a boundary's range.

Once formatted as an image, a human expert working with such data seems to use two levels of processing to carry out an interpretation. At a subconscious level, image segmentation is carried out automatically to identify characteristic features such as regions, boundaries, or texture. At a conscious level, more rule based reasoning employing a priori knowledge of the characteristics of the sonar device and the surrounding marine environment is used to accept or reject candidate features as resulting from a bona-fide object and to classify objects of known types.

To automate this task it appears reasonable to employ a knowledge based approach to integrate image processing and symbolic reasoning activities (corresponding to the subconscious and conscious levels of human processing) within a vision pyramid. Thus, the decision making associated with rejecting or selecting candidate features and with selecting image processing tools and parameters can be carried out explicitly. It further provides a framework within which subsequent classification and identification operations can be carried out to uniquely label these candidate objects, and allows for the integration of data (sensory or available a priori) from elsewhere.

17.5.2   Single Cell Knowledge Base For Interpretation

Previous work has used the BOFFIN implementation of a type 2 rational cell (Section 17.3) to implement and evaluate a sector scan sonar image interpretation knowledge base operating within a single cell [Lane 1986], [Russell and Lane 1986]. This has formed the basis for the distributed knowledge base used in the first cell distribution experiments. The knowledge base is capable of detecting and describing objects and shadows within a class of sector scan sonar images using 37 rule based and algorithmic knowledge sources. Typically the KS reason about the known environment and sonar characteristics to select appropriate parameters for signal processing KS and to infer hypotheses (e.g., the presence of seabed clutter) that cause particular image processing KS to trigger.

By way of example, Figure 17.7 shows a typical sonar scan derived from the UDI AS360 sector scanning device, with boxes overlayed showing regions in the image that have been identified and described as candidate objects or shadows. The scan is over 360 degrees on a 40m range setting and contains significant seabed clutter. The object regions correspond to a diving bell (top left), a diver with bubbles (bottom left), and a ridge on the seabed (middle right). The major shadow region corresponds to a seabed scar (middle right). The segmentations leading to these candidates are shown in Figure 17.8.

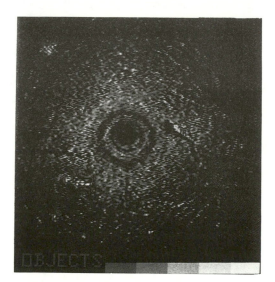 

Figure 17.7: Raw sector scan sonar image with candidate objects and shadows overlaid

Although capable of producing successful segmentations, the single cell knowledge base was slow to execute on both DEC and SUN minicomputers and did not demonstrate robust performance with incorrectly inferred hypotheses placed on the cell blackboard. This therefore provides the motivation for developing a distributed version of the knowledge base using a network of rational cells.

17.5.3 A Distributed Interpretation Experiment

For the initial experiments on distributed sonar interpretation, a horizontal partitioning of the vision pyramid implemented in the single cell knowledge base was chosen in preference to the complete hybrid architecture of Section 17.4. Thus, an FA/NA mode of interaction was chosen. This provided some early experience, and allowed the focus of activity to be concerned with validating the Global Network Language, and quantifying to some extent

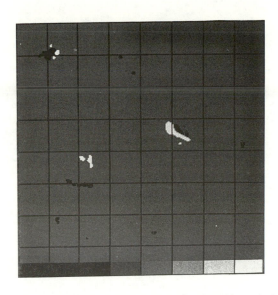

Figure 17.8: Segmentation of candidate objects (dark) and shadows (bright)

the processor loading and communication bandwidths involved. Because of the absence of cooperative interaction, the only available mechanisms for resolving uncertainty were those provided by BOFFIN within each cell. Thus, although partial solutions were allowed, they were resolved within each cell prior to transmission.

Four discrete blocks in the original knowledge base were identified, corresponding roughly to horizontal planes through the vision pyramid (Section 17.2). Cells were arranged such that cell 1 implemented the lowest pyramid level, and cell 4 the highest. This could equally be regarded as a four stage pipeline interconnection topology, thus allowing up to four sonar images to be processed concurrently. To provide an appropriate man-machine interface, a further cell was connected to each of the four interpretation cells (Figure 17.9).

To introduce some genuine parallelism into the implementation, a network of Sun workstations was employed to execute the cells, using a thick ethernet interconnect as the physical means of communication. Although we are developing the complete system for the distributed transputer architecture, using the Suns in the first instance provided a convenient starting point using existing software for relatively rapid prototyping. The complete system was displayed using the sunwindows environment (Figure 17.9). Concurrent operation of the cells could also be simulated on one workstation using the Sun's multitasking window environment.

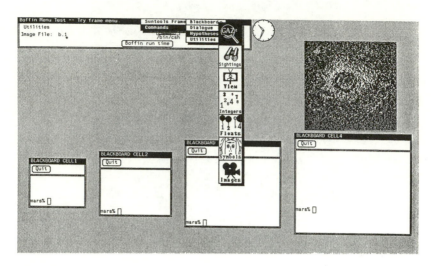

Figure 17.9: Distributed cell architecture with man-machine interface

17.5.4   Experimental Results

To ascertain the overall system speedup obtained and the communication channel bandwidths required using the FA/NA horizontal partitioning, the sonar image of Figure 17.7 was used at the base of the pyramid. In this way, single cell and multicell performance could be compared using a typical image.

Table 17.1 shows the processing time required by each cell to detect and describe the objects and shadows in the image. The total time taken to produce the first result is approximately 25 minutes. Thereafter subsequent results become available approximately every 12 minutes. There is therefore only a doubling in speed for the four cell implementation. This is a classic parallel processing result, arising because the cells do not operate in a coherent fashion (i.e., they are poorly load balanced) and hence one or more form a bottleneck. This produces inefficient operation where parallelism is not maximally exploited. The poor load balancing is a consequence of the approximately horizontal partitioning of the vision pyramid used to distribute the existing knowledge base (Section 17.2), illustrating the need for some vertical partitioning of the pyramid also. The imbalance of the processing times for each cell with respect to its position in the pyramid comes about because of the difficulty of partitioning the single cell knowledge base in an exactly horizontal way.

To ascertain the communication and inferencing overheads associated with the nearly autonomous interaction, the time taken to execute both the partitioned (therefore multicell) and unpartitioned (single cell) knowledge bases on a single workstation were compared. The

454

Table 17.1: Processing Time and Communications Required for Object Recognition

Cell	Processing Time (minutes)	Number of Input Processes	Number of Output Processes
1	4.08	44	42
2	8.42	42	42
3	11.82	42	40
4	1.00	40	42

time difference, and therefore overhead, was some 58 secs, of which the communication time needed to transmit some 170 hypotheses was estimated at 2%. The message passing scheme therefore appears to function well.

17.6   Other Robotic Applications

Thus far the hybrid architecture has been described for a computer vision application. However, the concepts behind the vision pyramid can equally be applied to any multisensor system where diverse types of information have to be processed, abstracted and combined. Thus, the hierarchy could have a variety of other applications, where cells at the lowest level are connected to a variety of sensors, instead of examining sections of an image. The FA/C and FA/NA mechanisms seem well suited to resolving ambiguities in such a system.

As a further development, robotic actuators could be attached to cells at the lowest level to replace the sensors. The implementation of cooperating robot subsystems now appears feasible. In addition, multisensor, multiactuator systems could be implemented using coupled hierarchies. However, this raises a number of research issues surrounding the need for tight feedback between sensor and actuator during closed loop control of the robot dynamics.

With this in mind, the experience gained by implementing the hybrid architecture for the vision application could have a substantial impact upon our multisensor, multiactuator knowledge based robotic activities in areas other than the submersible. Examples would be in cooperating robots performing an assembly task within a flexible manufacturing system workcell [Duffy *et al.* 1988] and in real time knowledge based process control [Leitch 1987].

17.7   Conclusions

This paper has presented a hybrid distributed problem solving architecture suitable for application to a range of knowledge based computer vision applications, of which the automatic interpretation of sonar data is an example. A description of the processing agent at the heart of the architecture (the rational cell) has also been presented.

Within the hybrid DPS hierarchy two forms of communication are envisaged, corresponding to the FA/C and FA/NA modes of operation. Horizontally (i.e., within a level) a cooperative strategy is employed where possibly inconsistent and incorrect partial results are passed between nodes in an iterative coroutine style of operation as a mechanism for resolving ambiguity. Vertically (i.e., between levels) a nearly autonomous strategy is employed, where each level is assumed to have the majority of information it requires locally, passing only complete results (that may also be inconsistent and incorrect) with associated confidence attributes.

Results have been presented showing the operation of the FA/NA mode of interaction in terms of processor loading and communication bandwidth. The following conclusions can thus be drawn concerning the approximately horizontal FA/NA partitioning of a single cell sonar interpretation knowledge base:

1. Partitioning the vision pyramid horizontally leads to a poorly load balanced system that does not maximally exploit parallelism. Some vertical partitioning of the pyramid is also required.

2. Implementing additional rational cells within a horizontally partitioned system need not impose significant communication and processing overheads.

3. The global network language (GNL) protocol and internal dictionary look up appear to be a successful mechanism for vertical intercell communication.

4. Partitioning a knowledge base designed for a single cell to exploit parallelism maximally may not be straightforward because of the way individual knowledge sources are conceived. The knowledge base should therefore be designed with the distributed implementation in mind.

The results from this initial work support some of the original assumptions upon which the usefulness of the hybrid FA/C, FA/NA approach depends, and we therefore feel justified in proceeding to the Transputer implementation. However, there are still many issues to be resolved both within each cell and in the cell interconnection strategy. These are briefly discussed in the next section. A more thorough discussion is left for future publication.

17.8 Future Work

Future work on the distributed problem solving aspects of the problem will concentrate on two areas. These are the cell internal architecture and the complete hierarchical structure.

Projects running in parallel are investigating improved signal processing tools for image processing and feature extraction, and a redesign of the structure of the sonar interpretation knowledge base to be more suitable for implementation in a distributed cell architecture.

17.8.1   Cell Internal Architecture

Experience with the current implementations of the type 2 cell internal architecture has shown that there are at least two generic areas requiring further research. These are (1) the stability and consistency of the cells' hypotheses, and (2) the responsiveness of the cells to external events.

Hypothesis Stability and Consistency

These problems affect the integrity of a cell's reasoning space, in that hypotheses are created that do not reflect the true status of the problem domain. Such hypotheses may mislead the cell down what are likely to be unproductive and incorrect solution paths. Of the two, the problems associated with hypothesis stability are the more severe.

At both the cell and network level there will be many complex chains of supporting hypotheses. It is possible for a designer to create a knowledge base where circular chains of self supporting hypotheses and knowledge sources occur during the normal course of inference (Figure 17.10). Once these *circularities* have been created they may remain even after removal of their original justification. Such circularities create "illusions" that constitute wasted processing effort and can lead to ill-considered actions. Furthermore, because of the fedback nature of these illusions, hypothesis attributes (e.g., confidence and value) may be unstable through time, exhibiting chaotic, oscillatory, or divergent behaviour.

If these problems are to be avoided either (1) the knowledge base must be checked off-line for circularities, by the knowledge base designer or by machine, or (2) the cells must keep track of the network of justifications for hypotheses at run-time, so that unnecessary cyclic triggering of KS can be stopped.

Due to the nonmonotonic nature of the environment about which cells reason, hypotheses will be asserted and then retracted or changed. If a hypothesis has been used as part of the justification for another hypothesis and the original hypothesis is changed or retracted, then a cell's reasoning space may become inconsistent. These inconsistencies will considerably increase a cell's search space and the time taken to reach its solution, but they are potentially less damaging than unsatisfiable circularities.

Both of the problems discussed above may be detected and eliminated by employing a truth maintenance system [Doyle 1982] to replace the existing belief revision system and

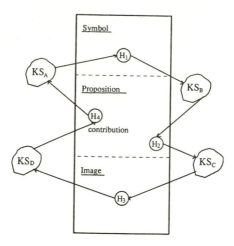

Figure 17.10: A circular chain of hypotheses and knowledge sources

maintain a network of justifications for asserted hypotheses. Such a system is computationally costly, but may actually increase the speed with which certain solutions are reached by reducing the search space and breaking oscillatory loops.

Responsiveness

Experience with the current implementations of cells has shown that they do not respond quickly to external events. There are two reasons for this:

1. Once a cell has initiated the execution of a knowledge source it must wait until that knowledge source has finished before it may reason about any external events that have occurred during the execution of that knowledge source.

2. Cells cannot adjust their inferencing to match the time available to achieve a goal.

The first problem may be solved by providing *preemptive* scheduling, which would allow cells to interrupt and suspend the execution of knowledge sources in favour of more urgent activity. This, however, introduces additional data consistency problems. Clearly, updates to hypothesis frames must be atomic. In addition, the metalevel focus-of-control KS must also take into account data dependencies between the preempting knowledge source(s) and the preempted knowledge source, when deciding whether to reschedule, restart, or abandon execution of the preempted knowledge source.

For the second problem, a cell may have to assess the time available to achieve a goal (if it is not explicitly stated in the goal) and trade-off precision of solution against inferencing time available. A cell's blackboard or reasoning space is partitioned into various levels of abstraction and knowledge sources are labeled according to the level at which they contribute. For quick responses, only the most abstract level would be consulted, while for a more detailed response and/or a response in which greater confidence was required, lower levels would be invoked. However, before a cell may select the appropriate level of inferencing it must know how much time it has to reach its solution. If this is not explicit in the goal then an ability to reason with time, such as that provided by Allen's temporal logic of intervals [Allen 1983] would facilitate the assessment of goal timings and selection of appropriate inferencing levels. Fuller discussions of the real-time aspects of knowledge based systems are given in [Chantler 1988] and [Laffey *et al.* 1988].

17.8.2 Pyramidal Structure

Future research on the pyramidal structure of Section 17.4 will broadly follow the architectural issues of Section 17.4.3. Of these, the important ones are felt to be

- the ability of cooperative problem solving to converge to a solution (rather than diverge, oscillate, or behave chaotically),

- the relationships that govern the optimum hierarchy dimensions and aspect ratio to exploit parallelism maximally while resolving, uncertainty

- the ability of the interaction strategies to successfully propagate the 3D world model to required cells in the network,

- the ability to implement a distributed truth maintenance system between agents with or without the need to communicate hypotheses' support structure, and

- the need to communicate metalevel information to maintain focus of control across the network [Corkill and Lesser 1983].

Acknowledgements

Numerous people have contributed to the development of this work. In particular, George Russell for illuminating discussions during the inception of the cell idea, and Keith Brown for contributing to regular group discussions on distributed problem solving. Thanks are due to Hugh Connor for software support during the long hours of system implementation, and to UDI Ltd., Aberdeen, Scotland, for supplying the sector scan sonar data.

This work is jointly funded by the Marine Technology Directorate Ltd., agents of the UK Science and Engineering Research Council, BP Petroleum Development Ltd., Shell UK Exploration & Production, Ferranti ORE Ltd., Honeywell Inc. (USA), and the Ministry of Defence—Admiralty Research Establishment.

References

[Allen 1983] J. F. Allen, "Maintaining Knowledge about Temporal Intervals," *Communications of the ACM*, Vol. 26, No. 11, 1983.

[Ballard and Brown 1982] D. H. Ballard and C. M. Brown, *Computer Vision*, Prentice Hall, 1982.

[Berry 1987] D. T. Berry, *A Knowledge Based Framework to Machine Vision*, PhD Thesis, Dept. of Electrical and Electronic Engineering, Heriot-Watt University, 1987.

[Chantler 1988] M. J. Chantler, "Real-Time Aspects of Expert Systems in Process Control," *Expert Systems in Process Control*, IEE Colloquium, March 1988.

[Corkill and Lesser 1983] D. D. Corkill and V. R. Lesser, "The use of Meta-level Control for Coordination in a Distributed Problem Solving Network," *Proc. 8th Int. Joint Conf. on Artificial Intelligence*, Vol. 2, August 1983, pp. 748–756.

[Davis 1982] R. Davis, "Report on the Second Workshop on distributed AI," *SIGART Newsletter*, April 1982, pp. 13–23.

[Davis 1980] R. Davis, "Report on the Workshop on distributed AI," *SIGART Newsletter*, October 1980, pp. 42–43.

[Davis and Smith 1983] R. Davis and R. G. Smith, "Negotiation as a Metaphor for Distributed Problem Solving," *Artificial Intelligence*, Vol. 20, 1983, pp. 63–109.

[Decker 1987] K. S. Decker, "Distributed Problem-Solving Techniques: A Survey," *IEEE Transactions on Systems, Man, and Cybernetics*, Vol. SMC-17, No.5, September/October 1987, pp. 729–740.

[Doyle 1982] J. Doyle, "A Truth Maintenance System," *Artificial Intelligence*, Vol. 12, 1982, pp. 231–272.

[Duffy *et al.* 1988] N. D. Duffy, J. T. Herd, and G. P. Philip, "A Structured Approach to the Control of Parallel Acting Cooperating Robots," *Proc. of 18th Int. Symposium on Industrial Robots*, 1988.

[Durfee 1987] E. H. Durfee, *A Unified Approach to Dynamic Coordination: Planning Actions and Interactions in a Distributed Problem Solving Network*, PhD Thesis, Dept. of Computer and Information Science, UMASS, September 1987.

[Durfee *et al.* 1987] E. H. Durfee, V. R. Lesser, and D. D. Corkill, "Coherent Cooperation Among Communicating Problem Solvers," *IEEE Transactions on Computers*, Vol. C-36, No. 11, November 1987, pp. 1275–1291.

[Eaves-Walton and Shippey 1987] C. Eaves-Walton and G. Shippey, "Digital Image Processing for Sidescan Sonar Data Analysis," *Proc. IERE 5th Int. Conf. on Electronics for Ocean Technology*, Heriot-Watt University, March 1987, pp. 203–209.

[Erman *et al.* 1980] L. D. Erman, F. Hayes-Roth, V. R. Lesser, and D. R. Reddy, "The Hearsay-II Speech-Understanding System: Integrating Knowledge to Resolve Uncertainty," *Computing Surveys*, Vol. 12, No. 2, June 1980, pp. 213–253.

[Fehling and Erman 1983] M. Fehling and L. Erman, "Report on the Third Annual Workshop on Distributed Artificial Intelligence," *SIGART Newsletter*, April 1983, pp. 3–12.

[Fennell and Lesser 1977] R. D. Fennell and V. R. Lesser, "Parallelism in Artificial Intelligence Problem Solving: A Case Study of Hearsay II," *IEEE Transactions on Computers*, Vol. C-26, No. 2, February 1977, pp. 98–111.

[Forgy *et al.* 1984] C. Forgy, A. Gupta, A. Newell, and R. Wedig, "Initial Assessment of Architectures for Production Systems," *Proceedings AAAI-84*, August 1984, pp. 116–120.

[Fox 1981] M. S. Fox, "An Organizational View of Distributed Systems," *IEEE Transactions on Systems, Man, and Cybernetics*, Vol. SMC-11, No. 1, January 1981, pp. 70–80.

[Genesereth *et al.* 1986] M. R. Genesereth, M. L. Ginsberg, and J. S. Rosenschien, "Cooperation Without Communication," *Proceedings AAAI-86 5th National Conference on Artificial Intelligence*, Vol. 1, 1986, pp. 51–57.

[Hanson and Riseman 1978a] A. R. Hanson and E. M. Riseman, "VISIONS: A Computer System for Interpreting Scenes," *Computer Vision Systems*, Academic Press, 1978, pp. 303–333.

[Hanson and Riseman 1978b] A. R. Hanson and E. M. Riseman, "Segmentation of Natural Scenes," *Computer Vision Systems*, 1978, pp. 129–163.

[Hewitt and Lieberman 1984] C. Hewitt and H. Lieberman, "Design Issues in Parallel Architectures for Artificial Intelligence," *Digest of Papers Compcon Spring '84: 28th IEEE Computer Society*, International Conference, 1984, pp. 418–428.

[Hillis 1985] W. D. Hillis, *The Connection Machine*, MIT Press, London, 1985.

[Homewood *et al.* 1987] M. Homewood, D. May, D. Shepherd, R. Shepherd, "The IMS T800 Transputer," *IEEE Micro*, October 1987, pp. 10–26.

[Huhns 1987] M. N. Huhns, ed., *Distributed Artificial Intelligence*, Pitman, London, 1987.

[Kanal and Lemmer 1986] L. N. Kanal and J. F. Lemmer, "Uncertainty in Artificial Intelligence," *Machine Intelligence and Pattern Recognition*, Vol. 4, North-Holland, 1986.

[Kornfeld and Hewitt 1981] W. A. Kornfeld and C. E. Hewitt, "The Scientific Community Metaphor," *IEEE Transactions on Systems, Man, and Cybernetics*, Vol. SMC-11, No. 1, January 1981, pp. 24–33.

[Laffey *et al.* 1988] T. J. Laffey, P. A. Cox, J. L. Schmidt, S. M. Kao, and J. Y. Read, "Real-Time Knowledge-Based Systems," *AI Magazine*, Spring 1988, pp. 27–45.

[Lane 1989] D. M. Lane, "Methodologies for Multi Sensor System Integration: Building Descriptions to Make Decisions," *NATO Advanced Studies Workshop on Kinematic and Dynamic Issues I*, Sensor Based Control, Tuscany, forthcoming book from Springer-Verlag.

[Lane 1986] D. M. Lane, *The Investigation of a Knowledge Based System Architecture in the Context of a Subsea Robotic Application*, PhD Thesis, Dept. of Electrical amd Electronic Engineering, Heriot-Watt University, 1986.

[Leitch 1987] R. R. Leitch, "Modelling of Complex Dynamic Systems," *IEE Proceedings*, Vol. 134, Part D, No. 4, July 1987.

461

[Lesser and Corkill 1983] V. R. Lesser and D. D. Corkill, "The Distributed Vehicle Monitoring Testbed," *AI Magazine*, Vol. 4, Fall 1983, pp. 63–109.

[Lesser and Corkill 1981] V. R. Lesser and D. D. Corkill, "Functionally Accurate, Cooperative Distributed Systems," *IEEE Transactions on Systems, Man, and Cybernetics*, Vol. SMC-11, No. 1, January 1981, pp. 81–96.

[Lesser and Erman 1980] V. R. Lesser and L. D. Erman, "Distributed Interpretation: A Model and Experiment", *IEEE Transactions on Computers*, Vol. C-29, No. 12, December 1980, pp. 1144–1162.

[Marr 1982] D. Marr, *Vision: A Computational Investigation Into The Human Representation and Processing Of Visual Information*, W. H. Freeman, 1982.

[Nii *et al.* 1982] H. P. Nii, E. A. Fiegenbaum, J. J. Anton, and A. J. Rockmore, "Signal to Symbol Transformation. HASP/SIAP Case Study," *AI Magazine*, Spring 1982.

[Robertson 1988] E. W. A. Robertson, *The Interface and Communications for a Distributed Knowledge-Based System*, MS Thesis, Dept. of Electrical and Electronic Engineering, Heriot-Watt University, 1988.

[Rosenschien and Genesereth 1985] J. S. Rosenschien and M. R. Genesereth, "Deals Among Rational Agents," *Proc. 9th Int. Joint Conf. on Artificial Intelligence*, August 1985, pp. 91–99.

[Russell and Lane 1986] G. T. Russell and D. M. Lane, "A Knowledge-Based System Framework for Environmental Perception in a Subsea Robotics Context," *IEEE Journal of Oceanic Engineering*, Vol. OE-11, No. 3, July 1986, pp. 401–412.

[Smith 1980] R. G. Smith, "The Contract Net Protocol: High-level Communication and Control in a Distributed Problem Solver," *IEEE Transactions on Computers*, Vol. C-29, December 1980, pp. 1104–1113.

[Smith and Davis 1981] R. G. Smith and R. Davis, "Frameworks for Cooperation in Distributed Problem Solving," *IEEE Transactions on Systems, Man, Cybernetics*, Vol. SMC-11, No. 1, January 1981, pp. 61–70.

[Yang *et al.* 1985] J. D. Yang, M. N. Huhns, and L. M. Stephens, "An Architecture for Control and Communications in Distributed Artificial Intelligence Systems," *IEEE Transactions on Systems, Man, and Cybernetics*, Vol. SMC-15, No. 3, May/June 1985, pp. 316–326.

[Submersible Symposium 1981] *Proc. 2nd Int. Symposium on Unmanned Untethered Submersible Technology*, University of New Hampshire, 1981.

D. M. Lane, M. J. Chantler, E. W. Robertson, and A. G. McFadzean
Intelligent Automation Laboratory
Department of Electrical and Electronic Engineering
Heriot-Watt University
Edinburgh, EH1 2HT
SCOTLAND

Chapter 18

The Cooperation of Experts in Engineering Design

Alan H. Bond

Abstract

The cooperation of specialists with distributed knowledge is examined, in the context of knowledge-based support for collaboration among different engineering departments in carrying out large design tasks. It is concluded that

1. each specialist department has its own private justification language, but interacts with another department using a common shared language.

2. there may be little shared knowledge, and the shared language may involve an abstracted subset of the private languages of the collaborators.

3. collaborative reasoning can be limited because of

   - *expression* problems, not being able to ask the right questions.

   - *rules of interaction* and protocol, arising from legalistic procedures or from proof strategy.

   - *performance* problems, not having sufficient resources, due to the complexity of resolving the distribution.

A simple model for collaborative reasoning is proposed that defines a collaboration strategy as a dialogue game.

463

18.1 Introduction

We consider the problem of the cooperation of a number of intelligent agents in producing an agreed design. We assume that the agents are experts in different areas of specialization, but that the final design or plan can only be found by contributions from all agents. We shall sometimes consider the case of two agents for simplicity, but in general there can be n agents.

We are studying this problem as an abstraction from common situations arising in manufacturing, which is a collaboration of several different kinds of engineer, who do not understand fully each other's areas of specialization. A classic situation is finding a design for a part that satisfies functional requirements and is also easy to manufacture. One can, in the simplest case, imagine two engineers, one an expert on functionality and the other an expert in production, collaborating to produce the best design. We can assume a nonantagonistic relationship; however, both agents must be convinced that the design satisfies their own specialized requirements and is also the best that can be achieved overall.

This type of situation, of two agents with disparate knowledge collaborating to produce a best solution satisfying to both, is quite ubiquitous. Consider for example the collaboration of a house owner and a construction contractor in deciding upon work for the improvement of the house, or a doctor and patient trying to diagnose a medical problem. It also occurs in hierarchical management organizations, where an administrative manager and a technical project leader collaborate to decide on project content, timescale, cost, personnel, etc.

This DAI problem is different from that of multiagent planning, which has been studied by [Georgeff 1987], [Rosenschein 1982], [Genesereth et al. 1984], [Konolige 1986], and others. In multiagent planning, one agent designs a plan to be executed by several agents. The problem is to devise a plan and then arrange that the agents synchronize order-dependent actions correctly and are correctly informed as they carry out the plan.

Our problem is almost the dual of this: several agents collaborate to produce a single plan. This resulting plan may be executed by some other single agent or it may be further parallelized and allocated to several agents, but this is not our concern. In a manufacturing organization, a design and a process plan for producing a part are found and established. It is then a problem for another part of the organization to use the process plan to produce the part and to work with the design in various ways, such as verification and inspection of parts produced and marketing of the part. The subsequent parallelization, distribution, and synchronization of work with the design and its production are often time-dependent, and are therefore separated from the initial generation of the design. A similar situation occurs in military planning, where several experts put together a military plan without considering

464

the details of its implementation or synchronization, which are left to the exigencies of the moment.

Other DAI problems, however, are similar and overlap the problem discussed here. VLSI design using a set of cooperating experts has been investigated by [Huhns et al. 1983]. Mutual plan construction is not well understood. It is confounded by disparity in goals and intentions, as well as in world knowledge. All the problems of multiagent planning exist, along with the problems of inconsistent world views due to distribution. [Durfee 1987] and [Durfee and Lesser 1987] have originated the idea of *partial global planning* as a mechanism to enable communicating problem solvers to incrementally construct mutually coherent plans. Added benefits may accrue by using multiple perspectives in the planning process at different levels of abstraction, as Hayes-Roth has suggested in work on the OPM system [Hayes-Roth 1985].

The problem of air traffic control can certainly be couched as a collaboration, where planes pool their knowledge, and may even produce individual plans that could be merged to produce an agreed plan. This type of thing has been described [Steeb *et al.* 1984], but has not so far been much developed. The DVMT architecture [Durfee *et al.* 1987] also involves the collaboration of agents with disparate knowledge, however this knowledge is usually simply data information of sensor values and interpretations at different spatial locations. Blackboard models [Erman and Lesser 1975] involve the collaboration of agents with disparate knowledge, however little negotiation or collaboration usually occurs.

Organizations seek to generate sound, relevant, and reliable information to support organizational decision making and action. According to Hewitt's model [Hewitt 1986], organizational reasoning takes place within small coherent modules that he calls *microtheories*. These correspond to the viewpoints held by individuals or groups or departments in the organization (and in fact, even individuals may reason using multiple microtheories). In general, microtheories will have some inconsistency with one another. Most office work will involve coping with these inconsistencies by collaboration, which involves negotiation among modules to deal with conflicts and inconsistencies between microtheories.

The purpose of our work in this paper is to explore the use of predicate logic in describing the collaboration of agents with disparate rather than inconsistent knowledge. However, it is likely that any disparity can lead to a conflict between agents [Bond and Gasser 1988]. The main problems arise just from the fact that knowledge is distributed among the agents, there is limited ability to express and represent problems communally, and there is limited ability to collaborate in attempting their solution. This work involves issues of formulation of collaboration so as to capture and describe the activities occurring in the types of collaborative situation described above. Theoretical issues arising in the use of formal logic in collaboration are the subject of a companion paper [Bond 1988].

The use of logic in collaboration has a distinguished philosophical history and involves positions that DAI could well embrace. "Disputation exhibits epistemological processes at work in a setting of socially conditioned interactions" ([Rescher 1977] page xii). Dialectic logic changes the orthodox egocentric notion of "how can I convince myself?" to the social and cooperative notion of "how can we convince each other?"

There has been some recent formal work in which dialectical schemes of disputation have been formalized as *dialogue-games* in [Hamblin 1971], [Hintikka and Saarinen 1979], and [Rescher 1977]. Note that these dialogue-games are different from and should not be confused with those of [Levin and Moore 1977], which are more familiar to DAI researchers. The dialogue-games approach is thus a candidate for representing the collaborative process we are studying, and some of the underlying approach and philosophy will be relevant. Work on dialogue-games, however, does not address the issue of disparity of the two agents' theories, which is a main concern here.

Another genre of theoretical approach is more concerned with rationality and probability [Cox and Willard 1982] [Hample 1982]. This connects in DAI with rational theories of negotiation [Sycara 1985] [Sycara 1985b] and in our case with the problem of finding an optimal, rather than logically valid, design.

The practical outcome of our work is to be a distributed knowledge-based system for the support of collaboration between different engineering departments in a manufacturing organization. Each department would have its own workstation with a knowledge base that it controls and maintains. The set of workstations would form a network, as shown in Figure 18.1.

18.2   Communication for Collaboration

Agents have disparate knowledge. We assume they will interact, in a predicate logic formulation, by sending goals or hypotheses to each other to be attempted. Each expert has a theory, which involves a vocabulary of predicate letters, function letters, and constant letters, and knowledge in the form of axioms. In order to communicate, the two theories must overlap, i.e., there must be a subset of the vocabularies that they share. It is not strictly necessary to have any axioms in common, indeed it is quite likely that no axiom will be shared (except basic mathematics and physics), since each specialist would have his own variant of a shared axiom, qualified in his own terms. Our emphasis is thus different from the mutual belief spaces of [Bruce and Newman 1978].

We also have to allow each agent to have part of their vocabulary that is not shared

466

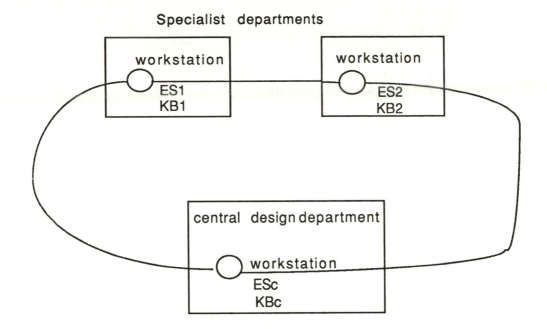

Figure 18.1: Support for collaborative design

with the other. These are used for, if you will, technical details that are important for the specialist in his own deliberations but are not used in communicating with the other agent. This is the language and terminology used in a particular specialized engineering department.

Since we need to define a shared argument language, we must allow closure under boolean operators and under quantifiers, and so we have a shared theory in predicate logic. We call the shared vocabulary the *commonality basis*, which is a set of predicate, functor and constant letters, with arities and possibly typed ("sorted"), arguments. The shared *argument language* uses these predicates with boolean combinations and universal and existential quantification. Every response must be expressed using the vocabulary of commonality in the language of argument. The private *proof language* may be different for each agent in that the proof of a statement may depend on different axiomatic bases for each agent. The noncommunal knowledge base or theory of each agent is a set of axioms involving a larger vocabulary. We diagram this in Figure 18.2.

A commonality basis and argument language have to satisfy certain conditions. For example, a logically valid argument by one agent in this language should be accepted as valid by the other agent. The axioms in the argument language are derived in the proof language of each. Further axioms can be created, during the collaboration, by proofs in

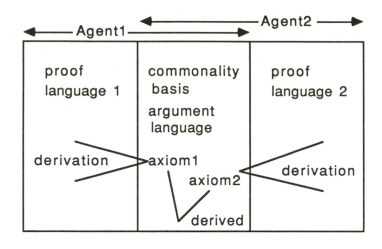

Figure 18.2: Commonality basis

the proof language in response to queries in the argument language. An axiom need not be atomic, but it will not have a proof in the argument language. We approach the problem in the spirit of open systems [Hewitt 1985], i.e., where we cannot make assumptions about the theories of other agents.

An illustrative example arises in our work on collaboration in wing section design [Bond 1988b]. Here a stress engineer and a producibility designer interact using a diagram on a CAD system. The stress engineer needs a solution that transmits loads well through the structure, and the designer needs a structure that is easy to fabricate using, for example, an automatic riveting machine. The criteria used by each specialist are private to them in that they are complex and concerned with their particular technologies. The internal proof language of the producibility designer concerns the use of the part and its production. For example, the joins must be compatible with known riveting gun types. Also rivet spacing must be kept constant or at least to a small number of different rivet spacings.

The internal proof language of the stress engineer concerns loads, stresses, transmission, and techniques for finding them. The stress engineer works privately with a finite element model that calculates load patterns satisfying differential equations derived from physical principles. These must match the load transmission properties of the sized geometry.

In aircraft design, there are many other specialists, each with his own technology and language. We show in Figure 18.3 the main specializations involved in the conceptual design phase of aircraft design and the main communication links. There are also noncentrally routed communications among specialists. The argument language is simply a drawing, that is, geometric elements and their relations, indications of what is right or wrong with a given geometry, and suggested changes in the geometry.

The main activity is that of refinement of the design, that is, the models are gradually changed from an abstract and approximate form to more detailed and specified forms. There are many different types of refinement operations, such as putting in detail within an envelope, making more precise numerical estimates, replacing lumped single elements by multiple elements, specifying surface geometry, sizing, and adding missing elements. The main collaboration occurs in the choices of refinements of the central model. There will also be some correctional suggestions, evaluations and changes at the current level of refinement. Figure 18.4 indicates the process of coordinated refinement that occurs.

We presume the aim of collaboration is to produce a design that is agreed to by each agent. This means that each agent has a proof (or "explanation" or "justification") of the statement with which he is satisfied. His proof may involve axioms and vocabulary from his internal logic as well as from the shared logic.

18.3 A Model of Collaboration

18.3.1 Model of One Agent

Let us take all agents to be of similar structure, so that all agents can make evaluations, set goals and make moves. There is an alternative model to this in which a central "designer" agent makes all the moves and is surrounded by n specialist critics, who observe the design search and send evaluations and goals to the designer.

We take the shared working data to be the design history and the current design. The design will be a relational structure with design elements and design relations. Any set of elements can have an evaluation associated with it. The current design also contains the *design rationale*, which is a goal graph whose leaves are either moves made or else subgoals to be satisfied. There will be a goal "focus," i.e., a designated subset of the goals. Moves can be design moves or else design goal moves, which generate goals or change the focus. The *design history* will be the sequence of moves made that change the current design and goal tree.

All agents will need the following types of actions:

goal $->$ subgoals

(sub)goal $->$ moves

situation $->$ evaluation or suggestion

evaluation $->$ goal.

An *evaluation* is a numerical evaluation associated with a set of elements; a *suggestion* is

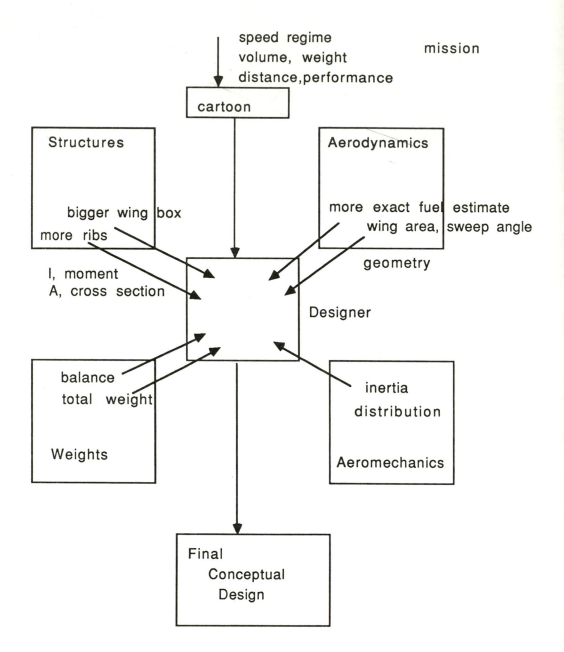

Figure 18.3: Specialists cooperating in the conceptual design phase

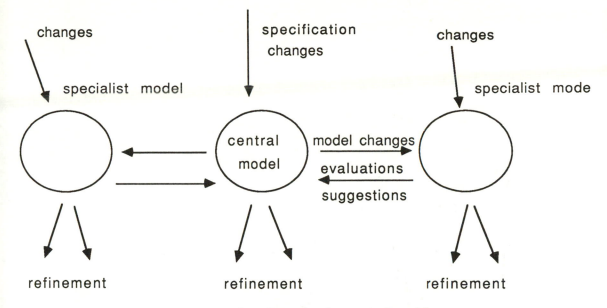

changes

specification
changes

changes

specialist model

specialist mode

central
model

model changes

evaluations

suggestions

refinement

refinement

refinement

Figure 18.4: Coordinated refinement of models

a suggested move. Suggestions can be constraints on proposed refinements or correctional requirements at the current level of refinement.

We use geometric models, which are sets of assertions in predicate logic. These include assertions about the existence of points, lines, faces, features, etc., and about relations that hold among them [Bond and Soetarman 1986].

18.3.2   Suggestions, Evaluations and Elaboration

We need to organize the collaboration rather than have a free-for-all. The type of coordination that is commonly used in design by a group of n agents is to have a single focus of attention that is shared by all agents. This basically serializes the search through the space of possibilities, but gains great savings in context switching, memory use, and version and hypothesis proliferation. The shared construction approach is depicted in Figure 18.5.

Individual suggestions are to be gathered from different agents for a given state of the central model. These will be *conjoined* into composite constraints or *joint suggestions*. Since we would like to find all individual suggestions, these will usually be a disjunction of conjunctions, so there is some question as to whether we need to use nonclausal representations [Bond 1988]. We also need each agent to evaluate the suggestions of others; although it may not be able to generate the suggestion, it can usually evaluate it. An evaluation can lead to conjoining the initial suggestion to further constraints by other agents. An example

471

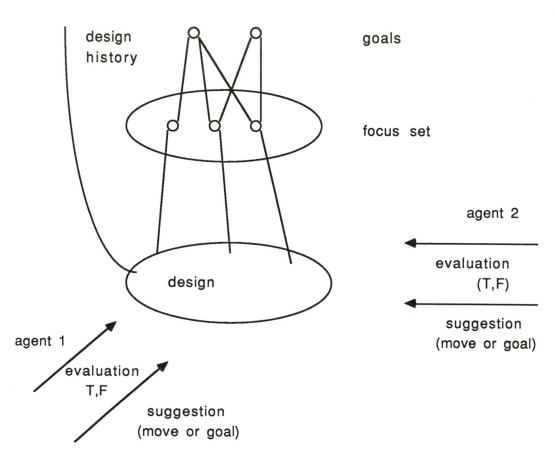

Figure 18.5: Shared construction approach

might be to introduce a tapering geometry for some structural members. Although this might not be introduced by a producibility specialist, he would have some evaluation to make as to the cost of forming the material and some additional constraints to be conjoined. This process can be treated as an explicit elaboration phase in the coordination strategy. But we can also, with some advantages, treat it as simply a further iteration of a coordination cycle, so that making model moves and elaborating suggestions are treated together and a control choice can be made among them.

In principle, constraints will be added until a unique geometric solution can be found, and at that time the designer can make a geometric move and change to central geometry. However, it is not always clear when this occurs. First, many constraints may be sufficient to give unique moves, particularly if inequality constraints are used. For example,

$x<3$ & $x\geq1$ & x a minimum yields x=1

However, further constraints can still be added by other agents, e.g.,

$x<2.5$

Conversely,

$x<3$ & $x\geq1$

are not sufficient. However, in general, there will be many global defaults such as minimizing cost that could translate into x a minimum.

18.3.3 Design Collaboration Strategy

The overall search strategy is to make the refinement as constrained and detailed as possible so as to generate a unique geometric change. However, it may still be necessary to backtrack to consider other alternatives upon failure of a joint line of reasoning. There seem to be three classes of control strategy available:

1. Arbitrary or "static", based on

    (a) lexical, temporal, or priority order of agents

    (b) random choices and parallelism

    (c) more complex criteria, such as complexity measures and priority of predicates.

2. Evaluative or "dynamic", based on

    (a) agents evaluate literals or conjunctions of literals of sets of clauses

    (b) agents evaluate partial, generative, or abstracted expressions

    (c) agents determine certainty of evaluation.

3. Empirical or "adaptive", based on empirical estimates of performance such as the effect on cost and value of the resulting design or the cost of the design process.

These interlocking issues are being investigated. A logic programming approach would primitively only apply to the first type of strategy; however, evaluative and adaptive strategies could be represented in terms of logic rules.

A simple coordination strategy would be

1. Start from a given central model

2. Each agent generates all individual suggestions, e.g., sets of clauses

3. These are globally conjoined to generate joint suggestions, shared by all agents. There may be a conflict within a joint suggestion. We must assume that the existence and nature of any conflict is agreed to by all agents, and does not depend on private knowledge.

4. Each agent generates evaluations of joint suggestions

5. A global control choice is made, using an agreed conflict and priority mechanism, to either elaborate a chosen suggestion, or to make a chosen geometric move. The mechanism could be, for example, to elaborate any unclear suggestions until clear evaluations are found; then take the strongest suggested unique design move; or else, if no clear elaboration or move, to take the strongest goal focus change. The conflict mechanism has to be not only agreed by all agents, but also it must be sufficiently unambiguous, and dependent only on shared knowledge, that they agree on the results of application of the mechanism.

6. if elaboration, return to step 3, if move return to step 1.

This is shown in Figure 18.6.

This strategy can be regarded as a kind of dialogue game [Levin and Moore 1977]. Agents collaborate in an expansion phase (diastole) of gathering and combining suggestions, and a contraction phase (systole) where suggestions are clarified and one joint action chosen.

It has the properties (1) that all agents consider the same thing, and it is assumed that it will not normally be necessary to reconsider the same state more than once, so all suggestions must be made while this state and goal focus are current, and (2) that the next move and state are in some sense agreed to by all agents, so that if a satisficing solution is found, then it can be committed to.

474

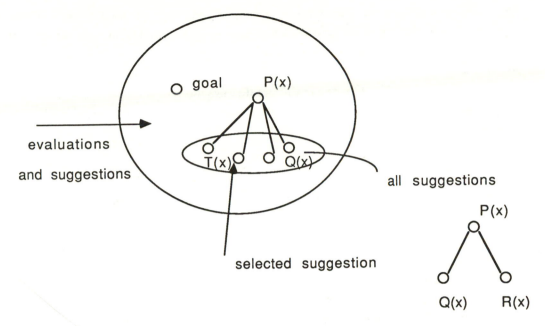

Figure 18.6: Pooled evaluation and suggestion strategy

The social responsibility to reveal all relevant suggestions in the current context corresponds to producing descriptions of all alternatives. In the denumerably infinite case, an agent should produce a generator expression that can be instantiated (using a remote "findall" for example) to give all the possibilities. This requirement makes demands upon the choice of argument language.

In the implementation of a network of interacting workstations, as there are problems with simply passing individual goals to each other for solution, we suggest as a model that the entire shared argument is passed back and forth during a collaborative dialogue. Since each agent can keep a record of what it has seen, and therefore has the complete proof tree of the shared argument, the only thing to be communicated is the current set of goals, with the current instantiations of any variables, and the dependencies between current goals and the immediately previous goals.

The interactions needed for the above collaboration strategy are (1) to make an evaluation of a goal or a design element (which is a statement), which can be true or false or can carry a numerical evaluation, and (2) to make a suggestion (a wff), which is a goal to be proved. So these map well onto the Prolog metaoperators; numerical evaluations can be represented as the values of additional arguments in wffs.

In a true open system, one agent cannot know, initially at least, another agent's reasoning strategy, so the use of an agreed dialogue game for collaboration requires at least that every potentially collaborative agent would understand the dialogue-game and how to get into and out of it. This strategy is consistent with the classical dialogue rules developed in [Lorenzen 1987]. Here the entire proof is available to both in the tableau, and the disputants work together on an active front of statements, in developing the tableau to closure or otherwise.

18.3.4   Example

An outline of an example of a correctional change to wing geometry during a conceptual design phase is as follows: from a given geometry, all agents create and update their own specialist models, perform analyses and produce results, which are fed back as suggestions in the shared language.

Suppose structures have "need bigger wing box" and aerodynamics have "need greater wing area" as suggestions. These will be precise statements giving a desired numerical value or bound. They are conjoined. T he first choice would be for each of these agents to elaborate this joint suggestion since they interact, so a final value of suggested new wing area and suggested wing box cross section would be found by iterating between the structures and aerodynamic departments. Aerodynamics may need to change the shape of the wing box to give the same lift/drag properties. Structures are mainly concerned with bending and twisting strength of the wing section. Suppose aerodynamics have increased the tapering at the rear of the wing. Then weights would now require, by conjoining a constraint, that 1g balance be restored. They may make two disjoint suggestions: to move the center of lift of the wings forward or to move the center of gravity of the plane back. Aerodynamics evaluates moving the wing forward as easiest, but the central designer vetos this with its evaluation. The second suggestion of moving the center of gravity of the plane backward by a specified amount can be solved by the designer by relocating the fuel tank. The set of suggested constraints is now stable under evaluation and has a unique geometric solution, and so a geometric move is made to change the central model.

Thus we see the main points of collaborative reasoning illustrated:

- goals are suggested by different agents that only they can suggest

- goals from different agents must be combined, initially by conjunction

- goals may need to be solved by other agents

- some goals may simply be failed or vetoed by other agents.

18.4   Design and Operational Issues

18.4.1   Optimality

We shall for the moment sidestep the issue of optimality of the resulting design. This involves a representation of the worth of a design and ways of dealing with comparability and conflict between the agents. We shall simply take the problem to be that of producing a design for which each agent has a convincing logical proof of validity in his own proof language.

18.4.2   Conflict

We shall avoid the problems of conflict and deception in collaboration and assume benign, nonantagonistic collaboration. This is in any case what happens in organizations. At a given organizational level, one department can assume that the information given by other departments is correct. Problems of competence and conflict of interest among departments are usually assumed to be dealt with at higher organizational levels.

18.4.3   Information Seeking

There may be many things that agent2 knows in the argument language that agent1 doesn't. Agent2 may either know or can derive them in his own proof language. We assume that agent1 can request such information. Agent1 is, however, limited to what can be expressed in the argument language. In principle, agent1 can elicit all statements that match any schema in the argument language, such as

$(\exists x)(metal(x))$ "what metals exist?"

$(\exists x)(metal(x) \ \& \ (\forall y)(x \neq y \ \& \ (strength(x) > strength(y)))$ "which is the strongest metal?"

$(\exists t)(\neg wifebeating(t) \ \& \ (\forall t1)(wifebeating(t1) => t > t1))$ "when did you stop beating your wife?"

We cannot however quantify over predicates, so we cannot ask if there exists any substance

$(\exists p)(p(a))$

unless we make it into a type

substance(a)

$(x)(metal(x) => substance(x))$

$(x)(plastic(x) => substance(x))$

It is hard to see how we can enquire under what conditions something takes place. However, this can emerge if we request a solution of a goal to make it take place; then the solution will give an answer. If we want to know more generally, then this may not be possible.

Hintikka [Hintikka and Saarinen 1979] [Hintikka and Hintikka 1982], for example, has been concerned with information seeking in dialogues; however, expression problems have not been emphasized. In Levin and Moore's dialogue-games in linguistics, information seeking is conducted through a specific dialogue game, which is controlled by a partially ordered set of goals. These goals must be in the common language; hence, a control regime using Levin and Moore's dialogue-games will probably suffer from the same problems we are discussing here, if formulated and implemented as computer mechanisms.

18.4.4 Learning

If we allow general learning to take place, where one agent can learn all the concepts that another has, then the disparity is a matter of performance and is harder to treat logically. We have to allow some information-seeking to occur, but this could be restricted to statements in the existing commonality basis. Thus we can probably separate learning as a separate effect. After each dialogue, the opponent has learned some new facts, and these could be

1. retained, or

2. erased, since time-dependent knowledge may not be useful.

We must allow temporary information accumulation during a dialogue, however.

18.4.5 Nonmonotonicity

The disparity issue we are considering does not necessarily involve nonmonotonicity [Ginsberg 1987]. However, most logic programming regimes use negation as failure and would become embroiled in this issue, particularly if any default assumptions are used. Since we must assume that new axioms are added to the shared knowledge during collaboration, and that the shared language involves abstraction from private languages, nonmonotonicity will be difficult to avoid.

18.4.6 Limitations of Collaboration

What limits the exercise of knowledge? Under what circumstances do we not get completeness under the union of the knowledge bases of the agents? Interacting agents may suffer from

1. *expression* problems, i.e., not knowing how to ask the right question

2. legalistic *rules* forbidding asking the other agent for evidence of a proposition (by convention, which could be official [court of law], or by agreed proof strategy)

3. *performance* problems, i.e., interrogation of the other agent may take a long time or require too many resources.

A strategy that is complete for one agent may not be for two agents, where, for example, each follows this strategy and each calls the other as a hypothesis solver. One can, for example, get circularities that would not occur in a single agent. In addition, there will be problems if both agents can generate the same set of solutions to a goal, but in different orders.

18.4.7 The Interaction Language

The *interaction language*, i.e., that used for the messages that are exchanged, could in principle and may need in practice to be richer than the argument language in which mutually convincing proofs are constructed. For example, it could include some metaoperators. One option is the user interface to Prolog, which provides three metaoperators
1. assert a wff into the workspace
2. attempt to prove a wff
3. find the next constructive proof and solution to the previously given wff.
In addition, there is the indication of success or failure of the attempt and the answer statement to the hypothesis. The interaction language, in the main, is simply the input of hypotheses as wffs in predicate logic and the output of solutions to these hypotheses as wffs in predicate logic.

18.4.8 Abstraction and Private Justification

The argument language may involve abstractions of the predicates that occur in the individual languages. One type of abstraction essentially forces a common argument to work with "package deals" made up from finer distinctions.

To give a simple example, suppose a customer and a mechanic are trying to decide how to fix a car. Suppose the customer privately can express the fact that the problem is that the idle-level is wrong, and knows that a tune-up fixes the idle-level, but only "tune-up" and not "idle-level" is in the common language. Suppose further that the mechanic knows about adjusting idle-levels and also adjusting distributors, and a tune-up involves doing both of these, but again "distributor" and "idle-level" are in his private language only, and only "tune-up" is in the common language. Then the customer wants his idle-level fixed, so he asks for a tune-up. The mechanic knows a tune-up means adjusting the idle-level and the distributor, but he cannot adjust the distributor because the distributor adjustment machine is broken, so he answers that he cannot do the tune-up, so the car cannot be fixed.

```
CUSTOMER                    COMMON              MECHANIC

idle-level                tune-up             idle-level
                                              distributor

tune-up => idle-level                 idle-level & distributor
                                             => tune-up
```

In this case, if the customer's and the mechanic's knowledge bases were merged, the problem would be solvable, but because the problem involves collaboration, since each has some essential knowledge, and because the solution involves reasoning jointly about something not expressible in the common language, the problem cannot be solved. (We think it reasonable to identify the customer's idle-level predicate with the mechanic's idle-level predicate in merging the knowledge bases.)

Private justification of a shared proof could be a very tall order, since it is saying that a proof in the abstracted theory should still be a proof in the full theory. In general, this is not true and it is very difficult to establish any implication whatsoever from a subset of a theory to the full theory. One very important question, then, is whether one can define a shared language so that shared justifications are valid in the private languages of the collaborating specialists.

If the shared language involves only statements that are valid in the private language, then the private language simply specializes the shared theory and shared proofs are valid privately. However, inevitably the shared statements will be abstractions, i.e., simplifications, which are not valid privately.

18.5   Summary and Conclusion

We have introduced the problem of collaborative reasoning, which differs from previously described DAI problems. It is however closely related to Hewitt's organizational problem solving using the notion of microtheories. We showed that this problem is general and widespread. We discussed the problem in the context of the collaboration of different specialized engineering departments in a manufacturing organization. We discussed the background of dialectic logic, which contributes to our philosophical basis for collaborative logic, in the entreaty *"How do we convince each other?"* We examined the constraints and issues arising in collaborative reasoning in practice.

The issues are that

1. Collaboration may involve very little shared knowledge, in practice.

2. Different languages are used for external collaborative argument and for internal justification, respectively.

3. There are limitations due to expression problems, rules of procedure, and performance.

4. Disparity cannot be resolved by learning.

We ignored issues of optimality of design and just considered logical validity. We noted that there are difficult issues of expression and of argument strategy.

We came up with a simple model of collaborative design, which has separate private languages for each agent and a shared argument language, a model of agents and a strategy for collaboration, defined as a dialogue game, and an interaction language involving the metaoperators needed to collaborate in this model.

This discussion has, we think, brought out many distinctions and issues involved in using logic for the support of organizational problem solving. There are problems arising from limitations of common language, limitations of justification, where shared justifications do not lead automatically to private ones, and requirements for a context in collaborative reasoning protocols and methods.

Acknowledgements

I should like to thank Bill Thompson, Rich Ricci, Dave Richardson, and Paul Ng of Lockheed Aircraft Company, Burbank, California, for discussions on wing-section design and on collaboration in manufacturing organizations in general. I should also like to thank Moses Tawil of Hughes Satellite Division, El Segundo, California, for discussions on engineering collaboration.

I am grateful to my colleague, Professor Les Gasser of the University of Southern California, for discussions on DAI issues and for a critical review of an earlier version of this paper.

I should also like to thank Dr. Michel A. Melkanoff, Director of the UCLA Computer-Aided Design Laboratory, for his encouragement and for providing the framework within which this research could proceed. The UCLA Manufacturing Program is supported by gifts and grants from many corporations.

References

[Barth and Martens 1982] E. M. Barth and J. L. Martens, *Argumentation, Approaches to Theory Formation*, John Benjamins, Amsterdam, 1982.

[Bond 1988] A. H. Bond, "Logic in collaboration," MEP Report 8819, University of California, Los Angeles, 1988.

[Bond 1988b] A. H. Bond, "Cooperation in Manufacturing Design," MEP Report 8820, University of California, Los Angeles, 1988.

[Bond and Gasser 1988] A. H. Bond and L. Gasser, "A Survey of Distributed Artificial Intelligence," *Readings in Distributed Artificial Intelligence*, Morgan Kaufmann Publishers, San Mateo, CA, 1988.

[Bond and Ricci 1988] A. H. Bond and R. Ricci, "The development and coordination of models in aircraft design," MEP Report 8821, University of California, Los Angeles, 1988.

[Bond and Soetarman 1986] A. H. Bond and B. Soetarman, "Integrating PROLOG and CADAM to produce an Intelligent CAD System," MEP report 8606, University of California, Los Angeles, 1986, to appear in *Software Practice and Engineering*.

[Bruce and Newman 1978] B. Bruce and D. Newman, "Interacting Plans," *Cognitive Science*, Vol. 2, No. 3, 1978, pp. 195–233.

[Cox and Willard 1982] J. R. Cox and C. A. Willard, *Advances in Argumentation Theory and Research*, American Forensic Association, 1982.

[Durfee 1987] E. H. Durfee, "A Unified Approach to Dynamic Coordination: Planning Actions and Interactions in a Distributed Problem Solving Network," PhD thesis, Department of Computer and Information Science, University of Massachusetts, Amherst, MA, September 1987.

[Durfee and Lesser 1987] E. H. Durfee and V. R. Lesser, "Using Partial Global Plans to Coordinate Distributed Problem Solvers," *Proceedings of the 1987 International Joint Conference on Artificial Intelligence*, 1987, pp. 875–883.

[Durfee *et al.* 1987] E. H. Durfee, V. R. Lesser, and D. D. Corkill, "Coherent Cooperation Among Communicating Problem Solvers," *IEEE Transactions on Computers*, Vol. C-36, 1987, pp. 1275–1291.

[Erman and Lesser 1975] L. D. Erman and V. R. Lesser, "A Multi-Level Organization for Problem Solving Using Many, Diverse, Cooperating Sources of Knowledge," *Proceedings of the 1975 International Joint Conference on Artificial Intelligence*, pp. 483–490, 1975.

[Genesereth et al. 1984] M. R. Genesereth, M. L. Ginsberg, and J. S. Rosenschein, "Cooperation without Communication," Technical Report HPP-84-36, Stanford Heuristic Programming Project, Stanford University, Stanford, CA, September 1984.

[Georgeff 1987] M. P. Georgeff, "Many Agents are Better Than One," Technical Report 417, SRI International, Menlo Park, CA, March 1987. An earlier version appears in *The Frame Problem in Artificial Intelligence: Proceedings of the 1987 Workshop*, Morgan Kaufmann Publishers, 1987.

[Ginsberg 1987] M. L. Ginsberg, *Readings in Nonmonotonic Reasoning*, Morgan Kaufmann, 1987.

[Hamblin 1971] C. L. Hamblin, "Mathematical Models of Dialogue," *Theoria*, Vol. 37, 1971, pp. 130–155.

[Hample 1982] D. Hample, "Modeling Argument," *[Cox and Willard 1982]*, 1982, pp. 259–284.

[Hayes-Roth 1985] B. Hayes-Roth, "A Blackboard Architecture for Control," *Artificial Intelligence Journal*, Vol. 26, 1985, pp. 251–321.

[Hewitt 1985] C. E. Hewitt, "The Challenge of Open Systems," *Byte*, Vol. 10, No. 4, April 1985, pp. 223–242, April 1985.

[Hewitt 1986] C. E. Hewitt, "Offices are Open Systems," *ACM Transactions on Office Information Systems*, Vol. 4, No. 3, 1986, pp. 271–287. Also in B. A. Huberman, *The Ecology of Computation*, Elsevier Science Publishers/North Holland, Amsterdam, 1988.

[Hintikka and Saarinen 1979] J. Hintikka and E. Saarinen, "Information-seeking Dialogues: some of their logical properties," *Studia Logica*, Vol. 38, 1979, pp. 355–363.

[Hintikka and Hintikka 1982] J. Hintikka and M. B. Hintikka, "Sherlock Holmes Confronts Modern Logic: Toward a Theory of Information-seeking through Questioning," In *[Barth and Martens 1982]*, 1982, pp. 55–76.

[Huhns et al. 1983] M. N. Huhns, L. M. Stephens, and R. D. Bonnell, "Control and Cooperation in Distributed Expert Systems," *Proceedings of the IEEE Southeastcon*, Orlando, FL, April 1983, pp. 241–245.

[Konolige 1986] K. Konolige, *A Deduction Model of Belief*, Pitman Publishers/Morgan Kaufmann Publishers, San Mateo, CA, 1986.

[Levin and Moore 1977] J. A. Levin and J. A. Moore, "Dialogue-Games: Metacommunication Structures for Natural Language Interaction," *Cognitive Science*, Vol. 1, 1977, pp. 395–420.

[Lorenzen 1987] P. Lorenzen, *Constructive Philosophy*, The University of Massachusetts Press, Amherst, Mass, 1987.

[Rescher 1977] N. Rescher, *Dialectics*, State University of New York Press, Albany, New York, 1977.

[Rosenschein 1982] J. S. Rosenschein, "Synchronization of Multi-Agent Plans," *Proceedings of 1982 Conference of the American Association for Artificial Intelligence*, 1982, pp. 115–119.

[Steeb et al. 1984] R. Steeb, D. McArthur, S. Cammarata, S. Narain, and W. Giarla, "Distributed Problem Solving for Air Fleet Control: Framework and Implementations," Technical Report N-2139-ARPA, Rand Corporation, Santa Monica, CA, 1984.

[Sycara 1985] K. P. Sycara, "Arguments of Persuasion in Labor Mediation," *Proceedings of the 1985 International Joint Conference on Artificial Intelligence*, 1985.

[Sycara 1985b] K. P. Sycara, "Persuasive Argumentation in Resolution of Collective Bargaining Impasses," *Proceedings of the Cognitive Science Society Conference*, 1985, pp. 356–360.

Alan H. Bond
Manufacturing Engineering Program
3066 Engineering 1
University of California
Los Angeles, California 90024

Chapter 19

Evaluating Research in Cooperative Distributed Problem Solving

Keith S. Decker, Edmund H. Durfee, and Victor R. Lesser

Abstract

Cooperative Distributed Problem Solving (CDPS) is a new field that has not yet established critical research mass, so relating and assessing individual research contributions is difficult [Huhns 1987, Decker 1986]. In this paper, we provide a framework for understanding the interrelationships of disparate research efforts in order to assess progress in the field. We evaluate progress in these basic issues by assessing the sophistication of CDPS systems on many different (and interdependent) axes, which when taken as a whole give a view of a system's overall sophistication. Our sophistication assessments are specified as a set of questions that relate to such things as the class of problem domains and environments that an approach can handle, the theoretical soundness of the approach, the software and hardware support provided, and how the approach addresses the important issues of CDPS themselves.

We explain the general goals of CDPS research, present questions pertinent to them, and describe a few research examples: the contract net, partial global planning, and proposed extensions to partial global planning. We evaluate these systems and discuss how the questions relate to the multiple goals of CDPS research, and how this methodology can be used to analyze the differences between the above systems.

19.1 Introduction

We broadly define cooperative distributed problem solving networks as loosely-coupled distributed networks of semiautonomous problem solving agents (or nodes). These agents each perform sophisticated problem solving and cooperatively interact to solve problems. When faced with a problem that could be solved more effectively through cooperation (perhaps because it requires expertise or information localized in different agents), the agents work together by identifying subproblems each should solve, solving them concurrently, and integrating their results (or at least ensuring that their results are mutually consistent). In most complex problem solving applications, subproblems are interdependent and overlapping, so agents must carefully coordinate their local problem solving actions, and must modify how they interact as circumstances change in the course of problem solving. This dynamic coordination must occur despite internode communication that is limited due to inherent bandwidth limitations or to the high computation costs of packaging and assimilating transferred information.

The basic issues that must be addressed in CDPS research include the development of

- theories for organizing CDPS systems in both small groups and large networks, providing guidelines for how domain and control problem solving tasks need to be distributed among agents based on the characteristics of the application, the agents, and the communications resources;

- paradigms for domain-level cooperation among disparate agents that can efficiently resolve inconsistencies and integrate results;

- methods for distributed control, permitting semiautonomous agents to work in a globally coherent manner despite uncertainty about the status of other agent's activities;

- guidelines for organizing or structuring the problem solving activities of individual agents so that they may be easily integrated into a CDPS environment, leading to novel problem solving frameworks (knowledge representations, inference techniques, and control architectures) that are more appropriate for use in CDPS systems than traditional techniques are;

- software infrastructures, in terms of languages and operating system features, that support the CDPS style of computing.

These issues center around how to achieve effective cooperation that balances the interdependent criteria of efficiently using processor and communications resources, reliability,

486

responsiveness to unexpected situations and real-time deadlines, and modularity. Effective cooperation requires resolving the uncertainties and inconsistencies that can arise between both long-term and short-term knowledge held by agents and exploiting the interdependencies among the agents' subproblems.

We evaluate progress in these basic issues by assessing the sophistication of CDPS systems along many different (and interdependent) axes, which when taken as a whole give a view of a system's overall sophistication; we view increasing sophistication as an indication of progress. Our sophistication assessments are specified as a set of questions, where each question has a set of answers that range from less to more sophisticated. Because the questions are subjective, and any strictly numerical means of recording, normalizing and summarizing the answers would result in a false sense of precision, we divide each set of answers into only three levels of sophistication (low, medium, and high). These questions relate to such things as the class of problem domains and environments that an approach can handle, the theoretical soundness of the approach, the software and hardware support provided, and how the approach addresses the important issues themselves. The questions are grouped into general goals, but each question often applies to more than one goal or issue. Since most research deals only with a subset of all the possible issues, not all questions may be applicable to a given theory, environment, or domain.

Our evaluation technique cannot be used to compare two entirely different research programs, since each will have different goals. Furthermore, if the goal of a project is to solve a specific domain problem, then extra sophistication is not always useful or welcome. This technique is most profitably used as a guide to whether a research program addresses *any* important aspects of CDPS, and as a guide to the progress of a particular research program over time.

Sections 19.2–19.10 explain the general goals of CDPS research and contain questions pertinent to them. Section 19.11 describes a few examples of CDPS research: the contract net [Smith and Davis 1981, Davis and Smith 1983, Parunak 1985], partial global planning [Durfee and Lesser 1987], and proposed extensions to partial global planning. Section 19.12 evaluates these systems and discusses how the questions relate to multiple goals, and how this can be used to analyze the differences between the above systems.

19.2   Goal: Limit Domain and Environmental Assumptions

One goal of CDPS research is to limit the number of assumptions that a CDPS theory has to make about the environment, or a CDPS architecture has to make about the problem domain. Even if the system was developed to solve a specific problem, the less assumptions made, the more generally applicable the system is to CDPS problems. The following questions pertain to the heterogeneity of the system, structural assumptions (about how the system is put together), and other domain and architectural assumptions. So the fewer assumptions that are made about the domain or the way the system is put together, the higher the rating.

19.2.1   How heterogeneous are the agents in your system?

Low: They are identical, or differ only in the resources available to them.

Med: They differ in the problem solving methods or expertise available at each node.

High: They share a common language, but no other assumptions have been made about the nodes.

19.2.2   What assumptions are made about the maximum number of agents in your system?

Low: There must be less than ten[1].

Med: There must be less than a hundred.

High: There can be more than a hundred.

19.2.3   How is problem solving knowledge shared among agents?

Low: Agents have identical knowledge bases.

Med: Agents' knowledge may differ, but mechanism/structure of knowledge is same (all frames or all logical assertions, etc.). Agent knowledge can be disjoint or overlapping.

High: Agents' knowledge is not just different, but may be *inconsistent* between agents. The structure of knowledge differs between agents. Algorithms or procedures may be entirely different.

19.2.4   How is short term knowledge and data that is acquired during problem solving replicated among agents?

Low: Each agent has identical short-term knowledge (data).

Med: Short-term knowledge (data) differs, and may be disjoint or overlapping.

High: Short-term knowledge (data) may be inconsistent between agents, or the representation/structure of knowledge is different at each agent.

---

[1] These numbers are derived from our experience with the DVMT.

19.2.5 How is the consistency of short term problem solving knowledge and data maintained?

Low: Cannot handle inconsistent short term knowledge or data, or provide concurrent access and maintain consistency by distributed database techniques.

Med: When necessary, can invoke a conflict resolution mechanism—inconsistencies are an extraordinary process in the course of problem solving.

High: Allow inconsistencies to occur and resolve them as a part of normal problem solving without a separate conflict resolution process.

19.2.6 How is the consistency of long term problem solving knowledge and data maintained?

Low: Cannot handle inconsistent long term knowledge or data, or provide concurrent access and maintain consistency by distributed database techniques.

Med: When necessary, can invoke a conflict resolution mechanism—inconsistencies are an extraordinary process in the course of problem solving.

High: Allow inconsistencies to occur and resolve them as a part of normal problem solving without a separate conflict resolution process.

19.2.7 Is the first solution obtained the correct one?

Low: Yes, it is correct and optimal.

Med: Either the system must obtain all solutions, or the system includes a mechanism for deciding when additional processing will not lead to a superior solution.

High: System attempts to trade-off optimality of a solution and other considerations, such as meeting a deadline.

19.2.8 Do the agents make any assumptions about the operating system?

Low: Have developed, and are dependent on, OS and hardware support, or have developed a new OS for the agent environment.

Med: Uses the OS supplied by the manufacturer in a nonportable way.

High: No assumptions made—OS independent (high on the domain independence scale but low on sophisticated system support scale).

19.2.9   Can the agents interact with humans as agents?

Low: No human interaction during problem solving.

Med: Some agents interact with humans in standard computer interface ways, but the humans are there only to give input to an agent and receive output.

High: The system is a *participant system*. Humans are actual agents, in that they can interact with computer agents just as other computer agents do. They appear as computer agents to each other and to the real computer agents.

19.2.10   Do you assume that new agents or communication paths can be dynamically added and deleted during problem solving?

Low: No, not dynamically.

Med: Communications paths, but not new agents.

High: New agents and new communication paths can be added and deleted dynamically.

19.2.11   Is problem solving continuous or discrete?

Low: System acts on discrete problems.

Med: System is in continuous operation, but individual problems are not related and do not usually occur simultaneously.

High: System is involved in continuous domain and control problem solving.

19.2.12   Has the system been evaluated in multiple domains?

Low: One domain.

Med: Two domains.

High: More than two domains.

19.3   Goal: Discover Paradigms for Building Cooperating Agents

We wish to build systems where agents can *cooperate* with one another to solve problems. This does not imply that the agents necessarily share the same set of goals, but rather that agents can coordinate effectively to approach common goals when they or their designers deem such actions appropriate. The questions here deal with interacting goals and conflicts between agents. The more the domains being pursued require cooperation, and the more the system supports it, the higher the rating (the more sophisticated).

19.3.1 How do the goals of your agents interact?

Low: Agents do not have goals, and interactions between agents are prespecified. Alternatively, each agent has separate, noninteracting goals.

Med: The system of agents is constructed with a shared set of high-level goals (the benevolent agent assumption was made). An agent's goals are derived from these. The low-level goals of two agents may constrain one another critically, but each agent can locally deal with such interactions.

High: Agents goals may interact destructively, and agents must interact with one another (or within some organizational structure) to resolve conflicts. A high-level goal may be shared serendipitously—agents recognize when goals interact and work towards positive outcomes of such goals (when this is possible and desirable) or try to outmaneuver and foil another agents goals (when this is possible and desirable).

19.3.2 Do you represent and reason about an agent's goals?

Low: Agents do not have goals.

Med: Agents' goals are implicit.

High: Agents' goals are explicitly represented and there are processes that make decisions based on goal interactions.

19.3.3 What range of collaboration is possible between agents?

Low: Agents act independently of one another, or in a fixed relationship.

Med: Solutions to one agent's subproblem may help, predict, or critically constrain the solution to another agent's subproblem.

High: Not only are there critical interagent constraints, but critical timing constraints in the actions of the agents. There may be undoable or nonreversible actions.

19.3.4 How are domain conflicts resolved?

Low: There are no conflicts or conflict resolution.

Med: Agents use a mutually known decision procedure or an arbitrator.

High: Agents negotiate by loosening of constraints of one or both agents. Agents may choose not to resolve some conflicts, or to use other methods if appropriate to the situation.

19.3.5 How do agents deal with nonreversible actions?

Low: Agent actions are always reversible, or any action that was possible in the past is always possible in the future (so there is no need to reverse actions).

Med: The agent handles the situation locally or appeals to a higher authority (other agent).

High: The agent will, depending on the situation, appeal to other agents or carry out the action and recover from the consequences. The agent tries to predict and avoid problems with nonreversible actions.

19.3.6 Can the prototypical problems (for which the system was designed) be solved without cooperation?

Low: Yes; although prototypical problems involve multiple agents, a centralized agent is used to solve them.

Med: Yes, but there are significant organizational, efficiency or fault tolerance reasons for solving them in a distributed fashion.

High: No, for some theoretical reason (bounded rationality, for instance) cooperation is necessary.

19.4 Goal: Develop Methods for Assuring Global Coherence

We wish to develop systems of agents that can react in a reasoned manner to the varied constraints of local, global, and partially global goals and input data. We wish to look at problems where an agent's local point-of-view crucially affects how that agent sees the global problem situation, and systems that can solve such problems. Global coherence addresses the problem of how members of a group can make sensible decisions that lead to problem solutions with only a limited amount of information. The questions in this section cover the types of information used and their availability. A system receives a higher rating if achieving a total, global view of the problem is not attempted or is impossible, and if an entirely local view is also insufficient for satisfactory results.

19.4.1 What is the range of nonlocal information that agents use to assure coherent behavior?

Low: No nonlocal information is used.

Med: Some nonlocal information can be accessed and used by each agent.

High: A wide range of nonlocal information, possibly in some abstracted form and including current, dynamic information, can be used by an agent for developing a partial global view.

19.4.2 Is predictive or constraining information available for the domain?

Low: No, subproblems and subtasks do not interact in any meaningful way, or the influences are known beforehand, and the system is hardcoded to handle them.

Med: Yes. The agents use such information as is available beforehand to help them act in a coherent manner with one another as a total system.

High: Yes. The agents can also develop this information dynamically as it occurs in any particular problem.

19.4.3 Do the priorities of goals or tasks change dynamically?

Low: There are no relative priorities of goals or tasks.

Med: The relative priorities are known beforehand, or are assigned by some organizational or other fixed procedural means.

High: Priorities change dynamically, and the system responds to those changes.

19.4.4 How does an agent decide if a solution to a subproblem is globally consistent?

Low: It doesn't try to; all solutions to subproblems are globally consistent.

Med: Solutions are constructed in one central location and a human or oracle is consulted.

High: The consistency of a solution is contingent on how it fits in with other solutions, the problem data, etc. Agents must look at the consistency of their solutions with these things; there is no central arbiter of acceptability.

19.4.5 How does the system deal with an overconstrained set of goals?

Low: This situation never occurs.

Med: There is a central arbiter that decides how to relax constraints, or there is a local algorithm that guarantees an acceptable, globally consistent solution, or there is a common procedure for prioritizing goals to achieve the most important as a subset.

High: There is no arbiter. Constraints are relaxed by mutual agreement. Agents may decide (perhaps negotiate) on precisely what level constraint relaxation should take place dynamically, as well as who should be involved in such a decision.

19.4.6 Does any agent need to develop a partial global view?

Low: Agents develop only a local view of the problem.

Med: Some or all agents must develop a complete, global view.

High: Agents must develop a partial global (nonlocal) view, but not a complete global view.

19.5 Goal: Theories of Organizational Behavior and Control

Another goal of distributed AI is that of Coordination Theory [Malone 1988]: how to effectively coordinate the activities of groups of computer and/or human actors. How do we organize such systems, especially if they are large? How do we control these systems? How do we reason about the control of the domain problem solving (if this is necessary)? How are problems broken down into simpler subproblems and solutions to these subproblems synthesized? More sophisticated systems are assumed to allow dynamic organizations and to reason on levels above the domain level (for example, reasoning about control).

19.5.1 Are multiple agents capable of solving a subproblem?

Low: No. There are specific agents for each subproblem.

Med: Yes and No. Some subproblems need special agents, but some don't, or multiple agents could have been used to solve a particular subproblem but were not.

High: Yes, multiple agents are capable and are used to solve a single subproblem.

19.5.2 How are tasks decomposed?

Low: Task decomposition is fixed at compile-time or system start-up, or tasks are inherently decomposed in the problem domain.

Med: Tasks are decomposed in a central location, or task decomposition is linked to task allocation (recursively).

High: A distinct, more complex, decentralized decomposition mechanism that is separate from the task allocation mechanism is used.

19.5.3 How are tasks allocated?

Low: Task allocation is fixed at compile-time or system start-up, or tasks are inherently allocated in the problem domain.

Med: Task allocation occurs using an organizational structure, or some other method where task allocation is fixed at the start of each individual problem.

High: Task allocation is dynamically opportunistic based on the availability of resources; a mixture of focused and open allocation.

19.5.4 How are results collected?

Low: There is no need to collect results, or result collection is the inverse of task allocation (it uses the same relationships).

Med: Result collection is independent of (and separate from) task allocation.

High: Result collection is independent and dynamically opportunistic (decided on during problem solving).

19.5.5 How autonomous is each agent in its actions?

Low: Agents have no autonomy whatsoever.

Med: Each agent is data directed and builds all of its goals locally (an "entrepreneurial" agent), or is goal directed and receives its goals from other agents (a "company" agent).

High: Each agent balances received and local goals in some reasoned manner.

19.5.6 How is network control distributed?

Low: It is not.

Med: In some fixed manner.

High: There is a control problem solving level that makes control distribution decisions.

19.5.7 How are network control problems resolved?

Low: They aren't resolved or there aren't any network control problems.

Med: By a central or otherwise known arbiter.

High: Through negotiation, or other mutual decision procedure among agents.

19.5.8 How are network control and domain problem solving related?

Low: There is no control problem solving.

Med: Control problem solving is tightly integrated with domain problem solving.

High: Control problem solving is done asynchronously from domain problem solving, possibly with a separate organizational structure.

19.5.9 What kind of organization is used?

Low: Master/Slave relationships between agents.
Med: A hierarchy or team.
High: Other, more complex organization (matrix?).

19.5.10 Can the organization or network control strategy evolve?

Low: No.
Med: It is fixed at the start of each problem.
High: It can change dynamically and opportunistically during problem solving.

19.5.11 How is network control related to domain control?

Low: No changeable local control mechanism.
Med: Network control is not strongly related to domain control.
High: Network control can effect changes and act in a synergistic fashion with local domain control (high in network control sophistication but low in domain independence).

19.5.12 Is there a network metalevel control component?

Low: No, or decisions are made at the start of a problem and are fixed thereafter.
Med: It allows fine tuning of network control.
High: It can cause a wide range of changes in network control dynamically and opportunistically during problem solving, and it is an integral part of the network control strategy.

19.5.13 Is predictive or constraining information available for control?

Low: Not present.
Med: Present but not used.
High: The information is present and affects the control of the system.

19.5.14 What other information is used for network control?

Low: None.
Med: Any of: information about individual tasks, organizational information, agent goals, or agent plans for accomplishing goals.
High: Several of the above.

19.5.15 What assumptions are made about the quality of network control information?

Low: It is assumed consistent and complete.

Med: Information is assumed to be consistent, but possibly incomplete, or it is marked with belief or other uncertainty measures.

High: No assumptions are made about incoming information (i.e., it can be inconsistent, incomplete, and uncertain).

19.5.16 Are there special mechanisms to handle large numbers of agents?

Low: No.

Med: The organizational structure of agents (limits communication).

High: Another, more complex mechanism, such as network control based on an abstracted view of groups of agents.

19.5.17 Has the network control mechanism been empirically evaluated?

Low: No we have not, or no network control mechanism is used.

Med: Evaluation will follow implementation, or is just beginning.

High: Yes, many experiments have been conducted and results have been published.

19.6 Goal: Guaranteed Responsiveness and Fault Tolerance

Another goal of distributed AI research is to use multiple agents to attack specifically the problems of real-time domains and fault tolerance. Many claims have been made that multiple agents can help in both of these problems. Several questions about hardware appear under later goals but also apply to this one. A system receives a higher rating if it includes facilities for problem solving in real-time (time-constrained) domains or for solving problems in spite of multiple kinds of failures.

19.6.1 Does the system assume that fault tolerance is important?

Low: No, it is not important.

Med: It is a desirable feature, but not strictly necessary.

High: It is a requirement, or a necessary feature because of our environment or domain.

19.6.2 Do you assume that multiple kinds of failures are possible?

[Possible types of failures: processors, memory, sensors, effectors, external resources, communications, software.]

Low: None.
Med: Several.
High: All.

19.6.3 Do you assume that redundant features are available?

[Possible redundant features: processors, memory, sensors, effectors, external resources, communications, problem solving knowledge.]

Low: None.
Med: Several.
High: All.

19.6.4 Do agents generate deadlines for tasks?

Low: No.
Med: Yes, at the start of a task.
High: Yes, deadlines can be introduced at any stage of processing.

19.6.5 Is predictive timing information available?

Low: All task times can be predicted accurately, or no time information is available.
Med: Timings are known or computed at various levels of accuracy at the start of problem solving.
High: Timing information is dynamically computed and adjusted during problem solving.

19.6.6 How do agents respond to task deadlines?

Low: They ignore or don't have them, or plan for them individually in the short-term.
Med: They have several means available, such as changing the priorities of tasks, reassigning them to different agents, etc.
High: Agents may modify the scope or extent of tasks in order to get them done on time, or do extra processing if they have extra time.

19.6.7 How are faults detected and handled?

Low: They aren't handled at all.

Med: Faults can always be detected and another processor assigned, or tasks are simply assigned redundantly to agents.

High: Agents communicate with one another about overlapping areas of responsibility in order to detect faults or decide to redundantly solve problems in different ways in order to check consistency of results.

19.7 Goal: Effective CDPS Communications Protocols

One research goal is how distributed agents may effectively communicate, even when their information may not be complete, consistent, or certain. How will agents talk to one another if they do not share common knowledge representations? How do agents find out who there is to talk to? Higher ratings are given for more complex and less constrained or prespecified communication protocols.

19.7.1 Do agents communicate functionally accurate information?

[Functionally accurate communication: agents communicate tentative results that may be incomplete, incorrect, or inconsistent with results produced by other agents [Lesser and Corkill 1981]]

Low: No. Only completely accurate information is communicated.

Med: Tentative solutions may be transmitted between agents, but nothing else.

High: Agents have some representation to transmit tentative solutions, predictive information, belief or confidence in that information, etc.

19.7.2 How syntactically and semantically rich is the communication language?

Low: Object-oriented message passing (context-directed procedure invocation) or other fixed low-level language.

Med: Fixed high-level domain language, possibly with domain and control concepts.

High: Dynamically expandable high-level language with domain and control concepts or natural language.

19.7.3 What information do agents use to determine the when, whom, and what of communication?

Low: Long-term, fixed knowledge.

Med: A combination of long-term, fixed knowledge and local knowledge developed during problem solving.

High: Nonlocal knowledge received from other agents (such as goals, tasks, or problem solving state), local knowledge, and long-term, fixed knowledge.

19.7.4 How do agents with different structured information communicate?

Low: Does not occur—all information is structured the same.

Med: Agents communicate such information without any special reasoning, or specifically avoid communicating such information.

High: Communications include information about structure to actively allow reasoning about such information.

19.7.5 How are the paths of communication specified?

Low: Agent communication paths are predetermined. For example, objects in an object-oriented language communicate by messages.

Med: Agents know who they may communicate with beforehand, but the order and contents of that communication are not prespecified.

High: Agent communication pathways are discovered as needed and used at the discrimination of the agent.

19.7.6 How are messages addressed?

Low: Broadcast to all agents (creates a scaling problem).

Med: Broadcast to small local groups, packet-switched, addressed, or point-to-point communications.

High: A full range of methods is available to use depending on the current situation.

19.8 Goal: Sophisticated Agents

Another research goal is to develop sophisticated agents to fill roles in a distributed system. What special properties or processes must an intelligent agent have in order to be part of a CDPS system? More sophisticated agents are those that extensively model other agents in the system.

19.8.1 What *a priori* knowledge do agents have about other agents?

Low: None, and they do not develop any.

Med: They know which agents have what domain knowledge.

High: They have models of the beliefs, actions, plans, and reasoning processes of other agents.

19.8.2 What knowledge do agents develop about other agents?

Low: None.

Med: They learn which agents have what domain knowledge, or notice changes in this or the organizational structure.

High: They model the beliefs, actions, plans, and reasoning processes of other agents.

19.8.3 Can agents deal with inconsistent, incomplete, and uncertain information?

Low: No, agents assume that they have consistent, complete, and certain information.

Med: Agents do the best they can with the available data, and may use a simple uncertainty system.

High: Agents have a complex belief system that can represent uncertainty, lack of knowledge, negative belief, inconsistency, second order uncertainty, supporting and refuting evidence, etc.

19.8.4 Do agents employ tacit bargaining and detect hidden agendas?

Low: No.

Med: They do employ such tactics as a manner of course, but they have no reasoning process for deciding when to apply them.

High: They choose to employ these and other complex actions when appropriate.

19.9 Goal: System and Hardware Support

One of the major research goals is to build software infrastructures, in terms of languages, environments, and operating systems, that support CDPS. The same applies to hardware infrastructure. Higher ratings are given to those systems that have better specialized system support in those areas. Note that this can lead to domain and environmental assumptions, but it is perfectly acceptable for a system to grow in software and hardware support sophistication while not becoming sophisticated in the sense of handling many different domains.

19.9.1 What happens when a single hardware failure occurs?

Low: System crashes.

Med: If the system notices what is occurring, or in some other limited cases, the system remains operational.

High: System always remains operational and reports the failure, but may work with decreased efficiency until the failure is fixed.

19.9.2 What is the likelihood of a hardware failure?

Low: Hardware failure seldom occurs during problem solving and is not of concern.

Med: Failures occur frequently enough that the issue must be addressed.

High: Multiple faults can occur frequently.

19.9.3 How do computational resources affect problem solving?

Low: They don't.

Med: Availability of resources will affect efficiency of the CDPS system.

High: System operates in real time, and computational resources must be used effectively and efficiently to generate solutions in time.

19.9.4 What special resources does the environment provide?

Low: No environment.

Med: One or two of: domain problem solving expertise, debugging, tracing, or explanation support.

High: All of the above, including a language for building CDPS networks.

19.9.5 What special resources do the operating system or hardware provide?

Low: Nothing special; just network communications protocols, etc.

Med: Distributed operating system, including protection and access mechanisms, load balancing.

High: Operating system provides access to load balancing, estimated process times, etc., for use by the CDPS system (high on the sophisticated system support scale but low on environment independence).

19.9.6 Are the goals, tasks, priorities, etc. of an agent used by the underlying system?

Low: Most of these things are procedurally represented.

Med: There are explicit, easily accessed representations of these things, but not really used by the operating system.

High: They are explicitly articulated and accessed or used by the operating system (high in sophisticated system support but low in environmental independence).

19.9.7 How far along is the implementation?

Low: Research proposal to paper design.

Med: Prototype to working research system.

High: System is in real-world everyday use.

19.10 Goal: Develop general and representative hard domain problems

Not only do we wish to understand exactly what assumptions we make about our domains and environments, but we also want to find truly hard problems that exhibit the usefulness and necessity of CDPS techniques. A problem gets a higher rating if it leads to a system that has one of the other goals mentioned earlier—the need for cooperation, the need to acquire nonlocal information in order to make informed local decisions, the possession of real-time or fault-tolerant characteristics, the use of multiple levels of reasoning, or the presence of complex communications.

19.10.1 What is the relative speed of communication versus the amount of local computation?

Low: Communication is extremely fast and cheap and does not result in a large amount of local computation.

Med: About an even tradeoff between communication and computation.

High: Communication is much more expensive, or cheap communication can result in a large amount of local computation. Perhaps security (or other) considerations preclude most communication, or force agents to communicate using a great deal of shared knowledge so that individual acts are hard to understand outside of the agents' mutual context.

19.10.2 Do all system tasks *have* to be completed?

Low: Yes.

Med: No, depending on the specific problem.

High: The problem requires a tradeoff to be reasoned about, between what tasks are completed and what is left out, depending on deadlines, priorities, etc.

19.10.3 Can this problem be solved in a centralized manner?

Low: Yes.

High: No.

19.10.4 Is there any advantage to having multiple agents solve the same subproblem?

Low: No.

Med: Yes, simple fault tolerance.

High: Yes, there are different ways to solve the problem that result in different quality solutions or the ability to double check results, etc.

19.10.5 Is there significant uncertainty involved?

Low: No.

Med: One or two of: the input data is incomplete, there is uncertainty in the reliability of the input observations or observers, there is uncertainty in the processes or heuristics used by agents, or uncertain information must be aggregated or summarized from multiple sources of differing reliabilities.

High: There are multiple sources of uncertainty.

19.10.6   Are overconstrained situations (in terms of unachievable domain goals) possible?

Low: No.
Med: Rarely. It is not a primary consideration.
High: Often. It is a feature of the problem.

19.10.7   How easy is it to find a solution to the problem?

Low: Easy. The search space is dense with solutions, or the search space is small.
Med: There are multiple acceptable solutions, but also many wrong ends.
High: Hard. The search space is large and solutions few or unique, or there are multiple solutions in a large search space, but they range in their acceptability.

19.10.8   How much empirical evaluation has been done of the domain problem solving capabilities?

Low: None.
Med: Evaluation is being performed in conjunction with implementation.
High: Extensive testing, in conjunction with domain experts or others, has been performed and the results published.

19.11   Example CDPS Systems

We have chosen to look at two well-known projects and a new research effort that we have just initiated. The first, CNET, is the contract net system developed by Davis and Smith for the vehicle monitoring domain [Smith and Davis 1981], [Davis and Smith 1983]. The second, PGP, is the partial global planning framework developed by Durfee and Lesser for the Distributed Vehicle Monitoring Testbed (DVMT) [Lesser and Corkill 1983], [Durfee and Lesser 1987]. The third (denoted here GPGP+) is our new research effort, which focuses on extending the PGP framework to other domains, especially real-time domains. We briefly describe the purpose and basic characteristics of each of these systems, and then compare them using our questions.

19.11.1   Contract Nets

Consider a network of loosely-coupled agents with various resources. If one of these agents receives a large problem to solve, then it has two choices: it can apply its own resources and solve the problem as best it can by itself; or it can decompose the large problem into smaller subproblems and convince other agents to pursue these subproblems. To make the best use of network resources, the agents should cooperatively solve large problems by assigning subproblems to suitable agents and working concurrently on these subproblems.

The contract-net protocol developed by Smith and Davis develops a framework for cooperating in this manner [Davis and Smith 1983]. Given a task to perform, a node first determines whether it could break the task into subtasks that could be performed concurrently. If it forms such subtasks, or it is locally unable to perform the initial task, then the node must coordinate with others to decide where to transfer tasks. It employs the contract-net protocol to announce the tasks that could be transferred and request that nodes that could perform any of those tasks submit bids. A node that receives a task announcement message replies with a bid for that task, indicating how well it believes it can perform the task. The node that announced the task collects these bids and awards the task to the best bidder. The contract-net protocol allows nodes to broadcast bid-requests to all others or to focus bid-requests to a likely subset of nodes. Nodes can also communicate about their availability, so that focusing information (and decisions about whether it is worth advertising a task in the first place) can be based on dynamic views of the network.

The contract-net protocol promotes control based on negotiating over task assignments to form contractor-contractee relationships. These relationships determine how nodes will act and interact, and allow them to coordinate their activities to work together effectively. Because nodes exchange information about tasks and availability, they make dynamic control decisions about how they will cooperatively pursue tasks. Thus, in applications where the principal mode of interactions between nodes fits into the contracting model, the contract-net protocol is an effective approach for controlling cooperation [Parunak 1985]. However, there are applications which do not fit cleanly into this model of cooperation: tasks may be inherently distributed among nodes, and coordination is not a matter of decomposing and assigning tasks but instead is a matter of recognizing when distributed tasks (or partial results) are part of some larger overall task (or result) and, when this is the case, how to interact to achieve the larger task (or result).

19.11.2 Partial Global Planning

Partial global planning [Durfee and Lesser 1987, Durfee *et al.* 1987] is a flexible approach to coordination that does not assume any particular distribution of subproblems, expertise, or other resources, but instead lets nodes coordinate in response to the current situation. Each node can represent and reason about the actions and interactions for groups of nodes and how they affect local activities. These representations are called **partial global plans** (PGPs) because they specify how different *parts* of the network *plan* to achieve more *global* goals. Each node can maintain its own set of PGPs that it may use independently and asynchronously to coordinate its activities.

A PGP contains an objective, a plan-activity-map, a solution-construction-graph and a status:

- The **objective** contains information about *why* the PGP exists, including its eventual goal (the larger solution being formed) and its importance (a priority rating or reasons for pursuing it).

- The **plan-activity-map** represents *what* the nodes are doing, including the major plan steps the nodes are concurrently taking, their costs and expected results, and why they are being taken in a particular order.

- The **solution-construction-graph** contains information about *how* the nodes should interact, including specifications about what partial results to exchange and when to exchange them.

- The **status** contains bookkeeping information for the PGP, including pointers to relevant information received from other nodes and when that information was received.

A PGP is a general structure for representing coordinated activity in terms of goals, actions, interactions and relationships.

When in operation, a node's PGPlanner scans its current network model (a node's representation of the goals, actions and plans of other nodes in the system) to identify when several nodes are working on goals that are pieces of some larger network goal (partial global goal). By combining information from its own plans and those of other nodes, a PGPlanner builds PGPs to achieve the partial global goals. A PGPlanner forms a plan-activity-map from the separate plans by interleaving the plans' major steps using the predictions about when those steps will take place. Thus, the plan-activity map represents concurrent node activities. To improve coordination, a PGPlanner reorders the activities in the plan-activity-map using expectations or predictions about their costs, results, and utilities.

Rather than examining all possible orderings, a PGPlanner uses a hill-climbing procedure to *cheaply* find a better (though not always optimal) ordering. From the reordered plan-activity-map, a PGPlanner modifies the local plans to pursue their major plan steps in a more coordinated fashion. A PGPlanner also builds a solution-construction-graph that represents the interactions between nodes. By examining the plan-activity-map, a PGPlanner identifies when and where partial results should be exchanged in order for the nodes to integrate them into a complete solution, and this information is represented in the solution-construction-graph.

To control how they exchange and reason about their possibly different PGPs, nodes rely on a **metalevel organization** that specifies the coordination roles of each node. If organized one way, the nodes might depend on a single coordinator to form and distribute PGPs for the network, while if organized differently, the nodes might individually form PGPs using whatever information they have locally. The partial global planning framework lets nodes converge on common PGPs in a stable environment (where plans do not change because of new data, failed actions, or unexpected effects of their actions). However, when network, data and problem solving characteristics change and communication channels have delay and limited capacity, nodes can locally respond to new situations, cooperating effectively even when they have inconsistent PGPs.

19.11.3 Generalized Partial Global Planning and other extensions (GPGP+)

We have begun new research thrusts in generalized partial global planning and extensions (GPGP+) to handle the issues of real-time and metalevel control. A major focus of the proposed work is the extension and generalization of the partial global planning architecture that was developed for network control in, and is closely tied to, the specifics of the DVMT. We want to generalize this PGP network control architecture so it is nonDVMT-specific; thereby creating a generic protocol for control of CDPS that is applicable to a wider range of tasks. This involves developing and implementing a protocol and associated algorithms through which the user can tailor this protocol by the implementation of domain-specific code.

Generalized partial global planning is useful for ensuring globally coherent behavior in any CDPS system. Each agent is assumed to have a set of goals and subgoals that it intends to achieve. These goals may be related in many ways, such as being ordered in time or being alternate methods of achieving a single supergoal. For example, Agent $\mathcal{A}$ has a plan for a goal that has two subgoals, G5 and G9, that are being handled by agents $\mathcal{B}$ and $\mathcal{C}$. Agent $\mathcal{C}$, while working on goal G9 along with its own goals, generates a plan that includes goal G17, that can only be handled by agent $\mathcal{B}$. Agent $\mathcal{B}$ cannot act in a globally coherent manner unless it understands how its goals (G5 and G17) are related. It is these relations that generalized partial global planning is based.

Generic Relations

To handle these interactions, we are developing a set of generic relationships that will allow us to plan for goals. This fixed set of primitive relations will be domain independent, but for some relations the act of determining if that relation holds will be domain dependent. These primitives can be used to build generalized partial global plans in systems that have nothing to do with the DVMT. Using these relations, we will rework and extend the PGP algorithms to handle the coherent network control of CDPS systems other than the DVMT (like Pilot's Associate). A high-level protocol will allow an agent to specify and maintain its goal, plan, or task structure and transmit that structure to other agents for coordination purposes. Much like contract nets provide a domain-independent task allocation mechanism, we will build a generic network control system that will provide support for domain independent objects (such as agents, goals, plans, and tasks) and relations among those objects. The system builder provides his domain problem solving control and his own domain relationships, as well as support for the recognition of domain independent relationships. The generic PGP system then uses these relationships to bring about coherent network problem solving behavior, as well as providing a framework in which to build the system.

Real-time Control

The creation of a generic PGP that is appropriate for a wide class of applications will also involve extending the current PGP architecture to handle the issues of real-time control and large networks. From our perspective, real-time network control means not only scheduling to deadlines both periodic and nonperiodic tasks, but also recognizing that for many applications there are trade-offs possible between the quality of the solution (e.g., certainty, precision, optimality) and the time needed to generate the solution. Often in real time situations planning is *reactive*, where the current situation mostly controls an agent's actions (the current situation may include both local and global information), rather than *reflective*, where a sequence of actions is planned in some detail before execution. This is because the agent must respond quickly, but more importantly, the agent may be too uncertain of the outcomes of its actions and of the changing world state to plan too far into the future. However, an intelligent agent will make use of periodic tasks, which occur in a predictable fashion, and known nonperiodic tasks, to build a opportunistic planning framework that can keep an agent from painting itself into a corner with purely reactive planning techniques, or from exhaustively planning uncertain future details with reflective planning techniques.

Metalevel Control

In addition to extending the PGP protocol for real-time, it needs to be extended to effectively handle large networks of tens to hundreds of cooperating nodes. Experimentally, we have found it both unnecessary and computationally expensive to do detailed planning of all possible node interactions. For example, in a large, geographically distributed sensor interpretation system that covers the entire nation, it would rarely be necessary to perform detailed coordination between a sensor interpretation node in New York and one in California. However, it is important for regional centers, such as those developing maps for the East and Midwest, to coordinate at a gross level, balancing loads in areas of overlapping sensing and developing expectations of future loading based on current observations. There is also the need to develop closer interaction among nodes at the boundaries of regions based on the dynamics of the situation. We will initially be exploring an approach to solving this large network coordination problem by using an abstract description of the work loads of a group of nodes. We will extend the PGP framework to handle this more abstract description and introduce multiple levels of abstraction into the PGP framework.

Both of these extensions to the PGP framework will involve adding some form of metalevel network control. Further need for metalevel control arises because the full range of sophistication and responsiveness of the PGP architecture is not always required. There is a computational overhead for PGP control that is not negligible; therefore, it should be used only in those situations where the benefits of sophisticated network control are warranted.

19.12 Comparisons

The previous examples can be used with the list of questions to show the state of some particular research from different viewpoints. The answer to each question denotes the position of a research project on some sophistication axis. Each project is placed at a low (−), medium (o), or high (+) sophistication. Our evaluations were assigned either on the basis of first-hand experience or from reading the literature—people with first-hand knowledge of a system might give different values for some questions.

Sometimes a project simply does not address the issue raised by a question. Such a system could have been marked low (−) because it does not deal with the issue, or high (+) because it does not preclude or prevent that issue from being solved, so anything is possible. Instead we use a fourth mark (?) to denote that the system in question does not deal with the issue, neither making restrictive assumptions nor providing sophisticated mechanisms. This mark can also be used when not enough information is available to answer the question.

19.2 Limit Domain and Environmental Assumptions	CNET	PGP/DVMT	GPGP+
1. How heterogeneous are the agents in your system?	+	o	+
2. What assumptions are made about the maximum number of agents in your system?	+	+	+
3. How is problem solving knowledge shared among agents?	?	o	?
4. How is short term knowledge acquired during problem solving replicated among agents?	?	+	+
5. How is consistency of short term knowledge maintained?	?	+	+
6. How is consistency of long term problem solving knowledge maintained?	−	−	−
7. Is the first solution obtained the correct one?	−	o	+
8. Do the agents make any assumptions about the operating system?	+	+	+
9. Can the agents interact with humans as agents?	?	?	?
10. Do you assume that new agents or communication paths can be dynamically added and deleted during problem solving?	+	+	+
11. Is problem solving continuous or discrete?	o	−	o
12. Has the system been evaluated in multiple domains?	+	−	−

511

19.3 Discover Paradigms for Building Cooperating Agents	CNET	PGP/DVMT	GPGP+
1. How do the goals of your agents interact?	−	o	+
2. Do you represent and reason about agent goals?	o	+	+
3. What range of collaboration is possible between agents?	?	o	+
4. How are domain conflicts resolved?	?	o	o
5. How do agents deal with nonreversible actions?	?	−	+
6. Can the prototypical problems (for which the system was designed) be solved without cooperation?	o	o	o

19.4 Develop Methods for Assuring Global Coherence	CNET	PGP/DVMT	GPGP+
1. What is the range of nonlocal information that agents use to assure coherent behavior?	−	+	+
2. Is predictive or constraining information present/developed for the domain?	o	+	+
3. Do the priorities of goals or tasks change dynamically?	−	+	+
4. How does an agent decide if a solution is globally acceptable?	−	+	+
5. How does the system deal with an overconstrained set of goals?	−	o	+
6. Does any agent need to develop a partial global view?	+	+	+

19.5 Theories of Organizational Behavior and Control	CNET	PGP/DVMT	GPGP+
1. Are multiple agents capable of solving a subproblem?	+	+	+
2. How are tasks decomposed?	o	+	+
3. How are tasks allocated?	+	+	+
4. How are results collected?	−	+	+
5. How autonomous is each agent in its actions?	o	+	+
6. How is network control distributed?	o	+	+
7. How are network control problems resolved?	−	+	+
8. How are network control and domain problem solving related?	o	+	+
9. What kind of organization is used?	o	+	+
10. Can the organization or network control strategy evolve?	−	o	+
11. How is network control related to domain control?	?	+	+
12. Is there a network metalevel control component?	−	−	+
13. Is predictive or constraining information present/developed for control?	o	+	+
14. What other information is used for network control?	−	+	+
15. What assumptions are made about the quality of network control information?	?	o	o
16. Are there special mechanisms to handle large numbers of agents?	−	o	+
17. Has the network control mechanism been empirically evaluated?	+	+	−

19.6 Guaranteed Responsiveness and Fault Tolerance	CNET	PGP/DVMT	GPGP+
1. Does the system assume that fault tolerance is important?	+	+	+
2. Do you assume that multiple kinds of failures are possible?	+	+	+
3. Do you assume that redundant features are available?	+	+	+
4. Do agents generate deadlines for tasks?	+	+	+
5. Is predictive timing information available?	−	+	+
6. How do agents respond to task deadlines?	o	o	+
7. How are faults detected and handled?	o	o	+

19.7 Effective CDPS Communications Protocols	CNET	PGP/DVMT	GPGP+
1. Do agents communicate functionally accurate information?	?	+	+
2. How syntactically and semantically rich is the communications language?	o	−	o
3. What information do agents use to determine the when, whom, and what of communication?	o	+	+
4. How do agents with different structured information communicate?	?	+	+
5. How are the paths of communication specified?	o	o	o
6. How are messages addressed?	+	+	+

19.8 Sophisticated Agents	CNET	PGP/DVMT	GPGP+
1. What a priori knowledge do agents have about other agents?	o	o	o
2. What knowledge do agents develop about other agents?	o	+	+
3. Can agents deal with inconsistent, incomplete, and uncertain information?	?	o	o
4. Do agents employ tacit bargaining and detect hidden agendas?	−	−	−

514

19.9 System and Hardware Support	CNET	PGP/DVMT	GPGP+
1. What happens when a single hardware failure occurs?	−	o	−
2. What is the likelihood of a hardware failure?	?	?	?
3. How do computational resources affect problem solving?	−	−	+
4. What special resources does the environment provide?	?	+	+
5. What special resources do the operating system or hardware provide?	−	−	−
6. Are the goals, tasks, priorities, etc. of an agent used by the underlying system?	−	−	?
7. How far along is the implementation?	o	o	−

19.10 Develop general and representative hard domain problems	CNET	PGP/DVMT	GPGP+
1. What is the relative speed of communication versus the amount of local computation?	+	+	?
2. Do all system tasks have to be completed?	−	o	+
3. Can this problem be solved in a centralized manner?	−	−	−
4. Is there any advantage to having multiple agents solve the same subproblem?	?	+	+
5. Is there significant uncertainty involved?	?	+	+
6. Are overconstrained situations possible?	−	−	o
7. How easy is it to find a solution to the problem?	?	o	o
8. How much empirical evaluation has been done of the domain problem solving capabilities of your system?	−	+	−

As was discussed earlier, each question may relate to more than one goal but appears only once in the set of questions. For example, Question 19.5.15 ("What assumptions are made about the quality of network control information?") applies to both Section 19.5 (Network Control) and Section 19.2 (Limiting Assumptions).

Sometimes, a question may have the opposite meaning for two goals. This is indicated in the table below by a bar over a bold number. For example, Question 19.9.6 ("Are the goals, tasks, priorities, etc. of an agent used by the underlying operating system?") is a question about both system support and limiting assumptions, with a "high" answer to

515

Question 19.9.6 implying high complexity in system support but low in limiting environmental assumptions.

The following table illustrates a mapping of questions to the goals (other than the ones they appear with) that they influence:

Limit Assumptions	$\overline{19.5.11}$,19.5.15,19.6.2,$\overline{19.9.5}$,$\overline{19.9.6}$,19.10.1
Cooperating Agents	19.2.1,19.2.3,19.2.5,19.2.6,19.4.5,19.5.1
Global Coherence	19.2.4,19.2.7,19.3.1,19.5.5,19.5.16,19.10.1
Network Control	19.2.2,19.3.3,19.10.1
Real Time & Faults	19.4.3,19.5.13,19.9.1,19.9.2,19.9.3
Communications	19.2.9,19.2.14,19.4.1,19.10.1
Sophisticated Agents	19.2.9,19.3.2,19.3.3,19.4.2,19.5.5
System Support	$\overline{19.2.8}$,19.2.14,19.5.17,19.10.8
Domain Problem	19.2.7,19.2.16,19.3.1,19.3.6,19.4.2,19.9.2

Now for each goal we can add up all of the low, medium, and high answers for the questions in that section *and* the related questions in the table above, ignoring the (?). Those evaluations can then be summarized as follows.

	CNET				PGP/DVMT				GPGP+			
	−	o	+	?	−	o	+	?	−	o	+	?
Limit Assumptions	2	1	9	6	3	6	8	1	3	2	9	4
Cooperating Agents	3	2	2	5	3	6	3	0	1	2	8	1
Global Coherence	7	2	2	1	0	4	8	0	0	0	11	1
Network Control	6	6	5	3	1	4	15	0	1	1	17	1
Real Time & Faults	4	3	4	1	1	3	7	1	1	0	10	1
Communications	1	3	3	3	2	1	6	1	0	2	5	3
Sophisticated Agents	1	5	0	3	1	3	4	1	1	2	5	1
System Support	6	1	2	2	4	2	4	1	6	0	3	2
Domain Problem	6	2	2	4	3	5	5	1	3	3	6	2

Evaluations such as this can be used in two ways. First, we can use then to compare the strengths, weaknesses, and different research thrusts of different CDPS systems. Secondly, and more usefully, we can use them to look at how new research will make advances in the field over older projects.

We can summarize the information in the above table by counting a (+) mark as a 1, a (−) mark as a −1, a (o) as a 0, and summing them. The table below shows the resulting values and the number of unanswered questions (?):

	CNET		PGP/DVMT		GPGP+	
	sum	?	sum	?	sum	?
Limit Assumptions	7	6	5	1	6	4
Cooperating Agents	-1	5	0	0	7	1
Global Coherence	-5	1	8	0	11	1
Network Control	-1	3	14	0	16	1
Real Time & Faults	0	1	6	1	9	1
Communications	2	3	4	1	5	3
Sophisticated Agents	-1	3	3	1	4	1
System Support	-4	2	0	1	-3	2
Domain Problem	-4	4	2	1	3	2

Looking at the table above as an aid to comparisons, we can see some large characteristics that point out the major differences between the evaluated systems:

- Although we felt that CNET made less assumptions about its domain than PGP, due to the uncertainty surrounding details of CNET this is only marginally apparent in the table.

- GPGP+ ranks significantly better than PGP or CNET on creating cooperating agents that can handle complex and sophisticated goal interactions, which is to be expected since one of the focuses of GPGP is to reason about the goals of agents so that they can cooperate more effectively.

- Both PGP and GPGP+ rank significantly higher than CNET in providing facilities for agents to act in a coherent manner, in creating sophisticated network control strategies, and in working in real-time and fault-tolerant situations.

- Little difference between the systems is seen in terms of communication protocols.

- PGP and GPGP+ rank marginally better than CNET in providing a sophisticated agent framework where agents reason about other agents explicitly. Perhaps more questions need to be aimed specifically at this area.

- PGP, as the most mature system presented, ranks higher than the others in system support and empirical evaluation.

- The domain problems of the PGP and GPGP+ frameworks show more promise than that of CNET, primarily because the vehicle monitoring problem that the DVMT solves [Lesser and Corkill 1983] was extended to make it more complex than the problem described in the CNET paper [Davis and Smith 1983].

517

The second way to use this data is to see how new work will extend the capabilities of the old. For example, besides the GPGP+ work described here, researchers are pursuing other work that will extend our abilities in building sophisticated CDPS systems. Work is being done on complex forms of negotiation and constraint relaxation between agents that will move us higher along the complexity axes in Questions 19.3.4, 19.4.5, and 19.7.4. Other work on reasoning with uncertainty will move us farther along on the axes of Questions 19.5.15, 19.7.1, 19.7.4, 19.8.3, and 19.10.5.

19.13   Conclusions

Cooperative distributed problem solving, like its parent field AI, is vaguely defined because it is precisely those problems that are ill-defined (admitting to no clear algorithmic solutions) that are of interest. Developing a set of questions for comparing and evaluating research projects is thus an ill-defined task in itself, where the lack of structure in the field leads to a sense of uncertainty about how to characterize the dimensions of the field. Ours is one of several attempts to chart these dimensions [Huhns 1987, Decker 1986, Smith 1985], and we feel it is the most complete to date for understanding and comparing similar projects, but as the field evolves, so will the questions. Indeed, many of the questions we ask in this paper were not and could not be considered in the early days of CDPS research when the field was even less defined.

Our hope is that our new research directions will serve to answer some questions and raise even more interesting new questions. As is clear from its description and comparisons among systems, our proposed work is intended to meet and often exceed the capabilities of past systems. Because it has yet to be implemented, however, we cannot realize the full implications of even more sophisticated cooperation among computers, in terms of their ability to achieve new results and to work more effectively with humans. Because our long term goal is to build computers that can intelligently work together and with us, we must continue to ask the questions put forth in this paper, and to extend this set of questions as we learn more about cooperative distributed problem solving.

Acknowledgements

We would like to thank Dr. Robert Simpson who inspired us to try to develop an approach to understanding how to measure progress in the field and discuss critically the scientific content of different research projects. We would also like to thank Dan Corkill, Dan Neiman, and the reviewers for their perceptive comments.

This research was sponsored, in part, by the Defense Advanced Research Projects Agency (DOD), monitored by the Office of Naval Research under Contract NR049-041.

References

[Davis and Smith 1983] R. Davis and R. G. Smith, "Negotiation As a Metaphor for Distributed Problem Solving," *Artificial Intelligence*, vol. 20, no. 1, January 1983, pp. 63–109.

[Decker 1986] K. S. Decker, "Distributed Problem Solving: A Survey," *IEEE Transactions on Systems, Man, and Cybernetics*, vol. 17, no. 5, September 1987.

[Durfee and Lesser 1987] E. H. Durfee and V. R. Lesser, "Using Partial Global Plans to Coordinate Distributed Problem Solvers," *Proceedings of the Tenth International Joint Conference on Artificial Intelligence*, August 1987.

[Durfee *et al.* 1987] E. H. Durfee, V. R. Lesser, and D. D. Corkill, "Coherent Cooperation among Communicating Problem Solvers," *IEEE Transactions on Computers*, vol. 36, no. 11, November 1987, pp. 1275–1291.

[Huhns 1987] M. N. Huhns, editor, *Distributed Artificial Intelligence*, Pitman, London, 1987.

[Lesser and Corkill 1981] V. R. Lesser and D. D. Corkill, "Functionally Accurate, Cooperative Distributed Systems," *IEEE Transactions on Systems, Man, and Cybernetics*, vol. SMC-11, no. 1, January 1981, pp. 81–96.

[Lesser and Corkill 1983] V. R. Lesser and D. D. Corkill, "The Distributed Vehicle Monitoring Testbed," *AI Magazine*, vol. 1, no. 3, Fall 1983, pp. 63–109.

[Malone 1988] T. W. Malone, "What is coordination theory?" *Proceedings of the National Science Foundation Coordination Theory Workshop*, February 1988.

[Smith 1985] R. G. Smith, "Report on the 1984 Distributed Artificial Intelligence Workshop," *AI Magazine*, Vol. 6, No. 3, Fall 1985, pp. 234–243.

[Smith and Davis 1981] R. G. Smith and R. Davis, "Frameworks for Cooperation in Distributed Problem Solving," *IEEE Transactions on Systems, Man, and Cybernetics*, vol. SMC-11, no. 1, January 1981, pp. 61–70.

[Parunak 1985] H. Van Dyke Parunak, "Manufacturing Experience with the Contract Net," *Proceedings of the 1985 Distributed Artificial Intelligence Workshop*, December 1985, pp. 67–91.

Keith S. Decker and Victor R. Lesser
Department of Computer and Information Science
University of Massachusetts
Amherst, MA 01003

Edmund H. Durfee
Department of Electrical Engineering and Computer Science
The University of Michigan
Ann Arbor, MI 48109